G000075141

WORLD TRADE ORGANIZATION

Dispute Settlement Reports

2008
Volume XVII

Pages 6715-7162

CAMBRIDGE
UNIVERSITY PRESS

CAMBRIDGE UNIVERSITY PRESS
Cambridge, New York, Melbourne, Madrid, Cape Town, Singapore, São Paulo,
Delhi, Dubai, Tokyo

Cambridge University Press
The Edinburgh Building, Cambridge CB2 8RU, UK

Published in the United States of America by Cambridge University Press, New York

www.cambridge.org
Information on this title: www.cambridge.org/9780521196376

First published 2010

Printed in the United Kingdom at the University Press, Cambridge

A catalogue record for this publication is available from the British Library

Library of Congress Cataloguing in Publication data

ISBN 978-0-521-19637-6 hardback

THE WTO DISPUTE SETTLEMENT REPORTS

The *Dispute Settlement Reports* of the World Trade Organization (the "WTO") include panel and Appellate Body reports, as well as arbitration awards, in disputes concerning the rights and obligations of WTO Members under the provisions of the *Marrakesh Agreement Establishing the World Trade Organization*. The *Dispute Settlement Reports* are available in English. Volumes comprising one or more complete cases contain a cumulative list of published disputes. The cumulative list for cases that cover more than one volume is to be found in the first volume for that case.

This volume may be cited as DSR 2008:XVII

TABLE OF CONTENTS

Page

**Canada – Continued Suspension of Obligations
in the EC – Hormones Dispute (WT/DS321)**

Report of the Panel – Annexes F and G 6717

CANADA – CONTINUED SUSPENSION OF OBLIGATIONS IN THE EC – HORMONES DISPUTE

Report of the Panel
WT/DS321/R

Adopted by the Dispute Settlement Body
on 14 November 2008
as Modified by the Appellate Body Report

LIST OF ANNEXES[*]

ANNEX F

COMMENTS BY THE PARTIES ON THE REPLIES OF THE
SCIENTIFIC EXPERTS, CODEX, JECFA AND IARC TO
QUESTIONS POSED BY THE PANEL AND COMMENTS
BY THE PARTIES ON THE OTHER PARTIES' COMMENTS

Contents		Page
Annex F-1	Comments by the European Communities on the replies of the scientific experts to questions posed by the Panel (30 June 2006)	6719
Annex F-2	Comments by the European Communities on the replies of Codex, JECFA and IARC to questions posed by the Panel (30 June June 2006)	6772
Annex F-3	Comments by the European Communities to the comments by the United States and Canada on the replies of the scientific experts to questions posed by the Panel (12 July 2006)	6789

---

[*]   This volume contains Annexes F and G to the Report of the Panel. Annexes A to E of this Report are to be found in volume DSR 2008:XVI.

Contents		Page
Annex F-4	Comments by Canada on the replies of the scientific experts, Codex, JECFA and IARC to questions posed by the Panel (30 June 2006)	6851
Annex F-5	Comments by Canada to the comments by the European Communities on the replies of the scientific experts, Codex, JECFA and IARC to questions posed by the Panel (12 July 2006)	6919

ANNEX G

TRANSCRIPT OF THE PANEL'S JOINT MEETING
WITH SCIENTIFIC EXPERTS ON 27-28 SEPTEMBER 2006

Contents		Page
Annex G	Transcript of the Panel's joint meeting with scientific experts on 27-28 september 2006	6955

ANNEX F-1

COMMENTS BY THE EUROPEAN COMMUNITIES ON THE
REPLIES OF THE SCIENTIFIC EXPERTS TO QUESTIONS
POSED BY THE PANEL

(30 June 2006)

A.   General Definitions

**Q1.   Please provide brief and basic definitions for the six hormones at is-
sue (oestradiol-17β, progesterone, testosterone, trenbolone acetate, zeranol,
and melengestrol acetate), indicating the source of the definition where applicable.**

EC Comments

Dr. Boisseau's reply does not consider any progress in toxicological knowledge
concerning these hormones, and in particular estradiol, since the 70th and 80th
JECFA reports. Since then new data concerning residues in tissue and their toxicological impact have been published. In his answer, he has only adopted a narrow regulatory definition. More specifically, as regards oestradiol, aromatization
of androgens in estrogens is also very significant in adipose tissue. In his definitions, the sites of production in the human body is limited to the primary source
and does not dwell on variability over the life span of an individual. Furthermore, his definition does not stress that Zeranol is a very potent estrogen.
Zeranol is not a "natural estrogen" that humans are exposed to. In fact, great care
should be taken to avoid the presence of fusarium molds in animal feed and especially in products for human consumption. As regards the implantation of
these hormones, he uses simple present tense ("the ear is discarded") when precisely this is not known nor it is sure that it happens in practice in all cases. He
should therefore have said that "the ear should be discarded at slaughter". Moreover, implantation can be made at the dewlap level, not only at the ear one, especially in case of multiple implantations. Furthermore, in some new recommendations of trenbolone use, it is possible to proceed to repeated implantation of
steers or heifers.

**Q2.   Please provide definitions for the following terms as they relate to the
hormones at issue, indicating the source of the definition where applicable:
anabolic   agents,   steroids,   steroidal   oestrogens,   parent   com-
pounds/metabolites, catechol metabolites, mitogenicity, mutagenicity, an-
drogenic/oestrogenic activity, genotoxicity, genotoxic potential, carcinogenicity, and tumorigenicity. In your replies, please be sure to identify and
describe any relevant differences between the terms.**

EC Comments

Dr. Boisseau's reply that "In my e-mail of 26/04/06, I have indicated that I did not think that I am in the position to reply to this question" calls into question the reliability of his answer to question no 1 and indeed to the other questions. As the EC has pointed out during the selection procedure, *Dr. Boisseau* does not posses any expertise on these substances, as he does not appear to have carried out any specific research on these substances during his professional life. *Dr. Boisseau* has explicitly admitted it in his e-mail to the Panel secretariat where he wrote: "*I did not join any publications as I have none on hormones*".

B.   Risk Assessment Techniques

Q3.   Please identify any international guidance documents relevant to the conduct of a risk assessment with respect to veterinary drug residues. Since when have they been available? Please also indicate if there is any relevant ongoing work at Codex.

EC Comments

The European Communities agrees with the statement by *Dr. Boisseau* that currently there is no international guidance document relevant to the conduct of a risk assessment with respect to veterinary drug residues and in particular the six hormones under consideration. Indeed, the documents to which *Dr. Boobis* refers to in his reply are *not* "assessment techniques developed by the relevant international organizations", in the sense of Article 5.1 of the *SPS Agreement*. They are informal ad hoc papers without any legal value. Moreover, when the European Communities evaluated these hormones, it applied its standard legislation for the evaluation of this type of substances, which complies fully with the general definitions of risk analysis as described in the Codex Alimentarius' latest Manual of Procedures.

Moreover, *Dr. Boisseau's* statement that "*the situation is similar in the European Union*" and that "*The CVMP has assessed all the pharmacologically active substances used in veterinary medecine without any written guideline about risk assessment*" is wrong. It is not the CVMP (Committee on veterinary medicinal products) which is responsible for these hormones when administered for animal growth promotion, but it has been the SCVPH (scientific committee on veterinary measures relating to public health). This latter Committee, and the European Communities in general, have been applying advanced principles and techniques of risk analysis which Codex Alimentarius is only now considering of formally putting in practice. See for instance the European Commission Decision 97/579/EC of 23 July 1997 which set up scientific committees in the field of consumer health and food safety which has established the SCVPH (OJ L 237, 28.8.1997, p. 18-23) and the Opinion of the Scientific Steering Committee on harmonisation of risk assessment procedures adopted on 26-27 October 2000, which can be found at http://ec.europa.eu/food/fs/sc/ssc/out82_en.html. These advanced principles of risk analysis have been routinely applied by the European Communities for quite some time well before 1997.[1] They were applied when the SCVPH evaluated these six hormones in 1999, 2000 and 2002, and have since then formally been restated in the relevant EC legislation, in particular Regulation (EC) No 178/2002 of the European Parliament and of the Council of 28 January 2002 laying down the general principles and requirements of food law, establishing the European Food Safety Authority and laying down procedures in matters of food safety, OJ L 31, 1.2.02, p. 1-24, in particular Article 6.

Q4.   The European Communities states that there is "no Codex standard specifically on the risk assessment of effects of residues of veterinary drugs" but a general one on microbiological assessment. Is this correct? Which guidelines or principles have been used by JECFA in the conduct of its risk assessments with respect to the hormones at issue? [see para. 192 of EC Rebuttal Submission (US case)].

EC Comments

As already explained above in its comments to the replies to question No 3, the European Communities agrees with *Dr. Boisseau's* reply that "there is no Codex standard specifically on the risk assessment of effect of residues of veterinary drugs". Neither the work of IPCS nor the Environmental health Criteria no 70 nor the monograph published in the WHO series no 43, mentioned by *Dr. Boobis* and *Dr. Guttenplan*, respectively, constitute legally binding "assessment techniques" for risk assessment in the sense of Article 5.1 of the *SPS Agreement*. The EC has been much more advanced than JECFA in the application of generally acceptable techniques for risk analysis, as explained in the references to the relevant EC legislation in the previous question No 3. The EC documents mentioned above, although publicly accessible, can be made available to the Panel and its experts upon request.

Q5.   Please briefly describe the three components of a risk analysis exercise (risk assessment, risk management and risk communication) and explain how they differ.

EC Comments

The European Communities submits that the Panel's question is of little relevance to the issues under consideration in the present proceedings. Indeed, the Panel's question appears to ignore the fact that the Appellate Body in the *Hormones* case has clarified that the term "risk assessment" in the *SPS Agreement* is wider in scope because it covers also evidence, considerations, objectives and

---

[1]   See, e.g., Commission Directive 93/67/EEC of 20 July 1993 laying down the principles for assessment of risks to man and the environment of substances notified in accordance with Council Directive 67/548/EEC, OJ L 227, 8.9.1993, p. 9-18.

factors that are also taken into account at the "risk management" phase.[2] Consequently, *the answers of all scientists* do *not* take into account the legal requirements of the *SPS Agreement* in this area, as interpreted by the Appellate Body. However, the European Comunities has in any case followed the three components of risk analysis, as explained above and in its reply of 3 October 2005 to question No 24 of the Panel.

Moreover, *none of the replies* by the scientists describes what is actually going on in Codex. The reality is that JECFA performs, most of the time, as it did with regard to these hormones, both risk assessment and risk management functions (something which *Dr. Boisseau* admits), thus the subsequent decisions/recommendations by the Codex Alimentarius Commission become a mere formality. Indeed, JECFA's reports and monographs are drafted in such a way as to leave practically no room to the members of the Codex Alimentarius Commission to decide on the appropriate level of health protection and the risk management options that are available to its members. That is another reason for which the European Communities decided that the Codex recommendations on these hormones could not achieve the level of health protection considered appropriate in its territory.

Q6.   Please briefly describe the four steps of a risk assessment (hazard identification, hazard characterization, exposure assessment and risk characterization) as identified by Codex, indicating any relevant sources.

EC Comments

The European Communities does not understand the relevance of this question for the purposes of these disputes and the corresponding replies of *Dr. Boisseau* and *Dr. Boobis*. This type of formal distinction between the various components of risk assessment are not mentioned in the *SPS Agreement* and they are clearly not legally binding, since they are not risk "assessment techniques" in the sense of Article 5.1 of the *SPS Agreement*. Moreover, as the Appellate Body has held in the *Hormones* case (at para. 181), to the extent these distinctions are used "to achieve or support what appears to be a restrictive notion of risk assessment" this has no textual basis in the SPS Agreement. More importantly, however, if these four steps are not formally identified in the risk assessment document of a member, this does not mean that the risk assessment of that member is faulty or scientifically unsound. For instance, the statements by the above 2 scientists appear to discard the relevance of some residues that are not pharmacologically active but may interfere with normal metabolic functioning of cells given their intrinsic chemical potential to form covalent adducts to biomolecules (trenbolone for example which gives a high level of protein adducts). Normally, this biological impact should be considered separately and in addition to the hormonal effects.

---

[2]   *See* Appellate Body Report in EC - *Hormones*, at paras. 181 and 206.

But until now, this has never been done by JECFA and the defending parties when they evaluated these hormones for animal growth promotion purposes. Hence, it is difficult in this context to know what is really a marker residue of a compound having some toxic impact that are not at all related to hormonal effects.

Q7. Please comment on the EC statement made in para. 140 of the EC Replies to Panel Questions that "which ever approach of a risk assessment is followed, they are all based on a deterministic approach to risk characterization [and that they] have serious limitations in non-linear situations, such as in the current case regarding hormones". Are these situations, in your view, addressed by the risk assessment guidance currently available from the Codex Alimentarius Commission? Have they been addressed in the 1988 and 1999 JECFA risk assessments of these hormones? [see Canada's comments in para. 72 of its Rebuttal Submission]

EC Comments

The European Communities notes first that *Dr. Boisseau* admits that "in 1987 and 1999, at the time of the assessment of oestradiol-17β, there was no risk assessment guidance available on this issue". Even so, he goes on to argue that neither in 1987 nor in 1999 JECFA considered this kind of non-linear situation, despite the fact that it had found in its 1999 report that "oestradiol-17β has a genotoxic potential." However, this approach of JECFA is scientifically unsound, as *Dr. Boobis* now accepts when he says that today "in practice, it is likely that as veterinary drug residues in food are avoidable by not using the drug, the Committee would have *declined* to establish an ADI".

The European Communities notes, however, that there are basic flaws in the replies of both *Dr. Boisseau* and *Dr. Boobis*. Indeed, the accumulation of so much new peer-reviewed evidence since 1999 establishes clearly that oestradiol-17β is a direct carcinogen and does not act only through hormonal receptors. In addition to the peer-reviewed studies mentioned in the 1999, 2000 and 2002 EC risk assessments, it would be appropriate to refer also to the work of Hari K. Bhat, Gloria Calaf, Tom K. Hei, Theresa Loya, and Jaydutt V. Vadgama: *Critical role of oxidative stress in estrogen-induced carcinogenesis*, published in the Proceedings of the National Academy of Sciences, Vol. 100 (2003) 3913-3918, demonstrating the necessary role of catechols of estradiol or other catechols (2/4-hydroxy-estradiol-alpha produced from estradiol-alpha, menadione) in induction of oxidative stress to induce tumors in the hamster kidney carcinogenesis model. See also the two papers by J. Russo and his co-workers: *17β-Estradiol is carcinogenic in human breast epithelial cells*, and *Estrogen and its metabolites are carcinogenic agents in human breast epithelial cells*, published in the Journal of Steroid Biochemistry & Molecular Biology, vol. 80 (2002) 149-162 and vol. 87 (2003) 1-25, respectively.

From a more systematic point of view, the views of *Dr. Boobis* can also be criticized because a threshold is a theoretical concept that provides the justification for the use of the NOAEL and thus the ADI. In the work of JECFA, the NOAEL is perceived as evidence of the practical revelation of a threshold. But a true threshold can only be established with an infinitely large group of animals: thus, the dose distance between the true threshold and the NOAEL cannot be established. In a genetically and phenotypically heterogenous human population, there is a risk from endogenous hormone – induced adverse outcomes. Additionally, there must be a distribution of both consumption of meat and hormone response sensitivity in the human population. We know that endogenous hormones in animals and humans are known to cause a wide variety of adverse effects from reproductive function to malignancies. These considerations demonstrate that some fraction of the population will be at higher risk for hormone-related adverse outcomes, no matter the dose, due to consumption of hormone-implanted meat. A number of publications, some of which have been submitted by the European Communities to this Panel, have explored the threshold concept and the activity of hormones at very low doses. These are:

Gaylor, D. W., Sheehan, D. M., Young, J. F. and Mattison, D. R.: The threshold dose question in teratogenesis (Letter). Teratology, 38:389-391, 1988.

Sheehan, D. M., and vom Saal, F. S.: Low dose effects of endocrine disruptors-a challenge for risk assessment. Risk Policy Report, 31-39, issue of Sept.19, 1997.

Sheehan, D. M., Willingham, E., Gaylor, D., Bergeron, J. M., and Crews, D.: No threshold dose for oestradiol-induced sex reversal of turtle embryos: How little is too much? Environmental Health Perspectives 107:155-159, 1999.

Sheehan, D. M.: Activity of environmentally low doses of endocrine disruptors and the Bisphenol A controversy: Initial results confirmed, in Proc. Soc. Exp. Biol. Med. 224:57-60, 2000.

Blair, RM, Fang, H, Gaylor, D, Sheehan, D. M.: Threshold analysis of selected dose-response data for endrocrine disruptors, in APMIS 109:198-208, 2001.

Q8.   Please describe the procedure followed by JECFA in the identification of ADIs and the development of recommendations on MRLs. Please identify and describe any steps that are taken in the risk assessment process to build a margin of safety into the final recommendation.

EC Comments

The replies of *Dr. Boisseau* and *Dr. Boobis* are theoretical statements with little scientific relevance as regards the safety of these hormones. For instance, the appropriate studies in humans would require a huge study population, and would be seriously confounded by medical treatments with hormones and environmental exposures to hormones. Also the conclusion that there is a threshold for hormone action in the absence of other sources of hormone cannot provide a sound scientific basis in order to conclude that endogenous hormones are below the threshold for all actions of the hormones. Therefore, added hormone from implanted beef should increase risk for endpoints that are already occurring from endogenous hormones. Appreciable risk is a subjective decision, as are the 10-fold safety margins. Because of the small numbers of animals on studies, the resolution is generally low.

More specifically, the evidence used by JECFA in the evaluation of these hormones is too old (dating from the 1970s) and has been obtained with outdated detection methods to be relevant today. *Dr. Boisseau* also writes that "*...taking into consideration the diversity of humans, resulting from the sex, age, race, which can lead to different sensitivity...*", but JECFA did not take the low endogenous levels and thus the high sensitivity of children into account. Also *Dr. Boobis* states that "*where there was an identifiable sub-group who might reasonably be expected to be more sensitive than the group in whom data were obtained, for example children relative to adults, an extra factor was applied.*" Indeed, the JECFA expert committee that examined these hormones did not include any physicians and child endocrinologists! It can be argued that for most chemical compounds, such as pesticides, the knowledge on their potential toxicity resides with toxicologists. However, when we are dealing with the natural hormones and compounds that directly affect the endocrine system, the knowledge on how they potentially can affect humans is a part of the daily work of paediatricians and other physicians. Thus, it is essential that persons with a medical background are present in the JECFA committee (see more on this below). *Dr. Boisseau* also writes something about low oral activity of 17β-oestradiol, but that is simply not scientifically correct as demonstrated below (comment in relation to question 43). For instance, oral contraceptives and some hormone replacement therapy are taken by the oral route and are shown to be very active. This demonstrates that oestradiol and progesterone are bioavailable through the oral route.

Q9. **Please confirm or comment on the following Canadian statement: "it is recognized that JECFA only allocates an ADI for a food additive or veterinary drug under review when JECFA considers that its scientific data base is complete and that there are no outstanding scientific issues". [see para. 68 of Canada Rebuttal Submission]**

EC Comments

The Canadian statement cannot be scientifically correct in the unqualified manner in which it is expressed and certainly is not correct as regards the six hormones under consideration. It would all depend on when JECFA's scientific data base is considered to be complete and that there are no outstanding scientific issue. For example, when JECFA evaluated in 1988 these hormones, it considered unnecessary to establish an ADI, presumably because it considered that there was no outstanding scientific issue. However, in its 1999 evaluation of the three natural hormones JECFA changed its evaluation and this time established an ADI. Both in 1988 and in 1999 JECFA's evaluation was based on the assumption that these substances act only through the hormonal receptors. However, this assumption is certainly incomplete and scientifically incorrect because it is today generally accepted that some of these hormones are genotoxic and can cause cancer directly. Furthermore, as already explained above, the ADI and MRLs that JECFA established in 1988 and in 1999 for the three synthetic hormones do not take into account the low endogenous levels and thus high sensitivity of prepubertal children. In conclusion, there are so many examples of cases where JECFA has set an ADI because it considered its scientific data base to be complete and that there were no outstanding scientific issues, but it had subsequently to change its mind in the light of more accurate reading of the evidence or more recent scientific data. A good recent example is the case of Carbadox, cited by the European Communities in paras. 150 and 151 of its 2nd Written Submission in the US Panel. It follows that the issue of when the scientific data base is complete can be very subjective and prone to many errors of which JECFA's assessments are certainly not immune.

Q10. In para. 129 and 168 of its Replies to the Panel Questions, the European Communities states that "JECFA's traditional mandate does not allow it to examine all risk management options but restricts it to either propose MRLs or not". Does Codex have risk management options other than (1) the establishment of an MRL, (2) establishing that an MRL is not necessary or (3) no recommendation?

EC Comments

The European Communities considers that the reply of *Dr. Boisseau* confirms that JECFA has a narrow mandate, even if it frequently oversteps its role and proposes also risk management measures, thus leaving practically no option to Codex Alimentarius Commission and its members than to follow its narrow recommendations to adopt or not an MRL. What is also important to note is that JECFA has not considered as part of its narrow mandate to examine whether there is any likelihood of misuse or abuse of these hormones and whether the identified risks to human and animal health from the use of these hormones for growth promotion by far exceed any potential benefits.

Q11. What should, in your view, be the components of a qualitative risk assessment, compared with a quantitative risk assessment? [see para. 82 of Canada Rebuttal Submission]

EC Comments

The European Communities agrees with the statement by *Dr. Cogliano*. The statements by *Dr. Boisseau* and *Dr. Boobis* are simply contrary to the findings of the Appellate Body in the 1998 *Hormones* case, where it held that a qualitative risk assessment is equally acceptable under the SPS Agreement and that it does not require the same type of analysis as a quantitative risk assessment. More generally, the issue of whether a threshold model or a non-threshold model is used is critical in determining risk. The literature on no-threshold cited above, in addition to the no-threshold models used for example for PCBs and dioxin, are more appropriate than the current procedures applied by JECFA. For instance, endogenous estrogens are active at inducing some responses in most, if not all, age and population groups. Additivity of exposure to endogenous and exogenous hormones will necessarily result in increased risk at any exogenous dose, no matter how low. Interestingly, the US EPA uses no-threshold models for non-genotoxic chemicals, such as dioxins and PCBs, due to a combination of very long half-lives and activity at very low doses. The European Communities submits that consumption of hormone-treated beef at regular intervals will provide continual or intermittent exposure of estradiol and other growth hormones and thus increase risk and undermine its high level of health protection from these substances.

Q12. How is scientific uncertainty addressed in risk assessments in general? With respect to the assessment of risks from the consumption of meat treated with the growth promotion hormones at issue, how has scientific uncertainty been considered by JECFA/Codex ? How does it differ from the way it has been considered by the European Communities in its assessment of risks from the consumption of meat treated with the growth promotion hormones at issue?

EC Comments

The European Communities disagrees with the statements by *Dr. Boisseau* and *Dr. Boobis* because of their extremely narrow understanding of the concept of scientific uncertainty. They both consider that scientific uncertainty is adequately addressed by JECFA when applying the so-called safety factors. There is however now almost universal agreement that this approach is not scientifically correct. A state of uncertainty may result from a number of factors, such as lack, incomplete or contradictory data. It is not the quantity but the quality of the data that is important. It is possible that an issue that was thought to be scientifically clear to become uncertain as more data become available. When scientific uncertainty is understood in this sense, this cannot be tackled with the application of so-called safety factors or margins, especially for countries that wish to apply a high level of health protection. For example, the genotoxic and carcinogenic potential of oestradiol-17β cannot be adequately addressed by the safety factors applied by JECFA, because the underlying scientific uncertainty about the mechanisms causing cancer are not amenable to quantification so as to be adequately addressed by the safety factors (there is always the risk of under-inclusion). Another example is that when JECFA evaluated the three natural hormones in 1988 and in 1999 and decide not to set a ADI and a MRL, it based its evaluation concerning endogenous production of these hormones by prepubertal children on very old data from 1974 (citing the paper by Angsusingha K. et al: *Unconjugated estrone, estradiol, and FSH and LH in prepubertal and pubertal males and females*, Journal of Clinical Endocrinology and Metabolism, 39: 63-68 (1974), as reported in the 32nd report of JECFA published in the WHO technical report series no 763, page 32). However, the data reported by Angsusingha et al. are no longer valid in view of the more recent findings with more accurate detection and measurement tools available (see the discussion in paras. 121-122 of the EC 2nd written submission in the US panel and the references thereto to the papers by Klein and Klein and by Anderson and Skakkebaek of 1994, 1999 and 2005, respectively).

It follows from the above that the statement by *Dr. Boisseau* that "for the three natural hormones, oestradiol-17β, progesterone and testosterone, JECFA has decided that the margin of safety deriving from the values of the established ADIs and from a maximum estimated intake of residue was such that it was not necessary to set up MRLs" is plainly wrong. His statement that the European Communities "did not consider any scientific uncertainty" is also false, because a careful reading of the 1999 risk assessment by the SCVPH shows that the reasons for which that scientific committee considered that oestradiol-17β is a proven carcinogen and that the uncertainty regarding the other five hormones (resulting from the lack of data or the presence of contradictory data) are properly explained and taken into account.

Dr. Boobis also made the equally false statement that: "… the EC assessment of the hormones did not go as far as including some of the considerations for uncertainty used by JECFA because of the conclusion that there was insufficient information to determine whether there was a threshold for the carcinogenic effects. However, for some of the compounds this was based on the results of a small number of non-standard tests of genotoxicity, with equivocal of very weak responses. It is not clear whether the EC applied *a weight of evidence approach* to evaluating the genotoxicity of all of the compounds, taking account the totality of the available data, as was the case by JECFA." Indeed, the three risk assessments of 1999, 2000 and 2002 by the SCVPH did consider the totality of the available data. In fact, *Dr. Boobis'* reply does not discusses at all that since 2002, the US authorities concluded that "steroidal estrogens are known to be human carcinogens based on *sufficient evidence of carcinogenicity in humans*, which indicates a causal relationship between exposure to steroidal estrogens and human cancer." For this reason, the US 2002 Report on Carcinogens (RoC) lists steroidal estrogens as known to be human carcinogens with the clarification that this listing now "supersedes the previous listing of specific estrogens in and applies to all chemicals of this steroid class." Moreover, in the same 2002 US Report it is stated that: "Veterinary use of steroidal estrogens (to promote growth and treat illnesses) can increase estrogens in tissues of food producing animals to above their normal levels."[3] So, the 2002 US Report on Carcinogenesis contradicts the allegations made by the US and Canada in these proceedings, which appear to be supported by Dr. Boobis, that the additional burden of residues coming from eating hormone-treated meat is so small that it would make no difference, compared to the level of endogenous production.

---

[3]   Available at http://ntp.niehs.nih.gov/index.cfm?objectid=72016262-BDB7-CEBA- FA60E922B 18C2540.

Furthermore, neither *Dr. Boobis* nor *Dr. Boisseau* mention the fact that the IARC has classified oestradiol-17β in Group 1 as carcinogenic to humans because there is sufficient evidence of carcinogenicity and progesterone and testosterone in Group 2B as possibly carcinogenic to humans. It is therefore a surprising statement by *Dr. Boobis* that the EC "*did not apply a weight of evidence approach to evaluating the genotoxicity of all of the compounds, taking into account the totality of the available data, as was the case by JECFA*", because it is precisely JECFA's evaluation that is based on old and outdated data and does not examine the totality of the available evidence. Moreover, the argument of *Dr. Boobis* that a WTO member has to apply a "weight of evidence approach" is legally incorrect. It is not very clear what Dr. Boobis means by this approach, but it must not be taken to mean that only the mainstream scientific views should be accepted or that such an approach could remedy the identified scientific uncertainty. Moreover, this approach would amount to forcing WTO members to dismiss or ignore minority scientific views, which has clearly been rejected by the Appellate Body in the 1998 *Hormones* case, where it held that:

> "Article 5.1 of the SPS Agreement does not require that the risk assessment must necessarily embody only the view of a majority of the relevant scientific community. In some cases, the very existence of divergent views presented by qualified scientists who have investigated the particular issue at hand may indicate a state of scientific uncertainty. In most cases, responsible and representative governments tend to base their legislative and administrative measures on "mainstream" scientific opinion. In other cases, equally responsible and representative governments may act in good faith on the basis of what, at a given time, may be a divergent opinion coming from qualified and respected sources. By itself, this does not necessarily signal the absence of a reasonable relationship between the SPS measure and the risk assessment, especially where the risk involved is life-threatening in character and is perceived to constitute a clear and imminent threat to public health and safety." (at para. 194 of the AB report)

On a more specific point, *Dr. Boisseau* is apparently committing the same error as the defending parties because he keeps referring to the "differences in the interpretation of data, as illustrated by the differing conclusions of the CVMP (1999) and the SCVPH (1999)", without knowing that the CVMP has evaluated *some* of the natural hormones in different preparations and for different purposes (therapeutic or zootechnical use) and its findings are not relevant for the use of the six hormones when administered for animal growth promotion (for which the competence to assess resided with the SCVPH).

C.   Assessment of Oestradiol-17β

Q13.   To what extent, in your view, does the EC risk assessment identify the potential for adverse effects on human health, including the carcinogenic or genotoxic potential, of the residues of oestradiol-17β found in meat derived from cattle to which this hormone had been administered for growth promotion purposes in accordance with good veterinary practice? To what extent does the EC risk assessment evaluate the potential occurrence of these adverse effects?

EC Comments

The European Communities is surprised by the affirmative tone in the statements by *Dr. Boisseau* and *Dr. Boobis* that the genotoxic effect of oestradiol-17β is associated with its hormonal activity, when JECFA itself was more cautious when stating that "the carcinogenicity of oestradiol-17β is *most probably* a result of its interaction with hormonal receptors" (emphasis added). Their statements become even more questionable in that they both do not take into account nor do they discuss the most recent and growing scientific evidence linking, directly or indirectly, oestradiol-17β and the other hormones with increased risk of cancer. Unlike what *Dr. Boisseau* states, there is growing evidence from in vivo studies, (e.g. by Bhat et al., already mentioned above, published in PNAS 100 (2003) 3913-3918) which has shown that estradiol is responsible for both initiation and promotion of tumors *in vivo*. Moreover, carcinogenicity of estrogens is primarily due to oxidative stress/DNA adduct formation caused by the catechols metabolites of estrogens. The role of receptor stimulation is only invoked in the promotion stage of carcinogenesis. For this reason, it is also necessary to consider estradiol-alpha as residues susceptible to be metabolised in consumer in catechol derivative with the same potency as estradiol to give adducts or to induce oxidative stress.

As already explained, it needs to be recalled again that estradiol has been classified as a Group 1 carcinogen by IARC and the results from numerous epidemiological studies support the association of elevated prolonged exposure to endogenous and exogenous estrogen with breast cancer. These studies are supported by studies in experimental animal models that not only include the Syrian hamster kidney model and mouse uterus model, referred to by *Dr. Guttenplan* in his response to Q. 14, but also the ACI rat (J. Endocrinology, 183, 91-99, 2004) and the ERKO/Wnt mouse (J. Steroid Biochem. Mol. Bio., 86, 477-486, 2003). In both of the latter models a clear dependence of the tumors on estradiol was shown and, in the latter model, the results show that the mammary tumors arise through effects of estradiol *not* mediated through the estrogen receptor (ER) since the mice lack ER expression.

So there seems now to be agreement that exposure to oestradiol-17β may increase the sensitivity to other carcinogens and thus increase the cancer risk (simultaneous or later in life). One more example is the ENU-mediated induction of endometrial adenocarcinomas (Takahashi et al., 1996),[4] where simultaneous exposure to oestradiol-17β significantly increased the yield of adenocarcinomas. More recently, the concept of tissue stem cells, as the cells where breast cancer originates, has led to a new concept linking breast cancer risk with the stem cell potential as a measurable variable of the 'fertile soil' for cellular transformation. It is suggested that low-dose estrogen exposure leads to increased proliferation of the tissue stem cells and, since it is hypothesised that the number of potentially carcinogenic tissue stem cells determines the risk of getting the cancer, thereby to an increased risk of breast cancer later in life. This aspect is not at all considered by these experts.[5]

Other adverse effects on human health have also been established. Thus, there are strong data linking administration of very low doses of oestradiol-17β to prepubertal girls to changes in growth pattern despite the fact that serum levels of oestradiol-17β remained below the detection limit (Lampit et al., 2002).[6] This may affect the risk for breast cancer later in life because it has been convincingly demonstrated that prepubertal growth rates significantly influence the breast cancer risk (Ahlgren et al., 2004).[7]

The European Communities also disputes the statements by *Dr. Boobis* that the EC's risk assessment used "speculative assumptions" about misuse or abuse of the product, that no adequate assessment of exposure following use according to GVP was undertaken, or that there was no attempt to estimate the potential occurrence of adverse effects in humans following exposure to levels of the hormones found in meat from treated animals. The experiments conducted by the EC and its findings are based on realistic conditions of use and demonstrate that GVP is frequently not respected in the defending members. The EC exhibits Nos 12, 16, 17, 52, 67, 68, 69 and 73 provide concrete evidence of abuse and misuse of these hormones by the both the US and Canada.

---

[4]   See Takahashi M, Iijima T, Suzuki K, Ando-Lu J, Yoshida M, Kitamura T, Nishiyama K, Miyajima K, Maekawa A.: Rapid and high yield induction of endometrial adenocarcinomas in CD-1 mice by a single intrauterine administration of N-ethyl-N-nitrosourea combined with chronic 17 beta-estradiol treatment, in Cancer Lett. 104:7-12 (1996).

[5]   *See* Smalley M., Ashworth A.: *Stem cells and breast cancer: A field in transit.* Nat Rev. Cancer. 2003, 3(11) :832-44, and Baik I., Becker P.S., DeVito W.J., Lagiou P., Ballen K., Quesenberry P.J., Hsieh C-C.: *Stem cells and prenatal origin of breast cancer.* Cancer Causes and Control 15: 517–530 (2004).

[6]   *See* Lampit M., Golander A., Guttmann H., Hochberg Z.: *Estrogen Mini-Dose Replacement during GnRH Agonist Therapy in Central Precocious Puberty: A Pilot Study.* The Journal of Clinical Endocrinology & Metabolism 87:687–690 (2002).

[7]   *See* Ahlgren M., Melbye M., Wohlfahrt J., Sorensen T.I.: *Growth patterns and the risk of breast cancer in women.* N. Engl. J. Med. 351:1619-26 (2004).

The European Communities agrees with the statement by *Dr. Guttenplan* that there are basically no direct epidemiological studies comparing matched populations consuming meat from untreated and hormone-treated cattle. However, apart from the ethical concerns, it is difficult to conduct such direct experiments in the presence of so many other confounding factors because of feasibility limitations for observational studies. This being said, it is common that in animal models used in carcinogenesis bioassays (rats and mice) one of the more sensitive tissues for tumorigenesis is liver. At the present time, however, the classification of chemicals as carcinogens does not require that the tumors produced in the bioassays are the same as would appear in humans; chemicals are classified as carcinogens when they cause a significant increase in tumors regardless of the tissue.

Q14. In your view, does the risk assessment undertaken by the European Communities on oestradiol-17β follow the Codex Guidelines on risk assessment, including the four steps of hazard identification, hazard characterization, exposure assessment and risk characterization with respect to oestradiol-17β?

EC Comments

The European Communities disagrees with the statement by *Dr. Boobis* because from a careful reading of the 1999, 2000 and 2002 risk assessment by the SCVPH it is obvious that it has followed the four steps of risk assessment when it carried out its qualitative risk assessment. That this is so is also confirmed by the statement by *Dr. Boisseau* although *Dr. Guttenplan* gives it a "mixed rating" in following the Codex guidelines which became available in 2003.

For the sake of completeness, however, it should also be clarified that *Dr. Guttenplan* has not considered the studies on the ACI rat and ERKO/Wnt mouse. The studies carried in experimental animal models do not only include the Syrian hamster kidney model and mouse uterus model, referred to by Dr. Guttenplan, but also the ACI rat (J. Endocrinology, 183, 91-99, 2004) and the ERKO/Wnt mouse (J. Steroid Biochem. Mol. Bio., 86, 477-486, 2003). In both of the latter models a clear dependence of the tumors on estradiol was shown and, in the latter model, the results show that the mammary tumors arise through effects of estradiol not mediated through the estrogen receptor (ER) since the mice lack ER expression. In addition, there are several additional models in transgenic mice where mammary tumor formation has been shown to be estrogen dependent.

D. Consumption of Meat Containing Hormones

(a) Carcinogenicity

Q15. Does the identification of oestradiol-17β as a human carcinogen indicate that there are potential adverse effects on human health when it is con-

sumed in meat from cattle treated with hormones for growth promotion purposes? Does your answer depend on whether good veterinary practices are followed? [see para. 206-207 of EC Rebuttal Submission (US case), para. 121 of EC Rebuttal Submission (Canada case), paras. 97-98 of EC Replies to Panel Questions, paras. 76-77, 150 and 155-156 of US First Submission, paras. 35-40 and 46 of US Rebuttal Submission]

EC Comments

The European Communities notes the different and in some parts contradictory statements by the four experts that replied to this question. It agrees with the reply of *Dr. Cogliano*. It also agrees that if GVP is not followed, the risk is even higher. For the benefit of *Dr. Guttenplan*, the EC would clarify that the term "potential" in the SPS Agreement has indeed been interpreted by the Appellate Body in the 1998 *Hormones* case to mean "possible" (at para. 185 of the report).

The position of *Dr. Boobis* and that of *Dr. Boisseau* is conditioned by their understanding that oestradiol-17β is causing cancer only through receptor mediated processes. This hypothesis is however scientifically no longer tenable in light of more recent evidence cited by the European Communities. Reading between the lines of their replies, however, these two experts also do not seem to deny completely the existence of possible adverse effects from residues in meat from animals treated with this hormone for growth promotion purposes.

Q16. Does the scientific evidence relied upon in the SCVPH Opinions support the conclusion that carcinogenic effects of the hormones at issue are related to a mechanism other than hormonal activity? [see para. 148 of the EC Replies to Panel Questions and paras. 35-40 and 46 of US Rebuttal Submission]

EC Comments

The European Communities disagrees with the statements of *Dr. Boisseau* and *Dr. Boobis*. For *Dr. Boisseau* there is only one other authoritative source of comparison, that is the JECFA reports, irrespective of the outdated nature of its reports and old data on which they are based. In his long reply, *Dr. Boisseau* interprets lack of data as lack of adverse effects. Is this really a valid approach that is followed by JECFA? *Dr. Boisseau* further criticises the SCVPH assessments on the ground that they did not include a "quantitative assessment" of the risk or that it did not establish its genotoxicity with data from experiments *in vivo*. *Dr. Boisseau* does not probably know that the Appellate Body has held that a *qualitative* assessment of risk is acceptable for the purposes of the *SPS Agreement*. Moreover, he does not consider the other more recent evidence cited by the European Communities showing the direct genotoxic potential of oestradiol-17β, progesterone, zeranol and most possible testosterone. As regards MGA and trenbolone acetate the evidence may be inconclusive but there are sufficient indications to treat them as such, despite the serious gaps in our scientific knowledge.

Amongst the flaws in *Dr. Boobis'* reply is that he criticises the EC assessment for not having evaluated these hormones "on a weight of evidence" basis. However, this type of criticism is scientifically inaccurate and legally inappropriate for the purposes of the *SPS Agreement* for the reasons explained in the EC's comments on the reply to question no 12 above. Moreover, he states that "*JECFA concluded that whilst oestradiol is a human carcinogen, its mode of action is such that there would be no appreciable risk of cancer at exposures up to the ADI*". JECFA's statement that there is no appreciable risk is a subjective expression, but it does confirm that there is excess risk due to added hormone. Again, "appreciable risk" is a qualitative and not a quantitative term, and thus fails to provide the necessary assurance that the EC's level of protection of no risk from residues of these hormones in meat will be achieved.

Dr. Guttenplan makes a more informed assessment of the scientific situation and concludes that the more recent evidence cited by the European Communities does support the finding that the genotoxic action of these hormones is not related only to their hormonal activity. Indeed, *Dr. Guttenplan* acknowledges that the evidence is now sufficient to support a role for the estrogen metabolites which include the genotoxic, mutagenic estrogen quinones in estrogen carcinogenicity (New Eng. J. Med., 354, 270-282, 2006).

Q17. Could you comment on Canada's statement t hat "the studies commissioned by the European Communities also failed to find evidence of "catechol metabolites" – that is the oestradiol metabolites identified as the source of the genotoxic potential – in meat from treated animals"? What would be the implication of an absence or presence of catechol metabolites? [see para. 102 of Canada Rebuttal submission, EC Exhibit 51A]

EC Comments

The European Communities agrees with the statements by *Dr. Guttenplan* and *Dr. Cogliano*. Indeed, it is known that, in contrast to humans, cattle do not efficiently metabolize estradiol to catechols and this apparently explains the very low levels of catechols in meat. Furthermore, the real problem is not to prove the presence of catechols as residues in edible tissues, but to determine the real part of estradiol, estradiol-alpha or estrone that will be metabolised in catechols in target tissues. Due to their structure, catechols metabolites eventually found as residues in edible tissue of treated cattle would exist more probably as glutathione conjugates and only a small part of them as glucuronides. Nevertheless, due to their chemical reactivity, catechols as such are not stable enough because they are already transformed in a more stable form. Therefore, more worrying from the human health point of view is the part of estrogens (estradiol, estradiol-alpha or estrone) which will be metabolised in catechol derivatives in target tissues. This is the reason for which it is necessary to perform a complete residue analysis with more powerful detection methods. Thus, as *Dr. Guttenplan* correctly states, the lack of catechols in meat does not imply that meat from estrogen-treated cattle is without risk for genotoxicity.

Indeed, it is important to keep in mind that in the ACI rat, mammary tumors were not induced by the administration of the catechol metabolites of estradiol, but only by administration of estradiol. Furthermore, the fact that exposure to the catechol metabolites does not cause mammary tumorigenesis does *not* necessarily negate the possibility that the catechol metabolites formed in mammary tissue play a role in mammary tumorigenesis. This is because administered metabolites may not reach levels in mammary tissue comparable to those achieved by metabolism of estradiol to the catechols within the mammary tissue itself. Analysis of both human and mouse mammary tissue has demonstrated the presence of catechol metabolites and conjugates of estrogen quinones with glutathione, the latter demonstrating that oxidative metabolism of estradiol to the catechols and their further oxidative metabolism to reactive estrogen quinones occurs in normal human and mouse mammary tissue (Carcinogenesis, 22, 1573-1576, 2001; Carcinogenesis, 24, 697-702, 2003).

As regards the statements by *Dr. Boisseau* and *Dr. Boobis,* they can only be explained by their lack of specific expertise on these hormones, as they have not carried any specific research on these substances in their professional life. Their statements therefore should carry no weight. Indeed, it should be recalled that during the 1997 panel report on hormones, one of the experts for the panel (Dr. G. Lucier) had stated:

> "For every million women alive in the United States, Canada, Europe today, about a 110,000 of those women will get breast cancer. This is obviously a tremendous public health issue. Of those 110,000 women get breast cancer, maybe several thousand of them are related to the total intake of exogenous oestrogens from every source, including eggs, meat, phyto-oestrogens, fungal oestrogens, the whole body burden of exogenous oestrogens. And by my estimates one of those 110,000 would come from eating meat containing oestrogens as a growth promoter, if used as prescribed."

However, the Appellate Body in 1998 denied evidentiary value to Dr. Lucier's statement for the reason that his opinion "... does not purport to be the result of scientific studies carried out by him or under his supervision focusing specifically on residues of hormones in meat from cattle fattened with such hormones ...". (at para. 198 of the 1998 Appellate Body report)

In this case, Dr. Boisseau has explicitly admitted that he has never carried any experiments on hormones and has published no scientific paper, and the same applies for Dr. Boobis who does not appear to have any publication on hormones either.

Q18. Please comment on the US argument that the European Communities fails to demonstrate through scientific evidence that oestradiol-17β is

genotoxic. Would your reply have been different at the time of adoption of the EC Directive in September 2003? If so, why? [see paras. 118-119 of EC Rebuttal Submission (US case), paras. 123-124 of EC Rebuttal Submission (Canada case), paras. 87-91 and 153-156 of US First Submission, paras. 35-40 and 46 of US Rebuttal Submission, and paras. 90-97 of Canada Rebuttal Submission]

EC Comments

The European Communities agrees with the statements by *Dr. Guttenplan* and *Dr. Cogliano*. The evidence both *in vitro* and *in vivo* was already strong at the time of adopting the EC Directive and it is even stronger now establishing the direct genotoxic action of oestradiol-17β. In support of *Dr. Guttenplan's* statement that the evidence for the genotoxicity of estradiol is now stronger, see *New Eng. J. Med., 354, 270-282, 2006.*

The question is not whether the European Communities has established that genotoxicity and cell proliferation would be induced by levels found in meat residues added to the pre-existing levels occurring in exposed humans, but whether the US and Canada have demonstrated to the requisite standard of proof that this adverse effect would not occur. They both assume (as does JECFA) that it will not occur, but they have failed to prove it, as has correctly been pointed out by *Dr. Cogliano*. As mentioned above, in the ACI rat model, the catechol estrogens did not cause mammary tumors; however, estradiol did cause such tumors in a dose-dependent response. Assuming greater bioavailability of estradiol and the fact that its oxidative metabolism to catechols and quinones occurs in various tissues as documented by their detection, the conclusion stated by *Dr. Guttenplan* that their absence in meat does not imply that meat from estrogen-treated cattle is without risk is correct.

The statement by *Dr. Boisseau* is beside the point, since the argument is hardly convincing that in 1999 JECFA established for the first time an ADI "in order to present in a more convincing way the outcome of its assessment". There is no trace of such an argument in the 1999 JECFA report which, it should be recalled, had found for the first time that "oestradiol-17β has genotoxic potential" (this admission was not in its 1988 report). Equally, the statement by *Dr. Boobis* lacks conviction because it is cast in cautious/conditional terms ("some, if not all, of the genotoxicity observed in vitro *would be expected* to exhibit a threshold..."). Again, *Dr. Boobis* appears to disregard the fact that evidence *in vivo* existed at the time that showed the direct genotoxicity of oestradiol-17β, which is reported in the 1999 SCVPH assessment and in the EC submissions to this Panel.

Q19. The European Communities states that "...it is generally recognized that for substances which have genotoxic potential (as is the case with oestradiol-17β) a threshold can not be identified. Therefore it cannot be said that there exist a safe level below which intakes from residue should be considered to be safe. Therefore the fact that doses used in growth promotion are low is not of relevance". Does the scientific evidence referred to by the

European Communities support these conclusions? Would your reply have been different at the time of adoption of the EC Directive in September 2003? If so, why? [see para. 201 of EC Rebuttal Submission (US case), paras. 120-122 of EC Rebuttal Submission (Canada case),paras. 73 and 86-98 of Canada Rebuttal Submission, paras. 87-91 and 153-156 of US First Submission and paras. 35-40 and 46 of US Rebuttal Submission]

EC Comments

The European Communities agrees with the thrust of the statements by *Dr. Cogliano* and *Dr. Guttenplan*. Indeed, it is true that there is no reason to expect a threshold to exist for a genotoxic chemical. After all, whether cancer will occur as a result of genotoxicity or hormonal action is from the regulatory point of view less critical, as the end result is the same: human cancer. As *Dr. Guttenplan* has stated, although DNA repair can occur, it presumably is occurring at all doses and the fraction of DNA damage repaired probably does not change at physiological levels, because the repair enzymes are unlikely to be saturated. However, would it not also be true that if the rate of repair were constant, an increase in the rate of formation of DNA damage would result in an increase in the time a mutagenic lesion remained in DNA? If this were the case, then there would be an increased likelihood for mutation if cell proliferation were occurring.

The arguments of *Dr. Boisseau* and *Dr. Boobis* that there is "no good evidence" that oestradiol is genotoxic *in vivo* or that it causes cancer by a genotoxic mechanism are unfounded. There are also a number of papers showing *in vivo* genotoxicity, some of which are already mentioned in the 1999 SCVPH report. Moreover, there are a number of scientific papers linking clearly elevated levels of 17β-oestradiol and other estrogens, at specific timepoints during development, to increased cancer risk (e.g. Hilakivi-Clarke L., Cho E., Raygada M., Kenney N.: *Alterations in mammary gland development following neonatal exposure to estradiol, transforming growth factor alpha, and estrogen receptor antagonist ICI 182,780*, in J. Cell Physiol. 1997 170:279-89). The levels of 17β-oestradiol in children are so low that *Dr. Boisseau's* statement cannot be accepted scientifically. In the EC's view, it is beyond doubt that there is a link between 17β-oestradiol exposure during development (pre- and post-natal) and the risk of breast cancer later in life and this is not only due to endogenous production.

Q20. In your view, how do the European Communities' conclusions above relate to the conclusion by Codex that "establishing an ADI or MRL for a hormone that is produced endogenously in variable levels in human beings was considered unnecessary"? To what extent, in your view, has JECFA's conclusion that oestradiol "has genotoxic potential" affected its recommendations on this hormone?

EC Comments

The European Communities notes that *Dr. Boobis*, after so many assumptions and hypothesis in his reasoning of which he offers no proof, arrives at the conclusion that:

> "... a modest incremental increase in oestradiol concentration from exogenous exposure (above the ADI) might conceivably perturb endocrine effects, depending on the physiological state. However, non-endocrine effects, such as genotoxicity, will depend on the circulating concentration of oestradiol and will not vary with physiological state. Hence, the natural variations in circulating oestradiol levels should have a much greater effect on any genotoxic response than the much more modest change that could arise from the hormone in meat from treated animals, at any conceivable level arising from its use as a growth promoter ...".

This reply of *Dr. Boobis* is based on his more erroneous underlying assumptions that oestradiol-17β is not genotoxic, that there is a threshold for residues in meat from animals treated with this hormone for growth promotion purposes, and that the rate of endogenous production by prepubertal children is as stated in the JECFA report. If these assumptions are false, as the available scientific evidence clearly demonstrates, then *Dr. Boobis'* statement – which is already a qualified one - would make no sense.

In any case, for the information of *Dr. Boisseau* and *Dr. Boobis*, the European Communities recalls that in the 1997 WTO hormones panel report (i.e. the first hormones panel), the US, Canada and JECFA were arguing that oestradiol-17β is not genotoxic, and this had influenced the findings of the 1987 panel report on these hormones. Since then, as the European Communities has been consistently arguing, the genotoxicity of oestradiol-17β is no longer seriously disputed and has now for the first time been accepted and written in the 1999 JECFA report re-evaluating the three natural hormones. But JECFA was not at all sure whether the genotoxicity of oestradiol-17β is due to its receptor-mediated action or by other direct mechanisms, because it uses in its 1999 report the soft terms "the carcinogenicity of oestradiol-17β is *most probably* a result of its interaction with hormonal receptors" (emphasis added). This contrasts sharply with the more affirmative and assertive statements to the contrary by both *Dr. Boisseau and Dr. Boobis*, who, by the way, have not done any direct experiments on these hormones in their professional life and so lack specific expertise.

More importantly, as the Appellate Body has held in the 1998 *Hormones* report:

> "... in most cases, responsible and representative governments tend to base their legislative and administrative measures on "mainstream" scientific opinion. In other cases, equally responsible and representative governments may act in good faith on the basis of what, at a given time, may be a divergent opinion coming

from qualified and respected sources. By itself, this does not necessarily signal the absence of a reasonable relationship between the SPS measure and the risk assessment, especially where the risk involved is life-threatening in character and is perceived to constitute a clear and imminent threat to public health and safety...".

Indeed, in this case *Dr. Boobis* is basing his arguments on so many assumptions and hypothesis in order to arrive at the conclusion that oestradiol-17β is genotoxic only through its hormonal activity; but can *Dr. Boobis* provide the necessary assurance to the responsible risk management authorities of the EC that the residues of these hormones in meat from animals treated for growth promotion will not increase the risk of cancer? Furthermore, can *Dr. Boobis* clarify whether he believes that the evidence on which the EC based its risk assessment on genotoxicity of oestradiol does not come from "qualified and respected sources"?

It is also noteworthy that *Dr. Boobis* does not comment on other relevant evidence, for instance the fact that the US authorities also concluded for the first time in 2002 that "steroidal estrogens are *known to be human carcinogens* based on sufficient evidence of carcinogenicity in humans, which indicates a causal relationship between exposure to steroidal estrogens and human cancer." For this reason, the US 2002 Report on Carcinogens (RoC) lists steroidal estrogens as known to be human carcinogens with the clarification that this listing now "supersedes the previous listing of specific estrogens in and applies to all chemicals of this steroid class." Moreover, in the same 2002 US Report it is stated that: "Veterinary use of steroidal estrogens (to promote growth and treat illnesses) can increase estrogens in tissues of food producing animals to above their normal levels."[8]

Dr. Boisseau and Dr. Boobis consider the assessments of JECFA as the Bible, although they know that the 1988 and the 1999 JECFA assessments are outdated by today's evidence and scientific standards. The European Communities has asked JECFA back in 1998 to withhold for a couple of years its assessment in order to take into account the new evidence which was then going to become available soon as a result of the studies that have been commissioned by the European Communities following the 1998 Appellate Body report in hormones. But JECFA for unknown reasons decided not to wait, despite the lack of any kind of urgency to review the three natural hormones in 1999. The European Communities hopes that JECFA will carry soon another assessment of these hormones on the basis of the most recent evidence available.

The European Communities agrees with the statements of *Dr. Cogliano and Dr. Guttenplan*. Indeed, the European Communities is arguing that a threshold cannot be established for the incremental human exposures that would be found

---

[8]   Available at http://ntp.niehs.nih.gov/index.cfm?objectid=72016262-BDB7-CEBA- FA60E922B 18C2540.

in meat residues because there can be no assurance – and the US, Canada and JECFA did not provide one - that these additional exposures may not increase cancer risk, especially for the most sensitive parts of the population (prepubertal children), taking also into account the other identified areas of concern, such as developmental effects.

Q21. Does the scientific evidence referred to by the European Communities demonstrate that the five hormones other than oestradiol-17β, when consumed as residues in meat have genotoxic potential? Does your answer depend on whether good veterinary practices are followed? Would your reply have been different at the time of adoption of the Directive in September 2003? If so, why? [see, *inter alia*, the SCVPH Opinions and paras. 63, 83, 89-91 and 93 of US First Submission, paras. 131-136 of Canada Rebuttal Submission]

EC Comments

The European Communities is puzzled by the dismissive statements by *Dr. Boisseau and Dr. Boobis*. It is noteworthy that the 1999 JECFA report, on which they so much rely, states that *"... equivocal results have been reported for the induction of single-strand DNA breaks and DNA adducts have been seen in vivo and in vitro in some studies..."* (see WHO, technical series report no 893, at page 61). Because it is said that progesterone is not found to be mutagenic, JECFA concluded that "*on balance, progesterone has no genotoxic potential*" (emphasis added). It is recalled that no such statement was available in the 1988 JECFA evaluation report on this hormone. So, unlike *Dr. Boisseau and Dr. Boobis*, JECFA was more prudent when rejecting the genotoxicity of progesterone in 1999. Since then, more evidence has become available, as explained in the submissions of the European Communities, which increases the likelihood of possible genotoxic effects of progesterone and the other hormones. The 1999, 2000 and 2002 risk assessment by the SCVPH provide enough evidence to demonstrate that genotoxicity and other adverse effects from these hormones are possible and that there are a number of uncertainties surrounding their mechanism of action to warrant further investigation. As *Dr. Guttenplan* states, their genotoxic potential may be weak but cannot be excluded. In particular, the evidence available to the US, Canada and JECFA on the basis of which these hormones were authorised for animal growth promotion purposes, which dates in most of these hormones since the 1970s, is today not complete nor adequate to respond, with the required degree of certainty, to the gaps in our scientific knowledge which have been clearly identified in the 1999 and 2002 evaluations by the SCVPH. It should also be recalled that the European Communities did not permanently prohibit these hormones as proven carcinogens, as it did with regard to oestradiol 17β, but on a provisional basis taking into account the numerous and serious gaps in our scientific knowledge which have been clearly identified in the SCVPH assessments. The relevant question therefore is whether these two scientists, who – it should be recalled have no specific expertise on hormones - contest that there exists at least some uncertainty regarding the genotoxicity and other possible risks from the residues of these hormones in meat that have been identified by the SCVPH?

As regards the respect or not of good veterinary practice, the increased presence of these hormones in meat from cattle presumably treated with preparations containing these hormones has the potential to affect the hormone levels, in particular in infants and prepubertal children, whose levels of serum are much lower than those used by JECFA, as the more sensitive RCBA assays now demonstrate.

Q22. How would you define *in vivo* DNA repair mechanisms? How effective or relevant are *in vivo* DNA repair mechanisms with respect to potential genotoxic effects from residues of the growth promoting hormones at issue when consumed in meat? Does your answer depend on whether good veterinary practices are followed in the administration of these hormones? To what extent does the scientific material referred to by the European Communities take into account these mechanisms in its evaluation of potential occurrence of adverse effects from residues of growth promoting hormones? Would your reply have been different at the time of adoption of the Directive in September 2003 and if so, why? [see para. 40 and 46 of US Rebuttal Submission, footnote 107 of US First Submission, and para. 89 of Canada Rebuttal Submission].

EC Comments

Dr. Boobis's reply summarises more or less accurately the difficulties authorities face with genotoxic substances by stating that: "...A major difficulty in the risk assessment of such compounds however, is the identification of the threshold for such effects. This is because they occur with low incidence, and experimental studies do not have the statistical power to determine the location of the threshold with any confidence. Thus, whilst recognizing the likelihood for a threshold for even genotoxic effects the risk assessor is faced with the impossibility of locating it. The conservative solution is to assume that the response is linear and that there is no dose below which exposure is safe." (references omitted) *Dr. Boobis* then goes on to deny direct genotoxic potential to residues in meat from these hormones. However, if his underlying assumptions concerning lack of direct genotoxicity are false, i.e. that oestradiol-17β is genotoxic and that there is no threshold for residues in meat from animals treated with this hormone for growth promotion purposes and that the rate of endogenous production by prepubertal children are much lower than those stated in the JECFA report, then *Dr. Boobis* should accept that DNA repair mechanisms are not sufficient to eliminate DNA damage.

Moreover, *Dr. Boobis and Dr. Guttenplan* appear to miss another important point. If the rate of repair were constant, an increase in the rate of formation of DNA damage would result in an increase in the time a mutagenic lesion remained in DNA. If this is the case, then there would be an increased likelihood for mutation if cell proliferation were occurring. *Dr. Guttenplan* states that "...most DNA damage by any agent is repaired and there is considerable redundancy in DNA repair, insuring that repair is effective. However, a small fraction of damage inevitably escapes repair ...". The implication of this should be that the unrepaired fraction would be increased with an increase in the rate of damage formation resulting from increased exposure to estradiol and the resulting estrogen genotoxic metabolites. In other words, a higher rate of damage may be accompanied by an increased fraction of unrepaired potentially mutagenic lesions.

The European Communities notes also the interesting statements by *Dr. Guttenplan* that "... there is no reason to assume that DNA repair processes involved in DNA damage produced by estrogen metabolites are any more or less effective than those involved in repair of other carcinogens ...", and that "... since it is not likely to be different for estrogen derived damage than other types of damage it is not really relevant [if this is not examined in detail by the SCVPH]. There is some evidence referred to in the SCVPH Opinions that error-prone DNA repair of certain estrogen derived damage can occur."

Q23. To what extent is it necessary or possible to take into account the "long latency period" of cancer in the conduct of a risk assessment, which is supposed to assess carcinogenic effects of these hormones when consumed in meat? Have the hormones in dispute been used as growth promoters over a sufficient number of years for an assessment of their long-term effects on human health to be made? [see para. 149 of EC Rebuttal Submission (US Case), para. 143 of EC Rebuttal Submission (Canada case)].

EC Comments

The European Communities notes the different and partly contradictory replies of the experts. It agrees, however, with *Dr. Cogliano and Dr. Guttenplan* that a sufficiently long latency period (at least 20 years) is extremely important. However, it is also true that such epidemiological studies will not be able to discriminate (or separate out) the true origin of cancer because of so many co-founding factors. This is admitted by both *Dr. Boisseau and Dr. Boobis*, thus undermining the position of the US and Canada that these hormones have been in use for a long time to be able to rule out their carcinogenic effects on humans. And *Dr. Boobis* concludes by stating that "...Hence, a negative result from such an observational study would not resolve the issue." However, the European Communities would recall the evidence cited in the 1999 SCVPH report – coming from the studies published by the IARC – showing that the frequency of breast cancer in countries where hormones are allowed is higher compared with countries where the hormones have not been used. Thus, this is just an indication that there might be a link between consumption of red meat and breast cancer.

Q24. To what extent is it possible to identify possible confounding factors causing cancer and attribute them to identified sources? What are the im-

plications of these factors for the conduct of a risk assessment evaluating the adverse affects caused by residues of growth promoting hormones in meat? Would your reply have been different at the time of adoption of the EC Directive in September 2003? If so, why?

EC Comments

The European Communities notes that the replies of all the scientists substantially agree with the EC position and the reasons for which it was not possible to carry out such an epidemiological study after the 1998 Appellate Body report in the hormones case. Moreover, their replies also undermine indirectly the position of the US and Canada that these hormones have been in use for a long time to be able to identify and, hence, rule out their carcinogenic effects on humans. However, the European Communities would recall the evidence cited in the 1999 SCVPH report – coming from the studies published by the IARC – showing that the frequency of breast cancer in countries where hormones are allowed is higher compared with countries where the hormones have not been used. This is of course no conclusive proof, but just an indication sufficient to raise concerns about the gaps of our knowledge in this area.

Q25. **To what extent do the three recent studies referred to by the European Communities confirm a risk to human health from the consumption of meat from cattle treated with growth promoting hormones? Please also comment on the EC statement that one of the studies "was carried out after the introduction of the ban on the use of hormones for growth promotion in Europe, which means that the subjects should have been exposed to hormone-free meat in their diet. This may further imply that it cannot be excluded that the risk of cancer may be further increased if meat treated with hormones for animal growth promotion were to be consumed". [see paras. 145-148 of EC Rebuttal Submission (US case) and paras. 139-142 of EC Rebuttal Submission (Canada case), footnote 97 in para. 147 of EC Rebuttal Submission (US case), and Exhibits EC-71,72,73]**

EC Comments

The European Communities notes the different and partly contradictory views expressed by the experts. *Dr. Boobis* dismisses the relevance of the studies cited by the European Communities for reasons that have to do essentially with what he calls the "weight of the evidence" approach. But as the European Communities explained before, this approach is not appropriate nor is it required under the *SPS Agreement*. It appears that *Dr. Boobis'* strongly held views - which it is worth recalling do not come from specific research he has conducted himself on these hormones - would only change if the evidence produced by the European Communities "confirms a risk to human health". *Dr. Boobis* is apparently not restrained in displaying such strongly held views, despite the fact that JECFA's evaluation is based on data from the 1970s – 1980s, when the experiments conducted by the industry then seeking regulatory approval in the US did not comply either with the kind of criticism now levelled by Dr. Boobis against the more recent evidence produced by the European Communities. In other words, *Dr. Boobis* is now demanding evidence of positive proof of harm, which the applicant pharmaceutical industry did not disprove (i.e. the lack of possible harm) with the data it submitted for regulatory approval in the 1970s and 1980s in the US.

Dr. Boobis apparently feels no restrain as an expert to state that: "*as long as exposure does not consistently exceed the ADI, there should be no appreciable risk to human health.*" But this is both speculative and unspecific. What is an appreciable risk? How do we interpret the qualitative term "no appreciable risk"? Is it 1% or 10% or some other value? And why would a scientific expert, who is supposed to do only a risk assessment, decide what is "appreciable" risk, a task reserved normally for the risk manager? Is it not normally the task of a scientific expert in a risk assessment exercise to explain the scientific evidence and see if there is scientific uncertainty? How confident can *Dr. Boobis* be when stating that: "However, as indicated elsewhere in my responses, the evidence is against an increased risk from such exposures". Would *Dr. Boobis* accept that there is some uncertainty surrounding his statements rejecting an increased risk of cancer from the residues of these hormones in meat? And would *Dr. Boobis* contest that the evidence with which he does not agree comes from reliable and credible sources?

Another example of the "absolutist" approach by Dr. Boobis is his comment on the EC epidemiological study making a correlation between meat consumption and colorectal cancer, showing an increased frequency in the US and Australia compared to Europe. But he dismisses these results because he relates the lower risk observed in Europe by linking it with a lower meat consumption in Europe. However, the numbers showing a lower frequency of colorectal cancer is only from Northern Europe, whereas the data for meat consumption is for all European countries combined. If so, would *Dr. Boobis* accept that this data might indicate that some uncertainty exists concerning the alleged by the US and Canada safety of hormone residues in meat treated for animal growth promotion?

The European Communities agrees with the comments of *Dr. Cogliano*, who rightly summarises the issues at stake. The European Communities also agrees with the careful and scientifically sound statement by *Dr. Guttenplan* concerning the study by *Liu S and Lin YC (2004)*, in that their "... observation was not previously reported ..." and that "... the study does suggest that additional tests of zeranol should be carried out." Consequently, the relevant legal question is who is to conduct these additional experiments and what should the regulatory regime be until their results become available? One of provisionally prohibiting or one of allowing the use of these hormones for growth promotion purposes?

Q26. Does the scientific evidence referred to by the European Communities, in particular any epidemiological studies, identify a relationship between cancer and residues of hormonal growth promoters? In its risk assessment of 1999, the European Communities makes reference to the higher

rates of breast and prostate cancer observed in the United States as compared to the European Communities. Can a link be established between these statistics and the consumption of meat from animals treated with the hormones at issue? Would your reply have been different at the time of adoption of the EC Directive in September 2003? If so, why? [see pages 17-19 of 1999 Opinion of the SCVPH and related Tables A4-A5 on pages 83-91]

EC Comments

The European Communities notes the different views expressed by the experts. What is important, however, is that there appears to be some consensus for the proposition – nicely summarised by *Dr. Cogliano* – that: "... *it is possible that differences in exposure to exogenous hormones can be one cause, but the data are not sufficiently specific to establish a link between these observations.*" Indeed, *Dr. Boobis* also states that: "*There is no scientific evidence demonstrating any association between consumption of meat from animals treated with growth promoting hormones and the risk of cancer in humans. There are some studies that are consistent with such an association, but there are several other possible explanations for the findings, some of which are more plausible than hormones in meat as being causal..*" (emphasis added). And *Dr. Guttenplan* states that: "... *However, the results are at least consistent with a possible effect of hormones on breast and prostate cancer ...*".

As already explained above, their replies undermine indirectly the position of the US and Canada that these hormones have been in use for a long time to be able to identify and, hence, rule out their carcinogenic effects on humans. It should also be pointed out that the European Communities cited this epidemiological evidence in the 1999 SCVPH not as an affirmative or adequate proof but just as an indication and possible explanation. In this sense, the three experts appear to agree, although at varying degrees. Furthermore, the plausibility of the EC argument is slightly reinforced by the fact that the differences in the cancer rates observed in the European Communities and US go in the expected direction in case of an effect, with higher rates in places where hormone-treated meat is consumed; and, similarly, the study of time trends is in agreement with the use patterns of these products in animal production. Again, the European Communities advanced this argument to demonstrate that the *scientific uncertainty* is growing concerning the harmless nature of the residues of these hormones in meat and to counter the arguments of the US and Canada that there is no uncertainty surrounding the safety of residues of these hormones.

(b)   Residue analysis

Q27.   How do the residues in meat from cattle treated with the three synthetic growth promoting hormones differ from residues in meat from cattle treated with the three natural growth promoting hormones at issue?

EC Comments

The European Communities wishes to stress that the difference in the residues is not only structural/chemical but also qualitative and quantitative. For instance, one of the studies by the EC (Stephany 2001, APMIS 109, 357-364) (see exhibits EC-49 and EC-19) gives some data on residues in meat samples from the US market. In the so called "HQ clean HFC US beef" study (i.e. hormone-free meat), an average 0.004 ppb of estradiol was found, whereas in the so called "M/LQ domestic US beef" study (i.e. hormone-treated beef) an average of 0.030 ppb estradiol was present. So this study indicates that the consumption of meat from the regular US market contains *7.5 times more estrogens than in meat from untreated cattle.* This is important and completely different information from that provided in the data from the controlled studies which were conducted in the 1960s, 1970s and 1980s by the pharmaceutical industry for the purpose of seeking authorisation of these hormones in the US and Canada (and on which JECFA based its evaluations in 1988 and in 1999).

Q28.   How do the hormones naturally present in animals, meat, or human beings differ from the residues in meat of the three natural hormones used for growth promotion purposes?

EC Comments

The European Communities would note that the statement by *Dr. Boisseau* is partially incomplete and partially false. First, no estradiol-alpha is produced endogenously by humans, whereas this is the main residue in the target tissue (liver) in cattle treated with oestradiol 17β. This metabolite, when ingested by humans, is highly susceptible to give catechols in target organs (colon, liver) which may react with nucleophilic compounds and induce some disruptions. Moreover, the hormonal effect of estradiol-esters which are found as residues in treated cattle are not examined in the old data submitted by the pharmaceutical industry for the approval of this hormone, despite the fact that we know that they are orally active and probably partially absorbed in the intestine lymph circulation.

The European Communities considers the statement by *Dr. De Brabander* very informative, in particular the statements the three natural hormones used for growth promotion purposes are synthetised (prepared) from plant material and that in plant material the $^{13}C/^{12}C$ ratio is different from the $^{13}C/^{12}C$ ratio of animals. Equally, the finding that the residues of the endogenously produced natural hormones in cattle are in the 17α form (inactive) while the use of the natural hormones for growth promotion purposes may lead to residues in the ß form (active form). The first of these remarks may provide a better understanding to the simplistic argument made by the US and Canada that humans are exposed to much higher burdens of residues from these hormones when eating natural products (e.g. broccoli) and they should not worry about the little increment they receive from eating meat treated with these hormones for animal growth promotion purposes.

Q29. To what extent do the SCVPH Opinions evaluate evidence on the actual residue levels of the synthetic hormones found in meat in their assessment of the risks from such residues? Are specific references provided as to how the evidence on residues relates to the observance of good veterinary practices or lack thereof? How do they compare with the MRLs set by Codex? [see paras. 165-176 of EC Rebuttal Submission (US case); pages 55-68 of the Opinion of the SCVPH of 30 April 1999 in US Exhibit 4, para. 144 of US First Submission, Exhibits US-6 and 7, footnote 46 of US Rebuttal Submission]

EC Comments

The European Communities considers that the statement of *Dr. Boisseau* is incorrect because the 1999 opinion of the SCVPH was structured in two levels: one making the analysis stated by *Dr. Boisseau*, but also a second one where an exposure assessment was nevertheless made to residues of the synthetic hormones (trenbolone, zeranol and MGA) in meat, in particular to underscore the point that the ADIs fixed by JECFA are most likely to be exceeded as regards specifically prepubertal children, taking into account their low levels of endogenous production. Specific reference can be made to paras. 165-176 of the EC's rebuttal submission and to the clearly marked sections of the 1999 SCVPH opinion. The European Communities not only considered the ADIs and MRLs set by JECFA but went even further and examined the tolerance levels recommended by the USA. Moreover, it is obvious, even from a cursory look at the 1999 and 2002 SCVPH opinions, as well as from the Exhibits EC-65, 67, 68, 69, 70 and 73, that the European Communities did examine the consequences from observance or lack thereof of GVP.

The statement by *Dr. De Brabander* confirms the EC argument that the data used by JECFA are not only too old but have also been obtained with methods that are no longer reliable today. This may also explain why the parties and JECFA have so strongly refused to provide those data to the European Communities and the Panel.

Q30. To what extent do the SCVPH Opinions evaluate evidence on the actual residue levels of the three natural hormones in meat in their assessment of the risks from such residues? Is it possible to compare these to the ADIs recommended by JECFA in 1999? Are specific references provided as to how the evidence on residues relates to the observance of good veterinary practices or lack thereof? [see paras. 120-123 and 155-164 of EC Rebuttal

Submission (US case), pages 33-54 of 1999 Opinion in Exhibit US-4, para. 144 of US First Submission, and 52ⁿᵈ JECFA Report in Exhibit US-5]

EC Comments

For the reasons already explained above regarding the synthetic hormones, the European Communities considers that the statement of *Dr. Boisseau* is also incorrect as regards the three natural hormones. Specific reference can be made to paras. 155-164 of the EC's rebuttal submission and to the clearly marked sections of the 1999 SCVPH opinion. The European Communities not only considered the ADIs and MRLs set by JECFA but went even further and examined the acceptable levels and tolerances recommended by the USA. Moreover, it is obvious, even from a cursory look at the 1999 and 2002 SCVPH opinions, as well as from the exhibits EC-65, 67, 68, 69, 70 and 73, that the European Communities did examine the consequences from observance or lack thereof of GVP.

The European Communities considers that the statement by *Dr. Boobis* is clearly wrong. In section 4.1.5 of the 1999 opinion, the SCVPH made a detailed exposure assessment both for the ADI established by JECFA and the acceptable levels and tolerance recommended by the US authorities. It is recalled that JECFA did not recommend MRLs for the different types of tissue, while the US has identified acceptable levels. Therefore, for comparative purposes and in order to be exhaustive, the SCVPH had to apply conversion rates. The result was that the ADI recommended by JECFA (0-50 ng/kg bw/day) is lower than that recommended by the US (102 ng/kg), as calculated by the SCVPH on the basis of the acceptable levels for individual tissues. However, both the JECFA and the US values are based on endogenous production by prepubertal children that the SCVPH found to be too high.

As the SCVPH found that the US acceptable levels and recommended tolerance will be exceeded by about 1,700 fold times, it was obvious that the JECFA ADI, which is lower than the recommended US tolerance, will also be necessarily exceeded. The SCVPH exposure assessment is made for prepubertal children, as the most sensitive part of the population. Moreover, the data used in section 4.1.5 of the 1999 SCVPH report are based on residue values that are assumed to result from administration of these hormones that respects use as authorised in the US ("GVP"). Indeed, Table A3 attached as Annex to the 1999 opinion uses the TMDI from the 1999 JECFA report. There is another section in the 1999 SCVPH opinion (section 3.3), which discussed the higher residue values that will result inevitably from misuse and abuse. It should also be added, that the same methodology and reasoning was applied for the other 2 natural hormones.

While it is admitted that an exposure assessment on natural hormones is a difficult task that has to cope with many uncertainties and may therefore not be as straightforward as desired, *Dr. Boobis* opinion that the European Communities did not carry out an appropriate exposure assessment is clearly not justified.

Q31. Please comment on the US statement that "concentrations of oestra-diol-17β in meat from treated cattle do not vary significantly from concentrations in untreated cattle, i.e., residue levels in meat from hormone-treated cattle are well within the physiological range of residue levels in untreated cattle. While tissue concentrations of oestradiol-17β in treated cattle may be slightly higher than those in untreated cattle, this increase is much smaller than the large variations observed in (reproductively) cycling and pregnant cattle and is thus well within the range of naturally observed levels." In your reply please take into account the US 11th Carcinogenesis Report where it is stated that "Meat and milk may contain estrogens. Veterinary use of steroidal estrogens (to promote growth and treat illness) can increase estrogens in tissues of food-producing animals to above their normal levels" and the statement by the European Communities that "meat consumption from pregnant heifers is exceptional as usually these animals are not slaughtered. [see paras. 51 and 144 of US First Submission and Exhibits US-6 and 7, para. 98 of EC Replies to Panel Questions, Exhibit EC-101, and paras. 2.3.2.3 of the 1999 Report of SCVPH]

EC Comments

The European Communities considers that *Dr. Boisseau's* reply accepts the US statement without much questioning. However, in the US statement there exist phrases which are imprecise and possibly misleading, such a "… do not vary significantly …", "… well within the physiological range …", "… may be slightly higher …". Neither the US nor *Dr. Boisseau* explain what is significant or what is the physiological range, as we know that the values for these concepts can vary substantially. For example, as explained by *Dr. De Brabander* in his reply to question no 27, one of the studies conducted by the European Communities indicates that the consumption of meat from the regular hormone treated meat market in the US contains 7.5 times more estrogens than in meat from untreated cattle. Moreover, *Dr. Boisseau* did not comment on the part of the question relating to the US 11th Carcinogenesis Report where it is stated that "Meat and milk may contain estrogens. Veterinary use of steroidal estrogens (to promote growth and treat illness) can increase estrogens in tissues of food-producing animals to above their normal levels." Indeed, in this 11th US report the terms "can increase estrogens in tissues of food producing animals to above their normal levels" do not explain by how much above their normal levels – supposing one could define such normal levels – could such an increase be. These issues are not unimportant, as the earlier comments of the European Communities on the absence of a threshold have demonstrated. Given the much lower levels of endogenous production of these hormones by prepubertal children, the European Communities considers that the reply by *Dr. De Brabander* rightly points out the increased risk which repetitive exposure to such higher residues can present to the most sensitive parts of the population.

Q32. Please comment on the conclusions of the EC risk assessment (Opinion of the SCVPH of April 2002) that ultra sensitive methods to detect residues of hormones in animal tissues have become available but need further validation. What is the significance of this with regard to identifying whether the natural hormones in meat are endogenously produced or are residues of hormones used for growth promotion purposes?

EC Comments

The reply by *Dr. Boisseau* is scientifically unsound. As is very well explained by *Dr. De Brabander's* statement, there is an urgent need to apply the latest analytical methods to determine the nature and level of the residues from these hormones and all their metabolites, in view of the widespread use of meat and meat products. Moreover, precisely because of the endogenous production of the three natural hormones, it is imperative that the analytical method used should be able to determine accurately the true origin of residues in meat and their magnitude (i.e. endogenous or exogenous source).

Q33. What were the reasons for the re-evaluation by JECFA of the three natural hormones in 1999? Were the residues data used for the three natural hormones in 1999 the same as those used in 1988? What additional information was used for the JECFA evaluation in 1999 of the three natural hormones which was not available in 1988? How did the conclusions differ? What led JECFA to establish ADIs for the three natural hormones? What are the implications of establishing ADIs? Why were JECFA's more recent recommendations not considered by the Codex Committee on Residues of Veterinary Drugs in Food? What is the status of these recommendations? [see paras. 96-97 of EC Rebuttal Submission (US case), paras. 79-80 of EC Rebuttal Submission (Canada case)]

EC Comments

The European Communities notes the conflicting replies of *Dr. Boisseau and Dr. Boobis* on the reasons for which JECFA decided to evaluate the three natural hormones in 1999 and on the significance of the establishment of ADIs for the first time.

The European Communities notes also the reply of *Dr. Boisseau* that the data on residues used in 1999 where the same as those used in 1988, in other words dated from the 1970s. As *Dr. De Brabander* correctly explains, these data should no longer be considered to be credible and reliable. It is therefore imperative that JECFA discloses to this Panel and the public the residues data it used in 1999 in order to verify in an open and objective manner the credibility and validity of its conclusion on the existence of a threshold, the lack of genotoxicity, etc.

Dr. Boobis admits that the 1988 evaluation was made by JECFA even without toxicological monographs, which means, *inter alia*, that for the two synthetic hormones – trenbolone acetate and zeranol – which have not been evaluated since 1988, JECFA's conclusions are no longer reliable. Moreover, *Dr. Boobis* accepts that: "…in the intervening time from the first to the second evaluation, it became clear that exposure to the natural hormones, albeit at levels appreciable higher that found in meat from treated cattle, could have adverse effects in humans. Hence, the implicit conclusion was that it was necessary to establish ADIs, to serve as health based guidance values. These could then be used as a benchmark for comparison with exposure via the diet." It is therefore remarkable that in the end JECFA did not recommend MRLs.

Q34. Please comment on the EC argument that the 1999 JECFA report based its findings on (a) outdated residues data and (b) not on evidence from residues in meat but on studies with experimental animals and on general studies of IARC. If the data were not new, did JECFA take this into account in its evaluation? What are the implications of using such data for the purpose of conducting a risk assessment? How reliable are extrapolations from animal studies to possible adverse effects on humans? How does this compare with the kind of data and studies used with respect to other veterinary drugs? [see para. 120 of EC Rebuttal Submission (US case), para. 102 of EC Rebuttal (Canada case)]

EC Comments

The European Communities notes that both *Dr. Boisseau and Dr. De Brabander* agree in that the data used by JECFA in 1999 are old (since well before 1987). *Dr. Boisseau* usefully clarifies that some of them have even not been published in peer-reviewed scientific journals, as has been consistently arguing the European Communities in these proceedings. However, the argument advanced by *Dr. Boisseau* to minimise the importance of their old nature is not scientifically sound. For example, *Dr. Boisseau* does not explain how would it be possible to integrate in the risk assessment procedure conducted by JECFA in 1999 the residues of estradiol-esters and estradiol-alpha given that their specific hormonal or metabolic characteristics were not examined at all in the 1988 data? Moreover, concerning estradiol-alpha, which is the main metabolite found in target tissue (liver) of treated cattle and which we know that it will be metabolised in catechol derivatives, no specific evaluation of this genotoxic mechanism of action has been performed by JECFA. Against this background, is it possible for Dr. Boisseau that the quality of the data used by JECFA in 1999 was scientifically credible?

As has been explained above, on the critical questions of genotoxicity and the existence of a threshold, the level of endogenous production of the natural hormones by pre-pubertal children, etc., JECFA's evaluation hinged on a number of instances "on the balance" of the evidence (e.g. on the genotoxicity of oestradiol, progesterone, zeranol, etc.). Can *Dr. Boisseau* provide an assurance to the European Communities that JECFA's conclusions would have not been different if more recent and accurate data were available to it?

Q35. Please comment on the European Communities claim that nearly all the studies referred to in the 2000 JECFA report on MGA date from the 1960s and 70s. Is this correct? Have subsequent reports of JECFA, prior or subsequent to the adoption of the EC Directive, also relied on the same studies? [see para. 171 of EC Rebuttal Submission (US case), para. 161 of EC Rebuttal Submission (Canada case), para. 55, including footnote 60 of US First Submission and Exhibits CDA-20, 33, 34, and 35]

EC Comments

The European Communities notes that both *Dr. Boisseau and Dr. De Brabander* agree in that the data used in 2000 by JECFA for MGA date from the 1960s and 1970s. The explanation offered by *Dr. Boisseau* is not valid for basic the same reasons as those stated in its comment to the previous question. For instance, the "low-dose" issue was not recognised in peer-reviewed literature before the mid 90s. Thus, all the research into possible low-dose effects has not been considered in the 2000 JECFA report. In the light of the new evidence provided by the European Communities in its risk assessment of 1999, 2000 and 2002, showing so many gaps and uncertainties in our knowledge on MGA, can *Dr. Boisseau* assure the Panel that all the relevant and necessary scientific aspects about the safety of MGA have been completely and properly analysed and assessed or is it rather fair to say that there is a need for further research because of scientific uncertainties?

(c)   Dose-response relationship

Q36. How would you describe a dose-response assessment? Is it, as suggested by Canada in para. 78 of its Rebuttal Submission, "widely, if not universally, accepted that adverse effects arising from hormonal activities are dose-dependent"? Is dose-response assessment a necessary component of hazard characterization? Or, is there an alternative approach which can replace the dose-response assessment. Is a dose-response assessment feasible/necessary for substances that are found to be genotoxic or to have genotoxic potential? [see para. 153 of EC Replies to Panel Questions, para. 200 of EC Rebuttal Submission (US case); paras. 143, 154, and 156 of US First Submission, paras. 70-74 of US Replies to Panel Questions, and paras. 34 and 37-40 of US Rebuttal Submission; paras. 76-82 of Canada Rebuttal Submission]

EC Comments

The European Communities agrees with *Dr. Cogliano's* statement that "dose-response assessment is not a necessary component of hazard characterization." This is also consistent with the Appellate Body's 1998 decision in the *Hormones* case that a qualitative assessment of the risk is acceptable under the SPS Agreement. The European Communities also notes that *Dr. Boobis* accepts that "in Europe and generally within JECFA, once a compound is identified as an in vivo

DNA-reactive mutagen, or as causing a carcinogenic response via a genotoxic mode of action, no exposure is considered without risk...". The European Communities also notes that the approach for such compounds that are known or assumed to exhibit no threshold in their dose-response curve, varies from one region to another, and this possibly explains the sharp difference between the parties to this dispute. What is also important to note is that there exist no internationally agreed guidelines on this issue, in the sense of Article 5.1 of the *SPS Agreement*. In the light of *Dr. Boobis* reply, the fact that the US and Canada have been arguing, on the basis of experience derived from their domestic practice, that the European Communities did not perform a dose-response assessment in this case is not really relevant.

Q37. Do JECFA or Codex materials confirm Canada's statement in para. 80 of its Rebuttal Submission that "... while international risk assessment techniques suggest that a dose-response assessment is optional for biological or physical agents when the data cannot be obtained, a dose-response assessment should always be conducted for chemical agents ..."? [see Exhibit CDA-25]

EC Comments

The European Communities notes that Canada's argument that "...a dose-response assessment should *always* be conducted for chemical agents..." is not a scientifically sound nor a legally binding proposition. Both *Dr. Boisseau and Dr. Boobis* appear to agree with the EC argument contesting Canada's proposition. Furthermore, *Dr. Boobis* states that JECFA may consider a dose-response unnecessary for genotoxic substances, although this – in his view- "is a very unlikely occurrence for a veterinary drug because, in general, producers tend to screen out genotoxic compounds during the development process." However, *Dr. Boobis* does not probably take into account the fact that the hormones at issue have been approved in the US and Canada in the 1970s and since then the pharmaceutical industry did not carry out any kind of screening and did not generate new set of genotoxicity data.

(d)   Sensitive populations

Q38. Please describe the range of physiological (or background) levels of the sex hormones in humans and identify the variations in these levels on the basis of age, sex group, and physiological stages.

EC Comments

The European Communities notes that *Dr. Boisseau* does not appear to contest the values stated in the SCVPH but rather whether the assays have been properly validated. However, it is not very uncommon in JECFA to use data from assays which are not yet properly validated. The European Communities believes that the values from JECFA for serum 17β-oestradiol levels in prepubertal children are not correct. JECFA originally used the limit-of-detection as the "real" level when they could not measure the levels (or find it in the old literature as explained earlier). JECFA apparently questions the very low values determined by Klein et al., 1994, and *Dr. Boobis* suggest using "newer data from Klein (Klein et al., 1998)". However, Klein et al., 1998 only reports values for girls with precocious puberty, while they in the paper still refers to the original data (Klein et al., 1994) for the levels in normal prepubertal girls.

Dr. Boobis also writes that the values from another ultra sensitive bioassay (Paris et al., 2002) suggest that the levels are significantly higher, however, that assay measures estradiol equivalents (includes other natural estrogens and anything that may interact with the estrogen receptor). Nevertheless, even if the values from Paris et al., 2002 are used, they are still less than 1/3 the values shown in the table. *Dr. Boisseau and Dr. Boobis* ask if the bioassays have been properly validated. However, JECFA used the limit-of-detection when it could not measure the real values, which is clearly not acceptable! The real values for serum 17β-oestradiol in prepubertal children still remain to be properly documented. Since it is not possible to make the calculation on daily production rates without knowing the serum levels and the metabolic clearance rate in the most sensitive segment (children), and JECFA considers such data essential for determining an ADI, it must be accepted that JECFA cannot set the ADI and MRL before the values are known!

Q39. Please comment on the SCVPH opinion stating that "any excess exposure towards oestradiol-17β and its metabolites resulting from the consumption of meat and meat products presents a potential risk to public health in particular to those groups of the populations which have been identified as particularly sensitive such as prepubertal children" [see para. 147 of the EC Replies to Panel Questions]

EC Comments

The European Communities notes that the replies of *Dr. Boisseau* conflict with those of *Dr. Sippel*. The European Communities agrees with *Dr. Sippel's* assessment, who demonstrates why there are a number of sources confirming the values mentioned by Klein et al, 1994 and 1999. *Dr. Boisseau's* reply is also false, because the SCVPH has performed – unlike JECFA which based its assessment on data from 1974 - the quantitative assessment taking account the lower endogenous production levels for pre-pubertal children from the most recent and reliable data (see also comments on previous question).

Q40. The European Communities states that "the levels of endogenous production of the hormones by prepubertal children is much lower than previously thought and this finding, which is subsequent to the 1999 JECFA report, casts serious doubts about the validity of JECFA's findings on the dose-response relationship..." Please comment on the methodology used by the SCVPH to support the conclusion that hormone levels are lower than

previously thought, and in particular comment on the validity of these methodologies and their conclusions. Would your conclusions have been the same at the time of adoption of the Directive in September 2003?

EC Comments

JECFA originally used the limit-of-detection as the "real" level when they could not measure the levels. Dr. Boobis suggest using "newer data from Klein (Klein et al., 1998)". However, Klein et al., 1998 only reports values for girls with precocious puberty, while they in the paper still refers to the original data (Klein et al., 1994) for the levels in normal pre-pubertal girls. *Dr. Boobis* also writes that the values from another ultra sensitive bioassay (Paris et al., 2002) suggest that the levels are significantly higher, however, that assay measures estradiol equivalents (includes other natural estrogens and anything that may interact with the estrogen receptor). Nevertheless, even if the values from Paris et al., 2002 are used, they are still less than 1/3 of the JECFA values shown in the table. The real values for serum 17b-oestradiol in prepubertal children still remain to be properly documented, although *Dr. Sippel* provides convincing explanations and arguments to accept as valid the results from the RCBA assay.

Q41. Why would individuals with the lowest endogenous hormone levels be at greatest risk? How would the risks for these individuals arising from hormones naturally present in meat differ from the risks arising from the residues of hormone growth promoters?

EC Comments

The European Communities considers that the replies of the experts confirm the basic concerns in the 1999 SCVPH risk assessment about the need to protect the pre-pubertal children, and *Dr. Sippel* has summarised correctly the reasons. The replies by *Dr. Boisseau and Dr. Boobis* as to whether the risk would be the same or different are not entirely convincing. For instance, concerning estradiol-17-esters and estradiol-alpha found as residues in treated steers (Maume et al, APMIS 109 (2001) 32-38, Maume et al, Anal Chim Acta, 483 (2003) 289-297), it would not be true that the risks are the same. It is preferable to establish a rigorous risk assessment evaluation by considering specific classes of residues. The European Communities considers that the most important studies available provide a bioavailability rate which is 10% or higher (see the 2nd EC Written Submission).

Q42. To what extent, in your view, has JECFA taken into account the particular situation of sensitive populations, in particular prepubertal children, in its risk assessments with respect to oestradiol-17β? Please compare the original data concerning endogenous production of natural hormones by prepubertal children upon which JECFA based its assessment and those used by the European Communities in its risk assessment. In your view, does the scientific material referred to by the European Communities re-

quire a revision of the Codex recommendation with respect to oestradiol-17β? [For the questions in this section, see paras. 121-122 of EC Rebuttal Submission (US case), paras. 103-104 of EC Rebuttal Submission (Canada case), Exhibits EC-88, 99, para. 42-45 of US Rebuttal Submission, paras. 84 and 159 of US First Submission, and for JECFA's work Exhibits CDA-11, 16, 17, 18, 39]

EC Comments

The European Communities notes the replies of *Dr. Boisseau and Dr. Boobis*, who incidentally have not carried out any research themselves on these hormones and so have no specific expertise, are very monolithic and one-sided. Their views are based again on the assumptions that this hormone is not genotoxic and that the rate of endogenous production by prepubertal children is correctly cited in the JECFA report. But if an over-estimation of endogenous levels and production rates would exist, as the more recent evidence demonstrates, then a revision would be immediately necessary. And there are so many other reasons to believe that the JECFA evaluation is scientifically wrong, as explained above (old and unreliable data, etc.), no reliance can be placed on the replies by these two experts.

(e)   Bioavailability

Q43.   Please define bioavailability, comment on the significance of bioavailability to assessments of risk, and on the degree of bioavailability of the residues of the hormones at issue when consumed in meat, taking into account parties' differing views on this matter. [see paras. 123-124 of EC Rebuttal Submission (US case), para. 105-106 of EC Rebuttal Submission (Canada case), paras. 100, 155-159 of the EC Replies to Panel Questions, paras. 32 and 41-42 of US Rebuttal Submission, paras. 69, 71, 88-89 and 146 of US First Submission, and para. 134 of Canada Rebuttal Submission]

EC Comments

The European Communities agrees with the summary on this question as stated by *Dr. Guttenplan*. Indeed, *Dr. Boisseau* writes "oestradiol-17β is inactive orally". This is simply factually wrong! Oestradiol-17β is routinely administrated to humans as a powder or in the form of pills that are taken orally. For example, in the study reported by Lampit et al., 2002, the girls were administrated 8 μg conjugated oestradiol-17β in the form of encapsulated powder. Moreover, in the "benchmark study" on oestradiol-17β performed in rats (Cook et al., 1998) the rats were orally dosed with oestradiol-17β. Thus, there are no doubts that oestradiol-17β is orally active.[9] It is also not disputed that no rigorous procedure has been used to assess hormonal risk concerning estradiol-ester, in particular on absorption via the lymphatic route. It is clear that estradiol and estradiol-esters are not devoid of effect when given orally (Paris et al, APMIS, 2001).

The European Communities has provided credible recent evidence that the bioavailability of estrogen is low but not insignificant (probably between 5 and 20%, if estrone is also taken into account). Moreover, the calculations presented in the SCVPH assessment clearly that suggest that even with low percentages of bioavailability of estrogen, the levels in meat could result in bioavailable estrogen approaching the daily production rate of oestradiol in pre-pubertal children. As *Dr. Guttenplan* states, this would represent a risk factor. Neither *Dr. Boisseau nor Dr. Boobis* provide a specific reply to this other than repeating the general and hypothetical assumptions of JECFA that their bioavailability "is rather low". It should also be noted that the bioavailability of the three synthetic hormones has not been determined by JECFA.

(f)   Good veterinary practice (GVP)

Q44.   Please define "good veterinary practice" (GVP) and/or "good practice in the use of veterinary drugs" (GPVD). What are the relevant Codex standards, guidelines or recommendations relating to GVP/GPVD? Please comment on the statement by the European Communities that the definition of the GPVD is "circular and hence problematic." [see para. 88 of the EC Replies to Panel Questions]

EC Comments

The statement by *Dr. Boisseau* that "Codex did not adopt any guideline on GVP aimed at minimizing the occurrence of veterinary drug residues in animal derived food" confirms what the European Communities has always been arguing. The European Communities recalls that the Appellate Body in the 1998 *Hormones* decision has held that:

> "... We consider that the object and purpose of the SPS Agreement justify the examination and evaluation of all such risks for human health whatever their precise and immediate origin may be. We do not mean to suggest that risks arising from potential abuse in the administration of controlled substances and from control problems need to be, or should be, evaluated by risk assessors in each and every case. When and if risks of these types do in fact

---

[9]   See Cook J.C., Johnson L., O'Connor J.C., Biegel L.B., Krams C.H., Frame S.R., Hurtt M.E.: Effects of dietary 17 beta-estradiol exposure on serum hormone concentrations and testicular parameters in male Crl:CD BR rats, Toxicol Sci. 1998 44:155-68.

> arise, risk assessors may examine and evaluate them. Clearly, the
> necessity or propriety of examination and evaluation of such risks
> would have to be addressed on a case-by-case basis. What, in our
> view, is a fundamental legal error is to exclude, on an a priori ba-
> sis, any such risks from the scope of application of Articles 5.1
> and 5.2 …". (at para. 206)

The European Communities also recalls that the inspections and measurements
of hormone residues in US meat made by the European Communities revealed
that hormones were found in what was supposed to be a "guaranteed hormone-
free beef", and that the levels of one of the hormones (MGA) were too high to be
achieved by the legal dosing. The European Communities has also performed
two specific risk assessments for the US and Canada that comply with the requirements laid down in para. 206 of the Appellate Body report mentioned
above (see in particular EC exhibits 67-73). Thus, there is specific evidence
proving that GVP is not followed by at least by some meat producers in the US
and Canada. The debate on this issue demonstrates, as *Dr. De Brabander* shows,
that there is an important difference between the theoretical assumption of re-
specting GVP and real life.

**Q45. In conducting a risk assessment of specific veterinary drugs, what
assumptions are made concerning GVP, if any? How, if at all, are risks that
might arise from the failure to follow good veterinary practice in the administration of veterinary drugs addressed?**

EC Comments

As *Dr. Boisseau* states, the Codex recommendations (whether ADIs or MRLs)
"are only meaningful in countries where GVP are effectively implemented."
There is, however, plenty and undisputed evidence that frequently GVP is not
respected in the US and Canada (although Canada appears to have a slightly
better record). However, as *Dr. De Brabander* rightly explains, the argument of
Dr. Boisseau is not correct that risk assessors cannot take into account possible
misuse or abuse in their assessment, as the 1999 and 2002 SCVPH opinions
have clearly demonstrated and as *Dr. Boobis* also admits in his reply to question
no 46.

**Q46. To what extent were risks from misuse or abuse assessed by JECFA
in its evaluation of the hormones at issue? In terms of the three synthetic
hormones at issue, how is GVP relevant to the establishment of MRLs by
JECFA?**

EC Comments

Although the theoretical description by *Dr. Boobis* is more or less accurate, the
important point is that the pharmaceutical industry did not carry out any systematic experiments on possible misuse or abuse of these hormones nor did it submit

such data to the US and Canadian regulatory authorities in the 1970 and 1980s when applied for the authorisation of these substances. The result is that also JECFA, which based its evaluation on the same old data, did not consider systematically the issue of possible misuse or abuse. This is a fundamental flaw in JECFA's assessment of these hormones.

As the European Communities has already explained, even the US authorities now accept (see e.g. the 2002 US Carcinogenesis Report) that the administration of these hormones to cattle, which presumably respects GVP, leads to residue levels that exceed the levels from endogenous production. This means that when misuse or abuse occurs the excess levels are inevitably going to be much higher. According to the studies cited by the European Communities, e.g. Exhibits EC-12 and 17 and 73, the level of residues in case of misuse or abuse by far exceed the ADIs recommended by JECFA and the acceptable levels and tolerances recommended in the US and Canada.

Q47. How significant are any differences in GVP in the European Communities, the United States, and Canada? Does the EC risk assessment take into account relevant control mechanisms with respect to GVP in place in the United States and/or Canada? If so, what are their conclusions?

EC Comments

The statement of *Dr. Boisseau* is partly false. The European Communities has carried out a specific assessment of the US and Canadian situation concerning respect of GVP (see EC Exhibits 67 and 68) and has taken into account the multiple sources of misuse and abuse that frequently occur there (see EC Exhibits 69 -70, and 71-72, 96, and 102-103). As *Dr. Boisseau* states these hormones are sold over the counter in the US and Canada, which means that there is in reality no way to control their possible misuse by the authorities there. The evidence available does show that such misuse or abuse occurs frequently, because these hormones are administered in combinations and the farmers have incentives to apply multiple doses.

Q48. To what extent does the scientific evidence referred to by the European Communities assess risks to human health from residues of misplaced implants or improper administration, i.e. when administered differently than indicated on the label of the manufacturer or contrary to GVP, of any of the six hormones? Would your reply have been different at the time of adoption of the EC Directive in September 2003? What are the potential hazards, if any, to human health of the use of large quantities, or doses higher than recommended, of any of the six hormones in dispute?

EC Comments

The criticism of both *Dr. Boisseau and Dr. Boobis* is based on their understanding that the European Communities did not perform a quantitative risk assessment, which they think is a necessary requirement for a proper risk assessment under the SPS. However, as the European Communities has explained several times in previous questions, this in not required under the *SPS Agreement* as interpreted by the Appellate Body. But as already explained, the European Communities has nevertheless performed a quantitative dose-response assessment in particular with regard to prepubertal children. As the exposure from residues in meat *treated with these hormones according to GVP* was found to lead to residues that exceeded several times the ADIs and MRLs, it is obvious that the higher levels of residues that will inevitably result from misuse or abuse of these hormones will also exceed the ADIs and MRLs recommended by JECFA.

Furthermore, *Dr. Boobis* states that "...the potential risk, i.e. the probability that effects would occur, would depend on a number of factors...". But as the European Communities has already explained, the risk and risk assessment under the *SPS Agreement*, as interpreted by the Appellate Body, is not the "probability" of the identified risk occurring but the "possibility" of the identified risk occurring under real conditions of use.

Q49. What analytical methods, or other technical means, for residue detection in tissues exist to control the use of the six hormones in dispute for growth promotion purposes in accordance with good animal husbandry practice and/or good veterinary practice? What tools are available to control the use by farmers of the six hormones in dispute for growth promotion purposes in accordance with good animal husbandry practice and/or good veterinary practice?

EC Comments

To the list of tools listed by *Dr. De Brabander* to control the possible misuse or abuse of these hormones, the European Communities would add that these hormones should not be sold freely on the counter but by veterinary prescription only. Of course all these apply only for the countries that would be prepared to assume that the possible risk would not undermine their chosen level of health protection.

Q50. Are there other measures available to the European Communities (other than a complete ban) which could address risks arising from misuse and failure to follow good veterinary practice with respect to the use of the hormones at issue for growth promotion purposes? Would your reply have been different at the time of adoption of the EC Directive in September 2003? If so, why?

EC Comments

The European Communities notes that the replies by *Dr. Boisseau and Dr. De Brabander* agree on the point that if GVP is not respected, then the importing country should have the right to restrict imports, even with a total ban, depending on the importing country's chosen level of health protection.

Q51. Does the material put forth by the European Communities regarding misuse or abuse of the hormones at issue in the United States and Canada call into question the potential applicability of Codex standards with regard to imports of meat from cattle treated with hormones from the United States and Canada?

EC Comments

The European Communities understands that the answer by *Dr. Boisseau* to this question is that the Codex standards would not be applicable. The European Communities also agrees with the statement by *Dr. De Brabander*.

(g)   Other

Q52. Do the risk assessment of the European Communities or any other scientific materials referred to by the European Communities demonstrate that a potential for adverse effects on human health arises from the consumption of meat from cattle treated with any of the six hormones in dispute for growth-promotion purposes? If yes, why? If not, what kind of evidence would be required to demonstrate such potential adverse affects? Would your response have been different at the time of adoption of the Directive in September 2003?

EC Comments

The European Communities considers that the statements by *Dr. Boisseau and Dr. Boobis* are scientifically incorrect because they are based on many assumptions and conservative interpretation of the available and constantly growing evidence that directly implicates these hormones in causing and promoting cancer and a number of other adverse effects in humans. If the views of these experts were to be adopted the prerogative of cautious public authorities to regulate risk in order to reduce or eliminate it would completely vanish. *Dr. Boisseau and Dr. Boobis* apply double standards because they require for the prohibition of these hormones evidence which the pharmaceutical industry did not provide nor did it even examine when it applied for the approval of these substances in the US and Canada in the 1970s and 1980s.

Dr. Boisseau states that: "… the kind of evidence required to demonstrate such potential adverse effects should be (1) toxicological data indicating that the values of the ADIs established by JECFA are not conservative enough, (2) data on residues in treated/non treated cattle and on daily production of hormones in sensitive individuals indicating that the hormonal residue intake associated with the consumption of meat from treated cattle is such that the established ADIs would be exceeded in the case of use of growth promoters." The European Communities submits that such data have been provided and taken into account in the 1999, 2000 and 2002 SCVPH risk assessment, which he has apparently not properly examined.

Dr. Boobis states again that: "… *the weight of evidence* is that the hormones are not genotoxic in vivo even at doses well above those that would be present in meat from treated cattle (…) However, all of the major reviews in this topic have concluded that *whilst there are data gaps*, there is no evidence that low level exposure is causing harmful effects in humans (…) However, it should be emphasised that on the basis of the information available, I would rate the risk of adverse effects in humans consuming meat from treated cattle *as minimal*." (emphasis added). So, according to Dr. Boobis conservative reading of "the weight of available evidence", which means that scientific views outside the mainstream or the majority held view do not count for him, it cannot be excluded that there is a risk, even though this is evaluated by him to be "minimal". However, he does not explain what is "minimal" risk, nor does he seem to pay any attention to the fact that the "gaps in our knowledge – which he admits exist – may indicate that there is scientific uncertainty with potentially disastrous consequences for the consumers.

The European Communities considers that *Dr. Guttenplan* has rightly summarised the issue: the evidence which the European Communities has presented suggests that "even with low percentages of bioavailability of estrogen, the levels in meat could result in bioavailable estrogen exceeding the daily production rate of oestradiol in prepubertal children". When the evidence is not to their liking, the US and Canada contest the accuracy of the assay originally employed for estrogens at the low levels found in children. However, they consistently refuse, as dose JECFA, to provide their old data in order to examine in an open and transparent manner the kind of assays used by the pharmaceutical industry in the 1970s and 1980s for the approval of these hormones in the US and Canada. But as *Dr. Guttenplan* rightly points out, recent reports indicate that "more recently reported levels used by the EC are accurate. In addition, levels in postmenopausal women were also very low." Moreover, he explains that: "For prepubertal children, even with the low bioavailability of estrogen along with and its low levels in meats, it appears possible that intake levels would be within an order of magnitude of those of the daily production rate. This is greater than FDA's ADI and suggests some risk to this population."

Q53. Please comment on the statement by the European Communities that the natural hormones progesterone and testosterone are used only in combination with oestradiol-17β or other oestrogenic compounds in commercial preparations? Would the systematic use of these and the synthetic hormones in combination have any implications on how the scientific experiments and the risk assessments are to be carried out? If so, have the scientific materials referred to by the European Communities or relevant JECFA reports taken into account the possible synergistic effects of such combinations on human health? [see sections 4.2-4.3 of the Opinion of the SCVPH of 2002 in US Exhibit 1]

EC Comments

The European Communities notes that both *Dr. Boisseau and Dr. Guttenplan* recognise that the statement by the European Communities is correct. *Dr. Boisseau's* reply is, however, partly false because it ignores the potential stimulatory estrogen receptor mediated effects of estradiol on cell proliferation which tend to be increased by progestins (see *New Eng. J. Med., 354, 270-282, 2006).*

Moreover, *Dr. Guttenplan* accepts that "... in principle the use of mixtures should complicate risk assessments/scientific experiments, as they would have to evaluate/investigate each component alone and in combination. This is a major undertaking as effects of individual agents may be additive, inhibitory, and synergistic or there may no effect." What is even more important, he acknowledges that "... it appears that no experiments on effects of combinations were performed, so some uncertainty exists there." The European Communities submits that this is still another kind of uncertainty that should be taken into account by the Panel in deciding whether the evaluations by JECFA are credible and reliable.

Q54. What is the acceptable level of risk reflected in the Codex standards for the five hormones at issue? How does this compare to the European Communities' stated objective of "no risk from exposure to unnecessary additional residues in meat of animals treated with hormones for growth promotion". [see para. 149 of EC Rebuttal Submission (US case)]

EC Comments

The European Communities notes that *Dr. Boisseau and Dr. Boobis* differ as to the acceptable level of risk reflected in the Codex standards for the five hormones at issue: the first argues that Codex's "... ADI represents the quantity of these residues which can be ingested daily by consumers over life time *without causing any problem* of health ...", but the reply of the second suggests that the level is "*no appreciable risk with daily exposure*". If one were to follow *Dr. Boisseau's* reply, then there is no doubt, and most of the experts have explicitly accepted it, that there is a risk although for some of them – like Dr. Boobis - this is viewed as "minimal". On the other hand, if *Dr. Boobis'* reply is followed, this would mean that Codex's standard recognises that there is an scientifically identified risk but recommends its members to follow it because it thinks (as a risk manager) that it is "not appreciable". If that were the case, however, Codex and the *SPS Agreement* cannot oblige a sovereign country to accept a risk, whether it is viewed as small, medium or big. This is the autonomous right of each member to decide and the Appellate Body has explicitly said that WTO members have the right to fix a level of protection of "zero risk".

For the benefit of *Dr. Guttenplan*, Codex has *not* set an ADI or an MRL for MGA yet, since no decision has been taken by the Codex Alimentarius Commission. So, no international standard exists for MGA yet.

Q55. Do the Opinions of the European Communities or other scientific materials referred to by the European Communities evaluate the extent to which residues of growth promoting hormones in meat contribute to what the European Communities calls "additive risks arising from the cumulative exposures of humans to multiple hazards, in addition to the endogenous production of some of these hormones by animals and human beings"? Would your reply have been different at the time of adoption of the EC Directive in September 2003? If so, why? [see para. 151 of EC Replies to Panel Questions, paras. 43-44 of US Rebuttal Submission, paras. 83-85 of Canada's Rebuttal Submission]

EC Comments

The European Communities disagrees with *Dr. Boisseau's* reply that its position is "a position of principle" or that it is based on economic grounds (as he implied with his reply to the previous question). The time, effort and money spent by the European Communities to clarify the scientific issues identified by the Appellate Body in its 1998 report on *Hormones* clearly establish that the EC's position and legislation are based on sound and up to date scientific grounds. The precautionary principle comes after proper consideration of the scientifically identified and analysed risk.

Dr. Boobis accepts that additive risks arising from the cumulative exposures is a scientifically sound approach and that can and is done in some cases. From his reply, one may infer that he accepts that this is not done by JECFA nor by the US and Canada. He only thinks this is not appropriate for these hormones because of his preconceived approach that there is a dose-response relationship (threshold) in the carcinogenic mode of action of these hormones.

The European Communities disagrees with the statements by *Dr. Boisseau and Dr. Boobis* for the reasons that have been developed extensively in its submissions and in some of its comments above. It urges the Panel to disregard their comments because they are purely theoretical and for the additional reason that they come from two experts that have never done any specific research on these hormones nor have they ever published something on these substances. Instead of criticising the risk assessment produced by the European Communities, these experts should have examined in their replies whether such an additive risk assessment ought to have been examined by JECFA in the first place before issuing the recommendation that the risk is "not significant".

The European Communities notes that *Dr. Guttenplan* would have liked to see much more evidence in the 1999 SCVPH assessment. To the extent this was not provided in 1999 and in 2002, this is not because of omission but because the state of scientific knowledge available by then – i.e. the gaps and scientific uncertainty clearly identified in those opinions – did not allow such an assessment to be completed.

Q56. Has JECFA/Codex considered in its risk assessment of the five hormones such "additive risks? Are there internationally recognized guidelines for conducting assessments of "additive risks"?

EC Comments

The European Communities disagrees with both *Dr. Boisseau's and Dr. Boobis'* replies. They provide no precise reference of where in the JECFA 2000 report it is stated that such a cumulative risk assessment was carried out. The European Communities understands that such a cumulative assessment of the additive risk has *not* been performed (and this is also what apparently *Dr. Guttenplan* believes, as words seem to be missing from his reply).

The European Communities notes that it has clearly been shown that the effects from exposure to different estrogens are additive; i.e. when several estrogens are given simultaneously at concentrations where none of them alone results in any detectable effects, the combined exposure leads to a clear effect. Thus, any additional dose will lead to an increased effect (Rajapakse N., Silva E., Kortenkamp A.: Combining Xenoestrogens at Levels below Individual No-Observed-Effect Concentrations Dramatically Enhances Steroid Hormone Action., Envir. Health Perspec. 110, 917-921 (2002); and Tinwell H., Ashby J.: Sensitivity of the Immature Rat Uterotrophic Assay to Mixtures of Estrogens, Envir. Health Perspec.112, 575-582 (2004)). Moreover, there are several hormonal preparations containing two hormones (estradiol plus trenbolone) and there are several publications in the animal science literature recommending different preparations in consecutive applications. Therefore, the additive risk needs to be carefully evaluated. For instance, trenbolone as such has a complex hormonal activity (at the same time progestin, androgen and glucocorticoid). Estradiol and trenbolone residues therefore may have 4 different hormonal activities.

The European Communities further notes that although there is agreement that "there is no international agreement on how to undertake a combined risk assessment of compounds acting by the carcinogenic mechanisms suggested by the EC for the hormones, i.e. genotoxicity via direct or indirect interaction with DNA", yet the performance of such a risk assessment is not impossible. The European Communities has tried to do such an assessment when the information available was sufficient, but could not complete it because of gaps in our scientific knowledge.

Q57. Canada comments that "one single molecule that the European Communities considers so dangerous from meat derived from animals treated with hormone growth promoters is suddenly not at all that dangerous when consumed from meat from animals treated for therapeutic or zootechnical purposes. The European Communities' concern about the genotoxic potential of oestradiol-17β suddenly and inexplicably disappears." To what extent are hormone treatments of cattle for purposes other than growth promotion, such as for therapeutic or zootechnical purposes, taken into account by the European Communities, if at all, in its assessment

of the cumulative effects from the consumption of meat containing residues of the hormones at issue? Would your reply have been different at the time of adoption of the EC Directive in September 2003? If so, why? [see para. 97 of Canada Rebuttal Submission; paras. 17-20 of US Opening Statement]

EC Comments

The European Communities considers that asking this question in the first place was unnecessary and irrelevant, because the Appellate Body did not find any violation from the use of some of these hormones for therapeutical or zootechnical purposes. As *Dr. Guttenplan* points out, the conditions imposed by the European Communities for such limited use are such that it would not be possible to undermine its chosen level of protection.

Therefore, the European Communities is consistent because the use of oestradiol for such purposes is now virtually terminated.

Q58. Please comment on the EC statement in para. 94 of the EC Replies to Panel Questions that "the only rationale that can be inferred from the available scientific data is that the higher the exposure to residues from these hormones, the greater the risk is likely to be", taking into account para. 105 of Canada Rebuttal Submission.

EC Comments

The European Communities needs to clarify that the quoted statement was made in response to the US and indeed Canadian argument that there is no risk from cumulative exposure to residue of these hormones in meat treated with one or several of these hormones for growth promotion purposes. Moreover, the statement is framed cautiously to say "is likely to be" precisely because such a complete cumulative risk assessment has not been carried out by JECFA and the other countries. Moreover, if the assumption of JECFA and of the US and Canada that there is a threshold is false, the relevance of the EC comment is a realistic eventuality. The European Communities has in fact provided the Panel with recent evidence (e.g. the papers by Dr. D. Sheehan, see Exhibit EC-87) which has showed the absence of such a threshold. It is indicative that none of the experts discuss it in his replies. The studies mentioned in these exhibits show that under the circumstance that the endogenous hormone is active, there can be no threshold unless metabolism is 100% effective before the dose reaches the target tissue. It is also noteworthy that none of the scientists discusses the reference made by the European Communities to the US 2002 Carcinogenesis Report which states as regards oestradiol that residues in meat from animals treated with hormones for growth promotion lead to levels higher than the endogenously produced ones. The question therefore is by how much and of what kind of biological and toxicological nature. In the EC's comments to previous questions, it has been shown that the level of residue formation in meat can be significantly higher and may contain residues from different metabolites. It seems therefore that the experts criticise the European Communities for making an assumption, but they are not apparently able to prove either that their own assumption is correct.

Q59. Does the scientific evidence referred to by the European Communities identify any adverse effects on the immune system from the consumption of meat from cattle treated with the growth promoting hormones at issue? Would your reply have been different at the time of adoption of the Directive in September 2003? If so, why? [see para. 132 of Canada Rebuttal Submission]

EC Comments

The European Communities notes the different views which the replies of the scientists display on this critical question. *Dr. Boisseau* accepts that such adverse effects have been identified, but faults the European Communities for not having conducted a "quantitative" risk assessment. *Dr. Boobis* continues with his line of argument that there is a threshold effect, which prevents this kind of adverse effects on the immune system from occurring. The point, however, is that neither the US nor Canada (and a fortiori nor JECFA) have identified such adverse effects because of the outdated nature of the data on which they based their assessments. The European Communities has offered some serious evidence, some of which appeared for the first time recently, and pointed to a number of gaps and uncertainty in our knowledge. This is recognised by *Dr. Guttenplan*, who states that "...there is evidence that estrogens can be involved in Lupus, rheumatoid arthritis, thyroiditis. In addition the development of allergies is thought to be at least partially related to estrogens. The studies in experimental animals also did not identify any immune-related effects, although it is not certain the types of possible effects in humans would be detected in experimental animals...". The question, therefore, is the degree of confidence by which the US and Canada (and JECFA) can ensure the Panel that such adverse immune effects are not possible to occur from residues in meat treated with these hormones for animal growth promotion. The European Communities thinks they have failed to do so to the required standard of proof.

Q60. Does the scientific evidence referred to by the European Communities identify and evaluate whether there is a difference in terms of potential adverse effects on human health from the consumption of meat from cattle treated with hormones for growth promotion purposes when these hormones are administered as feed additives (MGA) or implanted? Are you aware of any differences?

EC Comments

The EC contests the accuracy of the statements by *Dr. Boisseau and Dr. Boobis*. It is known that MGA is the only hormone that is administered as a feed additive, which confirms that the bioavailability of this hormone is rather high.

Moreover, it has been shown that MGA is highly lipophilic and accumulates in adipose tissue. The 1999 and 2002 SCVPH and exhibits EC-14, 16 and 19 have shown that the route of administration of MGA is conducive to misuse or abuse, as the residues of MGA detected in the US samples of meet were much higher than the levels which should have been normally expected (exhibit EC-16). The study mentioned in exhibit EC-16 has also shown that the residues in fat of oestradiol-17β increased by about 300% following labelled MGA treatment. The consequence of this is that given the tremendous "boosting" effect which MGA has on the residues of oestradiol in meat and the easiness by which its administration can be misused, the possibility to increase substantially the level of residues, and hence the risk of cancer, is significantly increased. This is not examined either by *Dr. Boisseau or Dr. Boobis*, who apparently have not read this material.

Hormone MGA has been in use in the US and Canada since the 1970s and it is interesting to note that JECFA has not been seized of a request to evaluate it until 2000. Yet, until today there is no Codex standard for MGA. It is also clear that the evidence upon which JECFA based its evaluation has not been made available to anyone, has not been published in peer-reviewed journals and it is outdated but today's standards. The most important evidence on MGA is the one generated by the EC following the Appellate Body 1998 hormones decision. This information is publicly available and demonstrates the gaps in our knowledge, the uncertainty surrounding this hormone and the multiple risks which the administration of MGA poses to human health.

As regards the risks from eating meat treated with implanted hormones, the evidence shows that non-removed implants contain milligrams of residues. These are 10^7 to 10^9 fold more residues than present in the peripheral tissue (pikograms per gram). The total dosage in an implantation site is therefore about a thousand fold higher than the residues in the whole carcass of the animal. There is no doubt that the risk from implanted hormones is in a completely different order of magnitude from the risk posed from untreated animals. *Dr. Boobis* makes again his unfounded statement that: "However, whilst this would lead to increased exposures, it is still unlikely this would exceed the ADI, and certainly not for any period of time. It is also an unlikely occurrence in view of the way in which the hormones are used and controlled." First of all, he has and provides no factual basis to argue that it is "unlikely" that misuse will exceed the ADI. Neither Codex nor JECFA have fixed yet an ADI, and even if they were to do it one day, he has now no data to suggest that it is unlikely to be exceeded. Moreover, it has already been shown that even the administration of MGA that does respects GVP leads to a tremendous "boosting" effect on the residues of oestradiol in fat and the attending risk of exceeding the ADIs is very high.

Q61. In your view and in the light of information provided by the parties as well as the work undertaken at JECFA and Codex, did the scientific evidence available to the European Communities at the time it adopted its Directive (September 2003) allow it to conduct an assessment (quantitatively

or qualitatively) of the potential for adverse effects on human health arising from the consumption of meat from cattle treated with (a) progesterone; (b) testosterone; (c) trenbolone; (d) zeranol; and (e) melengestrol acetate? Would your response differ in light of the scientific evidence provided which is subsequent to the adoption of the EC Directive?

EC Comments

The reply of *Dr. Boisseau* is surprising as the data available to the EC are mentioned in the 1999, 2000 and 2002 SCVPH assessments and the additional evidence from other sources is explained in the written submissions of the EC to the Panel and were provided as exhibits thereto. It is recalled that he has explicitly admitted that he has not done nor published any work on these hormones.

The reply by *Dr. Boobis and Dr. Boisseau* can only be explained by their exclusive reliance on the JECFA reports, which Dr. Boobis thinks represent the "weight of the evidence" that should be taken into account. This is probably not surprising, as they have both served in the JECFA panel that examined some of these hormones, although they both lack any specific expertise on these hormones, as they have not carried themselves any experiment on them when used for animal growth promotion purposes.

Their entire reasoning – whose objectivity and impartiality is therefore in great doubt for the reasons the EC has explained to the Panel during the expert selection procedure - is based on the assumption that there is a dose-response relationship (threshold), despite the accumulation of so much recent evidence showing that this assumption can no longer be valid for a number of these hormones, certainly for oestradiol 17β, progesterone, testosterone and zeranol. Their reasoning is also based on the idea that a risk assessment to be acceptable has to perform a quantitative analysis and assessment of risk even of aspects for which the available evidence is insufficient or there are total areas of gaps in our knowledge.

The EC considers that the reply by *Dr. Guttenplan*, as well as those by *Dr. Shippel, Dr. De Brabander and Dr. Cogliano* who have not expressed themselves on this precise question but this can be seen from their replies to the other questions, show that there is sufficient evidence which "does indicate that potential adverse effects exist for all of the hormones. However, the ability to make a risk assessment (qualitative or qualitative) does vary between compounds." (Dr. Guttenplan). The available evidence, at the varying degrees mentioned by *Dr. Guttenplan*, does establish that "… accurate ADI's cannot be established at this point", and that "… studies in experimental animals and studies on levels in beef are still needed." Most importantly, the EC agrees that "from the data available at the time of the Directive, the potential for adverse effects could not be ruled out."

Q62. Does the scientific evidence relied upon by the European Communities support the EC contention that the new scientific studies that have been initiated since 1997 have identified new important gaps, insufficiencies and

contradictions in the scientific information and knowledge now available on these hormones such that more scientific studies are necessary before the risk to human health from the consumption of meat from cattle treated with these hormones for growth promotion purposes can be assessed? Would your reply have been different at the time of adoption of the Directive in September 2003? If so, why?

EC Comments

The EC considers that its comments on the positions of *Dr. Boisseau and Dr. Boobis* to the previous question no. 61 are equally and fully applicable here.

It is difficult to grasp the idea of *Dr. Boisseau* for a temporary risk assessment, unless his statement was to be understood that the gaps and uncertainties identified by the EC in its risk assessment are such as to require further research and investigation.

As regards the long and dismissive reply by *Dr. Boobis*, who despite his lack of any specific expertise on these hormones tried to discredit all the studies mentioned by the EC, it is now clear on the basis of a more careful examination by a real expert of the same body of evidence that it would necessarily lead to the opposite conclusion. *Dr. Boobis'* comments on the studies generated by the EC are flawed in almost all respects.

For instance, he comments on the Leffers et al., 2001 study on the low-dose effects of Zeranol and other estrogens on gene expression in MCF7 cells. He writes: "Many of the changes will reflect the proliferative response to an oestrogenic stimulus". However, in the applied assay changes in gene expression were assayed after 24h exposure, whereas the first up-regulation of proliferation-sensitive genes becomes detectable after 36h exposure. Thus, the observed effects are a likely direct consequence of gene activation by the estrogen receptor, reflecting activation of the receptor by Zeranol and the other compounds. (see Jorgensen M., Hummel R., Bevort M., Andersson A.M., Skakkebaek N.E., Leffers H.: Detection of oestrogenic chemicals by assaying the expression level of oestrogen regulated genes. APMIS. 1998 106:245-51.)

Another example is that he dismisses the bovine metabolism of oestradiol-17β and oestrogenic potency of fatty acid residues on the unsubstantiated ground that "the difference in potency from the parent hormone is not very great or even apparent at low doses, where effects were minimal", where the opposite is rather true in the study cited. Another example is that he dismisses the relevance of the studies on misuse and abuse on the speculative ground that "... the probability that this would occur is extremely low". However, he has no evidence and provides no credible basis for that conclusion. Still another example is that he dismisses the relevance of the recent findings on the mutagenicity and genotoxicity of oestradiol-17β despite the fact that this has been shown both in vitro and now in vivo. The findings of the study he criticises for no valid reason have been largely confirmed in other recent studies supporting a role for the estrogen metabolites which include the genotoxic, mutagenic estrogen quinones in estrogen carcinogenicity (New Eng. J. Med., 354, 270-282, 2006). And the list of examples showing lack of specific knowledge or impartial presentation of the available evidence by *Dr. Boobis* is much longer.

Conversely, a more considered and objective view is to be found in the reply of *Dr. Guttenplan*, who provides some examples of the areas in which gaps and uncertainties have been identified and indicates some of the additional research that is required before the EC would be able to conduct a more complete risk assessment. The EC agrees with his comments.

ANNEX F-2

COMMENTS BY THE EUROPEAN COMMUNITIES ON THE REPLIES OF CODEX, JEFCA AND IARC ON QUESTIONS POSED BY THE PANEL

(30 June 2006)

Introduction

The European Communities appreciates this opportunity to comment on the replies of the international bodies to the questions posed to them by the Panel. The European Communities considers it necessary to recall the position it has already expressed to the Panel at the time it decided to ask questions from these bodies, namely that Codex and JECFA lack appropriate and transparent procedures for submitting this kind of comments and replies to other international organisations, such as the WTO dispute settlement bodies. In particular, replies and comments that come simply from the secretariat of those bodies, without following the legally required procedures for their internal elaboration and transmission, should be disregarded because they are likely to influence unlawfully the Panel's deliberations.

The European Communities notes that the comments submitted in these cases by those bodies do not explain whether the required internal rules and procedures for their adoption have been fully respected. Therefore, the European Communities requests the Panel to clarify this question with these bodies; in the absence of an adequate and legally sound reply – with precise references to the rules that were applied in the elaboration of their replies - the European Communities would request the Panel to disregard them.

Q1.   Please briefly describe the procedure for the elaboration and adoption of an international standard by Codex. What is the decision-making process for the adoption of an international standard?

EC Comments

The European Communities notes that according to Codex: "In the case of MRLs for veterinary drugs, submission of project documents is not required; instead, the Codex Committee on Residues of Veterinary Drugs in Foods (CCRVDF) prepares a priority list of veterinary drugs requiring evaluation or re-evaluation by JECFA, which is submitted to the Commission for approval." However, it is noteworthy that this procedure was not followed when JECFA decided to re-evaluate the three natural hormones in 1999, because the CCRVDF did not request such a re-evaluation.

The European Communities also notes the statement whereby: "The Commission attaches a great importance of achieving consensus at all stages of the elaboration of standards and that draft standards should, as a matter of principle, be submitted to the Commission for adoption only where consensus has been achieved at the technical level." However, the European Communities draws the attention of the Panel to the uncontested fact that the 1988 Codex standards for the five hormones (except MGA) were not adopted by consensus and the 1999 review by JECFA of only the three natural hormones were not even presented to Codex for adoption because the relevant committee [CCRVDF] decided not to consider them as it had not requested their re-evaluation.

Q2.   Please briefly explain the differences between Codex standards, codes of practice, guidelines, principles and other recommendations.

EC Comments

The EC has no comments at this stage.

Q3.   Please identify any international guidance documents relevant to the conduct of a risk assessment with respect to veterinary drug residues. Since when have they been available? Please also indicate if there is any relevant ongoing work at Codex.

EC Comments

As the European Communities explained by its comments to question no 3 of the Panel experts questions, its legislation complies with the *Working Principles for Risk Analysis for Application in the Framework of the Codex Alimentarius,* which where adopted by Codex in 2003, and these working principles were complied with in the assessment of the six hormones at issue and in the adoption of the Hormones Directive 2003/74/EC.

The European Communities further notes the statement that: "Following the adoption of the Working Principles, the Commission requested that relevant Codex Committees develop or complete specific guidelines on risk analysis in their respective areas for inclusion in the Procedural Manual...The two documents will be considered by the 30th Session of the Codex Alimentarius Commission in 2007 (after review by the Codex Committee on General Principles) for adoption and inclusion in the Procedural Manual." This statement confirms the EC position (see also its comments to question no 3 of the Panel experts questions) that until now there exist no guidelines on risk analysis for residues of veterinary drugs in the sense of Article 5.1 of the *SPS Agreement.* The consideration in 2007 of the two working documents does not mean that they will be adopted, if one were to judge from previous experience in the work of the Codex Committee on General Principles.

The European Communities also draws the attention of the Panel to the statement that the principles to be adopted one day will "...define the responsibilities of the various parties involved: the responsibility for providing advice on risk management concerning residues of veterinary drugs lies with the Codex Alimentarius Commission and its subsidiary body, the Codex Committee on

Residues of Veterinary Drugs in Foods, while the responsibility for risk assessment lies primarily with the Joint FAO/WHO Expert Committee on Food Additives (JECFA)." This confirms again the EC position (see also the EC Comments to question no 5 of the Panel experts questions) that such a clear definition of the responsibilities does currently not exist, and that in reality it is JECFA that is informally doing also the risk management, leaving practically no real risk management choice to the Codex members to adopt measures aiming to achieve a high level of health protection. This is clearly the situation in the case of the six hormones in dispute, since the old data used by JECFA and the way in which it drafted its reports (e.g. "genotoxic potential", "unlikely to be exceeded", "pose an insignificant risk", "MRLs considered unnecessary", etc.) in effect deprive the Codex members from applying a very high level of protection, which in the context of the WTO can be "no or zero (additive) risk" according to the Appellate Body.

The European Communities considers that the reply of JECFA confirms the EC position that there exists currently no international guidance documents relevant to the conduct of a risk assessment with respect to veterinary drug residues in food. What JECFA calls "key international risk assessment documents" are in reality nothing more than informal papers prepared for certain specific purposes and substances which were never presented for consideration and adoption by the competent decision-making bodies of Codex Alimentarius Commission and JECFA. They do not have, therefore the status of legally binding risk assessment techniques in the sense of Article 5.1 of the *SPS Agreement*. In fact, if such risk assessment techniques already existed, quod non, there would have been no need to start this kind of work in the CCRVDF in 2000. Indeed, the reply of Codex to the next question (No 4) confirms explicitly the accuracy of the EC position.

It should be further clarified that the above EC Comments do not intent to diminish the work that is being done in the framework of Codex and JECFA, which is of importance primarily for the countries which do not have in their internal legislation such rules and procedures on risk assessment. The informal technical work to which JECFA and Codex refer cannot, However, be invoked to resolve differences between the parties in a formal WTO dispute settlement with very serious legal, health and economic consequences for the parties to the dispute. This could be the case only when Codex and JECFA formally adopt some time in the future the relevant standards on risk assessment for this kind of residues of veterinary drugs in food. As the European Communities has explained with its comments on question no 3 of the Panel experts questions, its internal legislation on risk assessment applied to the six hormones in question is far more advanced than the informal working documents to which Codex and JECFA referred to in their replies.

Q4.   The European Communities states that there is "no Codex standard specifically on the risk assessment of effects of residues of veterinary drugs" but a general one on microbiological assessment. Is this correct? Which guidelines or principles have been used by JECFA in the conduct of its risk

assessments with respect to the hormones at issue? [see para. 192 of EC Rebuttal Submission (US case)]

EC Comments

The European Communities notes the reply of Codex that: "There is no adopted Codex standard or related text on the risk assessment of residues on veterinary drugs that provides guidance to governments (…) the CCRVDF in 2000 started develop texts on risk analysis principles (…) The documents may be adopted by the Commission in 2007". This statement confirms clearly the EC position that such standards or guidance are absent in the relevant legal framework. The European Communities also notes the Codex reply "[no] standard *or related text*", which clarifies that there is absence not only of standards but also of *guidelines and recommendations*, in the sense of Articles 3 and 5 of the *SPS Agreement*.

Q5. Please briefly describe the three components of a risk analysis exercise (risk assessment, risk management and risk communication) as defined by Codex and explain how they differ.

EC Comments

The European Communities has no specific comments other than to recall that its legislation, as applied to the six hormones, complies fully with the three components and actually goes further than the Codex work in progress. It is, however, true that there are some differences between the European Communities' and the US' and Canadian conception of these steps, as *Drs. Cogliano and Guttenplan* have explained in their replies, and the question is which philosophy will eventually prevail in the future work of Codex. The basic differences between the European Communities and the US and Canada reside, *inter alia*, in that the European Communities (i) is more strict with potentially genotoxic substances, (ii) does not always require a quantitative assessment of the risk (a qualitative assessment is acceptable when the data support it), (iii) pays more attention to scientific uncertainty and (iv) applies a higher level of health and environmental protection.

Q6. Please briefly describe the four steps of a risk assessment (hazard identification, hazard characterization, exposure assessment and risk characterization) as identified by Codex, indicating any relevant sources.

EC Comments

The European Communities has no specific comment at this stage other than to refer the Panel to its comments on question no 3 of the Panel experts questions.

Q7. Please comment on the EC statement made in para. 140 of the EC Replies to Panel Questions that "which ever approach of a risk assessment is followed, they are all based on a deterministic approach to risk characterization [and that they] have serious limitations in non-linear situations,

such as in the current case regarding hormones". Are these situations addressed by the risk assessment guidance currently available from the Codex Alimentarius Commission? [see Canada's comments in para. 72 of its Rebuttal Submission]

EC Comments

The European Communities notes the reply of JECFA whereby "(…) most risk assessments of chemicals today on a national and international level *are deterministic*, i.e. they use a point estimate for the toxicological endpoint and a point estimate for the exposure assessment (…) this is (…) often a necessity due to the information at hand. Uncertainties around these point estimates should be considered in the risk assessment process. The current risk assessment process, which includes consideration of sensitive subpopulations, is considered to be sufficiently conservative to be public health protective." The European Communities also notes the reply whereby "(…) increasing efforts are under way (…) to explore methods to perform probabilistic risk assessment, i.e. include distributions rather than point estimates in the risk assessment process (…) however probabilistic methods in the toxicological assessment are not yet internationally agreed and are not yet commonly applied (…) the outcome of a probabilistic risk assessment is much more difficult to interpret and apply by risk managers." More important is JECFA's comment that: "(…) the probabilistic or deterministic approaches can be applied, independent if a compound is assumed to act via a threshold mechanism, i.e. non-linear, or not. JECFA's assessment process is based on the mechanism of action of the compound to be evaluated, non-linearity *is assumed* if the adverse effect of a compound is caused via a mechanism with a threshold of effect. In such a case, as for the hormones, a no-effect-level can be determined from which an ADI can be established."

These comments confirm the EC point that JECFA assumes non-linearity, but dos not look for it nor does it attempt to prove it. If JECFA's guess about the mechanism of action of the hormones is wrong, as the evidence submitted by the European Communities shows, then its assumption of non-linearity (on safe threshold) is obviously wrong. It is recalled again that in the 1999 assessment, JECFA concluded that oestradiol 17 β has "*genotoxic potential*", it found that progesterone "*on balance*" is not genotoxic, and that the evidence on testosterone was *ambivalent*. This shows that a slight error when JECFA draws its balance of the evidence can be catastrophic for human health, as its was with so many substances in the past, and most clearly with the evaluation of *Carbadox* referred to by the EC in its rebuttal submissions (at paras. 150-152 of US panel).

The Panel would have to understand that these comments by the European Communities are not trivial. *Dr. Boobis* (like JECFA) came to the conclusion that these hormones are not genotoxic on the basis of the so-called "weight of the evidence" approach, meaning that in their view the majority of the evidence does not yet accept that they are genotoxic by a direct mechanism of action, and this is because on their view there are not yet enough experiments *in vivo*. This, how-

ever, is disputed by the European Communities on the basis of evidence conducted both *in vitro* and *in vivo*.

Finally, JECFA states that in its reports and in the toxicological monographs on
the safety assessment of the hormones it has"(…) used risk assessment principles
particularly targeted to the evaluation of such substances (…) [and has consid-
ered] (…) other relevant toxicological end-points, such as reproductive toxicity,
genotoxicity and potential carcinogenicity." The European Communities contests
the scientific accuracy and truth of this statement, because JECFA did not consider carefully many important end-points, such as the effects on pre-pubertal
children, on the immune system, endocrinological effects, etc. The European
Communities refers the Panel to the replies of *Drs. Cogliano, Sippel and Guttenplan* to the Panel questions in this regard.

**Q8.   Do JECFA or Codex materials confirm Canada's statement in para.
80 of its Rebuttal Submission that "... while international risk assessment
techniques suggest that a dose-response assessment is optional for biological
or physical agents when the data cannot be obtained, a dose-response assessment should always be conducted for chemical agents ..."? [see Exhibit CDA-25]**

EC Comments

The European Communities first likes to clarify that the question should have
not asked whether there are "JECFA or Codex materials" but "JECFA or Codex
materials that have been lawfully approved by the members of the Codex Alimentarius Commission". Furthermore, the European Communities considers that
there is no reason to evaluate differently chemicals as opposed to biological or
physical agents. The dose-response assessment can be done both qualitatively
and quantitatively, if the data so permit. The European Communities has done a
qualitative assessment in the case of these hormones. The difference is that
JECFA based its findings on a no-effect-level only, whereas the European Communities found also that there is no safe threshold.

**Q9.   Please provide definitions for the following terms: Acceptable Daily
Intake (ADI) and Maximum Residue Limit (MRL).**

EC Comments

The European Communities notes that the above definition from the 66 JECFA
meeting, which covers also metabolites and associated impurities, was not the
one followed when JECFA evaluated these hormones. Moreover, the definition
of an ADI does not mean that there is no risk, as the defending parties and
JECFA imply, but that there would be no "*appreciable* health risk". But whether
the risk is "appreciable" or not is for each WTO Member to decide. This is precisely the function of its desired level of health protect which can be no (or zero)
additive risk, and which is the level of protection applied by the European Com-

munities in the case of these hormones when administered for animal growth promotion purposes.

Q10. Please describe the procedure followed by JECFA in the identification of ADIs and the development of recommendations on MRLs. Please also identify and describe any steps that are taken in the risk assessment process to build a margin of safety into to the final recommendation.

EC Comments

The European Communities notes that according to JECFA, "(…) in setting ADIs, an attempt is made to take account of special subpopulations that may be exposed." However, as the European Communities has shown, this is not properly done in the case of these hormones because the data used by JECFA for the endogenous production by pre-pubertal children are no longer valid. Moreover, JECFA states that it "(…) uses the risk assessment process when setting the ADI, i.e. the level of "no apparent risk" is set on the basis of *quantitative* extrapolation from animal data to human beings." This statement contrasts with its statement to the previous question, where it claims that it performed a qualitative assessment. In any case, whether qualitative or quantitative, JECFA did *not* use in all of its calculations data from residues in meat from animals treated with these hormones for growth promotion purposes, as it is erroneously stated by the defending parties and the Codex and JECFA.

The European Communities also notes that JECFA "may recommend MRLs "not specified" or "unnecessary" when there is a wide margin of safety of residues when compared with the ADI (...)" and that "(…) JECFA may determine that MRLs cannot be recommended because of significant deficiencies in either residue data or available analytical methods or when an ADI is not established." It is crucial to note, however, that in the case of the three natural hormones JECFA did not specify MRLs because it found them "unnecessary". But this is utterly unscientific because there is no "wide margin of safety" for residues of these hormones given that it has been already established clearly that the endogenous circulating levels alone have been found to cause cancer for some individuals. It was, therefore, imperative for JECFA to evaluate the additive risk that the residues in meat from treated animals can pose to human health. This JECFA has failed entirely to do so, for the simple reason that there are currently no sufficiently powerful analytical methods to detect the origin of residues from the three natural hormones in meat, i.e. whether they are of endogenous or exogenous source. This is the only true reason for which JECFA did not specify MRLs in 1988 and in 1999, after it had found that an ADI had to be established. This is clearly stated in the 1988 evaluation of the three natural hormones by JECFA, where it is explicitly stated:

> "The Committee concluded that residues arising from the use of oestradiol-17β [and progesterone and testosterone] as a growth promoter in accordance with good animal husbandry practice are

unlikely to pose a hazard to human health. The Committee recognized that most methods of analysis for orstradiol-17β [and progesterone and testosterone] are radioimmunoassays, which usually have a large co-efficient of variation at the concentrations being measured. While these methods may be satisfactory for measuring oestradiol-17β [and progesterone and testosterone] levels in experimental situations, improvements would be needed if routine analytical methods for the control of residues were required. On the basis of its safety assessment of residues of oestradiol-17β [and progesterone and testosterone], and in view of the difficulty of determining the levels of residues attributable to the use of these hormones as growth promoters in cattle, the Committee concluded that it was unnecessary to establish an Acceptable Residue Level [i.e. an MRL]" (see WHO Technical Report Series no 763, page 19, 1988).

However, this passage from the 1988 JECFA report on the three natural hormones has now mysteriously disappeared from the 1999 JECFA report on these hormones without any explanation, other than that there is now "a wide margin of safety". So, JECFA finds itself now in the paradoxical situation of having for the first time to establish ADIs for the three natural hormones but is not in a position to fix MRLs for their residues! And the explanation it has offered was to say that they are "unnecessary". But are they really "unnecessary", given the endogenous production levels by prepubertal children and the widespread misuse and abuse of these hormones found in the US and Canada?

The European Communities would suggest to the Panel to ask JECFA to clarify its position on these precise points.

Finally, it is also interesting to note that according to JECFA "[A]s a general principle, the Committee will not normally recommend an MRL that results in residue levels that lead to dietary intake exceeding the ADI based on toxicological or microbiological considerations." The European Communities has demonstrated that there is such a clear possibility of the ADIs being exceeded routinely. As the European Communities has explained in its Written Submissions, this has been explicitly recognised also in the US Carcinogenesis Report since 2002, and it is confirmed by the replies of the experts to the questions of the Panel, in particular those of *Dr. De Brabander and Dr. Sippel.*

Q11. Please confirm or comment on the following Canadian statement: "it is recognized that JECFA only allocates an ADI for a food additive or veterinary drug under review when JECFA considers that its scientific data base is complete and that there are no outstanding scientific issues". [see para. 68 of Canada Rebuttal Submission]

EC Comments

The European Communities notes that there is a wide discrepancy between the theory and reality, in particular given the narrow mandate of JECFA, the potentially subjective interpretation of the data, and the opaqueness of its procedures and the data it uses in its assessments. JECFA's reply does not convince because it does not provide the data upon which it based its assessment for verification and peer-review by independent scientists.

Q12. In paras. 129 and 168 of its Replies to the Panel's questions, the European Communities states that "JECFA's traditional mandate does not allow it to examine all risk management options but restricts it to either propose MRLs or not." Does Codex have risk management options other than (1) the establishment of an MRL, (2) the establishment that an MRL is not necessary, or (3) no recommendation?

EC Comments

The European Communities notes that the replies of both Codex and JECFA confirm that the latter does not have the mandate to examine risk management options other than to propose or not ADIs and MRLs, and it has not been asked to consider such options when it examined these hormones. Moreover, both Codex and JECFA appear to have an extremely narrow understanding of what constitutes risk management: for instance, they appear to think that the question whether an identified (and characterised) risk is or is not "appreciable" is a risk assessment issue. This is not correct, as this issue is by definition a risk management question and it is a function of the chosen level of protection by the risk manager. A risk assessor's role, like that of JECFA, should be to identify only if there is a risk and to explain any scientific uncertainties that may surround its assessment. Its assessment of the risk may be qualitative or quantitative, but the decision whether a scientifically assessed risk (e.g. of cancer) is "significant" or "appreciable" is, strictly speaking, a risk management decision. It follows that JECFA does perform also risk management functions in the Codex system, despite its formal denial of doing so.

Q13. With respect to the data used in the evaluation of chemical substances, such as the hormones at issue, what are the data requirements for JECFA's work and how are they determined? Who provides data for such evaluations? Are any records/archives kept by JECFA? Do any confidentiality rules apply to data submitted to JECFA or should all data be publicly available? If confidentiality rules apply, in which circumstances? [see paras. 95-96 of EC Rebuttal Submission (US case), paras. 78-79 of EC Rebuttal Submission (Canada case), para. 123 of Canada Rebuttal Submission]

EC Comments

The European Communities would note the following statements by JECFA:

- "the data are mainly provided by companies who produce the compounds;
- the submitted data may be published or unpublished and should contain detailed reports of laboratory studies, including individual animal data;
- summaries in the form of monographs are helpful, but they are not in themselves sufficient for evaluation;
- the unpublished confidential studies that are submitted will be safeguarded and will be used only for evaluation purposes by JECFA;
- neither FAO nor WHO have facilities for storing printed data for long periods of time, so confidential data will either be returned to the submitter at the submitter's expense or destroyed after the evaluations have been completed;
- key material can be stored up to five years and will then be destroyed."

These statements confirm the EC position that JECFA has had access to the detailed reports provided by the industry, but failed to provide them to the European Communities. The European Communities has been asking for these confidential and unpublished data since 1999, so JECFA cannot pretend that it had destroyed them already at that time!

JECFA claims that "it is important to note that JECFA evaluations are completely publicly available, and a detailed description of the data evaluated is accessible through the monographs." But these monographs are not the original of the data used but processed and reworked information which does not enable scientists to verify the accuracy of the design of the study, of the experiments carried out, of the interpretations made and the conclusions drawn and for what reasons. The European Communities has not been asking for information regarding "the manufacturing process of substances, which are considered confidential for commercial purposes", but for the specific scientific studies (toxicological and residues analysis) in order to verify the scientific validity of these studies and the accuracy of the conclusions drawn by JECFA (and the defending parties). The European Communities has rendered public and provided its own studies to all the parties; therefore, it fails to understand why the US, Canada and JECFA (and Codex) continue to deny access to their own data.

The European Communities reiterates, therefore, its standing request to the Panel to order the production of their so-called confidential and unpublished data, if the credibility of their assessments and of this process is to be maintained. Otherwise it has to draw the necessary negative inferences from the failure to provide the requested data.

Q14. How are experts involved in JECFA's work selected? What are the selection criteria?

EC Comments

The European Communities simply notes that in the evaluation of the six hormones by JECFA have participated scientists who have no specific expertise on these hormones, like *Drs. Boisseau and Boobis*, since they have not worked on nor have published anything on these substances when used for animal growth promotion purposes. From the JECFA reply it is not clear to the European Communities whether the selection of JECFA's experts is as strict as that applied in the case of IARC (see its reply to Panel question no 22). The European Communities would ask the Panel to clarify further this point.

Q15. Please provide the definition of the term Good Veterinary Practice (GVP). Are there any relevant Codex standards, guidelines, or recommendations relating to GVP?

EC Comments

The European Communities notes that there is currently no definition nor guidelines on GVP in Codex and JECFA, as this is confirmed by the replies of *Dr. Boisseau and Dr. De Brabander* (question no 44 to experts).

Q16. Please provide an update on the status of international standards with respect to the six hormones at issue. What are the remaining procedures before the adoption of a standard on melengestrol acetate (MGA)? What is the timeframe for their completion?

EC Comments

The European Communities notes that the Codex standards on the five hormones were adopted by a very slim majority vote in Codex, despite the Codex' statement that decisions are taken by consensus. Indeed, the Codex standards were adopted in 1995 with 33 votes in favour, 29 votes against and 7 abstentions, that is by a minority of the members present and voting (see para. 4.77 of the 1997 Panel report, WT/DS26/R/USA, at page 39). Their assessment by JECFA dates of 1988. The Codex reply also confirms the EC position that currently there exists no standard for MGA.

Q17. Is the table in Exhibit CDA-32 outlining the chronology of JECFA's assessment of the hormones at issue and the resulting documentation complete?

EC Comments

The European Communities wishes to clarify that the 66th JECFA meeting (held 20 - 28 February 2006) deliberated on the MRLs previously proposed for melengestrol acetate. It did, however not consider any new data but limited itself to the correction of a calculation error. The EC highlighted this during the recent 16th Session of the CCRVDF that no original data were presented in the review (see ALINORM 06/29/31 paragraph 69).

Q18. What happens if new evidence or studies throw into doubt a Codex standard? What are the procedures for incorporating more recent developments into Codex work? Has the European Communities approached Codex for this purpose with respect to the hormones at issue in this case?

EC Comments

The European Communities notes the statement that "in the case of estradiol-17 beta, progesterone and testosterone, they were re-evaluated by the 52n JECFA (1999) at the initiative of the JECFA Secretariat", and that "the 12th CCRVDF (2000), in recognising that it had not requested the re-evaluation of the three substances and that the new MRLs recommended by the 52n JECFA did not differ significantly from the current MRLs, decided to not consider the new recommendation of the 52nd JECFA." There are many comments one can make on this statement. First, it is quite unusual for substances to be re-evaluated at the request of JECFA's Secretariat, despite the written request of one of its members (who represented at the time 15 countries) to postpone the re-evaluation for a couple of years in view of the expected new evidence that was about to become soon available. Indeed, most of the new evidence generated by the European Communities became available between 1999 to 2002. The European Communities would like to ask JECFA if this has ever happened in other cases. The European Communities has never understood what would have been the problem if its request for postponement were taken into account.

The European Communities notes that JECFA and Codex do not reply to the second part of the question. In any case, it is surprising that the same JECFA Secretariat, which used to be common with that of Codex, is now not proposing to review again these hormones, despite the wealth of the new evidence that became available from so many sources and the standing request by the European Communities.

It is also noteworthy that the CCRVDF did not adopt the 1999 assessment of the three natural hormones by JECFA, which may mean that this 1999 assessment is of no relevance for the purposes of these disputes.

As regards MGA, the European Communities has requested its re-evaluation on the basis of more recent scientific evidence.

Q19. What would be the procedures for requesting JECFA to re-evaluate its recommendations in light of new concerns/evidence? How would an amendment be adopted? Has the European Communities approached JECFA for this purpose with respect to the hormones at issue in this case? [see Exhibit EC-63]

EC Comments

The European Communities notes the statement by JECFA that the "European Union has not asked the JECFA Secretariat to bring their data referred to in the report of the 11th session of CCRVDF (see below point 1 of question 20) before JECFA for review." This is not correct because there is a standing EC request to review the hormones on the basis of the latest information available, including that generated by the European Communities.

Q20. What were the reasons for the re-evaluation by JECFA of the three natural hormones in 1999? Were the residues data used for the three natural hormones in 1999 the same as those used in 1988? What additional information was used for the JECFA evaluation in 1999 of the three natural hormones, which was not available in 1988? How did the conclusions differ? What led JECFA to establish ADIs for the three natural hormones? What are the implications of establishing ADIs? Why were JECFA's more recent recommendations not considered by CCRVDF? What is the status of these recommendations? [see para. 96-97 of EC Rebuttal Submission (US case), para. 79-80 of EC Rebuttal Submission (Canada case)]

EC Comments

The European Communities refers the Panel to its submissions and in particular Exhibit EC-63, which provides a more detailed account of the events with precise references to the original letters. It is unfortunate that JECFA states that it "decided to re-evaluate previous assessment when the Committee is made aware that there is new data which may be pertinent to the risk assessment of the substances in question", but failed to wait for the most important part of these data to become publicly available.

The European Communities draws the attention of the Panel to the statement that "most of the studies were the same", which confirms the EC position. The European Communities also notes that "a complete dossier submitted to the US Food and Drug Administration" was provided and that the "FDA kindly permitted the FAO expert to the Committee to search all their relevant files for data." This statement confirms again the EC position that the US and JECFA could have provided the same data also to the European Communities as it has been consistently requesting.

JECFA states that it performed "a more detailed thorough review of the validity of the analytical methods used in the studies and used only data generated using valid methods. It also performed more detailed statistical and graphical analyses of the data." However, since most of the data were the same old data, one wonders what kind of thorough processing JECFA now did, which it had failed to do in its 1988 assessment of the same data. This is all the more crucial given that the data in question are unpublished data of the 1970s. The European Communities recalls that this so-called "thorough review" seems to have been performed by Dr. Arnold, who has himself declared to this Panel during the selection procedures that he believes eating meet treated with these hormones poses "no in-creased health risk for consumers".

JECFA also states that "a few additional investigational studies were also re-viewed", but it does not explain which ones and how important they were for its assessment. JECFA further states that "since the FAO FNP 41/12 monograph provides all raw data used (in graphical form) and all the calculations performed, the document is also more transparent than the corresponding monograph pro-duced by the 32nd Meeting". The European Communities reiterates that it pre-cisely has been claiming for transparency in the JECFA proceedings, and a graphical presentation of the same old data is not what one would normally un-derstand by transparency.

JECFA states that "this conclusion was based on studies of the patterns of use of estradiol for growth promotion in cattle, the residues in animals, analytical meth-ods, toxicological data from studies in laboratory animals, and clinical findings in human subjects." The European Communities disputes that such detailed stud-ies have been performed and reiterates its standing request to be given access to these data or to be made available to the Panel and its experts for review.

JECFA further states that "at its 52nd meeting in 1999, estradiol-17β was re-evaluated to take into consideration any data that had been generated since the previous review and to make a quantitative estimate of the amount that could be consumed safely. The Committee established an ADI of 0-50 ng/kg bw on the basis of the NOEL of 0.3 mg/day (equivalent to 5 μg/kg bw per day) in studies of changes in several hormone-dependent parameters in postmenopausal women. A safety factor of 10 was used to account for normal variation among individu-als, and an additional factor of 10 was added to protect sensitive populations." This confirms that (i) JECFA did not consider residues in meat from animals treated with these hormones for growth promotion purposes, (ii) it based its ADI on "changes in several parameters in postmenopausal women" but not on the much lower rates of prepubertal children (as did the European Communities), and (iii) it sought to address these problems with the application of safety fac-tors!

The European Communities notes that statement of JECFA that "the 52nd JECFA performed a detailed theoretical intake assessment based on a worst case scenario (all animals are slaughtered at the time of the highest hormone levels - this time point differs largely from the time point at which the benefit due to the anabolic effect is greatest). In this assessment intake estimates for preferential meat eaters were performed on the basis of the hormone levels of treated animals in comparison with the corresponding levels in untreated animals and the addi-tional "burden" or "excess intake" was calculated. For total estrogens the highest excess intakes from approved uses calculated this way were in the order of mag-nitude of 30 – 50 ng/person/day. This range of intake is less than 2% of the ADI for estradiol-17β established by JECFA at the 52nd meeting. For certain experi-mental studies carried out with experimental combinations resulted in an excess intake of around 4% of the ADI." The European Communities would like to see the original of these underlying data, as the similar or more detailed studies and experiments in has generated itself provided different and in many cases much higher values (see e.g. Exhibits EC-16, 17, 18, 19, 34, 47, 52, 53 and 78). The same applies for testosterone and progesterone.

JECFA states that "hormone concentrations found in individual populations of treated animals, although they were typically statistically significant higher than untreated controls, were well within the physiological range of these substances in bovine animals. The data assessed and the worst case scenario calculations made indicated a wide margin of safety of consumption of residues from animals treated in accordance with good practice of use of the veterinary drugs containing the hormones in question. JECFA therefore concluded that there was no need to specify numerical maximum residue levels for the three hormones and recommended MRLs not specified in bovine tissues." This is an important statement that needs to be factually substantiated. The European Communities notes that the hormone concentrations found in treated animals were significantly higher than in untreated animals.

As for the reasons for which JECFA established in 1999 ADIs, the European Communities notes the statement that this was due to "the additional data reviewed and the need to establish an ADI as quantitative estimate for a safe oral intake. The exposure assessment performed would then allow the comparison of the estimated intake with the ADI." Thus, this confirms the EC position that it was the new evidence showing risk of cancer that led JECFA review its 1988 assessment. And if JECFA postponed its assessment until the new and more recent data generated by the European Communities were taken into account, it could have reached still another and arguably more accurate conclusion. In any case, it is clear that in 1999 JECFA did not establish ADI in order explain better its evaluation, as it is claimed erroneously by *Dr. Boisseau* (see his reply to Panel question to the experts no 18).

JECFA states that "sufficient new data from observations in humans were available to the 52nd JECFA which were suitable to derive ADIs." The European Communities does not know and has not seen these "data from observations in humans" and, if they exist, they are certainly different from the data it has generated itself with its own studies. JECFA should therefore provide them to the parties, the Panel and its experts for review. Moreover, the so-called "wide margin of safety" claimed by JECFA to exist is no longer credible in view of the "significantly higher levels" identified in treated animals and the need to establish ADIs, not to mention their direct genotoxicity and the other adverse effects established by the European Communities. Furthermore, the EC scientists rightly question why MRLs were not established in 1999, given that JECFA had felt nevertheless the need to establish ADIs. Was it for the alleged "wide safety margin" or simply because "of the difficulty of determining the levels of residues attributable to the use of this hormone as a growth promoter in cattle", as JECFA had admitted in 1988? But if the latter was the real reason, this means that JECFA did not carry out a quantitative dose-response assessment of residues in meat from treated animals under realistic conditions of use, as it is argued by the European Communities.

Q21. What is the mandate of the International Agency for Research on Cancer?

EC Comments

The European Communities has no specific comment at this time.

Q22. Who are the members of the IARC?

EC Comments

The European Communities has no specific comment at this time.

Q23. What are IARC Monographs? How are they prepared?

EC Comments

The European Communities notes the IARC statement that "when the epidemiological evidence is *sufficient*, the final evaluation is *carcinogenic to humans*, regardless of the experimental evidence. In other cases, the mechanistic and other relevant data are considered to determine whether the default evaluation should be modified, upwards or downwards. A subgroup of experts in cancer mechanisms assesses the strength of the mechanistic data and whether the mechanisms of tumour formation in experimental animals can operate in humans. The overall evaluation is a matter of scientific judgement, reflecting the combined weight of the evidence."

The European Communities would like further clarifications on the following points: Does the above statement mean that a substance can be classified in Group 1 even if there are no or a limited number of experiments showing genotoxicity in vivo? Moreover, in which of the different groups are genotoxic substances classified? How does IARC define genotoxic substances?

Q24. Please briefly explain the groupings that are used to categorize "potentially carcinogenic agents"? What are the implications when an "agent" is placed in one of the IARC categories?

EC Comments

The European Communities would like to request the following clarifications: 1) Would the IARC describe its assessments as risk assessments or as assessments that also include risk management? 2) When a substance is placed in Groups 1, 2A and 2B, what is the majority of IARC's members normally expected to do? To authorise or prohibit the substances in question? On what else does their decision depend? 3) Is the assessment performed by IARC a qualitative or a quantitative assessment of potential risk? 4) Is the IARC classification of various groups based on dose-response estimations under realistic conditions of use of the various substances? 5) Is the classification based only on experimental data in animals and extrapolations to humans or do they include also data from residues which such substances may leave in food?

Q25. Which of the six hormones at issue in this dispute (oestradiol-17β, progesterone, testosterone, trenbolone acetate, zeranol, and melengestrol acetate) have been evaluated by the IARC? Have any specific risks from the consumption of meat from cattle treated with these growth promotion hormones been assessed by the IARC?

EC Comments

The European Communities notes the statement that "Trenbolone acetate, zeranol, and melengestrol acetate have not been evaluated by IARC, nor have the risks from the consumption of meat from cattle treated with these growth promotion hormones", and would like the following clarifications: 1) Does it mean that IARC's evaluation of the three natural hormones covers also the specific risks from the consumption of meat from cattle treated with those hormones for growth promotion? 2) Can the IARC be more specific on the last part of the question? 3) Is it possible a pharmacologically active substance that is classified in Group 1 to ever lead residues in food of this substance to be classified into a different category? 4) If so, under what conditions can this take place?

Q26. How does the work of the IARC feed into the work of national regulatory agencies or international bodies, in particular with respect to assessments of risks from the consumption of meat from cattle treated with the six growth promoting hormones at issue in this dispute?

EC Comments

The European Communities would like IARC to clarify what it means by "as scientific support for their actions"? Does it mean that they can be used as risk assessments? Are they normally scientifically complete and adequate to be used as risk assessments? Could IARC be more specific and reply to the last part of the question concerning the consumption of meat from cattle treated with the six hormones or at least for the three hormones that it has assessed and classified?

ANNEX F-3

COMMENTS BY THE EUROPEAN COMMUNITIES TO
THE COMMENTS BY THE UNITED STATES AND
CANADA ON THE REPLIES OF THE SCIENTIFIC
EXPERTS TO QUESTIONS POSED
BY THE PANEL

(12 July 2006)

Introduction and general comments

1.   The European Communities thanks the Panel for the opportunity to comment on the other Parties' comments on the Panel's experts' replies. Before setting out its comments the European Communities would like to make two preliminary remarks of a general nature.

2.   First, the European Communities notes that the United States, in its comments, has chosen to follow its own structure in what may well be considered a full-fledged additional submission. Apart from the fact that reference is made to legal claims which the United States has not made anywhere (e.g. Article 5.6 of the *SPS Agreement*, see paragraph 5 of the US submission), the European Communities considers that this approach is confusing and of little assistance to the Panel and its experts as well as to the other parties. It is not surprising that the US has resorted to this tactic, as the replies of the majority of the experts support the scientific evidence and the arguments of the European Communities.

3.   In order to facilitate a structured debate, the European Communities will try to disentangle the misleading comments made by the United States. Also, for the same purpose, the European Communities makes but one set of comments, which addresses the Canadian and (as best as possible) the US comments following the order of the questions as asked by the Panel to the experts and the international bodies.

4.   Second, in light of the other Parties' comments on this general issue, it seems appropriate to briefly come back to the role of experts in these panel proceedings. As the European Communities has pointed out in earlier submissions (in particular in its submission of 15 March 2006), the purpose of the scientific questions and the role of the experts is to help the Panel understand the scientific issues involved. Neither the Panel nor the experts should aim to conduct their own risk assessment or to conduct a *de novo* review of the sanitary risks identified by the European Communities. The task of the scientific experts is to assist the Panel in assessing whether the scientific basis of the measure taken by the European Communities complies with the recommendations and rulings of the DSB in the *EC – Hormones* case. But the experts should not make comments on risk management options, since this is not their expertise or role. Therefore, the focus of the scientific questions should be to help the Panel understand the risk assessment conducted by the European Communities since the adoption of the

Panel and the Appellate Body reports in 1999. Unfortunately, as the European Communities has demonstrated by its comments of 30 June 2006, the replies of Dr. Boisseau and Dr. Boobis have not always complied with the above requirements.

A.   General Definitions

Q1.   Please provide brief and basic definitions for the six hormones at issue (oestradiol-17β, progesterone, testosterone, trenbolone acetate, zeranol, and melengestrol acetate), indicating the source of the definition where applicable.

5.   The United States and Canada have not referred to or commented in substance on the experts' (*Drs. Boisseau, Boobis and Guttenplan*) replies to this question.

Q2.   Please provide definitions for the following terms as they relate to the hormones at issue, indicating the source of the definition where applicable: anabolic agents, steroids, steroidal oestrogens, parent compounds/metabolites, catechol metabolites, mitogenicity, mutagenicity, androgenic/oestrogenic activity, genotoxicity, genotoxic potential, carcinogenicity, and tumorigenicity. In your replies, please be sure to identify and describe any relevant differences between the terms.

US comment

6.   The United States has not referred to or commented on the experts' (*Drs. Boisseau, Boobis and Guttenplan*) replies to this question.

Canada's comment

7.   The comments by Canada (at paras. 8-9) are not accurate. The statement that a substance (in this case oeastradiol-17β) "has genotoxic potential" does not mean that there is a "statistically likelihood" that it is carcinogenic (this is not what the European Communities has argued) but that on the basis of the evidence available, in particular *in vitro* studies, the genotoxicity of the substance is possible. This is not a theoretical statement but a frequent conclusion scientists make for this type of substances. In addition, in this case there is also *in vivo* evidence supporting that statement. *Dr. Boobis* and Canada may not like this evidence or would like to see more *in vivo* evidence before they are convinced, but this is irrelevant. The European Communities is entitled to rely on this recent and credible evidence if necessary to achieve its level of health protection.

B.   *Risk Assessment Techniques*

Q3.   Please identify any international guidance documents relevant to the conduct of a risk assessment with respect to veterinary drug residues. Since when have they been available? Please also indicate if there is any relevant ongoing work at Codex.

US comment

8.   The US comments on Question 3 are contained in paragraph 13 of its submission. The European Communities notes that there is general agreement among the parties that there is no internationally agreed risk assessment technique, within the meaning of Article 5.1 of the *SPS Agreement,* for the assessment of these hormonal substances. It is equally uncontested by all that there exists a number of documents which represent at most a practical understanding among some international experts on certain principles. These documents do not have any legal value under the *SPS Agreement* since they are not "risk assessment techniques developed by the relevant international organisations." In any event, the European Communities notes that neither the US nor the experts claim that the European Communities has not followed these.

Canada's comment

9.   Canada's comments (in particular at paras. 14-15) do not accurately describe the legal relevance of the documents to which it and JECFA have referred to. Canada states that many of the risk assessment techniques and methodologies "are also relevant to the risk assessment of veterinary drugs". However, these are no risk "assessment techniques" in the first place, in the sense of Article 5.1 of the *SPS Agreement* and, secondly, they cannot be applied by analogy to other kind of substances than for those for which they have been foreseen.

Q4.   The European Communities states that there is "no Codex standard specifically on the risk assessment of effects of residues of veterinary drugs" but a general one on microbiological assessment. Is this correct? Which guidelines or principles have been used by JECFA in the conduct of its risk assessments with respect to the hormones at issue? [see para. 192 of EC Rebuttal Submission (US case)].

US comment

10.   The US comments on the experts' replies to this question are contained in paragraph 13 of its submission. As stated above, these documents reflect the general discussion in the absence of an internationally agreed risk assessment technique and the presence of certain guidance documents. However, the United States misquotes *Dr. Boisseau* when pretending that he was referring to the "assessment of such drugs "[i.e. the hormonal substances in question] when stating that "it has been internationally harmonised through scientific conferences ...". *Dr. Boisseau* was not referring to the assessment as such, but to a "general ra-

tionale" on that assessment. Indeed, if there is some understanding among certain scientists on a general way of conducting a risk assessment, the European Communities applies this as much as any other country.

Canada's comment

11.   Canada maintains that, despite of the accuracy of the relevant EC statement "any suggestion that relevant risk assessment techniques or guidance developed by international organizations for the conduct of veterinary drug risk assessments do not exist is baseless".

12.   In the European Communities' view, Canada is misinterpreting the replies of *Dr. Boisseau and Dr. Boobis*. First, it should be underlined that both experts (and in addition *Dr. Guttenplan*) have confirmed the accuracy of the EC statement. Second, the existing general JECFA guidelines to which *Drs. Boisseau and Boobis* refer can not be taken – as Canada does – as a replacement of an international detailed Codex standard which alone would be of legal relevance under the *SPS Agreement*.

13.   JECFA might have produced certain internal guidelines on risk assessment for certain substances. However, it is a totally different matter to elevate internal JECFA papers, which have never been approved by Codex Members, into the rank of an international standard. Thus, Canada's insinuation and interpretation of the replies by *Dr. Boisseau and Dr. Boobis* is inaccurate and unacceptable.

Q5.   Please briefly describe the three components of a risk analysis exercise (risk assessment, risk management and risk communication) and explain how they differ.

US comment

14.   The United States has not provided comments on the experts' (*Drs. Boobis, Boisseau, Cogliano, Guttenplan*) replies to this question.

Canada's comment

15.   In summarizing the experts' replies, Canada reproduces *Dr. Boobis'* response and presents this as the common denominator of the experts. However, there are differences. For instance, in respect of the "risk assessment" *Dr. Boobis* introduces a concept of the "weight of evidence", which is not found in the replies by *Dr. Boisseau, Dr. Cogliano or Dr. Guttenplan*. These experts rather emphasize the risk assessment as an evaluation of risk (*Dr. Guttenplan*), a description of the "adverse effects of exposure of hazardous agents (*Dr. Cogliano*) or the "likelihood and the gravity of any unexpected unwanted effect for the consumer" on the basis of "scientific date, relevant with regard to assessing this risk" (*Dr. Boisseau*).

16.   These differences are important since *Dr. Boobis'* reply, which obviously suits Canada best, implies a margin of discretion in (or balancing and weighing

of) the scientific risk assessment procedure, based on the "weight of evidence", which is not the case for the other experts.

17.   Furthermore, as regards the risk management step, Canada again uses the language of *Dr. Boobis* reply and tries to "present" it as the common view of all experts. This is, in particular, interesting since *Dr. Boobis* refers in this context to "ensuring fair trade" which is not mentioned by any of the other experts. Instead, these experts refer to the use of other scientific criteria such as "economical, sociological, cultural" (*Dr. Boisseau*) or "legal mandates, technical feasibility, cost, equity, and social norms" (*Dr. Cogliano*). This is an interesting difference, because the concept of "fair trade" is not clearly defined and Canada and *Dr. Boobis* may have a different interpretation of this concept than for instance the United States, the European Communities or other experts.

18.   Moreover, Canada claims that all experts appear to support the so-called "functional separation" between risk assessment and risk management (at para. 20). Even if this were so, *quod non*, this is irrelevant for the *SPS Agreement*, because the Appellate Body has interpreted correctly its provisions in the 1998 *Hormones* case to partially overlap (at para. 181 of its report).

Q6.   Please briefly describe the four steps of a risk assessment (hazard identification, hazard characterization, exposure assessment and risk characterization) as identified by Codex, indicating any relevant sources.

US comment

19.   The United States refers to the experts' replies on this question in paragraph 14 of its submission trying to make again the erroneous point that the European Communities risk assessment did not engage in a hazard characterization because it did not evaluate a dose-response relationship. This is discussed in more detail below under Question 11.

Canada's comment

20.   Canada's summary of the experts' replies (Drs. *Boisseau, Boobis and Guttenplan*) concerning "hazard identification" is not accurate. According to Canada, "the experts" agree that hazard identification "involves the determination of *whether* an agent has the potential to cause adverse effects" (Emphasis added). However, this is not what *Dr. Boisseau, Dr. Boobis and Dr. Guttenplan* say. All of them do not define this step as to "whether" or not there are adverse effects. Rather, *Dr. Boisseau, Dr. Boobis and Dr. Guttenplan* define hazard characterization in respect of the identification of the different elements causing adverse health effects in humans.

21.   In respect of the "hazard characterization" it is not true, as Canada summarizes it, that all experts refer in their definition to a "dose-response assessment" or the determination of thresholds, i.e. an NOAEL or an ADI. Indeed, *Dr. Guttenplan* merely refers to the "quantitative and/or qualitative evaluation of the nature of the adverse health effects associated with the hazard" without referring

to a dose-response relationship or the establishment of whatever threshold. But even *Dr. Boobis* or *Dr. Boisseau* clearly condition the dose-response threshold aspects to "whether or not this is possible". Consequently, Canada's implied conclusion that these elements form an "integral part" of the risk assessment which the EC failed to complete are a serious mischaracterization of the experts' replies.

22.   As regards the definition of the "exposure assessment" Canada, again, does not provide a proper summary of the experts' replies even though it pretends that all experts have the same view. Canada uses the words of *Dr. Boobis* to define the exposure assessment as a step to evaluate "quantitatively" the exposure of consumers to veterinary drugs.[1] However, *Dr. Boobis and Dr. Guttenplan* refer explicitly not only to the quantitative aspects, but also to the "*qualitative* evaluation of the likely intake".

23.   In respect of the "risk characterization" Canada again generalizes from one expert reply and presents them as a common reply of all experts. This is obvious when Canada quotes *Dr. Boisseau's* statement whereby risk characterization "is not to assess qualitatively and quantitatively the likelihood and gravity of the adverse effects of consumers (…) but to protect consumer's health from any adverse effect associated with residues". In this context, Canada also pretends that all experts confirm that an MRL would be established. This presentation is simply wrong. In fact, neither *Dr. Boobis* nor *Dr. Guttenplan* refer to the "protection of consumer health from any adverse effects" and to the establishment of MRLs. Rather, both experts limit themselves to the qualitative and, where possible, quantitative determination, including attendant uncertainties, of the likelihood of occurrence or severity of potential adverse health effects. It follows, therefore, that *Dr. Boisseau's* reply contains a subjective judgement and a procedural step which is not supported by *Dr. Boobis and Dr. Guttenplan,* contrary to what Canada pretends. Moreover, Canada persists in its error to consider that it is the "probability" of occurrence of the adverse effect that counts, when the Appellate Body has clarified in the *Hormones* case that it is not the probability but the likelihood (or possibility) that is meant by Annex A(4) of the *SPS Agreement.*

Q7.   Please comment on the EC statement made in para. 140 of the EC Replies to Panel Questions that "which ever approach of a risk assessment is followed, they are all based on a deterministic approach to risk characterization [and that they] have serious limitations in non-linear situations, such as in the current case regarding hormones". Are these situations, in your view, addressed by the risk assessment guidance currently available from the Codex Alimentarius Commission? Have they been addressed in

---

[1]   Canada and Dr. Boisseau, however, differ on the food basket which according to Canada contains 300g muscle, whereas Dr. Boisseau refers to 500g muscle.

the 1988 and 1999 JECFA risk assessments of these hormones? [see Canada's comments in para. 72 of its Rebuttal Submission]

US comment

24.   The United States refers to the experts' replies to this question in paragraphs 15, 16 and 17 of its submission. Here again the US refers selectively to the "experts" views, when only *Drs. Boisseau and Boobis* appear to support what the US is arguing. Moreover, the basic error of these scientists, of the US (and Canada for this matter) and of JECFA is that they all argue that oestradiol is not genotoxic but acts only through hormone-mediated receptors. On the basis of this erroneous assumption, based on old and outdated data, they all come to the conclusion that there is a threshold dose below which there was no appreciable risk over a lifetime of exposure.

25.   This kind of statement by the US is surprising given that its own scientists no longer agree with this assertion. The US Carcinogenesis Report since 2002 has classified oestradiol as a proven human carcinogen (see Exhibit EC-101). Indeed, the above US report states *inter alia*:

> "The evidence is strong that estrogen carcinogenesis is mediated through activation of the estrogen receptor. *In addition, there is evidence that other mechanisms may play a role in the carcinogenic effects of estrogens in some tissues.* Prolonged estrogen exposure induces cell proliferation in estrogen-dependent target cells, affects cellular differentiation, and alters gene expression. *Although the molecular mechanisms responsible for estrogen carcinogenicity are not well understood, the evidence indicates that estrogen carcinogenesis is complex, involving proliferative effects and possibly direct and indirect genotoxic effects.* The relative importance of each mechanism is likely a function of the specific estrogen and of the exposed tissue or cell type and its metabolic state (Yager and Liehr 1996)." (emphasis added)

It is clear from the above excerpt that all the relevant US scientific institutions that have collaborated in the preparation of this Report have come to the conclusion that oestrogen acts not only through the estrogen receptors but, *in addition,* also by "other mechanisms". The report states also that "the evidence indicates that estrogen carcinogenesis is complex, involving proliferative effects and possibly *direct and indirect* genotoxic effects". This finding was made for the first time in the 2002 Report and is being repeated ever since. It is very strange that neither *Dr. Boisseau nor Dr. Boobis* commented on this, and it is even stranger that neither of the defending parties have ever said something about this, which clearly supports the EC assessment on this crucial point. Indeed, the European Communities is not doing other than what *Dr. Boobis* has described in his reply to Question no 7, namely that: "In practice, it is likely that as veterinary drug residues in food are avoidable by not using the drug, the Committee would have declined to establish an ADI".

Canada's comment

26.   The European Communities is again opposed to Canada's selective perception of the experts' replies. Canada merely pretends that "the experts confirm that JECFA was aware of "non-linear situations" and took these into account in conducting its risk assessment for the hormones at issue".

27.   However, *Dr. Boisseau's* reply is more nuanced than Canada would like to see. *Dr. Boisseau* replied that JECFA was aware in 1987 of non-linear situations but this was a general comment. In its reply, *Dr. Boisseau* only exemplifies this general awareness in respect of specific substances which are unrelated to the hormones in dispute and where at the time, JECFA concluded not to establish an effect-dose relation or to recommend an ADI.

28.   Yet, in respect of oestradiol-17β, *Dr. Boisseau* expressly states that "in its 32nd session held in 1987, JECFA did not address this kind of non-linear situation for oestradiol-17β (...)". Similarly, in 1999, according to *Dr. Boisseau*, JECFA "did not take into account consideration a non-linear situation in its risk assessment (...)". Against this background, Canada's presentation of *Dr. Boisseau's* reply on non-linear situations is unsustainable.

29.   Canada finds support in the statement of *Dr. Boobis*. But his statement and that of JECFA are scientifically unsound for the reasons already explained by the European Communities. Canada claims (at para. 31) that the European Communities has presented no evidence; however, this is not true because the evidence is there but Canada chooses to ignore it. For instance, Canada did not comment so far on the 2002 US Carcinogenesis Report quoted above.

Q8.   Please describe the procedure followed by JECFA in the identification of ADIs and the development of recommendations on MRLs. Please identify and describe any steps that are taken in the risk assessment process to build a margin of safety into the final recommendation.

US comment

30.   The United States does not refer to or comment on the experts' replies to this question nor to JECFA's and Codex replies to the same question (question 10 in questions asked to Codex, JECFA and IARC).

Canada's comment

31.   Canada's description of the expert replies demonstrates again a lack of precision and accuracy. Canada, for instance, refers to *Dr. Boobis* answer (to Question 54) that an ADI is a threshold "that will pose zero risk" to human health. However, in this reply, *Dr. Boobis* only refers to a WHO definition of an ADI whereby there would be "no appreciable risk with daily exposure over a lifetime". It goes without saying that the difference of "no risk" and "no appreciable risk" is considerable since the latter one involves a subjective judgement. Indeed, what may be "appreciable" to somebody may not be "appreciable" to others. Yet, in this sensitive hormones' discussion, these fine differences make a

difference. This is an issue of risk management, not of risk assessment, in the sense that *Dr. Boobis* cannot decide for the democratically elected governments in the European Communities what risk is "appreciable". It is, therefore, necessary to make the Panel aware of such rather blunt presentations of the experts' replies by Canada. Indeed, Canada is confusing its own subjective (policy) judgements with the remarks of the scientific experts.

32.   It may not come as a surprise that Canada's description regarding the experts' replies on MRLs is also misleading. First, it is inaccurate to say that "the experts have confirmed that the MRL is a management tool (...)" and that "if residues are within the MRL, then the ADI is unlikely to be exceeded and no adverse effects to human health are to be expected". First, only *Dr. Boisseau* refers in its answer to MRL but not the other experts. Second, Dr. Boisseau clearly states that a MRL is "an operational tool which offers a practical way to be sure that this ADI will not be exceeded". Conversely, contrary to what Canada describes *Dr. Boisseau* does not say "no adverse effects to human health are to be expected". Rather it appears that at this stage one would have to go back to the discussion whether an ADI poses "no risk" or "no *appreciable* risk". Moreover, Canada states (at para. 36) that JECFA has built into its calculations large safety margins. However, none of the points made by Canada here is correct, at least not in the case of these hormones. First, because JECFA did not consider all the metabolites for instance of oestradiol, like the esters. Indeed, *Maume et al.* have confirmed the presence of estradiol **esters** in meat of treated animals in an order of magnitude not very different to the free estradiol residues. But the estradiol esters is a totally new class of residues that have not been considered before in any risk evaluation. Their potential bioactivity may be much higher than the bioactivity of estradiol as such. The recent data provide clear evidence (1) for their existence after application of estradiol to cattle and (2) for their elevated oral bioactivity. Undoubtedly, these are important new data, and an accurate evaluation of the risk originating from steroid hormone esters will only be possible, if many more data become available. This includes the additional need to look for trenbolone esters and their bioactivity. (see *Maume D, Deceuninck Y, Pouponneau K, Paris A, Le Bizec B and Andre F (2001): Assessment of estradiol and its metabolites in meat, APMIS, 109:32-38*, Exhibit EC-47*). Second, because the bioavailability of these hormones has been seriously underestimated, and thirdly, because the so-called food basket can easily lead to residues intakes that by far exceed the endogenous production of these hormones, especially by pre-pubertal children.

Q9.   Please confirm or comment on the following Canadian statement: "it is recognized that JECFA only allocates an ADI for a food additive or veterinary drug under review when JECFA considers that its scientific data base is complete and that there are no outstanding scientific issues". [see para. 68 of Canada Rebuttal Submission]

US comment

33.   The United States refers to *Drs. Boisseau's and Boobis'* and to JECFA's replies to this question in paragraph 17 of its submission.[2] The US approves the statement by *Dr. Boisseau* about the quality and the quantity of the data used by JECFA. However, this is not surprising because the data used by JECFA are too old. Conversely, the data used by the European Communities are more recent and converge on this point with the statement of the US Carcinogenesis report which states that "... *Although the molecular mechanisms responsible for estrogen carcinogenicity are not well understood, the evidence indicates that estrogen carcinogenesis is complex, involving proliferative effects and possibly direct and indirect genotoxic effects ...* ". Thus, there is no doubt that there are several gaps in our knowledge but the new evidence available confirms the direct and indirect genotoxicity of oestradiol and of the other hormones.

Canada's comment

34.   Canada draws conclusions from JECFA's replies which are plainly wrong. JECFA was making a general and abstract statement on this point, but this tells us nothing of whether the ideal situation described in its reply is applicable in the case of these hormones, because JECFA's evaluations date from 1988 and are too old by today's scientific evidence.

Q10.   In para. 129 and 168 of its Replies to the Panel Questions, the European Communities states that "JECFA's traditional mandate does not allow it to examine all risk management options but restricts it to either propose MRLs or not". Does Codex have risk management options other than (1) the establishment of an MRL, (2) establishing that an MRL is not necessary or (3) no recommendation?

US comment

35.   The United States does not refer to or comment on *Dr. Boisseau's* and on Codex' and JECFA's replies to this question.[3]

Canada's comment

36.   The European Communities observes that, like the question itself, Canada's comments are confusing again what is a risk management measure in the terminology of Codex Alimentarius and JECFA and what this term should be understood to include in the *SPS Agreement*, as interpreted by the Appellate Body in the *Hormones* case.

---

[2]   Question 11 in questions asked to Codex, JECFA and IARC.
[3]   Question 12 in questions asked to Codex, JECFA and IARC.

Q11. What should, in your view, be the components of a qualitative risk assessment, compared with a quantitative risk assessment? [see para. 82 of Canada Rebuttal Submission]

US comment

37.   The United States does not refer to or comment on the experts' (*Drs. Boisseau, Boobis, Cogliano*) replies to this question.

Canada's comment

38.   Canada draws (at paras. 42-43) from the replies of the two scientists (*Dr. Boisseau and Dr. Boobis*) to this and to subsequent questions the conclusion that a risk assessment that does not include a dose-response assessment would be incomplete. However, as the other scientists who replied to these questions have explained, the European Communities has performed a qualitative (and where possible a quantitative) dose-response assessment. Moreover, Canada criticises (at para. 43) the relevance of the monographs produced by the IARC as a basis for conducting a dose-response assessment and cites in support the 1998 Appellate Body report in the *Hormones* case. However, the statement by the Appellate Body quoted by Canada is partly incorrect and partly irrelevant today. It is incorrect because the evaluation of substances by IARC, like the three natural hormones, have served for so many years responsible governments in their risk assessments and it is simply inaccurate and scientifically unsound to suggest that they do not provide a sufficient basis for a risk assessment. This is because the toxicological and other scientific evidence on which both the JECFA and the IARC base their findings *is the same*: they both decide on the carcinogenicity of a substance on studies conducted *in vitro* and *in vivo* and extrapolate from animal models to humans (if there is no direct evidence from experiments on humans). There is nothing in the JECFA data base and the methodology used by it which is different from the data on carcinogenicity and the methodology used by IARC. This is very important to understand. If there are residue data from meat treated with these hormones for animal growth promotion, IARC will use them in the same way as JECFA normally does. The difference is that JECFA has come to the conclusion that the three natural hormones are not genotoxic, which is not the conclusion reached by IARC on the basis of broadly the same toxicological evidence. But once JECFA had reached the conclusion that there is a safe threshold, it then used the residues data from treated meat in order to see if the presumed safe theoretical threshold would be exceeded. This, the IARC did not have to do, as the other direct and indirect evidence it examined supported the characterisation of these hormones as proven human carcinogens. Moreover, the most recent data cited and used by the European Communities and also those cited (for the first time) in the 2002 US Carcinogenesis Report confirm that oestrogen is genotoxic by direct and indirect mechanisms of action. Therefore, the data from residues in treated meat, to which para. 200 of the 1998 Appellate Body report refers, are irrelevant.

39.   It should however be stressed that, in any case, the 1999, 2000 and 2002 risk assessment conducted by the European Communities were based also on residues in meat treated with these hormones for animal growth promotion purposes, which were generated under realistic conditions of use, that is where GVP is respected but also where abuse or misuse could occur. These studies have shown that the resulting residues in treated meat are by far higher than the residue levels considered by the old and outdated studies on which the defending parties and JECFA based their findings. Moreover, the intake of residues from treated meat consumed by prepubertal children would exceed the ADIs and MRLs established by JECFA if the much lower levels of endogenous production of the three natural hormones is taken into account. That is why the European Communities considers imperative that these old data and the methods by which they have been measured and assessed should be provided to this Panel, its experts and the European Communities for a review. It is only then that a proper conclusion could be drawn on the accuracy and relevance of these old data for the risk assessment.

Q12.   How is scientific uncertainty addressed in risk assessments in general? With respect to the assessment of risks from the consumption of meat treated with the growth promotion hormones at issue, how has scientific uncertainty been considered by JECFA/Codex ? How does it differ from the way it has been considered by the European Communities in its assessment of risks from the consumption of meat treated with the growth promotion hormones at issue?

US comment

40.   The United States while referring to *Dr. Boobis'* reply to this question in paragraphs 17 and 20 of its submission[4] does not discuss or comment the issue of scientific uncertainty.

Canada's comment

41.   Canada makes again (at para. 46) the irrelevant argument that the European Communities is not consistent because it prohibits hormone-treated meat but allows the consumption of foods (e.g. milk, eggs, meat) containing some of these hormones at levels many times higher. But this argument has been made by both parties before the 1997 panel and has been rejected clearly by the Appellate Body in the 1998 Hormones report (at para. 221) as "an absurdity". So the European Communities wonders why Canada keeps repeating it.

---

[4]   There is no reference to Dr. Boisseau's reply to the same question.

C.   Assessment of Oestradiol-17β

Q13. To what extent, in your view, does the EC risk assessment identify the potential for adverse effects on human health, including the carcinogenic or genotoxic potential, of the residues of oestradiol-17β found in meat derived from cattle to which this hormone had been administered for growth promotion purposes in accordance with good veterinary practice? To what extent does the EC risk assessment evaluate the potential occurrence of these adverse effects?

US comment

42.   The United States refers to the experts' (*Drs. Boobis, Boisseau, Guttenplan*) replies to this question in paragraphs 19, 20, 21, 32, 37 and 84 of its submission. However, the underlying theme in all US comments is the fundamental error that these hormones, and in particular oestradiol 17β, are not carcinogenic because a safe threshold exists. This is a fundamental error on which the European Communities has already commented above (e.g. to Question no 7).

Canada's comment

43.   Canada's statement that the replies by *Dr. Boisseau, Dr. Boobis and Dr. Guttenplan* all indicate that the EC risk assessment "was deficient in one manner or another in its evaluation of the potential occurrence of adverse effects" is a very unqualified summary. In particular, *Dr. Guttenplan* has expressly stated that the European Communities has done a "thorough job in identifying the potential adverse effects on human health of oestradiol-17β" and that the European Communities has "performed thorough studies of residues levels in cattle, and the environment". Most importantly, Canada states (at paras. 49-51) that "there is no evidence that this [genotoxic] potential is realized in vivo (as opposed to in vitro)", that *Dr. Boisseau* disagrees with the European Communities "as do most other experts and international scientific bodies", and that the European Communities decision not to conduct a complete risk assessment "is not supported by the evidence". None of these statements is correct. The European Communities has shown that there is sufficient and constantly growing evidence from studies *in vivo* that show the direct genotoxicity of oestradiol 17ß and its catechol metabolites in animal and human tissue as well as the mutagenicity of oestradiol 17ß metabolites in experimental animals:

- Li et al. (2004) have demonstrated that the N7-guanine adduct (N7Gua) and the N3-adenine adduct (N3Ade) of E2-3,4-quinone (the putative carcinogenic E2 metabolite) were present in the DNA of the mammary gland of ACI rats after injection of 4-HO-E2 or E2-3,4-quinone (Exhibit EC – 121).
- Markushin et al. (2003) have detected the N3Ade (and in part N7Gua) adducts of 4-HO-E2 and 4-HO-estrone (E1) in the breast tissue of women (Exhibit EC – 118).

- Chakravarti et al. (2001) demonstrated mutations in the H-ras gene of SENCAR mouse skin after topical application of E2-3,4-quinone, and Chakravarti et al. (2003) found similar mutations in the mammary gland of ACI rats after administration of E2-3,4-quinone. The type of mutations in both *in vivo* animal systems can be explained by depurination of the N3Ade adducts. These experiments are reviewed in Cavalieri et al. (2006) (Exhibit EC – 48).

- Cavalieri et al. (2006) used the Big Blue® rat model to assess the mutagenicity of E2 and 4-HO-E2 *in vivo* and found both compounds to be mutagenic. The mutational spectrum observed for 4-HO-E2 was consistent with the formation and depurination of N3Ade adducts (Exhibit EC – 125)

44.   It should be noted that the magnitude of DNA adduct levels and mutagenic activities reported in these studies is not very high and seems to be much lower than encountered with most known genotoxins, which indicates that oestradiol may be a weak genotoxin. This may also be true for the other hormones and this may explain why standard genotoxicity assays show negative or borderline effects with these compounds. Moreover, the genotoxic activity of oestradiol 17β and its metabolites determined in rodent assays *in vivo* may be obscured by the diet, which usually contains high concentrations of phytoestrogens, e.g. from soy. It has been recently reported that several phytoestrogens induce the enzyme quinone reductase, which inactivates the quinones of catechol estrogens and thereby reduces DNA damage (Bianco et al., 2005, Exhibit EC – 124)).

45.   The question, therefore, is not that there is no evidence of genotoxicity *in vivo*, but rather how much evidence more is needed by the defending parties before they would be forced to reconsider their views, as did JECFA and Canada recently in relation to other substances, e.g. for Carbadox.

Q14. In your view, does the risk assessment undertaken by the European Communities on oestradiol-17β follow the Codex Guidelines on risk assessment, including the four steps of hazard identification, hazard characterization, exposure assessment, , and risk characterization with respect to oestradiol-17β?

US comment

46.   The United States refers to the experts' (*Drs. Boobis, Boisseau and Guttenplan*) replies to this question in paragraphs 19, 20 and 32 of its submission. In paragraph 19 of its submission, the United States claims that "the experts' responses confirm that, while the EC Opinions engage in hazard identification, the first step of a risk assessment, the Opinion fail to complete any of the remaining three components." The European Communities disagrees with the selective citation and the biased conclusions drawn by the US. *Dr. Guttenplan* has certainly supported the EC position on this point.

Canada's comment

47.   Canada's presentation that "Drs. Boisseau, Boobis and Guttenplan also agree with Canada that the EC failed to follow the Codex guidelines on risk assessments" and that "[t]he experts share Canada's concerns that the EC (and SCVPH) took significant and unjustified short-cuts in the conduct of its risk assessment" is plainly wrong.

48.   Neither *Dr. Boisseau nor Dr. Boobis or Dr. Guttenplan* make any specific comments on Canada's concerns. Thus, to present the experts' replies as if these had said: "Yes, Canada is right" is, to say the least, wishful thinking.

49.   More specifically, *Dr. Boisseau's* position can hardly be described as being "very critical of the EC's decision not to follow the Codex guidelines" as Canada presents it. *Dr. Boisseau* has explicitly stated that "[T]he European Communities does not indicate anywhere in its submission that it does not intend to follow the Codex guidelines on risk assessment including the four steps of hazard identification, hazard characterization, exposure assessment and risk characterization. On the contrary, the following indicates that the European Communities considers the same approach for assessing the risk associated with the residues of growth promoters." On that basis, how is it possible for Canada to describe *Dr. Boisseau's* position as "very critical on the EC's decision not to follow Codex guidelines"? Just the opposite is true.

50.   While it is true that *Dr. Boisseau* at the end of his reply has put in brackets a comment whereby "[t]hese two statements call for refining the exposure assessment of hormones residues" it is a complete mischaracterization by Canada to interpret this statement as a criticism that the European Communities should "not abandon the entire risk assessment methodology" and, even more, to take this conclusion as a confirmation of Canada's submission. Again, this is little more than wishful thinking by Canada.

51.   It is no surprise that Canada's comment on *Dr. Guttenplan's* reply is also more than selective. Canada refers to *Dr. Guttenplan's* alleged criticism on the European Communities' hazard characterization and risk characterization "for the same reasons advanced by others". The European Communities is wondering who are these others and on what basis Canada can make such an unqualified statement.

52.   On substance, Canada also completely ignores that *Dr. Guttenplan* has expressly stated that the "EC has been thorough in following Codex guidelines on hazard characterization and very thorough in exposure assessment." This indeed invalidates directly Canada's own statement whereby the "EC has done very little that resembles an exposure assessment".[5] In this context, the European Communities is also surprised about Canada's description that the European Communities has admitted "that it did not, because it could not conduct an expo-

---

[5]   See Canada's comments on expert replies, para. 54.

sure assessment". The paragraph 141 of the EC rebuttal submission quoted by Canada does not support this statement.

D. Consumption of Meat Containing Hormones

(a) Carcinogenicity

Q15. Does the identification of oestradiol-17β as a human carcinogen indicate that there are potential adverse effects on human health when it is consumed in meat from cattle treated with hormones for growth promotion purposes? Does your answer depend on whether good veterinary practices are followed? [see paras. 206-207 of EC Rebuttal Submission (US case), para. 121 of EC Rebuttal Submission (Canada case), paras. 97-98 of EC Replies to Panel Questions, para. 76-77, 150 and 155-156 of US First Submission, paras. 35-40 and 46 of US Rebuttal Submission]

US comment

53. The United States refers to the experts' (*Dr. Boobis, Boisseau and Guttenplan, Cogliano*) replies in paragraphs 34, 38, 42 and 43 of its submission. Conveniently, the United States does not comment on *Dr. Boisseau's* categorical statement regarding the dependence of his reply on the efficient implementation of good veterinary practices.

Canada's comment

54. From the outset, it should be noted that none of the experts "agree with Canada" on the effect of the carcinogenicity of oestradiol-17β. Indeed, none of the experts take any position on any statement made by Canada.

55. Canada's blunt summary of the experts' replies whereby "most of the experts conclude affirmatively that there would be "no appreciable risk" of adverse effects from exposure from this one minimal source of oestradiol 17β" is inaccurate as the experts differ considerably in their replies and most of them agree with the EC position.

56. *Dr. Boisseau* merely says that "oestradiol-17β (…) is not likely to produce adverse effects on human health when it is consumed in meat from cattle treated with hormones for growth promotion purposes". Yet, what is "likely" or not appears to be quite a subjective judgement. Moreover, even *Dr. Boisseau* explicitly subjects this view to the respect of good veterinary practices as otherwise all the work "to protect human health with regard to veterinary drug residues is meaningless".

57. *Dr. Cogliano* explicitly states that "the identification of oestradiol-17β as a human carcinogen indicates that there are potential adverse effects on human health when oestradiol-17β is consumed in meat from cattle treated with hormones for growth promotion purposes." This statement hardly supports Canada's

theory that the consumption of beef treated with oestradiol-17β does not entail an "appreciable risk".

58.   Furthermore, *Dr. Guttenplan* states that "if potential is taken to mean possible, then an adverse effect cannot be ruled out, but it is unlikely if good veterinary practices are followed". As *Dr. Boisseau, Dr. Guttenplan* thus refers to the likelihood of adverse human health effect. Yet, as can be seen from his reply (and it is also interesting to contrast this reply with *Dr. Boisseau's*), such an assessment contains a subjective judgement which justifies that in case of a political decision to take "zero risks" even the slightest minimal chance should be excluded. This is even more justified in this specific case where there are considerable doubts about whether GVP are always respected and which even according to *Dr. Boisseau* would render all the assumptions "meaningless".

59.   Finally, Canada argues that the EC evidence demonstrates that "multiple hormone implants resulted in residues that were still less than the ADIs." However, the data generated by the EC study in question (by *Daxenberger et al. 2000*) documented that the residues after improper use would exceed by far the ADIs.

Q16. Does the scientific evidence relied upon in the SCVPH Opinions support the conclusion that carcinogenic effects of the hormones at issue are related to a mechanism other than hormonal activity? [see para. 148 of the EC Replies to Panel Questions and paras. 35-40 and 46 of US Rebuttal Submission]

US comments

60.   The United States refers to the experts' (*Drs. Boisseau, Boobis, Guttenplan*) replies to this question in paragraphs 34, 36 and 50 of its submission. While pretending that all experts confirm the view that no scientific evidence supports the conclusion that the carcinogenic effects of oestradiol-17β are related to a mechanism other than hormonal activity, the United States has to admit, in the same paragraph (34) that *Dr. Guttenplan* has taken a much more nuanced view on this issue. The United States' interpretation of other statements made by *Dr. Guttenplan*, which allegedly suggest, that he links the carcinogenic effects to the hormonal activity, are simply erroneous. The European Communities has explained several times (also above in relation to question 13) that in 2002 there was sufficient evidence from experiments in vivo and this evidence is still growing further. In addition, there is evidence for the mutagenicity of oestradiol-17β as determined in cell culture. For example, Kong et al (Int. J. Oncology, 17: 1141-1149, 2000) reported on the mutagenicity of oestradiol-17β in V79 hamster ovary cells and recently Zhao et al., in a paper whose authorship included *Dr. Guttenplan* himself (Chem. Res. Toxicol. 19: 475-479, 2006, Exhibit EC-110), reported the mutagenicity of the 4-OH catechol metabolite of oestradiol-17β in BB Rat2 embryonic cells. In this study, multiple treatment of the cells with 50 to 200nM 4-OH oestradiol-17β induced mutations in the BB Rat2 cells in a dose response fashion, with a significant increase being observed

after 3 and 3 treatments at the 200nM level. The mutational spectrum resulting from 4-OH oestradiol-17β treatment was different than the "background" mutations seen in the control (untreated) cells further supporting the conclusion that the mutations were in fact caused by the 4-OH catechol estrogen. 2-OH oestradiol-17β did not induce mutations. These results support the difference in carcinogenicity difference between these 2 catechol metabolites and differences in their ability to cause transformation of normal human breast epithelial cell line MCF-10F as reported by Russo, et al. (J. Steroid Biochem. Mol. Biol. 87: 1-25, 2003, Exhibit EC-115). Furthermore, these results are particularly significant in that the 4-OH catechol metabolite of oestradiol-17β has been detected in the mammary tissue of mice in a model where mammary tumorigenesis is dependent on the presence of estradiol (Devanesan et al. Carcinogenesis, 22: 1573-1576, 2001 (Exhibit EC – 122); Yue et al. J. Steroid Biochem. Mol. Biol. 86: 477-486, 2003, Exhibit EC-90) and in human breast tissue (Yue et al. J. Steroid Biochem. Mol. Biol. 86: 477-486, 2003, Exhibit EC-90).

61.   With regard to the study by Chakravarti et al (Oncogene, 20; 7945-7953, 2001, Exhibit EC-48), which is criticised by *Dr. Boobis*, it should be explained that it detected mutations in the H-*ras* gene in the skin of SENCAR mice following dermal treatment with E2-3,4-quinone, with the specific nature of the mutations detected being consistent with the expected depurination of adenine due to the formation of an E2-3,4-quinone-Adenine adduct. This is relevant to the potential mutagenicity of estradiol in humans because: First, we know that oxidative metabolism of oestradiol-17β to the E2-3-4-quinone metabolite occurs in human breast tissue because E2-quinone adducts to glutathione have been detected (Yue et al. J. Steroid Biochem. Mol. Biol. 86: 477-486, 2003, Exhibit EC-90). Second, adducts of the E2-3,4-quinone with ademine and guanine have been detected in the mammary tissue of ACI rats injected into the mammary gland tissue with 4-OH E2 or E2-3,4-quinone (Carcinogenesis, 25:, 289-297, 2004, Exhibit EC-121). These findings are ignored by *Dr. Boobis* as well as by the US.

Canada's comment

62.   Unlike the US, Canada criticizes *Dr. Guttenplan's* support for the EC conclusion on the basis that he has not made an analysis on its own. However, Canada has obviously no difficulties in relying on *Dr. Boisseau* who, in turn is merely invoking (old) JECFA reports and who, therefore, has also not made an analysis on its own. Canada thereby applies a double standard just as it sees fit for its own purposes. In any case, the European Communities has explained above that *Dr. Guttenplan* has published together with other scientists several papers in peer-reviewed journals, the most relevant one a few months ago (Chem. Res. Toxicol. 19: 475-479, 2006, Exhibit EC-110) which has used the Big Blue® rat model to assess the mutagenicity of oestradiol-17β and 4-HO-E2 *in vivo* and found both compounds to be mutagenic. The mutational spectrum observed for 4-HO-E2 was consistent with the formation and depurination of N3Ade adducts.

Q17. Could you comment on Canada's statement that "the studies commissioned by the European Communities also failed to find evidence of "catechol metabolites" – that is the oestradiol metabolites identified as the source of the genotoxic potential – in meat from treated animals"? What would be the implication of an absence or presence of catechol metabolites? [see para. 102 of Canada Rebuttal submission, EC Exhibit 51A]

US comment

63.   The United States refers to *Drs. Boisseau's, Boobis' and Cogliano's* replies to this question in paragraph 44 of its submission and very conveniently omits any reference to *Dr. Guttenplan's* straightforward reply.

64.   Furthermore, its reference to *Dr. Cogliano's* reply is misleading as *Dr. Cogliano* does not conclude "that detectable levels of catechol metabolites were not formed from the parent compound", but rather concludes that "*the absence of catechol metabolites could imply either* (1) [the above] *or* (2) that some level of catechol metabolites was formed that the test methods were not sufficiently sensitive to detect it." (emphasis added) Indeed, as the EC has explained above (in relation to question no 13), there is sufficient and constantly growing evidence from studies *in vivo* that show the direct genotoxicity of oestradiol 17ß and its catechol metabolites in animal and human tissue as well as the mutagenicity of oestradiol 17ß metabolites in experimental animals.

65.   It should be noted that the magnitude of DNA adduct levels and mutagenic activities reported in these studies may not be very high. It seems indeed to be much lower than encountered with most known genotoxins, which indicates that oestradiol may be a weak genotoxin. However, this can also be true for the other hormones and this may explain why standard genotoxicity assays show negative or borderline effects with these compounds. Moreover, the genotoxic activity of oestradiol 17β and its metabolites determined in rodent assays *in vivo* may be obscured by the diet (Bianco et al., 2005, Exhibit EC-124).

66.   Finally, that oestrogen may be genotoxic by direct or indirect mechanisms of action is now admitted even by the US since its 2002 Carcinogenesis Report, cited above, and any argument now to the contrary by the US is necessarily not credible.

Canada's comment

67.   Canada takes issue with *Dr. Guttenplan* on the amounts of catechol metabolites by referring to "other experts'" confirmation. However, since Canada does not identify these other experts this is a rather unqualified remark. On substance, the European Communities finds it remarkable that Canada does not criticize *Dr. Guttenplan's* statement that even "the lack of catechols in meat does not imply that meat from estrogen-treated cattle is without risk for genotoxicity".

68.   Moreover, the European Communities would emphasize that, in the absence to the contrary, Canada obviously agrees with *Dr. Cogliano's* statement whereby "the presence of catechol metabolites would support the potential for

adverse effects to occur. The absence of catechol metabolites could imply either (1) that detectable levels of catechol metabolites were not formed from the parent compound or (2) that some level of catechol metabolites was formed that the test methods were not sufficiently sensitive to detect it." This is the most likely explanation, as stated above.

Q18. Please comment on the US argument that the European Communities fails to demonstrate through scientific evidence that oestradiol-17β is genotoxic. Would your reply have been different at the time of adoption of the EC Directive in September 2003? If so, why? [see paras. 118-119 of EC Rebuttal Submission (US case), paras. 123-124 of EC Rebuttal Submission (Canada case), paras. 87-91 and 153-156 of US First Submission, paras. 35-40 and 46 of US Rebuttal Submission, and paras. 90-97 of Canada Rebuttal Submission]

US comment

69.   The United States refers to *Drs. Boobis' and Cogliano's* replies to this question in paragraphs 35 and 44 of its submission and very conveniently omits to refer to *Drs. Boisseau's and Guttenplan's* replies. The latter's reply certainly does not "confirm" - as the United States claims (at paragraph 35) – "that the scientific evidence cited by the EC in its Opinions does not support the conclusion that estradiol 17β is genotoxic at levels found in residues in meat from cattle treated with growth promoting hormones." Quite to the contrary, *Dr. Guttenplan* confirms the existence of such evidence and states that "the evidence now is much stronger" citing a study of 2004.

70.   Moreover, the US argues (at para. 36) that the European Communities has failed to explain why its evaluation of estradiol 17β was not subject to a CVMP guideline requiring confirmation of an in vitro positive using an appropriate *in vivo* assay. This comment is disingenuous because the pharmaceutical industry, the defending members and JECFA, i.e. those arguing that these substances are safe, should produce the evidence showing that estradiol 17β is not genotoxic *in vivo*. The EC has fulfilled its obligations by funding a number of studies and also by collecting the growing evidence from experiments *in vivo* showing the direct genotoxicity of these hormones, in particular of estradiol 17β. It is now high time that the US (and Canada) stops criticising the European Communities for absence of evidence which itself did not have when it approved these hormones more that 30 years ago and makes an effort to prove what it preaches, that is that these hormones are not genotoxic by direct action. Instead of criticising the European Communities on the basis of purely hypothetical assumptions, the US should have tried to explain the statement from its 2002 Carcinogenesis Report which states:

> "The evidence is strong that estrogen carcinogenesis is mediated through activation of the estrogen receptor. *In addition, there is evidence that other mechanisms may play a role in the carcino-*

genic effects of estrogens in some tissues. Prolonged estrogen exposure induces cell proliferation in estrogen-dependent target cells, affects cellular differentiation, and alters gene expression. *Although the molecular mechanisms responsible for estrogen carcinogenicity are not well understood, the evidence indicates that estrogen carcinogenesis is complex, involving proliferative effects and possibly direct and indirect genotoxic effects.* The relative importance of each mechanism is likely a function of the specific estrogen and of the exposed tissue or cell type and its metabolic state (Yager and Liehr 1996)." (emphasis added)

Canada's comment

71.   Canada's interpretation of *Dr. Boisseau* reply is quite astonishing. First, Canada tries to construe from *Dr. Boisseau's* reply a difference for a substance having "genotoxic potential" and being "genotoxic". Yet, nowhere in his reply does *Dr. Boisseau* address this issue so that Canada can hardly take this response as support for its own theory. Moreover, Canada describes *Dr. Boisseau's* reply on the establishment of an ADI by JECFA in 1999 as "pointing to the need to place exposure to oestradiol 17β from this source into context." It will remain Canada's secret what it means by such a description, since *Dr. Boisseau* instead submitted that the ADI was established "in order to present in a more convincing way the outcome of its [JECFA's] assessment".

72.   In respect of *Dr. Boisseau's* reply it is also difficult to see how Canada can claim support for its assumption that oestradiol 17β is not genotoxic *in vivo*. He does not say so in his reply to Question 18 and even *Dr. Boisseau's* reply to Question 13 does not contain such a general statement.

73.   The comments by Canada (at paras. 72-73) are subject to the same criticism mentioned above for the statements made by the US. Indeed, the UK VPC constitutes quite a remarkable evolution on this point from its previous evaluation of these hormones in 1995, and it is certainly less categorical in its findings (it uses the terms "is likely") than Canada. Even so, however, the statement quoted by Canada (at para. 72) contrasts sharply with the findings in the 2002 US Carcinogenesis Report quoted above by the European Communities, which Canada has chosen to ignore.

Q19.   The European Communities states that "... it is generally recognized that for substances which have genotoxic potential (as is the case with oestradiol-17β) a threshold can not be identified. Therefore it cannot be said that there exist a safe level below which intakes from residue should be considered to be safe. Therefore the fact that doses used in growth promotion are low is not of relevance". Does the scientific evidence referred to by the European Communities support these conclusions? Would your reply have been different at the time of adoption of the EC Directive in September 2003? If so, why? [see para. 201 of EC Rebuttal Submission (US case), paras. 120-122 of EC Rebuttal Submission (Canada case), paras. 73 and 86-

98 of Canada Rebuttal Submission, paras. 87-91 and 153-156 of US First Submission and paras. 35-40 and 46 of US Rebuttal Submission]

US comment

74.   The United States refers to the experts' (*Drs. Boobis, Boisseau, Cogliano, Guttenplan*) replies to this question in paragraphs 37 through 40 of its submission. Its reading of *Dr. Guttenplan's and Dr. Cogliano's* replies is erroneous. On *Dr. Guttenplan*, the United States claims that he does not take a clear view on whether oestradiol 17β is genotoxic at level found in residues in meat from cattle treated with growth promoting hormones. *However, this is not what Dr. Guttenplan has said.*

75.   On *Dr. Cogliano*, the United States' claims that he "concurs [with *Dr. Boobis*] "noting that the EC's statement regarding the lack of a threshold has not been demonstrated by the scientific evidence." Quite to the contrary, however, *Dr. Cogliano* said: "The EC's statement that a threshold cannot be identified reflects their view of genotoxic mechanisms, just as the contrary statement that there is a threshold and that this threshold is above the levels found in meat residues reflects how Canada and the US view genotoxic mechanisms. Neither statement has been demonstrated by the scientific evidence, rather, they are different assumptions that each party uses in their interpretation of the available evidence."

Canada's comment

76.   Canada's statement that *Dr. Boobis' and Dr. Cogliano's* replies would support its own argument that for substances endogenously produced by human body there must be threshold is, at least, a challengeable conclusion. Indeed, neither *Dr. Boobis nor Dr. Cogliano*, who apart from this question obviously have a different perception about the genotoxicity of these hormones, do at all address this argument. Canada makes (at para. 74) the rhetoric argument that "humanity would have been wiped out by cancer millennia ago". This statement is highly unscientific. First, humanity did not use to eat meat treated with hormones, save for approximately the last 30 years and this only in the US (and a bit later in Canada). Secondly, the rates of cancer in general (including prostate and breast) are increasing, in particular in the US, where they are higher by about 20% compared to those in Europe. Third, as the European Communities has explained above, it may be that these hormones are weak carcinogens, which explains why they could not be detected by the old and most of the existing assays. But the rates of cancer observed today are a serious cause for concern. Furthermore, the implication of the Canadian claim that a substance that is produced endogenously cannot be carcinogenic when administered exogenously is incomprehensible.

77.   The same applies for Canada's claim (at para. 75 and 76) that even EFSA has recognised safe thresholds for genotoxic substances. This is simply not true because the EFSA opinion cited by Canada, although issued for another purpose,

simply states that the incidence of cancer may not be increased, but it does not state that there is no risk from such substances.

78.   Canada states (at para. 74) "that experts from around the world" contradict the EC' claim, but it manages to cite only the UK VPC and the JECFA reports. These are the "experts around the world". Canada fails however to cite the well known reports from the IARC – which as its name indicates is the best placed international institution on issues of cancer research and prevention – nor does Canada pay any attention to the US Carcinogenesis Report.

79.   It is clear from the replies of the experts that they are divided on this issue (2 against 2), but if the expected replies of the other 2 experts are added, then the majority of the experts agrees in substance with the EC position.

Q20.   In your view, how do the European Communities' conclusions above relate to the conclusion by Codex that "establishing an ADI or MRL for a hormone that is produced endogenously in variable levels in human beings was considered unnecessary"? To what extent, in your view, has JECFA's conclusion that oestradiol "has genotoxic potential" affected its recommendations on this hormone?

US comment

80.   The United States refers to the experts' (*Drs. Boobis, Boisseau, Guttenplan and Cogliano*) and JECFA's (to a related question)[6] replies to this question in paragraph 41 of its submission. The European Communities disagrees with the summary of the statements made by the US in that paragraph. That oestradiol 17β is carcinogenic by both direct and receptor mediated mechanisms is no longer in doubt (see the latest article by Cavalieri et al., 2006, see Exhibit EC-125). This has been stated also by the US since its 2002 Carcinogenesis Report to which the US fails to refer.

Canada's comment

81.   Canada draws an unjustified conclusion from the experts' replies whereby "Drs. Boisseau, Boobis and Guttenplan all consider the EC's conclusion about the absence of thresholds to be inconsistent with the Codex standards." Yet, the answers of these experts are much more nuanced than Canada presents. For instance, *Dr. Boisseau* only states that the "European Communities' conclusions are questionable". It goes without saying that there exists a difference between "inconsistent" (as Canada qualifies it) and "questionable". The same applies to *Dr. Boobis* who submits that the "EC conclusion on the absence of safety at any level of exposure is somewhat at odds with the underlying basis of the Codex conclusion regarding the need for an ADI or MRL". Again, if something is "somewhat at odds" it does not mean that it is "inconsistent". Finally, *Dr. Gut-*

---

[6]   Question 20 of the questions asked to Codex, JECFA and IARC is about …

tenplan merely states that the European Communities' conclusions above are "at variance" with those of Codex. It is difficult to see how this can be reconciled with Canada's statement that the EC's conclusions are "inconsistent" with Codex standard.

82.   In this context, it is also an unqualified assumption by Canada that "to the extent that most of the experts found the EC conclusions on the matter are un-supported by the evidence and are "questionable", they support the existing Co-dex standards." Indeed, the mere comparison between a Codex standard and a respective EC conclusion does not lend any support whatsoever about the value of this standard.

83.   Finally, the European Communities would take issue with Canada's un-supported conclusion that the "experts' answers also confirm that even though JECFA acknowledged that oestradiol 17β has "genotoxic potential", this ac-knowledgment did not generate concern about the safety of the substances and therefore did not affect its recommendation". Indeed, none of the experts makes any qualified statement to this effect and Canada's inference from the experts' replies is therefore completely baseless. At most, *Dr. Boobis* stated that "I do not believe that JECFA's conclusion that oestradiol has "genotoxic potential" af-fected its recommendations on this hormone (…)". As can easily be seen this is a mere unsubstantiated guess and personal opinion by one expert whereas the other experts remain mute on this issue. Thus, Canada's presentation is far from being an objective description of the facts.

84.   What is even more important is that the statements by *Dr. Boisseau and Dr. Boobis* are partial because they do not consider the totality of the available evidence, such as that mentioned by the European Communities and in particular the reports from the IARC and the US Carcinogenesis Report which have been made available to them. *Dr. Boobis* concentrates only on the JECFA reports, which are based on very old data.

Q21.   Does the scientific evidence referred to by the European Communi-ties demonstrate that the five hormones other than oestradiol-17β, when consumed as residues in meat have genotoxic potential? Does your answer depend on whether good veterinary practices are followed? Would your reply have been different at the time of adoption of the Directive in Septem-ber 2003? If so, why? [see, *inter alia*, the SCVPH Opinions and paras. 63, 83, 89-91 and 93 of US First Submission, paras. 131-136 of Canada Rebuttal Submission]

US comment

85.   The United States refers to the experts' (*Drs. Boobis, Guttenplan and Boisseau*) replies to this question in paragraph 50 of its submission. Overall, the experts' replies are much more nuanced than what the United States suggests when claiming that they all "confirm that the scientific materials cited by the EC in its Opinions do not demonstrate or support the conclusion that any of the five hormones has genotoxic potential or is carcinogenic by a mechanism other than

hormonal activity." As both *Dr. Boobis and Dr. Guttenplan* report, there are some data that indicate the possibility of genotoxic effects. The data are probably not "conclusive" (*Dr. Guttenplan*) and perhaps not "convincing" (*Dr. Boobis*) to everyone, but it is more than a sufficient and legitimate basis for a legislator acting on the basis of precaution to adopt provisional measures.

Canada's comment

86.   Canada's blunt statement that "Drs. Boisseau, Boobis and Guttenplan all refute the EC's claims about the potential genotoxicity of the other five hormones" is not supported by the experts' replies. For instance, *Dr. Boobis* merely states that "there is no convincing evidence that trenbolone acetate, MGA and zeranol are genotoxic". However, what is "convincing evidence"? In the same vein, *Dr. Guttenplan* refers to "no conclusive evidence" or "some evidence that certain of the hormones have genotoxic potential". Yet, what is "conclusive" or what means "some evidence"? Whatever it means, it can in any case not justify Canada's unqualified conclusion that there is no "potential genotoxicity of the other five hormones". Rather, their statements confirm the EC position that there are considerable gaps and uncertainties in our knowledge, which justify applying Article 5.7 of the *SPS Agreement* in order to achieve ones chosen level of health protection.

Q22.   How would you define *in vivo* DNA repair mechanisms? How effective or relevant are *in vivo* DNA repair mechanisms with respect to potential genotoxic effects from residues of the growth promoting hormones at issue when consumed in meat? Does your answer depend on whether good veterinary practices are followed in the administration of these hormones? To what extent does the scientific material referred to by the European Communities take into account these mechanisms in its evaluation of potential occurrence of adverse effects from residues of growth promoting hormones? Would your reply have been different at the time of adoption of the Directive in September 2003 and if so, why? [see paras. 40 and 46 of US Rebuttal Submission, footnote 107 of US First Submission, and para. 89 of Canada Rebuttal Submission]

US comment

87.   The United States refers to the experts' (*Drs. Boobis, Guttenplan*) replies in paragraph 31 of its submission. The US again misrepresents the views of the scientists, in particular those of *Dr. Guttenplan*, who stated *inter alia* that "a small fraction of damage inevitably escapes repair" and that consideration of this issue by the SCVPH is in fact irrelevant to the debate (even though he found some references in the SCVPH assessment that discussed this issue).

Canada's comment

88.   Canada spends again a number of paragraphs (at paras. 85-89) trying to interpret the experts' replies as supporting its views on this question. But as *Dr.*

Guttenplan has explained in his reply, there is no reason to believe that the repair mechanism in the case of these hormones would be different from what is happening in other instances. It is also inevitable that some DNA damage will remain unrepaired, as is the case with so many other direct genotoxic substances. As the 2002 US Carcinogenesis Report states: *"... prolonged estrogen exposure induces cell proliferation in estrogen-dependent target cells, affects cellular differentiation, and alters gene expression...[and that]...the relative importance of each mechanism is likely to be a function of the specific estrogen and of the exposed tissue or cell type and its metabolic state"*. This means that to go down the road advocated by the defending parties and *Dr. Boobis*, i.e. in trying to estimate how much of the DNA damage is likely to be repaired in time and what would be the carcinogenic potential of the damage left unrepaired would not be possible in view of so many specificities involved, supposing one could undertake this kind of estimation in a reliable way. That is why *Dr. Guttenplan* states that this issue is irrelevant for the debate on the genotoxicity of oestradiol and whether an ADI for such substances could or should be fixed.

Q23. To what extent is it necessary or possible to take into account the "long latency period" of cancer in the conduct of a risk assessment, which is supposed to assess carcinogenic effects of these hormones when consumed in meat? Have the hormones in dispute been used as growth promoters over a sufficient number of years for an assessment of their long-term effects on human health to be made? [see para. 149 of EC Rebuttal Submission (US Case), para. 143 of EC Rebuttal Submission (Canada case)].

US comment

89.   The United States refers to the experts' (*Drs. Boobis, Boisseau, Guttenplan and Cogliano*) replies on this question in paragraphs 57 and 58 of its submission.

90.   In Footnote 127 the United States is suggesting that there is no evidence of adverse effects after more than 20 years of consumption of beef from cattle treated for growth promotion purposes. However, as *Dr. Boobis* rightly concludes "... a negative result from such an observational study would not resolve the issue."

91.   Furthermore, the United States misinterprets *Dr. Guttenplan's* statement that "hormones in meat [...] have now been consumed for a sufficient number of years to observe strong or moderate increases in risk." The United States pretends that *Dr. Guttenplan* hereby suggest that there is no such evidence. However, the European Communities does not interpret in the same way Dr. Guttenplan's statement, quite the opposite.

Canada's comment

92.   Canada summarises the replies of the scientists in a partial way in paragraphs 90-93 to come to the conclusion that "... exposure to residues of hormones in meat from treated animals is only a small fraction of the overall expo-

sure to the substance from a variety of sources, including that produced endogenously within the human body ...". A careful reading of the replies of the scientists however does not support this conclusion. Indeed, none of the scientists explicitly said that the exposure is only "a small fraction", because it is not easy to estimate the level of the residues. For instance, the 2002 US Carcinogenesis Report simply stated that the use of these hormones for growth promotion increases the level of residues to above "their normal levels". The point therefore is that the two scientists cited by Canada have not and could not have come to the conclusion that the residues is a small fraction, not least because they do not know it and could not prove it (because of the background and other confounding factors).

Q24. To what extent is it possible to identify possible co-founding factors causing cancer and attribute them to identified sources? What are the implications of these factors for the conduct of a risk assessment evaluating the adverse affects caused by residues of growth promoting hormones in meat? Would your reply have been different at the time of adoption of the EC Directive in September 2003? If so, why?

US and Canada's comments

93.   The United States refers to the experts' (*Drs. Boobis, Boisseau, Guttenplan and Cogliano*) replies on this question in paragraph 59 of its submission and Canada in paragraphs 94-96. They both appear to accept (as do all the scientists) that there is now an association established between meat consumption and cancer, but they dispute that the evidence is there to clearly establish a causal link between the residues in meat from hormone-treated cattle and the high cancer incidence. But the European Communities has not argued it and does *not* take issue with the fact that it is difficult to establish that causal link. What is very important to note, however, is that the defending parties cannot make the argument that because the establishment of the causal link is difficult, there should be assumed that such a risk is insignificant or does not exist because the added burden is thought to be small. Furthermore, the defending parties can no longer make their simplistic argument that humans are exposed to hormonal residues from so many other sources, so a small additional exposure from the residues in treated meat would not make any difference. This simplistic argument has been made over and over again by the defending parties to the Panel and it is now clear that there is no scientific basis to this claim because they cannot establish the causal link of what they argue. However, the evidence is there, and it is indeed growing, associating high rates of cancer with meat consumption, and these rates of cancer are higher in the US than in Europe, and one day if the US and Canada would like to find out more about any possible causal link between the two so as to protect their people the same way as the European Communities does, it could undertake the studies which *Drs. Cogliano and Guttenplan* have suggested.

Q25. To what extent do the three recent studies referred to by the European Communities confirm a risk to human health from the consumption of meat from cattle treated with growth promoting hormones? Please also comment on the EC statement that one of the studies "was carried out after the introduction of the ban on the use of hormones for growth promotion in Europe, which means that the subjects should have been exposed to hormone-free meat in their diet. This may further imply that it cannot be excluded that the risk of cancer may be further increased if meat treated with hormones for animal growth promotion were to be consumed". [see paras. 145-148 of EC Rebuttal Submission (US case) and paras. 139-142 of EC Rebuttal Submission (Canada case), footnote 97 in para. 147 of EC Rebuttal Submission (US case), and Exhibits EC-71, 72, 73]

US and Canada's comments

94.   The United States refers to the experts' (*Drs. Boobis, Boisseau, Guttenplan and Cogliano*) replies on this question in paragraphs 61 through 63 of its submission. Contrary to what the United States suggests, the experts are far from "[agreeing] that the three studies demonstrate no such risk." While *Dr. Boobis* holds this view, both *Dr. Cogliano and Dr. Guttenplan*, on the contrary, confirm that these studies indicate or suggest risks. Indeed, as the European Communities has explained above, at least 2 out of the 4 scientists seem to agree that this kind of epidemiological evidence could provide indirect information indicating that there may be a causal link.

95.   It is therefore surprising the Canadian comment (in para. 102) that the European Communities is "manipulating a genuine scientific interest". This kind of manipulating tactic has been deployed by the defending parties since 1997, in their argument that the risk from residues in treated meat with these hormones is miniscule compared to the higher exposure of humans to intake from other natural foods (meat, broccoli, soya, eggs, etc.), a statement which the Appellate Body has dismissed as "an absurdity" in its 1998 *Hormones* report (at para. 221). Conversely, the EC argument has been supported by at least one panel expert in the 1998 *Hormones* case and appears to be considered relevant by two of the present experts. Indeed, it is recalled that during the 1997 panel report on *Hormones*, one of the experts for the Panel (Dr. G. Lucier) had then stated:

> *"For every million women alive in the United States, Canada, Europe today, about a 110,000 of those women will get breast cancer. This is obviously a tremendous public health issue. Of those 110,000 women get breast cancer, maybe several thousand of them are related to the total intake of exogenous oestrogens from every source, including eggs, meat, phyto-oestrogens, fungal oestrogens, the whole body burden of exogenous oestrogens. And by my estimates one of those 110,000 would come from eating meat containing oestrogens as a growth promoter, if used as prescribed."*

96.   However, the Appellate Body in 1998 denied evidentiary value to Dr. Lucier's statement for the reason that his opinion "... does not purport to be the result of scientific studies carried out by him or under his supervision focusing specifically on residues of hormones in meat from cattle fattened with such hormones ...". (at para. 198 of the 1998 Appellate Body report).

Q26.   Does the scientific evidence referred to by the European Communities, in particular any epidemiological studies, identify a relationship between cancer and residues of hormonal growth promoters? In its risk assessment of 1999, the European Communities makes reference to the higher rates of breast and prostate cancer observed in the United States as compared to the European Communities. Can a link be established between these statistics and the consumption of meat from animals treated with the hormones at issue? Would your reply have been different at the time of adoption of the EC Directive in September 2003? If so, why? [see pages 17-19 of 1999 Opinion of the SCVPH and related Tables A4-A5 on pages 83-91]

US comment

97.   The United States refers to the experts' (*Drs. Boobis, Boisseau, Guttenplan, Cogliano*) replies on this question in paragraphs 59, 60 and 63 of its submission. The United States' bold assertion that "the experts' responses confirm that the epidemiological studies cited by the EC in its Opinion fail to identify a link between hormone residues in meat and cancer" is once again a misrepresentation of what these experts actually stated. To take the example of *Dr. Boobis*, while he does state that "there is no scientific evidence demonstrating any association between consumption of meat from animals treated with growth promoting hormones and the risk of cancer in human," he qualifies that statement in the very next sentence pointing to the existence of "some studies that are consistent with such an association ..." (studies which admittedly he thinks have other possible explanations, some of which are more plausible than hormones in meat being causal). In the same vain, *Dr. Guttenplan* also concedes that "the results are at least consistent with a possible effect of hormones on breast and prostate cancer."

Canada's comment

98.   Canada submits that the breast and prostate cancer rates between Europe and North America are "relatively similar". However, on the basis of the figures mentioned by *Dr. Boobis* the difference would still be around 20% higher in the United States, which can hardly be described as "relatively similar". In this context, it is also amazing how *Dr. Boobis* minimizes the potential hormones treated beef on these differences by linking any difference rather to higher meat consumption. Apart from the fact that *Dr. Boobis* is just engaging in some "best guessing effort", it is undeniable that the higher meat consumption is intrinsically linked to higher hormones consumption. Thus, it defies any logic and

common sense, as *Dr. Boobis* does, to refer to one single figure on consumption but leaving aside the very fact that the higher consumption inevitably entails a higher intake of hormones.

(b)   Residue analysis

Q27.   How do the residues in meat from cattle treated with the three synthetic growth promoting hormones differ from residues in meat from cattle treated with the three natural growth promoting hormones at issue?

US and Canada's comments

99.   The United States and Canada do not refer to or comment on the experts' (*Drs. Boisseau, De Brabander*) replies to this question.

Q28.   How do the hormones naturally present in animals, meat, or human beings differ from the residues in meat of the three natural hormones used for growth promotion purposes?

US comment

100.   The United States does not refer to or comment on the experts' (*Drs. Boisseau, De Brabander*) replies to this question.

Canada's comment

101.   Contrary to Canada's view, *Dr. De Brabander's* opinion is not "much less clear". Rather, *Dr. Brabander* is very explicit and detailed in his reply suggesting that the residues in meat of the three natural hormones used for growth promotion purposes are not identical to the hormones naturally present in animals. What is even more questionable is that Canada criticises Dr. De Brabander's statement on the ground that "his position would be inconsistent with the detailed residue evidence reviewed by JECFA in its 1999 residue monograph. The monograph presents detailed data on hormone concentrations in various tissues, including muscle and fat, in untreated heifers and steers. Dr. De Brabander's suggestion in this regard simply does not withstand close scrutiny." Yet, as we know and as JECFA and Codex admitted openly in their replies – including that by Dr. Boisseau – the residue data used by JECFA in 1999 are essentially the same as those used in 1988 and that for the most part they date back to the 1960s and 1970s, whereas those used by *Dr. De Brabander* are the most recent ones. Therefore, the Canadian claim cannot be taken seriously. The European Communities reiterates once more its claim to the defending parties to provide their residues data and the Panel to request those data from JECFA and make them available to the experts, so that close scrutiny could indeed be exercised.

Q29.   To what extent do the SCVPH Opinions evaluate evidence on the actual residue levels of the synthetic hormones found in meat in their assessment of the risks from such residues? Are specific references provided

as to how the evidence on residues relates to the observance of good veterinary practices or lack thereof? How do they compare with the MRLs set by Codex? [see paras. 165-176 of EC Rebuttal Submission (US case); pages 55-68 of the Opinion of the SCVPH of 30 April 1999 in US Exhibit 4, para. 144 of US First Submission, Exhibits US-6 and 7, footnote 46 of US Rebuttal Submission]

US and Canada's comments

102.   The United States refers to the experts' (*Drs. Boisseau, De Brabander*) replies to this question in paragraphs 90, 91 to 93 of its submission. The US criticises *Dr. De Brabander's* reply as not being based on concrete evidence. The US further cites *Dr. Boisseau* as stating that "...older data is neither irrelevant or "bad" data simply due to its age. Rather, it is the quality and quantity of data that is important, and for the hormones at issue, a great deal of high quality data exists." As a general statement, the European Communities surely agrees with it. However, as regards the data on MGA used by JECFA date from the 1960s and 1980s, they are industry studies not published in any peer-reviewed journal, and have not been seen by anyone else except the US and JECFA (see Exhibit EC-127). Moreover, as long as these parties refuse to make them available for verification, it is legitimate for an expert and the European Communities to question their scientific quality and credibility, given that the more recent data produced by the EC studies and those available in open literature do not support the conclusions which the defending parties and JECFA pretend to draw from those old data.

103.   For these reasons, it is very inaccurate and misleading the comment made by Canada (at para. 111) that the methods used by JECFA are "modern" and validated ones. The problem is not only whether they are modern and validated but whether the residues which they are supposed to measure, if the MRLs were to be adopted one day by Codex Alimentarius, are taken with these modern methods or in the 1960s and 1980s when these so-called "modern" methods did not even exist. This is the point. Indeed, Canada (and the US) unjustifiably and incorrectly criticise the reply by *Dr. De Brabander* because he made his point as follows: "*At the time they are [the residues] produced (1987) there were no analytical methods available to quantify these residues at that concentration level in a correct way (methods as GC-MS-MS or LC-MS-MS)*". It is obvious, therefore, that Canada's comment (at para. 111) that "...his cursory conclusion is in stark contrast to the extensive evaluation of residue data conducted by JECFA. In particular, recent residue data from studies using "modern" validated methods (HPLC-MS, GC-MS and LC-MS) were assessed in the JECFA Residue Monograph for the 58th Meeting. All ten studies cited date from 1999 to 2002" is inaccurate because: First, JECFA in 2000 did not carry out any extensive evaluation of the data, it simply took for granted the old and unpublished data of the pharmaceutical industry; second, the ten studies cited in the 58th meeting of JECFA are those that will be used if the MRLs for MGA proposed by JECFA will be

accepted one day in the future by the Codex Commission, but they are clearly not those used to generate the data in the 1960s and 1970s.

104.   Moreover, Canada's summary of *Dr. Boisseau's* reply is misleading. *Dr. Boisseau* not merely stated that the SCVPH did not conduct a quantitative assessment but rather states more accurately that "[a]s, in its 1999 report, SCVPH concluded "that no threshold level and, therefore, no ADI can be established for any of the six hormones" (including the three synthetic ones), *there was no need for SCVPH* to conduct a quantitative assessment (…)." (Emphasis added). Obviously, it makes a difference if the SCVPH, as Canada insinuates, failed to do a quantitative assessment or, as *Dr. Boisseau* states there was a very good reason for SCVPH not to do such an assessment.

Q30.   To what extent do the SCVPH Opinions evaluate evidence on the actual residue levels of the three natural hormones in meat in their assessment of the risks from such residues? Is it possible to compare these to the ADIs recommended by JECFA in 1999? Are specific references provided as to how the evidence on residues relates to the observance of good veterinary practices or lack thereof? [see paras. 120-123 and 155-164 of EC Rebuttal Submission (US case), pages 33-54 of 1999 Opinion in Exhibit US-4, para. 144 of US First Submission, and 52nd JECFA Report in Exhibit US-5]

US and Canada's comments

105.   The United States refers to *Dr. Boobis'* reply to this question in paragraph 90 of its submission. No reference is made to *Dr. De Brabander's* reply. As the European Communities has noted in its comments of 30 June 2006 on *Dr. Boobis'* reply to this question, his position is incorrect because the SCVPH did perform the comparison of the ADI and MRL values proposed by JECFA with those generated by the EC studies that were reviewed by the SCVPH. In addition, the reply of *Dr. De Brabander* confirms the EC finding that the data used by JECFA are old and their validity can be questioned, until we are given the means to see and review them. The comment by the US (in para. 90) on the reply of *Dr. Boobis* is misleading, because it seems that both have not understood that JECFA reviewed old data that did not take into account realistic conditions of use of these hormones, unlike the data generated by the EC studies for the first time and examined by the SCVPH. *Dr. Boobis* asks the rhetorical question that "the frequency of occurrence of such misuse" is not stated. However, the studies cited at Exhibits EC-65, 67, 68, 69, 70 and 70-73 show that the higher the frequency the higher the risk will be. But in the case of prepubertal children the EC studies have clarified explicitly that even a unique occurrence or an occasional one would be sufficient to lead to residue levels in meat that would exceed by many times their endogenous production of these hormones.

106.   Since *Dr. Boisseau* referred back in his answer to this Question to his reply to Question 29, the same criticism on Canada's summary of *Dr. Boisseau's* statement applies here.

Q31.   Please comment on the US statement that "concentrations of oestra-diol-17β in meat from treated cattle do not vary significantly from concentrations in untreated cattle, i.e., residue levels in meat from hormone-treated cattle are well within the physiological range of residue levels in untreated cattle. While tissue concentrations of oestradiol-17β in treated cattle may be slightly higher than those in untreated cattle, this increase is much smaller than the large variations observed in (reproductively) cycling and pregnant cattle and is thus well within the range of naturally observed levels." In your reply please take into account the US 11th Carcinogenesis Report where it is stated that "Meat and milk may contain estrogens. Veterinary use of steroidal estrogens (to promote growth and treat illness) can increase estrogens in tissues of food-producing animals to above their normal levels" and the statement by the European Communities that "meat consumption from pregnant heifers is exceptional as usually these animals are not slaughtered. [see paras. 51 and 144 of US First Submission and Exhibits US-6 and 7, para. 98 of EC Replies to Panel Questions, Exhibit EC-101, and para. 2.3.2.3 of the 1999 Report of SCVPH]

US comment

107.   The United States refers to *Dr. De Brabander's* reply to this question in paragraph 96 of its submission. No reference is made to *Dr. Boisseau's* reply. The United States comments on the view taken by *Dr. De Brabander* that "there is no need to add more [hormonal substances] by artificial ways" stating that this is *Dr. De Brabander's* "personal opinion or policy statement." As a matter of fact, *Dr. Boisseau* seems to take the opposite view by referring to a "theoretical" of "no additional intake of residues [being] acceptable." What both experts express here, is indeed a policy statement, a policy statement of the kind the European Communities as a risk regulator has every legitimacy to make.

Canada's comment

108.   In its comments to the experts' replies, Canada again demonstrates its very selective perception of what the experts actually said. While it quotes *in extenso Dr. Boisseau* (who may be understood to support Canada's position) it basically ignores *Dr. De Brabander's* very critical remarks regarding the significant increase of estradiol-17β in human food if all animals were treated accordingly. The Panel would be well advised to take good note of *Dr. De Brabander's* response and to draw its own conclusions why Canada is unwilling or unable to comment on the serious questions in relation to animal welfare, environment and consumer protection as raised by *Dr. De Brabander.*

109.   More importantly, however, Canada resorts (in paras. 116-117) to its dear and old argument (in the absence of anything else) that "…in order appropriately to understand the risks associated with the use of growth-promoting hormones, one must view the exposure to these hormones in their overall context, including the wide exposure to natural hormones from other dietary sources and endoge-

nous production of natural hormones." However, this kind of argument has been clearly rejected by the Appellate Body in the 1998 *Hormones* case as "an absurdity". Moreover, the Appellate Body has also found that the occasional use of meat from pregnant cows or those treated for therapeutical or zootechnical purposes does not lead to arbitrary or unjustifiable discrimination and do cannot undermine the EC's level of health protection (at paras. 222-225 of its report).

Q32.   Please comment on the conclusions of the EC risk assessment (Opinion of the SCVPH of April 2002) that ultra sensitive methods to detect residues of hormones in animal tissues have become available but need further validation. What is the significance of this with regard to identifying whether the natural hormones in meat are endogenously produced or are residues of hormones used for growth promotion purposes?

US and Canada's comments

110.   The United States refers to *Dr. Boisseau's* reply to this question in paragraph 93 of its submission. No reference is made to *Dr. De Brabander's* reply. However, *Dr. De Brabander* states that "there are now new data available demonstrating that the pattern change of hormones by the application of the 'natural' hormones used for growth promotion purposes." This is in direct contradiction with *Dr. Boisseau's* statement that ultrasensitive detection methods would be "less useful in the case of the three natural hormones, which are endogenously produced by food producing animals." The United States seems to agree with *Dr. Boisseau's* comment without, however, commenting clearly on this contradiction. The basic point *Dr. De Brabander* was making in his reply is that the residue examined by JECFA were generated with the old methods and that new methods should be used now to re-evaluate them. This is in agreement with the position of the European Communities. *Dr. Boisseau's* reply is besides the point, because the new powerful and ultra sensitive methods will always be required in order to determine the origin of residues in meat, for example in order to determine whether is it endogenous or exogenously administered and whether there was an abuse or misuse.

Q33.   What were the reasons for the re-evaluation by JECFA of the three natural hormones in 1999? Were the residues data used for the three natural hormones in 1999 the same as those used in 1988? What additional information was used for the JECFA evaluation in 1999 of the three natural hormones which was not available in 1988? How did the conclusions differ? What led JECFA to establish ADIs for the three natural hormones? What are the implications of establishing ADIs? Why were JECFA's more recent recommendations not considered by the Codex Committee on Residues of Veterinary Drugs in Food? What is the status of these recommendations? [see paras. 96-97 of EC Rebuttal Submission (US case), paras. 79-80 of EC Rebuttal Submission (Canada case)]

US comment

111.   The United States refers to the experts' (*Drs. Boisseau, Boobis, De Bra-bander*) replies to this question in paragraphs 97 through 99 of its submission and also to Codex' and JECFA's replies on related questions.[7] Contrary to what the United States pretends there is complete dissent among the experts on the reasons why JECFA re-evaluated the three natural hormones,[8] and the Panel is referred here to the reply of JECFA which admits that the ADIs were set because of the new evidence that became available in the meantime.

Canada's comment

112.   It is not clear whether Canada's comment is fully consistent with its comment on Question 18. In this question Canada assumes that the "genotoxic carcinogen [of oestradiol] appears to have promoted at least in part JECFA's 1999 re-evaluation", whereas in its comment to Question 18 Canada denied that JECFA's establishment of an ADI was related to its finding about "potential genotoxicity", (see para. 71 last sentence).

113.   Moreover, what is interesting is that *Dr. Boobis* appears to recognise that "in the intervening time from the first to the second evaluation, it became clear that exposure to the natural hormones, albeit at levels appreciable higher than found in meat from treated cattle, could have adverse effects in humans". This is remarkable, as he admits that there is a problem of principle (despite all the talk about eggs, milk and broccoli etc.), and it appears to be rather a question of "how much" is acceptable (see also Canada's comment in this respect at para. 125, last sentence).

114.   Canada's comment (at paras. 127-128) apparently approving the explanations provided by JECFA and *Dr. Boobis* is inadequate. Indeed, after the CCRVDF refused to consider the 1999 re-evaluation of the three natural hormones, where ADIs were considered necessary in order to avoid the risk of cancer identified, the continued 1988 indication that MRLs are not "necessary" do not enable the countries using these hormones to see if the ADIs are reached or exceeded. It would therefore be imperative that JECFA and Codex review again all these hormones soon by taking into account all the latest evidence and data available, in particular, those generated by the studies sponsored by the European Communities.

Q34.   Please comment on the EC argument that the 1999 JECFA report based its findings on (a) outdated residues data and (b) not on evidence from residues in meat but on studies with experimental animals and on gen-

---

[7]   Question 20 in questions asked to Codex, JECFA and IARC.

[8]   Of course, there is agreement on the outcome of that evaluation, but that is not the question that was put to the experts. The outcome – JECFA finding that these hormones are safe for consumers – is a fact and not a matter of assessment.

eral studies of IARC. If the data were not new, did JECFA take this into account in its evaluation? What are the implications of using such data for the purpose of conducting a risk assessment? How reliable are extrapolations from animal studies to possible adverse effects on humans? How does this compare with the kind of data and studies used with respect to other veterinary drugs? [see para. 120 of EC Rebuttal Submission (US case), para. 102 of EC Rebuttal (Canada case)]

US comment

115.   The United States refers to *Dr. Boisseau's* reply to this question in paragraphs 49, 92 and 111 of its submission. No reference is made to *Dr. De Brabander's* reply. The reference to *Dr. Boisseau* is always the same namely his statement that "the quality and the number of the available data are more important than the dates at which these data have been produced." The European Communities has already commented on this statement, which it considers scientifically unsound (see EC comments on replies to question 34).

116.   The US further claims (at para. 111) that "[a]s noted by the United States in its Rebuttal Submission, and confirmed by Dr. Boobis' analysis above, even in the artificial scenarios developed by EC scientists, in most cases extreme misuse and overdosing of cattle with implants did not result in violative residue levels, *i.e.*, levels exceeding ADIs and MRLs." This statement is not correct because the new evidence generated by the European Communities does establish that the ADIs and MRLs will be exceeded by the residue levels resulting from misuse or abuse. Since the US (and on this point also Canada) keep arguing that extreme misuse did not result in violative residue levels, it is important to quote the conclusion from the relevant EC study (Exhibit EC-17) which states:

> "Treatement with zeranol and testosterone propionate, even after multiple application, does not cause any problems, as far as infringement of the threshold levels is concerned. Off-label application of trenbolone acetate and estradiol benzoate, however, may lead to illicit values. Exceeding of the MRL was found in the liver in one out of two animals after 3-fold and in two out of two animals after 10-fold dose of the 200 mg-trenbolone acetate-implant. Estradiol threshold levels were violated in the liver and in the kidney even after 3-fold dose of Synovex-H. Fattening of calves with the preparations Synovex-H and Synovex Plus lead to similar residue levels as after Synovex-H or Finaplix-H treatment of heifers".

117.   It is therefore misleading for the US to summarise the findings of the study in the way described above.

Canada's comment

118.   Canada completely fails to comment on *Dr. De Brabander's* reply. Instead, Canada merely looks for support in *Dr. Boisseau's* answer. However, con-

trary to what Canada tries to present as "what is generally accepted within the scientific community: that scientific data do not deteriorate simply because the passage of time", Canada would have been well advised to address *Dr. De Brabander's* statement whereby "[t]he implications of not using such (modern) data is that the results of the risk assessment are biased in favour of the "allowance" of hormones." Indeed, new data obviously may lead to different conclusions and it is, therefore, indispensable to update and review constantly scientific evidence. Canada obviously fails to do so.

119.   Furthermore, Canada also misrepresents *Dr. Boisseau's* answer concerning the assessment of hormones. *Dr. Boisseau* merely stated that "[f]or assessing the growth promoters, JECFA has used the same procedure it has used for all other veterinary drugs". Re-formulated by Canada this statement reads as follows: "[a]s the experts confirm, *the data* and process used for assessing the safety of hormones are the same as those used for other veterinary drugs" (emphasis added). Thus, Canada just by convenience adds the word "data" and it presents this as a commonly held view by "the experts" even though *Dr. De Brabander* (as the only other experts replying to this question) did not make such a statement. This is just another example on how Canada tries to manipulate the Panel in its presentation of the experts' responses.

Q35.   Please comment on the European Communities claim that nearly all the studies referred to in the 2000 JECFA report on MGA date from the 1960s and 70s. Is this correct? Have subsequent reports of JECFA, prior or subsequent to the adoption of the EC Directive, also relied on the same studies? [see para. 171 of EC Rebuttal Submission (US case), para. 161 of EC Rebuttal Submission (Canada case), para. 55, including footnote 60 of US First Submission and Exhibits CDA-20, 33, 34 and 35]

US comment

120.   The United States concedes that the experts (*Drs. Boisseau, De Brabander*) have confirmed that the studies relied upon date indeed from the 1960s and 70s (paragraph 49 f its submission). The United States relies on *Dr. Boisseau's* statement cited above (question 34), which the European Communities considers scientifically unsound for the reasons explained above.

Canada's comment

121.   Canada ignores *Dr. De Brabander's* reply for obvious reasons. But Canada appears also to accept that the data examined by JECFA in 2000 and again in 2004 for MGA date from the 1960s and 1970s.

(c)   Dose-response relationship

Q36.   How would you describe a dose-response assessment? Is it, as suggested by Canada in para. 78 of its Rebuttal Submission, "widely, if not universally, accepted that adverse effects arising from hormonal activities are

dose-dependent"? Is dose-response assessment a necessary component of hazard characterization? Or, is there an alternative approach which can replace the dose-response assessment. Is a dose-response assessment feasible/necessary for substances that are found to be genotoxic or to have genotoxic potential? [see para. 153 of EC Replies to Panel Questions, para. 200 of EC Rebuttal Submission (US case); paras. 143, 154, and 156 of US First Submission, paras. 70-74 of US Replies to Panel Questions, and paras. 34 and 37-40 of US Rebuttal Submission; paras. 76-82 of Canada Rebuttal Submission]

US comment

122.   The United States refers to *Drs. Boisseau's and Boobis'* reply to this question in paragraph 21 of its submission. No reference is made to *Dr. Cogliano's* reply. Contrary to what the United States claims there is no consensus among the experts on whether a dose-response assessment is a necessary component of hazard characterisation. Indeed, *Dr. Cogliano* takes the exact opposite view. Also, *Dr. Boobis* recognises that there may be differences in approach between Europe and the US and Canada as regards the assessment of compounds that have been "identified as an in vivo DNA-reactive mutagen, or as causing a carcinogenic response via a genotoxic mode of action."

Canada's comment

123.   Although all the experts, including the Codex and JECFA, agree that there are no legally binding risk assessment techniques in the sense of Article 5.1 of the *SPS Agreement* for this kind of substances, Canada makes the unsubstantiated statement (at para. 141) that the hazard-based approach would be inconsistent with the obligations under the *SPS Agreement* that a substance be evaluated for the "potential for occurrence" of an adverse effect. The European Communities finds nothing of this sort in the terms "potential for occurrence", as interpreted by the Appellate Body in the *Hormones* case, given also that a qualitative assessment of the risk is also permissible. In any case, the European Communities has carried out such an analysis of the likelihood of occurrence of the scientifically identified risk in the case of these hormones.

Q37.   Do JECFA or Codex materials confirm Canada's statement in para. 80 of its Rebuttal Submission that "...while international risk assessment techniques suggest that a dose-response assessment is optional for biological or physical agents when the data cannot be obtained, a dose-response assessment should always be conducted for chemical agents..."? [see Exhibit CDA-25]

US comment

124.   The United States does not refer or comment on the experts' (*Drs. Boisseau, Boobis*) replies to this question.

Canada's comment

125.   The European Communities considers that Canada's statement (at para. 142) that "in light of the universally held view that the adverse effects of hormones are dose-dependent", is erroneous because it is factually not true, as the evidence presented by the European Communities has demonstrated. Indeed, except JECFA and the 2 experts *Drs. Boisseau and Boobis* who participated in the risk assessment of JECFA, the majority view (which is growing steadily since 1999) is that expressed by the IARC and the 2002 US Carcinogenesis Report that these hormones act by direct and indirect mechanisms.

(d)   Sensitive populations

Q38.   Please describe the range of physiological (or background) levels of the sex hormones in humans and identify the variations in these levels on the basis of age, sex group, and physiological stages.

US comment

126.   The United States refers to *Dr. Boisseau's* reply to this question in paragraph 65 of its submission, in the context of its comments on the replies given on Question 40 (see below).

Canada's comment

127.   Canada pretends that *Dr. Boisseau* in his reply "raises concerns, as many others have done, about the reliance by the EC on a new 'ultrasensitive biosassay'". However, first of all, *Dr. Boisseau* has not expressed any "concerns" but he merely said that "[i]t would be important to know whether these new bioassays have been properly validated (…)". Thus, *Dr. Boisseau* has merely raised a question. Second, Canada refers to "many others" while, indeed, all other experts have not raised any concerns. Canada, therefore, is making a misleading general statement, which is not supported by the facts.

Q39.   Please comment on the SCVPH opinion stating that "any excess exposure towards oestradiol-17β and its metabolites resulting from the consumption of meat and meat products presents a potential risk to public health in particular to those groups of the populations which have been identified as particularly sensitive such as prepubertal children" [see para. 147 of the EC Replies to Panel Questions]

US comment

128.   The United States refers to the experts' (*Drs. Boisseau, Sippel*) in paragraphs 67 and following of its submission. Contrary to what is claimed by the United States, *Dr. Boisseau* does not state that "the EC has failed to assess this risk entirely." *Dr. Boisseau* merely takes the view that a quantitative dose-response assessment (as opposed to a qualitative one) would have been needed.

129. The United States discusses *Dr. Sippel's* reply to this question in great detail (in paras. 64-82). As regards the validation of the Klein assay, the principle of the yeast assay has been validated in an international comparative study of different assays for estrogens (Andersen et al., Comparison of short-term estrogenicity tests for identification of hormone-disrupting chemicals. *Environmental Health Perspectives*; 107 (Suppl. 1): 89-108, 1999, Exhibit EC-123), so this should not now be in doubt. Moreover, how can the US (and Canada on this point) claim that an assay cannot be used because it had not been properly validated, since it is clear that JECFA used old "historic" values for endogenous hormone levels in children that are clearly and undisputedly wrong because the old assays used (RIA) cannot measure such levels? Therefore JECFA used the LIMIT-OF-DETECTION as the "real values" in children, which is obviously wrong and scientifically unacceptable.

130. The US criticise the EC statement "any excess exposure..." but the concept of concentration additivity has been proven for estrogens, including the demonstration of "0+0 $\approx$ 0" (i.e. that two doses which alone do not produce any detectable effects, when added together result in an observable effect). Thus, any dose matters. On dose additivity see: Rajapakse N., Silva E., Kortenkamp A.: Combining Xenoestrogens at Levels below Individual No-Observed-Effect Concentrations Dramatically Enhances Steroid Hormone Action, in Envir. Health Perspec. 110, 917-921 (2002) (Exhibit EC – 116); and also Tinwell H., Ashby J.: Sensitivity of the Immature Rat Uterotrophic Assay to Mixtures of Estrogens, in Envir. Health Perspec.112, 575-582 (2004) (Exhibit EC – 112).

131. The US criticises (at para. 67) the reply of *Dr. Sippell* for "proposing a different result than his own research". However, the cited statement from *Dr. Sippell* is from a 2000 (published in 2001) study, and a lot has happened since then, including the publication of many of the cited papers. Thus, *Dr. Sippell* demonstrates his scientific integrity by adjusting his opinion according to the developing scientific research. This is contrary to for example *Dr. Boobis*, who repeatedly claims that his opinion has not changed since 1999, despite the publication since 1999 of so many papers on direct genotoxic action.

132. At para. 68 the US cites the study by Schmidt which shows an overall association between estradiol levels and postnatal breast development for the groups as a whole. But the study also shows large variations in estradiol levels, including a demonstration of breast development without measurable levels of estradiol. This emphasises the difficulty in measuring the very low estradiol levels, and the study clearly shows breast development, likely caused by estradiol, also in girls where the estradiol level cannot be determined by the RIA assay. Whether this is a pathological effect cannot be answered before the possible outcome of perturbed breast development (breast cancer) can be assayed (i.e. in 40-50 years), but recent research into the origin of breast cancer do suggest that changes in mammary gland development may play a significant role (see Baik I, Becker PS, DeVito WJ, Lagiou P, Ballen K, Quesenberry PJ, Hsieh C-C.: Stem cells and prenatal origin of breast cancer, in Cancer Causes and Control 15: 517–530, 2004).

133.   In para. 69 the US discusses the Lampit et al study, which clearly demonstrate an effect of the administrated estradiol on the growth of the children. However, the US criticises that Lampit et al., "fails to quantify the amount of estradiol that would be required to accelerate growth in normal children". However, this is a consequence of the lack of sufficiently sensitive assays, since Lampit et al. cannot measure the serum levels of estradiol, neither before nor after the administration of estradiol. Thus, Lampit et al. clearly show an effect of administrated estradiol, despite serum levels not reaching the current detection limit of the assays. This is very important and an extremely relevant finding which the US avoids to confront objectively.

134.   In paras. 70 and 71 the US advances a number of unscientific arguments. It is textbook knowledge that estradiol strongly influences the onset of puberty in girls. Is this questioned by the US and Canada? Given that it is beyond doubt that estradiol is the main determinant for the onset of puberty in girls, it seems reasonable that *Dr. Sippell* raises the possibility that exposure to excess hormones in the US may play a role for trends in puberty disorders.

135.   In para. 73 the US discusses the other publications cited. But in line with many other publications, the Felner & White paper clearly shows that a small amount of estradiol strongly affects breast development in children.

136.   The US statement in para. 74 contains many aspects that need clarification. First, there are several publications that show higher estrogen levels for twins (1.7 to 3 times higher in a twin pregnancy compared to a singleton pregnancy) (Kappel 1985; TambyRaja 1981; Ikeno 1985). Second, there are many publications showing lower estrogen levels in women with preeclampsia (Goldkrand 1978; Long 1979; Shibata 2000). Thus, in the absence of other risk factors for breast cancer that change in exactly the same way as the estrogen levels do in these groups, it is reasonable to correlate the changes in breast cancer risk to changes in the levels of the most likely cause for the changed risk, and that is the differences in estrogen levels. The US asks for mechanistic evidence. However, there are so many peer-reviewed papers relating breast cancer to estrogens. Moreover, the publication by Baik et al. 2004 (cited above) provides a possible mechanistic explanation, especially when combined with other publications linking the cells described by Baik et al. to cell types that are the prime candidates for being the cells-of-origin for breast cancer (for example, Petersen et al., 2003). See on *Estrogen levels in twin pregnancies compared to singletons*: B. Kappel, K. Hansen, J. Moller, J. Faaborg-Andersen: Human placental lactogen and dU-estrogen levels in normal twin pregnancies, Acta Genet Med Gemellol (Roma) 34 (1985) (1–2), pp. 59–65; R.L. TambyRaja, S.S. Ratnam: Plasma steroid changes in twin pregnancies, Prog Clin Biol Res 69A (1981), pp. 189–195; N. Ikeno and K. Takahashi: Studies on changes in serum estrone, estradiol, estriol, DHA-S, and cortisol and urinary estriol excretion, Nippon Sanka Fujinka Gakkai Zasshi 37 (1985) (1), pp. 99–106. See also on *Estrogen levels in women with preeclampsia*: W. Goldkrand: Unconjugated estriol and cortisol in maternal and cord serum and amniotic fluid in normal and abnormal pregnancy, Obstet Gynecol 52 (1978) (3), pp. 264–271; P.A. Long, D.A. Abell, N.A. Beischer:

Fetal growth and placental function assessed by urinary estriol excretion before the onset of pre-eclampsia, Am J Obstet Gynecol 135 (1979) (3), pp. 344–347; A. Shibata, A.Y. Minn. Perinatal sex hormones and risk of breast and prostate cancers in adulthood, Epidemiol Rev 22 (2000) (2), pp. 239–248; On *breast cancer* see: Petersen, O.W., Gudjonsson, T., Villadsen, R., Bissell, M.J., and Ronnov-Jessen, L: Epithelial progenitor cell lines as models of normal breast morphogenesis and neoplasia. Cell Proliferation 36, Suppl. 33-44 (2003).

137.   In para. 76 the US discusses the "Testicular dysgenesis syndrome" (TDS), which describes a HUMAN syndrome that is observed in the clinic! The relationship to animal studies is only made as an attempt to extrapolate possible reasons for the syndrome. In general, animal studies are designed to show effects in a small number of animals and, therefore, large doses are used in order to get effects in essentially all the exposed animals. However, it is a different situation for the human population where TDS-like symptoms are observed in a relatively small percentage of men. Thus, when genetic variation is taken into consideration, low-dose exposure of hundreds of millions of humans may in a small percentage of the exposed people lead to effects similar to those observed at high doses in all the animals in a small group of exposed animals. Moreover, humans are exposed to a mixture of compounds and it has been shown that the effects represent the sum of all the different exposures (i.e. concentration addition!).

138.   In para. 77 the US dismisses the effects of DBP because it "is a well known reproductive toxicant". However, DBP in an endocrine disrupter and acts by reducing the testosterone production in the Leydig cells of the testes and thereby DBP is an example of a compound that induces TDS-like symptoms via effects on the endocrine system, by lowering the testosterone levels.

139.   Unlike the US comments in paras. 79 and 81, it seems clear that *Dr. Sippell's* conclusion "exposure during pregnancy might result in severe transplacental virilisation of a female fetus" is reasonable, since it has been shown that trenbolone is about 3 times more potent that testosterone and given that trenbolone is extensively used as an androgen by body builders. This strongly suggests that trenbolone is a potent androgen in humans.

140.   Despite the US comments in para. 80, there are now several studies on the estrogenic potency of Zeranol (e.g. Guevel & Pakdel 2001; Liu & Lin, 2004) and all essentially report the same potency (which is similar to that of estradiol). The Leffers et al paper analysed the induction of several estrogen-regulated genes and found that different genes responded differently to the tested estrogens. However, the Leffers et al. paper did not measure cell proliferation and none of the analysed genes were proliferation-sensitive. The observation that DES and estradiol (and Zeranol) were equipotent depended on which genes were used for the analysis. The key finding in the Leffers et al. paper, which the US apparently fails or does not wish to accept, is that Zeranol is as potent as estradiol and that has now been confirmed by other studies. See in particular: Le Guevel R, Pakdel F: Assessment of oestrogenic potency of chemicals used as growth promoter by in-vitro methods, in Hum Reprod. 2001 16,1030-1036 (Exhibit EC – 108); and Liu S, Lin YC: Transformation of MCF-10A human breast

epithelial cells by zeranol and estradiol-17beta, in Breast J. 2004 10, 514-521 (Exhibit EC – 62).

Canada's comment

141. Contrary to what Canada asserts, *Dr. Boisseau* is not criticizing the "excess exposure" but merely asks for its assessment and comparison. In other words, by its reply *Dr. Boisseau* actually confirms that an "excess exposure" exists.

142. In its comments on *Dr. Sippell's* reply, Canada is making again an unqualified statement concerning the "controversial" bioassay methodology. However, Canada does not offer any supporting arguments for its blunt statement. Furthermore, Canada pretends that "the experts have contested" elsewhere the conclusions of the European Communities' quote. This is not true. Canada would be well advised to respect more accurately the various experts' replies instead of using an unqualified and misleading language in order to manipulate the Panel.

Q40. The European Communities states that "the levels of endogenous production of the hormones by prepubertal children is much lower than previously thought and this finding, which is subsequent to the 1999 JECFA report, casts serious doubts about the validity of JECFA's findings on the dose-response relationship..." Please comment on the methodology used by the SCVPH to support the conclusion that hormone levels are lower than previously thought, and in particular comment on the validity of these methodologies and their conclusions. Would your conclusions have been the same at the time of adoption of the Directive in September 2003?

US comment

143. The United States refers to *Dr. Boobis'* reply to this question in paragraphs 28, 65 through 67 and 83 of its submission. There is a discussion of *Dr. Sippell's* view on assay validation in paragraph 66 of the submission, on which the European Communities has already commented above.

Canada's comment

144. Canada refers to the "concerns" by *Dr. Boisseau* as expressed in its reply to Question 38. However, as already mentioned above, Canada is not accurately interpreting *Dr. Boisseau's* reply and it abuses the expert's response to pursue its own litigation objective. In the same vein, it is quite superficial when Canada, in paragraph 150, refers to "concerns highlighted by the experts about the SCVPH's use of this methodology". If at all, there is only one expert, *Dr. Boobis* who makes some critical remarks, while *Dr. Boisseau* remains neutral, *Dr. Sippell* supports the methodology and *Dr. Guttenplan, Dr. Cogliano and Dr. De Brabander* do not express themselves at this stage. Even more, *Dr. Guttenplan*, in his response to Question 52 states that: "[a]lthough the US and Canada question the accuracy of the assay originally employed for estrogens at the low levels

found in children, recent reports (…) indicate more recently reported levels used by the EC are accurate".

145.   Concerning the in vitro assay developed independently by Klein *et al* and F Paris *et al* to assay low amounts of receptor-active estrogens, it should be added to what has been explained above that these biological assays are not absolute in the sense that they should give precise and absolute values. Indeed, they are internally validated assays but not yet inter-laboratory comparison has been made. But even if one may consider that this is a drawback, the assay is very useful in that it is far more sensitive than any other spectro-physical assay based on mass spectrometry. Nevertheless, this inter-technique comparison will be performed rather soon thanks to the new generation of mass spectrometry based on Fourier-Transformed MS. This technological progress should be useful to perform the complete hormonal exploration (androgens, estrogens) in plasma of no- and pre-pubertal girls and boys and the results will be critical to the risk assessment exercise. Conversely, the JECFA evaluation was based on old and very questionable data that were not produced at that time by any spectro-physical method but only by radio-immunologic assays.

Q41. Why would individuals with the lowest endogenous hormone levels be at greatest risk? How would the risks for these individuals arising from hormones naturally present in meat differ from the risks arising from the residues of hormone growth promoters?

US comment

146.   The United States does not dispute the experts' (*Drs. Boisseau, Sippell*) replies to this question, which confirm the view taken by the European Communities that prepubertal children are particularly sensitive to hormones exposure.

Canada's comment

147.   As in its comments on earlier question, Canada claims support by "the experts" for the criticism on the Klein assay which, however, is not supported by the facts. Thus, Canada's criticism on the detailed reply by *Dr. Sippell* is completely baseless.

Q42. To what extent, in your view, has JECFA taken into account the particular situation of sensitive populations, in particular prepubertal children, in its risk assessments with respect to oestradiol-17β? Please compare the original data concerning endogenous production of natural hormones by prepubertal children upon which JECFA based its assessment and those used by the European Communities in its risk assessment. In your view, does the scientific material referred to by the European Communities require a revision of the Codex recommendation with respect to oestradiol-17β? [For the questions in this section, see paras. 121-122 of EC Rebuttal Submission (US case), para. 103-104 of EC Rebuttal Submission (Canada case), Exhibits EC-88, 99, paras. 42-45 of US Rebuttal Submission, paras.

84 and 159 of US First Submission, and for JECFA's work Exhibits CDA-11, 16, 17, 18, 39]

US and Canada's comments

148.   The United States refers to *Dr. Boobis' and Sippell'* replies to this question in paragraphs 67, 84 and 85 of its submission (no reference to *Dr. Boisseau*). In Footnote 178 of its submission, the United States dismisses *Dr. Sippell's* view that JECFA has not adequately taken into account the particular situation of sensitive populations, in particular infants and prepubertal children. The United States claims that it is unclear whether *Dr. Sippell* is familiar with JECFA's safety factors or whether/why he finds these factors to be inadequate. However, none of the US comments is valid because the so-called safety factors cannot substitute for the need of JECFA to review these hormones on the basis of the most recent scientific data, including in particular the direct genotoxicity and the low levels of endogenous production by prepubertal children.

149.   Similarly, Canada fails to address Dr. Sippell's detailed and supported criticism of the JECFA conclusions. The European Communities regrets Canada's selective perception of all experts' replies and to respond adequately to criticism on the use of hormones as growth promoters.

(e)   Bioavailability

Q43. Please define bioavailability, comment on the significance of bioavailability to assessments of risk, and on the degree of bioavailabilitiy of the residues of the hormones at issue when consumed in meat, taking into account parties' differing views on this matter. [see paras. 123-124 of EC Rebuttal Submission (US case), paras. 105-106 of EC Rebuttal Submission (Canada case), paras. 100, 155-159 of the EC Replies to Panel Questions, paras. 32 and 41-42 of US Rebuttal Submission, paras. 69, 71, 88-89 and 146 of US First Submission, and para. 134 of Canada Rebuttal Submission]

US comment

150.   The United States claims that "none of the experts' responses appear to indicate otherwise", when claiming that the European Communities has failed to take into account the low bioavailability of estradiol 17β in its assessment of that hormones (see paragraph 27 of its submission). This is plainly wrong as *Dr. Guttenplan* comes to the opposite conclusion when stating that: "[i]t appears that the bioavailability of estrogen is low but not insignificant (probably between 5 and 20%, if estrone is also taken into account. (Estrone is readily inter-convertible with estrogen). Calculations are presented in the above reference that suggest that even with low percentages of bioavailability of estrogen, the levels in meat could result in bioavailable estrogen approaching the daily production rate of oestradiol in pre-pubertal children (EC Rebut, para. 122). This would represent a risk factor (EC Rebut, para. 122)."

151.   Indeed, the United States tries to refute the view taken by *Dr. Guttenplan* by arguing that (1) he relies on materials cited by the European Communities that do not in fact demonstrate a higher bioavailability for estradiol 17β than previously thought, and (2) he miscasts as "paradoxical" a US argument relating to bioavailability (paragraphs 28 and following of the US submission).

152.   As for the first argument, it should be recalled that human beings are considered as having a monogastric physiology and, consequently, the large digestibility of nutrients should be clearly applicable. Therefore, for risk assessment purposes it is considered that digestibility and hence bioavailability of steroids ("primary bioavailability" or the amount of xenobiotics absorbed from a given matrix or formulation) and in particularly estrogens is more or less complete. In the absence of any specific study on bioavailability of steroids considering the low amounts of residues found in edible tissues of treated cattle, there is a need to consider this bioavailability parameter at its maximal value due to a complete intestinal absorption. This point has been formerly anticipated in milk-fed calves which have kept a seemingly monogastric physiology and for which the estrogens excretion is mainly achieved by urinary route, that is strikingly different from this obtained for ruminant physiology, which prove the important enterohepatic cycle and hence the very significant intestinal absorption of estrogens. This also explains the bioavailability of hormones present in gut, even if they are excreted by the biliary route. In addition, there is a need of common understanding of what is the definition of bioavailability of steroidal hormones, given the greatly varying degrees between gut, liver and peripheral tissues, due to the progressive metabolism of those hormones. Again, we need to consider that there is total intestinal absorption and a complete hormonal effect at least on intestinal cells and hepatocytes before their metabolic degradation. Therefore, it is very doubtful when JECFA and *Dr. Boobis* assume that an oral bioavailability of rate of 5% (Fortherby, 1996) is rightly used in order to assert there is a low hormonal effect of orally given hormones. This result may be only a comparative result of hormonal effect of two different administration routes on classically considered target tissues and is related to raw bioequivalence measured on a given target tissue, not the bioavailability. In the context of hormone residues in meat, no specific results have been obtained on the hormonal response of intestinal cells exposed to those hormonal residues neither on hepatic cells measurements have been carried.

153.   Some specific attention should also be placed on the different bioavailability rates of estrogens, considering that some are ingested as free or conjugates compounds (thus being easily hydrolyzed by gut microflora) and some other are lipophilic compounds (estrogen esters) and are susceptible to take the lymph route after intestinal absorption (see Paris et al, 2000). Therefore, this class of lipoidal estrogenic residues will partially escape the liver degradation step. This specific bioavalability of estrogen esters may explain why, even by oral route administration, they are about 10 fold more active than estradiol in inducing a significant uterotrophic response in the juvenile female rat model (Paris et al, APMIS 109 (2001) 365-375) (Exhibit EC-117). This has been taken

into account by the SCVPH, unlike JECFA and Dr. Boobis that seem to disregard it.

Canada's comment

154. Canada fails to address specifically the conclusion by *Dr. Guttenplan* whereby "calculations are presented in the above reference that suggest that even with low percentages of bioavailability of estrogen, the levels in meat could result in bioavailable estrogen approaching the daily production rate of oestradiol in pre-pubertal children (EC Rebut, para. 122). This would represent a risk factor (EC Rebut, para. 122)".

(f)   Good veterinary practice (GVP)

Q44. Please define "good veterinary practice" (GVP) and/or "good practice in the use of veterinary drugs" (GPVD). What are the relevant Codex standards, guidelines or recommendations relating to GVP/GPVD? Please comment on the statement by the European Communities that the definition of the GPVD is "circular and hence problematic." [see para. 88 of the EC Replies to Panel Questions]

US comment

155. The United States does not comment on this point and the replies given by *Dr. De Brabander and Dr. Boisseau* (on the discussion in paragraph 107 of its submission see below, question 45).

Canada's comment

156. Canada, regrettably, does not address *Dr. De Brabander's* reply on why the definition of the GPVD is considered to be "somewhat circular and hence problematic". Instead, Canada just reproduces a general statement by *Dr. Boisseau* although even *Dr. Boisseau* provides an interpretation which Canada, again, ignores.

Q45. In conducting a risk assessment of specific veterinary drugs, what assumptions are made concerning GVP, if any? How, if at all, are risks that might arise from the failure to follow good veterinary practice in the administration of veterinary drugs addressed?

US comment

157. In the context of this question the United States comments on the reply given by *Dr. De Brabander* in paragraph 107 of its submission dismissing the reference he makes to evidence of abuse of hormonal substances in the US. While the study referred to by *Dr. De Brabander* is certainly interesting, the European Communities would recall that it has undertaken its own studies to

assess the possibility of misuse and abuse in the US and Canada. It is on these studies that the EC risk assessment relies on.

Canada's comment

158.   Canada does not comment on *Dr. De Brabander's* pertinent response whereby "farmers (and vets) have indeed economic incentives to misuse growth promotion substance (implants or others)". The Panel may draw its own conclusion by this Canadian failure.

Q46.   To what extent were risks from misuse or abuse assessed by JECFA in its evaluation of the hormones at issue? In terms of the three synthetic hormones at issue, how is GVP relevant to the establishment of MRLs by JECFA?

US and Canada's comments

159.   The United States and Canada does not refer to or discuss in detail the experts' (*Drs. De Brabander, Boisseau, Boobis*) replies to this question.

Q47.   How significant are any differences in GVP in the European Communities, the United States, and Canada? Does the EC risk assessment take into account relevant control mechanisms with respect to GVP in place in the United States and/or Canada? If so, what are their conclusions?

US and Canada's comments

160.   The comments above under Question 45 apply here as well. In addition, Canada argues (at para. 182) that the comment of Dr. De Brabander that control mechanisms short of total ban is "deeply flawed". However, Canada - as well as the US – fails to discuss at all the numerous instances of abuse and misuse documented in the EC inspections in their territories, nor do they comment on the findings of the evidence reported in exhibits EC-67 to 73.

Q48.   To what extent does the scientific evidence referred to by the European Communities assess risks to human health from residues of misplaced implants or improper administration, i.e. when administered differently than indicated on the label of the manufacturer or contrary to GVP, of any of the six hormones? Would your reply have been different at the time of adoption of the EC Directive in September 2003? What are the potential hazards, if any, to human health of the use of large quantities, or doses higher than recommended, of any of the six hormones in dispute?

US comment

161.   The United States refers to the experts' (*Drs. Boobis, De Brabander, Boisseau*) replies to this question in paragraphs 103, 104 and 109 of its submission. As stated in its own comments, the conclusions reached by *Drs. Boisseau*

and Boobis rest on the assumption that a quantitative assessment is required. Indeed, *Dr. Boobis* concedes that this is not the view taken by the EC risk assessors, a remark which the United States conveniently omits to refer to or comment on. The US criticises the statements by Dr. De Brabander as not based on evidence, but as explained above in relation to Question 47 the evidence is provided in the relevant EC exhibits which the US has chosen to ignore.

Canada's comment

162.   The way Canada comments on the three expert replies is again an interesting and typical example on how Canada attempts to influence the Panel by a selective reproduction of only those expert replies which, in Canada's view', supports its position. However, instead of looking for comfort in replies that merely allegedly confirm its own position (which is a natural and convenient way of doing but insufficient in this case) Canada should have better addressed *Dr. De Brabander's* very critical conclusion whereby "more and more scientific data sustain the ban on the use of hormones: the economical profits resulting from using hormones does not balance the potential danger [in respect of, *inter alia*, animal welfare, environment and transformation of hormones] **in all of its aspects**" (emphasis in the original).

Q49.   What analytical methods, or other technical means, for residue detection in tissues exist to control the use of the six hormones in dispute for growth promotion purposes in accordance with good animal husbandry practice and/or good veterinary practice? What tools are available to control the use by farmers of the six hormones in dispute for growth promotion purposes in accordance with good animal husbandry practice and/or good veterinary practice?

US comment

163.   The United States does not refer to or discuss *Dr. De Brabander's* reply to this question. Moreover, as the European Communities has explained, these hormones are dispensed over the counter (OTC) in the US and Canada. In such a case the concept of GVP is not applicable and can be even misleading. Veterinarians are not involved in the whole process of distribution and administration of these hormones to animals since any farmer is free to use them at his will. Therefore, the initial statement by *Dr. Boobis* that "… it has been used as an anabolic agent in veterinary practice" is totally misleading as regards the realistic conditions of use of these hormones in the US and Canada. Moreover, the pinna of the ear is the only authorized site of application.[9] If this is not observed, the

---

[9]   See in the US the freedom of information summary, supplemental new animal drug application, NADA 140-897; Route of Administration: Subcutaneous implantation on the posterior aspect of the middle one-third of the ear by means of an implant gun; and freedom of information summary, supplemental new animal drug application, NADA 140-897, the Center for Veterinary Medicine has

depot goes directly into the edible part of the animal. Thus, it is more than surprising that this issue of utmost importance is not covered by any reply from the defending parties and the experts. *Dr. Boisseau* states that the administration of the implant is "… by subcutaneous implant to the base of the ear …". If this is so, this is already a serious misuse of these implants.

Canada's comment

164. The European Communities agrees that the additional information asked by Canada may be asked from Dr. De Brabander. The European Communities is confident that this also will support its position.

Q50. Are there other measures available to the European Communities (other than a complete ban) which could address risks arising from misuse and failure to follow good veterinary practice with respect to the use of the hormones at issue for growth promotion purposes? Would your reply have been different at the time of adoption of the EC Directive in September 2003? If so, why?

US comment

165. The United States does not refer to or comment on *Dr. De Brabander's* reply to this question, which is entirely supportive of the position taken by the European Communities.

Canada's comment

166. In its comments on *Dr. De Brabander's* reply Canada fails to see the difference between, on the one hand, the theoretical possibilities of control possibilities, as provided by *Dr. De Brabander* in his reply to Question 49, and the actual possibility to address risks arising from misuse and the failure to follow GVP and which, in *Dr. De Brabander's* view, can only be achieved by the European Communities through a complete ban. There is no contradiction between these two statements.

Q51. Does the material put forth by the European Communities regarding misuse or abuse of the hormones at issue in the United States and Canada call into question the potential applicability of Codex standards with regard to imports of meat from cattle treated with hormones from the United States and Canada? [For questions on GVP see the SCVPH Opinions in Exhibits US-1, 4 and 17, paras. 125-127 of EC Rebuttal Submission (US

---

concluded that, for these products, adequate directions for use by layperson have been provided and the products will have over-the-counter (OTC) status. Label directions are accompanied by pictorial diagrams and detailed instruction in plain language. The drugs are not controlled substances. The products' status remains OTC. The labelling is adequate for the intended use and has sufficient warnings/statements to prevent illegal use in veal calves.

case), paras. 107-109 of EC Rebuttal Submission (Canada case), para. 154 of EC Replies to Panel Questions, Exhibits EC-12, 67, 68, 69, 70, 73, 96, 102, 103, paras. 32 and 54-65 of US Rebuttal Submission, para. 75 of US First Submission, paras. 107-111 of Canada Rebuttal Submission, page 40 of Exhibit CDA-27]

US comment

167.   The United States refers to *Dr. Boisseau's* reply in paragraph 108 and comments on *Dr. De Brabander's* reply in paragraph 111 of its submission. The US relies again on the statements by *Dr. Boobis* (in paras. 109-110) to counter the evidence on abuse and misuse produced by the European Communities. But neither *Dr. Boobis* nor the US contest as such the accuracy of the scientific findings reported in those studies. *Dr. Boobis'* only claim is that (at para. 109) that the "probability" of these happening is "extremely low". However, what is "extremely low" is not defined nor is it true of course.

Canada's comment

168.   Canada draws the conclusion from *Dr. Boisseau's* reply that "in the unlikely event that GVP is not followed, the applicability of Codex standards is not put into doubt". However, *Dr. Boisseau* never said this. Rather, *Dr. Boisseau* explicitly agreed that "the European Communities is right to state that, in case of these different misuses/abuses, the exposure of consumers may be totally different" (*Dr. Boisseau's* reply to Question 48).

(g)   Other

Q52.   Do the risk assessment of the European Communities or any other scientific materials referred to by the European Communities demonstrate that a potential for adverse effects on human health arises from the consumption of meat from cattle treated with any of the six hormones in dispute for growth-promotion purposes? If yes, why? If not, what kind of evidence would be required to demonstrate such potential adverse affects? Would your response have been different at the time of adoption of the Directive in September 2003?

US comment

169.   Apart from a wholesale reference to *Dr. Boobis'* reply in footnote 41, the United States does neither refer to nor discuss the experts' (*Drs. Boobis, Boisseau, Guttenplan*) replies to this question.

Canada's comment

170.   Canada attempts again to mislead the Panel by drawing conclusions that are not warranted, in particular when it misstates (at paras. 197-198) the reply of *Dr. Guttenplan*. If to the reply by *Dr. Guttenplan* are added the replies from the

other 3 scientists who replied in their areas of expertise, then 4 out of the 6 scientists, in the view of the European Communities, agree with its scientific basis and the risk assessment it has conducted on these hormones. The European Communities would suggest that the Panel requests each of the experts to respond to this question for his respective areas of expertise.

Q53. Please comment on the statement by the European Communities that the natural hormones progesterone and testosterone are used only in combination with oestradiol-17β or other oestrogenic compounds in commercial preparations? Would the systematic use of these and the synthetic hormones in combination have any implications on how the scientific experiments and the risk assessments are to be carried out? If so, have the scientific materials referred to by the European Communities or relevant JECFA reports taken into account the possible synergistic effects of such combinations on human health? [see sections 4.2-4.3 of the Opinion of the SCVPH of 2002 in US Exhibit 1]

US comment

171.   The United States does neither refer to nor comment on the experts' (*Drs. Boisseau, Guttenplan*) replies to this question.

Canada's comment

172.   Canada's statement is, to say the least confusing. First, Canada pretends that *Dr. Boisseau and Dr. Guttenplan* "advise that the exposure to these hormones, both alone and in combination is so low that there is very little risk of any increase in the risk if assessed in combination". Yet, this description falls short by what *Dr. Boisseau* or *Dr. Guttenplan* actually stated. *Dr. Boisseau* merely states that "[c]onsidering that it has been established that progesterone and testosterone are not genotoxic, it is not likely that the testing of combinations of progesterone and testosterone with oestradiol-17β would have led to synergistic effects compared with those obtained from these individual substances". *Dr. Guttenplan*, for his part, states that "the use of mixtures should complicate risk assessment/scientific experiments, as they would have to evaluate/investigate each component alone and in combination. This is a major undertaking as effects of individual agents may be additive, inhibitory, and synergistic or there may no effect. It appears from the evidence submitted that, by far, estrogen is the major agent of risk and because the concentrations of all of the hormones in beef are so low, that they would be unlikely to affect the potency of estrogen. However, it appears that no experiments on effects of combinations were performed, so some uncertainty exists here".

173.   Against this background, Canada's conclusion that "once oestradiol 17β has been demonstrated not to have effects when used as a growth promoter, there is little risk that adverse effects would occur if used in combination with the other hormones" has never been stated by any of the experts.

Q54. What is the acceptable level of risk reflected in the Codex standards for the five hormones at issue? How does this compare to the European Communities' stated objective of "no risk from exposure to unnecessary additional residues in meat of animals treated with hormones for growth promotion". [see para. 149 of EC Rebuttal Submission (US case)]

US comment

174.   The United States does neither refer to nor comment on the experts' (*Drs. Boisseau, Boobis, Guttenplan*) replies to this question.

Canada's comment

175.   The comments by Canada about "theoretical" and "real" risk are again misleading, because the scientists (*Drs. Guttenplan, De Brabander and Sippell*) and the European Communities have identified a real risk from the consumption of residues in meat from animals treated with these hormones for growth promotion purposes. The existence of the real risk has been confirmed also by the US 2002 Carcinogenesis Report and it is simply a question of defining the appropriate level of protection – which is much lower in the US and Canada than in the European Communities – that has so far led the defending parties from ignoring the regulatory implications of that finding. This is not different from what has happened in the case of Carbadox a few years ago, when the defending parties were arguing this case in 1997 before the WTO. It is useful to recall here how Canada has explained its 360 turn on Carbadox in 2000, just 3 years after its persistent insistence in the WTO that Carbadox was a safe substance to use:

> "Carbadox is an antibiotic approved in the 1970s for use in swine to prevent and treat disease as well as to maintain weight gain during periods of stress, such as weaning. It has been shown that the drug, and the by-products of the drug that occur when the drug is metabolized in the body, can cause cancer in rats. However, when an appropriate withdrawal period (i.e stopping the administration of the drug before slaughter) is observed, the drug and its breakdown products are not found in the food derived from the treated animal. Carbadox was approved on the basis that this specified 35-day withdrawal period be strictly observed.

> However, *reports of misuse and accidental contamination*, combined with *a better scientific capacity* to detect breakdown products of carbadox, resulted in serious concerns about the safety of the product. The first reported incident occurred in the fall of 2000 when pigs at a farm in Quebec were accidentally fed carbadox and slaughtered without respecting the withdrawal period. All affected product was recalled and removed from store shelves and an investigation into the incident was launched. The investigation was

then broadened to review the use of carbadox throughout the Canadian pork industry.

In February 2001, responding to the European Union Fall 2000 audit of the Canadian Program for the Control of Residues, Canada made a public commitment to reassess the use of carbadox in pigs.

Based on the reassessment, Health Canada proposed to amend the Food and Drug Regulations to ban the sale of any drug containing carbadox for administration to food-producing animals."[10] (Emphasis added)

Q55. Do the Opinions of the European Communities or other scientific materials referred to by the European Communities evaluate the extent to which residues of growth promoting hormones in meat contribute to what the European Communities calls "additive risks arising from the cumulative exposures of humans to multiple hazards, in addition to the endogenous production of some of these hormones by animals and human beings"? Would your reply have been different at the time of adoption of the EC Directive in September 2003? If so, why? [see para. 151 of EC Replies to Panel Questions, paras. 43-44 of US Rebuttal Submission, paras. 83-85 of Canada's Rebuttal Submission]

US and Canada's comments

176.   The United States refers to *Dr. Boisseau's and Dr. Guttenplan's* replies in paragraphs 23 and 25 of its submission but fails to put in doubt the accuracy of *Dr. Guttenplan's* comments. The fact is that the decision of JECFA to set an ADI for oestradiol 17β was based on the alleged lack of evidence for *in vivo* genotoxicity and the seemingly safe use of oral contraceptives and postmenopausal estrogen replacements, implying the existence of a threshold for the carcinogenic effect of oestradiol 17β. But both situations are wrong and in any case have changed in the meantime, as there is now clear evidence for *in vivo* genotoxicity and evidence for an increased risk of cancer in women taking oral contraceptives and postmenopausal estrogen therapy. Even if a threshold would exist (which should not because of genotoxicity), the endogenous production of oestradiol 17β obviously exceeds that threshold, because we see oestrogen mediated cancer of the breast, endometrium and ovary in women. So any additional exposure to estrogens, e.g. from food, will inevitably increase the risk.

---

[10]   See at the website of Health Canada at: http://www.hc-sc.gc.ca/ahc-asc/media/nr-cp/2001/2001_88_e.html, visited on 11 July 2006.

177.   Moreover, as the EC has explained above, the US criticism that the EC statement "any excess exposure would increase the risk" is incorrect because the concept of concentration additivity has been proven for estrogens, including the demonstration of "0+0 ≈ 0" (i.e. that two doses which alone do not produce any detectable effects, when added together result in an observable effect). Thus, it is clear that any dose matters.

Q56. Has JECFA/Codex considered in its risk assessment of the five hormones such "additive risks? Are there internationally recognized guidelines for conducting assessments of "additive risks"?

US comment

178.   The European Communities suggests that it be clarified at the hearing where in its assessment JECFA is considering the issue of additive risks. United States refers to *Drs. Boisseau's and Boobis'* reply to this question in paragraph 26 of its submission, but again uses the idea of "trivial increase, something it is obviously unable to prove with scientific evidence. Indeed, quite the opposite is true. It has been shown that additivity of an exogenous dose to an endogenous hormone that is already causing responses will increase risk and have no threshold (see Hoel, D.G., Incorporation of background in dose-response models, in Fed. Proc. 39, 73-75 (1980)). Nonetheless, non-linearity (a threshold) is assumed.

Canada's comment

179.   Canada's comments on the expert' replies only tell half of the story. Indeed, Canada fails to see that *Dr. Boisseau* stated that for the synthetic hormonal growth promoters, JECFA/CODEX did *not* consider such "additive risks" probably because no internationally recognized guidelines for conducting assessment of "additive risks" exists. Canada's comment cites with approval *Dr. Boobis* reply. But the "additive" risk they both have in mind is quite different from the additive risk the European Communities has explained. For both of them, JECFA is supposed to take into account such risks through the mechanism of "safety margins" and default assumptions, which are obviously totally inadequate and scientifically inappropriate for this type of genotoxic substances.

Q57. Canada comments that "one single molecule that the European Communities considers so dangerous from meat derived from animals treated with hormone growth promoters is suddenly not at all that dangerous when consumed from meat from animals treated for therapeutic or zootechnical purposes. The European Communities' concern about the genotoxic potential of oestradiol-17β suddenly and inexplicably disappears." To what extent are hormone treatments of cattle for purposes other than growth promotion, such as for therapeutic or zootechnical purposes, taken into account by the European Communities, if at all, in its assessment of the cumulative effects from the consumption of meat containing residues

of the hormones at issue? Would your reply have been different at the time of adoption of the EC Directive in September 2003? If so, why? [see para. 97 of Canada Rebuttal Submission; paras. 17-20 of US Opening Statement]

US comment

180.   The United States refers to the experts' (*Drs. Boisseau, Boobis, Guttenplan*) replies to this question in paragraph 24 of its submission. Contrary to what the United States claims, *Dr. Guttenplan* does address the Panel's inquiry, i.e. whether the European Communities, in its Opinions, took these treatments into account in an assessment of cumulative effects. He states that the European Communities "does not really take [these] [...] into account in their risk assessment." *Dr. Guttenplan* then refers to the reasons why this is so and qualifies these as "a reasonable response."

Canada's comment

181.   Canada draws the wrong conclusion from the expert's reply when it purports that "the experts' advice indicates that the EC is trying to have it both ways: that hormones are genotoxic for some purposes and not others". Indeed, while *Dr. Boisseau* is questioning the logic of the EC's limited exception for the use of hormones for zootechnical and therapeutic reasons, *Dr. Guttenplan* expressly states its support for the EC' approach. This is not a question about the genotoxicity of hormones, as Canada tries to present it, but it is a pure risk management decision whereby in these limited circumstances it is assumed that the hormones will not enter into the food chain and, therefore, logically not present a risk to consumer's health. For this reason, it is by the way also an incorrect conclusion by *Dr. Boisseau* that this limited exception would raise questions regarding the overall approach taken by the European Communities. Indeed, the European Communities has always been pursuing the objective of health protection. This objective is not put into danger in case of the use of these hormones for zootechnical and therapeutic reasons, which in any case has been rejected by the Appellate Body back in 1998.

Q58.   Please comment on the EC statement in para. 94 of the EC Replies to Panel Questions that "the only rationale that can be inferred from the available scientific data is that the higher the exposure to residues from these hormones, the greater the risk is likely to be", taking into account para. 105 of Canada Rebuttal Submission.

US comment

182.   The United States refers to the experts' (*Drs. Boobis, Guttenplan, Boisseau*) replies to this question in paragraphs 24 and 25 of its submission. Quoting *Dr. Guttenplan* as referring to an "indeed very weak statement of the EC", it conveniently omits the rest of *Dr. Guttenplan's* statement who went on to say "[h]owever, the alternative would be to suggest a risk that might be wildly inac-

curate, due to the limitations imposed by the lack of solid data on levels of hormones in meat. Perhaps a better approach would have been to suggest several scenarios. These could be validated or disproved by subsequent studies." Thus, *Dr. Guttenplan* suggests that other alternative scenarios. The European Communities considers that the Panel may request *Dr. Guttenplan* to explain what other scenarios he has had in mind.

Canada's comment

183.   The comment by Canada (at para. 210) is also incomplete and partly false, because the European Communities has demonstrated that if the appropriate levels of endogenous production are taken into account, the ADIs set by JECFA will be reached and will be even exceeded easily.

Q59. Does the scientific evidence referred to by the European Communities identify any adverse effects on the immune system from the consumption of meat from cattle treated with the growth promoting hormones at issue? Would your reply have been different at the time of adoption of the Directive in September 2003? If so, why? [see para. 132 of Canada Rebuttal Submission]

US and Canada's comments

184.   The United States refers to the experts' (*Drs. Boobis, Boisseau and Guttenplan*) replies to this question in paragraph 86 of its submission. Canada discuss this in para. 211 of its submission. They both do not comment on the fact that there is a straightforward contradiction in the statements they quote. While *Dr. Boobis* denies that there is any evidence of adverse effect on the immune system, both *Dr. Boisseau and Dr. Guttenplan* acknowledge that there is such evidence.

Q60. Does the scientific evidence referred to by the European Communities identify and evaluate whether there is a difference in terms of potential adverse effects on human health from the consumption of meat from cattle treated with hormones for growth promotion purposes when these hormones are administered as feed additives (MGA) or implanted? Are you aware of any differences?

US comment

185.   The United States only refers to *Dr. Guttenplan's* reply to this question. In footnote 114 of its submission it states that *Dr. Guttenplan's* statement that MGA can be administered both as feed additive or implant is incorrect.

Canada's comment

186.   Canada's claim (at para. 212) that *Dr. Boobis* is right in arguing that misuse would "not occur in feed additives" is without any basis. The example of

Carbadox may be again useful, because this substance too was administered as a feed additive. But as the European Communities has explained above in relation to Question 54, Canada has admitted that its misuse has occurred and actually to such an extent as to lead it to ban this product also on this ground

Q61. In your view and in the light of information provided by the parties as well as the work undertaken at JECFA and Codex, did the scientific evidence available to the European Communities at the time it adopted its Directive (September 2003) allow it to conduct an assessment (quantitatively or qualitatively) of the potential for adverse effects on human health arising from the consumption of meat from cattle treated with (a) progesterone; (b) testosterone; (c) trenbolone; (d) zeranol; and (e) melengestrol acetate? Would your response differ in light of the scientific evidence provided which is subsequent to the adoption of the EC Directive?

US and Canada's comments

187.   As so often, the United States' claim that "*the* experts' responses confirm that the scientific evidence and information relating to the five hormones is sufficient to conduct an assessment" does not reflect the reality of what the experts have said. Indeed, only *Dr. Boobis* has taken this view (paragraphs 48 and 49 of its submission).

188.   *Dr. Boisseau* declines to comment on the question itself noting that "I don't really know what were the data available to the European Communities at the time it adopted its directive." Furthermore, *Dr. Guttenplan* takes a very nuanced and partly opposite view. As regards Trenbolone and Zeranol, he states that from the data available at the time of the Directive, the potential for adverse effects could not be ruled out. The United States tries to undermine this statement by pointing out that *Dr. Guttenplan* mistakenly thinks that trenbolone is an estrogen.

189.   However, *Dr. Guttenplan* may not be wrong completely as *Bauer et al.* have documented that trenbolone has three separate hormonal activities combined in one substance. It binds to the androgen receptor, progestin receptor and glucocorticoid receptor. This was not documented before. *Dr. Boobis* and certainly the US (at para. 49) in their statements still call trenbolene an androgen. The finding above is of clear relevance for the risk assessment of trenbolone acetate. If multiple hormonal activities are exhibited from one and the same compound, the potential of the synergistic activity has to be considered. See Bauer ERS., Daxenberger A., Petri T., Sauerwein H. and Meyer HHD.: *Characterisation of the affinity of different anabolics and synthetic hormones to the human androgen receptor, human sex hormone binding globulin and to the bovine progestin receptor*, in APMIS 108: 838-846, (2000)(Exhibit EC – 15).

190.   The European Communities would disagree however with the statement by *Dr. Guttenplan* that the evidence for MGA and its assessment "seems sound" and would like that the Panel requests *Dr. Guttenplan* to provide a more detailed

explanation of his statement on this point, taking into account in particular the new evidence produced by the European Communities.

191. The European Communities considers that also the other experts who have not expressed an opinion on this question should be requested by the Panel to take a position in their own areas of expertise, since it seems to the European Communities – from their replies to the other questions – that in their view the evidence available did not allow the European Communities to conduct a full and complete risk assessment.

Q62. Does the scientific evidence relied upon by the European Communities support the EC contention that the new scientific studies that have been initiated since 1997 have identified new important gaps, insufficiencies and contradictions in the scientific information and knowledge now available on these hormones such that more scientific studies are necessary before the risk to human health from the consumption of meat from cattle treated with these hormones for growth promotion purposes can be assessed? Would your reply have been different at the time of adoption of the Directive in September 2003? If so, why? [Please see the following references for the two questions above:

– **paras. 58-94 and 125-129 of US First Submission, paras. 28-32 of US Rebuttal Submission**

– **paras. 116-124 of Canada First Submission, paras. 74, 130-135 of Canada Rebuttal Submission (Exhibit CDA-23)**

– **paras. 108, 147, 162-169 of EC Replies to Panel Questions, paras. 143-174 of EC Rebuttal Submission (US case), and paras. 148-166 of EC Rebuttal Submission (Canada case)**

– **Exhibit CDA-32 provides a detailed table outlining the chronology of JECFA's assessment of these hormones and the resulting documentation]**

US and Canada's comments

192. The United States refers to the experts' (*Drs. Boisseau, Boobis and Guttenplan*) replies to this question in paragraphs 49 through 53, 90, 103, 109 and 110. As so often, it pretends that "*the* experts' replies" confirm its view where only one or two have done so and another one has taken the opposite view (paragraphs 51 and following). Indeed *Dr. Guttenplan* has listed a number of examples where the 17 studies have identified important gaps. The United States claims that the majority of those relate to oestradiol 17β and therefore are not relevant for the purposes of the provisional an on the other five hormonal substances (paragraph 52). This allegation is erroneous.

193. In particular, it is again useful to review some of the comments provided by *Dr. Boobis* for each of the studies funded by the European Communities in order to determine their relevance and the gaps and level of uncertainty they have established.

194.   Concerning the study "re: experimental studies in rabbits by Rajpert-De Meyts et al.", only a part of the study concerning metabolism and placental transfer has been published so far (Lange et al. Xenobiotica 2002). The results on the reproductive effects of Zeranol (ZER), Trenbolone Acetate (TBA) and Melengestrol Acetate (MGA) in rabbits exposed during development were summarized in a detailed report (by Rajpert-De Meyts et al.) sent to the European Communities in December 2001 with additional data supplemented in the spring 2002. The study has not yet been submitted for publication elsewhere for the following reasons:

- similar findings concerning the effects of ZER and Estradiol on spermatogenesis and epididymal reserves were previously published in another animal model (bull) by Veeramachaneni et al. Environ & Appl Toxicol 1988; 10: 73-81, thus this part of the rabbit study was only confirmatory;

- in the course of the rabbit study, hundreds of samples of tissues, sera and semen were collected and stored, and only a part of investigations have been completed due to lacking funds. Some ensuing studies are still in progress. The study will be submitted for publication when these investigations have been finalized.

195.   The evaluation of the *Lange et al.* study and the report (Rajpert-De Meyts et al.) by *Dr. Boobis* is one-sided. The sentence stating that *"there was no net accumulation of the compounds in fetal tissues"* is only partially true. The concentrations of the residues after MGA treatment were in fact higher in the fetal muscle than in the maternal muscle, the fact not mentioned by him.

196.   The unpublished part of the study of the exposure at three different developmental stages provided a wealth of data, which are dismissed by *Dr. Boobis* with a following statement: *"It is not clear whether the changes observed were consistent and hence compound-related as only a single dose was used for each compound "*. The report did, in fact, very clearly state that the study was preceded by a dose-finding pilot study that investigated three different doses of all three compounds. Because the higher doses caused extensive adverse changes, only the lowest doses were selected for the definitive study. Contrary to *Dr. Boobis'* statement - *"nor is it apparent whether the magnitude of all changes discussed reached statistical significance"* - a detailed statistical analysis was performed, with all significant changes at $p < 0.01$ and $p < 0.05$, showing effects of the anabolic steroid used, clearly highlighted in the report.

197.   Concerning the study "re: genotoxic potential of xenobiotic growth promoters and their metabolites", it is true that this study has not provided clear evidence for the genotoxicity of trenbolone, melengestrol acetate and zeranol in several in *vitro test* systems. However, the metabolism studies have clearly shown that all three compounds give rise to numerous hitherto unknown metabolites, which may or may not have adverse effects. Therefore, the value of this study is the demonstration that the fate of all three xenobiotic growth promoters in the organism may be far more complex than previously thought. Unfortunately, none of the novel metabolites could be structurally elucidated in the lim-

ited time period of the study, which prevented publication in peer-reviewed journals. Nonetheless, the structures of these novel metabolites and their biological activities need to be further studied in order to improve the risk assessment. The same applies to the observation of DNA adduct formation, though at low level, of trenbolone in rat hepatocytes by the post-labeling assay. Whether these adducts contain trenbolone or not, they should be further characterized in order to make sure they do not pose a risk.

198.   Concerning the set of studies "re: estradiol metabolism in cattle", *Dr Boobis* has well noticed the presence of estradiol-17-esters as tissular residues. Nevertheless, his comment does not integrate a possible different absorption route by the lymphatic circulation. This specific point has been demonstrated in the same set of studies in cannulated piglets. Concerning this specific class of estrogens, currently there is a gap in our knowledge of the extent to which they have some hormonal effect in peripheral tissue but also in intestine when ingested. Moreover, when considering the *in situ* catechol estrogens formation in target tissues of exposed consumers (in particular at the intestine level), there is still a gap about the complete residue information on the parent compound but also on the metabolites, specifically on estradiol-alpha. This latter compound gives the same DNA-adducts pattern from catechols as estradiol (Jouanin *et al*, Steroids 67 (2002), 1091-1099). This information is pivotal when considering the risk of genotoxicity of all estrogen residues, not only this of estradiol. It should be recalled that all residue data on tissular estrogen were obtained by a fully validated spectro-physical procedure, discarding any doubt on false positive signals. Such reference data were never obtained at this sensitivity and precision level with any other hormones considered before.

199.   As regards the criticism of *Dr. Boobis* of the Chakravarti et al. study concerning in particular the comment that the two major adducts formed by E2-3,4-quinone are N3Ade and N7Gua, it should be noted that both adducts are spontaneously released from the DNA (a process called depurination) but at different rates (Zahid et al., 2006): the N3Ade is depurinated much faster than the N7Gua. Therefore, the N7Gua may allow accurate DNA repair whereas the N3Ade may not be repaired properly and give rise to mutations of the type observed in the mutagenicity studies. What is important to stress, however, is that Chakravarti et al (Oncogene, 20; 7945-7953, 2001) has detected mutations in the H-*ras* gene in the skin of SENCAR mice following dermal treatment with E2-3,4-quinone, with the specific nature of the mutations detected being consistent with the expected depurination of adenine due to the formation of an E2-3,4-quinone-Adenine adduct. This is relevant to the potential mutagenicity of estradiol in humans. First, we know that oxidative metabolism of E2 to the E2-3-4-quinone metabolite occurs in human breast tissue because E2-quinone adducts to glutathione have been detected (Yue et al. J. Steroid Biochem. Mol. Biol. 86: 477-486, 2003). Second, adducts of the E2-3,4-quinone with ademine and guanine have been detected in the mammary tissue of ACI rats injected into the mammary gland tissue with 4-OH E2 or E2-3,4-quinone (Carcinogenesis, 25:, 289-297, 2004). So, *Dr. Boobis* criticism appears to miss the important point that

mutagenicity *in vivo* is now established thanks to this and the other studies cited by the European Communities in relation to Question 13 above.

200.   It follows that *Dr. Boobis* provides a partial and selective discussion of certain aspects of these studies. The importance of these studies is however not questioned. If some of the results obtained by some of these studies are not clear or unequivocal, this simply strengthens the EC position that important gaps in our knowledge have become available recently which made the completion of a risk assessment impossible in 2000-2002 and even today for the five hormones (except for oestradiol 17β)

ANNEX F-4

COMMENTS BY CANADA TO THE REPLIES OF SCIENTIFIC EXPERTS, CODEX, JECFA AND IARC TO QUESTIONS POSED BY THE PANEL

(30 June 2006)

TABLE OF CONTENTS

Page

I.   INTRODUCTION 6851
II.   COMMENTS ON THE RESPONSES FROM THE EXPERTS 6852
       A.   General Definitions 6852
       B.   Assessment of oestradiol-17β.. 6865
       C.   Consumption of Meat Containing Hormones........................... 6867
             (a)   Carcinogenicity.. 6867
             (b)   Residue analysis.. 6881
             (c)   Dose-response relationship 6890
             (d)   Sensitive populations 6892
             (e)   Bioavailability.. 6896
             (f)   Good veterinary practice (GVP) 6898
             (g)   Other 6906
III.   COMMENTS ON INTERNATIONAL ORGANIZATION
       REPLIES 6913
IV.   CONCLUDING COMMENTS 6917

I.   INTRODUCTION

1.   Canada is pleased to have this opportunity to comment on the responses to the Panel's questions of the experts and international organizations. Canada expresses its appreciation to the experts and international organizations for having agreed to participate in this proceeding as scientific and technical advisors to the Panel.

2.   The Panel has sought advice on the scientific and technical matters that arise in the context of the dispute between the parties over whether the European Communities (EC) has complied with the recommendations and rulings of the WTO Dispute Settlement Body (DSB) in *EC – Measures Concerning Meat and Meat Products (Hormones)*. In light of the nature of this dispute, the most relevant questions (and answers) are those that shed light on whether the scientific evidence relied upon by the EC supports its conclusions that there is a potential

for the occurrence of adverse effects from the consumption of meat from cattle that have been treated with oestradiol 17β, and that there is insufficient scientific evidence to conduct an assessment of the risks from consuming meat from cattle that has been treated by any of the other five hormone growth promoters (HGP).

3.   The responses provided by the experts and international organizations generally confirm the explanations of the scientific and technical issues provided by Canada in its previous submissions.[1] With some limited exceptions, these responses indicate that (1) the EC's regulatory opinions do not properly evaluate the potential for adverse effects to human health from residues of oestradiol 17β in meat from cattle treated when used for growth promotion, and (2) that the available scientific evidence is sufficient to conduct an assessment of the risks from consuming meat that has been treated with any of the remaining five HGP.

4.   The issues are complex, however, and Canada submits these comments with a view to further assisting the Panel in understanding these matters. Canada has sought to identify where the experts and international organizations agree with one another and with Canada's explanations of the scientific and technical issues, to reconcile any inconsistencies among the responses received, to elaborate on certain responses that require clarification or amplification, and to address advice by certain experts that is not supported by the available scientific evidence. In several instances, Canada suggests follow-up questions that the Panel may consider asking the experts at a later date.

II.   COMMENTS ON THE RESPONSES FROM THE EXPERTS

A.   General Definitions

Q1.   Please provide brief and basic definitions for the six hormones at issue (oestradiol 17β, progesterone, testosterone, trenbolone acetate, zeranol, and melengestrol acetate), indicating the source of the definition where applicable.

5.   Canada has no comment on the responses to this question provided by Drs. Boisseau, Boobis and Guttenplan other than to note that there does not appear to be any material disagreement concerning these terms.

Q2.   Please provide definitions for the following terms as they relate to the hormones at issue, indicating the source of the definition where applicable: anabolic   agents,   steroids,   steroidal   oestrogens,   parent   compounds/metabolites, catechol metabolites, mitogenicity, mutagenicity, androgenic/oestrogenic activity, genotoxicity, genotoxic potential, carcino-

---

[1]   Canada First Written Submission, at paras. 86-131; Canada First Oral Statement, at paras. 41-73; and Canada Rebuttal Submission, at paras. 45-146.

genicity, and tumorigenicity. **In your replies, please be sure to identify and describe any relevant differences between the terms.**

6.   Drs. Boobis and Guttenplan provide definitions of the terms identified by the Panel. While the responses appear to be consistent, Dr. Boobis' reply is more thorough and supported by references.

7.   A few key definitions warrant highlighting. According to Dr. Boobis, carcinogenicity is the "[p]rocess of induction of malignant neoplasms", or what is commonly referred to as cancer. Neoplasms, which are new and abnormal formation of tissue, can be malignant or benign. Malignant neoplasms (cancer) pose the greatest risk to human health. In contrast, mutagenicity is the "[a]bility of a physical, chemical or biological agent to induce heritable changes (mutations) in the genotype in a cell as a consequence of alterations or loss of genes or chromosomes (or parts thereof)." Mutagenicity does not necessarily lead to the formation of malignant neoplasms (cancer).

8.   Genotoxicity is the "[a]bility to cause genetic damage." Genotoxicity does not necessarily lead to mutagenicity, if the damage to the DNA is not inherited into the genotype of the affected cell. Genotoxic potential means that a compound "possesses characteristics such that it might be capable of causing genotoxicity (usually *in vivo*), based on considerations such as the results of tests in vitro." Dr. Boobis emphasizes that "[i]t remains to be determined whether genotoxicity is indeed expressed *in vivo*, i.e. that the potential is realized". Thus, "potential" does not refer to the statistical likelihood that the genotoxic mode of action will occur *in vivo*, but, rather that the genotoxic mode of action is theoretically possible.

9.   Combining these concepts, if a compound is only identified as having genotoxic potential, the compound is still several steps removed from carcinogenicity. The genotoxic potential will have to be realized *in vivo*, the genetic damage to the cell would have to be "fixed" into the genome created a mutated cell, the mutated cell in turn would have to replicate to form neoplasms, and the neoplasm would have to be malignant (cancer). Any one of these steps may be thwarted by the various effective and redundant defence and repair mechanisms.[2]

Q3.   Please identify any international guidance documents relevant to the conduct of a risk assessment with respect to veterinary drug residues. Since when have they been available? Please also indicate if there is any relevant ongoing work at Codex.

10.   This question was also posed to the international bodies (Question 3). Drs. Boisseau and Boobis, as well as JECFA and Codex, responded.

---

[2]   For a clear explanation of the relationship between genotoxic potential and carcinogenicity, see Dr. Boobis' answer to Question 19.

11.   Dr. Boobis, JECFA and Codex identify a significant number of relevant international guidance documents. A review of this documentation indicates that the development of risk assessment techniques by international organizations has been ongoing for decades. The International Program on Chemical Safety (a collaborative venture between the World Health Organization, the United Nations Environment Programme and the International Labour Organisation), as early as 1987, published a comprehensive guidance document entitled *Principles for the Safety Assessment of Food Additives and Contaminants in Food, Environmental Health Criteria 70* (EHC 70).[3] EHC 70 sets out principles and approaches to safety assessment for food additives and contaminants, consolidating of 30 years of JECFA experience. While not specific to veterinary drug residues, much of the detailed guidance is relevant to the risk assessment generally, including the assessment of veterinary drugs.

12.   Building on EHC 70 and recognizing that the assessment of veterinary drug residues can pose specific issues, the WHO and FAO have issued several guidance documents outlining risk assessment techniques and procedures specific to veterinary drug residues. These include:

- JECFA, *Procedures for Recommending Maximum Residue Limits – Residues of Veterinary Drugs in Food (1987 – 1999)*, (Rome: FAO/WHO, 2000) (JECFA Procedures);[4]

- WHO, *Residues of veterinary drugs in food – WHO procedural guidelines for the Joint FAO/WHO Expert Committee on Food Additives* (Geneva: January 2001);[5]

- WHO, *Residues of veterinary drugs in food – Guidelines for the preparation of toxicological working papers for the Joint FAO/WHO Expert Committee on Food Additives* (Geneva: August 1996);[6] and

- FAO, *Residues of veterinary drugs in food – FAO procedural guidelines for the Joint FAO/WHO Expert Committee on Food Additives*, (Rome: September 2002).[7]

13.   In addition to the above, Codex also identifies several relevant guidance documents, including the Statements of principles relating to the role of food safety risk assessment[8] and the Working Principles for Risk Analysis for Application in the Framework of the Codex Alimentarius Commission.[9]

---

[3]   The International Program on Chemical Safety, *Principles for the Safety Assessment of Food Additives and Contaminants in Food*, Environmental Health Criteria 70 (Geneva: WHO,1987); online: *http://www.inchem.org/documents/ehc/ehc/ehc70.htm* (Exhibit CDA-43).

[4]   Exhibit CDA-44 ("JECFA *Procedures for Recommending Maximum Residue Limits*").

[5]   Attached to JECFA's answers to the Panel's questions.

[6]   Exhibit CDA-45.

[7]   Attached to JECFA's answers to the Panel's questions.

[8]   Quoted in the answer by Codex to Question 3 addressed to the international bodies; reproduced in the *Procedural Manual of the Codex Alimentarius Commission* (15th edition), at p. 161.

[9]   Annex 6 to the answers by Codex.

14.   The JECFA *Procedures for Recommending Maximum Residue Limits* is a consolidation of JECFA's collective experience developing risk assessment techniques and methodologies for veterinary drugs from 1987 to 1999. This document confirms that many of the general risk assessment techniques and methodologies developed by international organizations are also relevant to the risk assessment of veterinary drugs.[10]

15.   As JECFA points out in its response to Question 3, there is a continuous effort to update and harmonize international level risk assessment techniques for chemicals. However, the fact alone that international risk assessment techniques are continuously subject to refinement and elaboration does not, *a priori*, suggest that existing international techniques and methodologies are inadequate or problematic.

Q4.   The European Communities states that there is "no Codex standard specifically on the risk assessment of effects of residues of veterinary drugs" but a general one on microbiological assessment. Is this correct? Which guidelines or principles have been used by JECFA in the conduct of its risk assessments with respect to the hormones at issue? [see para. 192 of EC Rebuttal Submission (US case)].

16.   The experts confirm the accuracy of the EC's statement referred to in the Panel's question. However, while the statement is technically correct, the experts confirm that the absence of a Codex standard does not imply an absence of internationally developed risk assessment guidelines or principles. Furthermore, the experts confirm that JECFA based its risk assessment of the hormones at issue on relevant international risk assessment methodologies and techniques.

17.   Specifically, Dr. Boisseau states in his reply that:

> In the conduct of its risk assessment with respect to the hormones at issue, as for all the other pharmacologically active substances used in veterinary medicine, JECFA has followed the general rationale used by all the countries which have assessed the safety of veterinary drug residues. This rationale has been internationally harmonised through scientific conferences and it is possible to say that there was an international non written agreement on this rationale.

18.   Referring to the documents identified in his response to Question 3, Dr. Boobis also confirms that JECFA relied upon a number of relevant guidance documents in its risk assessments of the hormones at issue. Moreover, Dr. Guttenplan acknowledges that the "principles for risk assessment...were

---

[10]   For example, a significant portion of the general toxicological data requirements that have been established for food additives and contaminants are equally applicable to veterinary drug residues. JECFA, *Procedures for Recommending Maxium Residue Limits*, at p. 3 (Exhibit CDA-44).

used in determining Acceptable Daily Intakes (ADI) for estradiol, progesterone, and testosterone."

19.   It is apparent from the experts' answers that international organizations have expended considerable effort in developing risk assessment techniques relevant to the assessment of veterinary drugs. Much of that effort has been the result of contributions from the EC's own Member States[11] and much of the resulting guidance used as a basis for decisions taken by European regulatory authorities, including the Committee for Veterinary Medicinal Products (CVMP). Thus, any suggestion that relevant risk assessment techniques or guidance developed by international organizations for the conduct of veterinary drug risk assessments do not exist is baseless.

Q5.   Please briefly describe the three components of a risk analysis exercise (risk assessment, risk management and risk communication) and explain how they differ.

20.   The responses of all four experts who replied to this question appear to be consistent with the response provided by Codex to a similar question posed to the international bodies (Question 5). In all cases, the experts and Codex identify a functional separation between risk assessment and risk management. In the context of food safety, a risk assessment is a scientific process in which data are evaluated and on this basis, together with the weight of evidence and expert judgment, a conclusion is reached as to the nature of the hazards, the potential risk to exposed individuals and the extent to which exposure is within those levels considered to be without appreciable risk.[12] The descriptions of risk assessment provided by the experts are consistent with the definition of risk assessment set out in Annex A(4) of the *SPS Agreement*, namely an evaluation of the potential for adverse effects on human health.

21.   Risk management, on the other hand, is the process of weighing policy alternatives, considering the risk assessment and other factors relevant for the health protection of consumers and for the promotion of fair trade practices, and, if needed, selecting appropriate prevention and control options.[13] This description of risk management is akin to the process of identifying and selecting SPS measures appropriate to the circumstances.

Q6.   Please briefly describe the four steps of a risk assessment (hazard identification, hazard characterization, exposure assessment and risk characterization) as identified by Codex, indicating any relevant sources.

---

[11]   For instance, the UK Department of Health and Social Security was instrumental in providing support for EHC 70.
[12]   See *e.g.* Dr. Boobis, at p. 12.
[13]   Codex, at p. 6.

22.   This question is the same as Question 6 addressed to the international bodies. Drs. Boisseau, Boobis and Guttenplan, as well as JECFA and Codex, respond to this question. Their answers reflect principles for the conduct of a risk assessment generally accepted by the international community.

Hazard Identification

23.   With slight differences, the experts and international bodies appear to agree that hazard identification involves the determination of whether an agent has the potential to cause adverse effects.

Hazard Characterization

24.   Again, with slight differences, the experts appear to agree that hazard characterization involves the quantitative and/or qualitative evaluation of the nature of the identified adverse effects caused by the agent. The experts agree that, where possible, hazard characterization should involve a dose-response assessment and a determination of whether a threshold can be established below which no adverse effects can be expected to occur.[14] The outcome of this step is the establishment of a No-Observed-Adverse-Effects-Level (NOAEL), from which an Acceptable Daily Intake (ADI) is derived. The experts' answers are consistent with JECFA's response that "[d]ose-response assessment is an integral part of each assessment and is an essential part of the hazard characterization step." As Canada has stated previously, central to this dispute is whether the EC's failure to complete this "integral part" of the risk assessment implies that the assessment conducted by the EC fails to meet the requirements of the *SPS Agreement*.[15]

Exposure Assessment

25.   In terms of exposure assessment, the experts confirm that the objective of this step is to evaluate quantitatively exposure by relevant population groups to the substance under review. In order to do so, risk assessors typically use a "food basket" which is based on "available intake data at the upper limit of the range for individual consumption of edible tissues and animal products".[16] The "food basket" used by JECFA is as follows:

---

[14]   Dr. Boisseau, at p. 5; Dr. Boobis, at p. 13.
[15]   Canada Rebuttal Submission, at para. 78.
[16]   JECFA, *Procedures for Recommending Maxium Residue Limits,*, at p. 31 (Exhibit CDA-44). Also see JECFA, *Evaluation of certain veterinary drug residues in food: Fifty-second Report of the Joint FAO/WHO Expert Committee on Food Additives*, WHO Technical Report Series 893 (Geneva: WHO, 2000), at p. 67 (Exhibit CDA-16).

Muscle	300 g
Liver	100 g
Kidney	50 g
Tissue Fat	50 g
Milk	1.5 litre
Eggs	100 g

26.   The Panel may wish to seek clarification from the experts on whether the food basket is adjusted to reflect estimated consumption by prepubertal populations.

Risk Characterization

27.   The experts all appear to agree with the Codex definition of risk characterization: a qualitative and/or quantitative estimation, including attendant uncertainties, of the probability of occurrence and severity of known or potential adverse health effects in a given population based on the three preceding three steps of a risk assessment. Dr. Boisseau specifics that:

> ... the goal of the risk analysis for these compounds is not to assess qualitatively and quantitatively the likelihood and the gravity of the adverse effects for the health of consumers associated with the veterinary drug residues they are exposed to through the animal derived food[,] *but to protect consumers' health from any adverse effect associated with these residues.* [emphasis added]

28.   The experts confirm that to achieve the goal of no adverse effects on human health, Maximum Residue Limits (MRL) are established. The purpose of the MRL is to ensure that the exposure to residues of the veterinary drug in question consumed in edible animal products does not exceed the ADI established for that drug.

Q7.   Please comment on the EC statement made in para. 140 of the EC Replies to Panel Questions that "which ever approach of a risk assessment is followed, they are all based on a deterministic approach to risk characterization [and that they] have serious limitations in non-linear situations, such as in the current case regarding hormones". Are these situations, in your view, addressed by the risk assessment guidance currently available from the Codex Alimentarius Commission? Have they been addressed in the 1988 and 1999 JECFA risk assessments of these hormones? [see Canada's comments in para. 72 of its Rebuttal Submission]

29.   The same question was put to the international bodies (Question 7). JECFA, Drs. Boobis and Boisseau respond. The experts confirm that JECFA

was aware of "non-linear situations" and took these into account in conducting its risk assessment for the hormones at issue.

30.   The assumption implicit in the EC's statement is that, in non-linear situations, no threshold can be established below which there is no appreciable risk. As the experts and JECFA point out, this is simply not true. JECFA explains that "probabilistic or deterministic approaches can be applied, independent [of whether] a compound is assumed to act via a threshold mechanism, i.e. non-linear" and "non-linearity is assumed if the adverse effect of a compound is caused via a mechanism with a threshold of effect." Thus the important issue is not linearity, as the EC has asserted, but rather whether a threshold mechanism operates and an ADI can be set. In deciphering the EC's logic, Dr. Boobis states that the EC's assertion presupposes a specific outcome to the risk assessment, i.e., that no threshold can be set below which no adverse effects occur. This is simply not true. JECFA explains that "[i]n such a case, as for the hormones, a no-effect-level can be determined from which an ADI can be established."

31.   In support of its "non-linearity" claim, the EC argues that "here, the risks are embedded in changes in exposure to biologically active molecules which may, within minute differences in their bioavailability, have dramatic effects, such as turning on or off complete developmental programs of the human genome, or inducing pathological conditions."[17] The EC presents no evidence that the minute increases in exposure to the hormones resulting from residues of growth promoting hormones in treated meat "turn[] on or off complete developmental programs of the human genone, or induc[e] pathological conditions." This is not surprising given that wide variation in background levels of hormones endogenously produced by humans and considerable exposure to dietary sources of hormones.

Q8.   Please describe the procedure followed by JECFA in the identification of ADIs and the development of recommendations on MRLs. Please identify and describe any steps that are taken in the risk assessment process to build a margin of safety into the final recommendation.

32.   This question is the same as Question 10 addressed to the international bodies. The description provided by the experts of the procedure followed by JECFA in the identification of ADIs and development of recommendations on MRLs appears to be consistent with JECFA's answer to Question 10. In terms of the steps taken in the risk assessment process to build in a margin of safety, Dr. Boobis describes similar steps in his answer to Question 12 when addressing scientific uncertainty. Canada would like to highlight the following:

---

[17]   EC Replies to Questions from the Panel, Question 24. at para. 140. The EC refers to no scientific evidence in support of this assertion.

Establishment of ADI

33.   The experts and JECFA have confirmed that the ADI is the highest quantity of residue that can be ingested on a daily basis over a lifetime that will not result in adverse effects to health, or, as Dr. Boobis states in response to a later question, that will pose zero risk.[18] The establishment of the ADI is a two-step process involving the determination of a NOAEL and the application of safety factors.[19] A NOAEL is established for each adverse effect. The NOAEL from the most sensitive adverse effect is used as the NOAEL for the substance.[20] "Safety factors" are applied to the NOAEL to take into account inherent uncertainties in extrapolating animal toxicity data to potential effects in human beings and variation in the human species.[21] The experts and JECFA confirm that JECFA typically uses a default safety factor of 100, representing a safety factor of 10 for extrapolation from animal to human species and a safety factor of 10 for diversity within the human population. Smaller safety factors may be justified in certain circumstances, such as where the NOAEL is derived from data from human studies. Extra factors may be applied in other circumstances such as where there is an identifiable sub-group that might reasonably be expected to be more sensitive than the group in which data were obtained (*e.g.*, children relative to adults).[22]

34.   In the case of the six hormones at issue, JECFA has established the following ADIs:

Hormone	JECFA Meeting	Exhibit #	Pg.	ADI	Safety Factor
Oestradiol 17β	52nd Meeting	CDA-17	60	0-0.05 μg/kg	100
Progesterone	52nd Meeting	CDA-17	62	0-30 μg/kg	100
Testosterone	52nd Meeting	CDA-17	64	0-2 μg/kg	1000
Trenbolone Acetate	34th Meeting	CDA-30	107	0-0.02 μg/kg	100
Zeranol	32nd Meeting	CDA-29	145	0-0.5 μg/kg	100
Melengestrol Acetate	54th Meeting	CDA-31	179	0-0.03 μg/kg	200

---

[18]   Dr. Boobis, answer to Question 54.
[19]   JECFA's answer to Question 10, at p. 6.
[20]   Dr. Boobis, at p. 15.
[21]   JECFA's answer to Question 10, at p. 6.
[22]   Dr. Boobis, at pp. 14-15.

Proposal of an MRL

35.   The experts have confirmed that the MRL is a risk management tool designed to ensure that exposure to veterinary drug residues does not exceed the established ADI. In other words, if residues are within the MRL, then the ADI is unlikely to be exceeded and no adverse effects to human health are to be expected.

36.   The experts and JECFA have set out various ways in which a margin of safety is built into the establishment of the MRL. In this regard, the risk assessor makes the following conservative assumptions:

- the parent substance and all its metabolites have the same potential toxicity unless demonstrated otherwise;[23]
- the parent substance and all its metabolites are considered to be bioavailable (or biologically active) unless demonstrated otherwise;[24] and
- the standard food consumption figures (the "food basket"), used to estimate exposure, overestimate actual consumption.[25]

37.   As can be observed from the foregoing, JECFA has developed risk assessment techniques that build into its risk assessments a significant margin of safety.

Q9.   Please confirm or comment on the following Canadian statement: "it is recognized that JECFA only allocates an ADI for a food additive or veterinary drug under review when JECFA considers that its scientific data base is complete and that there are no outstanding scientific issues". [see para. 68 of Canada Rebuttal Submission]

38.   The same question was put to the international bodies as Question 11. JECFA states in its response that "[i]f there are substantial data gaps and important information missing, JECFA *can not* establish an ADI." [emphasis added] This confirms Canada's statement quoted in the question was correct. Thus, given that JECFA established ADI for all six hormones at issue, it is reasonable to infer that the record was complete and sufficient for all hormones in question.

39.   The experts who responded to this question, Dr. Boisseau and Dr. Boobis, confirm that Canada's statement is correct as a general rule. Dr. Boobis identified a number of exceptions in which JECFA might issue an ADI without a complete dataset. As he explains, the "critical issue is whether a sufficiently cautious default can be adopted in the absence of certain information." He concludes that "JECFA would require a complete data base unless it could adopt default assumptions that would if anything lead to a more conservative risk assessment than would be the case otherwise".

---

[23]   Dr. Boisseau's answer to Question 13(B), at p. 10.
[24]   Dr. Boisseau, at p. 23; Dr. Boobis, at pp. 14-15.
[25]   Dr. Boisseau, at p. 7.

Q10. In paras. 129 and 168 of its Replies to the Panel Questions, the European Communities states that "JECFA's traditional mandate does not allow it to examine all risk management options but restricts it to either propose MRLs or not". Does Codex have risk management options other than (1) the establishment of an MRL, (2) establishing that an MRL is not necessary or (3) no recommendation?

40.   The same question was put to the international bodies as Question 12. JECFA's answer clarifies that its role is to conduct risk assessments. It will only consider the health impact of specific risk management options, if requested to do so by the Codex Committee on Residues of Veterinary Drugs in Foods (CCRVDF). The response by Codex to Question 12 indicates that it is not necessarily limited to the three risk management options listed in the question, and mentions the possibility of developing "codes of practice" through the CCRVDF.

Q11. What should, in your view, be the components of a qualitative risk assessment, compared with a quantitative risk assessment? [see para. 82 of Canada Rebuttal Submission]

41.   The experts with specific expertise on risk assessments of veterinary drugs explain that a qualitative risk assessment may be conducted under certain limited circumstances. Both Dr. Boisseau and Dr. Boobis agree that a qualitative risk assessment should comprise the main steps of a conventional risk assessment, including hazard identification, hazard characterization and exposure assessment. Both experts also agree that if the mode of action is such that a dose-response relationship cannot be established and, thus, no safe intake threshold can be set, then a quantitative dose-response assessment is not necessary. However, Dr. Boobis explains that even where the need for detailed dose-response analysis would be questionable, a risk assessment still needs "scientific rigour", a statement supported by the Appellate Body's description of the risk assessment process as characterized by "systematic, disciplined and objective enquiry and analysis."[26]

42.   Dr. Boisseau provides examples of where JECFA has based its conclusions on a qualitative risk assessment and declined to recommend an ADI (*e.g.*, chloramphenicol and nitroimidazole). Both Dr. Boisseau and Dr. Boobis also confirm in subsequent answers that, in respect of the hormones at issue in this dispute, a dose-response assessment can be undertaken and a safe threshold (ADI) can be established for each hormone.[27] Thus, it can be inferred that, according to internationally developed risk assessment techniques, a risk assess-

---

[26]   *EC – Measures Concerning Meat and Meat Products (Hormones)*, Report of the Appellate Body, WT/DS26/AB/R, WT/DS48/AB/R, adopted February 13, 1998, at para. 187 (*EC – Hormones*).
[27]   See answers to Questions 36 and 37.

ment for these substances that does not include a dose-response assessment would be incomplete.

43.   Dr. Cogliano also responds to this question with references to IARC's practice in developing its monographs. However, the type of assessment to which Dr. Cogliano refers only satisfies the first element of a risk assessment contemplated by the *SPS Agreement*, which includes both the identification of adverse effects arising from the substance at issue *and* the evaluation of the potential of occurrence of such effects. In this regard, it is important to recall the Appellate Body's conclusion regarding previous IARC Monographs relied upon by the EC in the first hormones dispute. After citing the Panel's conclusion that the IARC Monographs were "in the nature of general studies of…the carcinogenic potential of the named hormones" and have not "evaluated the carcinogenic potential of those hormones when used specifically *for growth promotion purposes*"[28], the Appellate Body, in *EC – Hormones*, concluded as follows:

> We believe that the above findings of the Panel are justified. The 1987 IARC Monographs and the articles and opinions of individual scientists submitted by the European Communities constitute general studies which do indeed show the existence of a general risk of cancer; but they do not focus on and do not address the particular kind of risk here at stake – the carcinogenic or genotoxic potential of the residues of those hormones found in meat derived from cattle to which the hormones had been administered for growth promotion purposes – as is required by paragraph 4 of Annex A of the *SPS Agreement*. Those general studies, are in other words, relevant but do not appear to be sufficiently specific to the case at hand.[29]

44.   It is also worth noting that Codex has estimated general principles in relation to the use of quantitative information. For instance, the Codex *Statements of principles relating to the role of food safety risk assessment* include requirements that "[f]ood safety risk assessment should be *soundly based on science, …* ", and that "[r]isk assessment should use *available quantitative information to the greatest extent possible …*" [emphasis added] Moreover, paragraph 20 of the *Working Principles for Risk Analysis for Application in the Framework of the Codex Alimentarius* restates the same principles while recognizing that a risk assessment may also take into account qualitative information. Paragraph 23 of the *Working Principles* also provides:

> Constraints, uncertainties and assumptions having an impact on the risk assessment should be explicitly considered at each step in the risk assessment and documented in a transparent manner. Ex-

---

[28]   *EC – Hormones*, Report of the Appellate Body, at para. 199.
[29]   *Ibid.*, at para. 200.

pression of uncertainty or variability in risk estimates may be qualitative or quantitative, *but should be quantified to the extent that is scientifically achievable.* [emphasis added]

Q12. How is scientific uncertainty addressed in risk assessments in general? With respect to the assessment of risks from the consumption of meat treated with the growth promotion hormones at issue, how has scientific uncertainty been considered by JECFA/Codex ? How does it differ from the way it has been considered by the European Communities in its assessment of risks from the consumption of meat treated with the growth promotion hormones at issue?

45.   Both Drs. Boisseau and Boobis explain the numerous ways in which scientific uncertainty is addressed in a risk assessment. Dr. Boobis' response is worth quoting at length:

> One way of dealing with uncertainty is [1] to default to the worst case in the absence of evidence to the contrary. Hence, the most sensitive relevant endpoint in the most sensitive species is used as the basis of the risk assessment. [2] In extrapolating to humans a default factor of 10 is used to allow for species differences, which assumes that humans are more sensitive than the experimental species. [3] A further factor of 10 is included for interindividual differences. These differences may be due to gender, genetics, life stage or other factors. [4] However, to some extent such differences have already been taken into account in the choice of endpoint, as this will usually represent the most sensitive lifestage, gender and to some extent genetics by using data from the most sensitive species. [5] Where there are additional uncertainties, such as no NOEAL or the absence of a non-critical study, an additional safety factor will be included, and this is almost always conservative, as when the data gaps have been completed, the appropriate safety factor is almost always less than that used to account for these data gaps. [6] The residue may be assumed to be all as active as the most active moiety, which is almost always a conservative assumption. [7] Dietary intake is based on conservative data for food consumption. [8] It is also assumed that all meat that could contain veterinary drug residue will contain the residue and that this will be present at the high end of the range (MRL or other appropriate level). [9] In respect of the ADI, the assumption is that intake will be at this high level for a lifetime, when in reality there will be occasions when little or no meat is consumed or that which is consumed contains less or even no residue. In their risk assessment of the hormones, JECFA applied all of these approaches to dealing with the uncertainty.

46.   Dr. Boisseau indicates that the EC "did not consider any scientific uncertainty", because it had decided as a matter of "principle" that it was not possible to establish an ADI for genotoxic substances. Clearly, however, this "principle" is one of selective rather than general application, if one considers that the EC knowingly allows its population to consume, without so much as a warning, the very same "genotoxic" substance (*i.e.*, oestradiol 17β) naturally present in many dietary sources (*e.g.*, milk, eggs, meat) and in oral contraceptives, at levels many times higher than that which would be present as residues of growth promotants.

B.   Assessment of Oestradiol-17β

Q13.   To what extent, in your view, does the EC risk assessment identify the potential for adverse effects on human health, including the carcinogenic or genotoxic potential, of the residues of oestradiol 17β found in meat derived from cattle to which this hormone had been administered for growth promotion purposes in accordance with good veterinary practice? To what extent does the EC risk assessment evaluate the potential occurrence of these adverse effects?

47.   Drs. Boisseau, Boobis and Guttenplan chose to answer this question, and all of them indicate that the EC's "risk assessment" (*i.e.*, the three SCVPH opinions) was deficient in one manner or another in its *evaluation of the potential occurrence of adverse effects* (whether carcinogenic, genotoxic or other) from the consumption of residues of oestradiol 17β in meat from treated animals.

48.   Dr. Boisseau acknowledges the general international agreement that oestradiol 17β is associated with "carcinogenic potential", but also confirms what Canada has explained in its submissions: that this potential is due to the hormonal effect of estrogens,[30] which requires "prolonged exposure to high concentrations" for adverse effects to occur. Exposure to residues of these hormones from meat from treated cattle does not generate the "high concentrations" considered by Dr. Boisseau and others to be required for these effects to occur.

49.   Dr. Boisseau further confirms that, despite the growing acknowledgement that oestradiol 17β may have "genotoxic potential", there is no evidence that this potential is realized *in vivo* (as opposed to *in vitro*). He points out that, as a result of what must be done to observe a genotoxic effect (*i.e.*, use far higher than realistic doses of the parent compound with an assumption that the toxicity is the same as that for residues), such tests are more useful for identifying modes of action than for assessing dose-response relationships. He therefore disagrees with the EC, as do most other experts and international scientific bodies, that no threshold can be set for substances for which "genotoxic potential" has been identified.

---

[30]   Canada First Written Submission, at paras. 95-97; Canada Rebuttal Submission, at paras. 90-96.

50.   Dr. Boisseau also shares Canada's concern that the EC did not conduct any "quantitative risk assessment" of other adverse effects, known to be dose-dependent, that would lead to the establishment of thresholds and ADIs that would differ from those established by JECFA. The quantitative assessment referred to here is not the same as that contemplated by the Appellate Body when it found that a risk assessment need not quantify the risk.[31] Rather, Dr. Boisseau refers to analyses of the dose-response relationship that is completely absent from the EC's opinions, but which is a crucial component of internationally accepted risk assessment techniques and is essential if the EC is to demonstrate that existing international standards are insufficient to achieve its appropriate level of protection.

51.   Dr. Boobis also cites the flaws in the EC opinions as a risk assessment, in particular that the analysis "focused primarily on hazard identification". He confirms what Canada has explained in its submission,[32] that there was "little in the way of hazard characterization and no independent exposure assessment". Without the data generated in these steps, which have been shown in responses to previous questions to be necessary components of a risk assessment, Dr. Boobis advises the Panel that "it was not possible [for the EC] to complete the risk characterization phase". Most importantly, Dr. Boobis indicates that the EC "essentially stopped" the assessment of risk after it concluded that no thresholds of exposure could be established. In light of the later responses of all the experts about the issue of thresholds,[33] this observation by Dr. Boobis is critical: it means that the EC decision not to conduct a complete risk assessment was based on a conclusion that is not supported by the evidence.

52.   For his part, Dr. Guttenplan similarly finds that the EC's evaluation of the potential occurrence of adverse effects is "weak", even as he accepts that the EC did identify potential adverse effects. However, identifying potential adverse effects (*i.e.*, the hazard identification) is only the starting point of a valid risk assessment. As for the remaining components of such an assessment, Dr. Guttenplan points to several deficiencies in the EC's opinions (*i.e.*, limited utility of animal models, absence of epidemiological studies, *etc.*) and concludes that "little can be inferred about the potential occurrence of the adverse effects".

Q14.   In your view, does the risk assessment undertaken by the European Communities on oestradiol 17β follow the Codex Guidelines on risk assessment, including the four steps of hazard identification, hazard characterization, exposure assessment and risk characterization with respect to oestradiol 17β?

53.   In addition to their responses to the more general question above, Drs. Boisseau, Boobis and Guttenplan also agree with Canada that the EC failed to

---

[31]   *EC – Hormones*, Report of the Appellate Body, at paras. 186-187.
[32]   Canada Rebuttal Submission, at paras. 76-85.
[33]   See Canada's comments below on the experts' responses to questions 16-19.

follow the Codex guidelines on risk assessments. The experts share Canada's concerns that the EC (and SCVPH) took significant and unjustified short-cuts in the conduct of its risk assessment.[34]

54.   Dr. Boisseau is very critical of the EC's decision not to follow the Codex guidelines, concluding that the EC's own science did not justify the abandonment of these guidelines. At most, Dr. Boisseau concedes that the scientific studies relied upon by the EC indicate that it should have refined its approach to assessing exposure to hormone residues, not abandon the entire risk assessment methodology. But as Canada has indicated in its submissions,[35] the EC has done very little that resembles an exposure assessment.

55.   Dr. Boobis states simply that the EC did not follow Codex guidelines (which include the four steps), adding that even if the EC concluded that oestradiol 17β was genotoxic – a conclusion with which Dr. Boobis disagrees in his response to Questions 15, 18 and 19 – the EC should still have followed all four steps.

56.   Dr. Guttenplan also finds it difficult to give the EC's risk assessment anything more positive than a "mixed rating". For many of the same reasons advanced by the others, Dr. Guttenplan finds fault in the EC's hazard characterization and risk characterization, the first because of the questionable relevance of studying hamster kidneys for the task at hand and the second because it is "qualitative at best", and not based on any data or confirmed by epidemiological studies. Moreover, Dr. Guttenplan's limited support for the EC's exposure assessment is left unexplained; he simply declares it to be "thorough", which is itself an odd declaration in light of the EC's own admission that it did not, because it could not, conduct an exposure assessment.[36]

C.   Consumption of Meat Containing Hormones

(a)   Carcinogenicity

Q15.   Does the identification of oestradiol 17β as a human carcinogen indicate that there are potential adverse effects on human health when it is consumed in meat from cattle treated with hormones for growth promotion purposes? Does your answer depend on whether good veterinary practices are followed? [see para. 206-207 of EC Rebuttal Submission (US case), para. 121 of EC Rebuttal Submission (Canada case), paras. 97-98 of EC Replies to Panel Questions, paras. 76-77, 150 and 155-156 of US First Submission, paras. 35-40 and 46 of US Rebuttal Submission]

---

[34]   Canada Rebuttal Submission, at para. 86.
[35]   Ibid., at paras. 83-85.
[36]   EC Rebuttal Submission, at para. 141; 1999 SCVPH Opinion, at p. 20 (Exhibit CDA-2).

57.   Drs. Boisseau, Boobis and Guttenplan all agree with Canada that the mere identification of oestradiol 17β as a carcinogen is not itself sufficient to conclude that there are potential adverse effects when consumed as residues in meat from treated animals. Not only is the evidence of the substance's carcinogenicity in general *not indicative* of carcinogenicity of the substance from a given source, but most of the experts conclude affirmatively that there would be "no appreciable risk" of adverse effects from exposure from this one minimal source of oestradiol 17β.

58.   The experts arrive at this conclusion following the tried and tested methods of the international scientific community. Dr. Boobis' explains the relationship between findings of carcinogenicity in general and adverse effects from this one source in particular by stating that "the entire basis of risk assessment in [*sic*] based on the fact that there is a relationship between dose and effect"; and second, that a "key consideration in the risk assessment is whether there is a threshold in the dose-response". Applying these two principles to oestradiol 17β, which is naturally produced in the human body, Dr. Boobis considers that the main task is to determine whether the additional exposure to hormones from meat from treated animals changes the circulating levels of the hormone. The answer given by JECFA (and not contradicted by the EC) is that it does not; therefore, even though oestradiol 17β is considered a human carcinogen when exposure is prolonged and significantly greater than the ADI, exposure to it from this single source does not present such risks.

59.   The experts do not agree on whether the answer would be different if good veterinary practice (GVP) was not followed. On the one hand, Drs. Boisseau and Guttenplan indicate that there might be a potential for adverse effects if GVP were not followed. As general answers, they are not really surprising. These experts are simply applying a general scientific principle that changes in assumptions in the course of predicting an outcome (*e.g.*, cancer) may change the prediction. While neither expert would guarantee that the outcomes would be the same if GVP had not been followed, they did not state categorically, nor could they have, that the failure to follow GVP *will* create the potential for adverse effects to occur. In fact, even the studies on this issue submitted by the EC demonstrate that multiple hormone implants resulted in residues that were still less than the ADIs.[37]

60.   Whereas the answers of Drs. Boisseau and Guttenplan are based on general principles about the effect of changing assumptions, Dr. Boobis deals more specifically with the conditions of exposure from the failure to follow GVP. He states that failure to follow GVP would only affect the cancer risk if it resulted in exposure levels above the ADI, and even then it would have to be on a "regular basis". Since he believes that neither of these conditions will be met, Dr. Boobis

---

[37]   Canada Rebuttal Submission, at para. 110 and Exhibit EC-52.

advises that the failure to follow GVP "would not be associated with any increase in risk of cancer".

61.   Dr. Boobis' response suggests an obvious point, but one worth emphasizing: that it is not the conditions under which the hormones are administered that cause adverse effects, but the resulting hormone exposure levels, which depend on many factors. This reinforces the Appellate Body's findings that the EC has to demonstrate through an assessment of the risk arising from the failure to follow GVP that it increases the risk of adverse effects.[38] As the advice from the experts confirms, the EC has not done so.

62.   For his part, Dr. Cogliano simply asserts, without explanation or support, that the identification of oestradiol 17β as a human carcinogen indicates consuming it via meat from treated cattle has the potential to cause adverse effects. His answer seems to suggest that he believes there is no threshold below which adverse effects will not occur, a point which he does not support and which is also contrary to the findings of JECFA, Codex and his colleagues who also answered this question. His point that adverse effects depend on the "presence of hormones in the meat that people consume" is also inconsistent with the fact that hormones are already present in meat regardless of whether it is derived from treated cattle or non-treated cattle.

Q16.   Does the scientific evidence relied upon in the SCVPH Opinions support the conclusion that carcinogenic effects of the hormones at issue are related to a mechanism other than hormonal activity? [see para. 148 of the EC Replies to Panel Questions and paras. 35-40 and 46 of US Rebuttal Submission]

63.   Drs. Boisseau and Boobis agree with Canada that any potential carcinogenic effects of these hormones are related to their hormonal activity, which is dose-dependent and exhibits a threshold exposure level below which these effects will not occur. More importantly, they agreed that the evidence relied upon by the EC does not support the conclusion that adverse effects will arise from anything other than the hormonal activity of these substances, such that existing international standards will be insufficient to meet the EC's level of protection.

64.   Dr. Boobis provides extensive analysis of the EC's controversial theory that carcinogenic effects of these hormones may be caused by a mechanism other than hormonal activity, in particular a genotoxic mechanism. Dr. Boobis acknowledges that some studies demonstrate that the hormones may be genotoxic *in vitro*, but categorically rejects, with supporting evidence, that this has been demonstrated *in vivo*. He advises that "guidelines for genotoxicity testing require confirmation of an *in vitro* positive result using an appropriate *in vivo* assay" for such *in vitro* positive result to have any validity. Dr. Boobis provides a number of explanations of why this *in vivo* confirmation is so critical, in par-

---

[38]   *EC – Hormones*, Report of the Appellate Body, at paras. 205-208.

ticular because the *in vitro* conditions that allow the genotoxicity to be observed do not contain the many defence and repair mechanisms that would exist *in vivo* to prevent cell damage from occurring. The failure to observe positive genotoxicity test results *in vivo* confirms that these defence and repair mechanisms operate to ensure that there is a threshold exposure below which genotoxicity will not occur.

65.   Only Dr. Guttenplan attempts to support the EC's conclusion, but he does so with no analysis of his own, choosing instead simply to cite the EC's regulatory opinions. In simply referring to the conclusions of the SCVPH, Dr. Guttenplan has in fact failed to adequately answer the question, which was not whether the SCVPH *had concluded* that there were non-hormonal adverse effects, but whether the scientific evidence relied upon by the SCVPH *supported* that conclusion.

Q17. Could you comment on Canada's statement that "the studies commissioned by the European Communities also failed to find evidence of "catechol metabolites" – that is the oestradiol metabolites identified as the source of the genotoxic potential – in meat from treated animals"? What would be the implication of an absence or presence of catechol metabolites? [see para. 102 of Canada Rebuttal submission, EC Exhibit 51A]

66.   Drs. Boisseau and Boobis confirm the evidence that catechol metabolites are largely absent in meat from treated animals, and that even if such metabolites were present in small quantities (which they acknowledged may be possible), it would not be enough to make the genotoxic potential of oestradiol 17β an issue with respect to residues in meat from treated animals.

67.   Dr. Boobis advises that the absence of catechol metabolites confirms the effectiveness of the mechanisms for detoxification and elimination of these metabolites *in vivo*. He further confirms that the formation of such metabolites in meat would only be relevant to the risk assessment if it were true that catechol metabolites were responsible for adverse effects and if it were true that there is no threshold for any effects for which they are responsible. In his response to this and other questions, Dr. Boobis advises that neither of these are the case, so the presence or absence of catechol metabolites preformed in meat does "not impact on the risk assessment".

68.   Dr. Guttenplan's seemingly contrary acknowledgement that "only very small amounts of catechol metabolites were detected" overstates the case. As other experts confirm in greater detail, the study commissioned by the EC that looked at the issue observed that "no metabolites coming from the catechol oestrogen biosynthesis could be isolated" and that "metabolic studies performed *in vivo* … and *in vitro*… failed to demonstrate a significant aromatic hydroxylation activity that would lead to catechol oestrogen derived metabolites".[39] In

---

[39]   Exhibit EC-51A, at p. 18.

other words, contrary to Dr. Guttenplan's claim, catechol metabolites have not been found in meat from treated animals, at least not in detectable quantities, and to the extent that they exist in undetectable quantities, they are not present in sufficient quantities to create a genotoxic potential. In light of the discrepancy between the explicit conclusions of even the EC evidence on this issue and the unsupported claim of Dr. Guttenplan, the Panel may wish to ask him to support his claim.

Q18. Please comment on the US argument that the European Communities fails to demonstrate through scientific evidence that oestradiol 17β is genotoxic. Would your reply have been different at the time of adoption of the EC Directive in September 2003? If so, why? [see paras. 118-119 of EC Rebuttal Submission (US case), paras. 123-124 of EC Rebuttal Submission (Canada case), paras. 87-91 and 153-156 of US First Submission, paras. 35-40 and 46 of US Rebuttal Submission, and paras. 90-97 of Canada Rebuttal Submission]

69.   Drs. Boisseau and Boobis both confirm Canada's explanation that the EC has failed to demonstrate that oestradiol 17β is genotoxic *in vivo*.[40] They acknowledge what other reputable international scientists and scientific authorities now see as the "genotoxic potential" of oestradiol 17β, but deny that this "potential" is relevant *in vivo* at doses to which humans are exposed from consuming meat from treated animals.

70.   Dr. Boobis reiterates his detailed analysis in response to Question 15 that sets out the many reasons for which genotoxic potential identified in *in vitro* will not be confirmed *in vivo*. In particular, he highlights the important point that the genotoxicity that has been "observed in vitro would be expected to exhibit a threshold." The EC's conclusion that there is no threshold below which genotoxicity will not occur runs directly counter to this advice, and is therefore not supported by the scientific evidence.

71.   Dr. Boisseau also highlights an attempt by the EC to misrepresent certain of JECFA's findings. In particular, he points to the EC's efforts to represent JECFA's findings about the "genotoxic potential" of oestradiol 17β, combined with its decision to establish an ADI, as a finding that oestradiol 17β *is* "genotoxic". Dr. Boisseau correctly points out in his answer to Question 13 that there is a difference between a substance having "genotoxic potential" and it being "genotoxic", confirming that JECFA has never considered that oestradiol 17β is "genotoxic". Dr. Boisseau then explains the rationale behind JECFA's decision to adopt an ADI in 1999, pointing to the need to place exposure to oestradiol 17β from this source into context. His explanation was confirmed by JECFA in its answer to Question 20. Citing exposure values identified by

---

[40]   See Canada First Written Submission, at paras. 95-98; also see Canada Rebuttal Submission, at paras. 86-98.

JECFA, Dr. Boisseau advises the Panel that exposure to residues of the three natural hormones remains a mere fraction of the ADI (conservatively estimated between 0.03% and 4.0%, depending upon the substance). In other words, the EC claims to the contrary notwithstanding,[41] JECFA's establishment of an ADI for the three natural hormones was not related to its findings about "potential genotoxicity". In fact, just the opposite is true: JECFA would not have established ADIs at all if it considered the hormones to be genotoxic *in vivo*.

72.   For their part, Drs. Cogliano and Guttenplan both suggest that the EC has demonstrated that oestradiol 17β is genotoxic, but neither of them does so with reference to supporting scientific evidence. Dr. Cogliano simply repeats the EC's assertion that it is, and endorses an excerpt from the EC Rebuttal Submission that was itself from a report of the UK Veterinary Products Committee (VPC).[42] However, the EC neglected to include, when quoting from that report, the very next paragraph, which concluded that:

> [a]lthough there is evidence that oestrogen metabolites may be directly genotoxic *in vitro*, *in vivo* their formation is affected by opposing activation and inactivation metabolic pathways, the presence of anti-oxidants and DNA repair capacity and thus it is likely this genotoxicity will have a thresholded response.[43]

73.   Even as Dr. Cogliano endorses the EC's selective quote from the VPC Report, he also appears to understand and accept the broader context of that quote when he admits that "it has not been established by the EC that genotoxicity and cell proliferation would be induced by levels found in meat residues added to the pre-existing levels occurring in exposed humans". This observation brings him in line with Drs. Boisseau and Boobis, who explain that there is a threshold exposure below which genotoxicity will not occur.

Q19.   The European Communities states that "... it is generally recognized that for substances which have genotoxic potential (as is the case with oestradiol 17β) a threshold can not be identified. Therefore it cannot be said that there exist a safe level below which intakes from residue should be considered to be safe. Therefore the fact that doses used in growth promotion are low is not of relevance". Does the scientific evidence referred to by the European Communities support these conclusions? Would your reply have been different at the time of adoption of the EC Directive in September 2003? If so, why? [see para. 201 of EC Rebuttal Submission (US case), paras. 120-122 of EC Rebuttal Submission (Canada case), paras. 73 and 86-

---

[41]   EC Rebuttal Submission (Canada case), at paras. 100-101.

[42]   EC Rebuttal Submission (Canada case) at para. 124. See also UK, Veterinary Products Committee, *Risks Associated with the Use of Hormonal Substances in Food-Producing Animals: Draft report of the UK Veterinary Products Committee*, May 2005 (UK VPC Draft Report), at p. 27 (Exhibit CDA-26).

[43]   *Ibid.*

98 of Canada Rebuttal Submission, paras. 87-91 and 153-156 of US First Submission and paras. 35-40 and 46 of US Rebuttal Submission]

74.   Drs. Boisseau and Boobis (and, to a lesser extent, Dr. Cogliano, but not Dr. Guttenplan) explicitly confirm the main point that Canada has made from the beginning of this dispute: that for substances that are endogenously produced by the human body, there simply must be a threshold below which no adverse effects are observed, or else humanity would have been wiped out by cancer millennia ago. This simple reality, repeatedly ignored by the EC, but stressed time and again by experts from around the world,[44] contradicts directly the EC's claim about the genotoxicity of the three natural hormones, and its corresponding claim that no threshold can be established.

75.   Even though JECFA acknowledged that oestradiol 17β may have genotoxic potential, it decided to establish an ADI. If there had been no threshold below which exposure to the substance would be safe, JECFA would not have been able to establish an ADI. More recently even, the European Food Safety Authority (EFSA) (the successor to the SCVPH) has recognized thresholds for genotoxic substances when it concluded that, "based on the current understanding of cancer biology there are levels of exposure to substances which are both genotoxic and carcinogenic below which cancer incidence is not increased (biological thresholds in dose-response)".[45]

76.   As pointed out by many of the experts in their responses, the consensus among the experts on the issue of thresholds is based not only on their scientific understanding of the modes of action of the substances but also on the absence of any epidemiological studies that demonstrate a relationship between exposure to hormones and adverse health effects.

77.   Dr. Cogliano's response does not directly address the question. He offers his view that the difference between the parties to the dispute is simply one of differing *assumptions* about the nature of genotoxic mechanisms. But the question is not about what Canada or even the EC *assume* about genotoxic mechanisms, but rather which assumption is supported by the science, in particular whether the "genotoxic potential" of these hormones exhibits a threshold below which it will not be realized *in vivo*. He also does not cite any evidence that supports the EC's conclusion that no such threshold exists.

78.   Dr. Guttenplan appears to be more explicit in his suggestion that the science relied upon by the EC supports its conclusion, but his answer is at the same time contradictory. In admitting that "repair enzymes are unlikely to be satu-

---

[44]   Not only do the experts relied upon by the Panel confirm this, but this conclusion has been confirmed by all international bodies that have addressed the issue. See, for example, VPC and JECFA.

[45]   EFSA, *Opinion of the Scientific Committee on a Request from EFSA Related to a Harmonised Approach for Risk Assessment of Substances which are both Genotoxic and Carcinogenic* (Request No. EFSA-Q-2004-020, adopted October 18, 2005) (*The EFSA Journal, 282, 1-31, 2005*), at p. 18 (Exhibit CDA-46).

rated" at physiological levels, he seems to suggest that there is a level at which repair will always occur. He then goes on to say that "[f]or any toxin the dose determines the risk". These two statements together suggest that at the dose to which consumers are exposed to oestradiol 17β residues from treated meat, the "genotoxic potential" of these hormones is not relevant. This is consistent with what the other experts have indicated: that there is indeed a threshold below which these hormones are safe.

Q20. In your view, how do the European Communities' conclusions above relate to the conclusion by Codex that "establishing an ADI or MRL for a hormone that is produced endogenously in variable levels in human beings was considered unnecessary"? To what extent, in your view, has JECFA's conclusion that oestradiol "has genotoxic potential" affected its recommendations on this hormone?

79. Drs. Boisseau, Boobis and Guttenplan all consider the EC's conclusions about the absence of thresholds to be inconsistent with the Codex standards, whereas it remains somewhat unclear what Dr. Cogliano thinks about this issue. However, to the extent that most of the experts found that the EC's conclusions on the matter are unsupported by the evidence and are "questionable", they support the existing Codex standards.

80. Dr. Boobis elaborates on the concept of "incremental risk"; first by clarifying what in his mind is the more important issue of whether low levels of exposure affect "circulating levels". He makes three important points: (1) homeostatic control mechanism combined with low bioavailability means there is a "range of exposures for which there are compensatory alterations in endogenous levels"; (2) depending on endogenous levels, which vary by physiological state, some increments in exposure may "perturb endocrine effects", but these exposures would have to be above the ADI; and (3) genotoxic effects, to the extent that they will occur at all, will respond more to the natural variations in endogenous levels than the small changes in these levels that might arise from hormones from meat from treated animals. All of these points support the conclusion that there are clear thresholds for exposure to exogenous sources of substances that are also produced endogenously in variable amounts.

81. The experts' answers also confirm again that even though JECFA acknowledged that oestradiol 17β has "genotoxic potential", this acknowledgement did not generate concern about the safety of the substances and therefore did not affect its recommendation. JECFA essentially did not consider that this "genotoxic potential" was relevant to the carcinogenic effects of oestradiol 17β, which it considered dependent on hormonal activity.

82. For his part, Dr. Guttenplan attempts to justify the EC's conclusion with reference to new "areas of concern, such as developmental effects". However, Canada has some difficulty understanding the relationship Dr. Guttenplan seems to be drawing between the purported inability to set thresholds for genotoxic substances and the identification of new concerns that appear to result from hormonal activity. Dr. Guttenplan seems to be using new concerns about one

type of adverse effect (developmental effects) to demonstrate that concerns about the occurrence of another type of adverse effect (genotoxicity) are justified. The Panel may wish to ask Dr. Guttenplan to elaborate on the relationship he suggests in this response.

Q21. Does the scientific evidence referred to by the European Communities demonstrate that the five hormones other than oestradiol 17β, when consumed as residues in meat have genotoxic potential? Does your answer depend on whether good veterinary practices are followed? Would your reply have been different at the time of adoption of the Directive in September 2003? If so, why? [see, *inter alia*, the SCVPH Opinions and paras. 63, 83, 89-91 and 93 of US First Submission, paras. 131-136 of Canada Rebuttal Submission]

83.   Drs. Boisseau, Boobis and Guttenplan all refute the EC's claims about the potential genotoxicity of the other five hormones. Drs. Boisseau and Boobis survey the various tests by which these substances failed to show genotoxicity (the former in his answer to Question 16), and Dr. Guttenplan simply states generally that there is "no conclusive evidence presented by the EC" that they have genotoxic potential.

84.   Whereas Drs. Boisseau and Boobis both indicate without qualification that the failure to follow GVP would not affect the "genotoxic potential" of the five hormones, Dr. Guttenplan's advice on this matter contradicts his advice given in response to other questions. In some of his other responses, he seems to support the EC's contention that no threshold can be established for substances that are genotoxic. At the same time, he provides in his response to this question that genotoxic effects will be "minimized by good veterinary practice". To the extent that the purported risks from failure to follow GVP are that cattle (and ultimately consumers) will be exposed to higher doses, Dr. Guttenplan seems to be suggesting a dose-response relationship between exposure to hormones and genotoxicity. The Panel could ask him to clarify his views on whether there is a dose-response relationship.

Q22. How would you define *in vivo* DNA repair mechanisms? How effective or relevant are *in vivo* DNA repair mechanisms with respect to potential genotoxic effects from residues of the growth promoting hormones at issue when consumed in meat? Does your answer depend on whether good veterinary practices are followed in the administration of these hormones? To what extent does the scientific material referred to by the European Communities take into account these mechanisms in its evaluation of potential occurrence of adverse effects from residues of growth promoting hormones? Would your reply have been different at the time of adoption of the Directive in September 2003 and if so, why? [see paras. 40 and 46 of US Rebuttal Submission, footnote 107 of US First Submission, and para. 89 of Canada Rebuttal Submission]

85.   Drs. Boobis and Guttenplan both extensively discuss the effectiveness of DNA repair mechanisms in what the former calls a "flexible and very efficient DNA repair process" and what the latter considers a mechanism with "considerable redundancy". They also both agree that the repair mechanisms that operate to repair the "considerable oxidative DNA damage" (Dr. Boobis) caused by endogenous processes are as effective for damage caused by exogenous agents.

86.   Importantly, Dr. Boobis points out that because of DNA repair mechanisms, the creation of DNA adducts does not in itself always indicate that mutations will occur, let alone malignant neoplasms (*i.e.*, cancer). He further confirms that the kind of DNA damage that might be expected from hormones from meat from treated animals (*i.e.*, active oxygen) is also the kind of repair mechanism that is "amongst the most efficient".

87.   For his part, Dr. Guttenplan makes some unsupported statements, in particular when he suggests that repair mechanisms are "not really relevant" to a risk assessment of oestradiol 17β because the repair will not be different than for other types of damage. He does not attempt to describe the "other types of damage" and whether repair of these other types of damage means that such damage does not lead to adverse effects. In the absence of a specific assessment of the effectiveness of the repair mechanisms for comparable types of damage, the statement that they are comparable is not helpful.

88.   Quite apart from the lack of clarity in Dr. Guttenplan's response, it is inconsistent with the more thorough advice provided by Dr. Boobis. The central issue differentiating JECFA's conclusion that even though oestradiol 17β has "genotoxic potential" it is possible to establish an ADI, on the one hand, and the SCVPH's conclusion that oestradiol 17β is genotoxic and therefore no threshold exposure can be determined, on the other, is the degree to which damaged DNA, if indeed it is damaged, is repaired and adverse effects avoided. Far from being "not really relevant", therefore, this issue is one of the most relevant issues to the resolution of the controversies surrounding the safety of these hormones. It is therefore also central to the issue of whether the EC has conducted a valid risk assessment.

89.   With respect to whether the EC had failed to take into account these repair mechanisms in its evaluation, Dr. Guttenplan considers that it failed to do so. Ultimately, to the extent that the SCVPH takes so many short-cuts in its opinions on the basis that the hormones are seen to be genotoxic, the failure to address the role of mechanisms that counter this genotoxic potential is a critical shortcoming. Ignoring such evidence results in a significant overestimation of the risk, to the point of concluding there are risks where none exist.

Q23.   To what extent is it necessary or possible to take into account the "long latency period" of cancer in the conduct of a risk assessment, which is supposed to assess carcinogenic effects of these hormones when consumed in meat? Have the hormones in dispute been used as growth promoters over a sufficient number of years for an assessment of their long-term effects on

human health to be made? [see para. 149 of EC Rebuttal Submission (US Case), para. 143 of EC Rebuttal Submission (Canada case)]

90.   There is both agreement and disagreement between the experts who answered this question (Drs. Boisseau, Boobis, Cogliano and Guttenplan) on the importance of cancer's long latency periods to the conduct of risk assessments that purport to identify cancer risks from hormones in meat. On the one hand, the experts tend to agree that the hormones in question have been in use long enough as growth promoters (a minimum of 20 years, according to some) for any long-term health effects to manifest themselves. On the other hand, they disagree about whether it is possible to positively identify the use of these hormones for growth-promotion purposes as the source of any observed adverse health effects. Dr. Cogliano does not weigh in on either of these points, confining himself instead to the observation that it is "definitely necessary" to take long latency periods into account in general, a point not disputed by any other expert.

91.   Dr. Guttenplan advises that it is possible to identify a relationship between hormones consumed in meat and carcinogenic effects, but he does not explain how this would be accomplished. He provides no information on how to account for the fact that the populations he says would be studied to observe the relationship would also be exposed to many other sources of hormones other than that consumed through meat from treated animals, such that it would be very difficult to identify any causal relationship between the effect and the specific source.

92.   Dr. Boobis is sceptical, but does seem to suggest that it might be possible with a well designed study involving "extremely large populations to detect any increase in cancer incidence". Dr. Boisseau is even more sceptical that a relationship can be identified with any certainty, finding not only that it is not possible to study such a relationship, but it is not even "useful". Drs. Boisseau and Boobis explain their scepticism in two separate, but related, ways: the former says it would be impossible to discriminate between different factors in allocating responsibility (see also the experts' responses to the next question on confounding factors); the latter says that since the risk from such a small dose is so minimal, "it is questionable whether an increase in risk, even if it existed, could be detected in exposed populations." In other words, epidemiological studies are of little use in risk assessments of hormones in meat from treated cattle.

93.   The answers from these two experts confirm again the essential point: that exposure to residues of hormones in meat from treated animals is only a small fraction of the overall exposure to the substance from a variety of sources, including that produced endogenously within the human body. Given the wide variety of sources of, and variability of exposure to, hormones, any correlation observed between exposure to hormones and adverse effects cannot be attributed to the single source of hormones that comes from residues of hormones in meat from treated animals. Nothing in the SCVPH's opinions, in the scientific evidence submitted by the EC, or in the answers of the experts supports a conclusion other than this.

Q24. To what extent is it possible to identify possible co-founding factors causing cancer and attribute them to identified sources? What are the implications of these factors for the conduct of a risk assessment evaluating the adverse affects caused by residues of growth promoting hormones in meat? Would your reply have been different at the time of adoption of the EC Directive in September 2003? If so, why?

94.   Drs. Boisseau, Boobis, Cogliano and Guttenplan all agree that it is extremely difficult to *attribute* causal roles to different confounding factors in the study of the causes of cancer, even as some of them advise that it is at least possible to *identify* what some of these factors may be. According to Dr. Boobis, this would be particularly the case in the circumstances of these hormones, where "the risk from the confounder is appreciably greater than the risk of the exposure of interest".

95.   To the extent that any of the experts respond to the second part of the question, they seem to suggest that the difficulty with attributing causality to a specific factor reduces the value of epidemiological studies in risk assessments of the nature under review here (*i.e.*, where the source of the agent under review comprises such a small amount of overall exposure and the adverse effects have multiple causes). Dr. Boobis offers the view that confounding factors do not affect the risk assessment, but the "interpretation of the data used in the risk assessment", which Canada understands to mean that all causal factors should be taken into account, and not just single factors.

96.   Contrary to advice from the experts that it is extremely difficult to isolate confounding factors in circumstances such as these, the EC has claimed that it has done just that. It has taken observed adverse effects and then has ascribed the cause of these effects to one source of hormones (that from meat from treated animals). In light of the advice from the experts, the EC has failed on two accounts: it has not observed adverse effects that can be co-related to hormones; and even to the extent that it has observed such effects, it has not investigated the role of hormones writ large, preferring instead to focus on the single source of hormones.

Q25. To what extent do the three recent studies referred to by the European Communities confirm a risk to human health from the consumption of meat from cattle treated with growth promoting hormones? Please also comment on the EC statement that one of the studies "was carried out after the introduction of the ban on the use of hormones for growth promotion in Europe, which means that the subjects should have been exposed to hormone-free meat in their diet. This may further imply that it cannot be excluded that the risk of cancer may be further increased if meat treated with hormones for animal growth promotion were to be consumed". [see paras. 145-148 of EC Rebuttal Submission (US case) and paras. 139-142 of EC Rebuttal Submission (Canada case), footnote 97 in para. 147 of EC Rebuttal Submission (US case), and Exhibits EC-71, 72, 73]

97.   Drs. Boisseau, Boobis and Guttenplan expressly deny that the three studies referred to by the EC confirm a risk to human health from exposure to hormone residues from meat from treated animals. Only Dr. Cogliano endorses the
EC's attempt to use these studies as evidence of risk from consuming hormones
from meat from treated animals, but he does so without any supporting evidence
or analysis.

98.   With respect to the study on zeranol[46], Drs. Boobis and Guttenplan both
indicate that the study was based only on *in vitro* experiments and therefore cannot be extrapolated to human exposure. They find it particularly difficult to extrapolate to exposure from meat consumption since the dose used in the study
was high, a point that even Dr. Cogliano acknowledges. In response to the observations of positive genotoxicity findings *in vitro*, Dr. Boobis notes that
"genotoxicity by this mechanism [redox cycling] should exhibit a threshold and
is also militated against in vivo by antioxidant defence systems and efficient
repair of oxidant-damaged DNA."

99.   With respect to the study on the relationship between intake of red meat
and colorectal cancer,[47] Dr. Boisseau simply refers to his general scepticism of
the ability of epidemiological studies to identify specific causal agents due to
confounding factors. Dr. Boobis is even more specific in dismissing the relevance of this study, noting that its results are not new, that they are consistent
across geographical area, and that even the authors point to possible explanations, such as the formation of mutagens during the cooking of meat and the
generation of nitroso compounds. He notes that the study provides "little support
for a contribution from hormones present in meat from their use as growth promoters … because the association is just as strong in regions where hormones
are not used as where they are used".

100.   Dr. Boobis is the only expert to make any detailed comments on the study
of the relationship between hormone replacement therapy and the incidence of
breast cancer.[48] He notes again that this study did not find any relationship that
had not already been observed in the past, and that had not already been acknowledged by JECFA. The real issue, therefore, is not whether there is such a
relationship, but whether that relationship has any relevance for the assessment
of risk from the consumption of hormones in meat from treated animals. On this
point, Dr. Boobis advises that it does not, because the "weight of evidence is
such that the hormones cause cancer by a mechanism exhibiting a threshold" and
the doses of hormones involved in this study were considerably higher than that
found in meat from treated animals.

101.   Ultimately, the experts' reactions to the specific quote from the EC (about
the studies having been conducted after the ban) capture the overall response to

---

[46]   Exhibit EC-73.
[47]   Exhibit EC-71.
[48]   Exhibit EC-72.

the EC's use of these studies. Dr. Boisseau considers that this comment "expresses a concern but does not provide any scientific evidence supporting this concern", whereas Dr. Guttenplan considers that it "negates any relevance to the possible connection of hormone-treated meat consumption and cancer". Dr. Boobis considers that the only way the timing of the studies would matter would be if it were proven that there were risks from hormones from meat from treated animals, which Dr. Boobis confirms again has not been demonstrated. Dr. Boobis is more pointed in his criticism of the EC's suggestion that "it can not be excluded" that there is greater risk. He advises that since the same statement can be made in the absence of any study whatsoever of the risk from hormones, this statement is "not scientifically defensible".

102.   These reactions highlight a tactic employed by the EC, namely, the manipulation of a genuine scientific interest in assessing the possible adverse effects arising from exposure to a substance in general (*i.e.*, hormones) to create specific and unjustified concern about possible adverse effects from one single and insignificant source of that substance in particular.

Q26. Does the scientific evidence referred to by the European Communities, in particular any epidemiological studies, identify a relationship between cancer and residues of hormonal growth promoters? In its risk assessment of 1999, the European Communities makes reference to the higher rates of breast and prostate cancer observed in the United States as compared to the European Communities. Can a link be established between these statistics and the consumption of meat from animals treated with the hormones at issue? Would your reply have been different at the time of adoption of the EC Directive in September 2003? If so, why? [see pages 17-19 of 1999 Opinion of the SCVPH and related Tables A4-A5 on pages 83-91]

103.   As with their responses to the previous questions related to the potential of epidemiological studies, Drs. Boisseau, Boobis, Cogliano and Guttenplan all agree that the studies relied upon by the EC, in particular the epidemiological studies, do not identify a relationship between cancer and residues of hormones from meat from treated animals.

104.   Many of the reasons they provide have already been discussed above, such as confounding factors, *etc.* The EC places considerable emphasis on statistics comparing breast and prostrate cancer rates between Europe, where hormones are banned for growth-promotion purposes, and North America, where they are not. Not surprisingly, while there may be some observable differences in rates between certain regions and ethnic groups, on the whole the rates are relatively similar. The experts agree that the differences that do exist are so slight as to be not statistically significant. To the extent that there are differences at all, Dr. Boobis cautions against inferring too much from geographical differences in cancer rates, because of what he calls an "ecological fallacy" (the belief that differences observed between groups will also be observed between individuals). More importantly, none of these studies relied upon by the EC included

assessments of data on hormone intake, so even if the differences were significant (and they are not) no link can be made between these statistics and the consumption of meat from animals treated with the hormones at issue.

(b)   Residue analysis

Q27.   How do the residues in meat from cattle treated with the three synthetic growth promoting hormones differ from residues in meat from cattle treated with the three natural growth promoting hormones at issue?

105.   The experts who respond to this question (Drs. Boisseau and de Brabander) agree that since the chemical structures of the three synthetic hormones (zeranol, trenbolone acetate (TBA) and melengestrol acetate (MGA)) are different from the structure of the three natural hormones (oestradiol 17β, testosterone, progesterone), the residues of the synthetic hormones in the meat of treated cattle will be different from the residues in meat from cattle treated with natural hormones.

Q28.   How do the hormones naturally present in animals, meat, or human beings differ from the residues in meat of the three natural hormones used for growth promotion purposes?

106.   Dr. Boisseau and Dr. de Brabander address this question. Dr. Boisseau states:

> The definition of residues encompasses both the parent substance and all the metabolites derived from this parent substance. Therefore, in the case of the part of residues of the natural hormones which consists of parent substances, there is no difference between hormones naturally present in food producing animals, meat or human beings. Metabolites of these natural hormones existing in cattle and meat are, obviously, the same. To my knowledge, there is no scientific evidence showing that the main metabolites of the three natural hormones existing in cattle and humans are not similar.

107.   For the sake of clarity, the Panel may wish to ask that Dr. Boisseau clarify whether the residues, both parent and metabolite, in meat from cattle treated with the three natural growth promoting hormones are the same as their respective endogenous natural hormones found in animals, meat or human beings.

108.   Dr. de Brabander's opinion is much less clear. First he states that "there are no differences", then he qualifies his statement with references to unspecified "ongoing research". He states that "[t]he residues of the natural hormones in cattle are in the 17α form (inactive) while the use of 'natural' hormones used for growth promotion purposes may lead to residues in the β form (active form)." If Dr. de Brabander is suggesting that residues of natural hormones in untreated cattle do not occur in the β (active) form, he is contradicting his own answer to

Question 31. There, he agrees that "residue levels in meat from hormone-treated cattle are well within the physiological range of residue levels in untreated cattle". Moreover, his position would be inconsistent with the detailed residue evidence reviewed by JECFA in its 1999 residue monograph. The monograph presents detailed data on hormone concentrations in various tissues, including muscle and fat, in untreated heifers and steers. Dr. de Brabander's suggestion in this regard simply does not withstand close scrutiny.[49]

Q29. To what extent do the SCVPH Opinions evaluate evidence on the actual residue levels of the synthetic hormones found in meat in their assessment of the risks from such residues? Are specific references provided as to how the evidence on residues relates to the observance of good veterinary practices or lack thereof? How do they compare with the MRLs set by Codex? [see paras. 165-176 of EC Rebuttal Submission (US case); pages 55-68 of the Opinion of the SCVPH of 30 April 1999 in US Exhibit 4, para. 144 of US First Submission, Exhibits US-6 and 7, footnote 46 of US Rebuttal Submission]

109.   Dr. Boisseau confirms that the level of residues is typically taken into consideration at the third step of the risk assessment process, namely the exposure assessment, after the ADI has been established. The purpose of evaluating the level of residues in food is to ensure that dietary exposure to the substance does not exceed the ADI. Dr. Boisseau confirms that the SCVPH did not "conduct a quantitative assessment of the exposure of consumers to the residues of [synthetic] hormonal growth promoters including the determination of the levels of residues in food from treated animals, the impact of the non observance of good veterinary practices on these levels and the comparison between these levels and the MRLs set up by Codex".

110.   Dr. de Brabander fails to directly answer the Panel's question. Instead, he appears to offer his own opinion regarding the inaccuracy of published concentrations of residues. Referring to Table 8 in the SCVPH 1999 Opinion[50], he indicates that residue levels for trenbolone are "extremely low...and serious doubts about their accuracy can be made." Table 8 is drawn in part from the extensive review of residue data contained in the JECFA Monograph to the 34th Meeting.[51] By quoting the JECFA data without qualification, the SCVPH does not appear to share Dr. de Brabander's concerns about the inaccuracy of the trenbolone residue data.[52] In any event, in contrast to the JECFA analysis, Dr. de Brabander fails to

---

[49]   JECFA, *Residues of some veterinary drugs in animals and foods*, FAO Food and Nutrition Paper No. 41/12 (Rome: FAO, 2000), at p. 38 (Exhibit CDA-17).
[50]   1999 SCVPH Opinion, Section 4.4.2, at p. 56 (Exhibit CDA-2).
[51]   JECFA, *Residues of some veterinary drugs in animals and foods: Monographs prepared by the Thirty-fourth Meeting of the Joint FAO/WHO Expert Committee on Food Additives*, FAO Food and Nutrition Paper, No. 41/2 (Rome: FAO, 1990), at pp. 88-100, in particular p. 96 (Exhibit CDA-38).
[52]   1999 SCVPH Opinion, Section 4.4.2, at p. 56 (Exhibit CDA-2).

provide a single reference for his conclusion that "concentrations may seriously be underestimated."

111.   Dr. de Brabander's statement that the MRLs set by Codex are high in relation to "modern analytical limits" is confusing. MRLs are a function of the ADI and are not set on the basis of detection methods, but toxicological data. As Dr. Boisseau states in response to Question 32, for control purposes, a validated analytical method need be only as sensitive as is necessary to detect residues at the established MRL. Thus, it makes little sense to assert that the MRLs are high unless there is evidence to suggest that the ADI is set too high. Moreover, Dr. de Brabander lists the MRL for MGA, an MRL that was recommended by JECFA as recently as February 2004 (62nd meeting). Dr. de Brabander appears to suggest that the analytical techniques used by JECFA in 2004 were not sufficiently "modern". However, his cursory conclusion is in stark contrast to the extensive evaluation of residue data conducted by JECFA.[53] In particular, recent residue data from studies using "modern" validated methods (HPLC-MS, GC-MS and LC-MS) were assessed in the JECFA Residue Monograph for the 58th Meeting.[54] All ten studies cited date from 1999 to 2002.

112.   Lastly, Dr. de Brabander indicates that "[a]s demonstrated in several documents a major part of the hormones used are excreted through the faeces (for MGA ca. 75%)..." It would be helpful if Dr. de Brabander could provide citations for documents to which he refers. In addition, for completeness, it would be helpful if Dr. de Brabander could provide corresponding statistics in relation to excretion for all the hormones at issue, synthetic and natural.

Q30.   To what extent do the SCVPH Opinions evaluate evidence on the actual residue levels of the three natural hormones in meat in their assessment of the risks from such residues? Is it possible to compare these to the ADIs recommended by JECFA in 1999? Are specific references provided as to how the evidence on residues relates to the observance of good veterinary practices or lack thereof? [see paras. 120-123 and 155-164 of EC Rebuttal Submission (US case), pages 33-54 of 1999 Opinion in Exhibit US-4, para. 144 of US First Submission, and 52nd JECFA Report in Exhibit US-5]

---

[53]   See JECFA, *Residues of some veterinary drugs in animals and foods: Monographs prepared by the Sixty-second Meeting of the Joint FAO/WHO Expert Committee on Food Additives*, FAO Food And Nutrition Paper, No. 41/16 (Rome: FAO, 2004) (Exhibit CDA-33); JECFA, *Residues of some veterinary drugs in animals and foods: Monographs prepared by the Fifty-eighth Meeting of the Joint FAO/WHO Expert Committee on Food Additives*, FAO Food And Nutrition Paper, No. 41/14 (Rome: FAO, 2002) (Exhibit CDA-35); and JECFA, *Residues of some veterinary drugs in animals and foods: Monographs prepared by the Fifty-fourth Meeting of the Joint FAO/WHO Expert Committee on Food Additives*, FAO Food And Nutrition Paper, No. 41/13 (Rome: FAO, 2000) (Exhibit CDA-37).

[54]   JECFA, *Residues of some veterinary drugs in animals and foods: Monographs prepared by the Fifty-eighth Meeting of the Joint FAO/WHO Expert Committee on Food Additives*, FAO Food And Nutrition Paper, No. 41/14 (Rome: FAO, 2002) (Exhibit CDA-35), pp. 56-59. All of the 10 studies cited by JECFA in this Monograph are from 1999-2002.

113.   Both Dr. Boobis and Dr. Boisseau confirm that the SCVPH did not itself evaluate evidence of actual residue levels of the three natural hormones in its assessment of risks from such residues.[55] In addressing the impact of GVP on residue levels in meat, Dr. Boobis explains that, while the SCVPH considered potential exposure following inappropriate use scenarios, "these data are limited in the absence of any information on the frequency of occurrence of such misuse in the use of the products in question." Moreover, he confirmed that "[i]t would have been possible to compare the SCVPHs estimates of exposure [in the misuse scenarios] with the ADIs derived by the JECFA but this was not done." Lastly, he concludes that the "ADI would have exceeded the exposure estimates for the three [natural] hormones." This advice supports the conclusion that the EC has not properly assessed the potential occurrence of adverse affects from the misuse of the natural hormones in question.

114.   Unfortunately, Dr. de Brabander fails to directly answer the Panel's question. Instead, he refers to "old" data for residue concentrations and concludes without any analysis that their "accuracy could be doubted." Rather than responding directly to the Panel's question, he discusses, amongst other things, the potential environmental effects of hormone residue in excrement and the side-effects of testosterone spray used to enhance a woman's enjoyment of sex.

Q31.   Please comment on the US statement that "concentrations of oestradiol 17β in meat from treated cattle do not vary significantly from concentrations in untreated cattle, i.e., residue levels in meat from hormone-treated cattle are well within the physiological range of residue levels in untreated cattle. While tissue concentrations of oestradiol 17β in treated cattle may be slightly higher than those in untreated cattle, this increase is much smaller than the large variations observed in (reproductively) cycling and pregnant cattle and is thus well within the range of naturally observed levels." In your reply please take into account the US 11ᵗʰ Carcinogenesis Report where it is stated that "Meat and milk may contain estrogens. Veterinary use of steroidal estrogens (to promote growth and treat illness) can increase estrogens in tissues of food-producing animals to above their normal levels" and the statement by the European Communities that "meat consumption from pregnant heifers is exceptional as usually these animals are not slaughtered. [see paras. 51 and 144 of US First Submission and Exhibits US-6 and 7, para. 98 of EC Replies to Panel Questions, Exhibit EC-101, and para. 2.3.2.3 of the 1999 Report of SCVPH]

115.   Dr. de Brabander offers qualified agreement with the US statement.

---

[55]   Dr. Boobis, at p. 33. Dr. Boisseau refers back to his answer to Question 29, in which he concluded that the EC failed to "conduct a quantitative assessment of the exposure of consumers to the residues of [natural] hormonal growth promoters including the determination of the levels of residues in food from treated animals, the impact of the non observance of good veterinary practices on these levels and the comparison between these levels and the [ADI] set up by Codex."

116.   Both Drs. Boisseau and de Brabander indicate that meat consumption from pregnant heifers is exceptional. However, this conclusion is at odds with the evidence considered by the UK Sub-Group of the Veterinary Products Committee.[56] The Sub-Group analyzed the effect on exposure to oestradiol 17β in meat from the termination of the Over Thirty Months Scheme (OTMS) in the UK, a program that removes culled adult cows from the food chain. The Sub-Group concluded that "the removal of these pregnant cull cows to the food chain [as a result of the OTMS] has reduced the quantity of oestradiol in the food chain by 37% ... which will be returned as the BSE controls are removed and the market returns to normal."[57] This is based on the assumption that 25% of slaughtered cows are in calf, at stages of pregnancy evenly distributed over the three trimesters.

117.   In a different vein, Dr. Boisseau's response to this question also supports Canada's basic point that the EC is attempting to divorce the use of growth-promoting hormones from their appropriate context and, as a result, presents a distorted assessment of the risks associated with the use of growth-promoting hormones. He states:

> Even if, accepting the substance of the EC comment [meat consumption from pregnant heifers is exceptional], it is possible to limit the physiological range of oestradiol 17β and of progesterone in cattle, it has nevertheless to be recognized that (1) consumers are exposed to these two natural hormones through their consumption of meat and milk from the different non treated food producing animals and, mainly as least for women, through their endogenous production, (2) this exposure cannot be avoided. *Therefore, the use of the concept of threshold in the risk assessment of the natural hormone residues is legitimate and the additional intake of residues of these natural hormones from the meat from treated cattle has to be considered in this context and not according to a theoretical "no additional intake of residues is acceptable".*[emphasis added]

118.   In essence, Dr. Boisseau advises that, in order appropriately to understand the risks associated with the use of growth-promoting hormones, one must view the exposure to these hormones in their overall context, including the wide exposure to natural hormones from other dietary sources and endogenous production of natural hormones. To posit that the risks arising from the use of HGPs are

---

[56]   UK, Sub-Group of the Veterinary Products Committee, *Executive summary and critical evaluation of the scientific reasoning and methods of argument adopted in the opinion of the Scientific Committee on Veterinary Measures Relating to Public Health which assessed the potential risks to human health from hormone residues in bovine meat and meat products*, October 1999 (Exhibits CDA-6, US-12).
[57]   *Ibid.*, at para. 56, pp. 19-20.

such that no threshold for acceptable intake can be established is simply irrational and scientifically unjustified.

Q32. Please comment on the conclusions of the EC risk assessment (Opinion of the SCVPH of April 2002) that ultra sensitive methods to detect residues of hormones in animal tissues have become available but need further validation. What is the significance of this with regard to identifying whether the natural hormones in meat are endogenously produced or are residues of hormones used for growth promotion purposes?

119.   The SCVPH's statement concerning ultra-sensitive detection methods appears to relate its discussion of analytical techniques set out in Section 4.1.1 of its 2002 Opinion. In that section, the SCVPH acknowledges that the "low number of samples does not allow a qualified validation of typical characteristics such as sensitivity, specificity, accuracy and reproducibility (study 1, study 8)."[58] The experts who answered this question appear to agree on the importance of validating analytical methods.[59] Dr. Boisseau states that "validation must be carried out in compliance with well defined and internationally accepted criteria". These criteria include accuracy, precision, sensitivity, specificity, reproducibility, and reliability.[60]

120.   In terms of the second part of the Panel's question, Dr. Boisseau explains that once an MRL has been established, the sensitivity of the validated analytical method need only be consistent with the values established by the MRLs. Analytical methods that are more sensitive, or "ultra sensitive," are redundant for control purposes.

Q33. What were the reasons for the re-evaluation by JECFA of the three natural hormones in 1999? Were the residues data used for the three natural hormones in 1999 the same as those used in 1988? What additional information was used for the JECFA evaluation in 1999 of the three natural hormones which was not available in 1988? How did the conclusions differ? What led JECFA to establish ADIs for the three natural hormones? What are the implications of establishing ADIs? Why were JECFA's more recent recommendations not considered by the Codex Committee on Residues of Veterinary Drugs in Food? What is the status of these recommendations? [see paras. 96-97 of EC Rebuttal Submission (US case), paras. 79-80 of EC Rebuttal Submission (Canada case)]

---

[58]   EC, Health & Consumer Protection Directorate-General, *Opinion of the Scientific Committee on Veterinary Measures Relating to Public Health on Review of previous SCVPH opinions of 30 April 1999 and 3 May 2000 on the potential risks to human health from hormone residues in bovine meat and meat products*, adopted April 10, 2002, Section 4.1.1, at p. 9 (Exhibit CDA-7). See also p. 21.

[59]   Drs. Boisseau and de Brabander.

[60]   JECFA, *Procedures for Recommending Maxium Residue Limits*, at p. 37 (Exhibit CDA-44).

121.   Three experts respond to this question. JECFA also responds to the same question asked of the international bodies (Question 20). JECFA indicates that it can decide to re-evaluate previous assessments when it is made aware that there are new data which may be pertinent to the risk assessment of the substances in question. The claim by the EC in *EC – Hormones* that it had new evidence showing that oestradiol 17β was a direct acting genotoxic carcinogen appears to have promoted, at least in part, JECFA's 1999 re-evaluation. Moreover, JECFA indicates that new studies had also been published for the other hormones. This is consistent with the advice of Dr. Boisseau.

122.   In terms of whether the residue data for the natural hormones used in 1999 were the same as those used in 1988, JECFA indicates that while most of the residue studies were the same, a few additional studies were reviewed. JECFA also states that it performed a more detailed review of the validity of the analytical methods used in the studies and used only data generated using valid methods.

123.   JECFA also confirms that in the 1999 evaluation new toxicological and epidemiological data for the three natural hormones were evaluated, a position that is supported by Dr. Boobis. JECFA is quite specific as to the new information that was not available to it in 1988 but was available and considered by it in 1999.

124.   In terms of whether the conclusions from the two evaluations differed, Dr. Boisseau confirms that in substance the conclusions remained the same. The risk assessment indicated a wide margin of safety for consumption of residues in meat from treated cattle. Hence, the establishment of numerical MRLs was not necessary to protect human health.[61]

125.   As to the reasons for establishing ADIs for the three natural hormones in 1999, JECFA refers to "[t]he additional data reviewed and the need to establish and [*sic*] ADI as quantitative estimate for a safe oral intake".[62] This is consistent with Dr. Boobis' explanation that in the intervening years between the first and second JECFA evaluations, it became clear that exposure to natural hormones, albeit at levels much higher than that found in meat from treated cattle, could have adverse effects in humans. The implicit conclusion was that it was necessary to establish ADIs as benchmarks to ensure that exposure to these hormones through dietary sources did not cause adverse effects observed in other areas.

126.   JECFA confirms that "the establishment of an ADI implies that there is a threshold of effect for such a compound, below which now [*sic*; read "no"] toxicological effects occur".[63] This conclusion is supported by both Dr. Boisseau and Dr. Boobis.

---

[61]   JECFA's answer to Question 20 (to the international bodies), at p. 18.
[62]   *Ibid.*
[63]   *Ibid.*

127.   As to the reasons for CCRVDF's not having considered JECFA's more recent recommendations in respect of the natural hormones, JECFA's answer to Question 20 (to the international bodies) includes a direct quote from the 12th CCRVDF report, which states:

> Recognizing that this Committee had not requested the re-evaluation of these substances and that the new MRLs recommended by the 52nd JECFA did not differ significantly from the current MRLs, the Committee decided not to consider these new recommendations.

128.   As Dr. Boobis explains, the result is that Codex continues to list the three natural hormones with an indication that MRLs are "unnecessary" for tissues from cattle.

Q34.   Please comment on the EC argument that the 1999 JECFA report based its findings on (a) outdated residues data and (b) not on evidence from residues in meat but on studies with experimental animals and on general studies of IARC. If the data were not new, did JECFA take this into account in its evaluation? What are the implications of using such data for the purpose of conducting a risk assessment? How reliable are extrapolations from animal studies to possible adverse effects on humans? How does this compare with the kind of data and studies used with respect to other veterinary drugs? [see para. 120 of EC Rebuttal Submission (US case), para. 102 of EC Rebuttal (Canada case)]

Outdated Residues Data

129.   Dr. Boisseau confirms what is generally accepted within the scientific community: that scientific data do not deteriorate simply because of the passage of time. He concludes that "the quality and the number of the available data are more important than the dates at which these data have been produced." Dr. Boisseau also confirms that it is standard practice for JECFA to determine the quality and sufficiency of the data under consideration in its assessment of substances, as well as the validity of the analytical methods employed.[64]

130.   In the specific case of the hormones at issue, Dr. Boisseau confirms that:

> JECFA has considered that the quality and the number of the available residue data were satisfactory and therefore the fact that these data were not new had no specific impact on its evaluation.

---

[64]   For a description of JECFA's approach to data quality, see EHC-70, at pp. 22-23. ("JECFA has always judged studies on their merits, the main criteria being that the study was: (a) carried out with scientific rigour, and (b) reported in sufficient detail to enable comprehensive evaluation of the validity of the results.")

131.   Thus, the EC's suggestion that old data are necessarily unreliable data is simply groundless. Obviously old data that have been generated using validated analytical methods are to be preferred over more recent data generated by unvalidated and widely ignored analytical techniques. At the end of the day, the expert advice supports Canada's position that sufficient scientific evidence exists to conduct a risk assessment for all six of the hormones at issue.

Type of Data and Extrapolations from Animal to Human

132.   It should first be noted that the EC's statement in paragraph 102 of its Rebuttal Submission makes little sense. Studies with experimental animals are always *in vivo* and cannot by definition be *in vitro*. *In vitro* studies are studies that are conducted in an artificial environment outside the living organism.

133.   To the extent that the EC's statement suggests that there is something unusual or inappropriate about making extensive use of studies with experimental animals and general studies by IARC, the experts' responses to this question demonstrate that such a suggestion is nonsense. Understandably, Dr. Boisseau expresses surprise with the EC's statements, stating:

> … it is the normal way for assessing the toxicological potential of a substance to take into consideration in vivo studies with experimental animals, in vitro studies and also reports already published by internationally recognized scientific organisations such as IARC.

134.   Where human studies are not available, which is typically the case, for ethical reasons, risk assessors resort to these other studies out of necessity. Extrapolations from animal studies to humans have been standard practice for many years and regularly applied by international and national agencies in the conduct of risk assessments for food additives and contaminants, as well as veterinary drugs. It should be emphasized however, that in the case of the natural hormones, JECFA made extensive use of data derived from human studies involving the three natural hormones, in addition to animal studies. Moreover, this statement is all the more surprising when one considers that the very type of studies that the EC appears to suggest are inappropriate are precisely the type of studies relied upon by the SCVPH.

135.   As the experts confirm, the data and process used for assessing the safety of the hormones at issue are the same as those used for other veterinary drugs. JECFA has applied well-recognized procedures and principles in conducting its various risk assessments for the hormones at issue. Rather, the EC has strayed from internationally recognized techniques and methodologies.

Q35.   Please comment on the European Communities claim that nearly all the studies referred to in the 2000 JECFA report on MGA date from the 1960s and 70s. Is this correct? Have subsequent reports of JECFA, prior or subsequent to the adoption of the EC Directive, also relied on the same studies? [see para. 171 of EC Rebuttal Submission (US case), para. 161 of

EC Rebuttal Submission (Canada case), para. 55, including footnote 60 of US First Submission and Exhibits CDA-20, 33, 34, and 35]

136. Dr. Boisseau's answer to Question 34 also applies to this question, namely, that the quality and quantity of data are more important than the date upon which the data were generated.

137. While the studies referred to in the 2000 JECFA Report on MGA date back to the 1960s and 1970s[65], JECFA assessed these data to determine whether the quality and quantity were sufficient to conduct its risk assessment. As Dr. Boisseau concludes, "JECFA considered a wide series of toxicological studies in its assessment, used as end point a non hormonal effect dose by far more conservative than a NOAEL based on tumorigenic effect and adopted a 200 safety factor to derive an ADI from this NOAEL."

(c)   Dose-response relationship

Q36. How would you describe a dose-response assessment? Is it, as suggested by Canada in para. 78 of its Rebuttal Submission, "widely, if not universally, accepted that adverse effects arising from hormonal activities are dose-dependent"? Is dose-response assessment a necessary component of hazard characterization? Or, is there an alternative approach which can replace the dose-response assessment. Is a dose-response assessment feasible/necessary for substances that are found to be genotoxic or to have genotoxic potential? [see para. 153 of EC Replies to Panel Questions, para. 200 of EC Rebuttal Submission (US case); paras. 143, 154, and 156 of US First Submission, paras. 70-74 of US Replies to Panel Questions, and paras. 34 and 37-40 of US Rebuttal Submission; paras. 76-82 of Canada Rebuttal Submission]

138. Two of the three experts who responded to this question (Drs. Boobis and Boisseau) confirm that a dose-response assessment is a necessary component of hazard characterization. While these experts also acknowledge that such an assessment may not be feasible or required for substances that are genotoxic *in vivo*, they both confirm that this exception is not absolute. Dr. Boisseau confirms that this exception only applies to xenobiotic substances (*i.e.*, those that are foreign to the human body) or to substances with "genotoxic potential" where it is thought that this potential can be expressed in *in vivo* conditions. At least for the natural hormones involved here, neither of these conditions is met such that a dose-response assessment should be skipped.

139. Dr. Boobis similarly describes at least two general sets of circumstances in which a dose-response assessment would still be conducted on substances thought to have genotoxic potential. First, if the mechanism of action of the

---

[65]   Exhibit CDA-37.

genotoxic effect was known, and it was of the type of mechanism that is known to exhibit a threshold (for example, substances with kinetic or dynamic causes, as well as those caused by reactive oxygen species), then a dose-response assessment is necessary. Second, if the mechanism of action of genotoxicity was known or assumed to be DNA-reactive, then this genotoxicity would need to be confirmed *in vivo* before it would be appropriate to dispense with a dose-response assessment. As we know from numerous sources, including the EC risk assessment itself, it has not been demonstrated that any of these six hormones have genotoxic potential *in vivo*. According to the experts, this requires that a dose-response assessment be conducted.

140.   Dr. Cogliano's short response suggesting a dose-response may not be required tells only half the story. His comments seem to be limited to circumstances involving a "hazard-based approach", without explanation of when such an approach is or is not appropriate. A hazard-based approach simply identifies whether a substance is *capable* of causing an adverse effect under certain conditions, and not whether such adverse effect would actually occur at given doses. This corresponds only to the "hazard identification" stage of a risk assessment (*i.e.*, whether a substance can cause an adverse effect) and disregards the hazard characterization stage, which includes an assessment of the dose required to provoke the identified hazard (*i.e.*, dose-response assessment).[66] Quite apart from the explanation from Dr. Boobis that a "hazard-based approach" is not appropriate for these hormones, it would also be inconsistent with obligations under the *SPS Agreement* that a substance be evaluated for the *potential for occurrence* of an adverse effect.

141.   Dr. Cogliano's view that a dose-response assessment is optional is inconsistent with his later view that it is "widely accepted that adverse effects arising from hormonal activities depend on the dose".

Q37.   Do JECFA or Codex materials confirm Canada's statement in para. 80 of its Rebuttal Submission that "... while international risk assessment techniques suggest that a dose-response assessment is optional for biological or physical agents when the data cannot be obtained, a dose-response assessment should always be conducted for chemical agents ..."? [see Exhibit CDA-25]

142.   Drs. Boisseau and Boobis confirm Canada's statement that international techniques require that a dose-response assessment always be conducted as part of an assessment of the risk from chemical substances such as the six hormones. Dr. Boisseau indicates that it would not be possible to establish an ADI, and Dr. Boobis indicates that it would not be possible to recommend MRLs, in the absence of a dose-response assessment. These opinions are confirmed by JECFA in its response to Question 8 to the international bodies. In light of the univer-

---

[66]   See Canada's comments on the experts' responses to Question 11.

sally held view that the adverse effects of hormones are dose-dependent, these answers are not at all surprising given the purpose of the dose-response assessment of determining as closely as possible the level of dose at which there is no response (*i.e.*, the NOAEL).

(d)   Sensitive populations

Q38.   Please describe the range of physiological (or background) levels of the sex hormones in humans and identify the variations in these levels on the basis of age, sex group, and physiological stages.

143.   In presenting various figures for background levels of sex hormones of different age groups in response to this question, Dr. Boisseau raises concerns, as many others have done, about the reliance by the EC on a new "ultrasensitive bioassay" (also referred to as the Klein assay). In light of the SCVPH's decision to revise downward by 100-fold the estimated physiological level of hormones in pre-pubertal boys and girls, and the significance of the conclusions it draws as a result, Dr. Boisseau raises the important point about whether this assay has been validated. More detailed discussion of the flaws of this methodology follow in Canada's comments on the experts' responses to Question 40.

Q39.   Please comment on the SCVPH opinion stating that "any excess exposure towards oestradiol 17β and its metabolites resulting from the consumption of meat and meat products presents a potential risk to public health in particular to those groups of the populations which have been identified as particularly sensitive such as prepubertal children" [see para. 147 of the EC Replies to Panel Questions]

144.   In his reply to this question, Dr. Boisseau confirms that the EC has failed to compare quantitatively the exposure to oestradiol 17β from meat from treated animals to that from meat from non-treated animals and other sources of oestradiol 17β. Without having conducted such a comparison, the SCVPH is unable to claim that such exposure is "excess", nor that, even if it is "excess", the amount of the excess would be sufficient to "present a potential risk to public health".

145.   While Dr. Sippell offers the view that the EC's claim is supported, the evidence he refers to largely involves the controversial, and yet-to-be validated, methodology for measuring background levels of oestradiol 17β (*i.e.*, the Klein assay). Quite apart from the fact that serious concerns have been expressed about the validity of this methodology,[67] the use of the methodology does not, on its own, support the conclusion that exposure to oestradiol 17β residues from treated meat amounts to "excess exposure", nor that it "presents a potential risk to public health". Almost all the studies cited by Dr. Sippell apply to oestrogen

---

[67]   See Canada's comments on Question 40.

in general, and not to residues of oestradiol 17β consumed via meat from treated animals.

146.   Therefore, when Dr. Sippell refers to "elevated estrogen levels", he provides no evidence whatsoever that such levels are achieved from the consumption of residues of hormones from meat from treated animals. On the contrary, to the extent that his greatest concern appears to be for exposure to oestradiol 17β during "early life" (*i.e.*, pre- and post-natal periods), Dr. Sippell provides no evidence for, nor even a plausible explanation of, exposure at this age to residues from meat products. Certainly a foetus/infant could be exposed via the mother, but since late pregnancy and early *post partum* are the periods of a woman's life where the natural oestrogen level is at its most elevated, the proportion of oestrogen exposure of the foetus/infant that would come from the consumption by the mother of meat from treated animals would be trivial.

147.   Moreover, a review of the full context of the quote cited in the question[68] reveals that it is based on conclusions that the experts have contested elsewhere in their replies. Citing disputed findings that metabolites of oestradiol 17β have "genotoxic potential", the SCVPH concludes that oestradiol 17β is both a *tumour initiator* as well *tumour promoter*. It then suggests that this conclusion is confirmed by epidemiological data and IARC's classification of oestrogen as a human carcinogen. On the basis of these findings, the SCVPH further concludes that "any excess exposure… presents a potential risk to public health". [69] However, in establishing the adverse effect threshold as "any excess exposure", the SCVPH offered no confirmed evidence of genotoxicity of the substances, nor any scientific support for its suggestion of a link between epidemiological data and its conclusions. The result is that the quote from the SCVPH's opinion is no more than speculation based on tenuous links drawn between unsupported conclusions.

Q40.   The European Communities states that "the levels of endogenous production of the hormones by prepubertal children is much lower than previously thought and this finding, which is subsequent to the 1999 JECFA report, casts serious doubts about the validity of JECFA's findings on the dose-response relationship..." Please comment on the methodology used by the SCVPH to support the conclusion that hormone levels are lower than previously thought, and in particular comment on the validity of these methodologies and their conclusions. Would your conclusions have been the same at the time of adoption of the Directive in September 2003?

148.   Drs. Boisseau and Boobis both share concerns about the methodology (an "ultrasensitive" recombinant cell bioassay (RCBA) developed by Klein and others[70]) that generated the underpinning the conclusion that endogenous levels of

---

[68]   1999 SCVPH Opinion, at pp. 74-75 (Exhibit CDA-2).
[69]   *Ibid.*, at p. 74.
[70]   *Ibid.*, at pp. 30 and 38.

hormones in pre-pubertal children are lower than previously thought. Dr. Boisseau's concerns about the absence of validation of this methodology are reflected in his answer to Question 38.

149.   Dr. Boobis echoes these concerns in a very comprehensive review of the issues surrounding this controversial methodology. While he acknowledges that endogenous levels may be lower than previously thought, Dr. Boobis expresses grave doubts that this is by the "orders of magnitude" suggested by the SCVPH, repeating Dr. Boisseau's concern when he says that the "reliability of the Klein *et al.* assay has yet to be determined". He points to a number of contradictory results in the use of this assay, including from the original inventors themselves, that at the very least suggests that it has not been adequately validated for use in a risk assessment.

150.   The concerns highlighted by the experts about the SCVPH's use of this methodology have been consistently cited by others as one of the flaws in the analysis of the SCVPH. For example, the UK Sub-Group Report early on expressed the concern that the Klein assays have not been appropriately validated. It expressed:

> ... concerns about the reliability of this analytical approach, which has been very little used in peer-reviewed publications other than by the originators of the assay, despite its initial publication in 1994. These concerns throw doubt upon the values derived by Klein *et al.* and therefore also on the conclusions of the [SCVPH] opinion.[71]

151.   Not only does the SCVPH fail to point out the obvious problems with the validity of the Klein data, but it ends up comparing apples with oranges. The 1999 SCVPH Opinion recognizes that "perhaps the hormone residues in beef, which are also low and which have also been determined by Radio Immune Assays (RIA) are equally variable and over representative of the actual hormone concentrations."[72] Thereafter, without acknowledging that it is using two different analytical techniques, the SCVPH goes on to compare concentrations of oestradiol in beef using RIA with concentrations in plasma using the Klein assay. As the UK Sub-Group Report concluded, "[t]his is inappropriate and may lead to a biased inappropriate perspective."[73]

152.   Most importantly, even the 1999 SCVPH Opinion calls the data produced by Klein *et al.* "experimental evidence", calling the data "insufficient" to form the basis of a sound risk assessment.[74] A few years later, the SCVPH itself concluded in its 2002 opinion that "[t]he obtained results suggest that the use of re-

---

[71]   UK Sub-Group Report, at pp. 26-28 (Exhibit CDA-6).
[72]   1999 SCVPH Opinion, at p. 30 (Exhibit CDA-2).
[73]   UK Sub-Group Report, at para. 96, p. 28 (Exhibit CDA-6).
[74]   1999 SCVPH Opinion, at pp. 38-9 (Exhibit CDA-2).

combinant yeast and rainbow trout hepatocytes to detect oestrogenic compounds is not justified in view of their lack of sensitivity."[75]).

153.   Contrary to the concerns expressed by at least two of his colleagues, Dr. Sippell seems to believe the recombinant yeast bioassay (RCBA) methodology constitutes a "quantum leap" in assay methodology. In support of this claim, Dr. Sippell cites a later study (Paris *et al.*, 2002) to suggest that the Klein RCBA has been validated. Interestingly, the research by Paris *et al.* was also cited by Dr. Boobis in support of his opinion that the Klein RCBA *had not been validated* by subsequent research because the research by Paris *et al.*, which in Dr. Boobis' mind is more credible, demonstrated that the Klein RCBA overestimated background oestrogen levels by up to 18 times. The Paris *et al.* results in fact were closer to the original data used by JECFA based on the RIA methodology. In light of these discrepancies, the Panel may wish to ask Dr. Sippell to clarify why he believes the Paris *et al.* results validate the 1994 Klein results.

154.   Dr. Sippell makes another ambiguous observation in his advice when he states that "the complexity of the [Klein] RCBA so far prevents its wider use for routine measurements in small serum samples from infants and prepubertal children". Canada understands this to be confirmation that there are very little reliable data related to the use of RCBA.

Q41.   Why would individuals with the lowest endogenous hormone levels be at greatest risk? How would the risks for these individuals arising from hormones naturally present in meat differ from the risks arising from the residues of hormone growth promoters?

155.   Drs. Boisseau and Boobis agree that although individuals with the lowest endogenous hormone levels are at the greatest risk from any adverse effects that might result from exposure to hormones, the exposure to hormones via meat from treated animals would not result in any change in the effect that would be expected from hormones from meat from non-treated animals, or any other exogenous source for that matter.

156.   Dr. Sippell suggests that the risks would be different, but he bases his assessment of "risk" on what he calls a "new threshold", which appears to be based on the results from the Klein assay. However, as the experts have advised in response to previous questions, this assay has not been validated sufficiently to support the kinds of conclusions that Dr. Sippell makes.

Q42.   To what extent, in your view, has JECFA taken into account the particular situation of sensitive populations, in particular prepubertal children, in its risk assessments with respect to oestradiol 17β? Please compare the original data concerning endogenous production of natural hormones by prepubertal children upon which JECFA based its assessment and those

---

[75]   2002 SCVPH Opinion, at p. 9 (Exhibit CDA-7).

used by the European Communities in its risk assessment. In your view, does the scientific material referred to by the European Communities require a revision of the Codex recommendation with respect to oestradiol 17β?

157.   Drs. Boisseau and Boobis both acknowledge the many ways in which JECFA takes into account the situation of sensitive populations. They point in particular to the use by JECFA in establishing the ADI for oestradiol 17β of an additional safety factor of 10 specifically for sensitive populations, in addition to the initial safety factor of 10 for variation between individuals. The resulting safety factor of 100 makes for a very conservative assessment of safe exposure. Dr. Boisseau confirms that the safety factors for some of the other hormones were even greater. Moreover, Dr. Boisseau highlights two additional safety factors: first, that the estimated exposure to the natural hormones from meat from treated animals amounts to a very small proportion of the overall exposure from all sources, and, second, the fact that the bioavailability of the natural hormones is quite low. The approach of JECFA builds in significant safety margins to take into account the situation of sensitive populations.

158.   Only Dr. Sippell expresses concern about whether JECFA's analysis adequately takes into account the situation of sensitive populations, but his concern is based on estimates of endogenous levels in these populations that have been generated by the Klein RCBA. As discussed above, however, this methodology has not been adequately validated, and the original results obtained by Klein have not been reproduced by others. In light of more credible measurements of endogenous levels of hormones, Dr. Boobis indicates in his answer to Question 40 that exposure up to the ADI established by JECFA would still be safe for sensitive populations. Nothing in Dr. Sippell's comments (other than a non-validated methodology) contradicts the analysis conducted by Dr. Boobis.

159.   Both Drs. Boisseau and Boobis indicate that the scientific material referred to by the EC does not require a revision of the Codex recommendation with respect to oestradiol 17β.

(e)   Bioavailability

Q43. Please define bioavailability, comment on the significance of bioavailability to assessments of risk, and on the degree of bioavailabilitiy of the residues of the hormones at issue when consumed in meat, taking into account parties' differing views on this matter. [see paras. 123-124 of EC Rebuttal Submission (US case), paras. 105-106 of EC Rebuttal Submission (Canada case), paras. 100, 155-159 of the EC Replies to Panel Questions, paras. 32 and 41-42 of US Rebuttal Submission, paras. 69, 71, 88-89 and 146 of US First Submission, and para. 134 of Canada Rebuttal Submission]

160.   The experts generally agree that bioavailability refers to the fraction of the substance that is available for systemic circulation. It is normally estimated by comparing the availability of a substance after oral administration with the

availability of a substance after intravenous administration (which is assumed to be 100% bioavailable). The experts also agree that only the bioavailable portion of the substance at issue can produce an adverse effect. As a consequence, only that portion of the substance that is bioavailable will be significant for risk assessment purposes.

161.   Dr. Boisseau and Dr. Boobis confirm that the natural hormones are either inactive orally or have low bioavailability (between 5% to 10%). These conclusions are supported by both JECFA[76] and CVMP.[77] The JECFA analysis is based on a review of the scientific literature on the absorption, distribution and excretion of oestradiol 17β set out in the Toxicological Monograph for the natural hormones prepared for JECFA's 52nd meeting.[78]

162.   Dr. Guttenplan indicates that the "bioavailability of estrogen is low but not insignificant (probably between 5 and 20%, if estrone is also taken into account[)]." He further indicates that the SCVPH in its 1999 and 2002 opinions questions the sufficiency and accuracy of the data relied upon by JECFA. However, Dr. Boobis places the concept of bioavailability, and by extension the SCVPH analysis, in its proper context. He states:

> However, low bioavailability does not necessarily increase the margin of safety (the ratio of ADI to actual exposure). This is because the effects of concern are usually determined following exposure by the route of interest, in this case oral. Hence, the ADI represents a "bioavailability adjusted" dose, just as the TMDI does. The consequence of this is that anything that increases bioavailability will reduce the margin of safety whilst anything that reduces bioavailability will increase the margin of safety. In the case of the natural hormones, changes in bioavailability are likely to be a consequence of changes in the enzymes of metabolism in the liver and/or small intestine.

163.   Thus, as the ADI is a "bioavailability adjusted" dose, for the purposes of establishing the ADI, it matters not that the estimated bioavailability of the substance is later revised. The ADI is based on the dose that represents the NOAEL,

---

[76]   See JECFA, 52nd Report, at p. 58. (Exhibit CDA-16). ("In general, oestradiol-17β is inactive when given orally because it is inactivated in the gastrointestinal tract and liver".)

[77]   European Medicines Agency, Committee for Veterinary Medicinal Products, *Report of the CVMP on the Safety Evaluation of Steroidal Sex Hormones in particular for 17β-Oestradiol, Progesterone, Altrenogest, Flugestone acetate and Norgestomet in the Light of New Data/Information made available by the European Commission*, EMEA/CVMP/885/99, December 1999, at p. 2 (Exhibit CDA-5). ("[T]he bioavailability of 17β-oestradiol esters after oral administration is low (3% as unchanged 17β-oestradiol), but it might be higher if estron, an estrogenic metabolite, is included".)

[78]   See JECFA, *Toxicological evaluation of certain veterinary drug residues in food: prepared by the Fifty-second meeting of the Joint FAO/WHO Expert Committee on Food Additives*, WHO Food Additives Series No. 43, (Geneva: WHO, 2000), Section 1.2.1 Absorption, distribution and excretion, at p. 45 (Exhibit CDA-11).

together with appropriate safety factors. Thus, even if the SCVPH is correct that the bioavailability of the hormones at issue is higher than previously estimated, a conclusion that Canada contests, this has no impact on the ADI. The ADI could be called in question if, for instance, studies demonstrate that the bioavailability of oestradiol 17β in residues in meat from treated cattle was higher than the bioavailability of the fine-particle oestradiol 17β used in the studies that formed the basis of the ADI. However, the EC has presented no evidence to this effect. Indeed, the evidence points in the opposite direction.

(f)   Good veterinary practice (GVP)

Q44.   Please define "good veterinary practice" (GVP) and/or "good practice in the use of veterinary drugs" (GPVD). What are the relevant Codex standards, guidelines or recommendations relating to GVP/GPVD? Please comment on the statement by the European Communities that the definition of the GPVD is "circular and hence problematic." [see para. 88 of the EC Replies to Panel Questions]

164.   Two experts, Dr. Boisseau and Dr. de Brabander, answer this question. Codex also answers a similar question posed to the international bodies (Question 15). The Codex definition of GPVD, with which both experts agree, is as follows:

> Good Practice in the Use of Veterinary Drugs (GPVD) is the official recommended or authorized usage including withdrawal periods, approved by national authorities, of veterinary drugs under practical conditions.

165.   In terms of Codex standards, guidelines and recommendations, Codex and Dr. de Brabander identify the Codex *Recommended International Code of Practice for Control of the Use of Veterinary Drugs (Codex Recommendations),*[79] although Dr. de Brabander does so only in passing. Instead of discussing the *Codex Recommendations,* Dr. de Brabander extensively quotes from what appears to be a code of ethics and principles of conduct for the Federation of Veterinarians of Europe (FVE). Two points need to be made. First, the FVE code is not an international standard, guideline or recommendation. Second, a code governing ethical conduct is of limited relevance to risk assessments of veterinary drug residues in meat.

166.   In contrast to the FVE, the *Codex Recommendations* addresses in detail such issues relating to the use of veterinary drugs as requirements for distribution, transport, and storage (*e.g.*, temperature, humidity, light, *etc.*); requirements on handling and administration (*e.g.*, dose, method of use); withdrawal periods;

---

[79]   Codex, *Recommended International Code of Practice for Control of the Use of Veterinary Drugs (Codex Recommendations)*, CAC/RCP 38 (Exhibit CDA-47).

disposal; and record keeping. Notably, the *Codex Recommendations* do not suggest that all veterinary drugs must be administered by a veterinarian:

> [w]hen the administration of a medicine is not under direct veterinary supervision, it is therefore essential that, after the diagnosis, clear instructions should be provided on dose and methods of use, taking account of the competence of the user performing the work and ensuring that the correct calculation of, and the importance of adhering to, withdrawal periods is fully understood.[80]

167.   Regrettably, neither expert discusses the detailed provisions of the *Codex Recommendations* or whether this document sheds light on the EC's claim that GVP is "somewhat circular and hence problematic." Canada shares Dr. Boisseau's concern that the EC's comment is less than clear. This concern may flow from the fact that the EC appears to be questioning a well recognized international practice, employed by its own agencies.[81] He posits that the EC means that the conditions of use of the veterinary drug may differ in a very significant way from one country to another. Here, Dr. Boisseau's answer to Question 45 is relevant.

168.   Dr. Boisseau states that JECFA and other national authorities conduct risk assessments of veterinary drugs using studies in which the drug under review has been administered according to officially approved conditions of use (*i.e.*, labelled instructions). Thus, he suggests that adherence to GPVD is intricately linked to compliance with approved conditions of use (*e.g.*, storage, dose and method of use, withdrawal periods etc.).

169.   The EC suggests that the circularity arises because "GVP is ... dependent upon what national authorities consider appropriate". This only becomes problematic if the conditions of use that underlie the studies relied upon by JECFA are more stringent than approved conditions of use at the national level. Consequently, it would be helpful if the experts could clarify whether the approved conditions of use in Canada for the hormones in question differ from the conditions of use underlying the studies that JECFA used to assess the safety of these hormones.

Q45.   In conducting a risk assessment of specific veterinary drugs, what assumptions are made concerning GVP, if any? How, if at all, are risks that might arise from the failure to follow good veterinary practice in the administration of veterinary drugs addressed?

---

[80]   *Codex Recommendations*, at para. 5, p. 1.
[81]   In this regard, see Dr. Boobis' answer to Question 46, in which he states "appropriate residues studies are those obtained after the normal use of the hormones, i.e. in accordance with GVP. This is the policy of all agencies and organisations involved in such activities (*EEC, 1990; EMEA, 2005; FAO, 2006*)."

170.   Both Dr. Boisseau and Dr. de Brabander indicate that in conducting a risk assessment it is assumed that GVP is followed.[82] Dr. Boisseau explains in greater detail that JECFA and other national authorities conduct risk assessments of veterinary drugs using studies in which the drug under review has been administered according to officially approved conditions of use. As discussed above, for the most part, use in accordance with GPVD means use in accordance with the approved conditions of use (*e.g.*, storage, transport, dose, method of use, withdrawal period).

171.   As regards the second part of the Panel's question, Dr. Boisseau indicates that it is very difficult for risk assessors to identify all possible permutations of misuse and abuse. In terms of the risks that might arise from the failure to follow GPVD, Dr. Boisseau states:

> It would not be appropriate also because it would not be ethical for the case where such data, being available, would lead to the conclusion of the risk assessment that, given a possibly wide margin of safety for a veterinary drug under review, the excess intake of residues associated with these misuses/abuses does not raise any problem of public health.

172.   Canada requests that Dr. Boisseau clarify whether he is suggesting that, with respect to the growth-promoting hormones at issue, such a wide margin of safety has been incorporated into the risk assessment that any misuse and abuse is unlikely to give rise to adverse effects for human health?

173.   Dr. de Brabander fails to respond to the Panel's actual question.

Q46. To what extent were risks from misuse or abuse assessed by JECFA in its evaluation of the hormones at issue? In terms of the three synthetic hormones at issue, how is GVP relevant to the establishment of MRLs by JECFA?

174.   Drs. Boobis, Boisseau and de Brabander respond to this question. Dr. Boisseau cites his answer to Question 45, implying he is of the view that the risks of misuse and abuse are not typically assessed by risk assessors such as JECFA. However, Dr. Boobis confirms that in several instances JECFA did consider the risks of misuse of some of the hormone growth promotants at issue, namely, zeranol and MGA.

175.   Dr. Boobis also states that the point at which misuse and abuse is relevant in the risk assessment is at the risk characterization stage, during which potential exposure is compared with the ADI. He also states that, where appropriate, one could consider other potential exposure scenarios, such as the misuse and abuse of the substance in question.

---

[82]   In the light of the answers to Question 44, Canada assumes that, when the Panel refers to GVP, it is actually referring to "good practice in the use of veterinary drugs" (GPVD).

176.   Drs. Boobis and Boisseau appear of the view that it is not for JECFA to monitor compliance with GVP. Dr. Boisseau's answer to Question 45 above, is supported by Dr. Boobis' response to Question 62 where he states that:

> [misuse and abuse] cannot be used as the basis for establishing MRLs. This is because whilst use according to GVP can be foreseen and regulated, it is not possible or appropriate to regulate any conceivable misuse or abuse, whether actual or hypothetical. Normally, the risk management strategy to deal with this is to ensure adequate surveillance of residues and to put in place a system of penalties for violation. This is the situation for veterinary drugs in all regions where they are subject to market authorisation, including the EU and the USA.

177.   Therefore, to the extent that the EC is suggesting that JECFA's risk assessment is somehow flawed because it failed to assess potential misuse and abuse, the EC is fundamentally misconstruing JECFA's role.

178.   Dr. de Brabander's answer is confusing and difficult to follow. First, he suggests that JECFA "denied" that there was misuse and abuse. Canada has carefully reviewed JECFA's reports and can find no example of JECFA "denying" such a possibility. In the light of the responses of the other experts, the Panel may wish to ask Dr. de Brabander to support this allegation. Second, he appears to draw illogical conclusions about the relationship between misuse and abuse and the establishment of MRLs. He states:

> If other substances (like zilpaterol or ZMA etc ...) or uncorrect [*sic*] use of implants are used the principle of the establishment of MRLs by JECFA is certainly unvalid [*sic*]

179.   As Drs. Boobis and Boisseau explain, MRLs are established on the basis of the normal use of hormones, *i.e.*, in accordance with GVP, and are set independently of potential compliance issues. In the light of this evidence, Dr. de Brabander's conclusion is questionable, to say the least.

Q47.   How significant are any differences in GVP in the European Communities, the United States, and Canada? Does the EC risk assessment take into account relevant control mechanisms with respect to GVP in place in the United States and/or Canada? If so, what are their conclusions?

180.   Drs. Boisseau and de Brabander respond to this question. Dr. Boisseau, although acknowledging that he did not think that he was in a position to answer this question, indicates that in his view the main problem for the EC is that HGPs in North America are sold over the counter without veterinary supervision. He further states that "it is not possible to say that the European Communities took into account relevant control mechanisms with respect to GVPs in place in the USA and/or Canada" in its risk assessment.

181. On the other hand, in answering this question, Dr. de Brabander appears again to confuse concepts by suggesting that the very use of growth-promoting hormones is contrary to the principles of GVP. However, as the *Codex Recommendations* reveals, GVP establishes principles governing the use of veterinary drugs, but does not prescribe which substances can be used and for what purpose.

182. As to relevant control mechanisms, Dr. de Brabander again fails to answer the Panel's question and instead postulates that "any control mechanism, that is only based on audits and paper work will not prevent farmers to use either uncorrect [*sic*] use of legal production aids either the use of other illegal growth promotors which are readily available in the US and Canada through the internet." Aside from the fact that Dr. de Brabander is straying from his area of expertise, the only evidence presented to support his assertion is a warning issued by Health Canada concerning athletic performance-enhancing products containing illegal anabolic steroids.[83] Although it is less than clear, Dr. de Brabander appears to imply that because anabolic steroids are used illegally in performance enhancing products in Canada, control mechanisms short of a complete ban would not prevent the misuse and abuse of HGPs. This logic is deeply flawed. A warning issued by Health Canada to protect Canadians from illegal anabolic steroids in bodybuilding drugs is hardly credible evidence of the existence or extent of the misuse and abuse of HGPs or an evaluation of relevant control mechanism.

183. Moreover, the illegal use of anabolic steroids by athletes has been a world-wide problem for decades. Much of the internet trade in illegal anabolic steroids originates in Europe, where controls over the distribution of these products are more lax.[84] The implication of Dr. de Brabander's logic is that, because these products are available in Europe through the internet, European farmers are misusing anabolic steroids in the husbandry of cattle.

Q48. To what extent does the scientific evidence referred to by the European Communities assess risks to human health from residues of misplaced implants or improper administration, i.e. when administered differently than indicated on the label of the manufacturer or contrary to GVP, of any of the six hormones? Would your reply have been different at the time of

---

[83] Health Canada, Advisory, *Health Canada advises consumers not to use unauthorized products containing anabolic steroids*, April 21, 2006; online at: *http://www.hc-sc.gc.ca/ahc-asc/media/advisories-avis/2006/2006_17_e.html.*

[84] US Drug Enforcement Agency, *Anabolic Steroids, A Dangerous and Illegal Way to Seek Athletic Dominance and a Better Appearance*, "For purposes of illegal use there are several sources; the most common illegal source is from smuggling steroids into the United States from other countries such as Mexico and European countries. Smuggling from these areas is easier because a prescription is not required for the purchase of steroids. Less often steroids found in the illicit market are diverted from legitimate sources (e.g. thefts or inappropriate prescribing) or produced in clandestine laboratories"; online at: *http://www.deadiversion.usdoj.gov/pubs/brochures/steroids/public/public.pdf.*

adoption of the EC Directive in September 2003? What are the potential hazards, if any, to human health of the use of large quantities, or doses higher than recommended, of any of the six hormones in dispute?

184.   Although Drs. Boisseau, Boobis and de Brabander all provide answers, only the first two respond to the question posed by the Panel in a comprehensive fashion. These experts agree that the EC failed to assess risks to human health from residues of misplaced implants or improper administration. Dr. Boobis states directly that:

> There was no attempt to evaluate the risks from the resultant exposures on misuse or abuse, either in the papers cited or by the SCVPH (2002) in their evaluation of these studies. Indeed, the SCVPH (2002) simply noted that "Therefore, these data have to be considered in any quantitative exposure assessment exercise", without undertaking such an exercise.

185.   For his part, Dr. Boisseau notes that the EC:

> ... is right to state that, in case of these different misuses/abuses, the exposure of consumers may be totally different. Once again, this situation is not specific to hormones as it applies also to all the veterinary drugs already assessed by JECFA, EU, USA or anywhere else in the world.

186.   These responses support Canada's explanation that the EC has failed to evaluate the potential risks to human health from the misuse or abuse of the growth-promoting hormones at issue.[85] The EC has simply identified the possibility that misuse or abuse could occur without having evaluated its frequency or the potential risk to human health in the event it occurs. As Dr. Boobis states:

> In my view, the potential hazards to the use of large quantities of the six hormones in dispute are those dependent on their endocrine activity, including cancer in hormonally responsive tissues. However, I should stress that this is their potential hazard. The potential risk, i.e. the probability that effects would occur, would depend on a number of factors. These include the magnitude of the exposure, the duration of the exposure and the life stage of the exposed individual. From the range of exposures likely from anticipated misuse or abuse the risks are likely to be very low.

187.   In his response to Question 62, reviewing the EC's additional research conducted since 1997, Dr. Boobis further states:

---

[85]   Canada Rebuttal Submission, at paras. 107-111.

> Taking account of all of these factors, the data generated by the
> EU research in question do not provide any indication that it is not
> possible to conduct a risk assessment of the hormones used as
> growth promoters. Nor do they provide any indication that even
> such misuse and abuse as investigated gives rise to undue risk
> from the resultant residues, as intake would only very rarely ex-
> ceed the ADI and then only on a rare occasion. [86]

188.   As Dr. Boisseau notes, the misuse and abuse of a substance could lead to
exposure scenarios different from those contemplated in establishing an MRL.
This applies to any veterinary drug, or indeed any substance for which an MRL
is established. If it were sufficient for a WTO Member simply to raise the possibility, without any evaluation, of misuse and abuse as a justification for a ban on
a substance, the obligation in Article 5.1 of the *SPS Agreement* to base an SPS
measure on a risk assessment would be rendered illusory, and the work of international scientific risk assessment bodies, such as JECFA or the Joint Management Pesticide Committee, could be largely irrelevant. Mere assertions that misuse and abuse may occur without any evaluation of the factors outlined by
Dr. Boobis on page 52 of his answers do not satisfy the requirements of a risk
assessment as defined by the *SPS Agreement*.

**Q49.   What analytical methods, or other technical means, for residue detec-
tion in tissues exist to control the use of the six hormones in dispute for
growth promotion purposes in accordance with good animal husbandry
practice and/or good veterinary practice? What tools are available to control the use by farmers of the six hormones in dispute for growth promotion
purposes in accordance with good animal husbandry practice and/or good
veterinary practice?**

189.   Only Dr. de Brabander responds to this question. He indicates that:

> There are a large number of analytical methods available to con-
> trol the use of the six hormones in dispute for growth promotion
> purposes. New methods are regularly presented in international
> conferences and in the open literature. In Europe a system of
> community reference (CRL) and national reference laboratories
> (NRL) is installed so that the analysis carried out by the field labo-
> ratories are kept up to the standards of the moment. If necessary I
> can provide the panel with a large number of methods but I don't
> think that is the purpose.

190.   As it would be helpful to understanding the issues in dispute, the Panel
may wish to ask Dr. de Brabander for a complete listing of available analytical
methods to detect residues in meat and meat products for each of the hormones

---

[86]   Dr. Boobis, at p. 52.

at issue as well as a complete description of the CRL and NRL networks to which he refers.

Q50. Are there other measures available to the European Communities (other than a complete ban) which could address risks arising from misuse and failure to follow good veterinary practice with respect to the use of the hormones at issue for growth promotion purposes? Would your reply have been different at the time of adoption of the EC Directive in September 2003? If so, why?

191.   Both Drs. Boisseau and de Brabander respond to this question. Dr. Boisseau makes a number of suggestions for addressing human health concerns arising from the failure by the exporting country to ensure compliance with GVP. He notes that a "[b]an is the last possible measure if all the other options have failed or have been proved ineffective."

192.   In contrast, Dr. de Brabander states that there are no measures possible other than a complete ban that could address the risks arising from misuse and abuse. This remark appears inconsistent with his earlier statement in response to Question 49 that "[t]here are a large number of analytical methods available to control the use of the six hormones in dispute for growth promotion purposes."

Q51.   Does the material put forth by the European Communities regarding misuse or abuse of the hormones at issue in the United States and Canada call into question the potential applicability of Codex standards with regard to imports of meat from cattle treated with hormones from the United States and Canada?

193.   Both Drs. Boisseau and de Brabander respond to this question. Dr. Boisseau refers back to his answers to Questions 45 and 48, implying that, in his view, the misuse and abuse of hormones used for growth promotion do not call into question the potential applicability of Codex standards. Dr. Boisseau earlier commented that the establishment of ADIs and MRLs are based on an assumption that GVP will be followed. Thus, in the unlikely event that GVP is not followed, the applicability of Codex standards is not put into doubt. Misuse or abuse may cause the residues of the substance in question to exceed the established MRL and may lead to exposure to the substance in excess of the established ADI, but it does not imply that the Codex standard is any less applicable. Questions of compliance with an MRL differ conceptually from whether the MRL is valid or applicable.

194.   Unlike Dr. Boisseau, Dr. de Brabander appears to confuse the applicability of a Codex standard with the consequences of misuse and abuse. Then, he refers to "older" experiments upon which the ADIs and MRLs were based and suggests that "scientific knowledge on residues, their link with animal welfare and the impact on the environment has increased considerably." With respect, it is somewhat difficult to follow Dr. de Brabander's reasoning in this regard and it is less than clear how Dr. de Brabander's response addresses the Panel's question concerning misuse and abuse. To the extent that Dr. de Brabander suggests that

the experiments on which the Codex ADI and MRL are based were "old" and no longer valid, he appears to be answering Question 34, on which Canada has already commented. Moreover, Dr. de Brabander's reference to his own study of the formation of boldenone has no bearing on the issue of misuse and abuse.

(g)   Other

Q52.   Do the risk assessment of the European Communities or any other scientific materials referred to by the European Communities demonstrate that a potential for adverse effects on human health arises from the consumption of meat from cattle treated with any of the six hormones in dispute for growth-promotion purposes? If yes, why? If not, what kind of evidence would be required to demonstrate such potential adverse affects? Would your response have been different at the time of adoption of the Directive in September 2003?

195.   Drs. Boisseau and Boobis both agree with Canada that the scientific evidence relied upon by the EC does not demonstrate that there are adverse effects from the consumption of residues of hormones through meat from treated animals. Dr. Boisseau states that the EC did not carry out a risk assessment, but, rather, simply "provided scientific data and hypothesis supporting its worries" about the safety of the hormones. In particular, he confirms Canada's explanation of some of the flaws of the EC's risk assessment when he notes that the SCVPH should have:

> integrated in its risk assessment the exposure of consumers to these hormones resulting from the consumption of hormone residues from animals which have not been treated by hormonal growth promoters and the [*sic*] from the daily production of these hormones by humans.

196.   Dr. Boobis echoes this evaluation of the EC's risk assessment and its scientific evidence when he advises that "none of the information provided by the EC demonstrates the potential for adverse effects for humans" from meat from cattle treated with hormones. More specifically, he adds that:

> [t]he studies on genotoxicity provide no convincing evidence of potential for harm in consumers. The weight of evidence is that the hormones are not genotoxic in vivo even at doses well above those that would be present in meat from treated cattle. As such, there would be no risk of such effects in human from such exposures. The carcinogenic effects observed are entirely consistent with a hormonal mode of action that exhibits a threshold that would be well above the intake arising from consumption of meat from treated cattle. Other effects of the hormones that have been observed either in experimental animals or in exposed subjects occur at doses much higher than those to which consumers would be ex-

posed via meat from treated cattle. As such, there would be no risk of such effects in humans from such exposures.

197. For his part, Dr. Guttenplan seems to suggest, but does not explicitly state, that the EC has identified the potential for adverse effects. However, his main concern is based on the SCVPH's conclusion that pre-pubertal children have lower endogenous levels of hormones, itself based on data obtained principally by the Klein assay. As discussed in Canada's comments on Question 40, there are serious doubts about the validity of this assay. Dr. Guttenplan's endorsement of the EC's conclusions about adverse effects suffers from the same shortcomings as those conclusions themselves: they both rely on scientific methodologies that have not been validated.

198. All three experts provide useful advice on the evidence that would be required to demonstrate adverse effects, such as toxicological data (Dr. Boisseau), residue data that show that consuming treated meat leads to any change in circulating levels (Drs. Boisseau, Boobis and Guttenplan), and specific epidemiological studies (Dr. Boobis). It is important to note that none of them suggests that the EC has demonstrated such evidence currently exists.

Q53. Please comment on the statement by the European Communities that the natural hormones progesterone and testosterone are used only in combination with oestradiol 17β or other oestrogenic compounds in commercial preparations? Would the systematic use of these and the synthetic hormones in combination have any implications on how the scientific experiments and the risk assessments are to be carried out? If so, have the scientific materials referred to by the European Communities or relevant JECFA reports taken into account the possible synergistic effects of such combinations on human health? [see sections 4.2-4.3 of the Opinion of the SCVPH of 2002 in US Exhibit 1]

199. Both Drs. Boisseau and Guttenplan, the only two experts that addressed this question, advise that the exposure to these hormones, both alone and in combination, is so low that there is very little risk of any increase in the risk if assessed in combination. They both acknowledge that it is oestradiol 17β that is the most potent, with the addition of the others not significantly changing this potency such that the risk would increase. Therefore, once oestradiol 17β has been demonstrated not to have adverse effects when used as a growth promoter, there is little risk that adverse effects would occur if used in combination with the other hormones.

Q54. What is the acceptable level of risk reflected in the Codex standards for the five hormones at issue? How does this compare to the European Communities' stated objective of "no risk from exposure to unnecessary additional residues in meat of animals treated with hormones for growth promotion". [see para. 149 of EC Rebuttal Submission (US case)]

200.   Drs. Boisseau, Boobis and Guttenplan all advise that the acceptable level of risk reflected in Codex standards is that there is no risk of adverse effects if exposure to hormones is kept below the established ADI. In that sense, as Dr. Boobis points out, the acceptable level of risk reflected in the international standards is identical to that purportedly sought by the EC through its ban.

201.   While Drs. Boisseau and Guttenplan both appear to suggest that the acceptable level of risk chosen by the EC is different than that embodied in the Codex standards, a close examination of their answers reveals that the difference to which they refer is that between theoretical risk and real risk, and not between acceptable levels of protection. That is, whereas the Codex standards indicate that there is no *real risk* if exposure is kept below the established ADI, the EC attempts to prevent even theoretical risk. Dr. Guttenplan confirms that the EC has not addressed the actual level of risk presented by consumption of meat from treated animals, only that there is a potential risk. Dr. Boisseau also advises that the EC will not accept "any risk, even theoritical [*sic*]".

202.   Dr. Boobis expresses the issue in slightly different terms that lead to the same result. He advises that there is no difference between the two levels of risk (which are otherwise identical in that they accept zero risk to consumers of meat from treated animals) but there is a difference in how the evidence has been interpreted. On the one hand, in light of its conclusions that *there is* a threshold below which no adverse effects will result, Codex has adopted a standard that will not result in risk. On the other hand, in light of its conclusions that *there is not* a threshold below which adverse effects will not result, the EC has adopted a measure that it considers will not result in risk. To the extent that the experts in their answers to other question advise that the EC has not demonstrated that there is not a threshold, the EC has also not demonstrated that the international standards is insufficient to achieve its acceptable level of risk, which is identical to that embodied in the international standards.

203.   The distinction made by the experts between theoretical risk and real risk is an important one in the context of this dispute also because it confirms that the sole reason for the EC to adopt a ban, rather than establish maximum acceptable exposure levels, was to avoid a theoretical risk, something that the Appellate Body has confirmed is not permissible under the *SPS Agreement*.

Q55. Do the Opinions of the European Communities or other scientific materials referred to by the European Communities evaluate the extent to which residues of growth promoting hormones in meat contribute to what the European Communities calls "additive risks arising from the cumulative exposures of humans to multiple hazards, in addition to the endogenous production of some of these hormones by animals and human beings"? Would your reply have been different at the time of adoption of the EC Directive in September 2003? If so, why? [see para. 151 of EC Replies to Panel Questions, paras. 43-44 of US Rebuttal Submission, paras. 83-85 of Canada's Rebuttal Submission]

204.   Drs. Boisseau, Boobis and Guttenplan confirm that the EC did not evaluate additive risks. Dr. Boisseau's answer suggests that he believes the EC's "position of principle" (that it would not accept even any theoretical risk) prevented it from even trying to assess the "additive risks". Dr. Boisseau only partly answers the question, in that he only assesses the EC's decision not to compare hormone levels in treated meat versus untreated meat; he does not comment on the EC's failure to compare the effects of hormones from treated meat to the effects from all other sources of hormones, including endogenous production.

205.   In the first sentence of his response, Dr. Guttenplan agrees that the EC did not evaluate "additive risks". It is not entirely clear, however, how his reference to the EC's comparison of exposure to hormones from treated meat and the background levels in prepubescent children is relevant to the evaluation of "additive risks". In fact, if anything the EC's selective evaluation of purported risks to sensitive populations from hormones from treated meat simply confirms that the EC has not evaluated "additive risks", because it has not conducted a similar evaluation of the risks posed by exposure from other sources of hormones, many of which are far greater than that from treated meat.

206.   For his part, Dr. Boobis distinguishes between "aggregate risk" (risk resulting from the aggregate exposure from all sources of a single substance) and "cumulative risk" (risk resulting from the cumulative exposure from all substances with a common mechanism of toxicity) and then confirms that the EC evaluated neither kind of risk. Dr. Boobis explains that one way to assess the "aggregate risk" from exposure to exogenous sources of substances that are also produced endogenously is to determine the tolerable upper intake level taking into account endogenous production, then determine whether exogenous sources change the circulating levels of the substances in the body. JECFA has essentially done this for the natural hormones when it assessed the exposure from meat from treated animals relative to the circulating levels and found that the former fell within the normal variation of the latter.

207.   Dr. Boobis acknowledges that a critical issue in assessing additive risks is whether there is a threshold below which adverse effects will not occur, something the EC argues is not the case with these hormones. As discussed previously, the EC's claim that there is no threshold for adverse effects from these hormones is simply not supported by the evidence. Therefore, its claim, from a "position of principle", that there are "additive risks" is similarly not credible in the absence of a quantitative evaluation of those risks. Indeed, the advice from the experts confirms Canada's identification of a critical flaw in the EC's claim that hormones from treated meat present an "additive risk": additive to what? In other words, what is the baseline risk from endogenous sources of hormones, or from other exogenous sources? Does exposure to hormones from meat from treated animals alter that risk? The EC does not ask, let alone answer, any of these questions, so it is difficult to see how its answer to the issue of additive risk can be legitimate.

Q56. Has JECFA/Codex considered in its risk assessment of the five hormones such "additive risks? Are there internationally recognized guidelines for conducting assessments of "additive risks"?

208.   Two of the three experts who responded to this question, both of whom are quite familiar with the work of JECFA, advised that JECFA does take into consideration "additive risk" (covering what Dr. Boobis refers to as "aggregate risk" but not "cumulative risk"). The manner in which JECFA does so is similar to the process described above in Canada's comments on the responses to Question 55. That is, because there is such a wide "margin of safety" (Dr. Boisseau) between the exposure from hormones from treated meat and the aggregate exposure from all other sources (both endogenous and exogenous) and because the increase in aggregate exposure from consuming meat from treated animals was considered to be "trivial" (Dr. Boobis), there would be no "additional risk" over that from background levels.

Q57.   Canada comments that "one single molecule that the European Communities considers so dangerous from meat derived from animals treated with hormone growth promoters is suddenly not at all that dangerous when consumed from meat from animals treated for therapeutic or zootechnical purposes. The European Communities' concern about the genotoxic potential of oestradiol 17β suddenly and inexplicably disappears." To what extent are hormone treatments of cattle for purposes other than growth promotion, such as for therapeutic or zootechnical purposes, taken into account by the European Communities, if at all, in its assessment of the cumulative effects from the consumption of meat containing residues of the hormones at issue? Would your reply have been different at the time of adoption of the EC Directive in September 2003? If so, why? [see para. 97 of Canada Rebuttal Submission; paras. 17-20 of US Opening Statement]

209.   Drs. Boisseau, Boobis and Guttenplan indicated that the EC did not take into account in its risk assessment the risks that arise from the use of these hormones for therapeutic purposes. Both Drs. Boisseau and Boobis share Canada's difficulty in reconciling the EC's conclusion that there is no threshold below which there are no adverse effects from hormones from treated meat and its authorization of the use of these substances for certain purposes and not others. Dr. Boisseau considers it a "problem of principle", whereas Dr. Boobis suggests that the only way this is justified is if one assumes that there is a dose-response relationship, something the EC rejects. Dr. Guttenplan fails to support his observation that the EC's explanation for why it allows such use is "reasonable". On the whole, the experts' advice indicates that the EC is trying to have it both ways: that hormones are genotoxic for some purposes and not others.

Q58.   Please comment on the EC statement in para. 94 of the EC Replies to Panel Questions that "the only rationale that can be inferred from the available scientific data is that the higher the exposure to residues from

these hormones, the greater the risk is likely to be", taking into account para. 105 of Canada Rebuttal Submission.

210. Drs. Boisseau, Guttenplan and Boobis all expressed in their own ways some difficulty with this statement by the EC. Dr. Boisseau suggests (with reference to his answer to Question 55) that this constitutes simply a "position of principle", one not supported by evidence that there are additive risks from higher doses of these hormones. Dr. Guttenplan simply offers that it is "indeed a very weak statement". His further suggestion that it is nonetheless better than an estimate of risk that is "wildly inaccurate" only reinforces Canada's concern that there is simply no basis for the EC to draw such a conclusion. Dr. Boobis confirms again that this statement is not supported by the evidence in that "within quite broad limits, higher exposure would not result in an increase in risk". Considering that hormone intake from meat from treated cattle represents only 1.5% of the ADI (the level below which there is no risk), it simply cannot be "inferred from the available scientific data" that exposure to more residues from meat from treated animals will lead to greater risk.

Q59. Does the scientific evidence referred to by the European Communities identify any adverse effects on the immune system from the consumption of meat from cattle treated with the growth promoting hormones at issue? Would your reply have been different at the time of adoption of the Directive in September 2003? If so, why? [see para. 132 of Canada Rebuttal Submission]

211. While the three experts that responded to this question all acknowledge that there can be adverse effects on the immune system from hormonally active substances, they all confirm that there is no scientific evidence that such effects will occur from exposure to doses of hormones that would be expected from residues in meat from treated animals. Dr. Boobis points to the "margin of safety" inherent in the dose relative to the background level; Dr. Boisseau indicates that the EC has not conducted the "quantitative risk assessment" that would be required to demonstrate risk from what are known to be dose-dependent adverse effects; and Dr. Guttenplan simply cites the absence of "definitive studies" (although he could have just as easily referred to the absence of "any studies") of low dose adverse immune system effects. All of the experts therefore confirm that for the EC to demonstrate that there are risks of adverse effects to the immune system from hormones from treated meat, it would have to demonstrate that such exposure would surpass the threshold at which such adverse effects would occur. It has not.

Q60. Does the scientific evidence referred to by the European Communities identify and evaluate whether there is a difference in terms of potential adverse effects on human health from the consumption of meat from cattle treated with hormones for growth promotion purposes when these hormones are administered as feed additives (MGA) or implanted? Are you aware of any differences?

212. Drs. Boisseau, Boobis and Guttenplan all indicate that the EC did not demonstrate that the potential for adverse effects differs depending on the route of administration. Only Dr. Boobis indicates that there may be a difference in effect as a result of misuse and abuse of implants, which would not occur in feed additives. However, he only acknowledges that the level of the exposure may be greater, and not that the level of risk of adverse effect necessarily would be greater. For the level of risk of adverse effects to be different, the exposure from one source of administration or the other would need to exceed the ADI, something that is quite unlikely to happen.

Q61. In your view and in the light of information provided by the parties as well as the work undertaken at JECFA and Codex, did the scientific evidence available to the European Communities at the time it adopted its Directive (September 2003) allow it to conduct an assessment (quantitatively or qualitatively) of the potential for adverse effects on human health arising from the consumption of meat from cattle treated with (a) progesterone; (b) testosterone; (c) trenbolone; (d) zeranol; and (e) melengestrol acetate? Would your response differ in light of the scientific evidence provided which is subsequent to the adoption of the EC Directive?

213. Both Drs. Boobis and Guttenplan indicate that sufficient scientific evidence was available to the EC to conduct a risk assessment of the five other hormones. Dr. Boisseau indicates that he is unaware of what the EC had available to it at the time, but goes on to suggest that it is never possible to eliminate all scientific uncertainty, and that the EC could have obtained any information it felt it did not have. Dr. Guttenplan specifically, and Dr. Boobis through reference to his other answers, both point to work done by JECFA as establishing that the data are complete enough to conduct risk assessments. It also seems to be the case, especially from Dr. Boobis' reference to his other answers, that since there is sufficient evidence to demonstrate the safety of oestradiol 17β , which is considered to be the more potent substance, the same type of data and principles of analysis that demonstrate the safety of this substance indicate that the other five hormones will also be safe.

Q62. Does the scientific evidence relied upon by the European Communities support the EC contention that the new scientific studies that have been initiated since 1997 have identified new important gaps, insufficiencies and contradictions in the scientific information and knowledge now available on these hormones such that more scientific studies are necessary before the risk to human health from the consumption of meat from cattle treated with these hormones for growth promotion purposes can be assessed? Would your reply have been different at the time of adoption of the Directive in September 2003? If so, why?

214. While Drs. Boisseau, Boobis and Guttenplan all indicate that new scientific evidence has raised new and interesting issues, they do not agree that this evidence suggests important gaps in the understanding of the safety of these sub-

stances. Dr. Boisseau does not believe that these new data are contrary to previous conclusions or that they make it impossible to conduct a risk assessment. Dr. Guttenplan suggests some new areas of potential study, but some of them are already answered (see, for example, Dr. Boobis' review of the effect of consuming meat from treated animals on blood levels of oestrogen); some of them are not necessary for the completion of a risk assessment; and at least one of them (epidemiological studies of consumption of treated versus non-treated meat) will never be able to demonstrate the linkages that Dr. Guttenplan would like to see (see discussion of confounding factors above). Dr. Boobis provides the most comprehensive assessment of the new scientific data, and addresses each and every study that the EC claims raise new scientific issues. As a result of his review, he concludes that the additional information "was often not definitive, sometimes it was not relevant, in some instances it confirmed or expanded upon previous knowledge".

III.   COMMENTS ON INTERNATIONAL ORGANIZATION REPLIES

Q1.   Please briefly describe the procedure for the elaboration and adoption of an international standard by Codex. What is the decision-making process for the adoption of an international standard?

215.   Canada has no comments to make at this time.

Q2.   Please briefly explain the differences between Codex standards, codes of practice, guidelines, principles and other recommendations.

216.   Canada has no comments to make at this time.

Q3.   Please identify any international guidance documents relevant to the conduct of a risk assessment with respect to veterinary drug residues. Since when have they been available? Please also indicate if there is any relevant ongoing work at Codex.

217.   See Canada's comments on the experts' answers to Question 3.

Q4.   The European Communities states that there is "no Codex standard specifically on the risk assessment of effects of residues of veterinary drugs" but a general one on microbiological assessment. Is this correct? Which guidelines or principles have been used by JECFA in the conduct of its risk assessments with respect to the hormones at issue? [see para. 192 of EC Rebuttal Submission (US case)]

218.   See Canada's comments on the experts' answers to Question 4.

Q5.   Please briefly describe the three components of a risk analysis exercise (risk assessment, risk management and risk communication) as defined by Codex and explain how they differ.

219.   See Canada's comments on the experts' answers to Question 5.

Q6.   Please briefly describe the four steps of a risk assessment (hazard identification, hazard characterization, exposure assessment and risk characterization) as identified by Codex, indicating any relevant sources.

220.   See Canada's comments on the experts' answers to Question 6.

Q7.   Please comment on the EC statement made in para. 140 of the EC Replies to Panel Questions that "which ever approach of a risk assessment is followed, they are all based on a deterministic approach to risk characterization [and that they] have serious limitations in non-linear situations, such as in the current case regarding hormones". Are these situations addressed by the risk assessment guidance currently available from the Codex Alimentarius Commission? [see Canada's comments in para. 72 of its Rebuttal Submission]

221.   See Canada's comments on the experts' answers to Question 7.

Q8.   Do JECFA or Codex materials confirm Canada's statement in para. 80 of its Rebuttal Submission that "...while international risk assessment techniques suggest that a dose-response assessment is optional for biological or physical agents when the data cannot be obtained, a dose-response assessment should always be conducted for chemical agents..."? [see Exhibit CDA-25]

222.   See Canada's comments on the answers from the experts to Question 37.

Q9.   Please provide definitions for the following terms: Acceptable Daily Intake (ADI) and Maximum Residue Limit (MRL).

223.   See Canada's comments on the answers from the experts to Question 8.

Q10.   Please describe the procedure followed by JECFA in the identification of ADIs and the development of recommendations on MRLs. Please also identify and describe any steps that are taken in the risk assessment process to build a margin of safety into to the final recommendation.

224.   See Canada's comments on the answers from the experts to Question 8.

Q11.   Please confirm or comment on the following Canadian statement: "it is recognized that JECFA only allocates an ADI for a food additive or veterinary drug under review when JECFA considers that its scientific data base is complete and that there are no outstanding scientific issues". [see para. 68 of Canada Rebuttal Submission]

225.   See Canada's comments on the answers by the experts to Question 9.

Q12.   In para. 129 and 168 of its Replies to the Panel's questions, the European Communities states that "JECFA's traditional mandate does not allow it to examine all risk management options but restricts it to either propose MRLs or not." Does Codex have risk management options other than (1) the establishment of an MRL, (2) the establishment that an MRL is not necessary, or (3) no recommendation?

226.   See Canada's comments on the answers from the experts to Question 10.

Q13.   With respect to the data used in the evaluation of chemical substances, such as the hormones at issue, what are the data requirements for JECFA's work and how are they determined? Who provides data for such evaluations? Are any records/archives kept by JECFA? Do any confidentiality rules apply to data submitted to JECFA or should all data be publicly available? If confidentiality rules apply, in which circumstances? [see paras. 95-96 of EC Rebuttal Submission (US case), paras. 78-79 of EC Rebuttal Submission (Canada case), para. 123 of Canada Rebuttal Submission]

227.   JECFA confirms in its response that "[u]npublished confidential studies that are submitted will be safeguarded and will be used only for evaluation purposes by JECFA", and that "confidential data will either be returned to the submitter at the submitter's expense or destroyed after the evaluations have been completed."

Q14.   How are experts involved in JECFA's work selected? What are the selection criteria?

228.   Canada has no comments to make at this time.

Q15.   Please provide the definition of the term Good Veterinary Practice (GVP). Are there any relevant Codex standards, guidelines, or recommendations relating to GVP?

229.   See Canada's comments on the responses from the experts to Question 44.

Q16.   Please provide an update on the status of international standards with respect to the six hormones at issue. What are the remaining procedures before the adoption of a standard on melengestrol acetate (MGA)? What is the timeframe for their completion?

230.   Canada has no comments to make at this time.

Q17.   Is the table in Exhibit CDA-32 outlining the chronology of JECFA's assessment of the hormones at issue and the resulting documentation complete?

231.   JECFA confirms that, with the addition of a reference to the 66th JECFA meeting held 20-28 February 2006 , at which meeting JECFA further deliberated on the MRLs previously proposed for MGA, Exhibit CDA-32 is complete.

Q18.   What happens if new evidence or studies throw into doubt a Codex standard? What are the procedures for incorporating more recent developments into Codex work? Has the European Communities approached Codex for this purpose with respect to the hormones at issue in this case?

232.   See Canada's comments on the answers by the experts to Question 33.

Q19.   What would be the procedures for requesting JECFA to re-evaluate its recommendations in light of new concerns/evidence? How would an amendment be adopted? Has the European Communities approached JECFA for this purpose with respect to the hormones at issue in this case? [see Exhibit EC-63]

233.   JECFA's response states that "[t]he re-evaluations of compounds follow the same procedure as an evaluation performed for the first time, with clear identification of the new data that were assessed." See also Canada's comments on the answers from the experts to Question 33.

Q20.   What were the reasons for the re-evaluation by JECFA of the three natural hormones in 1999? Were the residues data used for the three natural hormones in 1999 the same as those used in 1988? What additional information was used for the JECFA evaluation in 1999 of the three natural hormones which was not available in 1988? How did the conclusions differ? What led JECFA to establish ADIs for the three natural hormones? What are the implications of establishing ADIs? Why were JECFA's more recent recommendations not considered by CCRVDF? What is the status of these recommendations? [see paras. 96-97 of EC Rebuttal Submission (US case), paras. 79-80 of EC Rebuttal Submission (Canada case)]

234.   See Canada's comments on the answers by the experts to Question 33.

Q21.   What is the mandate of the International Agency for Research on Cancer?

235.   Canada has no comments to make at this time.

Q22.   Who are the members of the IARC?

236.   Canada has no comments to make at this time.

Q23.   What are IARC Monographs? How are they prepared?

237.   Canada has no comments to make at this time.

Q24. Please briefly explain the groupings that are used to categorize "potentially carcinogenic agents"? What are the implications when an "agent" is placed in one of the IARC categories?

238.   The Panel may wish to request further explanation from IARC regarding the considerations that determine the classification by IARC of a substance as belonging to Group 1, 2A or 2B, as well as the consequences or implications of such a classification.

Q25. Which of the six hormones at issue in this dispute (oestradiol 17β, progesterone, testosterone, trenbolone acetate, zeranol, and melengestrol acetate) have been evaluated by the IARC? Have any specific risks from the consumption of meat from cattle treated with these growth promotion hormones been assessed by the IARC?

239.   IARC's response states that it has evaluated the three natural hormones but not the three synthetic hormones. IARC's evaluation and classification of the three natural hormones appears not to have taken into account the different potential sources of these hormones and the different potential levels of exposure of individuals. Thus the kind of risk assessment that was conducted by JECFA was apparently not carried out by IARC. IARC does not respond to the question about the specific risks from exposure to residues of hormones in meat from treated animals.

Q26. How does the work of the IARC feed into the work of national regulatory agencies or international bodies, in particular with respect to assessments of risks from the consumption of meat from cattle treated with the six growth promoting hormones at issue in this dispute?

240.   IARC's response to Question 26 is the same as that to Question 25.

IV.   CONCLUDING COMMENTS

241.   The experts and international bodies have provided extensive advice on the scientific and technical matters at issue in this dispute. The experts' responses exhibited general agreement that the scientific evidence and information does not support the conclusions of the EC's evaluation of these six hormones. While this is the case for most of the issues addressed by the experts, several issues that are central to the Panel's review of the EC's evaluation warrant specific mention.

242.   In particular, the experts indicate that the scientific evidence does not support the following conclusions:

- that all or some of the hormones (but in particular, oestradiol 17β) present a risk of adverse effects (such as genotoxicity) that do not exhibit an exposure dose below which they will not occur (*i.e.*, a threshold);

- that exposure to the hormones from residues in meat from treated animals will be so significant in proportion to the endogenous hormone levels present in certain sensitive populations such that adverse effects will occur;

- that the exposure from this single source of hormones is sufficiently "additive" to the exposure from all sources of hormones to increase the risk of occurrence of adverse effects;

- that the failure to follow GVP will result in exposure to the hormones at doses capable of causing adverse effects and that the hormones are administered in Canada in a manner that fails to follow this GVP; and

- that the scientific evidence is insufficient to conduct an assessment of the safety of the five hormones other than oestradiol 17β.

243.   Canada looks forward to meeting with the experts and to the opportunity to discuss these and other scientific and technical issues in more detail.

ANNEX F-5

COMMENTS BY CANADA TO THE COMMENTS OF THE
EUROPEAN COMMUNITIES ON THE REPLIES OF THE
SCIENTIFIC EXPERTS, CODEX, JECFA AND IARC
TO QUESTIONS POSED BY THE PANEL

(12 July 2006)

TABLE OF CONTENTS

		Page
I.	INTRODUCTION	6919
II.	COMMENTS ON THE COMMENTS FROM THE EC ON THE RESPONSES FROM THE EXPERTS	6921
	A. General Definitions	6921
	B. Risk Assessment Techniques	6921
	C. Assessment of Oestradiol 17β	6926
	D. Consumption of Meat Containing Hormones	6932
	(a) Carcinogenicity	6932
	(b) Residue Analysis	6936
	(c) Dose-Response Relationship	6941
	(d) Sensitive Populations	6942
	(e) Bioavailability	6944
	(f) Good Veterinary Practice (GVP)	6945
	(g) Other	6949
III.	COMMENTS ON THE COMMENTS FROM THE EC ON THE RESPONSES FROM THE INTERNATIONAL BODIES	6953
IV.	CONCLUDING COMMENTS	6954

V. INTRODUCTION

1. Canada is pleased to have this opportunity to comment on the comments by the European Communities (EC) on the responses by the experts and by JECFA, Codex and IARC. Before turning to comments on the specific responses, several issues of a general nature raised by the EC warrant mention.

2.   First, the EC suggests in many of its comments that it is either Canada or the experts that need to demonstrate that adverse effects *will not* arise from consuming residues of hormones in meat from treated animals.[1] It is important to recall that it is the EC that has adopted bans on these hormones as growth promoters on the basis that they cause adverse effects, and it is the EC that has brought this case against Canada, alleging that these bans are justified under the *SPS Agreement*. Any suggestion by the EC that the burden is on Canada to prove that adverse effects will not arise runs contrary to the applicable WTO rules on the allocation of burden of proof. Similarly, any suggestion by the EC that the experts must demonstrate that such adverse effects will not arise demonstrates a misunderstanding of the role of the experts in these proceedings.

3.   Therefore, it is the EC – and not Canada or the experts – that must demonstrate that it has scientific evidence that supports its claim that adverse effects *will* arise from consuming residues of hormones in meat from treated animals. Consequently, the focus of the discussion should not be on the manner of adoption of the international standards and their scientific underpinnings but rather on the EC's opinions and whether they meet the requirements of the *SPS Agreement*.

4.   Second, the EC makes a number of assertions in its comments that that are accompanied by citations of articles that have not been filed as exhibits. Canada has been able to locate some of the articles, but not all of them and, accordingly, limits its comments to those it has been able to locate. However, to the extent that the EC refers to this material in relation to claims about scientific evidence that it is making for the first time, and then fails to provide the supporting material, the claims remain no more than unsupported assertions that should be given no weight by the Panel.

5.   Third, in its comments on certain experts' responses, the EC questions the relevance of the views of Dr. Boisseau and Dr. Boobis because, according to the EC, they did not carry out "experiments on hormones" and publish related scientific papers.[2] The *curricula vitae* of both these experts, which demonstrate extensive experience in the risk assessment of many veterinary drugs as well as other chemicals, and the quality of their replies, speak for themselves. While it is the EC's prerogative to disagree with the answers provided by any of the experts, there can be no doubt about the professional competence of Dr. Boisseau and Dr. Boobis that underlies their answers to the Panel's questions.

6.   Fourth, the EC tries to impugn the comments from Codex and JECFA, but not those from IARC, by questioning the legality of the transmittal of these comments by the Codex and JECFA Secretariats respectively to the Panel, without having complied with internal procedures that were not identified by the EC.

---

[1]   For example, see EC Comments on the Replies by the Panel Experts, in relation to Questions 18, 20 and 59 (EC Comments).

[2]   *Ibid.*, Questions 2, 17, 21 and 42.

It would not be appropriate for the Panel to inquire into the question of compliance with the internal rules of other international bodies. Also, the information provided by the Codex and JECFA Secretariats are matters of public record. In any event, it would be open to the EC to take any steps it deems appropriate within Codex and JECFA to deal with this issue.

7.　　Canada will address the EC's comments on the responses of the international bodies in Part III of this submission.

8.　　And finally, given the short time-frame for the preparation of these comments, the absence of comments by Canada on certain assertions by the EC should not, of course, be construed as agreement with such assertions.

VI.　COMMENTS ON THE COMMENTS FROM THE EC ON THE RESPONSES FROM THE EXPERTS

A.　General Definitions

9.　　In its comments on the experts' responses to **Question 1**, the EC quibbles with Dr. Boisseau's definition of the hormones at issue in this dispute. To the extent that the issues raised by the EC are relevant, Canada will address them below.

10.　　The EC's attempt to discredit Dr. Boisseau's response to **Question 2** by referring to his earlier indication of which questions he intended to answer is unjustified. Other experts, such as Dr. Cogliano and Dr. de Brabander, answered questions that they did not originally indicate they would answer; some of them in the end declined to answer questions they had earlier indicated they would answer. That is the experts' prerogative and nothing more should be read into an expert responding or not responding to particular questions.

B.　Risk Assessment Techniques

11.　　In its comments on the experts' responses to the Panel's Questions in this section (**Questions 3-12**), the EC raises several issues that warrant comment at this stage. These are:

- the meaning of the phrase "risk assessment techniques developed by the relevant international organizations", as found in Article 5.1 of the *SPS Agreement* and its relevance to this dispute;
- the relevance of the different mandates of the European Medicines Agency's Committee for Veterinary Medicinal Products (CVMP) and the Scientific Committee on Veterinary Measures relating to Public Health (SCVPH);
- the distinction between risk assessment and risk management;
- the meaning of "no appreciable risk";
- the distinction between qualitative and quantitative risk assessments and the relevance of this distinction to the meaning of "risk assessment" as found in the *SPS Agreement*;

- the existence of scientific uncertainty; and
- the relationship between weight of evidence and minority science.

"Risk Assessment Techniques" in Article 5.1 of the SPS Agreement

12. In its comments on the responses to **Questions 3, 4** and **6**, the EC attempts to dismiss the various international guidance documents identified by the experts and JECFA and Codex as being relevant to the conduct of veterinary drug risk assessments. In doing so, the EC distorts the meaning of the phrase "risk assessment techniques developed by the relevant international organizations" in Article 5.1 of the *SPS Agreement*.[3] The thrust of the EC submission is that unless an international guidance document is formally adopted by Codex it is not "legally binding" and therefore cannot constitute a "risk assessment technique" under Article 5.1 and is irrelevant.[4] However, the EC's line of reasoning is misguided. The question is not whether the "risk assessment techniques" are "legally binding" but whether the "risk assessment techniques" assist in determining whether the risk assessment at issue is "appropriate to the circumstances." For a risk assessment to be "appropriate to the circumstances", the WTO Member must "tak[e] into account the risk assessment techniques...". Failure to do so suggests that the assessment at issue is not "appropriate to the circumstances".

13. To the extent that the EC is suggesting by the phrase "legally binding" that "risk assessment techniques" must be formally established by one of the international organizations listed in Annex A(3) as a "standard, guideline and recommendation", the EC is incorrect. Had the Members intended such an effect, then they would have used "standard, guideline and recommendation" in Article 5.1. The fact that they did not implies this is not the case. The use of the term "technique" suggests that the treaty drafters were referring to the technical aspects of risk assessment methodology. Some "techniques" may be embodied in a formally established "standard, guideline, and recommendation", while others may not. The "risk assessment technique" must be "developed by the relevant international organization." Without question, Codex is a "relevant international organization". Given that Codex relies on the work of JECFA to conduct risk assessments and develop risk assessment techniques for food additives, contaminants and veterinary drugs, it can be inferred that JECFA is a "relevant international organization" for the purposes of Article 5.1.

14. In this case, "risk assessment techniques" developed by Codex include the four steps of the risk assessment process (hazard identification, hazard characterization, exposure assessment and risk characterization). Those developed by

---

[3]   Article 5.1 of the *SPS Agreement* reads in full "Members shall ensure that their sanitary or phytosanitary measures are based on an assessment, as appropriate to the circumstances, of the risks to human, animal or plant life or health, taking into account risk assessment techniques developed by the relevant international organizations."

[4]   See EC Comments, Questions 3, 4 and 6.

JECFA are embodied in EHC 70[5] and the JECFA Procedures.[6] More specific to this case are techniques such as the assessment of the quality and quantity of available study data, determination of pivotal studies and the NOAELs (No Observed Adverse Effects Levels), the conduct of the dose-response assessment, the selection of appropriate safety factors and the establishment of ADIs (Acceptable Daily Intakes). Therefore, assessments of veterinary drugs that fail to take into account these techniques are not, *prima facie*, "appropriate to the circumstances" and, therefore, do not satisfy the requirements of Article 5.1 and the definition of risk assessment in Annex A(4).

Relevance of the different mandates of the CVMP and SCVPH

15.   In its comments on responses to **Question 3**, the EC's attempt to discredit Dr. Boisseau's advice concerning the CVMP's ability to assess pharmacologically active substances used in veterinary medicine "without any written guideline about risk assessment" is confused and illogical. The EC appears to imply that techniques used by the CVMP in conducting risk assessments are not applicable to the work of the SCVPH on the basis that the SCVPH's mandate differs from that of the CVMP. This appears to be an indirect attempt to explain the differing conclusions reached by these committees in relation to adverse effects caused by the use of hormones in animal husbandry. However, the fact that these two committees assess different uses of the same substances has no bearing on the nature of the risk assessment techniques employed. For instance, the techniques adopted to determine whether oestradiol 17β is genotoxic apply regardless of the use to which the substance will be put. If oestradiol 17β, when used for therapeutic purposes, has a dose threshold, it is illogical to conclude that it does *not* have a dose threshold when used for growth-promotion purposes. The EC cannot escape from the CVMP's conclusion that oestradiol 17β is not genotoxic by referring to different committee mandates.

Risk Assessment/Risk Management

16.   The EC attempts, in its comments on responses to **Question 5**, to dismiss all the explanations provided by the experts of the three components of "risk analysis" by reiterating its previous arguments concerning the differing scope of, on the one hand, risk assessment as defined by the *SPS Agreement*, and, on the other hand, risk assessment as a component of Codex's risk analysis. As Canada has explained in detail in its Rebuttal Submission,[7] the EC is attempting to insulate its SPS measure, *i.e.*, its ban on all meat and meat products derived from

---

[5]   International Program on Chemical Safety, *Principles for the Safety Assessment of Food Additives and Contaminants in Food, Environmental Health Criteria 70* (Geneva: WHO, 1987) (EHC 70) (Exhibit CDA-43).

[6]   JECFA, *Procedures for Recommending Maximum Residue Limits – Residues of Veterinary Drugs in Food (1987 – 1999)* (Rome: FAO/WHO, 2000) (JECFA Procedures) (Exhibit CDA-44).

[7]   Canada Rebuttal Submission, at paras. 55-65.

treated animals, from Panel review by suggesting that the "wider" risk assessment contemplated by the *SPS Agreement* includes risk management considerations and that risk management is *a priori* non-reviewable because it is related to a WTO Member's autonomous right to set its appropriate level of protection.

17.   As Canada explained, the EC cannot escape the obligation in Article 5.1 of the *SPS Agreement* to base its measure on a risk assessment by claiming that a component of the risk assessment includes non-reviewable risk management considerations. The Appellate Body's statement that Article 5.1 was "intended as a countervailing factor in respect of the right of Members to set their appropriate level of protection"[8] implies that risk management and the autonomous right of each WTO Member to set its level of protection cannot be used to avoid the obligation in Article 5.1.

The concept of "Appreciable Risk"

18.   The EC arguments concerning "appreciable risk" are a direct challenge to one of the cornerstones of modern risk assessment techniques widely employed by risk assessment bodies at both the national and international level. The EC attempts to discredit this concept by asserting that it is "subjective", "qualitative" and "unspecific".[9] However, these arguments reflect a profound misunderstanding of this concept and its role in the risk assessment process.

19.   The phrase "without appreciable risk" is found in Codex's definition of ADI: "an estimate by JECFA of the amount of a veterinary drug, expressed on a body weight basis, that can be ingested daily over a lifetime *without appreciable health risk*".[10] To understand what is meant by "appreciable health risk", or "appreciable risk", one must consider the risk assessment process as a whole. On the basis of detailed scientific experimentation, observation and analysis of empirical data, a NOAEL is set for each observed adverse effect. The NOAEL represents the dose level at or below which no adverse effect is empirically observed or measured in the target organism.

20.   The NOAEL is then adjusted by safety factors to derive the ADI. If no effect is observed, then, logically, there is no observable or empirically ascertainable risk. Appreciable, in the sense used in the ADI, means observable, ascertainable or identifiable. Thus, far from being "subjective" or "qualitative", as the term is used by the EC, the identification of a lifetime daily intake that is "without appreciable risk" is based on quantitative scientific experiments that lead to objective, measurable observations. Indeed, the very purpose of the risk assessment methodology used by JECFA and Codex is to identify quantitatively the point at which risks are not observed or ascertained.

---

[8]   *EC – Measures Concerning Meat and Meat Products (Hormones)*, Report of the Appellate Body, WT/DS26/AB/R, WT/DS48/AB/R, adopted February 13, 1998, at para. 177 (*EC – Hormones*).
[9]   See EC Comments, Questions 8, 16, 25 and 54.
[10]   See Codex's reply to Panel IO Question 9 [emphasis added].

21.   When "appreciable risk" is properly understood, the EC's comments do not make sense. An ADI based on "no appreciable risk" implies that there is no scientifically identifiable or ascertainable risk if the daily intake is equal to or below the ADI. Of course, the ADI does not eliminate the theoretical uncertainty that always exists as "science can *never* provide *absolute* certainty that a given substance will not *ever* have adverse health effects".[11] However, this theoretical uncertainty, or hypothetical risk, is not the kind of risk that, under Article 5.1 of the *SPS Agreement*, is to be assessed.[12] Thus, assuming that good veterinary practice is followed, the difference between the level of risk inherent in an ADI and the EC's purported "zero risk" level of protection, is not ascertainable or identifiable risk, but theoretical or hypothetical and is not the kind of risk to be assessed under Article 5.1.

Quantitative and Qualitative Risk Assessments

22.   In its comments on the responses to **Questions 11**, **16** and **36**, the EC attempts to neutralize the evidence of Dr. Boisseau and Dr. Boobis concerning the distinction between quantitative and qualitative risk assessments by claiming that the Appellate Body has confirmed that qualitative risk assessments are "acceptable" under the *SPS Agreement*. However, as Canada explained in its Rebuttal Submission, although the Appellate Body concluded that a risk assessment need not establish a "minimum magnitude of risk" in order to be consistent with Article 5.1, it did not discuss qualitative and quantitative risk assessments, writ large.[13] Thus, the EC's attempt to deduce from this conclusion the more general proposition that a qualitative risk assessment is acceptable, *a priori*, under the *SPS Agreement* distorts the conclusions of the Appellate Body. The critical question is whether the risk assessment at issue evaluates the potential for adverse effects in a manner "appropriate to the circumstances ... taking into account risk assessment techniques developed by the relevant international organizations". If the nature of the substance is such that no threshold for adverse effects can be established, then a dose-response assessment is not necessary. However, when scientific evidence demonstrates, as it does in this case, that a dose threshold below which no adverse effects occur can be established for the substance in question, a risk assessment that fails to include a quantitative dose-response assessment would not be "appropriate to the circumstances."

The existence of Scientific Uncertainty

23.   In its comments on the experts' responses to **Question 12**, the EC attempts to impugn the use of safety factors to address certain types of scientific

---

[11]   *EC – Hormones*, at para. 186 [emphasis in original].
[12]   *EC – Hormones*, at para. 186.
[13]   Canada Rebuttal Submission, at paras. 81-82. Also see *EC – Hormones*, Report of the Appellate Body, at para. 186.

uncertainty.[14] It suggests that where new scientific evidence casts doubt on previous scientific conclusions, safety factors cannot adequately compensate for the resulting uncertainty. Whether this assertion is correct as a matter of principle is debatable; in any event, it does not apply in this case. As the experts have amply demonstrated, the "new" scientific evidence referred to by the EC does not call into question the scientific conclusions concerning the potential for adverse effects from residues of hormones in meat from treated cattle, particularly conclusions relating to their carcinogenic potential. The EC is simply trying to create scientific uncertainty where there is none.

The relationship between "weight of evidence" and minority scientific opinion

24.   In its comments on the experts' responses to **Question 12**, the EC highlights Dr. Boobis's use of the term of "weight of evidence" and seeks to equate the term with "mainstream scientific views". The EC further suggests that using a "weight of evidence" approach forces WTO Members to dismiss or ignore minority scientific views. These arguments reveal a misunderstanding of the term as used in the context of risk assessments. The term "weight of evidence" is a term of art used to characterize the interpretation of all scientific evidence relevant to the causal hypothesis under review, in drawing conclusions about causal relationships. Not all scientific evidence will be of equivalent importance, or weight, in providing information about presence or absence of a causal relationship. A "weight of evidence" approach involves assessing the relative strength and conclusiveness of all relevant data, including the quality of testing methods, size and power of study design, consistency of results across studies, and biological plausibility of exposure-response relationships and statistical associations. It is not equivalent to "mainstream scientific views", but is a process that should underpin the formation of scientific opinions generally, be they mainstream or minority, in order to ensure that they are scientifically sound. Dr. Boobis appears to use "weight of evidence" to indicate that the EC conclusions were not based on an evaluation of *all* pertinent scientific evidence, including an assessment of the relative strength of that evidence.

C.   Assessment of Oestradiol 17β

25.   The EC makes several comments on the experts' responses to **Questions 13** and **14** that warrant further comment. These include the EC's: 1) inaccurate and misleading descriptions of the adverse effects it purports to have identified; 2) exaggeration of the role of epidemiological studies in risk assessments of the kind appropriate to these circumstances; 3) repeated attempt to embellish scien-

---

[14]   The EC does not appear to suggest that the use of safety factors is inappropriate to address the scientific uncertainty arising from inter-species and intra-species variability. Had it done so, it would be challenging a fundamental risk assessment technique widely employed by its own scientific committees and regulators.

tific results to demonstrate *in vivo* genotoxicity from oestradiol 17β; and 4) un-justified reliance on several new scientific studies and its criticism of the experts for failing to take these into account.

Inaccurate and misleading descriptions of the purported adverse effects

26.   In response to the advice from the experts under **Question 13** that the SCVPH opinions do not amount to a risk assessment, the EC makes several confusing assertions about the nature of the adverse effects that it purports to have identified. In particular, on several occasions it uses interchangeably the terms 'carcinogenicity' and 'genotoxic effect', linking them both to the interaction of these hormones with hormonal receptors.[15] The EC's description of the issues is both wrong and misleading, so for purposes of restoring clarity to the issues it is useful to restate the basic controversy related to the potential carcinogenicity of these hormones and to summarize the advice of the experts.

27.   The claim made by the EC is that oestradiol 17β is carcinogenic because it both *initiates* tumours and *promotes* tumour growth, the former through a hypothesized genotoxic effect and the latter through interaction with hormonal receptors.[16] To the extent that the international scientific authorities and the experts consulted by the Panel agree with the general proposition that oestradiol 17β is carcinogenic, they unanimously attribute this effect exclusively to its interaction with hormone receptors.[17] At the same time, the experts have confirmed again that there is no scientific evidence demonstrating that oestradiol 17β initiates tumours through a genotoxic effect.[18]

28.   The distinction between these two *different* mechanisms of carcinogenicity is an important one because the findings of receptor-mediated carcinogenicity by JECFA, IARC and other scientific authorities have been exclusively attributed to circumstances involving *high dose exposure* to hormones, something that is clearly not a factor in exposure to dietary sources of hormones, including that from residues in meat from treated cattle. The EC's careless interchanging of the mechanisms of action and the role of dose is simply an attempt to confuse the scientific evidence related to carcinogenicity.

---

[15] See EC Comments, at p. 12 (Question 13).
[16] The EC's claim in its comments that the "*genotoxic effect* of oestradiol 17β *is associated* with its hormonal activity" [emphasis added] is simply nonsensical. *Ibid.*
[17] Canada's Rebuttal Submission, at paras 90-95.
[18] The EC's statement that the "carcinogenicity of estrogens is primarily due to oxidative stress/DNA adduct formation caused by the catechols [*sic*] metabolites of estrogens" is unsupported by any of the evidence submitted by the EC and is not supported by the experts. *Ibid.*

Role of epidemiological studies

29.   The EC on several occasions in its comments relies on the results of epidemiological studies,[19] in particular those conducted or sponsored by IARC, as well as those on which the 2002 US Report on Carcinogens was based, as the central support for its claims that it has identified and evaluated adverse effects from the consumption of meat from treated animals. In doing so, the EC vastly overestimates the role of epidemiological studies in risk assessments of the kind required in these circumstances, that is, of exposure to substances in such small doses.

30.   None of the studies cited by the EC purports to identify a relationship between cancer and residues of hormones from meat derived from treated animals. It is true that in 1987 IARC classified steroidal oestrogens as a Group I carcinogen on the basis of observed relationships between cancer and treatments using high doses of oestrogens.[20] However, the Appellate Body has already specifically rejected the claim that this classification demonstrates anything about the substances at issue here. In upholding the findings of the panel, it found that the IARC Monographs:

> constitute general studies which do indeed show the existence of a general risk of cancer [from oestrogen]; but they do not focus on and do not address the particular kind of risk here at stake - the carcinogenic or genotoxic potential of the residues of those hormones found in meat derived from cattle to which the hormones had been administered for growth promotion purposes - as is required by paragraph 4 of Annex A of the *SPS Agreement*.[21]

31.   Since that time, IARC further classified postmenopausal oestrogen therapy[22] and combined oral contraceptives[23] as Group I carcinogens, again on the basis of observed relationships between cancer and these treatments. However, what all of these classifications have in common is that they involve prolonged, high dose exposure to various forms of oestrogen. Therefore, the reasoning used by the Appellate Body in the above excerpt applies equally to the EC's invocation of more recent IARC findings, as well as to any use of other findings that are based on the results of epidemiological studies.

---

[19]   See EC Comments, at pp. 12 (Question 13), 20 (Questions 20), 23 (Question 23) and 24 (Question 24).

[20]   *EC – Hormones*, Report of the Appellate Body, at paras. 199-200. Also, the note attached to IARC's classification indicates that this "evaluation applies to the group of compounds as a whole and not necessarily to all individual compounds within the group" (online: http://monographs.iarc.fr/ENG/Classification/crthgr01.php).

[21]   *Ibid.*, at para. 200.

[22]   IARC, Vol. 91, Monograph No. 2, Section 5, *Combined Estrogen-Progestogen Menopausal Therapy* (Lyon, France: 2005) (Exhibit CDA-48).

[23]   IARC, Vol. 91, Monograph No. 1, Section 5, *Combined Estrogen-Progestogen Contraceptives* (Lyon, France: 2005) (Exhibit CDA-49).

32.   As the experts have confirmed,[24] it is simply not possible to draw *specific* conclusions about adverse effects from residues of hormones in meat from treated animals on the basis of epidemiological studies. For that reason, these kinds of studies have limited usefulness in a risk assessment of the nature required to justify the EC's measure. They may help in identifying possible adverse effects, but they reveal nothing about the potential for occurrence of such adverse effects from a single dietary source of hormones.

33.   The EC's claim that epidemiological studies, such as those on which IARC's classification of oestrogen as a carcinogen are based, support its claim is all the more surprising in light of its subsequent comment on Dr. Guttenplan's response to **Question 13**. The EC comments that it:

> agrees with the statement by Dr. Guttenplan that there are basically no direct epidemiological studies comparing matched populations consuming meat from untreated and hormone-treated cattle. However, apart from the ethical concerns, it is difficult to conduct such direct experiments in the presence of so many other confounding factors because of feasibility limitations for observational studies.

34.   In this statement, the EC acknowledges the absence of epidemiological studies that demonstrate that there are risks from consuming residues of hormones from meat from treated animals. More importantly, the EC acknowledges the significant limitations of such studies to support such a conclusion.

Embellishment of scientific evidence related to in vivo genotoxicity

35.   In its comments on the experts' responses to **Questions 7, 13** and **18**, the EC refers to several scientific studies in support of its claim that oestradiol 17β can cause genotoxicity *in vivo*. It is important to recall that the experts are very clear that evidence of *in vivo* genotoxicity, as well as evidence that the mode of action of genotoxicity is of a type that does not exhibit a threshold, are required to confirm findings of *in vitro* genotoxicity before it can be concluded that such genotoxicity is relevant to the development of cancer.[25] The studies cited by the EC do not satisfy these requirements.

36.   In the first study referred to by the EC, by Bhat *et al.*, the authors conclude that their data "provide evidence that oxidant stress plays a crucial role in estrogen-induced carcinogenesis". However, as Dr. Boobis has indicated in his responses, oxidative stress as a genotoxic mode of action is of a type that is universally considered to demonstrate a threshold response, due to the "efficiency of endogenous antioxidant systems".[26] Therefore, this study does not demon-

---

[24]   See experts' responses to Question 26.
[25]   See experts' responses to Questions 16, 18 and 19.
[26]   Dr. Boobis's response to Question 16. See also EFSA, *Opinion of the Scientific Committee on a Request from EFSA Related to a Harmonised Approach for Risk Assessment of Substances which are*

strate anything that was not already known, but simply confirms that genotoxicity can result from overwhelming the antioxidant systems with high doses of oestradiol 17β.

37.   In its comments on the responses to **Questions 16, 18** and **62**, the EC introduces, also for the first time, a review by Yager and Davidson that the EC claims confirms that the "evidence is now sufficient to support a role for the estrogen metabolites which include the genotoxic, mutagenic estrogen quinones in estrogen carcinogenicity." The first point is that this article is only a review of other studies so provides no new evidence on its own. Second, like the studies conducted by Bhat *et al.*, this review postulates an oxidative stress damage pathway for genotoxicity, which, as noted above, is considered to have a threshold.

New scientific material cited by the EC and the role of the experts' advice

38.   In its comments on the experts' replies to **Questions 13** and **14**, the EC cites a number of additional studies to support claims made in its comments and in earlier submissions. Some of these studies are introduced by the EC for the first time in its comments, very few of them were considered by the SCVPH in its opinions, and most of them do not support the specific claims made by the EC about adverse effects arising from residues of hormones in meat from treated animals.

39.   The EC introduces several new studies in an apparent misunderstanding of what the experts had been asked to do. In its comments on the responses to **Question 13** concerning whether the EC opinions evaluate the potential occurrence of adverse effects (a question that specifically asks the experts for advice on the 1999, 2000 and 2002 SCVPH opinions), the EC raises two entirely new claims about adverse effects that were not even cited in those original opinions.

40.   The first new claim is that "there seems now to be agreement" that oestradiol 17β increases the risk of "endometrial adenocarcinomas", citing a single study completed by Takahashi *et al.* in 1996, well before the completion of the EC's opinions. However, like much of the other scientific evidence relied upon by the EC, the Takahashi study examined adverse effects that result from exposure to oestradiol at doses above a certain threshold. The study presents no evidence that the levels of hormones that would be expected from meat from treated animals cause these effects.

41.   The second new claim is that oestrogen plays a role in the hypothesized relationship between stem cells and breast cancer, citing a recent study by Smalley and Ashworth.[27] However, a review of this study reveals that it did not

---

both Genotoxic and Carcinogenic (Request No. EFSA-Q-2004-020, adopted October 18, 2005) (*The EFSA Journal, 282, 1-31, 2005*), at p. 18 (Exhibit CDA-46).

[27]   See Smalley, M. & Ashworth, A., *Stem Cells and Breast Cancer: A Field in Transit* (2003) Vol. 3 online: www.nature.com 832-844.

even investigate the role of "low-dose estrogens" in tissue stem cell proliferation, but simply hypothesized a relationship between stem cells and breast cancer. Quite apart from the fact that the study failed to identify adult mammary stem cells, which it hypothesized led to breast cancer, there are many other sources of oestrogen that would affect proliferation of these stem cells far more than would dietary sources of hormones. In other words, the relevance of this study to a safety assessment of these hormones for these uses is questionable. The authors themselves indicate the hypothetical nature of their findings when they conclude that "these issues are going to keep the field of mammary stem cell biology occupied for many years to come".[28]

42.   The EC then goes on to present two additional studies, which were also not considered by the SCVPH, that it claims demonstrate a relationship between pre-pubertal growth and risk of breast cancer. The first study, by Lampit *et al.*, simply demonstrates that oestrogen replacement therapy for prepubertal children, already undergoing therapy to delay precocious puberty, resulted in changes to growth patterns. The EC attempts to combine these results with a second study, by Ahlgren *et el.*, that postulated a relationship, on the basis of epidemiological studies, between cancer and a number of other factors, one of which was prepubertal growth rates. The link that the EC is trying to draw between these two studies is, however, simply too tenuous to support the conclusion that the EC suggests.

43.   Similarly, in its comments on the experts' responses to **Question 14** on whether the EC's opinions on oestradiol 17β follow the four steps in the risk assessment set out in the Codex guidelines, the EC argues that Dr. Guttenplan failed to take into account two studies concerning the ACI rat and ERKO/Wnt mouse. That the question was not whether new scientific evidence supports the EC's claims, but whether the SCVPH opinions follow the four steps of a risk assessment seems to have been lost on the EC. The new studies referred to by the EC do nothing to undermine the "mixed rating" that Dr. Guttenplan gave the EC's opinions.

44.   The EC concludes its presentation of its new claims of adverse effects by lamenting that the new material was "not at all considered by the experts". However, the new material says nothing about meat from treated animals and, more importantly, the claims of adverse effects were not considered by the SCVPH in its opinions. Since the experts' role is not to review additional material and determine whether the hormones at issue pose a risk of adverse effects, the EC does not explain how any of this material – only introduced by the EC with its comments – is relevant to the issue of whether the SCVPH opinions amount to a risk assessment that is appropriate to the circumstances. The new studies do not change what the SCVPH did or did not do in its 1999, 2000 and 2002 opinions.

---

[28]   *Ibid.*, at p. 843.

D. Consumption of Meat Containing Hormones

(a) Carcinogenicity

45.   In its comments on the experts' responses to **Question 15**, the EC only explains half the story about the Appellate Body's interpretation of the term "potential". By suggesting that the Appellate Body found that a risk assessment need only identify whether adverse effects are "possible", the EC has attempted to reduce the requirements of a risk assessment to only its first step, the hazard identification.[29] To accept the simplistic definition of "potential" as "possible" eliminates the most important element of a risk assessment, that is, the *evaluation* of the potential for occurrence. In the entire context of the Appellate Body's ruling, such a narrow reading is not justified. The Panel may wish to ensure that the experts are aware of the full context of the requirements of a risk assessment under the *SPS Agreement*, as set out by the Appellate Body.

46.   In its comments on the experts' responses to **Question 16**, the EC again misrepresents the Appellate Body's findings related to quantitative versus qualitative risk assessments. Contrary to the EC's claim, nowhere did the Appellate Body make a finding as far reaching as a "*qualitative* assessment of risk is acceptable for the purposes of the *SPS Agreement*". As explained above,[30] what the Appellate Body said was that there is no requirement for a "risk assessment to establish a minimum magnitude of risk".[31] If the EC had identified that there was no threshold dose of hormones below which adverse effects would not occur, then it would be appropriate not to assess quantitatively the exposure. However, since the experts confirm that the EC has not demonstrated there are adverse effects that do not exhibit a threshold, the EC is required to evaluate exposure data. This requirement does not emerge from some general requirement to conduct a quantitative risk assessment, but rather from the need to *evaluate* the potential occurrence, even as this evaluation need not lead to the identification of a "minimum magnitude of risk".

47.   In its comments on the experts' responses to **Question 17**, the EC attempts to compare the advice provided by Dr. Boisseau and Dr. Boobis to that of Dr. Lucier that was disregarded by the Appellate Body in *EC – Hormones*.[32] The comparison is not appropriate. The advice that was disregarded by the Appellate Body related to Dr. Lucier's quantification of the risk of developing breast cancer from consumption of residues of hormones in meat from treated cattle as one in every million women in Canada, the United States and Europe. The Appellate Body disregarded this calculation because it was not the result of any study that supported the risk that Dr. Lucier calculated. In others words, his specific calcu-

---

[29]   According to the international techniques for risk assessments, this is the "hazard identification" stage. According to the Appellate Body, this is the "identification of adverse effects on human health".

[30]   See Canada's comments above, at para. 22.

[31]   See *EC – Hormones*, Report of the Appellate Body, at para. 186.

[32]   *Ibid.*, at para. 198.

lation of the quantum of risk was merely unsupported speculation. This is to be contrasted with the expertise and the advice of Dr. Boisseau and Dr. Boobis on the issue of the formation of catechol oestrogens in meat. These experts are not speculating a quantum of risk, but rather are providing their expert advice on basic biological processes well within their area of expertise developed over long careers of evaluating veterinary drugs and other chemical substances.

48.   With respect to the EC's comments on the experts' responses to **Question 18**, Canada has already commented above[33] on the EC's claim it has provided scientific evidence that oestradiol 17β is genotoxic *in vivo*. The EC then goes on to make the surprising and entirely unjustified claim that in any event it is Canada that must demonstrate that residues from hormones from meat from treated animals *will not* cause genotoxic effects. Quite apart from the fact that the EC makes no attempt to justify why Canada would bear such a burden, this assertion ignores some basic facts about this dispute: it is the EC that claims to have found evidence that the hormones cause adverse effects; it is the EC that has adopted an SPS measure to ban these hormones as a result; and it is the EC that now claims that this measure brings it into compliance with previous findings of non-compliance. As a result, there is no question that it is now the EC that bears the burden of demonstrating that its claims are justified on the basis of scientific evidence. It has not done so, and no attempt to shift the burden to Canada alters its failure to do so.

49.   In its comments on the experts' responses to **Question 19**, the EC claims that the mode of action of cancer is not relevant from a regulatory perspective. On the contrary, the mode of action is very relevant to regulators. It is also very relevant for purposes of compliance with obligations under the *SPS Agreement*, as the correct identification of the mode of action of cancer will determine whether a given SPS measure is justified by the science. If the mode of action is through hormonal activity, which clearly exhibits a threshold response, a risk assessment that ignores the existence of a threshold will not be "appropriate to the circumstances", and will not meet the requirements of the *SPS Agreement*. On the other hand, if the mode of action is through genotoxicity, regulators would be justified in eliminating exposure to the substance entirely if it were a type of genotoxic effect that did not exhibit a threshold.

50.   The experts have indicated in their responses that the carcinogenic potential of these hormones is related to their hormonal activity, and also that there is no evidence of genotoxic effect *in vivo*. As a result, SPS measures (*i.e.*, the EC's bans) that are based on an assessment that as a matter of principle assumes no threshold (*i.e.*, the SCVPH opinions) can not be considered to be based on an appropriate risk assessment.

51.   Furthermore, the EC's claims that there is also evidence of a relationship between exposure to oestradiol 17β during early development and the risk of

---

[33]   See Canada's Comments, Question 13.

breast cancer warrant further comment. The study cited by the EC in support of this claim does not specifically identify hormones from meat from treated animals as the source of exposure[34] and, more importantly, it only concludes that there "may be potential" for early hormone-induced changes to the mammary glands to be "prerequisites" for tumours. The EC therefore significantly overstates the case when it concludes that it is "beyond doubt" that there is such a link. In the absence of any evidence to support this assertion, it is simply that: an unsupported assertion. In any event, the EC does not explain the relevance of hormone exposure during early development to the experts' responses to this question, which is about the relationship between genotoxicity and the ability to establish dose thresholds.

52.   In its comments on the experts' responses to **Question 20**, the EC criticizes Dr. Boobis for basing his reply on "assumptions" and "hypothesis" that oestradiol 17β is not genotoxic and that a threshold can be set. However, Dr. Boobis's advice on the genotoxic potential of oestradiol 17β is based on far more than assumptions; it constitutes his reasoned conclusions based on his experience with the issues, his review of the scientific evidence and his expertise in the area. It is the EC that bases its SPS measure on an unproven hypothesis about genotoxicity.

53.   The EC also argues that it is "no longer seriously disputed" that oestradiol 17β is genotoxic, pointing again to the findings of JECFA on the matter. Canada has already addressed the significance of JECFA's findings of "genotoxic potential" in its own comments on the experts' responses to Question 20.[35] Nothing the EC has indicated in its comments changes the fact that if JECFA considered that oestradiol 17β were genotoxic, it would not have established an ADI for it.

54.   The EC also seems to believe that the issue is whether the JECFA assessments have now become outdated simply as a result of the passage of time. On the contrary, the issue is whether the EC has identified scientific evidence that the existing assessments, and the international standards based on them, cannot achieve the EC's level of protection, which is, in fact, the same as that embodied in the international standards. The focus then should be primarily on what the EC's "new" scientific evidence says about the safety of the hormones. On this point, the experts have not indicated that this new evidence changes the JECFA assessments.

55.   With respect to its comments related to **Question 21**, the EC again confuses the issues by responding to a question about the genotoxic potential of the other five hormones with reference to hormone levels in prepubertal children. This response seems to suggest that the EC believes that the genotoxic potential

---

[34]   In fact, as Canada has explained in its own comments on Question 39, there are many sources of oestrogen during early development, all of which would be far greater than residues of hormones from meat from treated animals. See Canada's Comments, at para. 146.
[35]   *Ibid.*, at paras. 79-82.

of these hormones is dose dependent and has a threshold below which it will not occur. By lumping together its claims that depend on doses and thresholds with claims that do not depend on doses and thresholds, the EC simply demonstrates that its arguments are internally inconsistent and contradictory.

56.   In its comments on the experts' responses to **Question 22**, the EC again refers to Dr. Boobis' "assumptions" about the genotoxic potential of oestradiol 17β, when in fact his advice is not based on assumptions, but on extensive evidence and opinion from the international scientific community that oestradiol 17β is not genotoxic *in vivo*.

57.   With respect to its comments on the issue of DNA repair mechanisms, the EC raises concerns never before raised by it or the SCVPH about an "increase in the rate of damage". It suggests that "if the rate of repair were constant", increases in the rate of damage caused from residues of hormones would lead to increases in the rate of unrepaired damage. Quite apart from the fact that it provides no scientific evidence to support the assertion that the rate of repair is constant, and apart from the fact that the experts have all said that there is considerable redundancy in the repair mechanism, even the EC acknowledges, by presenting the issue as a hypothetical, that its assertion is completely untested.

58.   In its comments on the experts'responses to **Questions 23** and **24**, the EC acknowledges what it failed to acknowledge in comments on Question 13 above, that "epidemiological studies will not be able to discriminate (or separate out) the true origin of cancer because of so many co-founding factors." It is not clear, however, why the EC believes that this acknowledgment undermines Canada's position, since Canada has never argued that epidemiological studies can prove that the hormones are safe. Rather, Canada has only ever argued that the results of epidemiological studies provide no information about causal relationships between adverse effects and consumption of hormones from meat from treated animals.

59.   The EC's additional comments on the IARC studies, on which it places so much emphasis in its response to Question 13, are also notable. Even though it misrepresents what those studies actually show,[36] it still has to acknowledge that "this is just an indication that there might be a link between consumption of red meat and breast cancer". In the end, it appears that the EC and Canada agree on the limited value of epidemiological studies in the conduct of a risk assessment appropriate to the circumstances of these substances.

---

[36]   The EC's statement that the IARC studies show that the "frequency of breast cancer in countries where hormones are allowed is higher compared with countries where the hormones have not been used" is misleading. If it is referring to IARC's classification of oestrogen as a Group I carcinogen, then the data relied upon in that conclusion did not distinguish between areas where growth-promoting hormones arre used and where they are not. In other studies, only a very selective reading of the data shows any cancer rate differences exist between such regions. To the extent these data show any differences at all, Dr. Boobis also cautions against "ecological fallacies" when interpreting such data.

60.   In its comments on the experts' responses to **Question 25**, the EC again attempts to impugn the data on which JECFA relied for its assessment that exposure to the hormones at levels below the established ADI would not lead to adverse effects. It again tries to claim that simply because the data are "old", they are no longer valid, without providing any scientific evidence that contradicts the conclusions of JECFA based on those data. Dr. Boobis has not imposed a higher standard on the EC than was imposed on JECFA; he is simply indicating that the EC has failed to demonstrate scientifically, either in the three additional studies or in any other studies, that there is a potential for adverse effects.

61.   The EC also again criticizes JECFA's level of protection of "no appreciable risk" as being subjective and qualitative. Not only is this criticism ironic in light of the EC's own defence of the appropriateness of "qualitative" risk assessments, but it is also wrong. As Canada has explained in its comments above on the EC's comments on risk assessment techniques,[37] "no appreciable risk" can be equally expressed as "zero observed risk". This is not 1% or 10% risk, as the EC suggests here, but is zero risk. This does not mean that there is no hypothetical risk; it simply means that no adverse effects have been observed to support a conclusion that there are risks. In other words, any risk that might be inherent in the expression "no appreciable risk" is simply a theoretical or hypothetical one.

62.   In its comments on the experts' responses to **Question 26**, the EC seems to shift position once again on the value of epidemiological studies. In earlier comments, it states that epidemiological studies confirm the existence of adverse effects; in other comments, it states that epidemiological studies cannot prove one way or another that adverse effects will occur; and now it states that it relies upon the results of epidemiological studies simply to demonstrate that scientific uncertainty is growing. The only thing that seems to be uncertain is what the EC actually believes is the value of such studies in support of its claims. The EC places considerable emphasis on the statements by several experts that the results are "consistent with" an association between hormone residues in meat and cancer outcomes. However, in light of the clear advice from the experts about the inability to separate confounding factors, finding that they are "consistent with" an association says very little about demonstrable association.

(b)   Residue Analysis

63.   In commenting on the responses to **Question 27** concerning residues of synthetic hormones, the EC asserts that the differences in residues are "not only structural/chemical but also qualitative and quantitative." What the EC means by "qualitative" is left unclear. In terms of "quantitative" differences, the EC refers to one of the 17 studies commissioned by the European Commission conducted by Rainer Stephany and the conclusions contained therein relating to the concen-

---

[37]   See Canada's comments above, at paras. 18-21.

tration of oestradiol-17β in meat from treated cattle.[38] However, concentrations of oestradiol 17β (a *natural* hormone) provide no information about quantitative differences in residues of *synthetic* hormones, which is the focus of this question.

64.   The study provides no support for the EC's suggestion that actual residue data for synthetic hormones differ from data submitted as a part of the authorization of synthetic hormones.

65.   In commenting on the experts' replies to **Question 28** concerning residues of synthetic hormones, the EC attempts to discredit Dr. Boisseau's reply by asserting that "estradiol-alpha", by which the EC presumably means oestradiol-17∀ (alpha), is a main residue found in the liver of cattle treated with oestradiol 17β and that this residue gives rise to human health risks. In the next paragraph, however, the EC cites Dr. de Brabander's conclusion that residues of endogenously produced natural hormones in cattle are in the 17α (alpha) form (inactive), while the use of natural hormones used for growth promotion "may lead to residues in the [oestradiol 17] β form (active form)". This latter conclusion suggests that, if indeed the EC is correct that oestradiol-17∀ (alpha) gives rise to human health risks (a bald proposition unsupported by any evidence), the risk comes from eating meat from *untreated* cattle. Dr. de Brabander does not suggest that meat from treated cattle contains a higher proportion of oestradiol-17∀ (alpha). Thus the EC's argument disproves itself.

66.   In commenting on the experts' replies to **Question 29** concerning residues of synthetic hormones, the EC asserts that the SCVPH considered ADIs and MRLs (Maximum Residue Limits) recommended by JECFA and "went even further and examined tolerance levels recommended by the USA." This statement is both inaccurate and misleading. For trenbolone acetate (TBA), the SCVPH did not even refer to, let alone consider, MRLs recommended by JECFA, choosing instead to compare tolerance limits set by the US Food and Drug Administration (FDA) to JECFA's ADI.[39] Whatever the merit of this approach, it says nothing about the appropriateness of JECFA's MRLs. Moreover, the SCVPH failed completely to address JECFA's conclusions, which are in part:

> The Committee recommended MRLs for β-TBOH in muscle and α-TBOH in liver of 2 µg/kg and 10 µg/kg respectively....These MRLs are not likely to be exceeded with good practice in the use of veterinary drugs.

---

[38]   Stephany, R., *Hormones in meat: different approaches in the EU and in the USA*, (2001) 109 (Suppl. 103) APMIS S357, at p. 361 ("Stephany Study") (Exhibits EC-49, CDA-12).

[39]   1999 SCVPH Opinion, at p. 57 (Exhibit CDA-2). Surprisingly, the SCVPH used temporary ADIs set by JECFA in 1987, as opposed to the final ADI set by JECFA in 1989. The final ADIs are found in JECFA, *Evaluation of certain veterinary drug residues in food: Thirty-fourth Report of the Joint FAO/WHO Expert Committee on Food Additives*, WHO Technical Report Series 788 (Geneva: WHO, 1989), at p. 62 (JECFA's 34th Report) (Exhibit CDA-19).

Conservative estimates using these MRLs and the daily intake values for edible tissues given in Section 2.6 indicate that the ADI for TBA of 0.02 μg per kg of body weight *should not be exceeded at any time after implantation of the drug*. The maximum concentrations of residues occur at 15-30 days after implantation and are below the recommended MRLs; *concentrations will be even lower at the usual withdrawal time of 60 days.*[40]

67.   Thus, even if withdrawal periods are not respected, the ADI would not be exceeded.

68.   In relation to zeranol, the SCVPH simply refers to the MRLs set by JECFA[41] and again compares them to the US FDA tolerances. This says nothing about whether the MRLs set by JECFA would lead to intake sufficient to exceed the ADI. Nor did the SCVPH evaluate JECFA's conclusion in its residue monograph for zeranol that "[t]he total residues [of zeranol] in liver, kidney, muscle and fat do not exceed 10, 2, .2 and .3 μg/kg, respectively, *at any time post-implantation*".[42] Again, even if the withdrawal periods were not respected, the ADI would not be exceeded.

69.   Lastly, in relation to MGA, the SCVPH did not consider the MRLs recommended by JECFA for MGA, let alone the detailed residue monographs for this substance.[43] It is worth noting that while the JECFA recommendations were made after the SCVPH opinions, they were made prior to the establishment of this Panel in January 2005.

70.   The foregoing demonstrates that the EC, through the SCVPH, did not consider whether actual residues of the synthetic hormones in meat from treated cattle would exceed the MRLs recommended by JECFA. It also failed to consider whether compliance with the MRLs recommended by JECFA would lead to an intake of residues in excess of the Codex ADI. Thus, in this regard, the EC has not provided a scientific justification for why established international standards would not meet its chosen level of protection.

---

[40]   JECFA's 34th Report, at p. 42 [emphasis added] (Exhibit CDA-19). The Residue Monograph for TBA prepared for the 34th Meeting of JECFA is found at Exhibit CDA-38.

[41]   JECFA, *Evaluation of certain veterinary drug residues in food: Thirty-second Report of the Joint FAO/WHO Expert Committee on Food Additives*, WHO Technical Report Series 763 (Geneva: WHO, 1988), at p. 28 (Exhibit CDA-18).

[42]   JECFA, *Residues of some veterinary drugs in animals and foods: Monographs prepared by the Thirty-second Meeting of the Joint FAO/WHO Expert Committee on Food Additives*, FAO Food and Nutrition Paper, No. 41/1 (Rome: FAO, 1988), at p. 46 (32nd JECFA, Residue Monograph for Zeranol) [emphasis added] (Exhibit CDA-39).

[43]   JECFA, *Residues of some veterinary drugs in animals and foods: Monographs prepared by the Fifty-eighth Meeting of the Joint FAO/WHO Expert Committee on Food Additives*, FAO Food And Nutrition Paper, No. 41/14 (Rome: FAO, 2002) (58th JECFA, Residue Monograph for MGA) (JECFA's 58th Report) (Exhibit CDA-35); and JECFA, *Residues of some veterinary drugs in animals and foods: Monographs prepared by the Sixty-second Meeting of the Joint FAO/WHO Expert Committee on Food Additives*, FAO Food And Nutrition Paper, No. 41/16 (Rome: FAO, 2004) (62nd JECFA, Residue Monograph for MGA) (Exhibit CDA-33).

71.   In commenting on the experts' replies to **Question 30** concerning residues of natural hormones, the EC again confuses and distorts the JECFA ADI. As will be discussed below,[44] although JECFA referred to background levels of circulating hormones, their daily production and metabolic clearance rates (MCR),[45] the ADI is not based on a calculation of endogenous production of natural hormones, but on the NOAEL. Therefore, even if background levels, daily production rates and MCRs of the natural hormones in prepubertal children are lower than first thought, the ADI would not be affected.[46]

72.   In commenting on the experts' replies to **Question 31** concerning the variation in physiological levels of natural hormones in meat from untreated cattle, the EC again presents inaccurate information. First, the EC inaccurately states that Dr. de Brabander refers to the EC study indicating that consumption of meat from treated cattle contains 7.5 times more oestrogens than meat from untreated cattle. Presumably, the EC is referring to the Stephany Study, cited earlier in relation to Question 27. However, Dr. de Brabander never once refers to this study, nor does he provide any quantitative estimate of the amount by which natural hormones in meat from treated cattle vary from meat from untreated cattle. Second, on a more substantive level, the EC inappropriately cites the average level of oestradiol 17β as opposed to the more appropriate median value, used by the author of the study. The author writes:

> From *ad random* studies in 1998 and 1999 with meat imported from the USA to the EU or obtained from the US domestic market (25-26) it is estimated that the median dietary intake of 17β-estradiol via a 250 gram steak of "Hormone Free Cattle" is less than 2.5 nanogram and via 250 gram "beef" of "Hormone Treated Cattle" is 5 nanogram. This has to be compared with the recently found median dietary intake of 17β -estradiol of 6.5 nanogram via a 50 gram hens egg....From this comparison the preliminary conclusion is that hens eggs are a major source of 17β (and 17α-estradiol in the daily "normal" diet.[47]

73.   Thus, residues of natural hormones in meat from treated cattle are only twice the median level found in meat from untreated cattle. Moreover, total residues of all oestradiol 17β in 250 grams of beef (approximately ½ lb) from *treated* cattle (5 ng) are less than that found in *one egg* (6.5 ng)! Not unexpectedly, the EC ignores this finding and the main recommendation of the Stephany

---

[44]   See Canada's comments below, at paras. 84-87.

[45]   JECFA, *Toxicological evaluation of certain veterinary drug residues in food: prepared by the Fifty-second meeting of the Joint FAO/WHO Expert Committee on Food Additives*, WHO Food Additives Series No. 43 (Geneva: WHO, 2000) (Toxicological Monographs for Oestradiol-17β, Progesterone and Testosterone), at pp. 51, 82 and 90 for each hormone, respectively (Exhibit CDA-11).

[46]   The EC's comments on misuse and abuse will be addressed later in these comments in the Section on GVP.

[47]   Stephany Study, at p. 361 (Exhibits EC-49, CDA-12).

Study that "[t]he 'hormones in meat problem' should be evaluated in relation to all facts about the actual total dietary intake of 'hormones', e.g. from meat(products), poultry, milk, dairy products, eggs, and fish(products) taking also into account the effects of various ways of food production and of 'household' cooking".[48]

74.   The above results and conclusions are consistent with those of the UK Sub-Group of the Veterinary Products Committee, which reviewed data relating to the natural occurrence of steroid hormones in a variety of food sources.[49] Those data included a study by Sonja Hartmann, et al., which concluded:

> Meat does not play a dominant role in the daily intake of steroid hormones…The main source of estrogens and progesterone are milk products (60-80%). Eggs and vegetable food contribute in the same order of magnitude to the hormone supply as meat does.[50]

75.   The Stephany and Hartmann studies support Canada's basic point that the risks associated with hormones for growth-promotion purposes cannot be appropriately evaluated without considering exposure to other sources of dietary hormones. The data also suggest that the EC's stated high level of protection for its citizenry, particularly prepubertal children, is more rhetoric than reality. One need only consider that few prepubertal children consume anything close to 250 grams (½ lb) of beef on a daily basis, while milk products and eggs are staples of a child's diet, to see that such claims ring hollow. Given the significance of other dietary sources of hormones in comparison with the trivial contribution from the use of growth promotants, the EC's purported concerns about genotoxicity and endocrine disruption, amongst others, begin to look less and less genuine.

76.   In commenting on the replies to **Question 32** concerning unvalidated detection methods, the EC criticizes Dr. Boisseau's advice as being "scientifically unsound." However, it is clear from Dr. Boisseau's reply that he is referring to the use of detection methods for determining compliance with MRLs. In that context, his statement that detection methods need only be sensitive enough to detect residues in excess of MRLs is scientifically accurate. To the extent that the "ultra-sensitive" detection methods referred to by the EC are intended to evaluate levels of naturally occurring hormones in a variety of food sources,[51] it

---

[48]   *Ibid.*

[49]   UK, Sub-Group of the Veterinary Products Committee, *Executive summary and critical evaluation of the scientific reasoning and methods of argument adopted in the opinion of the Scientific Committee on Veterinary Measures Relating to Public Health which assessed the potential risks to human health from hormone residues in bovine meat and meat products*, October 1999, at pp. 11-12 (Exhibit CDA-6).

[50]   Hartmann, S., *et al.*, *Natural occurrence of steroid hormones in food*, (1998) 62:1 Food Chemistry, at p. 18 ("Hartmann study") (Exhibit CDA-50).

[51]   It is unclear to what use the "ultra-sensitive" detection methods are to be put. However, one could infer from the introduction to Section 4.1 in the 2002 SCVPH Opinion that the intended use is

should be recalled that data on these levels currently exist and are before this Panel.[52] Unless and until new, more sensitive detection methods are developed and validated that call into question the accuracy of the current data, the current data should be accepted as accurate.

77.   In commenting on the experts' replies to **Question 33**, the EC implies that JECFA is keeping from the Panel and the public the residue data it relied upon during its 1999 review, thereby preventing an "open and objective" verification. One need only review the 50-odd pages of residue data summarized in the residue monograph prepared for JECFA's 52nd Meeting (summarized by Dr. Arnold from the German Federal Institute of Health, no less!) to appreciate the exaggerated and sensationalist nature of the EC's claim in this regard.[53]

78.   In relation to the EC's comments on the experts' replies to **Question 35** concerning MGA and whether "subsequent reports of JECFA, prior or subsequent to the adoption of the EC Directive, also relied on the same studies", it is important to recall that the MRLs recommended by JECFA in 2000 were only "temporary" pending the "receipt of information on an analytical method suitable for quantifying residues of melengestrol acetate in liver and fat tissue. This information is required for evaluation in 2002".[54] Indeed, as explained by Canada in its comments on the experts' answers (Question 29), a validated detection method was submitted and accepted by JECFA during its 58th meeting in 2002.[55] Contrary to the EC's view, these data are hardly "old" and "outdated".

(c)   Dose-Response Relationship

79.   In its comments on the experts' responses to **Question 36**, the EC again misrepresents the Appellate Body findings related to "quantitative" analysis, which Canada has already addressed in its comments above.[56]

80.   With respect to its further claim in its comments on that question that Dr. Boobis acknowledged that no dose-response assessment may be required, it is important to note that Dr. Boobis only accepted that to be the case if two conditions were present: 1) the particular mode of action for the genotoxic effect is of a kind that does not exhibit a threshold response; and 2) it is confirmed in *in*

---

to determine with greater precision the levels of naturally occurring endogenous hormones in the entire food basket.

[52]   See UK Sub-Group Report (Exhibit CDA-6); and Hartmann study (Exhibit CDA-50).

[53]   JECFA, *Residues of some veterinary drugs in animals and foods*, FAO Food and Nutrition Paper No. 41/12 (Rome: FAO, 2000), at 37-90, and 137-140 (Exhibit CDA-17).

[54]   JECFA, *Evaluation of certain veterinary drug residues in food: Fifty-fourth Report of the Joint FAO/WHO Expert Committee on Food Additives*, WHO Technical Report Series 900 (Geneva: WHO, 2001) (54th JECFA, Technical Report for MGA), at pp. 79-80 (Exhibit CDA-36).

[55]   See Canada's Comments, at para. 111. Also see JECFA's 58th Report, Residue Monograph for MGA, at pp. 56-59 (Exhibit CDA-35).

[56]   See Canada's comments above, at para. 22.

vivo tests.[57] As Dr. Boobis advised, neither of these conditions has been met in the case of these hormones when used as growth promoters.

81.   The EC then cites the absence of "internationally agreed principles" on when to conduct a dose-response assessment to justify its failure to have conducted one. However, the real issue is not whether the EC is required to do so under international risk assessment techniques but, rather, whether it is appropriate in these circumstances to fail to conduct a dose-response assessment in the course of a risk assessment. As Canada has argued elsewhere,[58] it is not possible appropriately to evaluate the potential occurrence of adverse effects from residues of hormones from treated meat without first knowing the dose at which such adverse effects will not occur.

82.   With respect to the EC's comments on the experts' responses to **Question 37** concerning whether a dose response assessment is necessary, it is sufficient to note that contrary to the EC's claim Dr. Boobis and Dr. Boisseau do not agree with the EC, but rather they agree with Canada's statement. To the extent that they describe any circumstances in which the statement would not be true, such as when genotoxicity is confirmed *in vivo*, those circumstances do not apply here. In fact, they clearly indicate that a dose-response assessment is critical to establishing an ADI and MRL.

(d)   Sensitive Populations

83.   In commenting on the experts' responses to several questions under this section, the EC makes a number of claims that reflect a misunderstanding of the relationship between the establishment of ADIs and the identification of background levels[59] and that rely too much on a single unvalidated measurement methodology (*i.e.*, the Klein recombinant cell bioassay (RCBA)[60]).

84.   The EC claims in its comments on the experts' responses to **Question 38** that JECFA cannot set ADIs and MRLs without accurate data on background levels. However, nowhere – at least, nowhere that Canada can find and the EC has not provided a source – is it indicated that JECFA considers data on background levels to be "essential for determining the ADI". On the contrary, the establishment of an ADI, and hence an MRL, does not depend at all on the identification of background levels. Rather, it depends on actual observations of adverse effects at given dose levels, to which appropriate safety factors are applied to protect against variation in sensitivity between different human populations.

---

[57]   See Canada's Comments, Question 36.
[58]   See Canada Rebuttal Submission, at paras. 80-82.
[59]   Canada understands that for the general purposes of the review of the scientific and technical material, the term "background levels" can be used interchangeably with "circulating levels" "endogenous levels" and "physiological levels".
[60]   Klein K.O., *et al.*, *Estrogen levels in childhood determined by an ultrasensitive recombinant cell bioassay* (1994) 94 J Clin Invest 2475–2480 (Klein RCBA).

85.   The general intention behind linking background levels with the establishment of ADIs for these hormones – which the EC does in almost all its comments in this section – is to create confusion between two distinct approaches to measuring exposure. On the one hand, there is the JECFA approach of identifying a NOAEL, applying safety factors and establishing an ADI, none of which depends on the identification of background levels. On the other hand, there is the EC's attempt to compare the proportion of intake exposure (which, incidentally, it never actually estimates) to background levels, and assert that if background levels are lower than once thought, the risk must therefore be higher simply because the ratio of intake (exogenous) dose to background (endogenous) levels would be higher.

86.   At no point, however, does the EC explain this relationship. Even if the EC demonstrates background levels are lower (which it has not), since JECFA's ADI approach is based on actual observed adverse effects regardless of the background level, a change in background levels is not relevant to whether adverse effects have been observed and therefore is not relevant to the ADI.

87.   To place this issue in a slightly different context, if no evidence exists that consuming an egg (which has 6ng of oestradiol 17β, an amount equivalent to that in 250 grams of beef from treated cattle) has adverse effects on the endocrine systems of prepubertal children, then studies using genetically modified yeast that suggest that the background levels of endogenous hormones in prepubertal children are lower than first thought, do not demonstrate that consuming an egg now has greater risk.

88.   The experts in their responses to **Question 41** have of course confirmed that populations with lower background levels are at greatest risk of adverse effects from exposure to hormones, and they have also confirmed that this is so because the proportion of exogenous hormone levels to endogenous exposure would be greater. However, this statement of basic physiology does not in itself confirm that even if it turns out that background levels are lower than once thought, the appreciation of the risk would be greater. New test results that suggest background levels are lower than once thought simply change the understanding of the levels themselves, and not the risks of adverse effects.

89.   In other words, for the purposes of establishing the ADI, the ratio that matters is not that between hormone intake and background hormone levels, but rather that between the background hormone levels of the populations used to identify the NOAEL and other subpopulations. And as the experts indicate in their answers to **Question 42**, JECFA already takes into account the expected lower background levels in sensitive populations.

90.   In its comments on the experts' responses to **Questions 38, 39** and **40**, the EC makes several confusing and unfounded assertions about the validity and importance of background level data generated by the Klein RCBA. First, in its comments on **Question 38**, it discounts the importance of validation of scientific methodologies in support of scientific conclusions, claiming that the ultrasensitive Klein RCBA need not be validated at all for the results to have any impor-

tance. There is no basis for such a claim. It requires more than one unvalidated attempt to generate competing data to cast doubt on the data generated by radio-immune assays (RIA). The claim that JECFA uses data from assays that have not been validated is also unfounded. JECFA goes to great lengths to validate the quality and precision of the data on which its recommendations are based. The EC did nothing to validate the data generated by the Klein RCBA.

91.   In its own comments on the experts' responses to **Question 39,** the EC seems to indicate that it does not even believe the Klein RCBA is valid, when it contradicts the comments it made on **Questions 38** and **40**. In its comments on these latter questions, the EC claims that the Paris assay results overestimate the levels compared to the Klein RCBA results. But in its comments on the question coming between these two, it supports Dr. Sippell's attempt to validate the Klein RCBA results with reference to a "number of sources confirming the values" generated by Klein. It seems to have been lost on the EC that the only "confirming" source offered by Dr. Sippell was that of the Paris assay. So, whereas the EC does not consider the Paris assay results to be credible enough to be used to demonstrate that Klein is *inaccurate* (as suggested by Dr. Boobis), the EC does believe that these results are credible enough for purposes of confirming that Klein is *accurate* (as suggested by Dr. Sippell).

92.   In the end, the EC itself dispels any doubt about whether it is convinced of the validity of new methodologies for measuring background levels, or the legitimacy of the data these have produced. It sums up its concerns in its comments on both **Questions 38** and **40** when it notes that the "real values for serum 17β-oestradiol in prepubertal children still remain to be properly documented". In light of the uncertainty about the validity of the new measurements and the continued legitimacy of JECFA's ADI approach – which does not depend on these measurements – the EC has not demonstrated that JECFA's recommendations need to be modified.

(e)   Bioavailability

93.   In its comments on the experts' responses to the only question of this section (**Question 43**), the EC makes the same mistake as it makes under the section on sensitive populations when it suggests that new information on bioavailability calls into question the validity of the JECFA-established ADIs. As Canada has already explained in its own comments on the experts' responses to the questions,[61] the actual amount of hormones that is bioavailable does not affect the validity of the ADI. Rather, the ADI is based on observed adverse effects from a given oral dose, which means that the ADI represents, in the words of Dr. Boobis, a "bioavailability adjusted" dose. The EC makes no comment on this concept. Instead, just as it does with the questionable re-evaluation of background levels, it also exaggerates the importance of what it considers "credible

---

[61]   See Canada's Comments, at paras. 162-163.

evidence" that the bioavailability of hormones might be higher than once thought. Neither issue, in the end, demonstrates that the international standards would not meet the EC's chosen level of protection.

(f)   Good Veterinary Practice (GVP)

94.   In the *EC – Hormones* dispute, the Appellate Body found that the EC did not submit a risk assessment "demonstrating and evaluating the existence and level of risk arising…from abusive use of hormones and the difficulties of control of the administration of hormones for growth promotion purposes, within the United States and Canada as exporting countries".[62] Thus, one of the central issues in this dispute is whether, this time around, the EC has actually evaluated the potential adverse effects on human health related to the failure to comply with good practice in the use of veterinary drugs (GVP). As explained by Canada elsewhere, the EC has not done so.[63]

95.   In its comments on experts' responses to questions in this section (**Questions 44-51**), the EC challenges the unequivocal conclusion of the experts that the SCVPH made "no attempt to evaluate the risks from the resultant exposures [from] misuse or abuse".[64] The EC claims that it indeed conducted a proper assessment of these risks, citing several exhibits to support its claim, the most important of which is the European Commission's *Draft Report on the Assessment of Risks of hormonal growth promoters in cattle with respect to risks arising from abusive use and difficulties of control.*[65] However, a close review of these exhibits reveals that the EC claim is profoundly flawed.

96.   It is important to clarify up front a few issues concerning GVP generally raised by the EC. First, with respect to **Question 46**, the EC's attempt to discredit JECFA's assessments of these hormones on the basis that JECFA did not assess potential misuse/ abuse is unsound. As explained by Dr. Boisseau, in recommending MRLs, JECFA assumes that GVP will be followed; for practical purposes JECFA does not examine potential compliance or control issues. While the failure to follow GVP *may* lead to residues that exceed the recommended MRL, and to a corresponding intake of residues in excess of the established ADI, such a failure does not undermine the validity of the MRL.[66]

---

[62]   *EC – Hormones*, Report of the Appellate Body, at para. 207.
[63]   Canada Rebuttal Submission, at paras. 107-111.
[64]   Response by Dr. Boobis to Question 48, at p. 42.
[65]   European Commission, *Assessment of Risks of hormonal growth promoters in cattle with respect to risks arising from abusive use and difficulties of control*, Draft Report by special working group of external private experts and European Commission officials, Brussels, 29 April 1999 (Commission Draft Report on Assessment of Risks of Abusive Use) (Exhibit EC-73). This document was exhibited for the first time in the EC Rebuttal Submission, despite the Panel's specific request to the EC to identify the documents that encompass the risk assessment for its permanent ban. See Questions from the Panel after the First Substantive Meeting, 3 October 2005, Question 16.
[66]   See Canada's Comments, Question 46.

97.   Second, in relation to **Question 48**, the EC's attempt to discredit Dr. Boobis's opinion by suggesting that he does not appreciate the distinction between "probability" and "possibility" as laid down by the Appellate Body is equally flawed.[67] The Appellate Body concluded that it is insufficient merely to identify the possibility of misuse/abuse, which is in effect all the EC did during the first *EC – Hormones* panel.[68] In correctly finding that the EC's assessment of this issue did not meet the requirements of a risk assessment consistent with Articles 5.1 and 5.2 of the *SPS Agreement*, the Appellate Body implies that a if WTO Member alleges risks to human health from failure to comply with GVP, that Member must evaluate the existence and level of risk arising from the abusive use of such a substance, not simply identify the possibility that such abusive use may occur.

98.   Third, compliance with GVP is not an end in itself, but only a means for estimating whether actual residues in meat from treated cattle exceed recommended MLRs and/or lead to intake in excess of established ADIs. The EC devotes considerable effort to the question of whether Canada and the United States can demonstrate to the satisfaction of the EC that compliance with GVP has been assured in their respective territories, while practically ignoring the more fundamental question of whether actual residues in Canadian meat from treated cattle exceed recommended MLRs and/or lead to intakes in excess of established ADIs.

99.   On a more substantive level, the EC's purported assessment of the misuse/abuse of hormones in Canada and the United States is based on a number of assumptions about both the occurrence of misuse/abuse and the risks to human health in the unlikely event that such misuse/abuse occurs. In terms of the former, the EC assumes that because there are economic incentives to using hormones for growth-promotion purposes (increased weight gain, greater feed efficiency, *etc.*), farmers will invariably misuse/abuse them in the absence of control measures as stringent as those applied in the EC. These assumptions may be based in part on the unfortunate fact that Europe has faced a "continuous series of residue scandals with illegal 'anabolic hormones' in cattle".[69] However, without concrete evidence, extrapolating illegal conduct in one's own jurisdiction to illegal conduct in another is unjustified.

100.   The notion that economic incentives will invariably lead to misuse/abuse does not reflect realistic conditions of use. It presupposes that farmers are irresponsible, concerned only about profit, and insensitive to issues of animal welfare and human health. Moreover, it assumes that weight gain is proportional to the amount of hormone administered (*i.e.*, increasing the number of implants increases weight gain and the corresponding economic benefit). This assumption is not valid. It also ignores the possibility that misuse/abuse can lead to perform-

---

[67]   See EC Comments, Question 48, at p. 40.
[68]   *EC – Hormones*, Report of the Appellate Body, at paras. 206-208.
[69]   Stephany Study, at p. 358 (Exhibits EC-49, CDA-12).

ance below optimum levels, negative effects on future reproductive performance and side effects such as vaginal and rectal prolapses. All of this demonstrates that the simplistic notion that "economic incentives" lead to misuse/abuse does not reflect realistic conditions of use.

101.   Similarly, the absence of control measures as stringent as those found in Europe does not imply that misuse/abuse is more likely. Control measures are typically proportional to the magnitude of the problem. There is simply no evidence that misuse/abuse of hormones in Canada is a problem sufficient to warrant the control measures that the EC appears to deem necessary.

102.   With those comments in mind, Canada will now turn to a detailed review of the assessment report contained in Exhibit EC-73. The EC asserts that higher risk flows from misuse/abuse of hormones in several ways: (a) misplaced implants, (b) off-label uses, (c) simultaneous multiple implants, and (d) black-market drugs.

103.   In terms of misplaced implants, the EC postulates that tissue from the site of application containing excessive concentrations of hormones may find its way into the human food chain. The EC then presents in Table 4 of Exhibit EC-73 hypothetical exposure scenarios for various elevated concentrations of hormones and concludes that there is a risk to human health from misplaced implants.[70] This risk can occur either because the ear into which the implant has been subcutaneously inserted may not be discarded or because implants may be incorrectly inserted in edible tissues, such as the neck muscle, shoulder or hind leg. In support of this concern, the EC cites one example from Canada that found residues in muscle tissue that could only be explained by improper placement of an implant or the application of unapproved intramuscular injections of liquid hormone preparations.[71] This anomalous result hardly constitutes compelling evidence of the frequency of misplaced implants. Other than this one example, there is no evidence that in Canada ears with implants are processed into food or that implants are inserted into other edible parts of the cow. The EC has merely identified a possibility, unsupported by any analysis of frequency of occurrence or assessment of the impact on human health in the unlikely event that such a possibility materializes.

104.   Canada notes that the risk of excessive concentrations of hormones entering the food chain is far greater when liquid hormone preparations are injected into the muscle of the animal (intramuscular injection). However, this is far more likely a problem in countries that ban outright the use of growth promotants than in North America, where subcutaneous implants in the pinna of the ear of cattle (middle third of the back-side of the ear) are permitted. In order to avoid detection, it is reasonable to assume that European farmers using illegal anabolic steroids would likely use intramuscular injections rather than pinna implants, as the

---

[70]   Commission Draft Report on Assessment of Risks of Abusive Use, at p. 15 (Exhibit EC-73).
[71]   Ibid., at para. 16.

latter can remain *in situ* for up to 120 days and are easier to detect.[72] Thus, the more realistic exposure scenario for the calculations presented in Table 4 of Exhibit EC-73 is excessive exposure from residues in edible tissues (muscle and fat) resulting from intramuscular injections, a practice far more likely in Europe than in Canada.

105.   In terms of off-label uses, the EC cites the presence of TBA and zeranol in veal calves (calves less than 45 days of age). This implies that some growth promotants may have been used earlier than recommended, but says nothing about the potential misuse of growth-promoting hormones later in the life of cattle.

106.   In terms of simultaneous multiple implants, the EC simply fails to present any evidence relating to the frequency of inappropriate multiple dosing in practice in Canada, a fact highlighted by Dr. Boobis.[73] Moreover, the EC's own studies confirm that, with most applications, even at doses 10 times the recommended level, residues remain below recommended MRLs,[74] a finding also noted by Dr. Boobis. Thus, even in the unlikely event of inappropriate multiple dosing, the EC's own evidence suggests that residues, for the most part, would remain below safe thresholds.

107.   Lastly, in terms of black-market drugs, the EC speculates that the economic incentives for using growth-promoting hormones "cannot exclude the emergence of a black market for less expensive or more effective substances".[75] The EC presents no evidence of illegal use of black-market drugs for growth-promotion purposes in cattle in Canada. Although the EC's own studies reveal that "[i]n the EU dozens of illegal hormones are used",[76] it is not logical to extrapolate the apparent problem with illegal hormone use in countries that outright ban *all* growth promotants to the North American context where growth promotants are permitted under specific circumstances. Indeed, the very availability of legal growth promotants in North America suggests that the likelihood of the misuse of illegal drugs would be much lower in Canada than in countries that prohibit outright any growth promotants.

108.   In conclusion, the EC's claim that it has properly evaluated the potential for adverse effects from the misuse/abuse, a claim contradicted by the experts, does not withstand scrutiny. In addition to being based on several flawed assumptions that do not reflect realistic conditions of use, the assessment simply

---

[72]   In the Stephany Study, the author suggests that in the EU the mode of application of growth promotants is intramuscular injection (Exhibits EC-49, CDA-12).

[73]   Dr. Boobis's reply to Panel Question 62, at pp. 50-51.

[74]   Lange, I., *et al.*, *Hormone contents in peripheral tissues after correct and off-label use of growth promoting hormones in cattle: Effect of the implant preparations Finaplix-H®, Ralgro®, Synovex-H® and Synovex Plus®* (2001) 109 APMIS 53-65, at pp. 382-383 (Exhibit EC-17).

[75]   Commission Draft Report on Assessment of Risks of Abusive Use, at para. 47 (Exhibit EC-73).

[76]   Stephany, R., *Hormones found in Meat Samples from Regular Controls in the European Union and from US Imports* (2000) Chemical Awareness: Issue 9, at p. 1 (Exhibit EC-19). Also see the Stephany Study, at p. 358 (Exhibits EC-49, CDA-12).

fails to evaluate the frequency of occurrence of misuse/abuse and the potential impact on human health in the unlikely event that misuse occurs. It does not satisfy the requirements for a risk assessment under Article 5.1 and 5.2 as set down by the Appellate Body in the previous Hormones dispute.

(g)   Other

109.   The EC, in its comments on the experts' responses to **Question 52,** again erroneously characterizes the advice of Dr. Boobis and Dr. Boisseau as based on "assumptions and conservative interpretation", and further that these experts hold the EC's opinion to a higher standard than that to which companies were held when they first received approval for the sale of the hormones as growth promoters.

110.   First, the advice from Dr. Boobis and Dr. Boisseau is based on far more than assumptions; it is based on their qualified expertise in their own areas of specialization. The EC may disagree with their advice, but that in itself does not mean it is based on assumptions. If any party in this dispute is making assertions unsupported by the scientific evidence, it is the EC itself, such as with its genotoxicity hypothesis and its reliance on unvalidated measurement methodologies.

111.   Second, the EC's accusation that Dr. Boisseau and Dr. Boobis are applying a double standard ignores the history of the evaluation of the safety of these substances. Quite apart from the standard of review to which the original applicants for approval of the hormones were held, the fact remains that the hormones have been repeatedly reviewed and approved by national authorities and international standards bodies, such as Codex and JECFA, on several occasions since the original approval. None of these subsequent reviews, all of which use the latest methodologies and scientific evidence, found that there was any evidence of adverse effects. On the other hand, it is the EC that now claims to have demonstrated that there are adverse effects. It is not only reasonable but legally necessary for the EC to demonstrate, with more than hypothesis and unvalidated methodologies, the potential for the purported adverse effects to occur. Far from being a double standard, this is simply holding the EC to the same standard.

112.   The EC also places considerable emphasis on a single statement by Dr. Boobis that the risks from consuming residues in meat from treated animals are "minimal". However, the EC conveniently ignores almost the entirety of the preceding paragraphs in Dr. Boobis's response, in which he states, *inter alia*, that: "*none* of [the] information provided by the EC demonstrates the potential for adverse effects in humans"; "[t]he studies on genotoxicity provide *no convincing evidence* of potential for harm in consumers"; "there would be *no risk* of ... [adverse] effects from ... exposures" from meat from treated cattle; and "there is *no evidence* that low level exposure is causing harmful effects in humans" [emphasis added]. Therefore, in light of Dr. Boobis's responses above to the issue of whether the EC has demonstrated the potential for adverse effects, it is quite clear what Dr. Boobis means when he uses the word "minimal".

113. The EC further endorses the responses of Dr. Guttenplan in a manner that is not supported by the advice of the other experts and the comments by the EC itself. The EC cites Dr. Guttenplan's support of the data generated by the Klein RCBA, despite the obvious concerns expressed about these data from all the other experts.[77] The EC then endorses Dr. Guttenplan's favourable reference to the Paris assay data to validate the Klein RCBA data, even though it stated that the former methodology was not appropriate to validate the latter methodology.[78] Finally, the EC cites these statements favourably without acknowledging that Dr. Guttenplan was simply saying that "more accurate methods of analysis could *now be used*" [emphasis added] to corroborate the EC's concerns, not that in fact they had been used or that the EC's concerns had been corroborated using these methods.

114. In its comments on the experts' responses to **Question 53**, it is sufficient to note that in quoting generously the response of Dr. Guttenplan, the EC tellingly failed to address the statement by him that "by far, estrogen is the major agent of risk and, because the concentrations of all the hormones in beef are so low, that they would be unlikely to affect the potency of estrogen". Dr. Boisseau made a very similar statement, which was also tellingly ignored by the EC.

115. The EC's comments on the experts' responses to **Question 54** are confusing and misleading. First, immediately after quoting Dr. Boisseau that the ADI represents the quantity of these residues that can be ingested daily "*without causing any problem* of health" [emphasis added], the EC concludes that his reply meant that "there is no doubt … that there is a risk", without explaining how the former idea supports the latter conclusion.

116. The EC then misrepresents Dr. Boobis's answer in the same manner when it interprets his statement that the "Codex standard [of no appreciable risk] is equivalent to the EC's stated objective of 'no risk from exposure to unnecessary additional residues…'" to mean that "Codex's standard recognises that there is an [*sic*] scientifically identified risk but recommends its members to follow it…". The EC again leaves unexplained how it justifies going from the former idea to the latter. Indeed, as Canada has explained above,[79] the concept of "no appreciable risk" does not mean that JECFA/Codex have identified some risk, even if minimal; rather, it means that any risk that might exist is purely hypothetical (*i.e.*, not observable). And as the Appellate Body made clear, a risk assessment cannot be based on hypothetical risk.[80]

117. In its comments on the experts' responses to **Question 55**, the EC disagrees with what the experts have to say, so it simply tries to change the subject. Instead of addressing the unanimous advice from the experts that the EC opin-

---

[77] See Canada's comments above, at paras. 89-92.
[78] See EC Comments, Question 38.
[79] See Canada's comments above, at paras. 18-21.
[80] *EC – Hormones*, Report of the Appellate Body, at paras. 199-200.

ions did not evaluate additive risks, the EC chooses to attack the integrity of the experts and the legitimacy of their opinions, and then diverts attention to whether JECFA conducted an evaluation of such risks. The attack on the experts is unjustified: first, because they were asked whether the EC had conducted such an assessment and not whether JECFA did; and second, since it is the EC that claims that there are additive risks, it is up to the EC to demonstrate that such risks exist. In any event, the experts did indicate that JECFA had evaluated additive risks and there were no concerns about such risks arising from meat from treated animals given the extremely low doses of exposure from this source.

118.   The EC then acknowledges that the SCVPH did not address additive risks "because the state of scientific knowledge available by then ... did not allow such an assessment to be completed". Given that the EC's justification for its bans relates to concerns about proven additive risks, it is nothing short of a remarkable admission that additive risks were not even assessed.

119.   The EC provides contradictory comments on the experts' responses to **Question 56.**[81] First, it provides that is has "clearly been shown that the effects from exposure to different estrogens are additive". Then it indicates that it "has tried to do such an assessment [of the additive risks] when the information available was sufficient, but could not complete it because of gaps in our scientific knowledge". Whichever it is, both of these statements are remarkable in light of the importance to the EC's justification of its bans of an assessment of additive risks. And to the extent that the studies cited by the EC say anything about additive risks from oestrogens, they still do not answer the question of whether hormones from meat from treated animals contribute to such additive risks.

120.   In its comments on the experts' responses to **Question 57**, the EC completely ignores the advice of two of the three experts that cast serious doubt on the EC's justification of its authorization of the hormones for therapeutic and zootechnical purposes. In declaring this question unnecessary and irrelevant by virtue of certain Appellate Body findings, the EC completely misses the nature of the experts' criticism of the EC use for these purposes. The issue is not whether there was a violation for authorizing these uses, but that the mere authorization itself undermines the EC's dramatic claims that no threshold for adverse effects from these hormones can be established. This is what leads Dr. Boisseau to call it a "problem of principle" and Dr. Boobis to indicate that this demonstrates the EC believes there is in fact a threshold response. Moreover, the claim that the use of oestradiol for "such purposes is now virtually terminated" does nothing to respond to the criticisms.

121.   Since the EC's comments on the experts' responses to **Question 58** merely demonstrate the degree to which its arguments rest on hypothetical situa-

---

[81]   It is also necessary to note the irony in the EC's criticism of the experts for failing to provide precise references in its answers.

tions and assumptions, nothing in its statements warrants further comment from Canada.

122. In commenting on the experts' responses to **Question 59** concerning the EC's non-existent evaluation of the potential for adverse effects on the immune system from residues of hormones consumed in meat from treated animals, the EC employs two diversionary tactics. The first is to indicate that the existing international recommendations that these substances are safe are based on "out-dated" data, not on the basis that the data have been superseded, but simply on the basis that they are "old". This line of argument ignores both the fact that the age of the data does not determine their currency and, further, that in any event the hormones have been repeatedly re-evaluated by JECFA as new information becomes available, and the recommendations have remained largely unchanged. The second tactic of course is to argue that it is not the EC that must demonstrate that these adverse effects will occur, but, rather, that it is Canada that must demonstrate that they will not occur. For reasons already discussed on many occasions, this claim is without merit.

123. In its comments on the experts' responses to **Question 60**, the EC comments at great length about the bioavailability of MGA as a feed additive and on the potency of consuming implants of the other five hormones that have not been removed, but in the end provides very little by way of relevant commentary on whether one route of administration leads to adverse effects that are any *different* from the other route. The EC goes on to challenge Dr. Boobis's comments about the risks from misuse and abuse of MGA implants. However, the EC seems to have understood him to be advising on the implanting of MGA, which is not an approved use, even though it was clear that he was referring to only those hormones that could be administered with implants. To the extent that the EC misunderstood Dr. Boobis's comments, its own comments are of little value.

124. In commenting on the experts' responses to **Question 61** concerning the sufficiency of the evidence to conduct a risk assessment of the other five hormones, the EC does little more than continue its direct attack on the objectivity and professionalism of Dr. Boobis and Dr. Boisseau. The participation in this process of experts that have extensive experience with the evaluations of JECFA of these substances only enhances the Panel's ability to understand the considerable scientific evidence related to the safety of these hormones. Far from lacking objectivity, these experts are best placed to advise the Panel on the sufficiency of the evidence to conduct a risk assessment according to the internationally agreed techniques employed by JECFA. In this case, they both indicated the evidence was sufficient to do so.

125. In commenting on the experts' responses to **Question 62**, the EC continues again its attack, this time singling out the comprehensive and informed review by Dr. Boobis of all of the new material provided by the EC. While the EC indicates that a "more careful examination by a real expert of the same body of evidence" led to the opposite conclusions to those offered by Dr. Boobis, it neglects to inform the Panel and Canada who this "real expert" is and why his or her anonymous views should be considered more authoritative that those offered

by the expert specifically chosen for the task. In any event, it is difficult to see how the EC could consider Dr. Guttenplan's one paragraph enumeration of gaps a "more considered and objective view" than the 11 pages of analysis offered by Dr. Boobis.

VII.   COMMENTS ON THE COMMENTS FROM THE EC ON THE RESPONSES FROM THE INTERNATIONAL BODIES

126.   In relation to the EC's comments on the responses by the international bodies to **Questions 1, 5, 16, 17, 18** and **19**, Canada will not comment at this time.

127.   In relation to the EC's comments on **Questions 3** and **4,** Canada refers to paragraphs 12-14 of this document.

128.   In relation to **Question 7,** Canada refers to paragraphs 23, 35-44, and 83-92 of this document.

129.   In relation to **Question 8,** Canada refers to paragraphs 35-44 of this document.

130.   In relation to **Question 9,** Canada refers to paragraphs 18-21 of this document.

131.   In relation to **Question 10,** Canada refers to paragraphs 12-14, 83-92, 116-118 of this document.

132.   In relation to **Question 11,** Canada refers to paragraph 77 of this document.

133.   In relation to **Question 12,** Canada refers to paragraphs 16 and 17, 18-21 of this document.

134.   In relation to **Question 13**, Canada refers to paragraph 77 of this document.

135.   In relation to **Question 14,** Canada refers to paragraph 5 of this document.

136.   In its comments on the responses **Question 15**, the EC continues to ignore the existence of the *Recommended International Code of Practice for Control of the Use of Veterinary Drugs*, of Codex, which was mentioned by Codex as well as Dr. de Brabander.

137.   In relation to **Question 20**, despite the explanation by JECFA that the three natural hormones had been placed on the agenda of JECFA in 1999 at the initiative of the JECFA Secretariat to ensure that all the latest information had been evaluated, the EC insists that, in its words, "most of the data were the same old data". The Panel may wish to ask JECFA for further clarification in this regard. Canada also refers to paragraph 77 of this document.

138.   In relation to **Questions 23, 24, 25** and **26**, Canada refers to paragraphs 29-34 of this document.

VIII. CONCLUDING COMMENTS

139.   As the above comments demonstrate, rather than address specifically many of the important concerns raised by the experts about the EC's evaluation of the safety of the hormones, the EC has chosen instead to attempt to create confusion about these issues. It has done so by presenting the responses of experts in a misleading and flawed manner; it has done so by misrepresenting the meaning of much of the scientific evidence and international guidance documents; and it has done so by attacking the professionalism and objectivity of the experts and the Secretariats of the international organisations.

140.   Canada is confident, however, that the Panel will see through these efforts and will keep the focus on the real issues, and on the legitimate scientific and technical material, on which it needs advice to decide this case. Ultimately, on the basis of the substance of the responses from the experts and the lack of substance in the comments by the EC, Canada is confident that the experts have provided sufficient advice to allow the Panel to conclude that the EC's bans are not justified by the scientific evidence.

ANNEX G

TRANSCRIPT OF THE PANEL'S JOINT MEETING WITH SCIENTIFIC EXPERTS ON 27-28 SEPTEMBER 2006

27 September 2006, morning

Chairman

1.   Good morning. I would like to welcome the parties, the Panel's experts and representatives of international organizations to this joint meeting of the two Panels; the Panel on *United States – Continued Suspension of Obligations in the EC Hormones Dispute*, referred to as WT/DS320, and the Panel on *Canada – Continued Suspension of Obligations in the EC Hormones Dispute*, referred to as WT/DS321. The experts with us today are Dr. Boisseau, Professor Boobis, Dr. Cogliano, Professor De Brabander, Professor Guttenplan and Professor Sippell. We have representatives from the secretariats of the three international institutions: the Codex Alimentarius Commission, the Joint FAO/WHO Expert Committee on Food Additives, known as JECFA, and the International Agency for Research on Cancer, known as IARC. The representatives are Dr. Angelika Tritscher, WHO JECFA Secretary, and Dr. Annika Wennberg, FAO JECFA Secretary, Dr. Kazuaki Miyagishima, Codex Secretary, and Dr. Cogliano, one of the Panel six experts, who is also head of the IARC's Carcinogen Identification and Evaluation Group.

2.   May I now invite the heads of delegations of each party to introduce themselves and the other members of their delegations. I would appreciate if you could submit the list of your delegations' members to the Panel secretary if you have not done this already. The European Communities first please.

European Communities

3.   Good morning. My name is Theofanis Christoforou. I am Principal Legal Advisor of the European Commission in Brussels and I will be functioning as the head of delegation for these two days. If you agree each member of the delegation will introduce himself or herself.

4.   Good morning. My name is Thomas Jürgensen – I work for the European Commission.

5.   Good morning. My name is Sybilla Fries. I am from the Legal Service of the European Commission, now based in Geneva.

6.   Good morning Chair. My name is Gudrun Gallhoff. I work for the European Commission Directorate General Health and Consumer Protection.

7.   Good morning. Brian Marchant of the Commission, working for DG Trade.

8.   Good morning. Lothar Ehring, European Commission, DG Trade.

9.   Good morning. My name is Lars Berner and I am with the EC delegation here in Geneva.

10.   Gentlemen, this was the delegation as such, the officials, lawyers and other advisors. Now we have a long list of experts with us and will also allow each one of them to present themselves, starting from Mr. Dan Sheehan.

11.   Daniel Sheehan from Daniel M. Sheehan & Associates.

12.   Annie Sasco from the University of Bordeaux, cancer epidemiologist.

13.   Manfred Metzler, Professor of Food Chemistry, University of Karlsruhe, Germany.

14.   Niels Skakkebaek, Medical Professor, Growth and Reproduction, Copenhagen University.

15.   Henrik Leffers, Microbiologist, Growth and Reproduction, Copenhagen.

16.   Professor François Andre from the National Veterinary School of Nantes, National Reference Laboratory for Hormones, Ministry of Agriculture.

17.   Alain Paris from National Institute for Agronomic Research. I specialize in metabolism of steroids.

18.   Professor Heinrich Meyer, Technical University of Munich. I am the Chair of biochemistry and physiology at the Technical University. Thank you.

19.   I am Professor Frederik Vom Saal of the University of Columbia, Missouri in the United States.

20.   With the delegation are also representatives of the member States of the European Community, and if you agree they will present themselves. Thank you.

21.   Jukka Pesola, Counsellor, Permanent Commission of Finland.

22.   I am Christian Forwick from the German Mission in Geneva.

23.   I am Sebastian Keyserlingk from the German Ministry of Agriculture.

24.   I am Anders Christiansen from the Danish Mission, Geneva.

25.   Luca Burmeister, Danish Mission to Geneva.

26.   Lukas Paul from the German Mission here in Geneva.

27.   Cédric Pène from the French delegation in Geneva.

28.   Blas Vicente, Spanish Mission in Geneva

Chairman

29.   Thank you. The United States please.

United States

30.   Good morning Mr. Chairman, members of the Panel. My name is Jay Taylor with the US Trade Representative's Office. To my left is Dan Hunter with the US Trade Representative's Office here in Geneva. To my right is Dr. Adele Turzillo with the Food and Drug Administration. To Adele's right is Steve Wolfson with the Environmental Protection Agency. To his right is Kelly Stange with

the Foreign Agricultural Service. To her right is George York with the US Trade Representative's Office here in Geneva. Across the table from George is Dr. Ralph Cooper with the Environmental Protection Agency. Next to Dr. Cooper is Rita Kishore with the US Department of Agriculture Food Safety and Inspection Service. Next to Rita is Dr. Richard Ellis, Consultant, formerly of the Food and Drug Administration. And next to Richard is Dr. Gregg Claycamp with the Food and Drug Administration. Thank you.

Chairman

31.　Then I give the floor to Canada.

Canada

32.　Thank you Mr. Chairman. I am Rambod Behboodi, First Secretary here at the Canadian Commission to the WTO. Counsel with me today who will argue this case are to my left Mr. Rob McDougall at the Trade Law Bureau, and to my right Mr. Kevin Thompson, also of the Trade Law Bureau of the Department of Foreign Affairs and International Trade. The rest of the members of the delegation, from the far left, there is Angela Webb who is the Paralegal, Dr. Don Grant who is adviser to the Government of Canada. Next to Mr. Thompson we have Dr. Jim MacNeil who is head of the Centre for Veterinary Drug Residues of the Canadian Food Inspection Agency. We also have Ms. Michele Cooper, First Secretary at the Canadian Mission and Mr. Vasken Khabayan, who is Second Secretary at the Canadian Mission, and across from me Mr. Evan Lewis of the Technical Barriers and Regulations Divisions of the Department of Foreign Affairs and International Trade, and Mr. Bill Bryson of the Department of Agriculture. Thank you.

Chairman

33.　Thank you. I would like to continue by introducing the members of the Panels. On my right is Ambassador William Ehlers, who is Ambassador of Uruguay to India. On my left is Madam Claudia Orozco, who is a former senior official of the Colombian Government and who is now working in Brussels as an independent consultant. And myself, Tae-yul Cho, serving as Chair of these Panels. I am Ambassador and Deputy Representative in the Korean Mission here in Geneva. The two Panels are composed of the same individuals and in agreement with the parties, we are holding a joint meeting with the experts consulted by the Panels.

34.　I would also like to introduce the Secretariat officials who will be assisting the Panel: Mr. Yves Renouf, Legal Officer to the Panel; Ms Xuewei Feng, Secretary to the Panel, and Ms Gretchen Stanton, Ms Serra Ayral and Ms Christiane Wolff from the Agriculture and Commodities Division of the WTO Secretariat. Finally I would like to inform the parties of the presence of Mr. Walters Nsoh, Intern in the Agriculture Division and Ms Esther Katende, an intern with the WTO Legal Affairs Division.

35.   As you all know, further to the parties' common request, the Panel has decided to hold this meeting with the experts open for observation by the public through a closed circuit TV broadcast. I would also welcome those who are observing this meeting from another room at this moment. I would like to remind the viewers who are observing this Panel meeting that tape-recording or filming during the Panel meetings by anyone other than the WTO Secretariat is not permitted. In order to ensure an orderly proceeding and as a courtesy to everyone, I also request everybody, including those participating in the Panel meeting and those observing the meeting of the Panel, to turn off their mobile phones during the whole meeting.

36.   In addition I would like to underline that the parties may request that the public microphones be switched off when any confidential material or information is being discussed. Finally, if the meeting is adjourned or suspended, I will specify the time at which it will resume for the benefit of those in this room, but also for those viewing this hearing from CR II.

37.   May I also remind you that the meetings of panels in the WTO are tape-recorded and that at today's meeting as well as the meeting of tomorrow, English/Spanish/French simultaneous interpretation will be provided in relation to the public broadcast of this hearing through closed circuit television into Room CR II at the request of the parties. So please be sure to use the microphones when addressing the Panel and above all, speak slowly. I would like to express my sympathy with the interpreters for this meeting considering its extremely technical nature. I would also like to remind the experts and the parties that there are constraints and difficulties of interpretation and therefore technical language will be properly interpreted only if it is delivered at the reasonable pace. To the extent possible, any prepared notes or statements should be shared with the interpreters so as to facilitate their task and ensure accurate interpretation.

38.   Turning to a brief history of the Panels' proceedings, I wish to recall that at its meeting of 17 February last year the Dispute Settlement Body decided in accordance with Article 6 of the Dispute Settlement Understanding to establish two Panels pursuant to requests of the European Communities. I further recall that the Panels held a joint first substantive meeting with the parties and third parties on 12-15 September 2005.

39.   After its first substantive meeting, the Panel decided on 20 October last year to consult with experts who have specialized scientific expertise on the issue arising in this dispute. In consultation with the parties, the Panel adopted working procedures for its consultations with scientific and technical experts. These working procedures were communicated to the parties on 25 November 2005.

40.   The Panel received suggestions from experts from three international organizations, namely, the Codex Alimentarius Commission, the Joint FAO/WHO Expert Committee on Food Additives, the IARC, and from the parties. Following consultations with the parties on the candidate experts, the Panel appointed, as I mentioned, Dr. Boisseau, Professor Boobis, Dr. Cogliano, Pro-

fessor De Brabander, Professor Guttenplan and Professor Sippell to serve as scientific experts in this dispute.

41. In accordance with working procedures and after having considered the parties' comments, the Panel sent questions to the experts and international organizations on 13 April this year. The experts were requested to reply in writing by 12 June 2006, and these replies were communicated to the parties. Comments and counter-comments received from the parties and the expert replies were also provided to the experts in July.

42. The purpose of today's meeting is for the Panel to obtain further clarification of the scientific issues and to discuss the experts' written responses to the questions. The parties will also be given an opportunity to discuss the responses of the experts to the questions.

43. This two-day meeting will proceed in the following manner. Before proceeding with an examination of the specific scientific issues under consideration, the Panel will first give an opportunity to each expert and international organization representative to introduce themselves and make some brief introductory remarks, in particular in light of parties' written comments on their specific responses to these questions. But please bear in mind that these remarks should be kept as general as possible since we will subsequently discuss each issue in more detail.

44. Afterwards, the Panel intends to hold its discussions under five areas which are linked closely with the specific sections included in the written questions of the Panel to the experts. I will clarify the specific areas in a moment. For each of the five specific areas, I will open the floor to the parties to ask questions to the experts based on the written information and comments received thus far, addressed either to a specific expert or to the experts in general. The Panel would also pose some questions either at the beginning or following parties questions, depending on the issue. Once the question and answer process has been completed for one area, I will invite the experts and international organization representatives to make some concluding remarks, if they so wish, before moving on to next area. In addition to the four predetermined areas, we have also foreseen a fifth area to address any other issues not covered by any of the four areas.

45. Concerning the questions by the parties to the experts, the Panel will proceed as follows. Under each section, the Panel will first give the European Communities the floor to ask questions to the experts. Thereafter, the United States and Canada will be given an opportunity to ask their questions to the experts, including any follow-up questions to those posed by the European Communities. After that, the European Communities will be given the opportunity to pose any follow-up questions to those posed by the US and Canada. The Panel is mindful that these are officially two proceedings and it will make sure that parties are given ample opportunities to ask questions necessary for a clear understanding of the facts. However, the Panel notes that the scientific issues are similar in both cases and would strongly encourage the parties to avoid duplicating

questions. Please all keep in mind that this meeting has been convened primarily to hear the views of the experts and that parties will have ample opportunities to express their views at our meeting next week.

46.　　Finally, once we have covered all the five specific sections, I would like to give each expert and international organization representatives an opportunity to make concluding remarks based on the discussions held by that time. I am not intending to invite parties to make any concluding remarks during this meeting since they will have the chance to discuss any relevant points further during the Panel's second substantive meeting with parties scheduled for next Monday and Tuesday.

47.　　I would like to underline that the Panel may ask follow-up questions at any time during the proceedings. Moreover, although the Panel or the parties may address a question to one or more specific experts, all experts should feel free to respond to specific questions if they so wish. In making any remarks, both parties and experts are requested to minimize redundancy with what they have already submitted to the Panel in writing. I would also like to remind you all that experts and international organization representatives are expected to answer scientific and technical questions; they must refrain from addressing any legal issues, such as questions of interpretation of the SPS Agreement.

48.　　I would also like to recall that the purpose of today's meeting is to take advantage of the experts' presence to allow the Panel to gain a better understanding of the scientific issues before us. The Panel's experts have been selected after extensive consultations. I would like to express the Panel's appreciation for their contributions and their presence today. I am confident that the parties will also make the best of their expertise during these two days.

49.　　Let me also clarify that the Secretariat staff will prepare a summary of all the information provided by the experts and international organizations in their written responses to the questions as well as a transcript of the information provided by the experts and international organization representatives in the meeting today and tomorrow. Each expert will be asked to review this summary and the transcript and to confirm its accuracy. These will be part of the Panel's reports on these disputes.

50.　　Last but not least, I would like to recall that we the Panel members do not have scientific expertise. Therefore I would like to ask the experts to bear this in mind in replying to questions and explain issues in layman's terms, providing information on underlying concepts as necessary. In order to get a clearer picture with respect to the six hormones at issue, I would also like to invite all those taking the floor to clarify which of the six hormones their question or reply applies to.

51.　　Now I would like to introduce the five areas that I referred to earlier. In order to facilitate a focussed discussion, the Panel would like to structure the meeting under four specific areas which relate to the Panel's original written questions: Area 1 relates to terms and definitions, which corresponds mainly to Section A of the Panel's written questions to experts; Area 2 is risk assessment techniques, which corresponds roughly to Section B of the Panel's questions and to some of the Panel's questions to international organizations; Area 3 is related to relevant scientific evidence, which corresponds roughly to Section D of the Panel's questions to experts; Area 4 relates to EC assessment of risks, corresponding roughly to Section C and some elements of Section D of the Panel's questions; and Area 5 is, as I mentioned, other – any follow-up questions that do not fit in the above categories.

52.　　In their replies, the experts may want to refer to various documents, including the parties' submissions and exhibits. These documents are either filed in the binders placed in the cupboard over there, or in the CD-Roms. The CD-Roms can be opened and viewed in the laptop computers near your seats. The Secretariat staff are ready to help you locate these documents if necessary.

53.　　Unless there are any comments or questions we can now proceed to hear the experts' brief introductory remarks. I will first give experts the floor in an alphabetic order, starting with Dr. Boisseau, which will be followed by the representatives of the international organizations. Dr. Boisseau, you have the floor.

Dr. Boisseau

54.　　Thank you, Mr. Chairman. Let me begin by apologizing for my voice – I caught a cold some time ago and I am afraid that my voice is not very clear, but I shall do my best to make myself understood. So, my name is Jacques Boisseau, and I withdrew from professional life four years ago. Before that, I directed the National Agency for Veterinary Medicinal Products (ANMAV) in France for 20 years. I was a member of the European Union's Committee for Veterinary Medicinal Products for 14 years and headed it for six years when it was still in Brussels. For 13 years I participated in all of the meetings of the JECFA, and had the honour to chair four of them and to be Vice-Chairman five times. Finally, for about 15 years I headed the French delegation to the Codex Committee on Residues of Veterinary Drugs in Food (CCRVDF). So, I specified in my curriculum vitae that in the above capacities, I had not done any scientific work on hormones, and that consequently, I had not published anything on the subject. I suppose that I have the honour to be part of this panel of experts thanks to my experience in assessing the safety of residues of veterinary drugs in food. I would like at this point to make three remarks that could be of help to the discussions that will be taking place over these two days.

55.　　The first comment is as follows: the experts have been given 64 precise questions, to which they were asked to provide precise answers. Consequently, I think that any comments on the replies of the experts, or criticism thereof, should focus on the replies in relation to the questions asked and not in relation to the questions that were not asked. Secondly, I think it is important that we should all have a common understanding of the risk analysis procedure. In other words, we should clarify together, and in agreement with each other, what pertains to the risk assessment procedure as opposed to the risk management procedure. We should be able, as well, to reach a common understanding of what a hazard is, and what a risk is. Finally, we should be able to adopt a common approach to what a qualitative risk assessment, is as opposed to what we might call a quantitative risk assessment. Finally – since I had meant to be brief – I think that we must clarify together the specificities of conducting a risk analysis for an endogenous substance as opposed to a risk analysis for xenobiotic substances. There we are, Mr. Chairman, thank you very much.

Chairman

56.   Thank you. Professor Boobis, please.

Dr. Boobis

57.   Thank you Mr. Chairman. My name is Alan Boobis. I am currently a professor of biochemical pharmacology at Imperial College London where I am also a director of the Department of Health Toxicology Unit. I originally trained in pharmacology at the University of Glasgow, but since 1976 have been involved in studies of xenobiotic metabolism of foreign compounds and in toxicology, particularly mechanisms of carcinogenesis of dietary contaminants. For the last 15 years I have played a role in national, regional and international advisory committees, as an independent member of a number of committees advising on the safety of chemicals, both pesticides, veterinary drugs and consumer products. I have published over 200 papers in peer reviewed journals, including a small number on issues of hormone research. I currently have two PhD students and a post-doctorate research fellow working on aspects of oestrogen toxicity.

58.   I have very few comments to make specifically about the issue at hand today because I hold myself ready to expand upon my responses to the questions. I would just make one general comment at this time which is that in risk assessment it is important to recognize that it is not possible to establish safety with absolute certainty. Safety is a concept which is related to the probability of harm, and this is the reason that we use terms like "no appreciable risk". In risk assessment we don't have a concept of zero risk, because in strict scientific terms of risk assessment, risk is considered as a probability – the probability of harm based on the hazard of the compound and the specific conditions of exposure to the agent under consideration. Thank you.

Chairman

59.   Thank you. Dr. Cogliano, please.

Dr. Cogliano

60.   Thank you, Mr. Chairman, members of the Panel. My name is Vincent Cogliano. I am the Head of the IARC Monographs Programme at the International Agency for Research on Cancer in Lyon, France. The IARC monographs are a system of expert scientific reviews where we convene international working groups of scientific experts to evaluate the potential carcinogenicity of a variety of agents. They started out looking at chemical agents but since then have evolved to look at occupational exposures, chemical mixtures, lifestyle factors,

physical and biological agents. Over the 35 year history of the Monographs Programme we have looked at over 900 agents and identified approximately 400 as potentially carcinogenic to humans, including 100 agents which are considered to be known to cause cancer in humans.

61.   I am here perhaps in a double role; partially in my role at the International Agency for Research on Cancer but also as a member of the expert committee. Before coming to IARC I worked for nearly 20 years at the United States Environmental Protection Agency in Washington, DC where I was part of the Office of Research and Development assessing the health hazards of chemicals found in the environment. I am not going to make at this time any particular statements about risk assessment or risk but I do stand ready to assist the Panel in any way I can in answering any questions that come up today. Thank you.

Chairman

62.   Thank you. Then I will give the floor to Professor De Brabander. Please.

Dr. De Brabander

63.   Thank you, Mr. Chairman. My name is Hubert De Brabander. I know that my name is difficult to pronounce for non-Dutch speaking people, but we'll do our best. Maybe you can give me a nickname or something if you want to address me. I am from Belgium, from Ghent University, from the Faculty of Veterinary Medicine. I am trained as a chemist and during my PhD in chemistry I also obtained a degree in environmental chemistry, and concern for the environment will stay with me for the rest of my life. Then I was offered a position at the Faculty of Veterinary Medicine and I am still there as Head of Department of the Department of Veterinary Public Health and Food Safety. Over the years I worked mostly on analytical chemistry, residue analysis. I did a second PhD in analytical chemistry of food (aggregaat hoger onderwijs) and also a PhD in veterinary sciences. As you see my background is in analytical chemistry, but over the years I have become a little bit "veterinized", I should say. What I can offer to the Panel is my background, my experiences with residue analysis and practical experience in control of legal and illegal compounds. Thank you.

Chairman

64.   Thank you. Professor Guttenplan.

Dr. Guttenplan

65.   My name is Dr. Guttenplan. I have a PhD in chemistry but I have been working in biochemistry and carcinogenesis for over 30 years. I also have a Masters in public health and environmental sciences. I have been teaching biochemistry for a number of years and have been involved in carcinogenesis for 30 years. In responding to the questions I found one of the most difficult points to evaluate was the word "potential". Many times it arose – this is a potential carcinogen, this is a potential hazard – and this comes back to the notion of risk;

almost any chemical can be toxic if the dose is high enough. I think this has been a very difficult area for the Panel to determine; what a dangerous dose is, and whether the doses of hormones that are in the cattle produce levels in humans that are dangerous. I am prepared to answer any questions during my responses throughout the day. Thank you.

Chairman

66.   Thank you. Professor Sippell, please.

Dr. Sippell

67.   Thank you, Mr. Chairman. I have prepared for introduction a few Power-Point slides.[1] (May I have the first one.) Yes, there you see my affiliation; I am the only one of the experts who is a medical doctor, more specifically a Professor of Paediatrics, and I have been running the Division of Paediatric Endocrinology and Diabetology for now more than 25 years and also running a relatively highly-developed paediatric endocrinology lab. Our speciality is to do refined steroid analysis in very small samples from children, from premature babies to adult individuals.

68.   (Next – just the first line of the second slide please.) I am a relative newcomer in the field and it is very interesting that this dispute has already been going on for more than a decade, and to my knowledge no paediatrician, let alone a paediatric endocrinologist, has been involved as a member of one of your expert committees. To my knowledge, neither has one of the very active scientific organizations been involved in these disputes, for example the Lawson Wilkins Paediatric Endocrine Society which serves North America, so not only United States but also Canada, or the European Society for Paediatric Endocrinology. This fact is incomprehensible and paradoxical in view of the fact that prepubertal children are indisputably the most sensitive and vulnerable members of the population.

69.   (Next point, yes, you can leave it there.) Children have the smallest body size but the longest life expectancy and I see (next please) my mission here as an advocate of and spokesperson for children and their specific needs. Just remember that children are not just small adults but something very special and they are our future, no doubt. Through my reading (can you go on) I got the impression that the validity of the supersensitive recombinant cell bioassay for oestradiol is a key issue in all the debate at stake. I would like to remind you that this supersensitive assay has been developed at the National Institutes of Health, the foremost and most refined research institution of the United States. And with our American colleagues – who in general really don't question the validity of this assay (can you go on please) the novel finding of significantly higher oestradiol levels – E2 stands for oestradiol, the female sexual steroid – in prepubertal girls

---

[1]   Dr. Sippell's slides are contained in Attachment 1 to this transcript.

than in boys readily explains fundamental features of human biology for the first time. Many questions that had not been answered before, basic biological questions, can be answered now by this quantum leap supersensitive assay of oestradiol in small biological samples. So for instance, the onset of puberty is on average one year earlier in girls than in boys. This is readily explained by a higher oestrogen input in girls endogenously, from the ovaries, which are not sleeping during pre-puberty but are active on a low level. The second aspect is the much faster bone maturation in girls than in boys, with a result that bone maturation is ready in girls on average at age 15, whereas it is mature at age 17 in boys.

70.   (Next point.) Lower adult height in women than in men by a mean of 13 centimetres – in all populations men are taller than women. This can only be explained by this higher prepubertal oestrogen secretion in girls than in boys. (Next.) The higher weight for height or body mass index in girls than in boys at start of normal puberty is also readily explained by this. We have evidence that oestrogen exposure increases weight, and you can see in the next slide a piece of our own research. You can see on the left-hand side in the yellow box plot were 50 girls with central precocious puberty, in some of them puberty started at age two already, and at diagnosis they were already two standard deviations in weight above the mean for age and sex. So oestrogen exposure – in these cases endogenous oestrogen supersecretion – leads to increased weight. And we have shown that treatment of this disorder does not increase weight – you can see that the BMI standard deviation score stays stable or goes down.

71.   (Next please, and I am coming to the end.) The incidence of central precocious puberty, as I told you, is about 10 times higher in girls than in boys. This is only explained by the fact that girls have prepubertally higher levels of oestrogen than boys. (Next.) I contrast, the incidence of constitutional delay of puberty is much more common in boys than in girls.

72.   (And then the last slide.) Ethical considerations – they should always be kept in mind. To investigate whether eating hormone-treated beef elevates oestrogen levels in prepubertal children, tests cannot be performed in healthy children, because this would involve physical and psychological injury to them. (And the next.) Epidemiological studies comparing adverse effects in mass populations – and I have read in some of the comments that this is advocated – in healthy children eating beef from hormone-treated and untreated animals to compare them would also be unethical. We have to protect children from unnecessary clinical trials. This is not only (can you go on) written in the Declaration of Helsinki, but also in all good clinical practice guidelines and in the recent EU Parliament ruling on better medicines for children. I thank you for your attention.

Chairman

73.   Thank you. I now request Dr. Miyagishima, the Codex representative, to take the floor.

Dr. Miyagishima

74.   Thank you, Mr. Chairman, and I thank all the members of the Panel for having given the opportunity to the Secretariat of the Codex Alimentarius Commission to be invited to this Panel hearing. The Codex Alimentarius Commission is one of the three international standards-setting bodies explicitly enumerated in Annex A of the SPS Agreement. The Codex Alimentarius Commission was established in the early 1960s by FAO and WHO as an intergovernmental body operating under the auspices of these two parent organizations. The core business of Codex is to set international food standards and other related texts with the objective of protecting the health of consumers and ensuring fair practices in food trade. Codex, by setting international standards, acts as an international risk-management body, if I put it in the overall framework of risk analysis. Codex, as such, does not undertake any risk assessments but draws on the work done by FAO/WHO scientific bodies in that respect. The membership of the Codex Alimentarius Commission is open to all member states of FAO or WHO. Currently the Codex membership counts 174 countries, thus covering more or less 99 per cent of the world's population. Codex has one member organization, the European Community, which made a formal accession to Codex in November 2003. Codex' highest decision-making body is the Codex Alimentarius Commission, which used to meet every year after the creation of Codex, then the Commission turned to a biennial meeting rhythm, and since 2003 the Commission is again meeting every year.

75.   The Commission adopts the final draft standards prepared by its subsidiary bodies, and Codex has 20-plus subsidiary bodies covering distinct speciality fields. In the 1980s, Codex decided to extend its activity area to cover the residues of veterinary drugs in food. Codex thus established the Codex Committee on Residues of Veterinary Drugs in Foods, known as CCRVDF. This Committee met for the first time in 1986 and continued to meet yearly until 1992; since then it is meeting more or less at the interval of 18 months. CCRVDF acts as a subsidiary body of the Codex Alimentarius Commission on matters related to the residues of veterinary drugs in food, and as mentioned earlier it does not conduct any risk assessments. It bases all recommendations that this Committee forwards to the Commission on the scientific advice given by JECFA. Of course JECFA covers a broader field than just the question of residues of veterinary drugs; it also covers food additives and contaminants and as such advises other subsidiary bodies of the Codex Alimentarius Commission.

76.   Mr. Chairman, this is a brief outline of the history and the mission of the Codex Alimentarius Commission, and I am willing to provide further clarification or supplementary information with regard to the written information we have provided. I would like to stress the fact that we represent – together with the joint secretaries of JECFA – our respective organs and we do not, in my case, represent directly the member states. I would be most happy to reply on questions regarding procedures and facts, but I am rather reluctant to make any comments on those questions requiring value judgements or any analysis or assessment of scientific data. Thank you, Mr. Chairman.

Chairman

77.   Thank you. May I now invite the JECFA representatives, Dr. Tritscher and Dr. Wennberg, to take the floor in turn and to make their introductory remarks.

Dr. Tritscher

78.   Thank you, Mr. Chair. My name is Angelika Tritscher; I am from the World Health Organization here in Geneva. And within the WHO I work in the International Programme on Chemical Safety. Within the Programme I am responsible for the Chemicals in Food Programme. The main part of this Chemicals in Food Programme is to be the scientific secretariat to international expert bodies that perform risk assessment on chemical residues in food. We have two expert bodies, JECFA and JMPR. JMPR is the Joint Meeting on Pesticides Residues, but it is not of relevance here. The other expert body, as already mentioned, is the Joint Expert Committee on Food Additives, which despite the name, as was already alluded to, deals not only with food additives but also with contaminants, natural toxins and veterinary drug residues in food.

79.   Very brief to my training: I myself trained in food science – I have a Masters degree in food science and a PhD in biochemical toxicology. However, as was already mentioned, I am not here in a role as a scientific expert. My role here in this Panel is to explain JECFA procedures and risk assessment methodologies and definitions as scientific secretary to the committee.

80.   Let me say a few words about JECFA, to explain what JECFA is. JECFA is an international independent scientific expert body. It is jointly administered by FAO and WHO. It is not a standing committee, so JECFA experts are invited for each meeting, depending on the compounds on the agenda and the tasks at hand. As was already explained, in the international arena of food safety, JECFA is the risk assessment body and does not deal by any means with risk management activities, which in the international arena are the responsibilities of Codex and its subsidiary bodies. As mentioned, JECFA is jointly administered by FAO and WHO, and FAO and WHO have complementary roles in administering this Committee and inviting respective experts. The role of the WHO secretariat, according to the role of the WHO, is to invite experts that perform toxicological evaluation of the available data and then together with FAO – and my colleagues from the FAO secretariat will explain in more detail the role of FAO and FAO experts overall – the risk assessment is performed. The WHO experts perform the toxicological evaluation.

81.   JECFA first met 50 years ago – the first meeting was in 1956 – which means JECFA predates not only me but also the Codex Alimentarius Commission. Over the years, JECFA has really laid the ground work by developing the principles for how risk assessment of chemicals in food is done nowadays, both on the international and on national levels. Besides laying the groundwork, there is continuous improvement over the years, as published in the reports of each JECFA meeting. All publications of JECFA are publicly available, which nowa-

days luckily means on the internet, but also in print. We publish reports of each meeting that give the precise description of the data that allow the conclusion. Then we have toxicological monographs, published in the WHO Food Additives Series, that give a detailed description of the full toxicological database, including the full reference list. So far to the transparency of the outcome of the JECFA procedures. I will be glad to answer any questions there may be regarding JECFA procedures, in particular risk assessment methodologies and so forth. And with this I would like to give over to my colleague from the FAO. Thank you.

Dr. Wennberg

82.   Thank you, Mr. Chairman. My name is Annika Wennberg, and as was said by my colleague Dr. Tritscher, I am the FAO JECFA Secretary. We work together; we have complementary roles to serve JECFA as the independent scientific committee in international settings. As was also mentioned, JECFA has been in place for some time, since 1956, and it actually started to evaluate veterinary drugs in 1987. The first meeting dedicated to veterinary drugs residues was held in 1987, and JECFA also started developing the general principles for the assessment of residues in veterinary drugs in food. Under the FAO constitution, JECFA is convened according to article 6, which lays down that the Conference of the Council of FAO may establish committees and working parties to study and report on matters pertaining to the purpose of the organization. These consist of individuals appointed in their personal capacity, because of their special competence in technical matters. Joint committees may also be established according to that article. This is the basis for the support of FAO to the work of JECFA.

83.   I myself have a PhD in nutrition and metabolism from the medical faculty of Gothenburg in Sweden. I have also been involved in evaluations of veterinary drugs in my previous position as employee of the Medical Products Agency in Sweden. But I am here in my role as the JECFA Secretary to respond to questions and clarifications that may be asked about the procedures and the principles of JECFA, not to respond to any questions on the substance matters. Thank you for inviting me and I will stop here.

Chairman

84.   Thank you all for your introductory remarks and particularly for their brevity. I think that concludes our introductory part of this morning's session, and I now turn to the main business of today, the consideration of specific issues in the five areas I mentioned. On the first area I would like to let you know that the Panel would first like to pose some questions related to certain terms and concepts and definitions. I will pose our questions one by one, and after listening to the replies from the experts and from the parties, I will move on to the next question.

85.   The Panel's first question is: Please explain the terms genotoxic, mutagenic and carcinogenic. How are they related? How do they differ? What

are the consequences if a substance is genotoxic, mutagenic and/or carcinogenic? I would welcome any replies from any of the experts present, please.

Dr. Guttenplan

86.   A genotoxic substance is one which damages DNA. Many genotoxic substances are mutagenic and many genotoxic substances are carcinogenic. Whether they pose a risk depends on the dose.

Chairman

87.   Dr. Boobis.

Dr. Boobis

88.   Just a further clarification of some of these terms. A carcinogenic compound is one that causes some abnormality of growth control and results in a tumour. It can arise from many different mechanisms. One of them is through direct damage to DNA, which is genotoxicity, and mutagenicity is a change in the sequence of the DNA caused by a genotoxin. So there are several different mechanisms of genotoxicity, some of them due to direct interaction with DNA.

Chairman

89.   My colleagues asked if you could speak a bit more slowly.

Dr. Boobis

90.   So there are many different mechanisms of genotoxicity, for example one can interfere with the mitotic spindle, which is the apparatus that determines how cells divide, or there could be direct modification of the DNA, which could lead to a mutation, a heritable change in the DNA. These mechanisms can give rise to cancer, but there are other possibilities, such as a mitogenic stimulus, something that stimulates the cells to divide. Perhaps random errors during normal replication can lead to the selection of cells which have a tumorigenic potential and could grow into a tumour. It is critical therefore in the risk assessment of something which produces cancer in an animal – which is simply a descriptive term, that is that we observe a tumour in an animal – that if possible we would determine the mode of action or mechanism leading to those tumours; and if the compound is shown to cause genotoxicity, if possible to determine how that compound caused genotoxicity. Not all genotoxicity is the same, because some of it is direct and some of it is indirect.

Chairman

91.   Thank you. I am wondering whether any of our colleagues in the Panel have …

European Communities

92.   Thank you, Chairman. Would you allow me to ask a clarifying question? The question is to the two scientists that have already expressed themselves, I think in particularly to Dr. Boobis. Dr. Boobis, in reply to question number two you have stated regarding genotoxic potential that the compound might be capable of causing genotoxicity, and then you say usually *in vivo*. You continue then to say it remains to be determined whether genotoxicity is indeed expressed *in vivo*. So there are a few words and each word of course changes specific meanings and significance. The question is, do we always need to find genotoxicity *in vivo*? Is it sometimes sufficient that we observe in large numbers of experiments genotoxicity *in vitro*, and are there examples of substances for which we have accepted that they are genotoxic on the basis of the large number of experiments *in vitro*? I don't quite understand what you mean, it remains to be determined whether genotoxicity is indeed expressed *in vivo*. Could you please elaborate and eventually …

Chairman

93.   Before I give the floor to Dr. Boobis, may I remind the delegations that we will have further opportunities to exchange our discussions on the specific issues relating to risk assessment techniques and so on. So why don't you confine your questions to the terms and definitions at this moment, and then I will move on to the discussions in detail on the specific issues later.

European Communities

94.   Chairman, my question then is simple. Do we always have to observe genotoxicity *in vivo* before we conclude that the substance is genotoxic? Thank you.

Chairman

95.   Actually, I do have a question. I have a question on what is the meaning of *in vivo* studies and *in vitro* studies. May I ask the experts to respond to this question first before they respond to the question put forward by the EC. Dr. Boobis.

Dr. Boobis

96.   Well, *in vitro* means outside of the body, usually in a cell-based system in a test tube or culture dish. *In vivo* means in the whole organism, the intact organism. And because of the many protective mechanisms, both metabolic and repair mechanisms, there is an accepted wisdom that the observation of a response *in vitro* in an isolated cell does not necessarily translate into a response in the whole animal. This is one of the reasons, as far as I am aware, that almost all test strategies for genotoxicity have in them a component that if one is performing a risk-based approach, one would seek to confirm a positive *in vitro* result with an OECD-accepted method *in vivo*, of which there are several.

Chairman

97.   Could you respond to the question by the EC?

Dr. Boobis

98.   It is pretty well embedded in that response, Mr. Chairman, that the potential is that there are indications of a positive *in vitro*, but that it is not actually described as an *in vivo* genotoxicant or a true genotoxicant with relevance to the risk of that compound until an appropriate study is conducted on mechanisms and an *in vivo* test to confirm that *in vitro* observation. There are examples of compounds which are clearly genotoxic *in vitro* where they are negative *in vivo*, and the risk assessment has proceeded on the basis that the genotoxicity is not expressed in the *in vivo* situation for one of a number of reasons.

Chairman

99.   Thank you. You wish to ask a question?

United States

100.   Thank you Mr. Chairman. Dr. Boobis, to follow up on your response, if I may. Could you please explain the relationship, if any, between genotoxicity and carcinogenicity? For example, if a compound is genotoxic, is it also carcinogenic?

Dr. Boobis

101.   This is the reason I tried to distinguish between, in a narrow sense, genotoxicity and mutagenicity. The answer to the question, is a compound that's genotoxic always carcinogenic is clearly no. There are a number of compounds that cause genotoxicity in *in vitro* tests by mechanisms which are not expressed *in vivo* because of repair mechanisms and detoxification by enzymes of xenobiotic metabolism. What is clearer is that a compound that is a mutagen, a direct-acting, DNA-reactive mutagen, is frequently a carcinogen. But to say that a genotoxin equates to carcinogenicity is not correct and is the reason we place such weight on understanding the mechanisms of genotoxicity and the relevance of observations *in vitro* to the outcome *in vivo*.

Chairman

102.   I also would like to remind the other experts that they are free to respond to any questions put forward by the Panel or by the parties. Regarding the parties' questions, I understand that each delegation has its own set of questions to be put forward to the experts on the terms and definitions. So I would appreciate it if you limit your questions at this moment to only those related to answers given by the experts, and then I will give the opportunity for each delegation to put forward its own set of questions to the experts under this particular item. Is this clear? OK. Then as a related question, we understand that experts' responses referred frequently to genotoxic and hormonal mechanisms. What does the term

mechanism refer to in this context? And also, as a follow-up question, how a hormonal receptor operates and what hormonal receptor really means. These are two related questions from the Panel. I would give the floor to any of the experts. Dr. Boobis.

Dr. Boobis

103. I propose, if you will, to answer the first half and perhaps one of the other experts can answer the second half. In terms of mechanism, there is this concept that has evolved during the last ten years or more, led by the International Programme on Chemical Safety and others, to try to understand carcinogenicity in a deeper way than simply the observation of abnormalities of growth, which is after all what a tumour is. And this has led to this idea of a mode of action, and a mode of action is a series of key events which are necessary to lead to the formation of the tumour, and these key events comprise the biological changes induced by the chemical and subsequent events which then lead to the development of cancer. In the case of a mechanism, it is the actual molecular events that are responsible for those changes. So a hormonal mechanism in that sense would mean that it is the endocrine or hormonal effect of the compound that leads subsequently to changes that result in the development of a tumour, whereas a genotoxic mechanism would be where there is a mechanism independent of the hormonal action that results in damage to the DNA directly that leads to the tumour. That is not to say that there aren't situations where both could apply, that there could be elements of more than one mechanism.

Chairman

104. Thank you. Dr. Cogliano, please.

Dr. Cogliano

105. Thank you very much. At the International Agency for Research on Cancer, the expert working groups have been using mechanisms to affect their evaluations of carcinogenicity for approximately 15 years. And the reason it is important to try to understand the mechanism if you can is that sometimes it lets you know that the events, the processes occurring in experimental animals, are relevant to humans, and in other cases it lets you know that the processes that are happening in experimental animals do not operate in humans. IARC has had experience in many cases elevating the concern because what is happening in experimental animals is relevant to humans, and in other cases it downgrades or discounts the evidence in experimental animals because it is not relevant to humans. These principles are spelled out in IARC's guidelines, called the preamble to the IARC monographs. I would also like to say that it is not always necessary to understand the mechanism. For example, many carcinogens, like asbestos, vinyl chloride, benzene were determined from epidemiological studies to cause cancer before anybody had any understanding of the mechanism by which they cause cancer. But when we do have an understanding of the mechanism, it helps

us put the experimental evidence in better context about whether it could be predictive of humans or not.

Chairman

106.   Thank you. Dr. Boobis.

Dr. Boobis

107.   I would just like to add that one of the reasons that such weight is placed on understanding the mechanism and mode of action is that it can inform interpretation of a dose response, and that of course is one of the issues at hand in this dispute. If we understand how the tumour arises, we can also understand what the likely nature of a dose response is.

Chairman

108.   Thank you. Dr. Guttenplan, please.

Dr. Guttenplan

109.   A part of the question was the effects of different mechanisms on carcinogenesis, and we have already talked about the genotoxic effects. That is the direct damage to the DNA. A hormonal mechanism results in enhanced growth or proliferation of certain cells that are responsive to the hormones. You could have an incipient or a single cancer cell that might not grow during the lifetime of the organism, but in the presence of a stimulus such as a hormone, that cell might grow and then become a tumour. So these are basic differences in terminology and that is another reason why mechanism is important, to understand how these different compounds act.

Chairman

110.   Thank you. Is any of the experts ready to respond to the second part of my question on what a hormonal receptor is and how it operates in terms of the hormonal mechanism. Dr. Guttenplan, please.

Dr. Guttenplan

111.   Yes there are certain cells – my nametag fell down on my controller and I am listening in French and talking in English – alright that sounds better. There are certain cells that have on their surface, if you will, acceptor proteins that can accept oestrogen, and when they accept the oestrogen, they then start to grow, and that's an oestrogen receptor cell, what we call an oestrogen receptor-positive cell. So they would normally grow at a very slow rate or not at all, but in the presence of oestrogen they are stimulated to grow.

Chairman

112.   Thank you. Any other follow-up questions? Yes, Dr. Boobis.

Dr. Boobis

113.   It is also, I think, relevant that the endocrine system, the system that the hormones act within, is a network of hormones and a network of receptors, and is part of the normal physiological control mechanisms of the body. These hormones evolved as one of the processes whereby we can function as organisms. They are signalling molecules which are transported in the blood from remote sites of production to their sites of action, so they differ from some other signalling molecules which are produced locally. The important thing about a hormone is that it is actually distributed by the blood and is an essential part of normal physiology. So we are looking in terms of hormones as residues against an existing background of hormonal activity, certainly for the endogenous hormones, sorry, the natural hormones.

Chairman

114.   Thank you. Dr. Sippell.

Dr. Sippell

115.   Yes, I would like to add that this network Dr. Boobis was alluding to is particularly sensitive in children, more sensitive than in adults. And this is very important also in the receptor levels. Some receptor function is really much different from adult individuals in order to allow growth and development at puberty.

Chairman

116.   Thank you. Dr. Guttenplan.

Dr. Guttenplan

117.   Yes, it is probably obvious to most people, but I just mention a few of the well-known oestrogen receptive organs, which are the breasts, the prostate, the ovaries and the uterus. And a somewhat different comment on genotoxic effects which Dr. Sippell brought to my mind is that genotoxic effects can be a lot more effective if the cell is rapidly dividing, so children represent an exceptionally sensitive population to genotoxic effects, too, not just hormonal effects on cell replication.

Chairman

118.   Thank you. But why is it causing only prostate and breast cancer, other than ...

Dr. Guttenplan

119.   Well, nobody is saying it only causes those, oestrogen is probably involved in ovarian cancer and uteran cancer.

Chairman

120. The next question is: what is marker residue? How is it established? And what is a bound residue? Why is it significant? Dr. De Brabander please

Dr. De Brabander

121. Would you repeat again the question, Mr. Chairman.

Chairman

122. What is a marker residue, how is established, what is a bound residue and why is it significant in this?

Dr. De Brabander

123. When a drug is given, or if a compound is given to a human being or to an animal, it is metabolized, and that metabolization is different according to the compound, also according to the species. When it is metabolized, it can be different for humans, it can be different for animals, it can be different in different animals, and if you want, and I go from the point of control, if you want to control that a given compound is administered, you have to look at the metabolite which you will find in a given matrix. What I call a matrix is urine, faeces, meat, whatever is available and you can measure. The marker residue is the residue which you will find. That is a general definition for me as control, it will be different if you look from a veterinary direction. And what is a bound residue? It can be a residue which is bound for example to tissues or to other compounds, so that you must use special techniques to extract it. Thank you.

Chairman

124. Before I give the floor to my colleagues, I will give the floor to Dr. Wennberg and Dr. Boisseau.

Dr. Wennberg

125. Thank you, Mr. Chairman. JECFA has also provided a definition for marker residue, which is in line with what Professor De Brabander has stated. It is a way to actually define what you want to analyse. It is the parent drug, or any of its metabolites, or a combination of these with a relation to the concentration of the total residues of the veterinary drugs in each of the tissues, i.e. the target tissues. What you want to measure is the level of the drug at any time between administration of the drug and the depletion of the residues to the safe level. So it means that to be able to recommend maximum residue limits which will be useful in the control of the safe use of the veterinary drug, you have to have a method, an analytical method, which measures a chemical substance which relates to the veterinary drug that has been administered, either the drug itself, or a combination of the drug and metabolite, or a metabolite of the drug which is formed in the body of the animal. The definitions of bound residues are the residues which cannot be extracted by the method used to measure the residues of

the drug in the tissue in question. There can be different ways of binding of chemical substances to various components of tissue, protein, fats, carbohydrates, etc., and the way to determine whether these residues should or should not be included in the residue definition is a matter to be determined on a case-by-case basis, depending on the behaviour of these bound residues, whether they can be released by enzymatic or other mechanisms, or whether they are actually completely bound and inactivated as such by their bondage to molecules in the tissue. Thank you.

Chairman

126.   Thank you. Dr. Boisseau.

Dr. Boisseau

127.   Thank you, Mr. Chairman. To begin with, a few words about marker residues. It is a challenge for those who perform evaluations to reconcile the frequent complexity of the metabolization of a substance, which can give rise to a multitude of derivatives of varying concentrations, and with the need for a simple control method. In other words, you have to be able to combine the two.

128.   The purpose of toxicological evaluation is to identify, in terms of a toxicological effect that is deemed relevant for the evaluation of the products, all of the residues including the parent substance and the metabolites associated with this toxic aspect. Most of the time, metabolism does not yield one single residue associated with the toxic effect. Thus, to keep the control simple, it is necessary to identify among the residues the one that can be considered a marker residue – in other words the residue that reflects, according to the time in a given matrix, the evolution of all of the residues of concern. Thus, there must be a constant quantitative relationship over time between the marker residue content in a given tissue and total residues of concern – i.e. that are of interest in terms of the toxic effect in question – taken as a whole. As it is not usually possible, however the modern methods used, to analyse different substances at the same time, it is much easier to follow a single residue, the marker residue, which must reflect, over time, the concentration in a given tissue of all of the residues of concern in terms of toxic effect.

129.   Now, as regards bound residues, these are what we call – and I do not wish to repeat what Doctor Wennberg has just said – residues that are covalently bound with macromolecules, and in that sense, are not bioavailable – i.e. they are not spontaneously available – as opposed to the so-called free residues, which are not bound to macromolecules. Since for the most part, these residues cannot be extracted, they are identifiable and quantifiable by so-called radioactive methods. Once the content of bound residues in a given tissue has been identified, we have to know what they signify, since the normal metabolism of a substance could lead to the complete degradation of that substance and the reincorporation of very simple monocarbonic elements, for example in the normal protein anabolism in particular. And where you have CO^2, for example, which is radioactive if it is the carbon of the CO^2 that is marked – it is not because this

CO^2 is reincorporated in a protein synthesis that it will necessarily pose a safety problem for the consumer. In other words, the mere identification of a certain bound residue content does not necessarily mean that these bound residues pose a problem. Thus, it is up to those conducting the toxicological evaluations – and this is not easy – to go further in the identification of theses bound residues, of their possible release according to the methods that Doctor Wennberg has just mentioned, to see if these covalent bindings could have an impact on the biology of the cell in which they have taken place. Thank you Mr. Chairman.

Chairman

130.   Thank you. I now give the floor to Madam Orozco – it is OK? Dr. Wennberg, would you like to take the floor? If that is not the case, Dr. Guttenplan.

Dr. Guttenplan

131.   I would suggest for bound, at least the way it is being discussed now, that there should really be a descriptive term there, covalently bound, because bound can be somewhat ambiguous. It just means that it is contained very strongly in a tissue, whereas covalently bound basically means that it is unavailable.

Chairman

132.   We have already heard some comments on bioavailability, but I would like you to further elaborate on what bioavailability is, and why is it relevant. Dr. Boobis.

Dr. Boobis

133.   Bioavailability is the availability to the interior; the systemic circulation of a compound, in this case via the oral route of exposure, and it can be less than complete because the material is not physically available, for example it is bound covalently to the food matrix, because it does not cross the intestinal wall easily, so absorption is incomplete, or it is metabolized either in the small intestine, the site of absorption, or the liver; because the peculiarity of the anatomy of the digestive system is that almost everything that is absorbed across the small intestine into the circulation first goes through the liver before it gets into the body, and the liver has a tremendous capacity to metabolize compounds. And so for some compounds, drugs and dietary chemicals, it is possible for the small intestine and/or the liver to metabolize to less active or inactive products some or even all of what is being absorbed. So this means bioavailability is less than 100 per cent, what is available to have a biological effect on the body is less than what was anticipated based on the administered dose or the ingested dose. And so in this assessment one would like to know how similar are humans to the experimental animals for example in terms of bioavailability.

Chairman

134.   Thank you. Dr. Sippell, please.

Dr. Sippell

135.   Again the special case in children regarding bioavailability, as an example for instance we paediatricians or paediatric endocrinologists know very well that a twentieth of the daily dose of the natural oestradiols being used in adult women is already effective in prepubertal girls in stimulating growth, weight development and inducing puberty. So bioavailability is certainly in children much higher in many instances than in adult individuals, and the problem is that pure bioavailability studies which tell us which compound is being absorbed to which extent in a two-year-old or three-year-old or four-year-old child are simply not available because they are unethical to perform in healthy children.

Chairman

136.   Thank you. Dr. Guttenplan.

Dr. Guttenplan

137.   Another way of expressing bioavailability is to compare the blood dose that one would obtain by injecting the compound intravenously compared to what one actually obtains when one ingests the compound orally. So if you get a much lower effect orally than you would intravenously, you have much less bioavailable compounds.

Chairman

138.   You wish to ask a question?

United States

139.   Just a clarification, Mr. Chairman. Dr. Sippell, you mentioned, referenced a daily dose in women, can you clarify what dose you are talking about or what sort of treatment of women you were referring to?

Dr. Sippell

140.   Daily replacement dose in women who for instance lack ovarian function.

United States

141.   And what would the quantification of that dose be? Is there an estimate of the level of that dose in terms of quantity?

Dr. Sippell

142.   I mean that's the amount necessary to replace endogenous oestradiol production which is not functioning or absent.

Chairman

143.   Thank you.

European Communities

144.   Chairman, clarification, what has been said previously by Dr. Boobis on this? Is it always necessary that – either through injection or oral absorption, in order to determine bioavailability – that the drug goes first through the clearing system, the liver, or is there another route which does not necessarily go through the liver? Is this also possible? And do you know if any of these substances enter the human body in that way?

Chairman

145.   Dr. Boobis.

Dr. Boobis

146.   There are other routes of course for absorption; a small amount will by-pass the portal blood supply, which is the one that goes to the liver. It is possible that something could be absorbed into lymphatics. It very much depends upon the physicochemical properties of the agent that is being absorbed. Of course early on oestrogens were trialled in adult patients for therapeutic purposes and it was apparent then, in those early studies, that there is a very substantial metabolism in the liver which made them unusable for nonhepatic targets in adult males, and this is the reason that they are given by other routes; to bypass that very extensive first-pass metabolism, pre-systemic, pre-absorption phase of metabolism. So there are data in adults. I mean I certainly take the point that has just been made by Dr. Sippell, that these data are not available in children, but in adults there are actually data in human subjects. But I would like to add an additional point about the ethical nature of the question of data gaps. There are studies that one could envisage to answer the question as to whether a child has similar or lower first-pass metabolism without giving a hormone. There could be oestradiol present in normal food; and we have done such studies on other compounds where it would be unethical to give the compound itself. But because it also occurs in low dosage as part of the natural diet it is possible with sophisticated analytical chemistry to design a natural experiment, which is that you just look at what is in the diet, measure what is in the blood and then determine whether there is any change. So one can think of experiments, if there is considered to be a data gap, to seek to address that data gap.

Chairman

147.   Thank you. Now the floor is for Madam Orozco.

Ms Orozco

148.   Yes, thank you. I had a question for Dr. Sippell, because I assume that something similar happens when you want to test or give drugs, medicines to

children. You have to know what is the bioavailability, so how do you find out the bioavailability of other substances?

Dr. Sippell

149.   That is indeed a very difficult question and there are special regulations to protect the integrity of children. You know, if they are not healthy, then you can do – with the informed consent of parents and guardians – you can do such studies, but you cannot take blood, for instance, just to study bioavailability. This is unethical.

Ms Orozco

150.   Just one question. How do you find out what is the bioavailability of medicines that are being developed for children?

Dr. Sippell

151.   Yes, that is a very very difficult question, and I am not a paediatric pharmacologist, but this is very much debated, how this can really be done. It cannot be properly studied as in experimental animals or in adult people.

Ms Orozco

152.   Do you know how it has been done until now? Because if one goes to any pharmacy one will find a cough syrup for children, and someone has studied how much is its bioavailability in the child, because we know that one spoon or two spoons would be enough or too much.

Dr. Sippell

153.   Most medications we prescribe or give to sick children are not licensed for, let's say, infants or young children, because there have never been done proper studies, as in adults. It is just by experience, by empiric, and that's a big big gap in our knowledge, that we for instance cannot do metabolic studies in infants or in small children. You know the access to their circulation is so difficult, and if some of you have ever done a blood puncture in a premature infant or so, its really very very difficult, and I am not aware of any big trials which can, or have been applied, to study these bioavailability factors.

Ms Orozco

154.   Just one last question. Nowadays a child, maybe two years old, might fall ill, might have an infection, might have a virus, and antibiotics are being suggested. So somehow until now someone has been able to find alternatives to find out more or less what bioavailability is, or at least to be able to estimate it drawn from something else. Do you know how?

Dr. Sippell

155. Exactly. We deduce from adults or from young adults, and of course observe any risks that are being observed, you know the reactions and so on, and in general this is of course explained to the parents and it's compassionate use, it's, as we call it, individual trial in a sick child. That's easy.

Ms Orozco

156. I am not asking about extreme cases, because there are situations where there is need to consent, but for example something which is daily occurrence, you go and you buy a syrup for coughing, or – it should not be, maybe, but it happens all the time – that antibiotics have been prescribed as a medicine, they are prescribed to a lot of children since a very early age, so it is common occurrence what I am talking about.

Dr. Sippell

157. This you can study of course with their metabolism, their absorbance and their bioavailability in sick children. You know that when a new antibiotic comes up, then of course we are doing studies in our patients. That is different from the healthy population in children. Do you understand what I mean?

Ms Orozco

158. Not really, because when a person, an adult, takes a child to a paediatrician because it's ill, the paediatrician will examine the child and conclude you need this or that. You go out from there, you go to a pharmacy, no one asks you anything; if it's known that that medicine at that dose is ok, there is no further clearance, so somehow the system has been able to identify ways to make sure to every consumer that it does not pose a problem. What I am trying to find out is: in the normal cases until now, how has society been able to estimate the absorption in a child?

Dr. Sippell

159. Just by guessing. Even the dosing is in many many instances pure empiric. In modern drugs its somewhat better, but in the past these old standard drugs have never been tested properly in clinical trials and therefore many of these drugs in Europe have lost their licence and have to be retested and this creates tremendous ethical problems. And that is a problem of paediatric pharmacology worldwide.

Chairman

160. I give the floor to Dr. Boobis first and then to the United States.

Dr. Boobis

161. Just in the interest of clarification, Chairman, I would like to make a couple of points. One is that it is important, when we are talking about children, we don't lump them all together, it is critical to recognize that an infant is not the same as a prepubertal child. There is a tremendous range of biology and physiology that changes from early childhood onwards to adulthood, and we have to treat them as distinct groups, and the effects of the hormones will vary as well depending upon the age. We don't use this term child to encompass everything under puberty.

162. And the second point is, it is actually possible for some compounds to design experiments that do not require you to take invasive measures. It is not necessary to take blood always to get some measure of what is in the circulation. Two examples would be a saliva sample, which could be acquired just by passive and non-invasive collection, and similarly the collection of excretions, particularly urine, where, if the compound is largely excreted as a parent or metabolite in the urine, one can get comparative information on bioavailability. So it is not always necessary to use invasive blood sampling techniques to get some indication of whether the compound is absorbed and the nature that the compound is absorbed in. It is just for clarification, if one is thinking about data gaps that might be filled in the future, for example. There are possible strategies that exist to do that.

Chairman

163. Thank you. The US.

United States

164. Thank you, Mr. Chairman. I think that Dr. Boobis just spoke to the point I wanted to raise. Thanks.

Chairman

165. Thank you. EC.

European Communities

166. Could we ask the representatives of the international organizations, in particular JECFA, whether this type of experiments for the residues of these substances which we are talking about here in children or in adults have been performed so that we know what one member of the Panel, Madam Orozco, was looking for, whether this has been done in this case, and why not. For example, when the United States has licensed these substances, why did it not look and why did it not perform these kind of experiments here for example. Thank you.

Chairman

167. Is the representative of JECFA ready to respond? You have the floor.

Dr. Tritscher

168.   I don't think we are in a position here to give the detailed response as to exactly what type of data were submitted and looked at by JECFA in individual compounds, that is not our role here. And I would like to point out that JECFA is not a regulatory authority, so we are not talking about drug registration; it is not a registration authority, which is very different. Studies as were just referred to would have to be partially done and submitted to a regulatory authority that registers drugs for specific drug uses. JECFA looks at scientific data, toxicological data and human data, epidemiologic or experimental studies of any kind that are submitted to the experts or that are publicly available in the published literature. And I am in no position now – I would have to go back to all the individual evaluations that have been done and that have been published in order to find out if any specific studies in children or young infants would have been performed. I am not aware of this.

Chairman

169.   EC.

European Communities

170.   Well, Madam, we are aware of what happened and we can tell you now; because, as you know, when JECFA evaluated these substances in 1988, all of the five substances, and in 1999 the three natural hormones and in 2000 for melengestrol acetate, we know from what we have seen that none of these experiments involved the kinds of experiments Madam Orozco was asking about. So we would appreciate if the member of JECFA goes back next week or the week after and has a look and can inform the Panel where this indeed has happened. We will give you the time to do that if necessary. Thank you.

Chairman

171.   Thank you. Dr. Tritscher please.

Dr. Tritscher

172.   With all due respect I am not sure what this really would contribute to go back on all these individual things if you already say that you also have an answer to that. The question is a different one to me: what is the relevance of this kind of study in light of the overall weight of evidence, in the light of the overall data that has been submitted and that has been looked at?

Chairman

173.   May I remind delegations again we are now on the first area, on terms and definitions, so I would like you not to go into discussions on the other specific issues. EC.

European Communities

174.   Chairman, this is all fine and we can let you go on asking questions, no problem, but please bear in mind that we will have other questions later on, and it is only for that purpose we intervene. We restrain ourselves from intervening really in order to give you the time which you think you need to clarify these questions, but we will have questions to ask on practically the same issues which are being discussed now. So with this understanding there is no problem from us of not asking questions now.

Chairman

175.   Thank you. It is quite clear to the Panel. Dr. Boobis you would like to – thank you. And the next question from the Panel is very technical and I don't even know whether I can pronounce the terminology correctly but I will try. Please explain the units used in measuring hormone levels, for example in Dr. Boisseau's response to question 38 of the Panel, in particular please explain ng per ml is or pg per ml, ng per person per day, microgram per day, and how they are converted. Dr. Boobis.

Dr. Boobis

176.   There are two main ways of expressing units – actually, I was going to introduce another unit which is micromoles, but I will stick to two at the moment. These are masses per unit volume, so the base would be grams per litre, where we have so much mass in grams per one litre of liquid. They are scaled to units of 10 according to the Système international, the SI units, so they go: micro is 10 to the minus 6 of a gram, nano is 10 to the minus 9, pico is 10 to the minus 12. In expressing dosages in an animal study or with respect to human exposure we often divide by the body weight, so we get so many nanograms per kilogram of body weight per day. So that is where the kilogram comes from, that is to normalize it to the weight, and that is because many effects scale from one species to another – although how much is open to discussion, but that is a scientific debate – on the basis of body weight. So, in other words, if we give a microgram to a mouse it is not equivalent to giving a microgram to a human, because a mouse is so small, so we divide by the body weight to get a body weight-normalized dose, which allows a better – not ideal, but better – comparison of dosage. I was going to introduce the micromole if you wish me to clarify that, which is based on molecular weight, so it essentially allows compounds to be compared on the basis of how many molecules of one to how many molecules of another. Because when you take a small molecule, one gram is going to represent more molecules than when you take a large molecule; and if it is interacting with a receptor it is the number of individual molecules that counts, not the absolute weight, so sometimes we express them in terms of moles. I agree it is a technical issue, discussion.

Ms Orozco

177. Just one clarification. This, for example, nanograms per millilitre – is it already normalized by body weight or is that a second stage?

Dr. Boobis

178. A separate stage. This is a concentration, nanograms per ml.

Chairman

179. Thank you. Dr. De Brabander please.

Dr. De Brabander

180. Thank you, Mr. Chairman. I used to teach analytical chemistry and residue analysis to veterinarians, so I developed something to help them understand these units and maybe it will help also the Panel, so it is just not technical. If you start from a lump of sugar which is approximately 6 grams and you put that lump of sugar in a can of coffee, which is approximately 0.6 litres, you have approximately 1 per cent. When you put it in a bucket of water, then you have 1 per cent, and we are familiar with that because in alcohol control we are in that unit, 0.5 per cent is the limit in Belgium. When you go down and you place the same lump of sugar in a truck which is bringing the gasoline to your home, you are in a range of what we say 1 ppm, one part per million, or 1 milligram per kilogram, or 1 microgram per gram. If you go down and you have it in an oil tanker then you are at a level of 1 ppb, or one nanogram per gram, that is to say one nanogram per millilitre. So if you go still down (you can go down and down further) then you go really to very very low concentrations, like if you can imagine that you have a soccer field and you have submerged it with water from 1 metre high, and you take 1,000 soccer fields and you put one lump of sugar in it then you are again a concentration factor of 1,000 times lower. Maybe that can help the Panel understand. It is not very technical, I know, but I try to make it comfortable for you.

Chairman

181. I agree with your point of view on layman's terms explanations, because it was much helpful for us to understand. Dr. Cogliano.

Dr. Cogliano

182. Thank you very much. I would like to address a little bit of the point about the difference between nanograms per millilitre and nanograms per person per day, because at IARC many times we look at all of the studies that are published in the scientific literature, and different investigators will report the doses in different ways, and we need to try to get some kind of common conversion. It helps us to understand, for example, why one study might be positive and another study might be negative. The positive study might have been conducted at 10 times higher dose, but the units are expressed differently. The third one there,

the nanogram per person per day, gives a good example of why you do want to perhaps normalize the dose, because a nanogram in an adult woman is very different than a nanogram in an infant per day. You could perhaps normalize it by body weight, but there might be other ways of doing it. The first unit that you have on the board, nanograms per millilitre, is a different way of normalizing it. It is the concentration in the blood, so it is one nanogram per millilitre of blood, and maybe that is an equivalent concentration, maybe it's not.

183.   This actually suggests also why mechanism is important. I think you heard earlier this morning from one of the experts that the rates at which cells are dividing is very important, if you have one nanogram per millilitre while cells are dividing very rapidly, that might have different effects than one nanogram per millilitre in an organ where the cells are not dividing very rapidly. So it is important to try to understand the mechanism, and which of these different units of concentration or dose or exposure is most relevant. Now frequently we don't know which is exactly the right one, and we make our best professional judgement on that. But I think – just to help everybody understand – the units that you have up there are really measurements of very different kinds, and it might take a mathematical model or a conversion formula to go from one to the other. But if we do know how to make those conversions, it can help us understand how a dose in different studies or in different populations might relate to each other.

Chairman

184.   Thank you. Dr. Guttenplan.

Dr. Guttenplan

185.   Just another way of maybe expressing what has been expressed before, a microgram per ml is one part per million, a nanogram per ml is one part per billion, and then if somebody consumes a ml of a compound that was one microgram per ml that person would consume one microgram of that compound for every ml. It may sound simplistic, but it might help people to understand some of these units.

Chairman

186.   Thank you. Dr. Boobis.

Dr. Boobis

187.   So just two additional points of clarification. Dr. Cogliano has already referred to the concentrations in blood, and the question was raised from the Panel earlier about normalization, they would not be normalized for body weight because – depending on the sensitivity of the receptor – it is the circulating concentration that determines response, and so one microgram per ml in a human and one microgram per ml in a rat are essentially equivalent. They may not give the same response, depending on the receptor, but they are equivalent because

they are distributed throughout the body. And the other point is that, on the nanogram versus picogram, just a simple point of explanation is that the reason we use these different terms, and it does cause a lot of confusion I recognize, is to avoid the situation of getting into a lot of zeros, so if one expressed something that in picograms was 0.00001, we would just convert it back down to the next appropriate unit, to make it a slightly more manageable number, and that happens in both directions, so it is a practical consideration there.

Chairman

188.   Thank you. Dr. De Brabander.

Dr. De Brabander

189.   Yes, for the benefit of the Panel I should also say that if you work with students, you learn that they have difficulties to work with those concentrations, they really need a training on that. You can put very difficult questions, and what may be interesting also for you is that you should not underestimate the psychological factor, which is coming with how you will say how the concentration is. For example, if you say it is "0.1 milligram per kilogram" it sounds less than if you said "100 micrograms per kilogram" – but both are the same. The psychological factor of expressing the concentration is very important and veterinary students should learn to see through that.

Chairman

190.   If there are no other follow-up questions, then the Panel's last question on this item is: what are xenobiotics? Dr. Boobis.

Dr. Boobis

191.   They are from the Greek root xeno, foreign; biotic, to the life, so they are compounds that are not produced naturally in the body, so they are a whole range of so-called foreign compounds. Usually we exclude from xenobiotics nutrients in the diet, so the essential nutrients in the diet like protein, carbohydrates etc. will not be classified as xenobiotics, but everything else, all the chemicals we are exposed to would be regarded as xenobiotics. It is simply a convenient way of lumping together an awful lot of different molecules.

Chairman

192.   Dr. De Brabander.

Dr. De Brabander

193.   I agree totally, but I would add to that, if you go through all animals and all human beings the definition of xenobiotic is a little bit different, because some components may occur naturally in some animals and not in other animals and not in human beings. We don't have to go into detail, but it can be confusing

if you speak about xenobiotic, it can be xenobiotic in one species and not in another one, and also in certain conditions.

Chairman

194.   Thank you for your clarification. This concludes the list of the Panel's questions on area 1, and I now give the floor to the parties to ask their own questions to the experts under this particular item. The floor is open. I will give the floor to the EC delegation first.

European Communities

195.   Thank you, Chairman. So in this broad area of terms and definitions we have one question first addressed to experts, in particular Dr. Boobis and probably Dr. Guttenplan. Dr. Boobis says in his reply to question number 2, where the definition of steroidal oestrogens is provided, at the end of his reply, that these substances – steroidal oestrogens – act through oestrogen receptors, and my question is: is it really the only way they act, is it only through oestrogen receptors, or do they act through another mechanism, one or more?

Chairman

196.   Thank you. Is Dr. Boobis or Dr. Guttenplan ready to respond? Dr. Guttenplan.

Dr. Guttenplan

197.   The evidence that oestrogens act through a non-receptor mechanism is not strong. There have been a lot of studies of what we call *in vitro,* in test tube studies, but there is some recent evidence that has not been published yet which pretty much confirms that oestrogens can act by a genotoxic mechanism in humans. However, the level is very very low and you need supersensitive instruments to detect it.

Chairman

198.   Dr. Boobis.

Dr. Boobis

199.   I think it is important that we recognize that there is a difference between what a given oestrogenic compound can do and what we mean by oestrogenicity. So we can argue or discuss whether oestradiol has various properties, but some of those properties may be additional to its oestrogenic activities. Oestrogenicity is a defined biological term and it functions through specific biological pathways, which is not to say that some compounds which are oestrogenic cannot have other properties. So I think we need to make a distinction, we cannot lump everything that is oestrogenic into one chemical class and say that it always has other properties. It is absolutely clear that not all oestrogens have any genotoxicity, not all of them, some of them do, some of them don't. It is probably not a

function of oestrogenicity that causes that effect, it is some other property that they have, in the case of oestradiol, it produces quinones; not all oestrogens can produce those structures.

European Communities

200.   Gentlemen, I recall, if I may say so, in a statement by Dr. Guttenplan, that these steroidal products, oestrogens, do not act only through the receptor, may they act through another means? And this is my question. Because in his reply Dr. Boobis only says they act through receptors, oestrogen receptors, which is in fact not true. There may be another way in which they act.

Chairman

201.   Dr. Boobis.

Dr. Boobis

202.   There are examples of oestrogenic antagonists, that were designed to interact with oestrogen receptors for therapeutic purposes, and these compounds have been studied using the most sensitive methods known to man for interaction with DNA, accelerator mass spectrometry, and have been shown to be negative. Now what that shows to me is that the oestrogenic structure *per se* itself does not necessarily lead to the capacity for genotoxicity. I am not saying that some of these compounds might not do that, but I think it would be inappropriate to regard that as a property of their oestrogenicity. That is the point I am making.

Chairman

203.   Thank you. Dr. Cogliano.

Dr. Cogliano

204.   I would like to say that last year the IARC monographs evaluated combined oral contraceptives and hormone therapy that combined oestrogen and a progestogen at the same time. And the expert working group concluded that both of these kinds of exposures clearly did have receptor activities, but that there was also some evidence of genotoxicity and that it was possible that they acted both through a hormone receptor mechanism and a genotoxic mechanism. The evidence was that it is obvious that they do have a hormonal effect, but the expert working group at IARC last year did conclude that these oestrogens and progestogens that are used in birth-control pills and in hormone therapy could have some evidence of genotoxicity as well.

Chairman

205.   Dr. Guttenplan.

Dr. Guttenplan

206.   Just to elaborate on what Dr. Boobis said. The oestrogenicity has no direct relevance to the genotoxicity of the compound – different effects. And I think of all the compounds and hormones that are possibly present in beef, the only one that might have genotoxic effects is oestradiol, and these would be very weak but they might still be there.

Chairman

207.   Thank you. Does the EC have more questions? EC.

European Communities

208.   I would like to ask the experts if they could restate or provide again their views on the mutagenicity in this case and how that relates to genotoxicity, in particular the DNA damage? And what is the role in that respect, and the conclusions we can draw, if a product is or is not mutagenic for the purposes of genotoxicity? Thank you.

Chairman

209.   Thank you. Dr. Guttenplan.

Dr. Guttenplan

210.   A mutagenic substance alters the structure of the DNA permanently and heritably. So DNA has if you would, an alphabet. If even one letter of that alphabet is changed, you have a permanent heritable change in that DNA, which will be transmitted to future cellular generations. Very few mutations actually are deleterious, most mutations are innocuous. And then of those that have deleterious effects, very few of them are in growth control genes. So the probability of a substance that causes mutations also causing, say, a cancer-causing effect would be very small. An agent that damages DNA is a potential mutagen. That damage is mainly going to be repaired, but if a little bit does not get repaired or is misrepaired – there are DNA damage responses that make errors when they repair – then you can get a mutation. So a substance that damages DNA may give rise to mutations and it may be carcinogenic. As was elaborated before by Dr. Boobis, there are many mechanisms by which chemicals can cause cancer, genotoxicity is only one of them.

Chairman

211.   Does that conclude the list of questions from the EC? I give the floor to the US. You have the floor.

United States

212.   Thank you, Mr. Chairman. The United States has only one question, so I will keep this brief. I would ask Doctors Boobis, Boisseau and Guttenplan, who

I think spoke on the terms and definitions section on similar issues, if you could please explain the difference between oestrogen and oestradiol 17-beta (17β).

Chairman

213.   Dr. Boobis

Dr. Boobis

214.   Oestradiol-17β is a specific compound. Amongst its properties it can bind to oestrogen receptors. Oestrogen is any compound with a steroidal structure that can bind to those receptors, so it is a class of compounds.

Chairman

215.   Thank you. If that is all from the US, then I give the floor to ... Are there any experts to add to the comments made by Dr. Boobis on this question before I give the floor to Canada? If there are none then I will give the floor to the delegation of Canada.

Canada

216.   Mr. Chairman, we have no questions at this time on the definitions. The discussions on the definitions has been very fruitful and clarified some of our questions. Thank you.

Chairman

217.   Thank you. We have 30 minutes to go before lunch break, but given the time constraints I would like to move on to the next item, that is risk assessment techniques. As was the case for the first item on terms and definitions, the Panel will pose some questions first and then invite the parties to pose their own question to the experts. The Panel's first question is composed of three parts; one is: how are ADIs and MRLs determined? and how do JECFA and Codex interact? The floor is open to answers by the experts.

Dr. Tritscher

218.   Thank you. I would like to start with the first part, on how ADIs are set, and the latter part I give over to my colleague. In this context I would like to refer to the basic document that explains how ADIs are set. I will make it very brief in my explanation, but it is explained in detail in Environmental Health Criteria 70, Principles for the Safety Assessment of Food Additives and Contaminants in Food, published by the World Health Organization in Geneva 1987. Again in the interest of time I will make it very brief and basic and then if there are additional questions I think I can explain later. ADI is an acceptable daily intake and is a chronic health-based guidance value. It denominates the amount that can be consumed over lifetime without appreciable health risk. As Dr. Boobis alluded to in the beginning, appreciable is not a legal term or any-

thing like that in this sense, it just denominates the basic concept in toxicology that there is no zero risk, there is always some level of risk.

219.   Now the accepted daily intake is established from the overall toxicological database. Experts review all available data, and since it's a chronic long-term guidance value the emphasis is on long-term studies. Mostly we talk about experimental studies from experimental animals that are treated under very defined circumstances and conditions with the specific compounds of interest. And from these studies no effect levels are determined; levels of exposure that do not lead to any adverse health effects in the test species. I have to add that sometimes of course there are also human data available that are also taken into consideration. From this no observed adverse effects level in the experimental studies it is then – with a number of uncertainty factors, or also called safety factors – extrapolated from experimental species, if we talk about animals, to the human situation. With another uncertainty or safety factor it is then taken into account that there is possibly broader variability in the response of the human population as compared to a more defined experimental setting, so that no observed effect level is divided by these combined safety or uncertainty factors in order to arrive at an acceptable daily intake level for the human population. Mr. Chairman, is this sufficient as a brief explanation for the Panel?

Chairman

220.   Yes, I suppose so. May I ask Dr. Wennberg?

Dr. Wennberg

221.   The acceptable daily intake is established by JECFA. To then go through the procedure which is used by JECFA since JECFA started to evaluate veterinary drugs, is to derive the MRLs from the data on the pharmacokinetics, the metabolism and depletion of the residues from the tissues after the last administration of the veterinary drugs in the animal in which the product is to be used. JECFA has developed a decision tree procedure to arrive at the maximum recommended maximum residue limit, which consists more or less of the following. As we were talking about the marker residue before, JECFA determines what is the most appropriate marker residue in the circumstances for the various tissues which have been chosen by JECFA to be included in a standard food basket to be consumed every day. This food basket consists of 300 grams muscle, which is meat, 100 grams liver, 50 grams kidney, 50 grams fat, 1½ litres of milk, 100 grams of eggs and 20 grams of honey – in the case of milk and eggs and honey, if the product is to be used in lactating animals, laying hens and honeybees, respectively.

222.   Then JECFA requires a study using a radio labelled compound, which means that the substance, the veterinary drug, is marked so that all the molecules of the substance can be found in an animal and compared to the amount of the marker residue which can be found by the analytical methods that I will come to later, which is used to analyse the marker residue. Then the recommendation of the MRL is an iterative process which has been described in our answer to ques-

tion number 9, in that JECFA tries to find the balance of the values where, given the depletion of the residue from the various tissues, which can be different, as a marker residue can remain longer in the liver or longer in the fat or longer in the kidneys. So for the practical purposes of using veterinary drugs, to establish a time where all the residues, if they were targeted for the specific food basket, would be below the ADI. So to try to balance the different levels of the total residues to the marker residue with the different concentrations at different time points in the tissues of concern, JECFA is making these calculations to make the best fit. And if, for example, the first calculation results in that the sum of all the total residues are significantly above the acceptable daily intake, then of course one has to adjust the calculations to arrive at final recommendations of the maximum residue limits for the marker residue, which if the drug is used according to good practice or use of the veterinary drugs, as defined by Codex, would result in the total residues being below the ADI. And then I could remind maybe the Panel and the rest of the experts and the parties that the food basket that has been chosen by JECFA is quite a substantial amount of food from animal original to be consumed every day. So in a sense it is also an over-estimation of the consumption of residues.

Chairman

223. Thank you. So who is going to respond to the second part? Dr. Miyagishima please.

Dr. Miyagishima

224. Thank you, Mr. Chairman. Let me briefly explain how Codex interacts with JECFA. As I mentioned in my introductory remarks, Codex is a risk-management body and, contrary to the perception which some people have according to which everything starts with risk assessment and then is followed by risk management, in the Codex/JECFA system the story starts with risk management, and the first component of risk management, called preliminary risk management activities. First of all, in the specialised Committee of Codex dealing with residues of veterinary drugs in foods, CCRVDF, the discussion takes place as to what compounds in what foods may pose public-health risks or may lead to barriers in international trade. And the Codex members in this Committee discuss, among themselves, on what compounds new work should be started within the Codex system. Of course they take into account various factors, such as whether the product itself is available as a commercial product, whether good agricultural practice has been established that goes with the use of the compound, whether there are sufficient amounts of scientific work that would warrant sound assessments by JECFA. When these conditions are considered to be met, then the CCRVDF puts the compound on what we call the priority list for evaluation by JECFA, and this is sent to JECFA for evaluation. You can put in this list compounds that were already evaluated by JECFA in the past, or you can put a new compound that has never been evaluated by JECFA; you can nominate a compound for which the Codex has already established an MRL, or

you can also include a compound for which no Codex MRL has been established. It is up to the CCRVDF to take various conditions into account and set priority for compound assessment.

225.   After JECFA has conducted risk assessment on these compounds, and when the result, including the recommended MRL, is sent to CCRVDF, CCRVDF usually sends or circulates the recommended MRL at step 3 of the Codex step procedure; that is the step at which government comments are invited. The comments made are considered and are looked at at a physical meeting of CCRVDF at step 4, and then MRLs usually follow the way through the final adoption at step 8; and of course at each step the Codex will have due regard to the scientific output of JECFA, but also take into account other factors that are deemed necessary to be looked at. And in this process there is interaction between Codex and the JECFA system. If Codex, namely CCRVDF, wants to have more information on certain issues, CCRVDF has the ability to ask those questions, either general or specific, to JECFA, and also Codex may request a particular type of risk assessment or scenario analysis and other kinds of supplementary information to JECFA, and it is up to JECFA to answer those questions. Thank you.

Chairman

226.   Thank you. I understand that Dr. Boisseau would like to add. Before I give the floor to Dr. Boisseau, may I give the floor first to Dr. Tritscher please.

Dr. Tritscher

227.   Thank you very much. Just to emphasize again the ADI and MRL and the interaction between JECFA and Codex. The ADI is established by JECFA; it is the outcome of the risk assessment, if you want, and it is not for discussion at the Codex, so that is a value that is established by the risk assessment body. The MRL as it is proposed by JECFA, is based on scientific studies and data that are made available to the expert body and that are evaluated by the risk assessment body, by JECFA, and then the MRLs are proposed to the respective Codex Committee, CCRVDF in that case. And then the risk management body, so the Codex, the CCRVDF is the risk management body, takes this proposal into account and can consider other factors in setting the final MRL. That is all it is, just to emphasize it again. Thank you.

Chairman

228.   Thank you for your clarification. Dr. Boisseau has the floor.

Dr. Boisseau

229.   Thank you, Mr. Chairman. I agree, of course, with what was just said by the three preceding speakers. I would simply like to add a few details. We are accustomed to saying that in order to determine an admissible daily intake, we perform an evaluation of the toxicological profile of the substance studied. In

fact, toxicology is a somewhat narrow term, since the experts will focus not only on the toxicological effects, but will be looking for all of the undesirable effects which, in addition to the toxicology, could include physiological and microbiological effects. And for each study concerning one of these aspects – toxicological, physiological or other – the experts establish an intake that has no effect, and depending on the nature of the undesirable effect observed, they will allocate to that intake which has no effect an appropriate safety factor which may range from ten to 1,000, enabling them to obtain a series of acceptable daily intakes. Finally, the committee – the CVMP or the JECFA – will select the most restrictive of these daily intakes, in other words the one that is most protective of public health. So it is important to take account of the great variety of tests involved and the fact that at the end of the day, the daily intake selected is the one which is most protective of public health. You will probably ask later on about the safety factors considered throughout the process of determining the ADI and the MRL, so I will not address that issue now.

230.   Let me add that usually, these toxicological studies are experimental studies that are conducted with the parent substance for practical reasons. But where feasible and justified in view of the toxicological profile of a given metabolite, this kind of study can also be conducted with a metabolite whose toxicological or pharmacological profile could make it the limiting factor in terms of the evaluation of the safety of the residues.

231.   Finally, I just wanted to add a word or two, if I may, on the distribution of the risk assessment and risk management tasks between the JECFA and the Codex. It is customary, in conducting a risk assessment of an environmental product, for the scientific committee to conclude its risk assessment with an indication of the probability of risk for a given population or sub-population. The residues of veterinary drugs are a somewhat special case, since we control the administration of veterinary drugs to animals, and the JECFA therefore goes beyond the mere appreciation of the risks, since that appreciation more or less stops with the determination of the ADI. With the determination of the MRLs, the JECFA is deliberately entering into the realm of risk management, since an MRL is a tool, a proposal to ensure that the ADI is not exceeded with regard to the standard food basket as mentioned a short while ago by Dr. Wennberg. This is a somewhat special case, since one can effectively manage the situation and the objective. The objective is not only to assess the risks, but also to minimise the risks to which consumers of foodstuffs of animal origin could be exposed.

232.   However, this does not detract from the JECFA's responsibility for risk assessment and the responsibility of the Codex Committee (CCRVDF) for risk management, since when it comes to MRLs, the JECFA, which is a competent scientific committee qualified to make proposals, makes proposals only, while the risk manager – in this specific case the CCRVDF – is the one that takes a decision. In other words, the fact that the JECFA makes MRL proposals on the basis of the competence of its WHO or FAO experts does not mean that it can be accused of interfering in risk management. It is the decision maker that manages the risk, i.e. the CCRVDF with the Codex member states. Thank you.

Chairman

233.   Thank you. Dr. Wennberg.

Dr. Wennberg

234.   Thank you, Mr. Chairman. Yes, could I just add a few comments, also regarding the possibility of temporary MRLs, or is that another question that you have? So JECFA will make full recommendations for quantitative values for MRLs if there is adequate data to do so and if this is in accordance with the ADI. There may be instances where there is enough information to recommend MRLs, but the analytical method to determine these MRLs has not been sufficiently validated to the use in control laboratories worldwide. In such instances, as the process in Codex is quite long, JECFA may recommend temporary MRLs, and providing an opportunity for submission of additional information to a next meeting or a future meeting of JECFA for evaluation of the validation of the analytical method. This has happened on occasion. Also the Committee of JECFA may recommend MRLs not specified, or unnecessary as it was termed in very old reports, where there is a wide margin of safety of residues when compared to the ADIs, and which would mean that it is not necessary to control this substance when it is used in accordance with good veterinary practice, because the values will never come anywhere close to the ADI. And finally, of course, if there is not enough information for JECFA, and there are deficiencies in the data available to the Committee, they will of course not recommend MRLs and they never have recommended MRLs if there is no ADI established.

Chairman

235.   What do you mean by temporary? When and under what conditions will temporary MRLs be terminated?

Dr. Wennberg

236.   Temporary MRLs are recommended with a qualification that if the specified information, which is also specified in the report, is not submitted within a certain timeframe, then the MRL will not exist anymore. So if the JECFA Secretariat does not receive the required information, the appropriate following meeting of JECFA will take the decision that a temporary MRL will be revoked. And this information is transmitted to the CCRVDF and Codex.

Chairman

237.   Thank you. As it is already ...

Ms Orozco

238.   Just one qualification please. What kind of criteria are brought into consideration when an MRL is being considered; information that is different than the one that has been taken into account by JECFA? What kind of other criteria or other information is it taken into account by Codex?

Chairman

239.   Dr. Miyagishima.

Dr. Miyagishima

240.   Thank you very much. Indeed, within the Codex system there has been a lot of discussion that took place to better delineate those factors that can legitimately be taken into account when Codex elaborates texts. In fact the Codex Alimentarius Commission adopted in 1995 a statement of principle concerning the role of science in the Codex decision-making process and the extent to which other factors are taken into account. There are four paragraphs and these statements are reproduced in the Codex procedural manual. Later, in the year 2001 there were additional criteria adopted by the Commission that assist in the consideration of those other factors referred to in these statements, and this text is also included in the Codex procedural manual. Basically, the factors that may be considered as relevant for the protection of the consumers' health and/or for ensuring fair practices in the food trade can be taken into account and they can be moved by any members of the Codex bodies. It is up to the CCRVDF and ultimately to the Commission to weigh those factors and incorporate and take account of them in making a final decision. One could give some specific examples but I would rather not mention them at this stage. Thank you.

Chairman

241.   US.

United States

242.   Thank you Mr. Chairman. Just a quick follow-up on the response of the representative from JECFA, just a point of clarification. Did JECFA make full recommendations for MRLs for each of the six hormones involved in this dispute?

Chairman

243.   Dr. Wennberg.

Dr. Wennberg

244.   Thank you, Mr. Chairman. Well, the six hormones which are the matter of this dispute, as far as I understood, are oestradiol-17β, progesterone, testosterone, trenbolone acetate, zeranol and melengestrol acetate, is that correct? OK. So JECFA evaluated the three endogenous hormones, the first three ones, and on three occasions; in 1981 only for general considerations; in 1987, concluding that an ADI was unnecessary; and in 1999, establishing ADIs for all these three hormones. At the same time, a complete residue evaluation of these hormones was performed and is available in FAO Food and Nutrition Paper 41/12, and concluding that it was not necessary, on the basis of the residue data, to recommend full MRLs for these three hormones. As regards trenbolone acetate,

JECFA evaluated this substance four times; in 1982, general considerations; in 1983, limited by good husbandry practice; and in 1987 and 1989, established first a temporary and then a full ADI. In the same way the residue data were evaluated and no MRLs were considered. No that is not correct. Can I have the lunch break to go back to the data and see about these three other substances, whether there were MRLs established for those?

Chairman

245. Sure. If you don't have the information now then you can do so. I would appreciate if you can respond to all the questions as briefly as possible. It is already 1 o'clock, so now I would like to have a lunch break and resume the discussions at 3 p.m. sharp in this room. I will see you all this afternoon at 3 p.m. Have a good lunch.

27 September 2006, afternoon

Chairman

246. [Beginning of tape] ... when our discussions were suspended, we were on the issues related to ADIs and MRLs and I believe that issues on this item, the risk assessment techniques, are at the heart of the discussions this afternoon. The Panel has a rather long list of questions, but as we understand it the parties are also very eager to put their own questions to the experts. I would like to be as brief as possible, not only in our answers and questions, but also I would appreciate if the experts will be very brief and succinct in their replies to the questions so that the parties can have more time to ask their own questions later.

247. The two follow-up questions regarding the first one I posed this morning also relate to ADI and MRLs, so I would combine these two questions together. My question is: does the ADI take into account the fact that some of the same hormones exist in other food and medicinal products and that therefore there are other sources of intake of the same compounds? The second one is: does the ADI take into account all uses of the hormones as veterinary drugs, including for example for zootechnical purposes? The floor is open for comments and replies, from JECFA first, and then I will give the floor to Dr. Boobis.

Dr. Tritscher

248. Thank you Mr. Chair. If I may ask, I happen to have slides on my computer that explain this and answer actually the two questions.[2] Just very quick, to the first question about the interactions of JECFA and Codex. This is illustrated here, but we have discussed, so JECFA as a risk assessment body interacts with the Codex as the risk management body. (Can I have the next slide please.) Now this illustrates what we actually do with the ADI and the exposure assessment,

---

[2]   Dr. Tritscher's slides are contained in Attachment 2 to this transcript.

and this is to answer questions (b) and (c) that was just raised, if JECFA, in setting the ADI takes account of all possible exposures, to simplify the two questions. As I mentioned briefly earlier, the ADI, the acceptable daily intake, is the outcome of the toxicological evaluation, and as was mentioned earlier by one of the experts, in the case of veterinary drug residues, its toxicological effects, physiological effects, pharmacological effects, as well as microbiological effects are considered, and from that an ADI is derived.

249.   Now the exposure assessment is then done separately from that, so in setting the ADI exposures are not considered. Exposure assessment is done separately in that the amount of the chemicals in the food times the amount of food consumed is considered, this is the exposure. And in the actual safety assurance you compare this estimated human exposure with the ADI, so if the estimated exposure is below the ADI, then the situation is OK, if the estimated exposure is above the ADI, then a risk management decision has to be taken. That can also be, from the risk assessment point of view, in the first step the refinement of the exposure assessment and so forth, so in an iterative process refining the exposure assessment and then comparing it with the ADI. Basically, and sure to answer the question, the exposure assessment is done separate of the ADI, so in a subsequent step the exposure has to be compared to the ADI in order to ensure safety of the overall food supply.

250.   Very quickly a few comments on the international field, so from the perspective of JECFA. The exposure assessment in the case of veterinary drug residues, as my colleague from the FAO explained earlier, is based on a food basket diet, so on a model diet. In a national setting, exposure assessments can be done in a more refined way, because more specific data for that country would be available, for example with food consumption patterns and so forth. So in the international field, in the case of veterinary drugs we work with model diets in order to assess the estimated human exposure and to compare it with the ADI. And also, then the estimated exposure is compared with the MRLs that JECFA proposes in order to ensure that they are compatible with the ADI and hence they are compatible with public health. I would leave it at that and would ask you if you have any additional questions.

Chairman

251.   Thank you. Dr. Boobis – ...yes, EC.

European Communities

252.   To change the subject a bit right now, because all of the things that you have not been told is that there is a lot of data that you can't get because you don't have enough animals to do the testing, in many cases, and so there are assumptions made, what the dose-response curves looks like when there is no data, so it's a guess. These assumptions are a weak scientific statement and there are dozens of these assumptions, and one of them is that there is a threshold, a dose below which there are no adverse effects. A threshold is a theoretical concept and it is difficult or impossible to actually measure, because there really are not

enough animals to be able to determine that there is a threshold or not. It would take thousands of animals and you could still find arguments that there are other data that suggest that these assumptions are not right. When there is a hormone that the body is making and is in circulation, and when you add more of the same kind of hormone, such as an oestrogen, you are just increasing the response that is already taking place, and in that case there cannot be a threshold. The threshold has already been exceeded by the concentration of hormones in the circulation. So this specific set of conditions results in dose-response curves that will have no threshold, and if there is no threshold, there is no safe dose, unlike the suggestion that there is an acceptable daily intake, and in a lot of cases an acceptable daily intake is legitimate, as long as there is not a counterpart to the chemical that you are giving and it does not exist naturally in the body, then you have the opportunity to at least justify an acceptable daily intake. But when those hormones are circulating and are already active and you add more hormones, particularly at lower doses, what you expect to get is an increase in the adverse effects, and under these conditions an ADI has no meaning whatsoever. There will be risk at any dose no matter how low, and both Fred and I have demonstrated that at experimental studies and we have nobody that has been able to tell us or to show us where what we have done experimentally, and what we have done in terms of our conclusion, no one has shown us that it is wrong.

Chairman

253.   US.

United States

254.   Thank you, Mr. Chairman. Two quick points, one a point of clarification. The United States was under the impression that this was the opportunity of the parties to ask questions of the experts selected by the Panel rather than presenting evidence of perceived situations ourselves in response to Panel questions. On the second hand I would refer back to the Panel's e-mail or letter of last week noting that the evidentiary record in the proceedings had in fact been closed but for a showing of good cause to present new evidence, and we would note that a presentation of evidence as we just heard could fall within the ambit of that letter. Thank you.

Chairman

255.   As I mentioned this morning, the purpose of this meeting is to request the experts to assist the Panel in discharging our duties as panellists, so it is quite clear to us. I also mentioned that parties will be given more opportunities to put their own questions at a later time in due course. So I would ask the delegation to limit their questions and comments or replies to those particularly related to questions put forward by the Panel. I give the floor to the delegation of Canada.

Canada

256.   Thank you very much, Mr. Chairman. First of all, of course we want the Panel to get as much information they can out of this process and out of the experts as possible, and we certainly are not in any position, we don't want to limit the flow of information to you. But in the same vein as the questions raised by my US colleague, and we support the point, I guess as a matter of clarification, you mentioned questions may be put, I would like to know whether questions also includes arguments and expert testimony by members of the delegation of one of the disputing parties? I think, to the extent that we are talking about questions, that presumes that we are not talking about arguments or running monologues, or we don't want to get into a debate or discussion with the experts at this point, it would seem to me.

Chairman

257.   Yes. As I made it clear in the opening statement this morning, the questions and comments have to be focussed on the information and replies given by the experts in written form. So I make it clear once again that the discussions that we are going to have this afternoon will also be focused on the information and comments and replies by the experts, without going further into the arguments on legal issues and those factual issues which have to be discussed next week on Monday and Tuesday. Is that clear to every delegation. OK. With that understanding ...

Ms Orozco

258.   Thank you, Mr. Chairman. I have a follow-up question to the information that has been presented by JECFA. In the case of hormones, for example, it is clear, as we have been told, that there are hormones in different types of food, so when you take establish the ADI, are you taking into account the level of hormones that there is from the consumption of every product that contains hormones in an endogenous way?

Chairman

259.   Dr. Boobis? JECFA, Dr. Tritscher

Dr. Tritscher

260.   Just very quick. In the MRL derivation, the experimental studies are done in the actual food-producing animal, as it's called, so by default you have the levels that are measured in these studies contain endogenous levels of hormones as well, so if you want, by default they are included in this consideration.

Ms Orozco

261.   Yes, but what I would like to understand is, it is the addition of all the hormones that you would intake in your diet, because I don't know if it is set by the product, by meat for example in this case, or if it takes into account all the

intake of hormones, because you eat different things. That was the first part of the question, and I'll just explain to you the second part of the question, so I don't have to repeat so many times. In the same vein, do you take into account the intake of a veterinary residue that would exist of the same compound because of other reasons, so we have also seen that there are veterinary drugs that use hormones that are used for zootechnical treatments. Is that reflected in any way in the ADI?

Chairman

262.   I would appreciate it if the replies would be right to the point, as succinct and as brief as possible, given the time constraint. OK?

Dr. Wennberg

263.   OK. Thank you, Mr. Chairman. Well, the questions that are asked to JECFA from the CCRVDF are particular questions on the assessment of a particular residue or a veterinary drug, and it is used according to good veterinary practice. It's also said that for JECFA to assess a veterinary drug, it has to be authorized at least somewhere in the world, so there has to be a national authorization somewhere. I think we have to make it clear once again that JECFA is not a regulatory authority that authorizes the use of drugs. So the questions that are asked to JECFA are related, in this case of the natural endogenous hormones, to their use as production aids in cattle. So what JECFA has evaluated is first of all the toxicological evidence which enables JECFA to set ADIs, which is irrespective of the exposure, as we have just heard. And following on from that JECFA evaluated the concentrations of the hormones, as evidenced by the residue depletions studies and taking into account the endogenous concentrations of hormones in the meat.

264.   Now, the endogenous concentrations of hormones in the meat are variable, and so its not possible to say that is X, Y or Z, because depending on the reproductive cycle of the animal, these levels vary. They can be high at certain times and low at certain times for the different hormones. So JECFA evaluated how much of the additional residues relating to the use of the hormones in question would represent in terms of the ADI, and we come to a very low figure, it's less than 2 per cent of the ADI for oestradiol, it's less than 0.03 per cent for progesterone and it's less than 0.2 per cent of the ADI for testosterone. That made the Committee conclude that it was not necessary to specify numerical MRLs and recommend MRLs not specified for these three natural hormones. Now, if you are using hormones, you can either use one hormone or you can use a combination, depending on what kind of effect you would like to have. These uses are to be authorized by national authorities. JECFA does not enter to efficacy of the use of these hormones.

265.   When you are using xenobiotic hormones which are not natural, these are also governed by national authorizations, how much you use and under which circumstances. And in these cases, as I was asked before the lunch break, I was going to come back with MRLs that JECFA had proposed, recommended for

these substances. So for these substances, ADIs were set specifically for these substances, so they are not put together with other hormones, because the effects that were evaluated in the toxicological assessment enabled the Committee to set an ADI for these specific substances. So you don't consider all different hormones with different kinds of effects and different types of profiles in the same evaluation. So if you use one hormone, that's the hormone that you are using at this time. There may be combinations but if they are authorized on a national level that's it. So for the three xenobiotic hormones, JECFA set full MRLs, recommended full MRLs for all three of them. This is available publicly and unless the United States want me to actually give you the levels, I will make my intervention shorter by not mentioning them. If you have any further questions I will be happy to answer.

Chairman

266.   Thank you. So are any other experts intending to add any more comments? EC.

European Communities

267.   Gentlemen, I think there are other more simple and I hope more clear ways to reply to the question. Now this is given in the reply of JECFA to question No. 10; it is already in your files. So you will see that JECFA says that they do not take into account data on the intended or actual use and consumption – the way the substances are going to be used or consumed, they don't take data into account. It is in the file. This is the reply to the question, the second of the questions. How they are going to be used and how they are going to be consumed; they don't take this into account. This is a purely generic toxicological study, without consideration of where they will be used for. A body with good veterinary practice or not, whether they would be misused or not, there would be more implants, in one implant there will be more hormones, one, two, three or not, this is not considered. As the doctor has said, it's only a single substance that is analysed.

268.   Now for the first question, again on the reply of JECFA to question number 10, you will see they speak about the so-called basket and whether there are intakes of the substances from other sources, and there you will see the basket consists mainly of steak, meat and muscle, meat and liver, meat and kidney and they have milk, eggs and honey, but of course it does not exhaust all the other possible sources which humans eat every day and from which intake of these hormones can come. This is the reply to the first question and it is explained also in the text. Thank you.

Ms Orozco

269.   Excuse me, an interruption just for completeness. What other sources are you thinking about? You say that there other ways in the diet of humans, other than the food basket of JECFA, what other sources do you have?

European Communities

270.   For example, speaking about butter, I can think of a list of substances a human eats every day. Some of them may contain more hormones, less hormones. Or other kind of meat. So these are things which – I understand it is difficult to devise a basket that is really representative, and the representative of JECFA has said they leave it to the national authorities to see, in each EC member State, in each country, according to the nutrition habits probably. If one country eats some substances a little more than what is in the basket, they would have to be reviewed, these calculations. But certainly humans one day eat not only 300 grams muscle, 100 grams of liver or 100 grams of kidney and so on. So there are certainly other sources from which we take in these substances. This is not disputed in the science. And if you allow me to clarify, in reply to what has been said by the representative of JECFA – this is very important – the toxicological analysis takes into account a substance individually. We will come back later to this. None of the implants as far as we know consist of one substance only, there is more than one substance. It means the majority of the implants contain more than one of these hormones together, and the data which they have examined, they don't take this into account. The toxicological data they take into account, they don't examine the possible additive or synergistic effects of these implants, and these possible effects they have not been examined because it is not done. It has not been done before by the countries that have authorized these substances, for example. Thank you.

Chairman

271.   Dr. Tritscher would like to add some more comments.

Dr. Tritscher

272.   Yes, I have to respond to that and clarify a couple of points that were not exactly correct in the intervention by the EC. (May I kindly ask you to put up a second slide, what I have on JECFA MRL, that is what it is called.) This is just a little graph, an illustration how JECFA does residue evaluations. Just to illustrate that it is based on specific detailed studies in the food producing animal. (Thank you, that's it.) As I said earlier, so you have detailed studies in respective animal species for what the veterinary drug is intended to be used for. So by default, and that is what I tried to say earlier, you consider endogenously occurring hormones as well as the additional treatment, that is by default, because that is what you measure in the end if you measure a synthetic hormone for example. So based on these studies, the residues, the MRL, is derived. And then from the studies, from the median residue level in these defined studies according to good veterinary practice – this is very important because it is incorrect what was said before, that this is not considered, it is considered. Only studies that are field trials and studies that are performed under good veterinary practice. And we have a small definition, but the problem here is that there is no internationally agreed definition. But from these studies the median residue level is taken for the intake assessment according to the model food basket, as was correctly said.

273.   Now this model food basket was constructed in a way to reflect exactly these commodities as animal-derived foods that may contain veterinary drug residues, and butter, for example, it is self-understanding that butter is covered by milk, because butter is milk fat. So there are all these different types of commodities that are covered in the model basket, in a way, to give you conservative – and conservative in our language means a high level – estimate, rather than going too low. And as I mentioned earlier, or what I tried to explain, is that JECFA has to consider a worldwide model, and I did by no means say that JECFA leaves it up to national authorities to do an exposure assessment. JECFA does do an exposure assessment based on this model diet, taking conservative assumptions to give them an idea of what the estimated exposure on the higher level could be. National authorities have the possibilities, based on refined data, to refine these intake assessments – to use data, additional data, that are adapted to, for example, national food consumption habits, or that are adapted to national registration for a specific purpose of this use of a veterinary drug, that is maybe only allowed in this country. So there may be additional exposure sources in a specific country that only that country can take into account, that cannot be taken into account if we have to give a recommendation on the international basis. Moreover, what this model basket reflects and the ADI reflects is a chronic exposure. We are not talking about somebody who eats half a beef on one day because there is a big wedding party somewhere, excuse me to talk like this, but just to say what we are trying to do here is to get a conservative – in a public health protective way – a model that is sufficiently protective over a lifetime exposure. And I think that are most of the comments I wanted to make now. Thank you.

Chairman

274.   Dr. Wennberg.

Dr. Wennberg

275.   Yes. I have two more comments to make on this. The first one is on this model standard food basket. It is internationally accepted; it is also used in the EU. And the second comment is that the studies performed in the field trials which were evaluated by JECFA reflect the use of these products also in combination, if it was the case that these were the authorised uses in the particular country. So for the endogenous hormones, the combination in terms of the exposure was evaluated, and the additional exposure, based on the use of these hormones compared to the endogenous one in relation to the ADI for each of the substances was calculated. So I do not consider that JECFA only looked at one single hormone in one single instance. The ADI is of course specific for each substance, because there are specific endpoints which have been used for the establishment of the ADI with the no effect level. So you cannot combine different hormones which have different endpoints in terms of toxicology and say that you can lump them together and say that if I use this and this and this I get an increased toxicity. You have to look at each of the hormones and their endpoints,

which is what the ADI is based on, to see whether there is a risk to public health or not.

Chairman

276.   Thank you. OK. EC please.

European Communities

277.   Mr. Chairman, I don't want to become polemic, but I think in the documentation of JECFA and Codex which we have seen, toxicological data, and the evaluations of combinations of implants have not been performed, as far as we know, not for all the substances which we are talking about here. So if the representative of Codex and JECFA think otherwise, we would like to see this paper. We have asked the United States and Canada to provide this paper; they didn't give them to us. So if they are claiming something, we need to see these studies, toxicological and residue studies, where they claim that the combinations of implants, where more than one hormone is contained and administered, has been performed. As far as we know they have not been done, not for all of them. If you allow me to come back on the first question replied by Dr. Tritscher, the basket, of course we have a basket similar to what Codex and JECFA have in their evaluation, but the point, I think, that the member of the Panel was trying to clarify is that we eat daily so many food products and otherwise which contain the same substances, or substances which have the same or similar toxicological effects and activities, and these of course are not taken into account. This is what we would like to clarify. There are so many other substances which have oestrogenic activity when they are consumed in food and this has not been examined. I don't know if it is feasible to be examined. I think it is difficult but it is not impossible and probably the countries which have authorized these hormones must have performed this before they authorized it. And later on we will give you precise reference to our assessment where we do mention this potential risk, possibly from these other sources. Thank you.

Chairman

278.   Dr. Boobis.

Dr. Boobis

279.   I don't propose to get into a long discussion at the moment on this issue, but I would just make the comment, since it has been raised, about the totality of exposure to oestrogenic compounds in our diet. There have been estimates of the total exposure to oestrogenic compounds, and by far the dominant source of those compounds is natural oestrogens which are produced by plants in our diet. These far outweigh the traces of oestrogens from other sources, either natural oestrogen coming from non-treated animals or the presence of growth-promoting hormones used to treat animals. That is not to say I have addressed the question of incremental risk, I assume that will come up later, but just to point out, in terms of the total burden of oestrogen exposure, this is a much broader question

than just the hormones coming from beef, it would open up the whole question of nutritional exposure as well.

Chairman

280.   If the JECFA representative is not in a position to clarify on the question posed by EC then can I ask the representatives to move on to the second part of the question. Am I right to understand that the second part of the question has not been fully responded?

Dr. Tritscher

281.   Could you please repeat the second part of the question?

Chairman

282.   Does the ADI take into account all uses of the hormones as veterinary drugs, including for example for zootechnical purposes? Dr. Boobis.

Dr. Boobis

283.   I tried to emphasize this, and I think the joint secretariat has made this point, but it bears repeating. There are two different questions here, and we have tried to answer the specific question. The ADI is derived from toxicological information. We can argue about the security of the conclusions, but it does not consider, nor should it consider, exposure or the use patterns. It is based simply on the toxicological properties and the biological properties of the compound itself. You then come up with a health-based guidance value, the allowable daily intake, that is then compared with exposure. And the second question which one might pursue, and I think we have been, is to what extent are all different exposures taken into account, but that is a separate question from the ones on the board, Mr. Chairman, which is that the ADI does not take account of other uses nor should it.

Ms Orozco

284.   Total exposure from food then should be taken into account during the exposure assessment?

Dr. Boobis

285.   Yes, indeed. That is where it would come in if it was going to be taken into account. It does not come down the left-hand side of Dr. Tritscher's diagram, which is the ADI derivation based on the toxicology, it comes down on the right-hand side, which is exposure evaluation. And then it becomes a risk management question as to how broadly are you going to include exposures other than those that arise from GVP, good veterinary practice, because of course JECFA bases its evaluations on the use of the compound according to good veterinary practice.

Chairman

286.   OK. I hope we can conclude the discussion on this question as early as possible. I will give the last chance to EC.

European Communities

287.   Chairman, I am afraid we cannot conclude these discussions because we have a number of other questions, but I would agree with the first reply of Dr. Boobis, that the way the ADI is performed by JECFA does not take into account other use of these hormones, like zootechnical or therapeutic use. The claim is that they cannot do it, or they don't want to know that they may be used in that way, fine, but for the purposes of your consideration this is true, they do not take any, and this actually has been said in the reply of JECFA, which if you wish I can read today. The second question is the reply of Dr. Boobis about where exposure from other sources has come in. If the reply of Dr. Boobis were to be true, then what JECFA does is not correct, and I think that the reply is somewhere in between. It is not as clear-cut as JECFA present it or Dr. Boobis would like to present it, because it all depends what these other sources are and what they contain. And if it is biological activity, in this case we speak about carcinogenesis, it has to be taken into account in the first step, in hazard identification, it is not only the in exposure assessment that we need to consider it. So I think we will have the opportunity, if we go down the questions later on, to clarify this instead of dwelling now on this issue in a generic manner. But if you allow me – because my questions relate to the two questions which you have asked, the first before the lunch break and the second now – if you allow me to have three follow-up questions on this.

Chairman

288.   Please do that at a later stage, as I mentioned earlier, because I think that the situation may be the same for other delegations too on the other specific questions.

European Communities

289.   Well, I think, if you allow, I will ask at least one question of the three I have.

Chairman

290.   OK. With the understanding of delegations, please go ahead.

European Communities

291.   Chairman, in the reply of Codex to question number 4, for your consideration I only read the first sentence: There is no adopted Codex standard or related text on the risk assessment of residues .... So what is being talked about here – there is no standard about how to do this risk assessment, techniques and how you set the ADI and MRL. These are the methods used and developed by

JECFA, but they are not presented in an assembly of an organ for adoption so that they become standards in the sense of the SPS Agreement. They are considered by some committees and JECFA and a few scientists, as they say, they are developed by individual persons who happen to sit on those committees and they thought that is the relevant model. But the truth is, and this is relevant for our case, there are no agreed international standards on how to do a risk assessment in that sense. The other questions I will keep for later on. Thank you.

Chairman

292.   Thank you for your cooperation. Is it on a procedural matter, Canada?

Canada

293.   I would simply – I did not hear a question there – but I would propose a question too. I think Drs. Boisseau and Boobis both spoke to the last point raised by the EC, on how safety assessments are conducted and the process by which that's done, and I wonder if they had any comments on the EC's last statement.

Chairman

294.   Can I give the floor to Dr. Boobis.

Dr. Boobis

295.   I think it is not entirely accurate to say that it was a few scientists at JECFA who developed risk-assessment methodology; this evolved out of the National Academy in the US. It has been developed by the International Programme on Chemical Safety and is the cornerstone of risk assessments by almost everybody. The four-step risk assessment paradigm, as we call it, – hazard identification, hazard characterization, exposure assessment and risk characterization – is very very widely use. It has been endorsed by essentially everybody conducting risk assessment on expert bodies. There has been lots of discussion about whether or not this is applicable to veterinary residues. The view widely held is that there is nothing fundamentally different about the philosophy of evaluating risk of a veterinary residue, as opposed to any other specifics about the exposure assessment; one has to work out the residues in meat from treated animals, but that is a technical detail, as opposed to the overall philosophy that underlies the strategy. So I think that it is not accurate to say that this is something that has been cooked up or produced by JECFA in an informal manner, it has been widely validated by many organizations. And in fact I believe it is in the Codex Manual as well, at least allusion to the general principles.

Chairman

296.   If Canada's point is not related to the procedural one, can I give the floor to the experts first, because I saw their flags were raised before you did. Dr. Boisseau and then Dr. Miyagishima.

Dr. Boisseau

297.   Thank you, Mr. Chairman. I am sorry, but there were many questions in rapid succession, and I wanted to take the floor following the statement by the European Union to the effect that ultimately, there were various utilizations that the ADI could not take into account. I think we have to be fairly precise on terminology, because otherwise we will be going round in circles like this for hours, without getting anywhere. The ADI has nothing to do with exposures, as Dr. Boobis quite rightly said. The ADI does not need to take account of exposures, it is the logical conclusion of a toxicological evaluation. By "toxicology", we may also mean "pharmacology" or any adverse effect. In any case, it is important that we bear this in mind. Now, we must not confuse the Theoretical Maximum Daily Intake (TMDI) with the daily amount ingested which is the sum of the amounts actually ingested from different sources, and we compare, as the joint secretariat said this morning, I think, the amount ingested with the ADI. So we must stop linking the ADI with the amounts ingested, otherwise I can see no way out.

298.   Secondly, regarding the standards and the protocol that we have just spoken of, there is currently a cascade protocol, so to speak. We have, today, a general structure for risk analysis and risk assessment. However, it is true that the JECFA applied this risk assessment to the consumer safety assessment of veterinary drug residues, with the exception of antimicrobials, for several years without a detailed assessment protocol – that work has been going on for a number of years within the JECFA. However, before the work was done, this protocol was perfectly well established in the minds of all those throughout the world who, at the JECFA or EU level (I am thinking of the CVMPs), use the same methods. Moreover, it was the same people working in the different bodies, so we can hardly say today that this work was done more or less according to the mood of the moment. There was a consensus on the way that this methodology for assessing the safety of veterinary drug residues should be applied. It was neither written, nor formally adopted, but the methodology was perfectly operational and universally accepted. Thank you.

Chairman

299.   Thank you. Dr. Miyagishima.

Dr. Miyagishima

300.   Thank you, Mr. Chairman. I would like to add some clarification as to what is meant by the Codex reply to question number 4. We did confirm that there is no adopted Codex standard or related text on the risk assessment of residues of veterinary drugs. When we call something a standard or related text, that means any text that is part of the Codex Alimentarius. The Codex Alimentarius is a collection of adopted standards and related texts that are there for guidance or for use by governments. In this particular case the Codex relies on JECFA, and Codex uses primarily MRLs as a tool for risk management. Codex in this

sense has not attempted to provide guidelines for governments to conduct risk assessment, because JECFA does the business.

301.   This is the reason why the document on risk assessment policy and the whole risk analysis framework related to the work of CCRVDF, which is now in elaboration, is not meant for inclusion in the Codex Alimentarius even if after it has been adopted by the Commission in the future. It will be eventually included in the Codex Procedural Manual, because the document describes the way the Codex interacts with JECFA. So the scope of the document has no links with the guidance Codex intends to provide to governments. This is the reason why the Codex replied that there is no risk assessment guidance within the Codex Alimentarius. In other areas such as microbiological risks in foods, the Codex has taken a different approach, and the Commission adopted risk assessment guidelines which have been included in the Codex Alimentarius. But with the approach the CCRVDF has taken, and the Codex Commission has taken so far, there has been no need for providing guidance to governments directly in terms of risk assessment techniques. Thank you.

Chairman

302.   Thank you. EC – sorry, I forgot that the Canadian delegation has raised its flag. Canada.

Canada

303.   Thank you, Mr. Chairman. It is always illuminating and interesting to listen to my friend Mr. Christoforou, so I didn't want to deprive him of the podium. But I think, as this exchange demonstrated, in fact it was immediately after the intervention of my American friend who put the statement into the form of a question, we can actually have a very fruitful contribution from the experts when instead of making statements and arguments we put simple questions to them. And I hope that my EC colleague will respect your guidance and in fact your initial statements about the way this process is to be made, which is that at this point instead of making arguments it's better to simply put clarification questions. And if later on, on Monday and Tuesday, we have arguments to make, we will make them. Thank you.

European Communities

304.   Chairman, there are two clarifications, and I will not continue this now. It is another thing to speak about the four stages of risk assessment to which Dr. Boobis has referred, risk identification, risk characterization, dose exposure, risk characterization, that is true. But here we were not talking about these four steps of what is a risk assessment and how to do it, we were talking about the ADI, and the maximum limits. For this concept Dr. Boisseau says there were a few scientists, it was probably already before considered and was taken into account in JECFA, but there are no internationally agreed standards about this concept. This is what I want to clarify. The question was relating to ADI and MRL not only four steps. With this we agree, of course, and we claim we can

follow these four steps of the risk assessment, but that was not the point, if you allow me to clarify. The second question is: Dr. Boisseau himself has said there are no agreements to the national standards, in JECFA or otherwise, how to define this concept of ADI and MRL. There are questions one may ask about the details or some other important aspect of this, so that is what I wanted also to clarify. Dr. Boobis said that it all started from the United States National Academy publications, this is all fine. But for you to understand, there is the Codex Alimentarius Commission, which is the members of the committee adopting texts, where the four steps of risk assessment have been presented and have been adopted and have been accepted. That's fine. But in JECFA there is no plenary of members of the WTO, for example, where they meet, and they take the papers of JECFA, and they say yes, they are well done, and we accept and adopt them. This does not exist in JECFA. And all these papers, as I said, they are publications without legal status in terms of the SPS Agreement. I think that it is as simple as that, I don't want to confuse the scientists about this, and I certainly would agree with my colleague from Canada that we would have the time to clarify this on Monday and Tuesday; simply then, on Monday and Tuesday, the experts will not be here, so we need to take advantage of their presence here as well. Thank you.

Chairman

305. I would ask the representative of JECFA to respond to that question, not in the context of the legal analysis of the SPS Agreement, but in the context of the work you are doing in JECFA and Codex. I give the floor to Dr. Tritscher.

Dr. Tritscher

306. Thank you. Again, it's not correct the way it was just presented by the representative of the EC, because specifically the ADI concept, how it is defined, and how this arrives, and how to go about to get to an ADI, is exactly described, as I said earlier, in the Environmental Health Criteria document No. 70, Principles for the Safety Assessment of Food Additives and Contaminants in Food. This is the document that was elaborated by a large group of international scientists convened through the International Programme on Chemical Safety. It is a consensus document of an international independent expert scientific panel published in 1987, and this is the basis on how to derive an ADI. An ADI cannot be derived if you don't follow the risk assessment steps as they were defined, so you cannot disconnect an ADI from the risk assessment procedure, the defined steps of hazard identification and hazard characterization. So again, this was not a correct statement. You cannot devise an ADI without following risk assessment steps. Generally this is the basis, and any of the national expert bodies, regional expert bodies, use exactly the same principles and the same methodology, let it be the European Food Safety Authority, former SCF committee, let it be the US FDA or whoever. This is the basis for this IPCS document published at WHO in 1987 and every follow-up from this. Going to JECFA – JECFA is not just a handful of people sitting there and having fun. JECFA is a scientific

peer review panel, independent scientific experts that are an international peer review panel. Everybody talks about peer review now. So what JECFA does, they use all the evidence that is available, scrutinize and discuss it to come to a conclusion, based on all the available evidence. Again JECFA works on a consensus basis to the extent possible; if it is not possible there will be a minority opinion presented. That has not been the case to my knowledge in the veterinary drug field; in the 50 year history of JECFA it only happened twice. So it is the highest level expert body in this field that performs a peer review of all available information. And just saying it is a handful of people sitting together doing something, sorry if I am reacting like this, but I find this rather offensive towards the experts that dedicate their time to do this work in the international context for public health protection purposes. Thank you.

Chairman

307.   Dr. Miyagishima.

Dr. Miyagishima

308.   Thank you, Mr. Chairman. I will be very brief. I just wanted to clarify that there is an internationally agreed document that governs the whole framework of risk analysis within Codex, which is the Working Principles for Risk Analysis for Application in the Framework of the Codex Alimentarius. This text was adopted in 2003 and is now part of the Codex Procedural Manual that applies not only to the work of the Commission but all subsidiary bodies. And as Dr. Boisseau mentioned, CCRVDF has now finalized the document called Risk Analysis Principles Applied by the Codex Committee on Residues of Veterinary Drugs in Food, and this document is awaiting the final endorsement by the Commission. But it does not mean that CCRVDF is now trying to reinvent the wheel; basically this document describes the standing practice applied by CCRVDF from its inception. Of course, risk analysis is a continuing process and Codex is trying to evolve with more fine-tuning about risk analysis, but basically this document describes the ongoing and established practice followed by CCRVDF. In essence, the basic framework of how JECFA does its work and how its work is treated by Codex has not changed substantively since the beginning of the Codex work in this area. Thank you.

Chairman

309.   Thank you. I think the replies are good enough for the Panel to clarify all the issues at hand. So now I would like to move on to the next question, that is purely procedural in nature again. The question is: How does the work of IARC feed into the work of JECFA and Codex? How was this done in the case of hormones at issue? May I ask this question to Dr. Tritscher or Dr. Cogliano? Dr. Cogliano.

Dr. Cogliano

310.   IARC convenes its own working groups to evaluate the carcinogenicity of various agents. They have evaluations of steroidal oestrogens as carcinogenic to humans, non-steroidal oestrogens as well, and also oestrogen as used in hormone therapy, and oestrogens and progestogens in combination, as they are used in hormone therapy or in oral contraceptives. There is also an evaluation of oestradiol-17β as carcinogenic in experimental animals, and there is an evaluation of testosterone as carcinogenic in experimental animals. IARC publishes those in the form of monographs, and they are available to be used by JECFA or any other body that is interested in making a decision about those agents.

Chairman

311.   Has the representative of IARC ever been invited by JECFA to the Committee meetings?

Dr. Cogliano

312.   I have not personally been, but Jerry Rice, my predecessor, might have been. I was there for something about expert advice, but I have not been there to evaluate any chemicals.

Dr. Tritscher

313.   IARC is also a WHO organization. We invite the IARC representative to JECFA meetings every time when there are contaminants and relevant substances evaluated. We are not talking about food additives in the context of IARC. What IARC does; IARC does cancer classification, so in the IARC assessments the focus is on the carcinogenicity or potential carcinogenicity of the compounds. How the work feeds in was already basically answered. IARC publishes their work in monographs, so does JECFA, and we base – depending on which one comes timely first is the starting point of the work of the other, so we take each other's work into consideration. Thank you.

Chairman

314.   Thank you. Dr. Boobis.

Dr. Boobis

315.   To expand on that a little bit, when JECFA discussed the hormones, the natural hormones, for the fifty-second meeting there was a staff member of IARC present who was an adviser, a temporary adviser, and we were fortunate that we had access not only to the published reports, but some of the information about to be published, and in fact, if you read the technical documents from JECFA, it was made clear that the IARC evaluation and some of the information they had put together formed an important part of the deliberations of the Joint Committee.

Chairman

316. Thank you. EC.

European Communities

317. Chairman, I have one question to both representatives of JECFA, actually Codex as well, and the International Agency for Research on Cancer. The International Agency for Research on Cancer has classified, as you know, oestrogen and oestradiol in the first group, which is the proven carcinogens of humans, and they have classified the other two in the second category, group 2A and 2B. So I would like to ask JECFA, how it is possible, since they are interacting, these two international organizations, that JECFA comes to the conclusion they are not proven carcinogens – I am speaking about oestradiol – whereas the International Agency for Research of Cancer has come to a different conclusion. I would like to know: is it because they use different data, do they use different toxicological studies, do they take other considerations into account which make for this different outcome? Because I guess you would like to know as we do, since we take the advice of these two groups into account, which one of the two to follow. One says oestradiol is a probable carcinogen, the other says no, there is a threshold, there is no risk. I simplify, but this is the end result. Thank you.

Chairman

318. I see many flags raised, so I will give the floor the JECFA first, and then Codex, and then Dr. Boobis.

Dr. Tritscher

319. Thank you. There are many things mixed up now in this statement. So JECFA and IARC are doing two different things. First of all I have to clarify that JECFA never said oestradiol is not a carcinogen, you will not find this anywhere in any JECFA publication. IARC does, as I said, cancer classification; it is a totally different thing than what JECFA does in doing risk assessment, and my colleague from IARC will explain what it means, what their work really means to cancer classification. A compound being a carcinogen does not preclude it from a safety assessment being performed and an acceptable daily intake or tolerable daily intake being set. Again, those are not mutually exclusive things. Sorry, let me say it like this: JECFA has evaluated several compounds that have carcinogenic properties and have still been able to set an ADI or a TDI.

Ms Orozco

320. Sorry, can I interrupt you there for asking you for an example of other compounds in a similar situation.

Dr. Tritscher

321.   Contaminants in food like the chloropropanols for example, monochlor-propandiol and DCP. I think I will leave it at that in the interest of time, because I know that ...

Chairman

322.   Thank you. Dr. Miyagishima.

Dr. Miyagishima

323.   Simply to say that there is no standing or institutional linkage between the Codex system and the IARC. Of course, to the extent that the work of IARC is beneficial to the work conducted by the Joint FAO/WHO bodies, such as JECFA, it is up to JECFA to draw any useful elements from the work of IARC. But there is no direct link between Codex and IARC. Thank you.

Chairman

324.   Dr. Boobis and Dr. Cogliano.

Dr. Boobis

325.   Well, it is just to emphasize the point that in the view of JECFA it is necessary to consider the mechanism and mode of action for the carcinogenicity, because, as we alluded to earlier, there are many different ways in which one can generate a tumorigenic response. I am sure tomorrow we will discuss exactly how oestrogens cause cancer, but as a philosophical point at the moment, just to clarify the point that Dr. Tritscher made, simply because a compound causes experimental cancer in an animal, or even at high doses in humans, does not necessarily and automatically mean that it is not possible to establish a safe level of exposure. JECFA sought to do that for the hormones. One can argue whether it came to the right conclusions, but it was on the basis of consideration of the mode of action and the mechanism of the carcinogenicity. As already stated, at no point did we ever exclude evidence which was readily available at that time, in 2000 and 1999, that in humans at certain levels of exposure oestrogens could cause cancer in endocrine sensitive tissues.

Chairman

326.   Thank you. Dr. Cogliano.

Dr. Cogliano

327.   I put my flag up just to make one correction. IARC has classified oestradiol 17β as possibly carcinogenic based on sufficient evidence in experimental animals. The agents that are known to be carcinogenic in humans are the steroidal oestrogens, non-steroidal oestrogens and various oestrogen-progestin combinations as used either as birth-control pills or menopausal therapy.

Chairman

328.   Thank you. EC.

European Communities

329.   Chairman, I think it would be useful if we take a little bit of time on this issue, because it is interesting to know the scientific basis upon which the International Agency for Research on Cancer re-examine partly the same documentation that is available, the toxicological studies and the profile in the mode of action in these substances. And I understand by reading the International Agency for Research on Cancer monographs that they consider that oestradiol, oestrogen and oestradiol-17β not only act through receptor mediation but also they consider them to be genotoxic. This problem, this toxicological assessment of this substance and the other natural hormones – I need to clarify, the International Agency for Research on Cancer, it has not examined the synthetic hormones, but they have examined the three natural. Partly the same studies have been evaluated by JECFA as well, and as you see, they dispute, they go through – if you take and read the opinion of JECFA and Codex subsequently, which is taken out and published – they go through the data, but the ultimate conclusion is that oestradiol has a genotoxic potential, but they do not define it as genotoxic in the sense that the evidence is sufficient. As Dr. Cogliano has said, they thought the evidence was sufficient to define as carcinogenic in humans. So I am still wondering and I would like, as a lawyer, and I hope you as well, to know why on this crucial aspect the International Agency for Research on Cancer comes to a different conclusion for oestradiol, and they also come to different conclusions for progesterone in particular and testosterone as well, than the conclusions obtained by JECFA. I am not trying to fudge the issues, no. But the truth is that part of the scientific documentation is examined by the two bodies, and the conclusions and toxicological conclusions they reach are very important, and I have the feeling, and we have the feeling here, that they are not getting to the same conclusion on that aspect. Dr. Boobis said that he does not, JECFA does not dispute that oestradiol is carcinogenic, fine, but the method by which we define oestradiol as a possible human carcinogen is also important, and I hope it is clear what I am asking the two or the three delegates to clarify. Thank you.

Chairman

330.   The Panel's intention in putting forward these questions was purely procedural, as I mentioned, and I think the comment you made is rather stretching out to the substantive issues to be discussed later on, in due course, through exchanges of questions and answers on different issues. I hope we can conclude discussion on this question here and then come back, if necessary, in due course. OK. Then the next question of the Panel is rather broad in concept, or which may capture the broader picture of the issues at hand. The question is: how much scientific evidence is needed for a valid risk assessment? What is normally done if data in a specific area are incomplete? How is scientific uncertainty addressed? The floor is open to any expert to respond. Dr. Boisseau.

Dr. Boisseau

331. Thank you, Mr. Chairman. There are two hypothetical possibilities here: either the necessary scientific data is lacking to the point where the risk assessment cannot be completed – in which case the required data is requested so that the risk assessment can be continued; or a committee, the JECFA – but it could just as well be the CVMP – considers that the necessary data has been gathered and is available, but since there is an element of uncertainty in any piece of scientific data owing either to the experimental protocol used or the obsolescence of the method used, or with the number of animals involved, it uses safety factors to ensure that the evaluation results in proper protection of public health. Thank you.

Chairman4

332. Thank you. Any other additional comments from the experts. If there are no follow-up questions from parties, then can I move on to the next, please. Madam Orozco.

Ms Orozco

333. I would like to ask a follow-up question, because I am not quite sure. The question has two elements that we would like to clarify: What would be the procedure when the data is incomplete? And what would be the procedure when there is uncertainty about the science?

Chairman

334. Dr. Tritscher.

Dr. Tritscher

335. Again, very quick, to the completeness of the database; if you want to look at chronic intakes or setting an ADI of course you need sufficient long-term studies that allow an extrapolation or an assessment of the compound. If it is a compound like the hormones, with hormonal effect, you would definitely require reproductive and developmental studies to check specific effects. Again, what Professor Boobis mentioned a couple of times already is that JECFA puts great emphasis on the mode of action of the compound. That's part of the first question, sorry that I am going back, but then the rest is better understood. To the question how much scientific evidence is needed, it is not a check box, it is not a list that then is then just checked off. There are certain basic studies that need to be available; over and above that, it is on a case-by-case basis. Depending on the toxicological profile or the suspected profile of the compound, you would require certain studies. If these studies are not available, if there are significant – now I am going to the follow-up question – if significant data gaps are identified by the Committee, then these have to be clearly identified. For example, there is concern for reproductive effects, however there is no reproductive study performed, that would preclude a safety assessment on that compound, and it would

be clearly identified what the significant data gaps are, and the conclusion would be that there cannot be a safety assessment performed on this compound if there is a significant data gap. If the data gaps are considered to be minor, in the sense that a safety assessment could be performed to still be public health protective, however additional data would be required, then there is the option to set a temporary ADI, and then there would be a specific definition of what additional data would be required in order to fill these minor data gaps. A temporary ADI usually has a limited lifespan, meaning the data requirements would have a date attached to them. If a temporary ADI is set, so minor data gaps that are clearly identified are there, then what usually happens is that there are additional safety factors, uncertainty factors, added on to have an extra level of safety added and to take this additional uncertainty into account. Thank you.

Chairman

336.   Dr. Wennberg and then the EC.

Dr. Wennberg

337.   Thank you, Mr. Chairman. Just short on the residue part. I already alluded to the requirements related to the data needed to perform an evaluation of the residue in the animals in question. When I was talking about how to set MRLs – I am not going to go into that any further – and similarly applying, which I also mentioned before, is that if there are minor gaps in the validation of the analytical method to be used in residue control, for example, JECFA could consider to set temporary MRLs, but we already talked about that.

Chairman

338.   EC.

European Communities

339.   Chairman, two brief statements and I think we can be more concrete. If you look at the 1987, 1988 evaluation by JECFA of the three natural hormones, they thought at the time that they had a complete set of data, they made the evaluation, but they did not fix an ADI because they thought the data was complete and there was no risk, because of the wide margin of safety, as they call it. JECFA has re-evaluated the three natural hormones again in 1999, and they came to a different conclusion, that this time it was necessary to fix an ADI, because data apparently changed, were more complete. Now, the United States, in its reply to the comments made by the experts and by the European Community, interprets why JECFA fixed in 1999 an ADI is because the data were now complete. This is the terminology, I can find the correct quotation if necessary. Whereas the reply of Dr. Boisseau, why they fixed an ADI for the first time in 1999, is in order to be more convincing. I can find the correct quotation as well. So there is quite an uncertainty in the way JECFA proceeds. The point is, and this comes to the second question asked by Madam Orozco – practically there is no room to take into account uncertainty in JECFA, because they think that they

can address uncertainty through the so-called safety factor. By applying the so-called safety factor, sometimes it's 100, 200 or 1,000 times, they think they can take into account uncertainty in the data, but at least the way we understand scientific uncertainty is different. And I would like to know instances where – if there are, there are really very few, very very few in the history of JECFA – where they came to the conclusion that for a substance we do not have sufficient data to propose an ADI or an MRL. And I should give you another example which is also pertinent in this case, the case of carbadox, and I will only mention it and not go on into the details. We were arguing the data were not sufficient in 1996, nevertheless JECFA proposed a provisional, as they call it, a provisional ADI and MRL, and ten years later on Canada, for example, has agreed that the data were not enough and were wrongly interpreted. So I think these questions are very important. Is there any room in the JECFA procedure and the risk assessment to take into account scientific uncertainties what the real scientists understand what is scientific uncertainty? And our feeling is that there is very limited room for that and I don't thing they actually do it. Thank you.

Chairman

340. Thank you. US.

United States

341. Thank you, Mr. Chairman. I again had a very difficult time discerning a question in the last statement by the EC, but there were quite a lot of factual assertions made in the course of that "question". I was wondering if, maybe we could open up the EC's comments to the experts who have spoken on the issue of ADIs and the JECFA/Codex/IARC work. So I would propose that Doctors Boobis, Boisseau, Cogliano and Dr. Tritscher respond to several of the factual statements made by the EC in its last comments.

Chairman

342. Well, before I give the floor to the experts, may I remind you again this is the session for the Panel to put the questions, and we are allowing the parties to ask additional questions in relation to those questions posed by the Panel. So we are not going to make any statements from the Panel or from the parties at this particular moment, and I would urge the delegations to refrain from making any statement and rather focus on the questions put forward by the Panel and replies given by the experts. With that I will give the floor to Drs. Boisseau and Boobis.

Dr. Boisseau

343. Thank you, Mr. Chairman. I will try to keep my reply to the EC intervention brief. Science is a discipline which is constantly evolving. When we manage to resolve a problem, we generally find that there is another problem hidden behind it, and so on ad infinitum. The assessment of the safety of veterinary drug residues is a pragmatic system, because the proper use of veterinary drugs depends on its conclusions. We need to be able to decide, at any given moment,

whether we should think of reconsidering an assessment in the light of scientific developments. But we cannot constantly delay that decision, or otherwise it can turn into a Sisyphean challenge. When the EU speaks of these scientific uncertainties, it is the general protocol that is being called into question. We must understand that the committees, the JECFA and the CVMP, work on the basis of the data available. Where do these data come from? Generally from the industrialists that provide them. In the end, there is very little, relatively speaking, in the way of data, from independent bodies. So ultimately, it is going to be necessary, in the light of the information available – if it is sufficient – to make proposals that it will be up to the Codex to accept or reject. If not, none of what we call old molecules will ever be evaluated and they will have to be withdrawn from the market, since no one will support them. The same applies to the developing countries. There are substances which are very important for the developing countries, but which represent a minor market. Most of the time, although their files are not complete the JECFA tries to conduct these evaluations on the basis of the data available and using appropriate safety factors to recommend ADI and MRL standards to the CCRVDF, that guarantee public health. Thus, I think it is important to remember that the approach is a pragmatic one.

344.   As regards what happened in the re-evaluation of natural hormones in 1999, I maintain what I wrote, namely that during the preceding re-evaluation, the margin of safety between what might have been envisaged as an ADI and the daily amount ingested seemed to the JECFA to be such that it did not appear necessary to determine ADIs, and its conclusion at the time was: ADIs not necessary; MRLs not necessary. It emerged that there was a problem of communication, because as a result this margin of safety did not appear; and the JECFA, of its own accord – this was not requested by the CCRVDF – reverted to this evaluation, for which, in fact, it had access to a whole data package. Please excuse me, I made a mistake in my previous reply: there were indeed new data in connection with the data package which the FDA placed at the disposal of the JECFA, and which helped, as it were, to determine more precisely this margin of safety between an ADI that was established at that time and the theoretical daily intake of residues. The JECFA once again determined that it was not necessary to establish the MRLs since the margin of safety was still sufficient. In other words, the evaluation remained unchanged, and it is not really the availability of new data that led the JECFA to reconsider its previous evaluation – it was only that the JECFA wanted to be more transparent, more explicit. The CCRVDF did not want to take account of this new re-evaluation which yielded the same results and which it had not itself requested. Thank you.

Chairman

345.   Thank you. Dr. Boobis.

Dr. Boobis

346.   Just from my own personal perspective, and I am not necessarily speaking for JECFA or anybody else here, I think it is probably fair to say that when

conducting a risk assessment, we are not really looking to see if a data package is complete as to as much as whether it is adequate for the purpose, because I agree entirely with everything that Dr. Boisseau has just said, that science moves on, and it would be complacent for a risk assessment body to assume that it knew everything about a substance at a particular point in time. We have to work within the available information, and the question we ask is: do we have sufficient information at this point to conduct a risk assessment? – not: is the data complete and are there no scientific questions remaining to be answered. And I would add that there are numerous examples in the JECFA monographs of substances where it was not possible to establish an ADI on the basis of incomplete data; that has been done on several occasions.

Chairman

347.   Thank you. Dr. Tritscher.

Dr. Tritscher

348.   I would like to comment on the aspect of uncertainty and if or if not uncertainty is taken into account by JECFA assessments. It is correct that scientific uncertainty is difficult to quantify very often, and the scientific community is still debating. There is a lot of debate currently going on to better quantify uncertainty in the database, to give a better information to the risk manager as to the confidence on the conclusions that are reached. As the delegate of the EC said, real scientists even have problems to define scientific uncertainty. The experts working in JECFA are also real scientists and they also have problems with that. However, it is always taken into account and, very briefly, there are two aspects that need to be separated out, that is uncertainty and variability. Uncertainty is what we don't know, and variability is variation in a response between individuals, between species. Those are two different concepts and both need to be considered. Uncertainties as to extrapolations from model systems to the real-life situation and so forth, they are taken into account by safety factors that are also called uncertainty factors. Now there are default factors that have been used by everybody, by all the expert bodies since the inception of the invention of the ADI, and now increasingly efforts are undertaken to go away from default uncertainty factors to data-derived uncertainty factors, meaning to put more science into the derivation of these factors to take account of true uncertainties, if possible, if the data are available. That is the concept of the chemical specific adjustment factors. Again, a concept that was developed by Andy Renwick, I think, originally, but the International Programme on Chemical Safety has published on that and the Expert Committees like JECFA and JMPR are trying to apply this concept where possible, meaning where data are available to extrapolate, for example from the animal to the human situation. So it is factually entirely incorrect to say that JECFA does not take uncertainty into account. Thank you.

Chairman

349. Thank you. I think the comments just made by Dr. Boobis and Dr. Tritscher have already answered the Panel's next follow-up question, but I would appreciate it if any other experts would further elaborate on this particular question, that is: how would you distinguish between insufficiency of science evidence and scientific uncertainty? Could you rephrase your comments in more clear terms to distinguish between these two concepts. Dr. Cogliano.

Dr. Cogliano

350. Yes. I want to start by agreeing with Dr. Boobis's comment that it is not so much a matter of being incomplete. But I would also point out that there are several kinds of uncertainty. There are uncertainties as to, for example, what is a null-effect level in animals, or a safe dose; or how would you extrapolate between animals and humans. There are also wider uncertainties about – are the animals predictive at all of humans, or is a single chemical fed to an animal predictive of the human situation? There are very different levels of uncertainty and I think that the way some types of uncertainty are addressed is by trying to quantify them, by trying to get data derived from chemical-specific uncertainty factors. Some forms of uncertainty are addressed by general assumptions, like we will assume animal results are relevant to humans unless we had the data to show otherwise. So that is another approach to dealing with uncertainty, to take a conservative approach and say that we will assume that these study results are useful. And I think that as risk assessment evolves there are more and more questions that are asked. We are now asking more questions; once we understand the mechanisms we start to ask: what is the range of variability in human populations and who is likely to be more susceptible? These are concepts that IARC monographs are trying to address more in the future, but they had not really been questions that were routinely asked 20 or 30 years ago. I think that what we do with uncertainty does evolve over time and there are different forms of uncertainty that do get different approaches. Some are very quantitative and some are much more qualitative. I think I will leave it at that since more specific questions – it's a very broad-ranging field, I think, to try to really answer in a few words. I think there can be whole books written on uncertainty and how to deal with it.

Ms Orozco

351. Simply, if you have similar explanation as to what is or what's not sufficiency of scientific evidence?

Dr. Cogliano

352. Let me try to answer that in the context of the monographs. If we don't have epidemiological studies, good epidemiological studies, we will say we have inadequate information, and then the evaluation will proceed looking at the animal studies. If we have good bioassays, we will make our conclusion that some-

thing is probably carcinogenic or possibly carcinogenic or not based on the animal studies. If we don't have good animal studies or good human studies, we have inadequate information, and we would end with saying we cannot classify this substance. So we do want to have either epidemiological studies or animal bioassays. Now let's shift to the mechanism field. If we don't have a good mechanistic understanding, that will not stop us from classifying the substance; we will classify the substance based on the human and the animal studies, even if we do not understand the mechanism. So having epidemiology or animal bioassays, that's a requirement to come up with a classification. Not having mechanistic studies – its nice to have that, it contributes to our understanding, but it does not stop us from a classification. So I guess you could say what we need, and IARC usually has, are some animal bioassays or some epidemiological studies and then we will proceed with a classification. If the rest of the database is somewhat lacking, that does not affect the classification. Now I should mention that IARC does not come up with safe levels of exposure and uncertainty factors. So our uncertainty analysis is really different from what JECFA would do or someone else trying to come up with a safe level for consumption in foods.

Chairman

353. Let me put this question to all of the experts. If there is scientific uncertainty, would you all agree that there is always insufficiency of scientific evidence, or, even if there is scientific uncertainty, may there be a situation where scientific evidence is sufficient in terms of risk assessment? Dr. Boobis.

Dr. Boobis

354. I will try and answer that question in a slightly different way, if I may, which is just following on from the comments of Dr. Cogliano. Where there is scientific uncertainty, we would tend to adopt a worst case default in extrapolating the data to take account of that, so we will use the most sensitive endpoint in the most sensitive species for the extrapolation purposes of a risk assessment, assuming that it is relevant to humans and assuming that humans are going to be more sensitive than animals. Now that is a fairly conservative assumption, based on the totality of scientific information available to us at this time. The insufficiency of scientific evidence, I would say, as has been indicated, could be trivial, it could be that just one test is not there and we can fill in, but it could be substantial. For example, there might not be a reproductive toxicity study for a compound that women of child-bearing age would be exposed to, in which case we would consider that a major insufficiency of data, not a scientific uncertainty, just an absence of data, and we would not proceed without filling that data gap. So I think they are rather different issues; one we can handle with taking conservative defaults, for the other we really need information to allow us to proceed.

Chairman

355. Thank you. Dr. Boisseau, Dr. Cogliano and then Dr. De Brabander.

Dr. Boisseau

356.   Thank you, Mr. Chairman. I am afraid it will be difficult to reply to the question you have just asked. I can repeat what I said, namely that if there is a major insufficiency of scientific data, as Dr. Boobis just mentioned, we cannot go any further in the evaluation of the safety of residues of veterinary drugs. There are other cases where scientific uncertainty with regard to less important data would not prevent a conclusion from being reached with a safety factor that would provide for adequate protection of public health. Beyond that, it is impossible to draw up a table with two columns showing what constitutes insufficiency and uncertainty. All we have is specific cases, we can provide the odd example. We could speak of insufficiency in the case of suspicious results of short-term mutigenicity tests without a supplementary carcinogenicity test or without any studies involving radio-labelled elements for a tissue depletion or a metabolism study. That is an insufficiency. We can give you a few examples, but there will always be cases that do not fit the examples. The reply that I am tempted to give you is that a distinction must be drawn between an individual evaluation, whatever the competence of the expert involved, and a collective evaluation conducted by a committee of competent experts, be it the JECFA, the CVMP, or another committee. We must not underestimate the notion of collective evaluation. When 30 or so experts reach a consensus that there is an insufficiency of data or that a scientific uncertainty can be managed through safety factors, I think that we can be fairly confident – this is a collective approach.

Chairman

357.   Thank you. Dr. Cogliano.

Dr. Cogliano

358.   I was going to respond. I think similarly – it really depends on what the question is, for example: does tobacco cause cancer? I think the answer is unequivocally yes. Are there uncertainties or are there things we don't know, for example I was asked the question earlier, am I going to get cancer if I smoke for only five years, or only one year, or only two cigarettes a day? We don't really know exactly the shape of the dose-response curve. But we do know enough to know that from a public health point of view tobacco is definitely harmful and we should take steps to curb smoking. There are always going to be uncertainties or things we don't know at the fringes. What happens if we smoke and we also work in a dusty environment, what happens if we smoke and we have vitamin deficiencies, these are the niceties that scientists will say are uncertainties, and there are things that we would like to know more about. So I think when you are asking about insufficiency of evidence it is really: insufficient for what purpose, and what is the question you are trying to ask? In some cases the data set can be absolutely conclusive that tobacco is harmful, but without necessarily answering every single question: what about in combination with this or in combination with that or two cigarettes a day? So yes, keep in mind the purpose, and data sets

are always sufficient to answer some questions and there is always more that you could know if you wanted to answer everything.

Chairman

359.   Thank you. Dr. De Brabander.

Dr. De Brabander

360.   Thank you, Mr. Chairman. As you know, I am layman in that area of risk assessment, but in answering this question I really want to make some remark on a question which is important to me and perhaps for the whole system. I agree that science grows continually, we always have new evidence. I also agree that there are internationally recognized items to make the risk assessment for veterinary drugs, but when you as a human being take medicine, or you give a veterinary drug to an animal, it is in order to cure it from a disease, and when you take a medicine, you always balance the profit of taking a medicine against the risks, because every medicine has its side effects, against the profit of being healed. So the question I ask: by scientific uncertainty, if you are using hormones, what is the counterbalance of using hormones except of profit, money?

Chairman

361.   Thank you. Any other – EC.

European Communities

362.   Thank you, Chair. A simple question. In the view of all experts, perhaps, and whoever wants to reply on this: is direct genotoxicity of oestrogens an issue on which there exists scientific uncertainty?

Chairman

363.   The floor is open. Dr. Cogliano.

Dr. Cogliano

364.   Yes, I think there is scientific uncertainty. One of the exhibits you have was the summary of the most recent monograph meeting on the oestrogen/progestogen combinations, either as birth-control pills or as menopausal therapies. And as I mentioned earlier this morning, a hormonal mechanism is clearly operating, but there was some evidence that there could be genotoxicity operating; it's not as strong. It was not the entire working group that put a lot of credence in it, but enough members of the working group thought that there was some possibility of genotoxic action that our summary does have a paragraph for each of those two types of exposures that mentions that there could be some genotoxic activity as part of the cancer mechanism. I think that is an area of continuing research and obviously more will be known later.

Chairman

365.   Thank you. Dr. Guttenplan.

Dr. Guttenplan

366.   I think qualitatively one can say that there is very little uncertainty in the fact that oestrogen is genotoxic, however quantitatively I think there is a lot of scientific uncertainty. I don't think we can really estimate the risk at this point from such low levels of genotoxic effects.

Chairman

367.   EC.

European Communities

368.   Mr. Chairman, I think that this is a very important question and we may replicate the examples where we would like to ask the scientists, all of them, where there is scientific uncertainty and where it comes from. Does it come from the lack of sufficient evidence, as you say in your question, or does it come from, as I would put it, from evidence which is there on the table but it is conflicting? One does not agree with the other evidence? And I think there is a very important causal relationship between these two concepts. Our suggestion is – and I would like to see if the experts agree or disagree – we would say, and we have said in our submissions to the Panel, if the evidence is insufficient, then I think practically always there will be scientific uncertainty, because the evidence is not sufficient. Dr. Boobis has said: if it is a major insufficiency; but it is a value judgement, whether the insufficiency is small, higher or major. Our suggestion to go about this issue is, if the data are not sufficient, there is scientific uncertainty. But this is not all, and it is not the most important in this case as well, because as Dr. Cogliano and Dr. Guttenplan have said, qualitatively there is no doubt that oestrogens are genotoxic or carcinogenic, but the evidence is not sufficient in terms of quantity. And there we will also propose to the Panel – and if the experts agree or disagree they can say so – but when there are conflicting interpretations of the evidence that is available, still we will argue that there is scientific uncertainty. Thank you.

Chairman

369.   Thank you. I think the EC's comments are somewhat related to the questions that the Panel are going to put forward later, so I would appreciate it if the experts would respond to the EC's comments when they respond to the Panel's questions, and then I will give the floor to the US.

United States

370.   Thank you, Mr. Chairman, I want to interject. I feel with the last question from the EC we have strayed into the scientific evidentiary discussions of tomorrow, and I just wanted to raise that point clearly. The EC's assertion that these

hormones function by a genotoxic mechanism at relevant exposure levels is critical to their arguments, and I would propose either the United States can go forward with its questions on genotoxicity and the scientific evidence, or that we hold back until tomorrow at the time the Chair had set aside to discuss the scientific elements of the case.

Chairman

371.   OK. In connection with that comment, may I propose to the delegations: why don't we go through all the Panel's questions as quickly as possible, and then based upon the answers and replies and comments from the experts on all these questions put forward by the Panel we can have more structured discussions by the parties, more elaborate questions on these basic discussions. So that we do not duplicate or repeat discussions we had already. I think that would be a more structured way of debate for today and tomorrow. So I would request the understanding of the delegations by way of refraining from putting many additional follow-up questions on the issues at hand. Are there any comments or replies from the experts? Dr. Boobis.

Dr. Boobis

372.   I appreciate your comments, Chairman, and will not enter into discussion about the evidence. I just wanted to make a general point, which is that it would be a mistake to think that risk assessment results in the complete and absolute agreement of everybody in the risk assessment. The nature of the evidence available on science in general is such that we will never get a uniform interpretation. What happens generally is that there is a consensus and if necessary the adoption of defaults which are conservative to allow us to move forward. Seeking unanimity on the interpretation of all the data is futile because it will not happen.

Chairman

373.   Thank you. Let me put the Panel's next follow-up questions, two questions at the same time. The first is: at what step in a risk analysis is a determination made whether the available evidence is sufficient to undertake a risk assessment? The second is: at what step of risk analysis does one factor in the level of protection to be achieved by an SPS measure? Any expert? Dr. Boobis.

Dr. Boobis

374.   Could I just ask you, Chairman, to repeat the second half of that question?

Chairman

375.   The second one is: at what step of a risk analysis does one sector in the level of protection to be achieved by an SPS measure? I would rephrase the last part of the second question as: by a health protection measures, instead of SPS measure. Dr. Cogliano.

Dr. Cogliano

376.   I would actually still like to clarify that. It seems to me the level of protection is something that was discussed earlier as part of risk management, and I
am not sure that it is part of the risk assessment. Well, risk analysis, then, is a
new term we have not talked about. We have talked in terms of risk assessment;
is risk analysis being used to mean risk assessment?

Chairman

377.   I don't want to go into the detailed legal issues which will be the focus of
our discussion next week, but there is a difference in the terminology of risk
assessment and management, and there is a broader concept of risk assessment,
risk analysis, so I think it would be better to avoid that discussion at this time,
and I give the floor to Dr. Tritscher.

Dr. Tritscher

378.   So at what step in the risk analysis is a determination made about the sufficiency of the data to undertake a risk assessment? In the ideal case you would
have a step that's called problem formulation, when you really formulate the
question, what is the concern, what is the question that the risk assessor should
answer, which is followed. Now, there are different terms used – a preliminary
risk profile – this is a step where you really look what kind of data are available.
Now in the international field, in the context of JECFA and Codex, these steps
have not been formalized as such, not in that level of detail, the way I have just
described it. What happens is, the Codex Committee, CCRVDF, poses fairly
simple, if you allow me to say it that way, a simple questions to JECFA, asks
JECFA to perform a safety assessment or a risk assessment on a specific veterinary drug when used according to good veterinary practice. And at that point it
goes over to the risk-assessment body, and the risk-assessment body, JECFA in
that case, puts out a call for data and performs literature searches, the experts
perform literature searches on all publicly available date. Now in the concrete
case of JECFA, in the preparation of the meeting, a designated expert reviews
the available database and prepares what we call a draft working paper as a basis
of the discussion of the Committee at the meeting. If at that point the expert determines that the data are insufficient to allow an assessment, that would be recorded as such, and why the insufficiency is there, or what other significant data
there is. So the working paper would lay that out, and then, when the actual
JECFA meeting takes place, the Committee would discuss that as such. So to
answer the first question, in the context of the JECFA/Codex system – in what
step of the risk analysis paradigm – in this case it is at the risk assessment step.
So JECFA makes that decision if the database is sufficient, as it concerns us, as
opinion of an international expert panel.

379.   At what step of the risk analysis does one factor in the level of protection? Now the level of protection is a term that comes from the microbiological
area and is not as such used that much in the chemical area and in the context of

chemicals in food, also veterinary drugs we are now talking about, where the risk assessment is performed to set an ADI. What that actually means, what an ADI is, what is done is to set a level of no apparent risk on the basis of the available data. So it is a little bit like an acceptable level of protection, like some other agencies or authorities or expert bodies do, in a sense, that one additional cancer case in a million population would be an acceptable level of risk. This is clearly a risk-management decision. The risk manager would have to define this for the risk-assessment body, to go to a certain level of protection. If we are talking about an ADI, setting of an ADI, this is not the concept. What the concept behind there is, to set – again, I repeat – a level of no apparent risk. This is a chronic acceptable intake level without – this famous term – appreciable health risk.

Chairman

380.   Thank you. Dr. Miyagishima.

Dr. Miyagishima

381.   Thank you, Mr. Chairman. I will speak only to the first question because I still have some difficulty in understanding the meaning of the second question. The determination, or any judgement as to the sufficiency or insufficiency of data to undertake risk assessment, may well take place within the risk-assessment programme. For instance, JECFA may come to a conclusion that the scientific data is insufficient to undertake a complete risk assessment, and they may abort their undertaking at that stage. There are also cases where the risk managers, in this case the Codex Alimentarius Commission, may already foresee the insufficiency of scientific data and yet the Commission may still ask the JECFA to attempt to undertake a risk assessment, or the Commission may decide not to waste the resources of JECFA and opt for another risk management options that would not require stringent risk assessment, for instance the development of a code of practice, rather than numerical standards, could be an option. There may be other options. I must say that there are cases where risk managers make some judgements on this point. Thank you.

Chairman

382.   Thank you. Then could you also explain what a deterministic approach to risk assessment is, and what other approaches are there? And in relation to that: what is a so-called hazard-based approach, and under which circumstances is that approach used? I would welcome the replies from the experts to these comments in combination. If there are no specific – Dr. Tritscher.

Dr. Tritscher

383.   I can try to give you the very very brief description, but there are also written comments to the deterministic versus probabilistic, if this is what is meant in this sense. I am sorry, but sometimes it's not that clear what is really behind the question. Deterministic approach to risk assessment means that we

are using point estimates – high-level consumer, mean-level consumer – on the exposure assessment, individual points on the dose-response curve, whereas probabilistic takes distribution into account – like I explained earlier, you have variability in responses, and to take this into account is a much more complex way of doing risk assessments. I am not aware that even on the national level really probabilistic risk assessments are performed. This is highly complex and is not routinely done. Increasingly probabilistic exposure assessments are done, meaning where one takes into account the variation of levels of different chemicals in food and the variation of consumption patterns, variation in portions of what people eat. That is increasingly taken into account; whereas when it is just a point estimate, what is the mean level of occurrence, what is the mean portion size. Taking also probabilistic approaches into account on the toxicological side, if you would think about the graphs that I had, so that, going down the left arm of the graph, taking also distributions into account is highly complex and definitely not done routinely, and – other than, let's say, in the scientific experimental field – I am not aware that this is done in the regulatory field. Again, on the international basis, in the context of JECFA we are basically bound to use deterministic approaches, because we basically have to cover scenarios for the whole world. However, again, having said this, the increase in the efforts now, at least on the exposure assessment, we try to take distributions into account. And I do not understand the second question, what is the hazard-based approach. Any risk assessment starts with the hazard, it is the hazard-based approach, so apologies, I do not understand the question.

Chairman

384. As I understand it, that terminology was used by one of the experts or parties in their replies or submissions, which I cannot identify for the moment. Dr. Boobis.

Dr. Boobis

385. Well, I suspect, what Dr. Tritscher has just explained is exactly what I understand by deterministic versus probabilistic, but I have a suspicion that something different is meant here. Obviously we are trying to get to a different place, so that deterministic is where we use point estimates, conservative assumptions, but the underlying assumption, based on analysis of the data, is that there is a point at which one can reach a safe level of exposure, an acceptable level of exposure, and so that is the basis for arriving at an ADI based on point estimates. One could do it in different ways, probabilistic, which is much more complex. But I think that what this is to be contrasted with is the idea that there isn't a safe level of exposure and what one could use under such circumstances is what is called quantitative risk assessment, extrapolating down levels of exposure, where one gets to a level where there is still a risk, but the risk, in the view of the risk manager, is considered acceptable. Now that is not an approach that JECFA has used before for veterinary drug residues. A hazard-based approach, I would imagine, is a qualitative risk assessment, if you like, where one stops once

one has identified a hazard that is deemed unacceptable. So, for example, the compound is shown to be direct-acting genotoxicant; this is considered unacceptable at any level of exposure, permitting exposure would not be appropriate, and then one stops the risk assessment at that point. So it does not need to take account of exposure, because any level of exposure is deemed to be of concern. There are some who argue that certain other endpoints, such as certain types of neurotoxicity, would fall into that category as well. There are intermediate positions, which is that even if there is such a hazard, one could think about what is the margin of exposure, or what is the exposure with respect to the so-called threshold of toxicological concern. These are newer strategies which have been designed to deal with endpoints which may not have a discernible threshold, but where some exposure may be unavoidable, for example a contaminant, and so we have to determine whether we need to prioritize resources to bring exposure down to lower than that. The issue of veterinary drug residues, which are compounds that are added intentionally to animals, is a wider discussion and I won't even enter into that here because it is outside of the thrust of the question.

Chairman

386.   I think I did understand the issues but could you repeat once again, but in a much briefer way, the difference between deterministic and probabilistic approaches.

Dr. Boobis

387.   I am not sure that that is helpful here, Mr. Chairman. The deterministic approach is to use single estimates of, for example, the toxicological no observable adverse effect level, the exposure level etc. One uses conservative assumptions for those values. The probabilistic approach is to take distributions of those values and try to get closer to the real world situation. We are not all exposed to the highest level of residues our entire lifetime and with the sensitivity of the most sensitive animal, and the most sensitive endpoint. So we can use distributions of those values, multiply them together, and say the probability of an individual lying on the curve is X, very low, medium, high, whatever. And then that requires the risk manager to take a decision as to a percentile of the population they wish to protect, because you never reach a 100 per cent on a distribution curve.

Chairman

388.   Thank you. If there are no other follow-up questions, let me put the next question. If a substance is genotoxic, can a threshold be established? If there are any substances for which no threshold can be established, how does this affect the conduct of a risk assessment for such a substance, and what happens to the four steps? Dr. Boobis.

Dr. Boobis

389.   There are substances for which there are thresholds for genotoxicity; it depends on how it causes the genotoxicity. For example, it may be acting indirectly through the apparatus that allows cells to divide, the so-called spindle apparatus, which is actually a protein which allows the DNA to segregate during cell division. And it has been shown that inhibition of that process has a clear threshold, and there are some pesticides which have been regulated accordingly. It is deemed that it is possible to adopt a deterministic approach for such compounds, with an allowable daily intake because there is a threshold. Most thresholds are demonstrated experimentally, mechanistically and *in vivo*. Whether there is a threshold can be established on the basis of scientific evaluation of the underlying mechanisms but not just on the observable data. I think it would be fair to say that the conduct of the risk assessment would depend upon the purposes of the risk assessment. If it was a contaminant, there would still be the need to proceed to determine where is the level of exposure relative to the level of concern. If it was a veterinary drug residue, then one might consider that it would not be acceptable to allow a non-thresholded compound to be present in the diet. But it is very much at the discretion and direction, I would say, of the risk manager as to how one would proceed.

Chairman

390.   When it comes to the question of establishing a threshold, what is the difference between a genotoxic substance and a substance with genotoxic potential? When a substance is genotoxic, by definition, and is there any possibility of not being able to set a threshold?

Dr. Boobis

391.   Yes, absolutely. If it was shown to be a direct-acting genotoxicant which caused mutation, and there was an indication that that also occurred *in vivo,* then it's very likely one would conclude that it was not possible to identify a threshold. There are one or two rare examples of compounds which are direct-acting genotoxicants, which because of metabolic reasons there is considered to be an *in vivo* threshold, but they are very very rare. As I said before, and as others have said on this side of the table, it very much depends on examination of the underlying data and the scientific interpretation of that data as to where one gets to in considering the significance of genotoxicity, and whether or not one can establish a threshold for that compound. There are no absolutes in this.

Chairman

392.   Dr. Guttenplan.

Dr. Guttenplan

393.   Most genotoxic compounds that we know of now are of the type that directly damage DNA and cause mutations, and they don't exhibit a threshold. In

terms of risk assessment then, the critical factor would be exposure. If exposure is near zero, then whether there is a threshold or not, it does not make a difference, you are not exposed, there is no risk. But determining the exposure is then critical in the case of a compound that exhibits no threshold. Now many of these genotoxic compounds, from what we can determine in animals, do not have, and this was discussed before, a linear dose-response curve. So determining risk from a compound without a threshold, where you don't know the dose response at the low levels, requires a fairly high level of extrapolation, and there is going to be a larger uncertainty, and that is one reason for the uncertainty factors.

Chairman

394.   Thank you. Any additional questions from the Panel.

Ms Orozco

395.   I would please ask Mr. Guttenplan to repeat what he has just said, because I am trying to think through, and I am not sure that I did understand.

Dr. Guttenplan

396.   Well, let me see if I can recapitulate. Yes, the type of genotoxic agent that damages DNA and causes mutations, as opposed to the spindle-active compound that has a threshold, is not going to have a threshold. And then its risk is largely going to be determined by how effective it is as a genotoxicant and the exposure level. If you are not exposed, or the exposure is very low, then the risk may be insignificant. However – yes.

Ms Orozco

397.   Sorry to interrupt, but if I allow you to end, then I will ask you to start again. Exactly this is the point where I lost you. If the premise is that a genotoxic substance can create damage to DNA, why do you say that at low exposures that changes?

Dr. Guttenplan

398.   I didn't say it changes. I said that there may be no appreciable risk. We have naturally occurring substances within our bodies that cause DNA damage, they are always there. Oestrogens may be in that class of compounds. We live with this. You cannot do anything about that background. That small amount that comes from a genotoxic agent if the exposure is very low may be insignificant in comparison to the natural background.

Chairman

399.   Thank you. If there are no other additional follow-up ... Dr. Cogliano.

Dr. Cogliano

400.   Can I try the same thing with an example we had two years ago at IARC, with formaldehyde, and that's again another substance that is carcinogenic to humans. It is genotoxic and there was a lot of discussion about what is the shape of the dose-response curve as you get down to lower doses. And when you have no threshold basically it means your dose-response curve goes down in some shape, but it does not go hit the x axis and be flat. A threshold means your low dose is a flat 0, and then it goes up after some threshold dose. No threshold means that as soon as you leave zero you are going to have some risk. Now, so what Dr. Guttenplan said, at very low doses, you also have very low risk. Now the question is, we don't really know, there is uncertainty about the shape of the dose-response curve at the lowest doses, and this is what came out in the modelling that was discussed at the IARC meeting on formaldehyde. Possibly you could have a dose-response curve that goes linear all the way down to zero. Possibly you could have a dose-response curve that is very steep at high doses and then at low doses it still goes down in a straight line, or you could have something that is curved all the way down but it is still slightly above zero for any finite dose. The point is, we don't have studies that are powerful enough to tell us what is happening at the lowest of the low doses. So there is some uncertainty. But when you have no threshold, it means you are not looking for a dose where you are absolutely safe, what you are looking for is a dose where you have some low level of risk. And you do your best to try to describe that dose-response curve as low as you can, but at some point you still have uncertainty and you cannot with any degree of confidence say what is the shape in this very very low range. Does that help any?

Ms Orozco

401.   Up to your last sentence there I got it. You were saying – and thank you for the effort too, to explain this important element – if there is a threshold, it means that a dose that is lower than your threshold does not pose any apparent risk?

Dr. Cogliano

402.   That's right. The risk curve is flat up to a threshold dose, and then it begins to rise, so below that dose, yes, your risk is zero.

Ms Orozco

403.   So why is it important to know what happens below that dose?

Dr. Cogliano

404.   That's if you have a threshold, it's not important to know; but if you cannot establish a threshold, you may have some level of risk, and we were really talking about cases where we cannot establish a threshold and there is uncer-

tainty about whether the dose-response curve is going down with some undefined shape, and how low is that risk at the lowest of doses.

Ms Orozco

405.   And when is it that you cannot establish a threshold? Is it because of the mechanism?

Dr. Cogliano

406.   Yes, the mechanism gives us clues as to whether something has a threshold. I think it has been stated by a couple of people that a direct-acting mutagen is not likely to have a threshold.

Chairman

407.   I think my follow-up question is also related to the question which has been responded to just now. Would you clarify the difference between linear and non-linear situations, which are referred to by the parties? When would it not be feasible to set this threshold below which there is no appreciable risk?

Dr. Cogliano

408.   Linear simply means the dose-response curve goes down at low doses at a straight line. Its not a straight line all the way up to past 100 per cent risk, its going to level off. But at low doses, linear means the risk is proportional to dose, and at any level of dose higher than zero there will be a risk higher than zero. Non-linear means the curve has some other shape and that's what is really problematic, because at those low doses, we don't have enough animals or our epidemiological studies are not big enough to observe what happens at one picogram of exposure. With a typical animal study with 50 animals, the lowest you can observe is a 2 per cent risk. With an epidemiological study that's got 10,000 people, the lowest you can observe is the one in 10,000 risk, but you still don't know if there is some lower level of risk at lower exposure levels. So the problem is that when you have a non-linear dose-response curve, you really don't know the exact shape at low doses, and that's where we get into what Dr. Boobis had said; we take conservative assumptions and try to predict what is the worst it can be, because we really can't precisely specify what the risk is there, so we say, well, the highest it could be is this, and then a risk manager has to decide if that is an acceptable level of risk, given all of the other factors that a risk manager thinks about.

Chairman

409.   Even in the linear situation could there be a situation where the threshold cannot be established?

Dr. Cogliano

410.   In the linear situation we do not have a threshold. Threshold means it's flat at zero and then starts to go up, like a hockey stick perhaps, it's flat against the ice and then it goes up to the person's hand. Linear means it is just a straight line from the origin of the graph and there is a risk at the lowest of doses. Now that risk can be very very very small, and if exposure is very very very small the risk is very very very small, but the risk is not zero. I think that is the distinction between linear and a threshold kind of response.

Chairman

411.   It may be linear, but it never hits the bottom, zero. After all it has to be flat at some point.

Dr. Cogliano

412.   I don't think there is consensus that it has to be flat at some point. I think that is one of the scientific arguments a lot of risk assessors have, about whether everything has a threshold or not. I think there is a consensus that there can be low levels where risks are very very low, and some people will say the risks are zero.

Chairman

413.   Dr. Guttenplan?

Dr. Guttenplan

414.   Yes, the problem is in the second question. That question says: when would it not be feasible to set a threshold below which there is no appreciable risk? And that is the question; what do you consider appreciable? One in a million, one in a thousand?

Chairman

415.   Well, actually, that is the Panel's next question (laughter). Let us go directly on to that question: what is appreciable risk, no appreciable risk, no apparent risk, zero risk, no additive risks, no adverse effects – what are the differences between all these terms?

Dr. Guttenplan

416.   Lets see all the terms and then (laughing). As far as what is an appreciable risk, I think that is up to the risk management to decide, what they consider appreciable and acceptable. If there are many compounds with additive risk, and if you have several compounds, each has a risk, and each risk is independent, then they are additive.

Chairman

417.   But if the appreciable risk is a concept related to risk management rather than the risk assessment, then it could vary depending on the level of protection chosen by each country.

Dr. Guttenplan

418.   Exactly, yes.

Chairman

419.   Then there would be no objective criteria at all. It could vary from zero to ...

Dr. Guttenplan

420.   In performing a risk assessment you can come up with a number, but which number in terms of risk a country wants to use is up to their own individuals, is up to their own risk managers.

Chairman

421.   Dr. Boobis.

Dr. Boobis

422.   I think part of the confusion is the innate self-preservation of scientists who don't want to commit themselves to absolutes. Most of those terms there generally have similar meanings, no appreciable risk, no apparent risk, zero risk, no adverse effects, maybe not the one no additive risk, we can talk about that later. And I will just try to explain why it is we use this term quite frequently, no appreciable risk. First of all, it is true, the level of protection is set by the risk manager, in that by usage and by adoption there is an implicit if not explicit level of protection for a thresholded residue, and that is how we set the ADIs as has been explained, based on default assumptions on the safety factors that are in common use. This provides, de facto, a certain level of protection. That level of protection, to this date, has been accepted by the risk manager as being appropriate, because they accept the risk assessments, and the assumptions that are in those risk assessments are clearly laid out, if we are using a safety factor default of 100 in the absence of other information. We don't call it zero risk usually, we call it no appreciable risk, and I am talking here only about compounds which have a threshold. And the reason we call it no appreciable risk is because of the two extrapolation factors we talked about, one to extrapolate from experimental animals to humans, and one to allow for human variability.

423.   And we are really talking about two different thresholds. The first threshold is the threshold in a dose-response curve, and really we have been talking about that largely today, that is when we talk about thresholds, that somewhere on the dose-response curve we reach a low dose and there is no response below

that dose. But the second threshold is a population threshold, that within a population there is a variability in sensitivity, and that second threshold is the one that makes toxicologists and risk assessors reluctant to say zero risk, because we cannot say with absolute certainty, within a population of 6 billion human beings at the present, that there is not somebody somewhere under a given set of particular circumstances that might not be ultra-sensitive, so we hedge our bets if you like and say no appreciable risk. We are protecting a very very large percentile if not the entire population. I would stress, however, this does not mean to say we are not protecting certain sections of the population such as the young or the elderly, because they are definable groups and the risk assessment takes account, to the extent it can, of such subgroups within the population. We can discuss how we do that, I assume later today or tomorrow, but I am talking about a rare sensitive individual, not the population.

Chairman

424.   OK. We also have related questions on the terms such as additive risk, additional risk, aggregate risk and cumulative risk. So would you explain further the differences.

Dr. Boobis

425.   Additive risk. Could we maybe have those terms – OK. Aggregate risk and cumulative risk have come to mean something by definitions that were devised by the US. They defined what is meant by aggregate and cumulative risk, it is not an intuitive meaning, it is not a meaning that would automatically be understood from the words themselves, so I must stress that. So what we mean by aggregate risk is, simply by convention, a lot of people use the term in that way, the same for cumulative risk, so that is just to clarify that. Aggregate risk in the sense that it has been defined under the Food Quality Protection Act, where this came from, is the risk from all sources of exposure to the same substance. We were talking earlier about, if we think of just oestradiol, all the different possible sources of exposure to oestradiol; if we were doing an aggregate risk assessment, we would add up all those sources together. A cumulative risk is thinking about substances which might act on the same target, so, in the case of hormones, all possible oestrogenic substances acting on the oestrogen receptor, we would have to think about exposure to all of those compounds by all different routes, and find some way of combining them. You would not just add up the amounts, because a phyto-oestrogen is going to be a lot less potent than oestradiol; diethylstilbestrol is more potent than oestradiol, so you have to normalize them for potency, which is a technical issue in respect of conducting a cumulative risk assessment. Additive risk is additional risk or risks over and above the background level of risks that already exists.

Chairman

426.   So all these terms are not necessarily limited to the problems arising from the long latency period.

Dr. Boobis

427.   No, they don't relate to it at all.

Chairman

428.   OK, thank you.

Ms Orozco

429.   Just one question. Aggregate risks – that was for Dr. Boobis.

Chairman

430.   OK, we will continue to the next question and then come back to this question again. Our next question is: what are the components of a qualitative risk assessment compared with a quantitative risk assessment? Could you please clarify whether in your view the four steps of risk assessment as defined by Codex and JECFA are not applicable for qualitative risk assessment? Maybe this question could be addressed particularly to Dr. Cogliano. The EC indicated that it has carried out a qualitative dose-response assessment. We would appreciate it if the experts could provide their views about this argument, and probably the EC may also want to respond to this particular part of the question.

Dr. Cogliano

431.   I would say qualitative risk assessment could be described as what IARC does when we come up with a determination that an agent is carcinogenic to humans or probably not carcinogenic to humans. It's simply the statement that a hazard does exist, without trying to further characterize that hazard as to dose level or duration of exposure of susceptible populations. This qualitative risk assessment can be a more quantitative risk assessment that could include developing dose-response relationships, establishing levels where you don't see adverse health effects, measuring exposure and comparing the exposure to the dose-response curve. So I would say, any time you are starting to get into dose-response curves and into exposure levels, you are getting into the quantitative risk assessment; the qualitative risk assessment is just the establishment of whether a hazard exists, whether something causes cancer.

Chairman

432.   You have a question?

Mr. Ehlers

433.   Well actually, and I thank you for that answer, it goes on to the last part of our question. It would seem then that to say that a qualitative risk assessment, if it is qualitative, then a dose response is a contradiction, because a dose response requires quantitative, and that is why this part of the question was put in.

Can you carry out a qualitative dose-response assessment if the dose is quantitative by nature? That is what we are trying to get at.

Dr. Cogliano

434.   When IARC does its qualitative evaluations that end up in simply a statement that an agent is carcinogenic or possibly carcinogenic, or probably not carcinogenic, it does look at dose-response relationships because, for example in an epidemiological study or an animal study, if high levels of exposure give you higher levels of risk, that increases your confidence that you do have a carcinogen. If you had a dose-response curve that went up and down, you are not sure what you have. And so we do look at dose-response relationships. What distinguishes qualitative from quantitative risk assessment is how the conclusion is expressed. IARC expresses the conclusion by saying this agent is carcinogenic to humans or this agent is probably carcinogenic to humans, but we don't get into if it's a dose-response relationship that's linear, that there's a safe dose; that's part of the quantitative risk assessment later. So I think I would refine my first answer by saying that the difference between qualitative and quantitative is how you express your conclusions, and if your conclusions have any element of a safe dose, dose-response curve, susceptible populations, then I think you have gotten into a more quantitative assessment.

Chairman

435.   So the same requirements and steps and components should be applied to the qualitative risk assessment even though their conclusion may be made in the form of a qualitative decision rather than quantifying?

Dr. Cogliano

436.   I would express it this way. The qualitative risk assessment is the first of the four steps, it's the hazard identification phase. When IARC says this agent is carcinogenic to humans, we have identified a hazard. If IARC says this agent is probably not carcinogenic to humans, we have made a hazard statement that this agent probably is not a hazard, at least for cancer.

Chairman

437.   Do you mean that when it comes to a qualitative assessment, stopping at the first step of the four steps could satisfy the requirements of risk assessment? I will give the floor to Dr. Boobis and then ...

Dr. Cogliano

438.   I think there are cases where calling something a carcinogenic hazard has led an agency to make a decision just on the qualitative element alone. But I think many agencies still prefer to see a quantitative risk assessment that they will then carry out, based on the exposures in their country, to determine what to do. The reason IARC does the qualitative assessment only is that we really don't

have the resources or the expertise to identify all the types of exposures in every country, and there does seem to be a need for an authoritative statement about what is carcinogenic and what we don't feel right now is carcinogenic. But then the next step is for national agencies or local agencies to look at their local exposure situation and compare it with a dose-response relationship or safe dose and make a determination about whether some action should or should not be taken.

Chairman

439.   If we follow your views, then there would be no need to get into the exposure assessment by way of doing qualitative or quantitative dose-response assessment.

Dr. Cogliano

440.   In some cases no. I would say for example cigarette smoking; I am not aware of any dose-response assessment that says your risk per cigarette you smoke is X. I think the totality of the evidence about smoking, that it causes, I think, 16 different types of cancer in the most recent IARC monograph, and just the consistency of positive results everywhere, I think is enough to have caused action to be taken. But smoking obviously is a very extreme case about having a lot data and a case where qualitative assessment is in itself sufficient to take an action.

Chairman

441.   Thank you. Dr. Boobis and Dr. Tritscher.

Dr. Boobis

442.   Well, I think that it does depend upon why the risk assessment is being conducted and what the risk manager requested, and in the case of a veterinary drug residue, one is seeking to determine whether residues at the level that occur in the diet are considered to be without appreciable harm or risk. And if a mechanistic consideration led to the conclusion that the hazard was such that the dose response was going to be linear, there is no threshold as we discussed just before, then it might be that one would stop the risk assessment at that point. But that would be an unusual circumstance, and in most circumstances one would want to understand the relationship between the hazard and the level of exposure that was occurring. For that reason one would progress at least to a semi-quantitative evaluation of the exposure and risk, rather than just stopping at a simple identification of hazard.

Chairman

443.   Dr. Guttenplan.

Dr. Guttenplan

444.   Yes. The comment was made, if you have a dose-response curve for an animal, you have a quantitative dose, why isn't that a quantitative risk assessment. Usually when you are testing a carcinogen in animals, you will test in both sexes at several doses and often in several species, and you will get different dose responses in each one of those. So just having a number for a particular animal species is not enough to produce a quantitative risk assessment.

Chairman

445.   We have ten minutes before 6 o'clock so I think the Panel has – OK sure.

Ms Orozco

446.   Sorry, I go back to something that was being mentioned, the aggregate risk. If you talk about evaluating aggregate risk, what that does is to modify the scope of the risk assessment, if I understand you well?

Dr. Boobis

447.   It does indeed, because one of the big questions that has to be asked is how widely do you cast the net for all exposures? Do you include therapeutic application of the same drug used in deliberate administration to patients? Whose responsibility is it to take account of all the different sources of exposure? And these are very difficult questions, and on the international scene are particularly problematical because the totality of exposure will vary with the circumstances of the region, and that is one of the reasons that it has been very difficult up till now to conduct aggregate risk assessments globally. And I would add we are still struggling with this, we have not answered these questions yet, we have not reached solutions yet.

Chairman

448.   EC.

European Communities

449.   Gentlemen, I would not intervene, since you say the EC, that we have carried out a quantitative dose-response assessment. And I would request the scientists tonight that they have a look at our risk assessment and we can take up the subject tomorrow. We said we have carried out a dose response, in particular for the children, and I would request the scientists to have a look at our 1999 first risk assessment. We have done this for all the hormones, the six hormones. It is on page 36, 37 and 38 for oestradiol and there are corresponding pages for the other hormones, and then we can take up this issue tomorrow. I am not posing a question now, but I would request, because it is not true that we have carried out only a qualitative dose-response assessment. We explain we have examined the ADIs and the rest proposed by JECFA and those levels demanded by the US. We have tried to go through this dose-response quantitative assessment,

in particular for children. As far as the genotoxicity of these substances, it is true we have made a qualitative dose-response assessment. But it is not true we did not try to do a quantitative risk assessment, and I give these pages for oestradiol but there are comparable pages for each of these six hormones. They are in our 1999 first risk assessment. They are in the documentation of all the experts. So please have a look tonight to see. We did not stop at the hazard identification, that's not true.

Chairman

450.   Well, we are here not to make a decision, we are just getting advice from the scientific experts. I was expecting to see the representative of JECFA, Dr. Tritscher raised her flag on this question. We are wondering whether JECFA has done qualitative or quantitative assessments for these hormones at issue, and I am wondering whether JECFA agrees that the hazard identification alone equals a qualitative risk assessment.

Dr. Tritscher

451.   Thank you. I had actually taken down my flag because I thought that we had clarified or had moved on, but it really addresses the last point here on the slide and we may have contributed in our response a little bit to the confusion in this context. So it is in the context of dose-response assessments, and dose-response assessment is an integral part of each risk assessment. Now this can be done qualitatively or quantitatively, and I tried to explain what we mean with that. In a qualitative sense, a dose-response assessment is simply determination of a no effect level. One looks at all the measured effects, identifies the dose where one sees an adverse effect, goes one step lower, the next dose lower is the no effect level. The outcome is a number, in that sense it is quantitative, that may be the confusion, but it is not doing a complete quantitative mathematical dose-response analysis, taking all the points of the dose-response curves into account. This is what we meant with the quantitative dose-response assessment. But even a derivation of a no-effect level and derivation of an ADI considers dose-response assessment, but not in a mathematical quantitative modelling way. Sorry if that raised any confusion in that context. Regarding the six hormones, JECFA did identify the no-effect levels and derived an ADI, so in the terminology, the way I introduced it, which may be a little bit misleading, this would be a qualitative dose-response assessment.

Chairman

452.   Am I right to understand your comment as saying that even in the qualitative assessment you have gone through all these four steps of risk assessment?

Dr. Tritscher

453.   Yes; that is the short answer. Hazard identification is not a risk assessment, a risk assessment comprises the four steps, and one can simplify it, the hazard identification and hazard characterization steps are often done together,

or can be done together. This is the toxicological assessment, again, the left arm; the right arm is the exposure assessment. The integration of the outcome of these two assessments is the actual risk characterization step and yes, JECFA has done this.

Chairman

454.   Thank you. Dr. Boisseau.

Dr. Boisseau

455.   Please excuse me, Mr. Chairman, but I had raised my flag following the Panel's question on cumulative risk. In Dr. Boobis' example, the cumulative use of the same substance as an additive and as a veterinary drug theoretically poses a complex risk assessment problem. In practice, there may be no problem. I think we need to be fairly pragmatic, because whereas a growth promoter may be used repeatedly or even continuously, the same substance used for therapeutic purposes may only be used on a one-off basis. The evaluation of the safety of residues is something which, according to the ADI definition, is done on a long-term basis. In other words, supplementary ingestion of residues in connection with the one-off therapeutic administration of veterinary drugs is relatively less important in terms of exposing consumers to the residues of that substance. Furthermore, we must not forget that therapeutic application is not oblivious of public health. There is what is known as the waiting time. Consequently, the possible supplementary ingestion of a given substance administered therapeutically can often be considered negligible. Thank you.

Chairman

456.   Thank you. Dr. Miyagishima.

Dr. Miyagishima

457.   Thank you, Mr. Chairman. The Codex Commission as such does not conduct any risk assessment, but it has expressed its position on risk assessment, and this is found in the Codex Working Principles for Risk Analysis for Application in the Framework of Codex Alimentarius. Paragraph 20 of this document states that risk assessment should be based on all available scientific data. Risk assessment should use available quantitative information to the greatest extent possible. Risk assessment may also take into account qualitative information. Therefore I think that one could interpret this phrase as the desire of the Codex Commission that risk assessors use as much quantitative information as possible, whether it is in the framework of what can be seen as a qualitative risk assessment or quantitative risk assessment. Thank you.

Chairman

458.   May I give the floor to Dr. Guttenplan before I give the floor to EC.

Dr. Guttenplan

459.   The term cumulative risk assessment has come up, and one way that could be interpreted is the accrual of damage or mutations; if one is talking about a genotoxic substance over time. One can estimate, for instance, for certain number of years smoked you will increase your risk of lung cancer by a certain amount, or for a certain number of years of taking oestrogen replacement therapy you will increase the risk of breast cancer by a certain amount. So this is an example of a cumulative risk assessment. The longer you are exposed the greater your risk.

Chairman

460.   EC has the floor.

European Communities

461.   Chairman, just a quick clarification and a question to JECFA. When you identify a substance as being directly genotoxic, do you go on in your risk assessment or you stop at hazard identification? Thank you.

Chairman

462.   Dr. Tritscher.

Dr. Tritscher

463.   It depends, it is very difficult, again, to answer very generally on these questions, it depends very much on the mechanism, again, as was explained in detail further. With respect to oestradiol, since this was the example used in this context, and I have to correct a statement that was made earlier by the EC, JECFA stated in the report of the fifty-second meeting that the Committee, JECFA in that case, concluded that oestradiol has genotoxic potential – it is worded that way on purpose, because of the scientific uncertainty that was alluded to earlier by the experts, and I am not in a position to comment on the content there. And in that case, the risk assessment was taken further in the sense that all other information is being looked at, in particular with compounds that have a genotoxic potential. One has to, of course, as a next step look if there are cancer bioassays, does the chemical cause cancer in animal studies, in the long-term studies or not. So it is the totality of the information that has to be taken into consideration before drawing any final conclusions.

Chairman

464.   EC.

European Communities

465.   Sorry, I did it on purpose not to ask specifically about oestradiol, because the views of JECFA are known as genotoxic potential on this one. If you without uncertainty identify a substance as being directly genotoxic, do you then go on?

Dr. Tritscher

466.   Yes, again, the answer is exactly the same. One has to take the totality of the information into account.

European Communities

467.   Gentlemen, the question is if you follow the four steps if the substance – we are not talking now for this question for oestradiol – in general, if you come to the conclusion, and we are not talking about uncertainty, if you come to the definite conclusion that a substance is genotoxic, would you still go on doing the four steps?

Dr. Tritscher

468.   I would say yes. It depends on what level of detail you go into. But now I have to, apologies for the time, but I have to explain a little bit longer, because its very different if we are talking about compounds that are added to foods for a specific purpose, or if we talk about unintentional and potentially unavoidable contaminants, that is a very different story. But traditionally in the food safety assessment area for compounds that have been added intentionally to food, veterinary drug residues, pesticides, what have you, if there is in *in vitro, in vivo* studies a clear-cut conclusion that the compounds are genotoxic, and traditionally no formal risk assessment was performed in a sense, not quantitating it and so forth, but the recommendation, and I guess that is what you want to hear now, that's what you are alluding to, is invoking the so-called ALARA principle, meaning that exposure to compounds that are unwanted in food should be reduced to as low as reasonably achievable. Again, one has to differentiate between unintentional compounds and intentional compounds, to say very briefly, and it is up to the risk management to make decisions on the regulatory level what to do to reduce exposure. For example, with compounds that are added, like veterinary drugs, one can make different legislative ruling than for example for contaminants.

469.   Now going back to the contaminants, JECFA as well as EFSA, the European Food Safety Authority, and then together in a joint EFSA/WHO effort, is trying to go a step further to get away from this ALARA principle, to give more advice to the risk managers for contaminants in food that have genotoxic and carcinogenic properties, which includes compounds where you cannot necessarily make the link; there are genotoxic properties, carcinogenic properties, not necessarily linking that the carcinogenic mechanism, the carcinogenicity has to be provoked by genotoxic mechanisms. In order to give better directions to the risk managers as to which compounds are really of public health concern – so

where to put your efforts, for management measures, for public health protection, the concept of the margin of exposure has been now formalized. I want to say it is not a new concept, but formalizing it, which compares certain effect levels for model studies with the estimated human exposure, and the larger the difference between those two, the lower the public health concern. By formalizing this approach, this allows comparison between different compounds, and gives some indication which are of more concern to health than other compounds. But having said this, I have to emphasize again this is a concept that JECFA applied or developed a formalized approach now, and it is applied only to contaminants. Thank you.

Chairman

470.   Even if in seven minutes it's already 6 o'clock, I think this is a rather important issue, so I will continue until we complete discussion on this particular issue this evening. I am wondering whether interpreters are available until that time.

Interpreter

471.   Could you tell me how long you might expect to last, how much longer you would like us to be here? I will have to check. I think that is alright but I will check with my superior. Thank you.

Chairman

472.   May I request each one of the experts to be as brief as possible in his or her response to this question. Dr. Boobis.

Dr. Boobis

473.   Briefly, just from an independent scientific perspective, regardless of whether I participate in JECFA or not, if I was talking about a veterinary drug which was generating a residue and were evaluating that compound and it was shown to be a DNA reactive mutagen which was expressed *in vivo*, I would consider it unnecessary to proceed with the risk assessment, with a proviso that for any reason the risk manager did not ask for some scenario evaluation. For example, it might be that there was a particular essentiality for that compound and the risk manager might say well, what is the margin of safety, along the lines Dr. Tritscher has just outlined, it would be possible to conduct a risk assessment on that basis.

Chairman

474.   Thank you. I saw many flags raised a few minutes ago. EC.

European Communities

475.   Gentlemen, we are grateful for the intervention of Dr. Boobis, because on the basis of what we have been hearing from the representative of JECFA, then

an exposure assessment in that situation, that means where you had a genotoxic substance, defined and uncontested, you only need to count how many people will die definitely, and the question is why you are supposed to do it, because this is the question, why you are going to go along with the risk assessment if you know that the substance is genotoxic? And by the way, I would like to ask, how are you going to do it since you don't know if there is no threshold there? So I appreciate the intervention, because it clarified the situation.

Chairman

476.   Thank you. Dr. Boobis.

Dr. Boobis

477.   I regret that I have been misrepresented, Chairman. I have chosen my words with extreme care – I would like to repeat, I said a DNA reactive mutagen. I would also like to point out, although we have not got into this yet, when JECFA evaluated the specific compound in question – and what my answer was was a general answer – the specifics are that they did not conclude that that compound was a DNA reactive mutagen, which is the reason why JECFA was able to proceed with this risk assessment, it felt it was appropriate to do so. These are different scenarios. As I stressed before, and I do again, it depends entirely upon the conclusions that an evaluation of the data lead to as to how you proceed.

Chairman

478.   Thank you. Dr. Boisseau, and I will conclude

Dr. Boisseau

479.   Yes, thank you Mr. Chairman. I simply want to mention, since we are speaking of general principles, that it is obvious that if a product has been shown to be mutagenic following a series of tests, it will be mutagenic for the target animal. But we are not talking about a target animal, we are talking about the consumer, so that the risk remains for the consumer to the extent that the mutagenic product is present as a residue. Imagine a parent substance that is definitively mutagenic but that is completely metabolized: I have in mind carbodox, for example. The substance, which is toxic as such, may not ultimately generate toxic residues in the foodstuff. So the evaluation must always be comprehensive, and indeed, stopping an evaluation as soon as a hazard has been detected, without trying to evaluate the possible risk for public health, is a procedural shortcut that could lead to an erroneous assessment of the risks without necessarily providing a comprehensive and reasoned view of the case as a whole.

Chairman

480.   Thank you. We do have some more questions that, I am sure, will be asked by the parties, because some them have already made comments in relation to conflicting evidence on the table and so on. So I would rather stop our discussions this afternoon here and see you tomorrow morning at 10 o'clock in this room. But before I adjourn the meeting – excuse me, there was a request from my colleague in the Panel to go on. Instead of getting into the question and answer session again, on the remaining questions, I just want to put the questions verbally so that you can consider these questions for the discussion tomorrow morning in responding to the questions posed by the parties.

481.   Our question was on the weight of evidence approach, which was, to my knowledge, used by Dr. Boobis, and the remaining two questions are: please comment on the EC statement in its comments on question 19, where it states that it has a standing request to review the hormones at issue. The last question is about Codex and JECFA. In response to question 3, Codex makes reference to ongoing work regarding risk analysis principles applied by the Codex Committee on Residues of Veterinary Drugs in Food and risk-assessment policy for the setting of MRLs in food. Do you expect major changes to Codex/JECFA work in this area once these documents are adopted? These are the remaining questions for your consideration at tomorrow morning's session.

482.   Thank you for your cooperation, and I particularly appreciate the patience and cooperation of the interpreters for staying with us until this time and I hope you will have a good evening and see you tomorrow morning at 10 o'clock sharp in this room.

28 September 2006, morning

Chairman

483.   Good morning. I hope you all had a good sleep last night and, for those who have travelled a long way from another continent, recovered from the jet-lag, I hope.

484.   This morning we are going to continue the remaining questions on area 2. As you may recall, before we adjourned the meeting yesterday afternoon, the Panel read out three questions, the question, Nos. 18 and 23 and 24, which you might have noticed on the screen, but we believe that 24 has already been answered by JECFA representative, so I hope we can start with the experts' replies to the Panel's questions 18 and 24.

485.   For your reference I will read out the questions once again: could you please explain what the weight of evidence approach is? And the other one is: please comment on the EC statement in its comments on question 19 where it states that it has a standing request to review the hormones at issue. These are two remaining questions of the Panel on which we expect the replies from the experts at the beginning of this morning's session. And then, as I mentioned in my opening statement yesterday morning, the Panel will invite parties to pose

their own questions to the experts on the area 2 items. And on area 3, the Panel has the intention to let the parties go first with their own questions and then the Panel will follow up the questions already posed by the parties. And I would like to remind the delegations that we have a time-limit to finish our business until the end of this session. And also I would like the delegations to know that one of the JECFA representatives, Dr. Tritscher, has a prior engagement this afternoon, so she has to leave after the lunch break. So we have to finish our discussions on the remaining questions under area 2 and, if possible, all the questions under area 3, that is scientific evidence, and there are many JECFA-related issues even under area 3. So I hope we can conclude our discussions on area 2 and area 3 this morning so that we can move into the remaining areas, that is EC's risk assessment and others. So, all in all, time is very constrained, so I hope the parties will be very strict in selecting the questions of their own, so that they can economize the time given during the remaining meeting today. Before Dr. Tritscher leaves this afternoon, parties are requested to pose questions on JECFA-related issues this morning, even if that falls into the category under area 3, that is scientific evidence. I am not sure whether I was quite clear to the delegations.

486.   OK, with that understanding may I ask the experts to respond to the Panel's questions on Nos. 18 and 23. Dr. Boobis.

Dr. Boobis

487.   Mr. Chairman, I would like to address the issue of weight of evidence. The weight of evidence is the evaluation of the available information about a particular toxicological endpoint, taking into account factors such as the adequacy and number of available studies and the consistency of results across studies. It is not an issue of seeking to weight one person's opinion against another. It is a specific situation where one is faced with a large body of information on a particular endpoint, and we can talk about, for example, genotoxicity. Where there are multiple tests of genotoxicity, and the results of those tests are not entirely consistent, a weight of evidence approach requires an examination of the quality of each study individually – because sometimes the studies will not all be done to the same standards – and the consistency across those studies, and then eventually an evaluation of what is the totality of the evidence telling us about that endpoint. Thank you.

Chairman

488.   Thank you. Any others – Dr. Boisseau.

Dr. Boisseau

489.   Thank you, Mr. Chairman. I would like to support what has just been said by Dr. Boobis concerning the genotoxicity and mutagenicity tests. In fact, these tests currently pose a double problem, I think. Over the past twenty years, the number of such tests has increased considerably, with the inevitable result that since we are using a greater number of tests to study a substance, the chances of

our ending up with a positive result obviously increase accordingly. The second problem is that these tests, which have flourished over the past few years, have not always been validated according to internationally accepted criteria – so that whereas fifteen years ago when a committee of experts considered the results of a series of what was usually four tests, two *in vitro* and two *in vivo*, where there were one or two positive tests it was not too difficult to declare the substance genotoxic or mutagenic, today we always have one or two positive tests and two or three dubious tests out of a total of fifteen; and when the tests used have not necessarily all been validated, it is easy to understand that the willingness of a committee of experts to declare the substance genotoxic or mutagenic is not very strong. Thank you Mr. Chairman.

Chairman

490.   If there are no other additional comments, then shall I move into the next – OK, then I will open the floor for EC.

European Communities

491.   Thank you. Without wishing to prolong the debate, I would like to ask the scientists which have responded and also the other scientists which have not taken the floor: the United States 2002 National Carcinogenesis Reports have classified oestrogen and oestradiol as capable of causing direct and indirect damage, cancer. This is part of the file we have submitted to the Panel and you must have it. Is it clear? The question then is: in your conception of the weight of the evidence approach, where would you place this United States National Carcinogenesis Report? Why is it not part of the weight of the evidence?

Chairman

492.   Dr. Boobis.

Dr. Boobis

493.   The report on carcinogenicity of the United States is the consequence and evaluation of the data, it is a conclusion. The weight of evidence approach requires a de novo evaluation of the data, so you don't use somebody else's conclusion in a weight of evidence approach. You may ask the question why does one reach a different conclusion, that is a perfectly justifiable question, but it is not appropriate to take other people's conclusions in a weight of evidence evaluation of the data.

Chairman

494.   US and then EC.

United States

495.   Thank you, Mr. Chairman. I would like to follow up on Dr. Boobis's comments and on the EC citation to the 2002 US report on carcinogens, and ac-

tually this is a question to Dr. Boobis with a short lead in. The EC has cited this report as evidence that steroidal oestrogens *per se* are known to be human carcinogens, and as you might be aware if you have looked at this report, the conclusions rely heavily on an evaluation conducted by IARC in 1999 entitled Post-Menopausal Oestrogen Therapy. Dr. Boobis, if you are familiar with the US report on carcinogens and these IARC monographs, can you comment on the relevance of these reports to the specific risk alleged by the EC, which is that posed by oestradiol 17 β residues in beef and beef products?

Chairman

496. Dr. Boobis.

Dr. Boobis

497. I am certainly familiar with the IARC evaluation and familiar to some extent with the RC. As I understand it, the conclusion was that oestradiol-17β was a likely human carcinogen; but neither of those reports, as I understand it, said that genotoxicity was the mode of action. And, based both on the evidence of other bodies and also on its own primary evaluation of the epidemiology – because at that meeting there were distinguished international epidemiologists present who did their own evaluation of the world's literature on the possibility of a risk of cancer from exposure of humans to oestradiol-17β – JECFA accepted at that time that was a risk. But, and it is a very big but, the conclusion was that this was not associated with genotoxicity. And critical to the JECFA evaluation was the relative level of exposure, and the conclusions of JECFA were based on an evaluation of the exposure that was likely to occur from the use of the hormones in beef-producing animals.

Chairman

498. Thank you. EC.

European Communities

499. Thank you, Chair. A simple question, going back to the weight of evidence and the explanation given by Professor Boobis. I would just like to know whether you mean to say that the weight of evidence approach involves interpretation of data of the kind you have explained in your reply to question 52. Thank you.

Chairman

500. Dr. Boobis. Is Dr. Boobis ready to respond?

Dr. Boobis

501. In fact, the IPCS report to which I refer did use a weight of evidence strategy. I was using weight of evidence in a narrower sense in my earlier response in that we were very much focussed – and this is common practice when

one is dealing with multiple studies on the same endpoints, or related endpoints, one has to have some process to determine what is the consensus picture of that data set. This is not a question of what people think and minority opinions, it is a question of looking at the data, and we had an expert genotoxicity person with us at that meeting to help us to evaluate the quality of the studies and the likelihood of outcome. Now when one looks at genotoxicity testing, some tests are more prone to artifactual results than others. So an Ames test, the bacterial test for mutagenicity, is generally a very reliable indicator of DNA damage, because there are few ways in which one can generate an artifact if the test is done to a reasonable standard. If one looks at some other tests, toxicity and other methods of interfering with a cell can influence the endpoint, so it is very important that one looks under the conditions of the protocol of the study as to the reliance that one is placing on the endpoint of that study. When one looks at 100 studies of genotoxicity, for most compounds one can find the odd positive, even for a genuinely negative substance. And so that is what I mean by the weight of evidence. If you have 99 negative studies all done well, one study done badly which gives a positive, what is the weight of evidence? The compound is negative. I am not arguing this is the case with oestradiol-17β, is was not quite as clear-cut, but using a weight of evidence approach, the committee was able to reach a conclusion as to what the genotoxicity was telling us, and that was the case for many other organizations that have looked at the body of evidence available for this compound's genotoxicity. There is an element of interpretation of the quality of the study, I accept, but that is why you have experts on the evaluation committee.

Chairman

502.   EC.

European Communities

503.   So Dr. Boobis and also the other scientists, do you accept that different groups of scientists can view the same set of data and reach different conclusions to that question?

Chairman

504.   Dr. Boobis.

Dr. Boobis

505.   The simple answer is yes, one can always get different interpretations with the same dataset, but some datasets are more likely to give a consistent answer than others for most people, if that makes sense. So the example I gave earlier of 99 good studies giving a negative, or let's put it the other way around, 99 good studies giving a positive and one bad study giving a negative, one would hope that the vast majority of people looking at that dataset would reach the same conclusion. It is just possible that somebody would say that the negative study is the one we should put the weight on.

Chairman

506.   Let me give the floor to Dr. Guttenplan and Dr. Boisseau first.

Dr. Guttenplan

507.   Yes, I guess I want to answer some of the questions. I think it is probably fair to say that most of the agencies that look at or have looked at these compounds or other compounds use a weight-of-evidence approach. I think that is true of the National Toxicology Program Report on Carcinogens, it is certainly true of the IARC monographs. It means that you get a lot of experts together and they look at the positive and the negative studies, they consider multiple interpretations, they try to weigh which studies should contribute most to the evaluation and come up with a reasonable judgement. Also, as Dr. Boobis said, it is possible for different groups of experts to come to different opinions. That is why we invite groups of experts, so that we are not too dependent on any one person's opinion. And in most cases when the IARC monographs programme looks at data, they do have a consensus, although there are cases where the dataset is sufficiently mixed that there is a close vote. So there are some cases where the overall signal about whether something is carcinogenic is an issue. I don't think that is the case with steroidal oestrogens, I think many bodies have said that steroidal oestrogens are carcinogenic. I think that the next level down of questions is: How is it carcinogenic? Is it carcinogenic through a hormonal mechanism, through a genotoxic mechanism, only one of them, possibly a mixture of both? And I think that there is some uncertainty and there is some difference of opinion among the experts. So in that case it is possible for different groups of people to reach different evaluations.

Chairman

508.   Thank you. Dr. Boisseau.

Dr. Boisseau

509.   Thank you, Mr. Chairman. I would go along with what was just said. The fact is that expert committees are currently issuing different opinions in the area of genotoxicity, perhaps because they are focusing more on the results. I am convinced that if we brought together competent and independent experts and if they began by objectively evaluating the validity of the methods, there would be far fewer problems with the results that those methods produce. I do not think that we place enough emphasis on the validity of the methods. Secondly, to favour consensus, it is important to know what these short-term mutagenicity or toxicity tests can produce and what they cannot produce in order to avoid erroneous interpretations depending on the results obtained. Clearly these techniques are used with large quantities of the substance that have nothing to do with residue content. This is particularly true of *in vitro* methods: they are conducted in conditions which do not reflect the fate of a substance in an organism, determined by pharmacokinetics and the metabolism – they are merely screening

tests, and nothing more. They cannot, under any circumstances, lead to a determination of dose effects, and at best, they can only provide information on the mechanisms of action. Thus, if the experts focus on the validity of the methods, on what these methods can produce and what they cannot produce, I am convinced that there would be much more consensus on the interpretation of the results of the methods. Thank you.

Chairman

510.   I have a procedural question. What if there are conflicting views, half and half, or almost half and half, among the experts participating in the JECFA Committee? What is the decision-making process in that case? Do they still make conclusions on the issues that do not provide any sufficient scientific evidence, or avoid making decisions and refer it to the next committee or to a later stage? Dr. Boobis.

Dr. Boobis

511.   First of all, Chairman, this is a hypothetical question, because it has not occurred. I want to make that clear. The JECFA Committee – at least as far back as 1997 – have been able to reach an agreed position on all the questions before them. In the event that there was a disagreement, there would be two possible options – one would be not to proceed further and seek further evidence, and the other would be, as has been indicated already by the secretariat, if the majority was of one view and a minority was of another view, to issue a so-called minority opinion or minority report as well, which reflects a contrary view on the interpretation of the data. As I said earlier, this has not happened, there was unanimity. Generally what happens is that there is a discussion, there may be varying interpretations of a dataset, the experts get together over the period of a meeting and explore the various possibilities, bringing new information, or new insights and reach a common position, and that has worked generally very successfully in the evaluation of the compounds over the last 10 years I have been involved in JECFA. Thank you.

Chairman

512.   Are all these decisions made by consensus, or sometimes by voting?

Dr. Boobis

513.   At JECFA the decisions have always been made by consensus, to my knowledge no vote has been necessary.

Chairman

514.   Dr. Tritscher.

Dr. Tritscher

515.   Thank you. I have to explain a little bit what I did not do in the beginning, what the role of JECFA is within the WHO Constitution. JECFA is an Expert Committee, and expert committees are the highest level scientific expert groups that exist within the WHO Constitution, and there are very strict rules for scientific groups. And as I said, an expert committee is the highest-level committee with very stringent rules with respect also to the selection of the experts and so forth. With regard to decision-making, it is the basic documents of the WHO which lay out the rules for expert committees, which are convened to develop a recommendation to the Director General for his or her decision. It is made very clear that scientific decisions are not subject to vote, that is very clear. And as Professor Boobis said, your question is indeed a hypothetical one because the whole purpose of an international expert committee is to reach a conclusion. If theoretically there would be a situation where you have a 50/50, 60/40 or very close decision, and then it is in the discretion of the Chairman on how to proceed. If it appears that no consensus opinion will be reached, then that subject would not be concluded on. If there is a minority, then there are also very clear rules, and there is the option that if it is not possible to reach consensus, a minority opinion can be expressed, and has to be expressed, if there is no consensus. And again, this minority opinion is published in the report, with the names of the experts having this minority opinion and a clear description of their rationale and their opinions. Thank you.

Chairman

516.   Dr. Wennberg.

Dr. Wennberg

517.   Thank you, Mr. Chairman. Yes, as I was explaining yesterday, the existence of scientific committees is also laid down in the basic text of the Food and Agricultural Organization of the United Nations, and as Dr. Tritscher explained, the same rules apply to the experts which participate in expert committees called by FAO to help the international scientific committees to elaborate on scientific issues. And may I also say that as far as the expertise is concerned, there is a transparent procedure in how these experts are called upon, are selected, are put on rosters which are agreed by the Director-General of FAO and by the member countries from where these experts are coming, and the experts have to sign a declaration of interests for every meeting in which they participate, and these declarations of interests are filed by the Organization. Thank you.

Chairman

518.   Thank you. EC.

European Communities

519.   Chairman, can I make a short statement instead of a question, or it is both. A clarification for Dr. Boobis. In the United States 2002 carcinogenesis report, is it not true that they examined and declared oestradiol as a direct and indirect genotoxic substance? They have also said, and I can read, veterinary use of oestradiol estrogens to promote growth and treat illness of animals can increase oestrogens in tissues of food-producing animals to above their normal levels. This is in the report. They didn't make just a general finding, they have linked it to the residues from meat of animals treated with hormones for growth promotion, it is written in the text. And later on we come to the more precise question of the growth response. Thank you.

Chairman

520.   US.

United States

521.   Thank you, Mr. Chairman. I think you know that the issue that the EC has raised is one that we can discuss on Monday of next week when we discuss these issues. But I would note that the statement made by the EC is nowhere linked, in that report, to the carcinogenic effect that the EC seems to be alluding to. So just as a point of clarification, and perhaps any of the experts who have read the report would like to speak to that issue.

Chairman

522.   OK. Question 23 regarding the EC statement that it has a standing request to review the hormones at issue has not been answered by the experts or the JECFA representatives. Dr. Miyagishima.

Dr. Miyagishima

523.   Thank you, Mr. Chairman. Yesterday I explained briefly how the Codex Committee on Residues of Veterinary Drugs in Foods operates, but please let me reiterate what I explained yesterday a little bit, and answer the question posed. CCRVDF uses the so-called priority list as a means of communication with JECFA. Prior to each meeting of CCRVDF, the Codex Secretariat circulates or distributes a circular letter to all Codex members and observers, and this circular letter invites any nominations of compounds for evaluation or re-evaluation. The comments or proposals received in reply to the circular letter are usually considered by an ad hoc working group that meets the day prior to the beginning of the CCRVDF session. The discussion and conclusions of the ad hoc working group are presented to the plenary session of CCRVDF where the final decision takes place as to what compounds should be included in the priority list and then communicated to JECFA.

524.   Now, with regard to the five substances for which the Codex established MRLs, that is, oestradiol-17β, progesterone, testosterone, trenbolone acetate and

zeranol, the only reference found in the reports of CCRVDF is the intervention made by the European Commission – which was an observer at that time, participating in CCRVDF – on behalf of the European Community, at the eleventh session in 1998. The European Community requested that the re-evaluation of these five substances that was being scheduled in 1999 be deferred to a later session of JECFA, in view of substantial studies that were being prepared by the European Union at that point of time. Since 1999, CCRVDF has met five times, as I explained, at the interval of approximately 18 months. In the reports of CCRVDF, there is no record of proposals, either from the European Community or from member States of the European Community, to include these five substances in the priority list for re-evaluation by JECFA. With regard to melengestrol acetate, it was included in the priority list for recalculation of MRLs and TMDI by the fifteenth session of CCRVDF that met in 2005. However, the request did not come from the European Community, but came from an industry observer present at the meeting. These are the records found in the reports of CCRVDF, and given the fact that Codex rules or internal procedures allow for any member to go on record for any decisions taken by CCRVDF contrary to its wish, it is unlikely, reading from the reports of CCRVDF, that a request was made from the European Community for re-evaluation or evaluation of these substances. Thank you.

Chairman

525. Thank you. Madam Orozco.

Ms Orozco

526. Thank you, Mr. Chairman. I have two follow-up questions, one to the EC, as to what they means by a standing request to review the hormones at issue, because that has been stated in some of your documents. I would like clarification as to what the actions are, or how this request has been submitted. And second, I have a follow-up question to the Codex representative as to what was the answer, and the reasons for the answer to that intervention by EC requesting postponement of the re-evaluation. Thank you.

European Communities

527. Mr. Chairman, I can be very brief on this. We have sent to the Panel Exhibit No. 63, where we have attached the exchange of letters we had with the JECFA and Codex secretariat. In the last letter, the reply of the joint secretariat, it is stated that we had been requesting JECFA to postpone the re-evaluation of 1999, which nobody has requested. It was coming from the secretariat themselves, which is a very rare procedure to apply. And we have requested them to postpone because the new data was coming. And they have replied to this letter that once the new data becomes available we will review them, and they conclude we will be happy to place again these substances on the agenda of a future meeting of JECFA. And the issue was left there. We never said after the re-evaluation don't do it, it was there on the table since we were communicating on

this question since 1999. It is true we didn't put it on a priority list subsequently, but the understanding was, at least this is how I understood it, that when the new data become available, they will review that. And the truth is, when they presented the 1999 evaluation to the Codex Committee, they said we did not ask you to re-evaluate, and they didn't consider that. So I think it would be reasonable, in the light of these letters which we have exchanged, and the promise that they will be happy to place again these substances on the agenda, they would have done it. That is all, it's no more than that. Thank you.

Chairman

528.   Thank you. Dr. Miyagishima.

Dr. Miyagishima

529.   Thank you, Mr. Chairman. Just to complement my previous intervention by saying that the latest session of CCRVDF actually met earlier this year, and there was a circular letter, Codex circular letter 2005/43, was circulated in September 2005 to invite nominations for compounds for evaluation, with a deadline of 28 February 2006. No replies were received from any member or observer. Thank you.

European Communities

530.   Excuse me. I have the question for Codex and for JECFA as to what was the answer to the intervention made by the EC observer referring to the deferral of the re-evaluation.

Dr. Miyagishima

531.   The request from the European Commission made at the eleventh session of CCRVDF was duly recorded in the report of that particular session and as such it was brought to the attention of the JECFA secretariat, and that was the action taken by the Codex side.

Chairman

532.   Thank you. Dr. Wennberg.

Dr. Wennberg

533.   Thank you, Mr. Chairman. The JECFA secretariat and the exchange of the letters that was talked about – the reason why JECFA put the substances on the agenda of JECFA was that there was new important epidemiological data that had become available since these substances had been evaluated in 1987. The JECFA secretariat may place any substance on the agenda for re-evaluation, even though no outside request has been received. It is not permissible that the JECFA secretariat should postpone a re-evaluation of a substance when new important information has come to the attention of the secretariat – let's make that clear. The second point I would like to make is that the procedure to put

substances on the agenda of JECFA, through the CCRVDF, is open to all members of Codex and even observers, as we have heard. So it's not because there is a letter responding to this request for postponing a re-evaluation that the secretariat would issue a call for data for re-evaluation of the substances when there is no explicit request from a member of Codex to do so. The procedures have been very well explained by Dr. Miyagishima and they are followed by everybody. The secretariat never received any information on the studies, the studies themselves, or the study report from the EC. Thank you.

Chairman

534. Thank you. Dr. Tritscher.

Dr. Tritscher

535. Just to add to what my colleague already said, it's really that there are three main routes or main ways for a compound to get on the agenda of JECFA; through the priorities working group in CCRVDF, but also requests from FAO and WHO member States can be brought forward directly to the JECFA secretariat with the request for evaluation or re-evaluation, with justification, data availability and this kind of information. And the third is that the JECFA secretariat can re-schedule the re-evaluation of a compound if they are made aware that there is significant new data available. What that requires usually is that these data are really made available, not just saying that there are new data, here it is, but there has to be a very clear list of what type of data, to allow, with the help of experts often, to judge if this is justified, if the data are significant enough to justify a re-evaluation. And it is not correct that this is an extremely rare procedure. Sorry, there is one other way for compounds to be nominated for evaluation; it is actually through specific FAO and WHO programmes themselves. It is commonly the case that, for example for the WHO drinking water guideline programmes, compounds are requested for evaluation through JECFA or through JMPR for pesticides. And although the main route for nomination of compounds for evaluation is through the Codex Committee, it is not correct to say on the other side that it is extremely rare; it really happens frequently. Thank you.

Chairman

536. We now invite the delegations to pose their questions. Starting with EC.

European Communities

537. Thank you, Chairman. So we move now to another area.

Chairman

538. Another area, you mean area 3, or are we still in the risk assessment techniques? Have you exhausted all your questions on item 2? Do the US and Canada have any questions on risk assessment techniques? Canada.

Canada

539.   Thank you, Mr. Chair. Our questions are just clarifications on some of the answers that have been provided. First for Dr. Cogliano. You said yesterday that IARC conducts qualitative risk assessments in that it stops after identifying a hazard. You also said that it's qualitative because of the way it expresses its conclusion as possibly carcinogenic or a known carcinogen. My question is, then, can you use the qualitative conclusions of a JECFA monograph to evaluate the potential for occurrence of the hazard that is identified for given exposure scenarios? Perhaps – you are going to answer that one first then.

Chairman

540.   Thank you. Dr. Cogliano.

Dr. Cogliano

541.   It is true, the IARC monographs do stop with a statement that something is carcinogenic or probably not carcinogenic to humans. That can be enough, depending on the structure in which you make a decision. The monographs on different forms of tobacco were enough for WHO to conduct its framework convention on tobacco control. It does not give you dose-response information about what is happening at lower doses; it will simply tell you what are the substances for which carcinogenicity should be considered, and then different decision-making authorities will have to decide whether that evidence is sufficient for them to make a decision, or whether they do need to conduct further analysis.

Chairman

542.   Thank you. Canada.

Canada

543.   On its own, then, the conclusion is not useful for evaluating occurrence in a specific exposure scenario though, is that what I understand? It might lead other authorities to determine in specific circumstances whether there is a risk that that particular hazard would occur.

Dr. Cogliano

544.   Yes. Other authorities would need to determine whether there is a risk. Now occurrence is a different matter. Occurrence simply means is there some exposure to the chemical through some particular pathway. The IARC monographs do attempt to identify the different types of exposures people encounter, whether it is occupational exposure, whether something is found in food, whether something is widespread in the environment; so the monographs identify occurrence, but not the specific levels of exposure in a particular population. There are a lot of terms, like occurrence, exposure, risk and I'm trying to be precise here.

Chairman

545. Thank you. Is that all Canada?

Canada

546. I have just two more questions. Dr. Boobis, you explained the difference between deterministic approaches and probabilistic approaches to risk assessments. I wonder if you could comment further on – I think in fact you did comment on – which approach is more often used, but if you could further comment on which is the more conservative of the approaches.

Chairman

547. Dr. Boobis.

Dr. Boobis

548. In terms of the toxicological side, the hazard side, of risk assessment, the probabilistic approach has only very rarely been used. We almost always use a deterministic approach. In terms of the exposure side, the majority of risk assessments have also used deterministic approaches, although increasingly people are using probabilistic approaches. Where data have been obtained, it is quite clear that almost always the deterministic approach is more conservative than the probabilistic approach, and sometimes by orders of magnitude.

Chairman

549. Thank you. Canada.

Canada

550. A final question then, Mr. Chairman, and this would go to the representatives of the JECFA secretariat, or I guess any other expert that is familiar with the operation. In light of the suggestion by the EC in its comments that JECFA takes for granted all the unpublished data from industry, I wonder if you could describe the steps that JECFA takes to verify the quality and sufficiency of the preparatory data it receives from industry. Thank you.

Dr. Tritscher

551. Thank you. I don't understand what is meant with taking for granted, maybe that has to be explained later if I am not addressing what is actually meant with that. When compounds are put on the agenda, the JECFA secretariat publishes a call for data on the internet that goes out publicly to everybody. With compounds that are commercially produced and sold, very often important toxicological information is proprietary information and is not publicly available. This information is submitted by the company to the JECFA secretariat, and JECFA requests the complete study reports, so not the summaries or the conclusions or what have you, but the complete detailed individual reports with all the

details, individual numbers, individual data, completely the whole set of information. And in addition, all the experts perform literature searches using standard techniques in order to, in addition to the non-publicly submitted information, to take into account everything that is publicly available in the public domain as relevant scientific information. The data that are submitted are scrutinized in detail by the JECFA experts, in particular with respect to quality of the study. There are criteria with respect to good laboratory practice that are very well defined. Modern newer studies have a statement to that effect, a legal statement, quality assurance statements, statements regarding good laboratory practice in their study reports. All those studies before these methods were implemented very often do not have such official quality-assurance statements and so forth. And then it is the responsibility of the experts to scrutinize in detail the study reports, if current good laboratory practice techniques have been followed. That means characterization of the test material, appropriate analytical methodology and any kind of really basic information that is available. If this is not available, if it is concluded that a study was not conducted according to what would be called good laboratory practice; it does not necessarily discredit the study as such. Sometimes these studies can still contain important information, in particular if you talk, as was explained earlier, in the context of the weight of evidence approach. Sometimes such studies still give important information, but one would not base an evaluation on such studies. It is in the overall context of evaluating the whole database. And again, all the data that are submitted are scrutinized in detail, checked for accuracy and then summarized and described in detail. I hope this addresses the question.

Chairman

552.   Canada.

Canada

553.   That concludes our questions on item 2. Thank you.

Chairman

554.   Thank you very much. May I now invite the EC to pose questions on item 3, scientific evidence. Please go ahead.

European Communities

555.   Thank you, Chairman. I would like to come back to the issue of the most sensitive segment of the population, in particular prepubertal children, and I would like to ask Dr. Sippell, for example, whether the values which we have seen yesterday on the screen from JECFA are the values for prepubertal girls and boys which are their actual production rate, daily production rate, or whether they are based on the detection limits of the assays used for the calculation.

Chairman

556.   Dr. Sippell.

Dr. Sippell

557.   As far as I could see the official production rates, and it is difficult to calculate exact production rates in prepubertal children because first you have to have a true level of endogenous production, blood levels, so that you can calculate the production rate. They have been based on the, so to speak, traditional levels measured by radio immuno assays, and usually by radio immuno assays without prior extraction. We all know that the sensitivity of such procedures is not enough compared with more modern techniques, so to speak, the extractive procedures involving radio immuno assays, but even more modern molecular base techniques like recombinant cell bioassays, of oestrogen, oestradiol or oestrogen activity. And these, as I have pointed out in my answers to the Panel, are significantly below the levels previously thought, and by that the production rate now is significant lower. And this of course implies that any risk from exogenous sources, for example beef treated with hormones, treated with oestradiol-17β, is much higher.

Chairman

558.   Thank you. EC.

European Communities

559.   You have also made reference yesterday to the latest method in the USA to calculate the daily production rates, and you made a reference to the assay of the group of Klein which became relevant after the evaluation made by JECFA, so does this in your view put in doubt the validity of the values given in JECFA, and I am precise as to the potential risk for prepubertal children from eating meat treated with hormones for growth promotion. It's an important point to clarify in my view. Thank you.

Chairman

560.   Dr. Sippell.

Dr. Sippell

561.   Yes, that's indeed the case. This ultra-sensitive assay has been recently confirmed, its validity has been confirmed by another lab, you know the Klein methodology. The main author is George Chrousos, by the way, who was for many many years director of the children's section at the National Institutes of Health, and this new supersensitive assay has been confirmed by another laboratory which also is very well-known and considered to be very thorough and applying good laboratory practices, of course; that is the lab of Professor Charles Sultan in Montpellier, and coming to quite similar levels and, as I said yesterday in my introduction, many basic biological features can only be explained by the

validity of these supersensitive oestradiol assays. There is no other explanation among scientists, among paediatric endocrinologists, than very very low levels, significantly higher levels of secretion in prepubertal girls, significantly higher than in prepubertal boys. Therefore there is no doubt, as I told yesterday already, there is no doubt among the scientists, also in the United States and Canada, that this is really the case, and this supersensitive assay is not being put into doubt really by the experts I have been speaking to. Therefore, there really is concern that the exogenous load from, for instance, oestradiol-17β, might be significant.

Chairman

562. I will give the floor to the US and then back to EC.

United States

563. Thank you, Mr. Chairman. Just as a point of clarification, to the best of our knowledge the Klein assay has not been used subsequent to its 1994 publication for regulatory purposes. But beside that point, I think there are two important questions here, one of which I would like to pose to the experts generally, which is: what does it mean when an assay is validated? And I think the follow-up to that is an appropriate question for Dr. Boobis, which is: given the considerable debate in these proceedings regarding blood levels of oestradiol in prepubertal children, and given the EC's heavy reliance on the Klein assay which purportedly shows lower circulating levels of oestrogen, I was wondering if in Dr. Boobis's opinion the Klein assay indeed establishes that circulating oestrogen levels in prepubertal children are lower than previous reported, and whether that assay has indeed been validated by the evidence that is on the record? So a two-part question, one to all the experts – what does it mean to validate an assay? and then secondly – has the Klein assay indeed been validated? – to Dr. Boobis.

Chairman

564. Is any expert prepared to answer the first part of the question? Dr. Guttenplan, please.

Dr. Guttenplan

565. If an assay has been confirmed independently in a number of laboratories, I would consider that validated.

Chairman

566. Dr. Boobis.

Dr. Boobis

567. I am not an expert on residues, and there are people here who can speak on this better than me, but as I understand it, in residue analysis the process required for assay validation to measure and analyse biological samples for regula-

tory purposes is fairly well defined and consists of a number of steps, such as ruggedness, precision, sensitivity, reproducibility, transferability, availability of standards, etc. etc. There is a procedure which the chemical societies have agreed internationally, that before an assay can be described as validated, as opposed to fit for purpose, these are different things, that for validation it has to undergo this procedure which has been recognized as a systematic analysis of the different performance characteristics of the assay.

Chairman

568.   Dr. De Brabander, please.

Dr. De Brabander

569.   Yes, I agree with what Dr. Boobis said, it completely described what validation is of a analytical method. Of course I don't have experiences with assays for very low amounts of oestrogen in blood, we don't work in blood, but it is completely described. The most essential thing is specificity – that you are really measuring what comes up, and in that respect yesterday we talked about qualitative and quantitative methods in risk assessment, we have the same nomenclature in analytical chemistry, qualitative and quantitative methods, and both are always mixed. Every quantification needs a qualification; you must be sure of what you are counting; the specificity of the method is extremely important. And also, if you have a qualitative method, you get always a signal and you get some kind of quantification, but it is only qualitative and again, you will have to fit the rules for quantification, a calibration curve etc. etc. I can put at your disposition a number of papers on validation, but I don't think we will start a discussion on validation as it is strictly described.

Chairman

570.   Thank you very much. Any other experts? US.

United States

571.   And then, just as a follow-up, if in Dr. Boobis's opinion the Klein assay has indeed been validated by any of the evidence that is on the record.

Dr. Boobis

572.   Not to my knowledge. I would just comment on my concerns about the Klein assay. There is a review published in the Journal of Paediatric Endocrinology and Metabolism in July of this year by the Klein laboratory, or with Klein as an author I should say, and it states in the review summary: prepubertal boys have oestradiol levels of 0.4 plus or minus 1.1 picograms per ml – which is somewhat higher than the level that was reported in the 1994 paper, which was 0.08 picograms per ml, that is significantly different. Now the Klein assay uses a recombinant assay in yeast with the human oestrogen receptor and therefore it is not specific to oestradiol-17β; if it is, there is something strange about the biol-

ogy, because one would not imagine that that receptor could discriminate between different oestrogens with absolute certainty, because otherwise the whole concept of oestrogenicity would not work. There are extraction procedures in the assay which might help select out certain compounds or others. Having looked at the characteristics of the assay, I find it extraordinarily difficult to understand why that assay would be so specific, or so sensitive, to oestradiol as opposed to other oestrogen agonists. There are other assays based on the recombinant oestrogen receptor; one of them utilizes a mammalian cell, not a yeast cell, and it is by Dr. Paris's laboratory. They have reported, using this assay, levels of oestradiol, of I think a couple of picograms per ml, yes, 1.44 picograms per ml. So we can see now that using these recombinant assays there is a variation from below 0.1 to 0.4, to 1.4, so that my view, having looked at these data is that, first of all, the recombinant assay has not yet been validated adequately, but secondly there is evidence, when one looks at these data, to suggest that the circulating levels of oestradiol in male children are lower than previously thought, I would accept that, but I would not think they are as low as in the original publication by Klein *et al,* because there have been numerous publications since then using a variety of assays which suggest that the levels are certainly higher than those very low levels first reported.

Chairman

573.   Can I give the EC and then Dr. ...

European Communities

574.   Gentlemen, I think we have a different interpretation of the data, and we will review references made by Dr. Boobis and will reply to that on Monday and Tuesday, but we understand that all the latest assays, and the one mentioned by Dr. Sippell later on, from the professors in Montpellier, they confirm that the level of oestrogen is much much lower, many more times lower than the ones reported in the JECFA report. There is no doubt, and even Dr. Boobis in his reply says in the first sentence of his replies that there is no doubt today that the levels are much lower. This minor difference to which he has made reference, they are not statistically different important differences, they are minor differences which sometimes you observe in the assays, and if you normalize the assays, you will see the values you expressed in the different assays, you will see there is no doubt about it, that it is significantly lower. But I have to move on from that debate and come back again to Dr. Sippell, and other scientists may come in, for example. In the risk assessments which the European Communities has performed and which you have in your files – and I refer to our 1999 and again to 2002 assessments – do you think that the European Communities has attempted to evaluate the risk for the prepubertal children from exposure to these hormones, taking into account these latest values which have been measured by the most sensitive assays?

Chairman

575.   Dr. Sippell.

Dr. Sippell

576.   I think that the risk is, and I have read several papers on that and also from my clinical experience, that as I pointed out yesterday, the levels probably are still lower than what has been measured by a radio immuno assay, and that the recombinant assays, they might differ, but they are with a lot of indirect evidence much closer to the truth than the traditional assays that we are all using nowadays in a routine lab. And if you calculate, then the exposure certainly is much higher if you have the low levels with the recombinant assays as a basis, and therefore I think some people have calculated that as little as 10 grams of meat ingested per day for a prepubertal boy might be or will be above his own production rate, and this is something one should consider.

Chairman

577.   Excuse me, I don't think the US questions have been fully answered, so may I invite experts other than Dr. Boobis to add their comments on the first part of the US question and then move into the second part of the question. Is there any expert who is willing to add comments on the first part, on validated or not.

Dr. De Brabander

578.   Well, as I said, there are rules for validation and normally if a lab performs well it is controlled by some organization. I don't know, I tell just for Belgium, you have the Belgian accreditation system, and labs who work in accreditation regularly have inspection from auditors. I have experience with that because I am an auditor myself, trained as an auditor, and when I go to a lab and they have qualitative methods (of course you don't test every method every time) I ask samples to be analysed. For example if it is urine and they have a method for testing urine, I ask them to prepare some samples of urine and I ask the components and then I take out amounts of the components and put them into the urine and then say do the test and show me the results. And then you can say that your method is validated. Of course, there are rules on paper – but in practice you can see if it works. And if it does not work, you can get the feedback to the lab – that's not in order, you should do that; that being the validation. It is not that you just have paperwork, there is control, and if you have a lab that works on GLP or accreditation, you have laboratory control on the results. In addition, maybe what was said, that a method is good when it is done in two labs, we use that also, performing analysis in two labs, and you see that for us chemists is it normal that if you get, for example, one ppb in one lab and two ppb in another lab, that's nearly the same. They are using slightly different procedures and it is

within the variation of the method. And there is also evidence for that; there is a curve published by Horwitz, from the United States, who says that the uncertainty goes up when the concentration goes down.[3] The lower the concentration, the more difficult. Of course, you can understand that it is really impossible to have exactly the same figure. So the figure may vary a little bit within ranges, giving the same results.

Chairman

579.   One follow-up question. In order for this scientific data by one laboratory to be validated, do we need a kind of endorsement by another laboratory or a number of laboratories on the same data?

Dr. De Brabander

580.   No, it is not necessary, you have different systems, like I said, you have an accreditation organism who control that your lab is accredited. Within the accreditation you are also obliged to do ring tests. There are organisms who will prepare samples with certain amounts of components, the laboratories that are accredited need to analyse those samples and produce results. If your results are outside of a certain z-score[4], as they call it, outside the normal range, you are alerted, and if you come, during an accreditation audit, you can ask: can you give me the results of your ring test, how have you done for that component, how have you performed for that component, you can control that. And that's not another laboratory, that's an organization who controls it. I hope that answers your question.

Chairman

581.   Dr. Boisseau.

Dr. Boisseau

582.   Thank you, Mr. Chairman. Yes, I would like to confirm what Dr. De Brabander just said. However, we are talking about two different things here. We need to draw a proper distinction between the accreditation of a laboratory and the validation of a method. Dr. De Brabander has just spoken of an accreditation, and I have nothing to add to what he said. But, the question that was asked concerned the validation of a method. Dr. Boobis had reminded us of all the internationally recognized criteria for validating a method, and as Dr. De Brabander said, it is well known that the lower the target in terms of concentration, the greater the uncertainty and the lower the reproducibility and the reliabil-

---

[3]   W. Horwitz, L.R. Kamps, K.W. Boyer, J.A.O.A.C. *63* (1980) 1344-1354. (Reference provided subsequently).

[4]   In statistics, a standard score (also called *z*-score or normal score) is a dimensionless quantity derived by subtracting the population mean from an individual (raw) score and then dividing the difference by the population standard deviation. (Explanation provided subsequently).

ity of the method – this is well known. There are two ways of validating a method: there is intra-laboratory validation, which takes place within one and the same laboratory, i.e. it is the same laboratory that repeats a certain number of dosages at different periods with different technicians, and if the results fall within an accepted range, the validation takes place within the laboratory. But more importantly, there is inter-laboratory validation, in which a certain number of laboratories are selected within the framework of what is known as a circular test, and the method is tested for precision, reproducibility, reliability, and what is also known as strength to see if it is exportable from one laboratory to another. Thank you Mr. Chairman.

Chairman

583.   Thank you. Ambassador Ehlers has a follow-up question.

Mr. Ehlers

584.   Thank you very much. The question has basically three elements. The first one is: do these hormones accumulate in the body or does the body eliminate them in total or in part? If so, do the adverse effects depend on this accumulation or not? And thirdly, if they do, then if you start with a lower endogenous level, would you not say that the risk also diminishes? Thank you.

Chairman

585.   Dr. Boobis.

Dr. Boobis

586.   The hormones don't accumulate to any appreciable extent in the body because of the natural production of similar or the same hormones, and these hormones would not be able to function if they accumulated in the body. So we have evolved mechanisms to allow the turnover of the hormones. All hormones have to have a turnover so that we can switch on and switch off the signalling pathway as necessary to off-regulate or down-regulate the target receptor system, and that would be true of the xenobiotic exposure to the hormones as well, because once they are in the body, the natural hormones are indistinguishable from the native hormones and would be eliminated by the same processes.

Chairman

587.   Dr. Sippell.

Dr. Sippell

588.   Again, the special situation in children before puberty – there is evidence that for instance secretion of sex steroids is pulsatile on a very very low level and that the sensitivity of the organism is such that these extremely low levels are being picked up and being recorded in the centres, in the hypothalamus, so in the brain, and also in the pituitary for regulation, also for imprinting. And we

know that prepubertal boys or prepubertal girls, in case of oestradiol, are particularly sensitive to very very low exogenous levels of oestrogens. We have, for instance, the natural example of Turner syndrome girls who lack ovaries and thereby ovarian function and thereby have no endogenous oestrogens. And we know that with as little as 25 nanograms per kilogram body weight per day we can promote growth in these poorly-growing girls. So I think if you make the point that levels are very low, then at the same time sensitivity is of course adjusted to these low levels, which has to be taken into account also for exogenous exposure.

Chairman

589. Yes please …

Mr. Ehlers

590. Yes, thank you, I followed that explanation and there is part of my question that has not been answered yet, maybe somebody can do it. That is – since the body eliminates, then there is no accumulation, or if it is only temporary until the body has done its work, the adverse effects then do not depend on that. But you were trying to say that the fact of starting at a lower level does not diminish the risk but it keeps it at the same rate.

Chairman

591. May I give the floor to Madam Orozco to follow-up on the question.

Ms Orozco

592. Would there be any comments to the follow-up question of my colleague before I change the subject? Because I would ...

Chairman

593. I will give the floor to the US first and then the EC. EC.

European Communities

594. When we started the meeting, if we think of a fair distribution of time, I think they have been asking quite a lot of questions and we don't have the time to ask our questions.

United States

595. I think this is a very quick question if the Panel will indulge. Yes, it is related to Dr. Sippell's response. Very quickly for the members of the expert panel who have had experience in JECFA, that is Dr. Boobis, Dr. Tritscher, Dr. Boisseau, Dr. Wennberg, I am wondering, does JECFA in its evaluations take into account populations such as prepubertal children or sensitive populations, and how do they do that?

Dr. Tritscher

596. It's a basic principle of every risk assessment to take – it's a general re-mark – to take into account sensitive subpopulations, it's a basic principle. Be-cause that is the part of the population that you want to protect with what you are doing, and this is based on the availability of data, what is taken into account. But it is definitely it's the goal of the risk assessment to identify who would be the most susceptible, the most sensitive part of the population, and that is the part of the population that the risk assessment is targeted to.

Ms Orozco

597. Just a quick follow-up question: how was it done in the 1990 evaluation?

Dr. Tritscher

598. I cannot respond to that question. I am not entitled to respond to that, sorry.

Chairman

599. Dr. Boobis.

Dr. Boobis

600. The Committee had available to it studies conducted in developing ani-mals, where one of the assumptions is, based on research and scientific informa-tion, that the basic physiology of the test species that were used has a similarity to that in humans, and based on an evaluation of effects in those sensitive life stages, together with the other available information, the Committee concluded that it had been possible to evaluate the risks to all susceptible populations.

Ms Orozco

601. One more question, Dr. Boobis. How was the endpoint chosen in the 1990 evaluation?

Dr. Boobis

602. One of the hallmarks of a toxicological evaluation is that we don't focus on a specific endpoint because of the concern that we would miss something. So we use, as much as possible, to start with a so-called holistic approach, so we look at the totality of effects, evaluating multiple endpoints for the possibility of a compound-related effect. So in this case we looked at reproductive outcomes, we looked at the developmental effects and we looked at a range of other effects that were the normal hallmarks of reproduction and development in an animal.

Ms Orozco

603.   Just one more question. The ADI that has been established – is that protection enough if you would take into account the new data about sensitivity of prepubertal children?

Dr. Boobis

604.   I have done a calculation, which was in my responses to the questions, based on what I consider a consensus concentration that was somewhat higher than the lowest concentration, but was still significantly lower than that originally reported, and I calculated that the ADI would still be protective. I should add that what has not been mentioned so far is that we should not just take the external exposure and assume this translates into an internal dose or concentration. There are two factors which go against this. One is the pre-systemic metabolism we mentioned earlier – I think it was assumed this was 100 per cent in the EC evaluation, sorry, zero per cent, it was all absorbed. Whilst I accept that it is likely lower than in an adult, it will be very unlikely to reach zero per cent, particularly after the first week of life, and there will not be exposure to the hormones in meat in the first week of life as I understand it. And the second is that the hormone is not circulating completely free, a very appreciable amount is bound to sex hormone binding globulin and other proteins and there is good evidence that only the non-bound form is able to cross cell membranes and interact with the oestrogen receptor, and so that will reduce the circulating concentration as well. So that one has to consider those aspects in the evaluation.

Chairman

605.   OK. Canada wanted to ask a related question quickly and then we move back to EC.

Canada

606.   Yesterday there was some discussion about the extent to which the human population is exposed to exogenous sources of hormones in their diet, and Dr. Boobis yesterday indicated that there was a significant amount of exposure to oestrogens or to phyto-oestrogens or oestrogens in plant material, and my question then to the experts is: in establishing the ADI, is the extent of exposure to exogenous hormones taken into consideration, particularly in the diet of a prepubertal person, and is there any evidence that in the normal food, a diet with a normal food consumption, that prepubertal boys are at risk from exposure to exogenous hormones?

Chairman

607.   Thank you. Dr. Sippell.

Dr. Sippell

608. I can be very brief. I believe that nobody has ever investigated this probably, also due to the fact that this is extremely difficult, also ethically, as I pointed out yesterday.

Chairman

609. OK. One more.

Canada

610. Dr. Sippell, in 2001, I believe, you co-authored an article that was looking into precocious puberty and you indicated, I believe, in your conclusion that there was no evidence in the literature that exogenous exposure to oestrogens led to pseudo puberty, which is to be distinguished from central puberty. But I wonder if you could elaborate on that conclusion that there was no evidence in the literature to suggest that exogenous exposure to oestrogens cause precocious puberty?

Dr. Sippell

611. Yes. This was, as you just said, more than six years back – I think that meeting was in 1999 –and this was a review article, so we combined a little bit of our own research with the opinions published in the periodic review literature. And at that time we came to that conclusion. Since then the acceptance of the significance of the supersensitive oestradiol assays within paediatric endocrinology increased tremendously because, as I said before, it for the first time gave an explanation for basic physiological peculiarities which we did not understand before, and therefore there has been really a change of our understanding since then, and therefore my opinion now is quite different from that opinion in the one review article you cited.

Chairman

612. I will give the floor to the EC.

European Communities

613. Chairman, I said that I had two related questions to ask. First, it is not disputed that oestradiol produces a number of metabolized and other substances when administered to animals, and quite a substantial part of this is in the form of this so-called fatty esters, or lipoidal esters, which are thought to be eight times more potent than oestrogen itself, and we know that from the review of JECFA papers that the potential risk from these esters have not been taken into account in order to measure the effects on the humans when they are administered This goes back to Dr. Boobis, to what he said. He explained how they have taken into account the prepubertal children. Here we are not talking about developing animals, that's not the point, the point here we are talking about is developing human beings, boys and girls, and we cannot extrapolate from developing

animals, which we know nothing about their organism, and draw a conclusion about human beings which nowadays it is internationally agreed, and Dr. Boobis has also said, that is at a much lower level of production. By the way, we have gone through the JECFA report and we didn't see any reference to developing animals. They have done the classical type of tests which are on animals, as they do it, and so all this is really questionable, and if there is any different view, then all the scientists can take the floor. The most important metabolite, which accumulates in the fat of meat, the fatty esters, which are more important, they are not taken into account. You cannot extrapolate for young animals, here we are talking about human beings, and this has not been done. And Dr. Sippell has confirmed, and if you would like to intervene, if you wish to explain why this is significant, and I posed the question in the beginning, we have provided the evidence, it is our 1999 and 2000 risk assessments. We have tried to estimate what would be the effects on prepubertal boys and girls, taking into account these recent findings from the residues in meat treated with hormones, under normal exposure conditions. And here we are talking about normal exposure conditions, we are not talking about other kinds of exposure which make up from misuse and abuse, we will come back to that later on, that is not the question. Here we are talking about normal exposure conditions. Thank you.

Ms Orozco

614.   I would like to ask, because I think it is a very important issue that is being touched right now and it was asked before, and I would like to hear answers from as many experts as we have, as to whether the EC evaluated the risk to prepubertal children from the exposure of eating meat from treated animals. I think that is a very important question for the parties and for the Panel on which to hear views from the experts, please. And I am talking about the risk assessment, that is the three Opinions that have been submitted by the EC and the supporting studies, I think that is the limit of their assessment for the purposes of this exercise.

Chairman

615.   Dr. Boobis.

Dr. Boobis

616.   The EC estimated the possible exposure of prepubertal children to food-derived hormones making a number of assumptions which we could debate here; they were certainly conservative, let's put it that way. For example, that everything that they were exposed to would be absorbed into the circulation – that is a conservative assumption, you could not get more than that but you could certainly get less than that. But what was not done was to consider what would the actual risk be, this was an exposure evaluation, I could not find in the documentation what the adverse effect that they were comparing that exposure to would be. So certainly they have done an evaluation of potential exposure, with certain assumptions, but I could not see how that was a complete risk assessment in

those populations. Just to add, if they wish to refer to page 70 of technical document 43 of JECFA, you will find reference to the reproductive toxicity studies that were available for evaluation.

Chairman

617. Turning to the JECFA recommendations, how would you comment on Dr. Sippell's response indicating that scientific material referred to by the EC requires the revision of the Codex recommendation with respect to oestradiol. In the replies of Dr. Sippell to the Panel's question 42 there was a statement that scientific material referred to by the EC requires the revision of the Codex recommendations with respect to oestradiol. This a comment by Dr. Sippell. Are any other experts willing to add their own comments on this statement? If none, EC.

European Communities

618. Chairman, I think we can provisionally make a little connection to this issue by making reference to the dose response, which is also important to understand, because children indeed are a very sensitive segment of the population, this is not disputed, and it is not disputed that they have much more lower level of endogenous production. And it has been said yesterday, for example, that here we are not talking about zero risk because the risk is non-appreciable, but the concept non-appreciable does not mean zero risk. There is some risk and we have heard that it is not possible to calculate it exactly because the shape of the curve is not clearly defined, we don't know how it is defined. We have evidence and the scientists which are around me can take the floor if they wish to explain in more detail. The question is the following: we know and we have observed – the scientists and experts and the studies which we have submitted to the Panel and in our risk assessment – with the exposure already to the background levels, endogenously produced, we observe a biological action, several biological actions on the organism of young children. Some of them may lead even to cancer, this is not also disputed. So the question is: since we know this already and we have evidence, a few molecules, one or two or three, in the experiments already initiate the cells to grow and proliferate and divide, the question is how does this enter into the risk assessment of JECFA in this particular case of residues in meat from animals treated with hormones for growth promotion? This is a very specific question. Because we have tried to take this into account in our risk assessment and came to the conclusion which is now in our documentation. The point I make is I don't want to fudge the issue, this is taken into account on page 70. It is very precise, knowing that a very small, limited number of molecules, one or two, have a biological action on the organs of young boys and children. Why was this not taken into account when JECFA has evaluated these hormones? And is this an important element to take into account in the light of the new evidence which is now available, for example, by JECFA?

Chairman

619.   Dr. Boobis first and then US.

Dr. Boobis

620.   Chairman, I must seek clarification. I am not clear yet whether the question relates to the DNA reactivity of oestradiol or to the hormonal effects of oestradiol. So far, what Dr. Sippell was talking about, as I understand it, was the hormonal effects. The genotoxicity argument is an additional argument and I was not clear in my own mind as to what was being asked by the EC.

Chairman

621.   Would you like to clarify first?

European Communities

622.   Chairman, the debate about the genotoxicity data is separate indeed, in our statement, what we are discussing here is about the hormonal effects, the effects through the hormone receptors' mediation.

Chairman

623.   Thank you. Dr. Boisseau.

Dr. Boisseau

624.   Thank you, Mr. Chairman. When it comes to the hormonal effect on pre-pubertal children exposed to hormone residues, and I am speaking of natural hormones, I think we need to recall the context of these discussions and to separate oestradiol, for example, from a xenobiotic, because when we say that an adult or young person is exposed to residues, we need to know what residues we are talking about. Since there is an endogenous production in the animals consumed for which we need to make allowances, what we are talking about is the additional residues linked to the treatment. Even if there is no treatment, there is in any case a basic level of residues that are natural. So what I want to know is, in view of these well-known variations in residues that are naturally present in meat, what is the risk already identified in connection with these residues alone and what is the additional risk linked to the supplementary residues resulting from the treatment. Oestradiol must not be treated as a xenobiotic on an all or nothing basis. The problem of oestradiol is that whether or not there has been treatment, we are still exposed to residues, and we must not forgot those residues.

Chairman

625.   US.

Mr. Ehlers

626.   Thank you. That is similar to what I was going to ask, not only about beef but about other sources, eggs or vegetables or others that also have hormones that come into our – or to children's, for that matter – diet. Do we have to stop their consumption of all of those also? Because if the effect is very great by just a few molecules, then it is not only the beef that is treated with these hormones, but all other sources should also be stopped. Do we have to set an age limit for consumption of any beef, any eggs, any broccoli or whatever other source of these hormones exists in nature?

Chairman

627.   Any experts? Dr. Guttenplan, please.

Dr. Guttenplan

628.   Not a direct answer but a clarification. When the term "a few molecules" is used, that really is a simplification. It is not a few molecules, it's a small number of molecules per unit of whatever unit, usually its weight that you are talking about. So it isn't that if you have one or two molecules you are going to have a biological effect, it's basically a low concentration, I think this is what the EC is referring to, and not a few molecules.

Chairman

629.   But still the question remains to be answered. No expert? Dr. De Brabander please.

Dr. De Brabander

630.   I cannot comment on risk assessment because I am not a specialist in risk assessment, I would just comment on the broccoli Mr. Ehlers mentioned. You know that for young children all kinds of these things should not be given because they contain some natural thyreostats which are not good for young children – for thyroid function, yes. Some food should be forbidden for young children, including broccoli.

European Communities

631.   Chairman, here the point is that there is no valid reason to overburden the human body, in particular of young children, with other sources, exogenous sources of these substances if it is not necessary. Normally we do it with children when it is for medical treatment, when there is a necessity; here there is no necessity to do it. But I would like to ask Dr. Guttenplan, and his qualification was very useful, this small quantity of molecules that you said, would they be present taking into account the ADI which has been fixed and the MRLs, if that quantity has just been fixed by JECFA, would that be sufficient to agree that a small number of molecules can indeed initiate or promote cancer? Would that be sufficient in the small quantity which has been defined as an ADI or an MRL?

Dr. Guttenplan

632.   You are asking whether the ADI that is currently accepted is sufficient to protect against cancer. Is that the question?

European Communities

633.   Yes, we have turned the question another way. My question was: if we agree that a small number of molecules, not one, two or three as you said but nevertheless a small set of molecules, can indeed initiate biological action, cells brought into separation and division, would the quantity which is included in the ADI from the residues in meat treated with hormones, would that quantity of molecules that can come from the absorption of these residues be sufficient to give rise to this kind of biological action when eaten?

Dr. Guttenplan

634.   If you are talking about cancer, I don't believe there is a risk from consumption below the ADI for cancer. Those low levels might have a greater effect on developmental abnormalities in children though – I think Dr. Sippell has commented on that already.

European Communities

635.   So you would agree that there would be other developmental effects on children, but probably you don't know if that will be leading eventually to cancer?

Dr. Guttenplan

636.   I don't think that the levels that produce developmental effects in children, that might produce developmental effects in children, would be sufficient to induce cancer later in life.

Chairman

637.   Dr. Boisseau would like to add?

Dr. Boisseau

638.   Thank you, Mr. Chairman. Very quickly, the statement by the European Communities that there is no reason to overburden an intake of residues clearly has to do with risk management. Here, we are talking about risk assessment, and I think it is important to separate the two concepts. When we say that a few molecules could possibly generate tumours, excuse me for saying so, but we are talking of induced hormonal cancers. I think that there is currently a consensus that cancer associated with hormonal activity can give rise to a threshold, so we must stop speaking of a few molecules, since in the case at issue, we are not talking about induction, we are talking about genotoxicity, in other words promo-

tion. And I think that there is a consensus on the fact that there is a threshold effect: this has been confirmed in writing by many committees. Thank you.

Chairman

639.   The focus of our discussion at this point of time is scientific evidence in terms of risk assessment in general. Dr. Wennberg would like to ...

Dr. Wennberg

640.   Just to recapitulate what I was saying yesterday about the additional residues that could be calculated from the residue depletion studies, where there were animals which were treated and animals that were not treated, the concentrations of the three natural hormones were analysed – what the excess amount of hormone would be in the beef – and compared to the ADI. The figures which are in the JECFA report and also in our report to the Panel say that the total oestrogen highest excess would be in the range of less than 4 per cent of the ADI, so that is a very small amount of the ADI. For the progesterone, the additional residues from the treatment would be 0.003 per cent of the ADI for progesterone, and for testosterone it would represent around 0.2 per cent of the ADI for testosterone. So we are talking about, in these studies, where there were control animals and treated animals, where there was variability in the natural hormonal discharge from these animals, that it is quite a small amount which could be considered additive to the natural background levels.

Chairman

641.   Thank you. Yes.

European Communities

642.   I would like to ask the representative of JECFA, do you know the date of these studies? Since when do they date? Because we know that these data date from the 1970s and 1980s. Could you give us the date of the studies to which you refer? We have been asking for this data, to see them.

Dr. Wennberg

643.   These studies are available publicly reviewed by the committee with individual animals so you could have studied them all by yourself in FAO Food and Nutrition Paper 41/12. These are studies which were provided to the committee by the Food and Drug Administration of the United States and were the studies that were used for the authorizations for particular products containing these substances. If you consider that these studies were not sufficient for the authorization of these hormones in the United States, I think you should ask the questions to the United States. Thank you.

Ms Orozco

644.　Excuse me, I have a follow-up question, please. What is the date of the residues data JEFCA used in the re-evaluation report of 1999? Or maybe, because we don't need a list of all the information used, but maybe to cut short the question, did you have new residues data for the 1999 re-evaluation? Did you use any residues data that was not used before?

Dr. Wennberg

645.　Yes, as I was saying, for the 1999 evaluation the data that was reviewed, that was not reviewed before, was the complete set of residue depletion studies that were provided by the Food and Drug Administration of the United States. Now these had not been evaluated before by JECFA.

European Communities

646.　Chairman, on this point, because this is important. I refer, and it should be in the records of the Panel, to Canada's Exhibits 17, which is the residues analysis monograph prepared for the 1999 evaluation by JECFA. It is on the record. Canada's Exhibit 17 and I refer to pages 88 and 89, where the studies upon which the evaluation was based are cited. And I don't see any of these studies cited here that it is more recent than 1989, they all date to 1979, 1982, and quite a number of them are undated and unpublished, so presumably they date from the 1970s and 1980s. I don't see any studies of the date which the representative of JECFA and Codex cite now. It is on the record.

Mr. Ehlers

647.　Thank you very much. I would like to add another point to this. First of all, of course, what is at stake here is not the JECFA studies themselves but rather the EC risk assessment, that is what we have to study. But perhaps the question more likely should be whether since the 1999 study to now new information has come to light that would question, undermine or require that a re-evaluation be made now in the light of new information that has appeared since that re-evaluation of 1999. So this would be my question to everybody. Has new information come to light, new studies, that would indicate that the basis for the 1999 re-evaluation has changed so much that a new evaluation is needed now? Thank you.

Chairman

648.　Thank you. In addition to that I am posing this question to JECFA: whether or not the new data available in the 1999 assessment were publicly available since that time? In order to know what was the reason why the EC has not received all these data materials since that time.

Dr. Wennbe4rg

649.   Thank you, Mr. Chairman, but I think that we are in the wrong, reverse sort of situation here. It is not for JECFA to submit data to the EC, it's for the EC to submit data to JECFA if they want JECFA to evaluate anything. So the data which are the basis for these percentages that I was quoting before are available in the report of JECFA, so they are available to everybody and not only to JECFA. That is the point of JECFA, to publish the evaluations.

Chairman

650.   Does this include the new data that is not those produced in the 1960s and 1970s?

Dr. Wennberg

651.   Well, as I now look at the reference list, many of these studies are from the 1980s and some are from late 1970s, some are not dated, but it's not true to say that they are all from the 1960s and 1970s. But may I also say that even if they were older, if the methodology that was used, and if the methods had been validated properly, there is no reason to discredit any studies because they were done a long time ago.

Chairman

652.   But my question was that JECFA said that new data were also reviewed and that all those data were publicly made available. I am wondering whether those new data were also publicly made available. If that is the case, then there is no reason why the EC is continuing to claim that it has not received any new data other than that from the 1960s and 1970s.

Dr. Wennberg

653.   The data that was evaluated by JECFA in 1999 as concerned the residues part are the data which had not been previously evaluated by JECFA. JECFA does not produce studies themselves, JECFA receives data from various sources, as we have explained before, from companies, from governments, from other institutions perhaps, and so what JECFA received and evaluated in 1999 was the complete residue dossier for these particular products, which are mentioned by name here in the report, from the Food and Drug Administration in the United States to JECFA. That was new data. It does not mean that all this data was produced in 1999, it means that the data was made available to JECFA for this evaluation, and there are studies from 1986, I read here in the reference list, 1979, 1982, 1983, 1989 and so on and so forth. I don't think I have to go further on this issue.

Chairman

654.   Dr. Tritscher.

Dr. Tritscher

655.   I would like to add just some general comments. As we have explained in our response to question No. 13, I refer to page 12 in our response, all documents from JECFA are published and are publicly available in the public domain, all JECFA assessments, and I think that is one of the features of JECFA, to write very detailed monographs with very detailed descriptions of the database and complete references. In general, all these documentations are available within a timeframe from 8 to 12 months after the meeting, as printed versions. Due to this lengthy editing and printing process, we make draft monographs available to interested parties, to member states, based on requests, earlier if so done. With respect to data that are looked at again, JECFA does not create data as such, it reviews data. The call for data is always published approximately one year ahead, so the planning for each JECFA meeting starts approximately one year ahead. There is a public call for data out, where it is detailed very clearly what kind of substances are evaluated, for what purpose and what type of data the Committee would want to have. And just posting things on the Internet is a very passive way, so there are additional means of distributing this call for data, in particular through the Codex distribution lists. Member States, parties here, they are all represented at the respective Codex committee meetings, and they do receive via this means also the call for data. We cannot actively go out and retrieve, so it is the responsibility of the member States to provide available information, and that is then submitted to the secretariat, to the relevant expert and reviewed. Thank you.

Mr. Ehlers

656.   Yes, I would just like to make sure, since nobody answered specifically what I asked, I take it then that the answer is there is no new scientific information that would fundamentally change what was already analysed in the 1999 review.

Chairman

657.   EC.

European Communities

658.   Mr. Chairman, I don't think one can draw this conclusion. I think the scientists should speak, each and every one of them, on this question, because it is very important. There should be no conclusions by default, I would guess.

Mr. Ehlers

659.   That is why I put in those terms to see if I could actually.. .

European Communities

660.   Could you put the question in a negative way so that we could also see the reaction of the experts, there might be another way of putting the question, please.

Chairman

661.   Dr. Cogliano and the US and Canada.

Dr. Cogliano

662.   The way the conclusion was just summarized by the Panel would not be my conclusion. We were not asked as experts to review all the scientific data that has become available since 1999, so I cannot make a conclusion. I certainly cannot make a conclusion that the data are sufficient for a new evaluation, or that the data are not sufficient for a new evaluation. That is not what the experts were asked to look at. I would say that it is normal that as new scientific data becomes available all different kinds of international bodies do take new looks at the data every few years. We have seen, I think, the hormones were evaluated in the mid-1980s and then in 1999, so there seems to be that every 10 years or so there might be an accumulation of new data that warrants a new evaluation. But we were not specifically asked to look at the data and I don't think that any of us can really comment, or at least I cannot comment on the adequacy of the new data.

Ms Orozco

663.   But most likely you have received all the information that has been submitted by the parties and drawn on the information that everyone has received from what has been submitted to the Panel. Is it your opinion that there is new information or is it your opinion from the review of all of that information that there is nothing new that merits a new assessment?

Dr. Cogliano

664.   Speaking from the monograph meeting on hormones last year, these are again birth-control pills and hormone therapies at higher levels, there did seem to be some emerging data on genotoxicity for these hormones at those levels of doses. There seems to be lower levels of hormones in prepubertal boys than had been believed 10 or more years ago, there seems to be data about what might be happening at extremely low concentrations that contribute to uncertainty of the dose-response curves. Now whether those would fundamentally alter the ADI or change any conclusions, I think that is why you convene an expert group to evaluate all of that, and I don't think, I wouldn't feel comfortable making a snap judgement, that it is or is not sufficient to conduct a new evaluation. There do seem to be some new data but that's typical of all science. Scientists take the current state of knowledge and ask the next question, and at some point the answers may change, but I don't know if we are at that point at this time.

Chairman

665.   OK. US.

United States

666.   Thank you, Mr. Chairman. I think I glean from the Panel's question that the Panel was asking about residue studies in animals and whether new data had been put on the record regarding that aspect of the EC's risk assessment. I would like to ask the experts who have reviewed the data, has the EC put forward scientific evidence that supports the conclusion that previous residue data looked at by JECFA, for example, is no longer adequate or sufficient to assess the risk of the three hormones?

Chairman

667.   I will give the floor to the experts first and then EC.

Dr. Boobis

668.   To my knowledge I have not seen any new information on residues data on the hormones following their use according to good veterinary practice. There have been some new data on their use according to abuse scenarios and we need to discuss the relevance of that later I assume. But in terms of the standard residue package which forms the basis for a risk assessment, as far as I know there are no new data, and there are no reasons to believe that the data that JECFA evaluated were not appropriate for that purpose.

Chairman

669.   Thank you. Dr. De Brabander.

Dr. De Brabander

670.   Yes, Mr. Chairman, I think we all agree that there are no new data, and I just speak for the analytical part, the concentrations of the components etc. are produced in the years 1980, 1986 maybe, and it is a fact that analytical methodology in the years from 1986 on until now increased considerably, and it is not only the limit of detection which is decreased but also the separation power of components. You are able now to separate much more components from each other than in those days, and there are some examples, and I don't wish to go into analytical details, but you separate components in what we call a chromatogram, a series of peaks, and one peak can stand for one component but can stand also for two or three components, and if the analytical methodology improves, we see that suddenly a peak that was thought to be one component can split into two or three, and you can have three other components with different properties. I cannot, and it was not our job, and it is not possible just on paper, say the analytical data are not valid from that time, but you cannot be sure that they are valid because they are produced with methods which are not modern. It is not because they were validated in that time that they are still valid, because

validation is a continuous process each time, that's why we as laboratories have to perform a new ring tests each year. We don't like that, we have to do it to keep up our performance, otherwise you say we perform one ring tests, OK, we are good for 50 years. That is not the case, we have to do it constantly, improve our methods and constantly improve our performance.

Chairman

671.   US. Is it directly related?

United States

672.   Dr. Boisseau has spoken of the issue of "old" data and whether "old" data is by nature bad data in his responses to the Panel's question. I though that would be a good follow-up to Dr. De Brabander's response.

Chairman

673.   EC.

European Communities

674.   Thank you Chairman. So Dr. De Brabander, if I have understood well, you are saying that these data which are old, from the 1970s and 1980s, because we have new, more powerful and more accurate analytical methods, their validity is in doubt because they are old and they have been measured with measurement methods which are by today's standards not credible, are not accurate. Is that the conclusion?

Dr. De Brabander

675.   That is my conclusion. I cannot say that the data are bad, I don't say that, I just say you don't know that they are good, and you have to check them with modern analytical methods, but nobody performs that; we will not do experiments with melengestrol acetate because we don't have the means, we don't allow it and why should we do that, it is not our task.

Chairman

676.   Yes. I would like to remind the delegations that we have 30 minutes before lunch break, but I have not given the opportunity to the other delegations so far to put their own questions. I am wondering whether the EC has exhausted, or almost exhausted, their list of questions under area 3?

European Communities

677.   We have not exhausted the questions Chairman, but I can consider that the delegations ask one of their questions and then we can take the floor, if you agree.

Chairman

678.   If you have – I see, OK. Dr. Boisseau first.

Dr. Boisseau

679.   Thank you, Mr. Chairman. I wish to speak very briefly on the validity of the results obtained with methods that were used 20 years ago. What the Commission said is true as regards the results that are at the level of the limits of detection of the methods previously used. But once the results obtained are clearly over the limits of detection, what counts is the precision of the method and its reproducibility. The fact that the method used to provide these results is old is irrelevant to the extent that they have been validated. Indeed, we need only concern ourselves with the uncertainty that we may have regarding the very low values at the level of the limits of detection. Thank you.

Chairman

680.   Dr. De Brabander, please.

Dr. De Brabander

681.   On an analytical point, I would agree with what Dr. Boisseau says on veterinary drugs and xenobiotic agents, but not for hormones which are also naturally present and in the company of a lot of very similar components. You force me to go into a technical question, but a lot of molecules have the same molecular mass, it means that they weigh the same, but they have different structures and they are not easy to separate. So I know for a certain component like AED (androstenedione) and beta-boldenone we have to do a special procedure, separate them first in a liquid chromatogram and afterwards in a gas chromatogram, to separate the two components from each other, because you cannot otherwise distinguish them. That was technically not possible in the 1980s, so again I do not say that the data are not correct, I cannot say that because I have not examined them. You have got to be sure that you are correct, and it's not just the limit of detection, it is also the specificity, meaning the separation power of components has increased considerable since that year.

Chairman

682.   Dr. Wennberg.

Dr. Wennberg

683.   I think that maybe this is the final comment on this issue with the analytical methods. These methods which were used are also described in the report. The methods that were used were radioimmunoassay methods, which are very specific for the compounds in question at the time that they were used. I don't want to go into the technical details here, but I think it is for the parties to argue whether these data are acceptable or not. For JECFA in 1999 they were evaluated and accepted.

Chairman

684. I see all the experts are waving their flags, starting with Dr. Boobis.

Dr. Boobis

685. I just want to make a point about specificity and that is the problem that Dr. De Brabander has just alluded to, which would in fact result in more conservative assumptions. That is, if you have cross-reactivity of your antibody detection system with something else, if that is not more potent than oestradiol or the analyte and it is hardly likely that it would be, then you over-estimate the residue present, so you are over-estimating your exposure. So while it is true that modern, very sophisticated analytical methods might allow you more precise estimates, my prediction is that the specific analyte would go down, not up.

Chairman

686. Thank you. Dr. De Brabander, please.

Dr. De Brabander

687. Yes, it is a possibility that concentrations go down, but there is also a possibility that they go up by other means. I had a colleague, I won't mention his name, neither the country, which has very very bad experience with radioimmunoassays. They did a radioimmunoassay and they say that animals are positive. They questioned the analysis, they did a separation and it was something else which caused a response on the radioimmunoassay. Radioimmunoassays are indeed – selectively but you can have cross reactions, you can have systems where the concentrations go down. Then I gave the explanation of modern methods, even in modern methods you have (in mass spectrometry, for instance) a phenomenon which is called ionization suppression. It means that when the component goes into the machine, it is not ionized and you don't see it and you underestimate the concentration. If you do a better separation, that ionization suppression is gone and you see the component and its real concentration. You have both: concentrations going down, concentrations going up, for modern methods corresponding with older methods. But again I would say I would not comment that the data are not valid, I don't know, and we don't know if they are valid.

Chairman

688. Thank you. Dr. Sippell.

Dr. Sippell

689. I can only agree with what was just said, and this applies particularly for the first period after birth. For neonates, for infants and for young children a standard commercially-available radioimmunoassay is not able to pick up the real concentrations, because there are numerous other cross-reacting steroids, for instance, that will really obscure the real concentration, for instance for oestra-

diol-17β. And therefore you have to do an extraction, you have to subject the extracts to a separation method, liquid column chromatography or HPLC, and then you have to quantitate, you can do that by either radioimmunoassay or by a gas chromatography and I think at the moment the new development is tandem mass chromatography, where you can have these separation procedures repeatedly and then, as Dr. De Brabander said, you separate many peaks and can quantitate them accordingly. And I think the analytical methodology is consistently improving right now and therefore one should really look to the new data.

Chairman

690.   Dr. Boobis.

Dr. Boobis

691.   Mr. Chairman, the point has already been made that science moves on, probably in few areas more than analytical chemistry, where the advances in mass spectrometric techniques have been truly remarkable. But I would like to put in a point of pragmatism here. It is not possible to re-evaluate the residues data of veterinary drugs and pesticides every year, or every two years. The EU itself has a periodic review programme of pesticides which takes 10 years before a compound is rescheduled, and it probably takes longer because of the need to generate the data, so we have to live with the methods that are available. They have been validated, the immunoassays that were used at that time were validated for their purpose, which is not to say that there are not newer, better methods, but they were validated at the time, they were adequately fit for purpose. I would make the point that a method that is used to measure low levels of oestrogens in infants is a different question from a method that is being used to measure resides in food. The analytical challenges are quite different and the methods that were developed in the 1980s for the residues were fit for that purpose, and that is what they were used for. If you ask the question about the circulating concentrations, that is a different issue. So in terms of the residues the methods were suitable. We reviewed the data in 1999. It would be unrealistic to expect a complete new residues data package to be generated over a period of a few years because analytical methods had advanced. At an appropriate period of time in the future new data may be generated and it would not be unreasonable at that time to look again at the exposure data.

Chairman

692.   Thank you – OK.

European Communities

693.   But there are part of the file which the European Communities submitted to the Panel, and it is provided to you, Exhibits number 7 up to 43, among those Exhibits a number of papers precisely provide new data about the residues in meat from animals treated with these hormones for growth promotion. But not only that, these new data have been generated with the latest methods of detec-

tion and measurement, the most recent ones to which Dr. De Brabander has made reference. So then the question is why these new data which are available and produced with the latest methods available are not sufficient to lead JECFA to do a new evaluation? This is the first question. And why would the European Communities, who has performed such a risk assessment on the basis of those data, be considered not to be part of the latest data available that have to be taken into account, as were the old data of the 1970s and 1980s which were submitted to Codex? Thank you.

Chairman

694.   Can I give the floor to Canada first and then to Dr. Wennberg?

Canada

695.   Thank you, Mr. Chair. I have a question for the experts who have been involved in JECFA and it is a question of clarification between the type of data you use in a residue monograph and the type of data you use in a toxicological monograph, and whether or not advancements in analytical techniques that relate to the type of data you would use in a residue monograph would have an impact on the data used in the toxicological monograph, which is the monograph from which the ADI is recommended. So a distinction between the two types of data-set, the dataset you would use for a toxicological monograph and the data set you would use for the residue monograph, and whether or not advancements in the analytical techniques, the types of studies you would do for residue mono-graphs would have an impact on the type of studies that are looked at in the toxicological monograph from which the ADI is derived.

Chairman

696.   OK. Dr. Tritscher.

Dr. Tritscher

697.   Thank you. Going back to the graph I put up yesterday, the toxicological evaluation and the residue evaluation and then the exposure assessment are two different parts of the risk-assessment procedure, and there are different datasets underlying these procedures. In the case of veterinary drugs, for the residue stud-ies there are metabolism studies, residue-depletion studies and so forth in the food-producing animal, so it is a different species, we are talking about cows, pigs, for whatever purpose the specific veterinary drug is registered. For the toxicological studies you have a completely different dataset and you look at normal test animal species, rodents in most cases, and in the case of the specific hormones we are talking about there were a lot of human data that were looked at in a toxicological study. There is some overlap, in particular with respect to metabolism studies for comparative purposes. If the metabolism is comparable in the test animal species, in the rodents, to what happens in the field, in the real application of the veterinary drugs of the food-producing animals. I think I will leave it with that.

Chairman

698.   Would you be quick please.

Dr. Wennberg

699.   First, I would like to respond to what the EC said about their data. As far as I can consider from the JECFA secretariat point of view, as I mentioned before, there was never any request from the EC to have these data evaluated. Secondly, it was up to the scientific experts which were appointed by the Panel to review the exhibits which were submitted by the different parties, so that does not have anything to do with JEFCA *per se*. And the final point I would like to make is that for the residue data that was evaluated in 1999, can I remind everybody that what was analysed was both the endogenous and the exogenous substances together, together with the metabolites that results from the elimination of the substances from the body of the animals, and there was no difference between what the natural production was as compared to what was administered. So there were quite high levels normally, so the point about low levels and more sophisticated techniques in this sense does not make any difference to the evaluation, because the levels were high in both cases and they were slightly higher in some instances when hormones were given, but the background level was quite high in both the control animal and the test animals. Thank you.

Chairman

700.   Dr. Miyagishima, would you like to ...?

Dr. Miyagishima

701.   Thank you, Mr. Chairman. I just wanted to make sure that the Panel is clear about the different roles of Codex and JECFA. As far as Codex is concerned, it has a built-in mechanism that would allow it to put in question the adopted MRLs, and in that case the procedure is through the inclusion of the compound in the priority list for re-evaluation. And the initiative should be taken by a member, and it is not for the Codex secretariat or other parties to take the initiative. Thank you.

Chairman

702.   So having heard what the JECFA and Codex representatives mentioned, I think it is quite clear that it is for the members and not the secretariat themselves to request the new data to be evaluated by JECFA, Codex, right? That is quite clear. Canada please.

Canada

703.   Yes, that's fine, our question was adequately answered. Thank you.

Chairman

704.   So we have only 15 minutes to go before lunch break, but as I believe that a large portion of the EC questions have already been addressed, I will give the same opportunity to the US and Canada during the remaining time of the morning session and the afternoon session, and then come back to the remaining questions from the EC, if necessary, and others too. OK. I will give the floor to the US.

United States

705.   Thank you, Mr. Chairman. A question to the experts who have spoken on the issue of genotoxicity of oestradiol-17β. I wonder, does the scientific evidence relied on by the European Communities in its Opinions support the conclusion that oestradiol-17β is genotoxic *in vivo* at levels below those associated with a hormonal response?

Chairman

706.   The floor is open for comments from the experts. Dr. Boobis.

Dr. Boobis

707.   I find it difficult to be persuaded that the evidence indicates such, because we have to be clear that the question of the genotoxicity of oestradiol-17β has been tackled in a number of different ways. Firstly, it used a variety of end-points, a variety of test systems *in vitro* and a variety of endpoints *in vivo*, but more particularly it has used precursors of the presumed genotoxic metabolite. Quite frequently what has been administered is not oestradiol, it's one of the metabolites or the quinone product to an *in vivo* situation or even *in vitro* situation, and it is those metabolites that have generally given some indication of a positive result. Now it is my view that the genotoxicity of oestradiol *in vitro* functions other than by a DNA reactive mechanism of the parent or metabolite, that it may be through redox cycling, generating reactive oxygen species or per-oxidative products, and that as a consequence one can overcome in-built protective mechanisms of detoxication and repair by adding a high level, relative to the parent, a high concentration of the metabolite. So what happens is that you by-pass a de facto threshold by giving that metabolite. And that is in my view what happens *in vivo* when these metabolites give a positive. These positives are not of, as I understand it, a mutational response, they are a genotoxicity response, and so I would say that I have yet to be convinced that oestradiol 17β at low concentrations is capable of producing a genotoxic response *in vivo*.

Chairman

708.   Thank you. Dr. Guttenplan, please.

Dr. Guttenplan

709.   There is recent evidence where they have detected the DNA adducts, that means damaged DNA products that have been produced from the reaction of oestradiol with DNA in the urine. As far as I know this data is only submitted for publication. However, the levels are extremely low and I question whether such low levels have any significance with respect to cancer-inducing properties.

United States

710.   Thank you, Mr. Chairman. As a follow-up, I think, to Dr. Guttenplan's comment, to the experts who have opined on this issue in writing, does the scientific evidence relied on by the EC in its opinions support the conclusion that oestradiol-17β is carcinogenic at levels found in residues in meat from cattle treated with the hormone for growth promotion purposes?

Dr. Boobis

711.   I can be very brief, Chairman. I would say no, that I am not persuaded by the evidence presented that the levels present of oestradiol-17β in cattle treated for growth promotion have the capacity to produce cancer in those so exposed.

Chairman

712.   Thank you. Dr. Guttenplan, please.

Dr. Guttenplan

713.   We were asked to comment on potential, and the potential is there, but I think I agree with Dr. Boobis that in actual practice or in actual situations the risk is minimal.

Chairman

714.   Thank you. EC.

European Communities

715.   Chairman, can I have a follow-up to a specific point, just to clarify. So is it correct to understand then that we cannot say that there is no risk, but the risk is small, minimal as you say, but the risk is not zero?

Dr. Guttenplan

716.   The risk is not zero. We really cannot calculate such low levels, but it might be less than one in a billion. But we were asked to calculate on potential, and I have a problem with that word potential in my responses. So it is almost like saying is it possible, yes almost anything is possible, but in a real situation – is it likely to occur at a significant level? – no.

European Communities

717.   Thank you. This is, I think, an important clarification. Here we are talking about the residues from meat treated with hormones for growth promotion, and the reply was that the risk is not zero, it is small and it cannot be evaluated. So we are not talking about zero – I think it is important to clarify for the Panel and then come back with the question. In the previous panel which has examined the substances in 1998 there was another expert in the place where you now sit by the name of George Lucier, and he made an evaluation at that time that there would be a risk of one in one million from residues in meat, but then the subsequent Panel and Appellate Body reports said that his conclusion does not come from concrete examples, from concrete experiments he himself has conducted. So this statement which has been made is very important. The conclusion that the risk is not zero comes from residues in meat treated with growth hormones; it is small but we cannot calculate it. Could you please confirm this.

Dr. Guttenplan

718.   Yes, that's right. It is small, we cannot calculate what it is. I might also say that every time we cook meat we produce new carcinogens, so every time we consume meat we are increasing the possibility that we will get cancer from the meat, but the likelihood is very small.

Chairman

719.   Let me give the floor to Dr. Boisseau and Dr. Boobis and then back to the United States.

Dr. Boisseau

720.   Thank you, Mr. Chairman. Concerning this carcinogenic potential associated with the hormonal properties of oestradiol, we come back to a general problem. When we carry out long-term carcinogenicity tests on animals, in order to be able to see anything, we have to use heavy doses which have nothing to do with the residue content in foodstuffs; if we used quantities more or less similar to the residue content, we would see nothing at all. In other words, as with the short-term mutagenicity and genotoxicity tests, we use high contents, and where there is a carcinogenic effect, we establish a relationship between the dose and the effect in the chosen experimental area. Once this has been done, and if indeed there is a dose/effect relationship, the problem becomes complicated, because we have to extrapolate from this experimental area to small doses in order to figure out whether there is a threshold and to determine the potential effect associated with a small dose. And at that point, we simply do not know what to do. Consequently, the JECFA like other committees, uses the principle of the safety factor. It is true that this is rather a simplistic system, and the truth is that it is open to criticism, because depending on the slope of the effect/dose ratio, the same safety factor will provide different levels of protection. But, as Sir

Winston Churchill once said about democracy, it may not be an ideal system of government, but the other systems are worse.

721.   Indeed, the mathematical extrapolation models will give you very different results based on the same data, depending on the model chosen and the criteria taken into account. So in the end, the pragmatic system that is used is worth what it is worth: it may not be perfect, but it is just as good as many others. Accordingly, when we say, as I have just heard, that when we have an effect/dose ratio following a carcinogenicity study and we cannot say that the risk is zero at low doses, the fact is that we simply don't know, we cannot say that it exists, nor can we say that it does not exist. So in order to protect itself and to protect public health, the JECFA opted for a safety factor of 1,000, in general, a figure which I think does provide guarantees – but we cannot make any claims, we cannot provide proof, nor can we cause alarm among populations, because in these cases we are not dealing only with hormones, there is all the rest, all the work that has been done by the JECFA for other substances, the work that has been done at the European Union level, since everybody works in the same way. So we have to be careful about casting doubt on a general working method in the case of hormones, because there is no reason to stop at hormones. We would have to cast doubt on everything that has been done over the past twenty years. Thank you.

Chairman

722.   Dr. Boobis.

Dr. Boobis

723.   Thank you, Mr. Chairman. I wanted to make rather similar points and I will be brief. First is that my view is that the risk of cancer from the levels of oestradiol in its use according to GVP as a growth promoter is such that it is not appreciable. This is the definition of ADI, so I believe the threshold approach and safety-factor approach, which is widely used for compounds which are not direct-acting genotoxicants, is appropriate for this compound. And as Dr. Boisseau has pointed out, when we say not appreciable, it is because no risk assessor worth his salt is going to say zero risk, an absolute guarantee of safety. This underpins all risk assessment. If the policy makers, the risk managers, would seek an assurance of zero risk, then they should provide the methods to generate that assurance. These are not known yet and it is not clear to me how you would ever conduct a risk assessment and guarantee that, without ensuring zero exposure, and of course that would cease all use of all compounds where there is any risk whatsoever, and they all have some risk. Thank you.

Chairman

724.   Thank you. Let me give the floor to Canada because I have seen the flag being raised since long time ago.

Canada

725.   Mr. Chairman, if indeed the EC has a specific follow-up question rather than a running monologue and argument with the experts we can wait for their question and then we will pose our own question.

European Communities

726.   Thank you, Mr. Chairman. It is not going to be a monologue but it's a precise question. Dr. Boobis, thank you for clarifying that non-appreciable does not mean zero, it is a small risk. But supposing it is one in one million, supposing that will come from residues in meat treated with hormones for growth promotion in accordance with good veterinary practice. Is this what you said?

Dr. Boobis

727.   I would rather that words were not put in my mouth, Chairman. I tried to give my answers as precisely as possible, I hope they were clear. What I said was that there was a very low risk, I did not say it was one in a million, it could be much less than that.

European Communities

728.   But it is not zero.

Dr. Boobis

729.   I am talking about a potential, not necessarily a real risk, I am saying we cannot give an absolute assurance of the absence of risk. If that was possible I would be very enthusiastic that a risk manager would provide the methodology where that could be done for any compound whatsoever. It is the underlying principle of all risk assessment, within the EU and within JECFA and within all other organizations that conduct risk assessment of chemicals. I will not go into the details of risk-assessment methodology here, but one of the questions was did they use state of the art risk-assessment approaches at JECFA, and the answer is yes we did, and those approaches are still generally accepted worldwide as the most appropriate way of evaluating the risks of compounds to which humans are exposed.

Chairman

730.   Thank you. The floor is for Canada now.

Canada

731.   Thank you, Mr. Chair. Recalling the discussion of yesterday about the components of the risk assessment, and in particular the circumstances in which a dose-response assessment should be conducted. As a result of the absence of evidence that several experts have just indicated about the genotoxicity of

oestradiol, is it your opinion that a dose-response assessment should be conducted in a risk assessment of oestradiol in this case.?

Chairman

732.   Dr. Boobis and then Dr. Boisseau.

Dr. Boobis

733.   Based on the weight of evidence evaluation of the genotoxicity of oestradiol – and I just wanted to clarify a point, I don't think that anybody on this side of the table has denied that oestradiol is an *in vitro* genotoxicant, there is no good evidence that it is mutagen, but it is certainly a genotoxicant *in vitro* – but based on the weight of evidence, the view certainly of JECFA was that that was due to a mechanism likely to have a threshold and therefore it would be appropriate and necessary to conduct a dose-response analysis of the *in vivo* responses, because any underlying mechanism would have a threshold in the view of the experts present.

Chairman

734.   Thank you. Dr. Boisseau.

Dr. Boisseau

735.   Thank you, Mr. Chairman. Let me just say a few words on the zero risk concept mentioned by the Communities. I merely wish to recall that, at least as concerns substances that are authorized and deliberately included as additives or as veterinary drugs, i.e. administered to animals, this zero risk concept was abandoned at least 20 years ago. It is valid today only for prohibited products for which, indeed, the most sensitive analytical method must be used to ensure that there is no fraud. So if I understood properly, as regards oestridiol and the carcinogenic risk associated with a hormonal effect, it is thought that extrapolation to low doses does not enable us to eliminate the least risk; but in that case, I repeat what I already said this morning, we must not lose sight of the characteristics of oestradiol, to name but one hormone, which is not a xenobiotic but for which part of the residue is a natural result of the physiology of animals. So that if we infer that zero risk for the most minute quantities or oestradiol residues does not exist, then once again, what are we speaking of? Should we prohibit the consumption of bovine meat on the grounds that without treatment it will make a contribution in terms of oestradiol that could, if I follow this reasoning, generate a risk, however minute, but in any case not zero? Once again, even if we forget about the administration of oestradiol, the risk, however small, already exists in normal meat. We must bear this is mind, and this involves a quantitative evaluation of the risk, since even where oestradiol is not administered to animals we would – and I say this in the conditional tense – be exposed to that risk.

Chairman

736.   I will give the floor to Dr. Tritscher and Dr. Boobis.

Dr. Tritscher

737.   Thank you. I would like to make some general remarks and clarifications regarding dose-response assessments. The point to differentiate here is what we discussed already yesterday, I am sorry if I repeat something, but the difference between a qualitative and a quantitative dose-response assessment. A quantitative dose-response assessment requires extrapolation to the low dose range outside of the observed experimental studies. And this extrapolation down to low exposure levels requires a number of assumptions that go into a mathematical modelling to describe the shape of the dose-response curve in the low exposure range. And if this is possible or not with a reasonable level, an acceptable level of uncertainty and acceptable level of assumptions that go in, totally depends on the data that are available. It is not dependent on the compound, it is exclusively dependent on the quality and appropriateness of the data as a first instance. In this context I would like to point out that there is a lot of discussion regarding dose-response assessment and low-dose extrapolation in particular. And the International Programme on Chemical Safety has held an international expert consultation on dose-response assessment in general, and the experts define a six-step procedure for dose-response assessment where the first, maybe the first three, I don't have the exact layout now in my head, but the first three are in line, they end with the NOAEL and the ADI, because this is a dose-response assessment where no extrapolation to the low dose range outside the observable range is done. But then, depending on the quality of the data, the reliability of the data, you can do low-dose extrapolation. However, any low-dose extrapolation is mathematical modelling, it's the best-guess estimate. But this would allow a quantitative estimate of a risk, again, a quantitative estimate of a risk at a certain exposure level. But to achieve that quantitative dose-response assessment, you have to have the appropriate data, and I do not believe that in the case of the hormones the appropriate data are there.

Chairman

738.   Thank you. Dr. Boobis.

Dr. Boobis

739.   I just wanted to emphasize this generality of the acceptability of the concept of no zero risk. This is the EMEA's definition of an ADI for establishing maximum residue levels of veterinary medicinal products in foodstuffs of animal original, exactly congruous to the issue we are talking about. The ADI is the estimate of the residue, expressed in terms of micrograms or milligrams per kilogram of body weight, that could be ingested daily over a lifetime without any appreciable health risk. So the EMEA, an organ of the European Union, has ap-

parently not been able to come up any more than we have at JECFA or anybody else has, with a methodology that can guarantee the absence of any risk.

Chairman

740.   Quickly, very quickly.

European Communities

741.   Well, for the benefit of Dr. Boobis I should clarify the EMEA is just a sub-organ of the European Commission and it evaluates the substances for therapeutic treatment only, not for growth promotion. So this statement has no relevance whatsoever for the residues of meat treated with hormones for growth promotion. This is the role of EFSA. But Chairman if you allow …

Dr. Boobis

742.   Does that mean that we can have zero risk in other circumstances, and could I ask the EC to provide a reference to where the methodology is so that I can apply it in my work?

Chairman

743.   Excuse me, it is already five minutes past 1 o'clock and the interpreters won't be available from now on, so if you all agree, then, shall we resume our discussion in the afternoon with more questions by the US? The meeting will start at 3 pm here in this room.

28 September 2006, afternoon

Canada

744.   Chairman, I have a point of order to make, and the point of order arose as a result of the brief display of what appeared to be a new piece of evidence on the projector. As I think I mentioned yesterday, we have seen this exercise as the Panel's chance to explore the issues to the extent possible with the experts. We have already exchanged through letters and through clarifications with you how we thought we might proceed, particularly in respect of the kind of argumenta-tion and evidence that might be put before you, and you have already provided that answer and you have reiterated that answer yesterday morning. Over the last two days I think we have exercised considerable restraint in raising procedural objections whenever we have had statements more in the nature of arguments rather than questions; but I think it really is important to keep on track. What was on the screen we have not seen before, to that extent it is new evidence, and if the EC proposes to put forward new evidence, then we want a ruling from you that that provision of new evidence is simply not permitted. You have already provided that, you have already stressed that yesterday, and at this point I think it should go beyond a reminder, and it should be a ruling from the Chair. Thank you Sir.

Chairman

745.   Thank you.

European Communities

746.   I would like to make a point. This point can be made orally, it can be made better by means of a diagram, and it is in response to comments made by scientists this morning, it is not new evidence. If the Canadian delegation thinks that this will be considered as new evidence they have not seen, we can make the point orally. We thought that this way it was easier to understand the point which we would like to make. And it is in response to what has been said by scientists, so we are not submitting new evidence; it is the natural development of the dialogue in this room that we would like to make this point. As I said, we can make it orally, we can make it through diagrams so everybody understands what one of our scientists said. That's all.

Chairman

747.   Thank you. US has the floor first and then Canada.

United States

748.   I would just make a quick point, Mr. Chairman, and then I am happy to move on with our questions as well. It is hard to say that a piece of evidence is responding to a question when there is a prepared power point slide, and I think, whether the evidence is oral or via some visual aid, I have to support the discussion of Canada on this issue.

Chairman

749.   Canada.

Canada

750.   Thank you, Mr. Chairman. I wish to underline that a point presented by scientific experts on the European Commission delegation is either expert testimony or it is new evidence to the extent that it is there to challenge what the scientific experts of the Panel have put forward. If the EC has a question to ask on the basis of what is on the record it may do so, but if it is a new point, then it is either extra testimony by the EC's delegation, or new evidence, and that is not permitted. Thank you, Sir.

Chairman

751.   OK. EC.

European Communities

752.   Maybe a point of clarification to the Canadian delegation. The Canadian delegation was referring to a paper quoted by Professor Sippell this morning, of

2001. I am not aware of this being on the record. Maybe Canada wants to comment on this.

Chairman

753.   US.

United States

754.   The paper by Dr. Sippell was actually cited in the US comments on the experts' comments, so it is on the record.

Chairman

755.   Yes, you have the floor.

European Communities

756.   Professor Boobis this morning has made a reference to a new paper by Klein, which we didn't know, and we have now found the data. Are we not allowed to make a comment on that? I don't understand what is the purpose of this meeting if we cannot comment upon something which has just been referred to.

Chairman

757.   Before I answer that question, would you respond to the point made by the Canadian delegation just before, whether it is a testimony of the experts of the EC delegation or new evidence?

European Communities

758.   Chairman, it is neither of the two. It is just a question through a means of presentation, or made orally; it is neither new evidence nor extra testimony.

Chairman

759.   So, with that understanding, would Canada and the US delegation agree to the EC delegation moving on with their oral presentation on whatever issues they have, with or without the videotape screen?

Canada

760.   Two points, Mr. Chairman. I understand first of all that as a matter of procedure I think the US is going to go next in questioning. It's impossible in advance of hearing the question to say whether we agree with the question as either expert testimony or a quote, unquote point. I don't know what that means. But very simply, if a point is being raised from outside of the record to question or to impugn what the experts have said, and we have not had notice of it, then we cannot respond to the point that is being raised by EC. That is the whole point of the procedural rules that are in place. So all I can say is that for your benefit, and to allow the process to go forward, we can agree to hear the ques-

tion. We will reserve however our right to raise a point of procedure and then at that point to ask you to disallow the question. If that would help the process to go forward we will go along with that.

Chairman

761.   To my understanding, whether to take a certain argument or presentation of the views or materials as evidence is up to the Panel. I don't know whether we as a Panel have to make a ruling on that procedural point at this particular point in time, but whether to accept it as evidence or argument or whatever will be decided by the Panel. So in order to prevent this process from being suspended or interrupted I hope the EC delegation will be very clear on this point so that US and Canada can agree on proceeding from here on. Would you further clarify on the point made by the Canadian delegation once again.

European Communities

762.   Chair, to be deadly honest with you, I have not fully understood the point. Is the Canadian delegation saying that the EC cannot make its own experts or part of the delegation intervene to provide a scientific view on issues that have been discussed here? Thank you.

Chairman

763.   I don't think that is the point. Canada has the floor.

Canada

764.   I agree with you Mr. Chairman, that is not the point.

Chairman

765.   EC.

European Communities

766.   Would the Canadian delegate care to restate his point please.

Canada

767.   Mr. Chairman, it's very simple. We see something on the display we have not seen before; the other experts here have not seen it before; we cannot respond to that. Now whatever it is, a point, piece of evidence, argument, expert testimony by one of the experts, we have not seen it before; we cannot respond to it. I don't know if the experts have seen it before. Something is being brought into this process from outside of the record and that is the simple point that we are making. If the experts on the EC delegation hear something that the Panel's experts are saying and they disagree; if there is something that they have said that does not fit within the record, then they impugn that, but they cannot bring in something that they have not seen before, that is simply not in accordance with the rules.

European Communities

768.   Before you rule, can I provide a way out. We don't insist, we don't want to delay these proceedings any more, so we will not show this slide, but we would appreciate if we had the time later on for one minute to make the point orally, like we have been making comments orally the whole day yesterday and today, and we have not seen the comments nor heard Canada's comments and the arguments they were going to make orally either, we don't know what they are going to say now. We are in the same situation. So just to avoid the problem and avoid any delays, we are not going to show the slide in this instance to please and satisfy the Canadian delegation. Thank you.

Chairman

769.   I think that is a quite positive response from the EC delegation, and I would like to remind all the delegations that the purpose of this meeting, as I mentioned in my opening statement yesterday, is to get the advice of the experts which the Panel has invited, for the Panel to get their understanding of the scientific and technical issues at hand. In that context, I think we are here to pose any questions or comments to the experts to get their understanding and advice, not in the form of a presentation of materials on evidence or whatever you may call it, so I hope delegations in putting questions do not get into the kind of exercise of presenting new evidence or new materials or new data. With that understanding, can the US and Canadian delegations agree that the EC delegation may have the chance to make their point a little bit later during our discussion this afternoon. And I will give the floor to the US delegation, as I mentioned this morning, because we have been stopped during our discussions when the US delegation was posing their questions. OK. US, you have the floor.

United States

770.   Thank you, Mr. Chairman. Continuing on with the questions, I would like to shift gears and discuss the five other hormones at issue in these proceedings. To the experts with experience in risk assessment, who spoke on this issue in their answers: does the scientific evidence relied on by the European Communities in its opinions support the conclusion that it is not possible to complete a risk assessment for those hormones?

Chairman

771.   The floor is open for comments or responses from the experts. EC.

European Communities

772.   Thank you, Chairman. It's a question of order, I think. This is a risk management question, I think. This question, as it is posed, requires the scientists to say whether as risk managers we can do a risk assessment. I don't have any objections that the US poses this question, but he needs to pose it as a question

addressed to risk scientists during the risk assessment, not to the risk managers. Thank you.

Chairman

773.   Before giving the floor to the US, let me ask the experts whether they have any views or comments on this point. The question was posed to the experts first. Dr. Boobis.

Dr. Boobis

774.   I cannot speak for the EC, and I think what has just been said is quite correct. I can speak for JECFA in which I participated, and in our view we had enough information to complete a risk assessment. I don't know if that is helpful, but that was the situation when we looked at the available data on those five other hormones.

Chairman

775.   Thank you. Dr. Cogliano.

Dr. Cogliano

776.   I think the way I would look at questions like this is that it is possible to complete risk assessments up to a certain point. IARC could do assessments of those, but IARC's risk assessment stops with the hazard identification and a statement about whether or not these hormones are carcinogenic. JECFA's assessment then continues to develop an ADI, which involves looking at the animal studies, selecting the dose where they think there are no observed adverse health effects, considering everything they can and dividing by safety factors. That's another more detailed risk assessment than IARC does. A further level of detail in risk assessment would be to do a dose-response curve down to lower doses and try to predict what would happen at very low levels, what would be increased risk, if there is any. And I think most people here have been very reluctant to say that you can extrapolate the dose-response cures and get any kind of precise level. So I think when we sometimes say can you complete a risk assessment, I think you cannot just say a risk assessment, but a particular type of risk assessment. I think you can complete a risk assessment that's an ADI style of risk assessment, you cannot complete a risk assessment that's a full dose-response curve and try to get a prediction of risk at very low exposure levels.

Chairman

777.   OK. US.

United States

778.   Then perhaps a good way to follow up would be to ask: does the scientific evidence relied on by the EC in its Opinions support the conclusion that any

of these five hormones is carcinogenic at levels found in residues in meat from cattle treated with the hormones for growth promotion purposes?

Chairman

779. Dr. Boobis.

Dr. Boobis

780. My view would be that, given the information that was available, it would have been possible to conclude that there was no evidence that at the levels present in meat these compounds would represent a risk of cancer in individuals so exposed.

Chairman

781. Thank you. Any other comments? EC.

European Communities

782. Chairman, I would not like to ask a question now, but would I have the chance to cover this point later on, if you allow me, so that I give the chance to the Canadian delegation to continue?

Chairman

783. If it is a one-time question then I would give the floor to the EC delegation now, but if you have to continue on then I will come back later.

European Communities

784. Well, I think we would like to ask Dr. Boobis and eventually the other scientists to clarify what kind of risk we are talking about. Is it the same as we were talking before, no appreciable risk, or no risk at all? I don't want necessarily to come to generate all this discussion again, but we argue that here we are not talking about a theoretical risk, we are not talking about zero risk, we are talking about a risk which has not been measured, which is difficult to quantify. This is the point and this is, I think, useful to clarify because there are different legal regimes that we apply for oestradiol and the other five hormones. Thank you.

Chairman

785. Dr. Boobis.

Dr. Boobis

786. In the case of the five hormones and oestradiol, the risk we are talking about is based on a view that there is a threshold for any carcinogenic response and therefore it is possible to apply the safety-factor approach widely used in the determination of an ADI, and whatever the ADI definition is by whoever wishes

to set it, these compounds fall into that category. I will not use the words no appreciable risk because it has been persistently misrepresented.

Chairman

787. Thank you. US.

United States

788. Thank you, Mr. Chairman. I only have a couple more questions. To the experts who evaluated the EC's risk assessment, does the scientific evidence, including epidemiological studies put forward by the EC in its opinion, support the conclusion that other human health risks, such as effects on the immune system, are posed by consumption of residues of these five hormones in meat from cattle treated for growth promotion purposes?

Chairman

789. Before I give the floor to any experts I saw Dr. Guttenplan raising his flag before. I give the floor to Dr. Guttenplan.

Dr. Guttenplan

790. With respect to the five additional hormones, if we said that there is no appreciable risk from oestradiol, then the five other hormones have a much less than appreciable risk, because I see no evidence in whole animal studies that any of those compounds have genotoxic or carcinogenic effects.

Chairman

791. I will give the floor to Dr. Boobis first.

Dr. Boobis

792. Chairman, if there is a follow-up to that, I was going to answer the next question.

Chairman

793. Is Dr. Boisseau going to answer the question now or is it related to the question put forward by the US.

Dr. Boisseau

794. Thank you, Mr. Chairman. I simply wanted to associate myself with what was just said following the question by the Communities, so that there is no need to repeat what Dr. Boobis said concerning the conditions for establishing an ADI threshold. However, there is an additional safety factor which Dr. Wennberg spoke of this morning, I think, namely that the exposure of a consumer to residues is considerably less than the dose that would be acceptable in terms of the ADI. In other words, we must not forget that aside from the safety factor that has

been determined and that is used to determine an ADI, there is another safety factor, since the dose, the TMDI, the dose that is in fact ingested, is far lower – somewhere around 4 per cent for oestradiol – than the dose that would be tolerated in terms of the ADI. We must not forget this other safety factor which minimizes the risk, if indeed there is such a risk.

Chairman

795.   I am wondering whether there is any other expert who is ready to respond to the US question, not the EC one. US.

United States

796.   I would simply reiterate, Mr. Chairman, my other question, Dr. Boisseau and Dr. Guttenplan spoke eloquently to the issue of level of risk. But as to whether the EC has actually produced any scientific evidence that supports a conclusion that any of these five hormones are going to pose other health risks when used for growth promotion purposes in cattle.

Chairman

797.   Thank you. Dr. Boobis.

Dr. Boobis

798.   I have seen no evidence that from the levels present in meat following the use of the five hormones according to good veterinary practice, that there is a risk to human health.

Chairman

799.   Thank you. Any other expert wishes to respond? EC.

European Communities

800.   Chairman, I think now is probably the point we would like to make with the diagram, we can make it orally on this precise question, so instead of making it later on, probably you will give us a minute or two to make this question; it relates to this precise point.

Chairman

801.   Can I ask the EC delegation to do that in the form of posing questions rather than giving a presentation?

European Communities

802.   My name is Frederik Vom Saal and I am a professor of biology at the University of Missouri. I appreciate the opportunity to address the Panel and the experts, and the first issue relates to what was just said, and I would like to ask Dr. Sippell who works with the system a question. We see in animal studies that

very small differences – and when I say small in terms of free oestradiol levels 0.05 parts per trillion, that is 0.05 pictograms per ml of oestradiol – are related to differences in prostate size in animals, and it suggests that very small background differences in oestrogen are related to differences between individuals, and we know that individuals have different levels of oestrogen and different response to them, and when we give extra oestrogen to these animals, the amount of response of the animal is greater in the animal with the greatest amount of background level of oestrogen, and that shows that there is in fact no threshold, because the endogenous amount of hormone is already above the threshold and the added amount of hormone in again a phenomenally small amount, below a part per trillion, is detectible against this very small background amount. So I would ask Dr. Sippell whether he really believes that when you are eating meat that has oestrogens in it, is the background level against which it is operating to be considered zero the way it is in a typical risk assessment in calculating an acceptable daily intake, or is the endogenous amount already above threshold and any amount added to that is just going to add to the risk and the types of effects caused by the endogenous hormone? Is this a question that you can answer?

Chairman

803.   Dr. Sippell.

Dr. Sippell

804.   It is, of course, difficult to answer such a question as a clinician, but from the experience we have with the low levels, I mentioned this several times before, with the extremely low levels that have been measured by these new recombinant assays, it is conceivable really that this extra burden of oestradiol poses a risk to very small children and particularly prepubertal boys, and this is in line with the very very high sensitivity of prepubertal children to oestrogens induced for other purposes. I mean, lets say, I mentioned the example of Turner girls, whom you treat with really minute amounts of oestradiol.

Ms Orozco

805.   I would like to take advantage of your knowledge to pose a question. If such minute amounts of additional oestrogens create an appreciable or more than appreciable risk in your view, why we don't we seem to see effects in prepubertal children or at a later stage in their lives from eating eggs, meat and milk?

Dr. Sippell

806.   That's actually an excellent question. One of the important parts of the answer to that is to ask whether there have been changes in human health trends over the past 50 years associated with the beginning of the use of the very large number of different types of estrogenic chemicals that children are now exposed to that they weren't before World War II when most of these chemicals began to

be used. And if you look at human health events such as breast cancer and related diseases (for instance, gonadal cancer, genital malformation).

Ms Orozco

807.   So that we talk about the same things, I am not talking about chemicals and residues of chemicals, but I am talking about the hormonal component that it is naturally present in food derived from animals.

Dr. Sippell

808.   I guess my response to that would be that they are part of a mix of additional chemicals that humans are exposed to now that were not being used 40 years ago, and it is not really possible, for somebody in epidemiology for instance, to state the added risk, the increase in the incidence in breast cancer, in prostate cancer, in obesity – all of the types of things that are related to oestrogen are only associated with one particular source, but each of these sources of oestrogen increase the risk. Each of them independently and they add together, and everything you do to reduce one of those sources of risk reduces the overall risk. So the answer to your question is the evidence from human health trends that practically every oestrogen-related disease has increased, associated with the use of these types of chemicals in products.

Chairman

809.   I will give the floor to Dr. Boobis and Dr. Sippell and Dr. Boisseau to respond.

Dr. Boobis

810.   Mr. Chairman, just in the interest of clarity I would like to make a brief point, which is that the issue of the effects of endocrine disrupting chemicals found in our environment is one of the most complex and controversial issues in biology today. There is absolutely no clear consensus among scientists; very reputable scientists have different perspectives because the heterogeneity of the data is extreme. There have been a number of international respected reviews which have reported that they could find no direct evidence of harmful effects. I recognize that the absence of evidence is not evidence of absence, which is why I choose my words carefully, but I just wanted to say that we are opening up a very major issue which, as an expert on this group, I have not had the opportunity, nor was I asked, to explore in response to the questions addressed. I would also add that it does not appear to me that the EC used such a consideration in their risk assessment; I can find nowhere reference to some of these papers which were published prior to the EC risk assessment.

Chairman

811.   Thank you. Dr. Sippell.

Dr. Sippell

812.   In view of the fact that we just lack epidemiological studies in children eating normal meat to be compared with those eating hormone-treated meat, we can at the moment rely only on indirect evidence. And if we talk to our American paediatric endocrinology colleagues, they always report us, and this has been published, that the mean age of start of puberty in girls is lower in the United States – particularly in the not so well-off children, particularly those from black background and Hispanic background – than in Europe. Everybody here in the room knows that the problem of childhood obesity is the highest in the United States on earth, and it is increasing in Europe now, but luckily at a lower rate, and there are some other not so obvious indirect pieces of evidence.

Chairman

813.   Thank you. Dr. Boisseau.

Dr. Boisseau

814.   Thank you, Mr. Chairman. Just a question for the scientist who spoke for the Communities. He said that there was a trend revealed by an epidemiological study. In his view, is there an actual correlation between this trend and the use of growth hormones in the country of which he was speaking, given that over the past 20 years, although consumption of meat has been steadily increasing, people have been living longer and longer? Is the epidemiological study to which he refers discriminating enough to be able to establish a correlation between the observed effect and the cause?

Chairman

815.   EC.

European Communities

816.   That's an interesting question. Of course in many epidemiological studies establishing carcinogenic effects is very difficult. But one of the important issues is that associated with the use of these chemicals. There have been very recent trends, such as what was just pointed out by Dr. Sippell – a change in the incidence of puberty which is clearly oestrogen driven, and changes in obesity that have been related to oestrogen. And so associated with the use of these chemicals in beef we do have public-health data that suggest an increase in incidences of abnormalities, and again I agree with Dr. Boobis, the absence of evidence cannot be taken as evidence for the absence of harm, and we have to be careful when studies have not been done to assume that that means that there is no effect. [change of speaker.] Chairman, for the benefit of Dr. Boobis, can I refer him to our risk assessment of 1999, it is on page 20 of our risk assessment, under sections 2.3.2.3, where precisely Professor Vom Saal is cited for his research in the risk assessment, his name appears in the risk assessment, and there is precisely the title of this section is called "The Issue of Dose", and we go through

this argument in our risk assessment, so it is not true that we have not included that in our risk assessment, and it goes on for two pages. It is on page 20. Thank you.

Chairman

817.   Dr. Boisseau would like to have the floor.

Dr. Boisseau

818.   Thank you, Mr. Chairman. Just a quick word on what Dr. Sippell said concerning the clear trend towards obesity among children in the United States. He also pointed out that the situation was getting worse in Europe, in the countries where growth hormones are prohibited and are not used. This brings me back to my question concerning the capacity for discrimination of epidemiological studies, since under two different systems – an American system where growth hormones are used and a European system where they are not used – we note that when it comes to obesity in children there may be a delayed effect in Europe, but the trend is similar.

Chairman

819.   Dr. Sippell.

Dr. Sippell

820.   But the obesity trend in Europe is at a much much lower rate, so the data from the (US) Centre for Disease Control – I think most of you are familiar with that map of the United States, where year by year the colour is getting darker in almost every state of the United States, in virtually every state. If you compare this with Europe, the rate of progression is much higher (in the USA).

Chairman

821.   Before we further proceed, as I mentioned, given the time constraint I may not be able to give you a coffee break during this afternoon's session, but for your information, the snack bar will be open for services for us from 5 to 5.30 so please feel free to get coffees during our conversations. OK. And for your information, three of our experts have to leave this evening by 7 o'clock so I hope we can conclude our discussions by 6, but not beyond 7 o'clock at all. With that I will give the floor to EC.

European Communities

822.   Chairman, we have promised to the Panel that we will do our best to finish indeed by the time you have alluded to, but there may be questions we really would like to ask, and you appreciate that this is an important occasion to clarify these issues. If we don't manage by then, what are we going to do?

Chairman

823.   So that I hope all the delegations will cooperate with the Panel and experts so that we can complete the discussions before some of the experts leave. Without your full cooperation we cannot finish our business.

United States

824.   Shall I continue with questions, Mr. Chairman?

Chairman

825.   Please, US, go ahead.

United States

826.   I only have one more question, actually, to keep things short, and it was interesting that there was a long debate on oestradiol when the question I asked was about the five provisionally banned hormones, and they are not involved in this debate whatsoever. To the experts who have opined on this issue, do any of the scientific materials presented by the EC in its opinions support the conclusion that bovine ears containing hormone implants enter the human food supply in the United States? If so, what is this evidence?

Chairman

827.   Can I ask any of the experts to respond. There seems to be none

European Communities

828.   Is it part of any of our areas of expertise to be able to trace what happens to bovine ears in the United States. I mean it is not in my area of expertise.

United States

829.   Perhaps I can clarify it, Mr. Chairman. The EC in its 1999 opinion has a section under its misuse section that claims there is a risk from implants in bovine ears being processed into the human food supply, and I am wondering if the experts are aware of any evidence put forward in that Opinion that supports that hypothetical situation?

Chairman

830.   No experts ready to respond. Dr. Boobis.

Dr. Boobis

831.   I could find no direct evidence for such an occurrence. I found studies which explored the implications should it occur, but I could find no direct study of such an occurrence. I am not an expert and I could not say how this would be done, but in reading the literature provided, the materials provided, I could not

find a specific study in which that had been investigated with the results presented.

Chairman

832.   Thank you. EC.

European Communities

833.   Chairman, probably the scientists have not understood, and if you allow me I would like to come in on this point because I think that it is an important point. We have submitted a number of Exhibits to the Panel and they are also mentioned in our risk assessment. The point is whether there are estimations or not how sure are we today that good veterinary practice is always respected in the United States, and in the evidence we have provided there are instances where good veterinary practice has not been observed. We have done specific inspections in the United States by our veterinarians; they came up with a written report which has been submitted to the United States and Canada, they are aware of this report, that identifies clear instances of the use and misuse, and I can refer to Exhibits 50, 52, 65, 67, 68.

Chairman

834.   Is that question posed to the experts or to the US delegation? I am afraid that the experts may not be in a position to respond to that question. Canada.

Canada

835.   I don't want to cut off the US questions, if the US has any more questions or any follow-ups. We have a number of questions, with your permission.

Chairman

836.   OK. Please go ahead, Canada has the floor.

Canada

837.   I think we are going to start with a follow-up on this point. [change of speaker] Yes, Dr. Boisseau in his answer to one of the definitions under the terms and definitions section indicated in describing these hormones that the hormones are implanted in the ear and that the ear is discarded, and the comment of the European Communities on this was that he should have said the ear should be discarded. But I wonder if Dr. Boisseau could give some explanation as to the operating procedures, if you will, in a slaughterhouse that are typically adopted so as to prevent or minimize the extent to which contaminants enter the food chain. And here perhaps not just a reference simply to the ear but to other types of contaminants like faeces, hair, hide, and those sorts of things.

Chairman

838.   Thank you. Dr. Boisseau.

Dr. Boisseau

839.   Thank you, Mr Chairman. I apologize, but since I am neither a veterinary doctor nor an inspector, I am unable to answer that question. I am terribly sorry.

Chairman

840.   Canada.

Canada

841.   OK. We have a couple of other questions on a separate issue. [change of speaker] Thank you, Mr. Chair, I have to take us back a little bit in the discussions, my apologies for reverting to an earlier question that came up only indirectly in some of the answers from the experts; it might be important to get some more information on this. In the comments from the experts they referred to homeostatic control or what might be also referred to as balancing systems. Perhaps a few experts could comment on the function of those balancing systems and further describe the implications of these systems for low doses of oestradiol received from meat from treated animals. Thank you.

Chairman

842.   Thank you. Any comment? Dr. Boobis, please.

Dr. Boobis

843.   Well, as indicated earlier, the endocrine system of which the estrogenic system is part plays a critical role in a number of physiological functions and Dr. Sippell has described some of these very clearly. We have also heard that we are subject to natural oestrogens in our diet and we have been for a long time. We have also heard that oestradiol levels can vary or fluctuate, and because of the criticality of the signalling system, it is important that the body is able to balance the levels of oestradiol against that required to produce the responses necessary. And so in general terms there is a system of checks and balances where the turnover of the hormone – any excess hormone tends to be balanced out to some extent. That is part of the role of the binding hormones, sex hormone binding globulin SHBG, it binds a large percentage of the free oestradiol in the circulation normally. And so the homeostasis is a way of preventing extraneous sources from completely unbalancing a tightly regulated system. That is just a general description, I am not saying that that is always the case under all circumstances at all life stages, but that is a general description of the homeostatic regulation of these systems.

Chairman

844.   Thank you. Dr. Sippell.

Dr. Sippell

845.   I only agree, but there are instances and reports, of course case reports, not epidemiological studies, that for instance children who are exposed to oestrogen-containing ointments, for example, which are being wrongly prescribed, and I have observed personally such cases, young girls get breast development and get a growth spurt and have changes in their behaviour and after this effect has been detected and the cause of that effect has been stopped, then, because the body and the hypothalamus of course react to the withdrawal of this exogenous source very sensibly, then this young girl enters into central precocious puberty, which then creates another problem. So precocious pseudo puberty caused by oestrogens from outside, if this is being stopped then the body reacts with central precocious puberty, and this to our understanding might be the underlying mechanism why chronic low-dose oestrogen exposure to prepubertal children might result in an early onset of puberty. And, just to give you another example, several other observations have been made with DDT exposure in young children that have been adopted (from the Third World) to European countries, and in them also a high incidence of precocious-central puberty has been observed, after withdrawal of this exogenous oestrogenic compound.

Chairman

846.   Dr. Boobis and then to Dr. Guttenplan.

Dr. Boobis

847.   I just wanted to make a comment, Chairman, about the observational studies suggesting changes in, for example, the instance of precocious puberty and how that might be associated with the levels of hormones in meat. But as any epidemiologist would be happy to explain, there is a serious danger in trying to compare disease trends in two different countries because of the substantial differences that can exist. It is always possible to point to one factor and say it might be responsible, and of course it might be, we cannot say, but that is one of the reasons that in a risk assessment we tend to base our conclusions on evidence and not on speculation. And in the case, for example, of US versus Europe, we can all point to very many differences, any number of which can explain differences in disease trends, and it's impossible to say that it is due to levels of the hormone, and in fact it is less likely to be due to that than to some other clearly discernable differences between those populations. And on the homeostatic question, I would just add this is very much a question of dose. Toxicity or adverse effect is sometimes described as the breaking of homeostasis, you exceed the level within which the body is able to compensate by homeostatic regulation and then you begin to generate adverse effects.

Chairman

848.   Dr. Sippell.

Dr. Sippell

849.   Very briefly. If I understand the literature correctly all these homeostatic experiments have been derived from adult individuals, and not from prepubertal or very young children, and I wonder whether these mechanisms are the same in the young child as they are in the adult. And you just said, those case reports have been put together by speculation, this is really not the case, the levels have been measured in these individuals, in these patients, because they are patients and we are allowed to measure at least in them.

Chairman

850.   With the understanding of Dr. Guttenplan, may I give the floor to Dr. Boobis to respond first.

Dr. Boobis

851.   I certainly did not suggest that the case reports were speculation. I am talking about the differences in trends between the US and Europe, and that the linkage is the growth hormones in meat. That is speculation because we have no evidence for that. It might be biologically plausible speculation to some, but it is speculation; there is no direct evidence for that.

Chairman

852.   Thank you. Dr. Guttenplan please.

Dr. Guttenplan

853.   I actually was going to respond to the homeostatic question, but just to comment on Dr. Boobis's last comment. Maybe it is not speculation, but often, the term that's used is it's consistent with. So yes, the trends, the time trends in different countries are consistent with the effect of oestrogens, but they are consistent with a lot of other trends too. So I would not say it's speculation, but on the other hand there is certainly no direct evidence that one particular component is responsible for a time trend in oestrogenic or prepubertal effects. With respect to the homeostatic control, at least in experimental animals it's very easy to exceed that. There have been many studies published on animals where oestrogens were administered by all different routes, and you get oestrogenic effects. So homeostatic mechanisms act, but they are not 100 per cent effective.

Chairman

854.   EC.

European Communities

855.   Chairman, on this point, I think it was a very useful clarification by Dr. Guttenplan. So do I understand correctly then, when you say it is consistent with, that means it is one possible explanation why we observe it. We cannot say

this is the only one, but it can be one of the explanations why. That is your statement?

Dr. Guttenplan

856.   That is correct.

European Communities

857.   Thank you.

Chairman

858.   Thank you. I am sorry, sometimes I don't notice the flag of the Canadian delegation. I give the floor to Canada now.

Canada

859.   Thank you. We don't usually tend to be as noisy as some of our friends. I just wanted to ask a point of clarification. First of all I should say that in the Canadian diplomatic service Brussels is usually known as a 10 kilogram posting; that is to say that in the first year on average everyone who gets posted there adds about 10 kilos. I am not sure that this is anything to do with levels of hormones in Belgian beef, but it may have something to do with the levels of butter. The question I had was with respect to Dr. Sippell's instances and reports; I understand that he mentioned something about children who are exposed to oestrogen-containing ointments, and I'm far from being an expert in this area or indeed even remotely close to being a scientist, but I gather that ointments are a different means of getting a particular drug into your system than eating something, considering that there is, well, the intestinal tract that about 9 meters long and things happen to it in a different way than when you put an ointment on. So I wonder about the relevance of that, and the other thing of course is that I go back to what Dr. Boobis mentioned and Ms Orozco, that these oestrogens or oestrogen-like compounds can be found in many green plants. I mean is there any observation, any instance of a boy turning into a girl as a result of eating too much broccoli? You know, that is the kind of information that perhaps we are lacking. But my specific question was to Dr. Sippell in respect of the ointment. Is there not a difference between ointments and taking something orally?

Dr. Sippell

860.   May I answer to that very briefly. Oestradiol-17β is a highly lipophilic substance which means that it is being absorbed almost 100 per cent by an infant's skin, more than by the intestinal tract. And this is long known to paediatricians and to endocrinologists, and as a matter of fact for instance testosterone replacement in adult men now is being done by topical gels and creams and ointments.

Canada

861.   Thank you, Dr. Sippell, you have made exactly the point I wanted to make. Thank you.

Chairman

862.   Thank you. Does this exhaust the list of questions from Canada?

Canada

863.   In light of the discussion about consistent with and relationships between a consumption of hormone residues in meat from treated animals and the early-on set of puberty, if I recall correctly there was some mention of the fact that the incidence of early puberty in females of African-American descent was higher than in other sub-populations, and my question is: is there any evidence to suggest that this sub-population consumes more hormone-treated meat than other sub-populations? And if the evidence was that they didn't consume more, that they consumed on average the same, then would that not be evidence that the exposure to hormone-treated beef is consistent with a conclusion that it has no impact whatsoever on the early onset of puberty, because the early onset of puberty is occurring for other reasons?

Chairman

864.   Dr. Sippell.

Dr. Sippell

865.   Unfortunately there are no epidemiological data to prove or to discard this very question, but there is indirect evidence. There has just been a new study in Germany where they compared the eating habits of children in different levels of the population, high-income, middle-income, low-income families, and they found out that children from low-income families consumed considerably more junk food, so-to-speak, and also higher amounts than an average-income-family child or a high-income-family child. For instance because they don't even have a common meal at home. Unfortunately we don't have such scientifically-sound data, but this might very well relate it with the increasing obesity. And we also know that fat tissues really aromatize, so convert androgens from the adrenals to oestrogens. So those (fat) kids have an additional source of oestrogens entering (from increased adrenal androgens) that turns them into early puberty.

Chairman

866.   Dr. Guttenplan.

Dr. Guttenplan

867.   Just as I mentioned the term consistent with, I would say studies or at least the statistics among the black and Hispanic community are inconsistent

with the hypothesis that oestrogen in beef is responsible for prepubertal and other oestrogenic effects, because I would guess, and I am not sure about this, that consumption of beef by lower socioeconomic status individuals is lower, because beef is expensive. If you look at what is ordered at McDonalds, it is French fries and Coca Cola.

Chairman

868.   Thank you. Our discussion is going too far beyond the issues of our constitution here, the focus of our discussions is whether or not the scientific evidence is sufficient in terms of risk assessment of hormone-treated beef consumption. So I think in order to focus our discussion on the subject at hand, I hope the delegations and parties and experts may not go beyond this range of discussions here.

Ms Orozco

869.   Mr. Chairman, in order to bring back the discussion to the problem that we need to solve, I would like to come back to a question that was raised, I think, by the United States some moments ago, and I would like to ask the experts if they can please one by one express opinions, because the time is running and you will go away and we will have to decide, and we need your best judgements. With respect to the five hormones, progesterone, testosterone, trenbolone, zeranol and melengestrol acetate, was the existing evidence, the existing scientific information sufficient to complete the risk assessment? We started to answer that question, and I would like to go back to that question, and in those cases where you think the information was not enough, if you can identify what in your view would be missing, or if the information would be enough to complete the risk assessment. I think Dr. Cogliano was answering and was explaining that it depends on what type of risk assessment. The type of risk assessment that we have in mind is the completion of four steps that are common to risk assessments nowadays. So I would really appreciate if we can go back and try to address those two points of that question.

Chairman

870.   The floor is open. Dr. Cogliano.

Dr. Cogliano

871.   I would say that if you are going to do a JECFA-style ADI, the data are sufficient to do all four steps of the risk assessment. If you wanted to do a low-dose prediction of risk at levels you might find in hormone-treated meat, the data are not sufficient because you cannot estimate that dose-response curve with any kind of certainty. I think I would like to get away from the idea "is something sufficient to show a risk from a particular kind of low-dose exposure", because I think in many cases, in industrial chemicals for example, we get data from occupational studies or from high-dose experimental studies, we conclude that a risk is possible at lower doses and we take action without asking the question – do

we have evidence that eating fish from the Hudson river is going to increase your burden of something? People don't often do studies at very low levels; we know what we know about hormones often from high-dose studies in animals, or from large studies in human populations, generally of people who have taken higher doses. I think that I see a disconnect in the way the scientists like to talk about something and the way the lawyers can phrase questions, because I can answer that, no, the data do not demonstrate that there is a risk from consuming hormone-treated meat. I can also say, yes, the data are consistent with the possible risk, and I think it is the way these questions are phrased. I go back to your question about: are the data sufficient to do a risk assessment? If I were to assume a threshold exists, the data are sufficient to do the kind of – take a no-effect level and divide it by 100 or 1,000. If I were not to assume a threshold, the data are not sufficient for me to describe the low-dose risk and to predict whether it is one in a billion or one in 5 trillion; what the risk is from eating hormone-treated meat, because I cannot estimate that dose-response curve. That's more the way I would think about it: in the language of science rather than phrasing a question to elicit a yes answer or a no answer.

Chairman

872.   Dr. Boobis.

Dr. Boobis

873.   In my opinion there are sufficient data on all of these hormones to perform a risk assessment and the data support it. In deterministic risk assessment, which means there is no requirement to extrapolate to very low levels of exposure, we can establish an ADI and compare this with the estimated human exposure, and when this was done, the exposure, as you heard from the JECFA secretariat, is only a tiny fraction of that ADI, and so the risk assessment was possible.

Chairman

874.   Thank you. Dr. De Brabander.

Dr. De Brabander

875.   Yes, Mr. Chairman, I was a little bit, more than a little bit, surprised about the question put by the United States about the implants in the ear. If implants in the ear should enter the food chain, that should not be very well, I think. But it was linked to good veterinary practice and the application of good veterinary practice, and there was put in evidence, and I cite EC-12 here, that meat which was imported from a hormone-free programme in the United States and analysed in European labs still contains hormones, first, and secondly contains hormones which were not allowed for the type of animal. Those are facts. So I would ask – I am not in a position to ask questions to you, I think, Mr. Chairman – you could ask, if there are such findings in an hormone-free programme, what should be the findings in a not hormone-free programme? And that is the question. All we

heard from JECFA is all the data we are talking about, I won't go into risk assessment because I am not a specialists in it, but it always said it has to be according to good veterinary practice, and here clearly shown from data, from evidence, that even in an hormone-free programme good veterinary practice is not followed. So can we be sure that good veterinary practice is followed in a not hormone-free programme? And as I answered, there are more products that can be used for growth-promotion than just hormones, and it can add an effect above the hormones. And if there is no monitoring for them, how can you be sure that they are not being used and that good veterinary practice is used?

Chairman

876.   On this point? Thank you.

European Communities

877.   Well, I would like to ask, because it is part of the evidence. Dr. De Brabander, if hormones, for example in the United States – we know they are sold over the counter. Really, is that good veterinary practice in your view?

Dr. De Brabander

878.   In my view not. Normally in Europe we have a very strict regulation and that is one of our problems in the laboratories, that it practically causes a lot of paperwork for us to have just a standard for analyzing samples. If we would have all the standards, 20 milligrams, 10 milligrams of them, which would not be enough to anabolize a fly or mouse or something alike and it can just be used for analytical purposes. We have to fill in piles of papers and in other places they are sold freely.

Chairman

879.   Thank you. Do you want the floor now?

United States

880.   I don't want to get in the way of Madam Orozco's question - this is sort of a distraction from that. The United States looks forward to speaking of these issues probably on Monday, when we get into the evidence that has been provided here today. I would make two comments though, one of which was the United States question whether implants in ears had found their way into the food chain. This is a conclusion, a scenario that the EC's 1999 opinion postulates. There simply is no evidence of that. There is nothing there in the Opinion that demonstrates this conclusion. Now if occasional situations where the US hormone-free programme had incidences of meat that was outside of normal ranges, the United States, we feel, and as we are ready to discuss on Monday, has a very robust system, and finding problems, addressing problems, and taking care of them within a regulatory structure, I think, is the utmost attempt to achieve good veterinary practice, rather than evidence against achieving good

veterinary practice. And again I look forward to going into that in great detail. I would note that on the other hand the EC, which has chosen to ban these materials, has a well-documented black market for their use per the Stephany paper that the United States has presented. So, when we talk about failure of good veterinary practice, I think this is a fairly complex discussion that maybe these most recent comments oversimplified a little bit.

Chairman

881.   I will give the floor to Canada.

Canada

882.   Yes, I would like to ask a follow-up question to Dr. De Brabander's comments, and that is: are you familiar with the Canadian Food Inspection Agency National Chemical Residue Monitoring Programme, and have you had an opportunity to review the results of that Programme for, let's say, the last five years?

Dr. De Brabander

883.   No, I'm not, that is simple. I am a chemist, I am working in a lab, involved in routine control, I'm not inspector, a veterinary inspector, and not a European inspector, but there are.

Canada

884.   So you don't have any expertise to share with this Panel as to the control mechanisms in place in Canada to minimize or to prevent misuse and abuse of these hormones.

United States

885.   We will just follow-up, Mr. Chairman, and ask the same question of the US system of controls.

Dr. De Brabander

886.   I think the question is beyond our role as an expert. As an expert we have been asked to examine the papers, and my role is not going inspecting in the United States, neither in Canada. But evidence is here. I was involved in problems with the import of American pork meat. I was asked by the USDA to perform some analysis and some studies on that phenomenon, from which there was evidence from urine that also pork should be treated with hormones. That I have practical experiences in.

Chairman

887.   I think Canada has been interrupted so many times while you were posing questions; I am wondering whether Canada has exhausted its list of questions.

Canada

888.   We just have one more question on detection methods of residues and perhaps we can ask this question. I think this question follows on one of the Panel's question and it was answered by both Dr. De Brabander and Dr. Boisseau. And the question is that if you have a Codex MRL, a maximum residue limit that has been adopted by Codex, and you have a detection method that is of a sufficient limit of quantification so as to be able to detect residues at that MRL, so for instance an MRL of 10 micrograms per kilogram, and your detection method has a limit of quantification, about, say, half that, 5 micrograms per kilogram, the fact that you have developed more sophisticated analytical methods that now have a lower limit of quantification, lets say a limit of quantification now of 1 microgram per kilogram, does that mean that the other type of detection method, assuming that it was fit for purpose, that that other detection method is no longer fit for purpose? That's my question.

Dr. De Brabander

889.   That goes into very technical details of analysis, technical terms like recovery. What is recovery? Recovery is if you take a piece of meat and you mix it with methanol for example and you add hormones to it, how much do you recover. And that is very dependent upon your analytical technique, and in most cases when you do that your recovery is low, so if you have an MRL of 10 and your recovery is less than 50 per cent, you cannot detect a residue at all. It's that simple. Furthermore, you should be certain that you detect the component in the right form. Certain components may be bound, maybe in another form than you detected. You must be sure that you free them, so it is a question which you can hold a conference on, I think, and maybe I should take a comparison with cars. If you drive at 100 kilometres an hour and you drive it with a car which just is able to get that maximum speed limit you are not comfortable, but if you drive a Ferrari or another racing car who can get up to 220 kilometres, then you drive safely at 100. It's a little bit the same with the analytical technique, if you have an analytical technique that is capable of 1 ppd or 0.5 ppd comfortably, then you can more easily and more correctly measure your MRL. I hope I was clear in that for you.

Chairman

890.   Dr. Sippell.

Dr. Sippell

891.   And this is just the follow-up to answer your question regarding the situation in children. We just don't have yet everywhere where it would be necessary the methodology, the analytical tools to measure as sensitively as we should do it, and therefore I think that the data available are insufficient. And I also already said before that due to ethical constraints I don't expect that we will get the data we need to answer these questions in the near future.

Chairman

892.   Dr. Boisseau.

Dr. Boisseau

893.   Thank you, Mr. Chairman. I would like to revert to the question concerning the methods of analysis. I have already answered, but since the question has re-emerged, I'll answer once again. We have to decide what we are talking about. The initial hypothesis was that there was an adequate method to control the established maximum residue limit, i.e. that this method must have been validated. This means, in particular, that the limit of quantification is compatible with the ADI value. I am not speaking of the limit of detection, which is lower, but rather of the limit of quantification. Moreover, this method needs to meet a certain number of criteria defined by the ISO standards such as reliability, reproducibility, precision, linearity in a given range of concentration etc. Assuming this method of analysis has been validated, it must also be practicable. Since any analysis has a cost, it is not necessarily a good idea to choose an ultra-sophisticated method, since what counts is to be able to ensure that the controls are economically reasonable. So if a method meets all of the criteria, there is no point in using a more recent and more sophisticated method. If other laboratories choose to use such methods, that is fine with me, but if a control laboratory is operational and produces good results for the control of that MRL with a method that may be ten years old but that works, I see no reason why it should be changed. The point of the MRL is that it offers the possibility of stopping this rush towards ever-better performance of methods of analysis, since analysts, like scientists, appear to have an infinite capacity to improve, to do more, to be more precise, to be more sensitive, and in general, this means higher and higher costs. Where there is no need, there is no point in investing in that area.

Dr. Boobis

894.   I wanted to come back to this question of the sufficiency of information and the correct comments from one of my colleagues that it is highly unlikely we will be able to get information in children of the sort that would be suitable for a risk assessment because of ethical reasons. And this is for oestrogenic or hormonally-active substances. I just want to reflect on the implications of that, because it implies we cannot proceed with a risk assessment without information that cannot be achieved or acquired, and that if we add to that the argument that there is no bottom end to the dose-response curve for oestrogen, and we look at the range of compounds and the range of potencies of hormonally active substances – this is a very diverse and wide-range of materials – does that imply that it is impossible to conduct a risk assessment on any of those materials? I do not believe that is the case. I believe that with a fundamental understanding of biology and appropriate model systems we can make intelligent deductions about the likely risk to the population. That is not to say that there may not be some gaps in scientific knowledge and that there may be severe gaps, but the implication that we can never proceed without information in the target population of chil-

dren means that we are going to be completely blocked from dealing with these compounds, and these compounds, as I said a minute ago, are an extraordinarily wide range of compounds, because we have this idea that there is no zero risk for an endocrine-active material.

Chairman

895.   Thank you. Dr. Miyagishima first.

Dr. Miyagishima

896.   Thank you, Mr. Chairman. I would like to clarify that the terms of reference of Codex on residues of veterinary drugs in foods currently include consideration of methods of sampling and analysis for the determination of veterinary drug residues in foods. And there is a document called Compendium of Methods of Analysis Identified as Suitable to Support Codex MRLs. This is not a document which is located in the Codex Alimentarius in a strict sense, but this is a list of methods that are considered to be useful for governments to check that residues in food samples are in compliance with the Codex MRLs. Currently in this compendium there are no methods mentioned for the determination of oestradiol, progesterone or testosterone. This is consistent with the fact that there are no numerical MRLs in place within the Codex Alimentarius. However, this compendium recommends method of analysis for trenbolone acetate and zeranol, for which there exist Codex MRLs, and for melengestrol acetate, for which the draft MRL is currently at step 7 of the Codex elaboration procedure.

Chairman

897.   Thank you. Dr. De Brabander.

Dr. De Brabander

898.   Just a small clarification, Mr. Chairman, on what Dr. Boisseau said about the MRL. He said that the MRL was installed to stop the race for lower concentrations. Am I correct? And I thought hearing from the JECFA that the MRL was really based on toxicological evidence, it had nothing to do with an analytical technique. I was not aware that they want to stop chemists of doing our work better and better.

Chairman

899.   Thank you. No comments from the experts, then I will give the floor to EC.

European Communities

900.   Chairman, I would like to take the floor and ask Dr. Boobis – because in his reply to question 64, precisely as he has said, and it is very important in my view to understand, that the level obtained in a residual risk has never been quantified, but is considered to be acceptable to society. So – if I say something

wrong, please, Dr. Boobis, correct me – that means he is making a value judgement for himself. He accepts that the residual risk has never been quantified, but he then goes on, every scientist, not a risk manager, every scientist to suggest that this is acceptable to society. And my simple question is: do you think it is a proper position to take of the scientists who are supposed to do a risk assessment in the strict sense? For example this is mentioned in the Codex Manual of Procedure. If I have misinterpreted what you wish to say please clarify it. Thank you.

Dr. Boobis

901.   I will clarify. You completely misrepresent what I said and misunderstood my meaning.

European Communities

902.   Could you explain then what is the meaning of what you said?

Dr. Boobis

903.   Because the risk assessments of JECFA are adopted by Codex, it is implicit that they as risk managers have accepted and established the level of risk that is acceptable for society. This is nothing that JECFA says; it uses a procedure which is acceptable throughout the world, is used by the EU itself to establish ADIs. Implicit in that procedure is therefore the recognition of the level of risk that is represented by that process. It is not my judgement, it is the judgement of risk managers, I am simply interpreting what the risk manager's conclusions must be to allow us to do the risk assessment according to the principles that have been accepted throughout the world. And I stress again, I am not making a value judgement here.

Chairman

904.   Thank you. Dr. Boisseau.

Dr. Boisseau

905.   Because the question that has been asked is really quite important in terms of principles, I would like to back up what Dr. Boobis has just said. The experts in the JECFA, in particular – but the same applies to the CVMP – do not define a socially acceptable level of risk. They have a working method which uses – within the framework of a deterministic approach – a certain number of safety factors. I note, moreover, that although I made this suggestion yesterday, there was no mention of the chain of safety factors used throughout the procedure up to the determination of the MRLs. There is a whole series of factors, and it is a shame not to bear them in mind, because this would perhaps give us a better idea of the protection provided by the method used by the different scientific committees. Once again, the scientist in charge of risk assessment does not determine beforehand what a socially acceptable risk is, and it is not his job to do so. He makes recommendations on the basis of a methodology which, although

not written out, is known to all and used everywhere. At the Codex level, the CCRVDF (the risk management body), fully aware of the method, was perfectly capable of accepting or not accepting the ADIs or the MRLs. We need to distinguish, when it comes to risk management, between those who make the proposals and those who end up deciding. The risk managers are those who decide – they are not the ones who propose. The same is true in other agencies, such as the AFSSA (French Agency for Food Safety), where I worked. As the Agency responsible for assessing all risks connected with food, it often made proposals with respect to management, but it was ultimately the Ministry that decided, and never was the AFSSA criticized for the proposals it may have made in the area of risk management.

Chairman

906.   Well, before I give the floor to the delegations, I would like to remind all the delegations that discussions should not escalate to the point of making any offensive remarks in the posing of questions. And I believe that the parties have exhausted their list of questions by now. If that is the case, then I will give the floor to my colleagues in the Panel so that we can also pose questions on area 3, and with that understanding I am wondering whether – the US still wants the floor? OK. Canada has the floor.

Canada

907.   Thank you. We just have a couple of more questions for Dr. De Brabander, and this is in relation to your comments that in your opinion there are economic incentives to illegally use hormones, and I would just like to ask you a few questions on this. At one point in your advice you indicated that hormones can negatively affect behaviour, and my question to you is if you add increasing amounts of hormones to cows, does that increasingly affect their behaviour? And I believe you have mentioned at one point that it makes the cattle more aggressive. So does increasing the amount of hormone increase the level of aggressivity?

Dr. De Brabander

908.   I think that is a little bit more than I said, what you take out of my words. I said that hormones may influence behaviour, and there are experiments, not with cattle but with rats, where hormones were added which made them more aggressive. That's right, that's known, that's facts, just facts. I don't know of experiments of a dose-response curve of aggressivity against hormones, and certainly not in cattle. Such experiments we would not do in Europe, not in Belgium, because of ethical reasons. For each animal experiment we have to do we also have to fill in a couple of papers, a number of papers. Luckily at our school we have our own ethical committee, a committee which is controlled, which assesses what experiments must be done, what can be done. I cannot answer your question because it is too far gone, the only thing I said is they really will influence behaviour and that is known in test animals.

Canada

909.   Thank you. My question was: if you add more, do you expect to see some sort of a relationship between the effect of behaviour and the amount of hormones, so that if you add more hormones, if you multiply the dose, if you add considerably more hormone than what is recommended, whether this is likely to have an adverse effect on the level of aggression in the animal?

Dr. De Brabander

910.   That is too a complex question to answer here on the floor, I think. I think it is a subject for a research programme, and certainly there are people who would like to carry out that programme, but we cannot answer that. I have just said they have an influence on behaviour, that's qualitatively, quantitatively that's not to answer at this moment.

Canada

911.   OK. Thank you. I just have another question for Dr. De Brabander. Do you know whether or not the administration of hormones or the overdosing of hormones has an effect on the carcass grade quality – and by that I mean the quality grade of the meat, grade A, US grade A, US double grade A, triple grade A? I take it that the grade is related to the amount of marbling, to the amount of fat distribution, in the carcass. Does administering more hormones than is recommended have an impact on that grade?

Dr. De Brabander

912.   Yes. That is also difficult to answer having studied these papers. What I have said is not the addition of more hormones, what I said was there are other components, and I mentioned here zilpaterol, a beta agonist of the third generation which is legal in Mexico, and I mentioned an experiment with zilpaterol I was looking at literature for zilpaterol because we have to monitor it and bring it into line with other beta agonists monitoring programmes. We found out that experiments with zilpaterol were done, and to my surprise the blank animals were not blank animals, but were animals treated with the regular US hormones and they had an extra profit. So if you ask: are there incentives to use other growth promoters, yes there are, and the same incentives that's the same everywhere in the world: money.

Chairman

913.   I think it is our turn, but before I give the floor to my colleague, the floor is for the EC. A quick question.

European Communities

914.   Chairman, I would like to say that we have a couple of questions more to ask on this area. I don't know if now is the moment or later.

Chairman

915.   Yes, please go ahead.

European Communities

916.   Thank you. That question relates to the discussion ... (end of tape) ... concerning the genotoxicity and whether the evidence which we have, which is reported in our risk assessment and subsequent papers which we have submitted, of genotoxicity *in vivo* – because Dr. Boobis has made a statement just before the break saying that in his opinion the evidence is not convincing, I think that is more or less what he has used. So I would like on this precise point, because he made a reference to some papers, to give the floor, with your permission, to one of our scientists to make a short statement and then probably ask a question on this precise point – it's Dr. Metzler. Thank you.

Chairman

917.   There is a question to be posed to Dr. Boobis? OK go ahead.

European Communities

918.   Thank you, Mr. Chairman. It has been stated that there is not sufficient evidence for the mutagenicity of oestradiol and its metabolites *in vivo*. Before I go into this question, let me just reiterate that we all agree, I think, that, first, the DNA-directed mutagenicity of oestradiol is not due to the oestradiol molecule itself but to one or several of its metabolites which need to be formed. Secondly, these reactive metabolites, which bind to DNA, causing DNA adducts, are weak mutagens, as has been shown in *in vitro* studies. Despite this fact, to my knowledge there are three studies demonstrating *in vivo* mutagenicity of these metabolites and also of oestradiol, one study in mice and two studies in rats. As Dr. Boobis has correctly stated, in most of the studies the metabolite under suspicion for causing mutagenicity has been tested, but in one of the studies in rats, also in addition to this metabolite, E_2, oestradiol itself has been administered to the rat and led to an increased mutation frequency in the mammary gland. So there are three *in vivo* studies on the mutagenicity of oestradiol and its metabolites. And let me just add one little piece of *in vivo* evidence; there is a paper that has demonstrated that the very adducts of reactive oestradiol metabolite that have been shown mutagenic in cell culture studies *in vitro* is present in the human target tissue, the human breast. These adducts have been demonstrated to be there, and this demonstrates, in my view, that even in normal women these adducts are formed, and in my view obviously any additional oestradiol would increase the frequency of these *in vivo* adducts. Thank you.

Chairman

919.   Dr. Boisseau – US first.

United States

920. Thank you, Mr. Chairman. I would just make one point. If the experts are going to respond to this, I would hope that they would discuss the levels of hormone that were used in the studies that were just were referred to. I think we may find that the levels used in these studies are exponentially higher or greatly higher than those that are relevant to the subject matter at hand, which is hormone residues in meat, but I leave that to the experts if they are indeed going to respond to this statement. Not to the EC's expert but to ...

Chairman

921. Right, thank you, that is clear. I will give the floor to Dr. Boisseau first and then to Dr. Boobis.

Dr. Boisseau

922. Thank you, Mr. Chairman. When we revert to this series of short-term tests to suggest, or conclude, that oestradiol is associated with genotoxicity, potential genotoxicity or mutagenicity, this means that we credit oestradiol with the capacity to induce tumours through a channel other than the hormonal effect. Since the short-term tests are screening tests, these hypotheses, which are perfectly valid with respect to the results of the short-term tests, need to be confirmed through studies on animals, experimental carcinogenicity studies. So this leads me to a question for Dr. Boobis, who is a specialist in this area: have the experimental carcinogenicity tests – 18 months on mice and two years on rats – been able to identify the appearance or increase of tumours in non-hormonally-dependent tissues which are predictive of the same tumours in human beings? In other words, did any tumours appear or develop in non-hormonally dependent organs in animals whose physiological and metabolic characteristics were such that what was taking place in animals was predictive of what could take place in human beings? Thank you Mr. Chairman.

Chairman

923. Thank you. Dr. Boobis.

Dr. Boobis

924. I was just concerned to identify the three studies mentioned by the EC, so that I can look at them. You mentioned three studies that were positive *in vivo*, I would like to know what they were. Thank you.

European Communities

925. May I answer that question? They were cited in EC Exhibit 125, so they have been provided.

Dr. Boobis

926.   Authors of those papers, to help me find them?

European Communities

927.   The first author is Cavalieri, and I think Professor Guttenplan is also on the author list. I am sorry, there are a number of authors and I cannot remember all of them but there are seven or ...

Chairman

928.   Dr. Boobis, do you need some time? Dr. Boobis, I think the secretariat may provide you with the relevant materials. OK. So in the meantime, can I give the floor to the EC to respond to the question put forward by Dr. Boisseau? Dr. Boisseau please.

Dr. Boisseau

929.   Excuse me, Mr. Chairman. I had directed my question to Dr. Boobis, and not to the Communities.

Chairman

930.   Thank you.

Dr. Boobis

931.   Chairman, what I have in front of me at the moment is EC 125, an unpublished review. Is that correct?

European Communities

932.   The draft you have is the prepublication available for the internet and it has been published and it has appeared in the meantime, in August 2006.

Chairman

933.   Thank you.

European Communities

934.   It's a review and it contains also original data on later pages.

Chairman

935.   Please go ahead, Dr. Boobis.

Dr. Boobis

936.   I have not had time to evaluate these date. This is a recent review, I hear that it came out less than six weeks ago, I have not been in my office for much

of that time, I have not had time to read this paper. If possible I will look at it and maybe be able to have a comment in the next half hour.

Chairman

937.   Thank you very much. I would appreciate it if you could do so. Does the EC want the floor?

European Communities

938.   I think we are satisfied with the reply and we would appreciate it if there is a reply later on. Thank you.

Dr. Boisseau

939.   Thank you, Mr. Chairman. Without wishing to harass Dr. Boobis, could I ask him please to answer the question that I directed to him – or perhaps he did not hear it; he may have been looking at the documents that he had just received from the Communities.

Chairman

940.   Before I give the floor – Canada has the floor.

Canada

941.   My apologies for interrupting the flow of discussions. It is simply a point of clarification. My colleagues tell me that the document as published may well be slightly different or different in certain key aspects, however way one looks at it, from the documents as a draft that has been put in evidence. So I just want to confirm whether in fact those who are familiar with the published version can guarantee to us, talking about appreciable risk, if they can guarantee to us that the document as published is in fact the one that we have in our possession, or alternatively what the differences are. We would like to know if in fact the reference made is to the published article or to the draft article. You will forgive the confusion here, but I think a better precision is probably useful, and we don't want Dr. Boobis to review a document that in fact may not be the document to which reference is being made.

Chairman

942.   I think regarding that question we can benefit from the response or comments by Dr. Guttenplan, because he was one of the co-authors. We can ask Dr. Guttenplan to clarify on that point later maybe. Is the US point also related to this one?

United States

943.   Simply to say that I was going to try to assist Dr. Boobis in his search. I think a relevant section to look at is section 5.2.1 in that study. There are a couple of paragraphs there that might shed some light on the methodology and how

it actually relates to this dispute. That assumes I am looking at the unpublished version that – oh I am looking at a published version, I am not sure which version the EC's Exhibit is.

Chairman

944.   EC has the floor.

European Communities

945.   Chairman, if you see with our comments on the comments of the parties which we have sent on 12 July, it is all these papers cited by Dr. Boisseau, Dr. Metzler, they are cited there in our comments to question 13. So this has already been sent to the Panel, and the other papers as well, at least on 12 July when we submitted these papers. You will see them clearly cited, all the three papers have been mentioned. Thank you.

Chairman

946.   Thank you for that clarification. I am afraid that Dr. Guttenplan was out of the meeting room for around ten minutes, so I am wondering whether he has followed the discussions so far?

Dr. Guttenplan

947.   No, I haven't.

Chairman

948.   Maybe the EC can briefly explain what he mentioned again.

European Communities

949.   Well I can answer that question, I think, if I understood correctly. What has been submitted in May or June or in July was the pre-publication, and the pre-publication means it is not a draft, but it's the final paper that appears on the internet, because the Journal where it is published usually appears two or three months later. So it is identical and it has appeared in the Journal now in August and I would be happy give you the reference, which is volume 1766, pages 63 to 78, Biochem. Biophys. Acta., as is already on the pre-publication.

Chairman

950.   So, until we reach the time when Dr. Boobis is ready to respond to that particular point, shall we move on to the next item on EC's risk assessment? If we have wound up the discussions on area 3, I will give the floor to the EC first to put questions on section 4. EC has the floor.

European Communities

951.   Chairman. With your permission, while Dr. Guttenplan was away, I think a member of the Panel, Madam Orozco, has posed the question on the sufficiency of the evidence, and I think practically all the scientists have replied, I thought, except Dr. Guttenplan, if I am not mistaken. So could you please make sure that we have the views of all the experts on this issue, and probably, if I may suggest, that Madam Orozco repeats the question again if possible. Thank you.

Ms Orozco

952.   Yes, Mr. Chairman and the experts who are assisting the Panel, I posed a question and I would appreciate answers as complete as possible, because we have a situation where the European Communities has stated that in their view they did not have sufficient evidence, sufficient information, to be able to carry out a full risk assessment on the five hormones other than oestradiol-17β. I have posed the question and I have asked your views as to whether or not the information that is available is sufficient to carry out the four-step risk assessment that we are talking about.

Dr. Guttenplan

953.   These are the five hormones in addition to oestradiol? I don't know about a full risk assessment, but I think there is enough data to carry out a risk assessment as Dr. Cogliano refers to.

Ms Orozco

954.   Because the terms are not always used in the same sense, what we are talking about is the four steps of a risk assessment, or a risk assessment that for some good reason does not have them, but in principle we are talking about a risk assessment that would have a hazard identification, that would have a hazard characterization, that would have an exposure assessment and that would have a risk characterization step. Whether or not the information that is available would be enough. If not, what is it in your view that is missing to be able to carry out a full risk assessment?

Dr. Guttenplan

955.   I think there is sufficient information out there.

Chairman

956.   Thank you. Dr. Boisseau.

Dr. Boisseau

957.   I am going to answer along the same lines as Dr. Guttenplan, in that the method usually applied by the JECFA is considered satisfactory because it is a

deterministic method. Now, if we are talking about a probabilistic method with effect–dose extrapolation to low doses, the data may not be sufficient. Consequently, my reply to Mrs Orozco's question is that my answer depends on the method applied by the JECFA.

Chairman

958.   Thank you. Dr. Boobis.

Dr. Boobis

959.   I have a comment on one of the studies that were referred to recently. Would you be prepared to listen to that now? A comment on one of the genotoxicity studies that were referred to a moment ago. This is an *in vivo* study of oestradiol. I note that it was a high dose – it was toxic – and that the mutational spectrum, which is a very important measure of the underlying mechanism whereby the interaction with DNA was occurring, was not significantly different from the control animals, and that the 4-hydroxy-oestradiol, which was the presumed metabolite, as Dr. Metzler has just pointed out – a possibility that the parent is not itself responsible but a metabolite – had a quite different mutational spectrum. So my view would be that this study is not sufficient at the present time to override the conclusions that we had come to earlier, that low doses of oestradiol do no cause a mutagenic response *in vivo*.

Chairman

960.   Thank you. Dr. Guttenplan please.

Dr. Guttenplan

961.   The mutational spectrum for 4-hydroxy-oestradiol was different in the control.

Dr. Boobis

962.   I stipulated that the mutational spectrum for 4-hydroxy-oestradiol was different from the control, but that of oestradiol was not, and if the hypothesis was that the effect of oestradiol in producing that response is through the 4-hydroxy metabolite, the anticipation would be that there would not be a very big difference in the mutational spectrum; there was.

Dr. Guttenplan

963.   Well, we don't know how much of the oestradiol gets converted to the 4-hydroxyoestradiol, and it has been detected *in vivo,* or at least the conjugates have, in breast tissue from human women, and we know that that gives a different mutational spectrum than the control.

Chairman

964.   Thank you.

Dr. Boobis

965.   Could I just respond, please? But the problem I am having, Chairman, is that the compound we are concerned about is oestradiol. I can find no difference in the mutational spectrum, which is a signature of the response to the DNA, from the control. So it may be exaggerating something that is going on naturally, and I would repeat that the dose of oestradiol used in these studies was so toxic that not all the animals actually survived.

Dr. Guttenplan

966.   Yes, this is a common problem with any toxicological study, you have to increase the dose in order to see something that is significant in the animals, you don't have enough animals to do the experiment if you were to use an environmental dose. So this is nothing different than what is done in usual toxicological studies.

Dr. Boobis

967.   There have been guidelines established for dose setting in studies in which mutational responses have been observed *in vivo*. I do not believe that any of those guidelines recommend going up to doses which are lethal. There is supposed to be some slight evidence of toxicity at the top dose, but by no means lethality, so this would be a heroic study.

Dr. Guttenplan

968.   4-Hydroxyoestradiol was not toxic though, just oestradiol alone, and often this is what you do, you test the presumed active metabolite. And this is often done, this is classical studies in metabolism of benzpyrene, as you are familiar, which were eventually done with the end product.

Chairman

969.   One last chance for Dr. Boobis.

Dr. Boobis

970.   I agree entirely with what was just said. In the case against benzpyrene, however, the parent compound and the metabolite produced the same mutational spectrum, therefore confirming the likely involvement of the metabolite in the response. Here, when we see a different mutational spectrum, the interpretation for me is: something else is going on; and it certainly does not confirm, it by no means confirms, the involvement of that metabolite. It may be that there was too low a level, but these data cannot be used to confirm that metabolite's involvement in response to the parent compound. That's all I was saying.

Chairman

971. Well, we have spent more than two hours already and we still have the most important issue of our consideration this afternoon, so I think it is better for us to move on to the next section on the EC's risk assessment, and then I will give the floor to the EC first to ask questions to the experts. You have the floor, EC.

European Communities

972. One question I would like to ask the experts, and in particular probably Dr. Guttenplan or Dr. Boisseau, is that, as we know these substances, the implants contain several of these hormones that, as we were told, they practically never are administered as a single substance, and Dr. Boisseau in his reply has confirmed that. The toxicological evaluation was made on an individual substance. Now how important do you think it is to know the possible synergistic effects, given that the actual administration of these implants involves more than one of these hormones? Thank you.

Chairman

973. Thank you. Dr. Guttenplan.

Dr. Guttenplan

974. I think that the biological effects of oestradiol so overwhelm the other effects that I would not be concerned with any synergistic effects.

Chairman

975. Is any other expert prepared to respond? If none, the EC has the floor.

European Communities

976. Chairman, it is not entirely clear how the current section differs from the previous one. In your instructions, your indications, you said section (c) and part of section (d), so I would like to discuss a specific aspect of the EC risk assessment which was discussed under the previous section. If you allow me to ask a question to Dr. Guttenplan.

Chairman

977. Sure. There is no clear-cut dividing line between these two areas. You can put whatever questions you feel are necessary.

European Communities

978. Thank you. It is just that, if I understood correctly, Dr. Guttenplan, you said that the scientific evidence on the five hormones was sufficient to conduct a risk assessment. In your reply to questions 61 and 62 you actually state differently, so could you explain the differences? There is a whole bullet-point list of

gaps you have identified, and in your reply to question 61 you speak of an assessment for melengestrol acetate which seems sound for example. Could you explain?

Dr. Guttenplan

979.   That means that the risk assessment was alright.

European Communities

980.   Would you care to elaborate on the gaps you have identified and question 62?

Dr. Guttenplan

981.   Yes, on subsequent reading I could not find anything to indicate adverse effects, and I now think that risk assessment is alright.

European Communities

982.   Can I reformulate the question? Because I think probably we have an issue of understanding each other. Can I ask, Dr. Guttenplan, whether your reply to question 61 is correct as you see it today?

Dr. Guttenplan

983.   Well, I said the ability varies between compounds, but that does not mean you can't make a risk assessment, it just means the accuracy of the risk assessment is different.

European Communities

984.   You also say, for example, that it does not appear that accurate ADIs can be established at this point.

Dr. Guttenplan

985.   Well accurate means – if it's not accurate, there is just a larger range, but you can still do a risk assessment.

Chairman

986.   I will give the floor to the US.

United States

987.   Thank you, Mr. Chairman. Dr. Guttenplan actually spoke to our question, which was whether these particular items he had identified in this question actually prevented the conduct of a risk assessment, which is entirely separate from whether there are certain small gaps, whether you can actually conduct a proper risk assessment.

Chairman

988.   EC, please, go ahead.

European Communities

989.   Chairman, we have asked previously a question about the fact that the hormones are administered in combinations containing more of these hormones, and only Dr. Guttenplan has replied. Probably Dr. Boisseau would like to give a reply. Would it be necessary to have an assessment that takes into account the real administration of these hormones and not the individual compounds in question?

Chairman

990.   Dr. Boisseau, please.

Dr. Boisseau

991.   The same type of study was conducted for trenbolone, which, if I recall, is administered jointly with oestradiol, and no particular potentiation effects emerged. These studies of combinations of hormones were not conducted for all hormones. The JECFA considered that since the receptors were not the same and the biological properties were not the same, the prospects of a hormonal potentiation effect through the action of another hormone was unlikely. So if I am not mistaken, toxicological studies were made only for trenbolone. That is all I can say.

Chairman

992.   Thank you. I would like to thank Dr. Wennberg and Dr. Miyagishima for their contributions and presence in this meeting. I would like to let the delegations know that they are leaving. Thank you. The floor is for the EC again.

European Communities

993.   Chairman, I would not ask a question now; we will wait for the other part before we intervene.

Chairman

994.   OK, good news. US has the floor.

United States

995.   Thank you, Mr. Chairman. A question for all of the experts who have looked at the EC's risk assessment and have comprehension of the four steps of risk assessment; hazard identification, hazard characterization, exposure assessment and risk characterization. In light of these components, have you identified any deficiencies in the EC's opinion relating to oestradiol-17β?

Chairman

996. Thank you. Any volunteers? Dr. Boobis.

Dr. Boobis

997. Well, in looking at the four stages of risk assessment, as we have heard earlier, for various reasons the EC evaluation tended to focus more on the hazard identification side. There was some hazards characterization but it was not completed and, as far as I could gather, there was no independent exposure assessments undertaken. And so, from the perspective of the four stages, it would certainly not be regarded as a complete risk assessment.

Chairman

998. Dr. Boisseau?

Dr. Boisseau

999. I concur with Dr. Boobis.

Chairman

1000. Thank you. EC?

European Communities

1001. Can we follow up on this? Dr. Boobis, is your reply based on the assumption that there would be a threshold, so that your reply would actually not apply in the case of direct genotoxicity?

Dr. Boobis

1002. That is partially correct, but I would have anticipated some exploration of the type of genotoxicity and whether it did have a threshold, and that does not seem to have been carried out very rigorously and there was not what I call the weight of evidence, a sort of balancing of the quality of the studies and the endpoints that they were responding to.

Chairman

1003. Dr. Boisseau.

Dr. Boisseau

1004. Thank you, Mr. Chairman. We always seem to come back to the problem of thresholds. Once again, short-term tests that can show a genotoxic or mutagenic potential are not intended for determining thresholds. If we really want to know whether this potential is real, it needs to be confirmed by long-term carcinogenicity tests. So I come back to my question to Dr. Boobis: in the long-term tests on mice and rats, was it possible to identify tumours in non-hormonally dependent organs that could confirm a mutagenic potential observed in short-term tests, and if so are such tumours in non-hormonally dependent animal organs predictive of what could happen in human beings?

Chairman

1005. Thank you. Dr. Boobis.

Dr. Boobis

1006. Apologies, Chairman, I did not catch that question to respond to earlier. From my knowledge, the studies in rodents have not shown any target tissues for carcinogenicity which are not hormonally dependent and that these tissues are targets one would have anticipated for an oestrogenically active substance. That is the factual evidence.

Chairman

1007. Do these answer the question by the US?

United States

1008. Yes, Mr. Chairman, thank you.

Chairman

1009. No further questions from the US? What about Canada?

Canada

1010. No further questions from Canada.

Chairman

1011. Thank you. I give the floor to the EC.

European Communities

1012. Thank you, Chair. On this last reply of Dr. Boobis we would like to intervene, and I would like to give the floor to Dr. Alain Paris who would like to respond to this please. [Change of speaker.] Out of courtesy towards Dr. Boisseau, I am going to speak in French. I am surprised at the division that has appeared, with regard to the action of oestrogens and their effects, between what passes through the oestrogen receptors and what passes via genotoxicity phenomena. To revert to the genotoxicity phenomenon, this is essentially a random process; and I wonder about the deterministic approach, as mentioned earlier, which would appear to be more efficient than the probabilistic approach, in that the deterministic approach, in my opinion, is incapable of taking account of all of these random phenomena.

Chairman

1013. Thank you. Dr. Boisseau.

Dr. Boisseau

1014. Thank you, Mr. Chairman. I am no specialist in these areas, but reverting to what you said, and I agree with you, a phenomenon based on genotoxicity or mutogenicity is random, which means that this genotoxic potential, if it exists, should, in a carcinogenicity study, provoke tumours which should concern a certain number of tissues in a random manner and not only those which are hormonally dependent. Hence my question earlier on, which was answered. For the moment, the only tissues affected by the development of tumours are hormonally dependent. This does not support the idea of a non-hormonal genotoxic-type mechanism. Finally, the statistical evaluation of the effect of small doses is another problem.

Chairman

1015. Thank you. Dr. Guttenplan please.

Dr. Guttenplan

1016. The genotoxic effects, at least the mutagenic effects, are also dependent on cell proliferation, and sometimes they are extremely dependent on cell proliferation, so that hormonally-sensitive tissues in the event of a random distribution of a genotoxic effect are going to show the first genotoxic effects. So it is not surprising that you see effects in animals in hormonal-sensitive tissues. Of course one could make the same arguments for a non-hormonal mechanism, too. On the other hand, one could make the same argument on a hormonal model as a genotoxic model, but even the hormonal model is dependent on mutagenic effects; it is just spontaneously occurring and not as a result of the oestrogen.

Chairman

1017. Dr. Boobis, would you like to ...? EC has the floor.

European Communities

1018. If you allow us to come in on this again, Alain Paris. [change of speaker.] Probably, the tumours that are detected, with regard to the administration of oestrogens, are revealed in a terminal stimulation process, and here we are combining initiation and promotion phenomena, knowing that promotion is extremely dependent on the oestrogen receptor. But this comes on top of the very premature initiation phenomenon which takes place via the activation, the bioactivation of the oestradiol molecule or its principal metabolites that will be found as residues, particularly oestradiol alpha.

Chairman

1019. Thank you. Dr. Boobis ... The United States have the floor.

United States

1020. I don't mean to interrupt Dr. Boobis, I was just going to note that I failed to discern a question in the statement that was just made and refer back to Canada's statement from earlier in the meeting regarding submission of evidence, and whether we are asking questions of the panel of experts that the Panel has comprised or whether the parties are providing evidence through their own experts at this point. Thank you.

Dr. Boobis

1021. I was going to make a somewhat similar comment. We are getting into the realms of interpretation of data. My view is that the data are interpretable as a non-mutagenic genotoxicity *in vivo,* if there is any response, with a threshold. Others have chosen to interpret the data differently. I was asked here for my opinion, my scientific opinion, based on the totality of the evidence. That is my opinion. So when we get into a discussion about the relevance of initiation and promotion in endocrine tumours, it critically depends upon the interpretation of the effects seen of these compounds. As I have just said, my view is that they do not support an *in vivo* initiation mechanism.

Chairman

1022. Thank you. Dr. Cogliano.

Dr. Cogliano

1023. Thank you. I think the comment that a lot of this is a question of interpretation, as Dr. Boobis has just said, is actually the heart of the scientific disagreement that we see here. I actually am not competent to tell whether there is or is not a threshold, but I can tell from my long experience in risk assessment that that is the fundamental scientific argument that is going on here. And so to be as helpful as I can to the Panel, the JECFA assessment felt that a threshold could be assumed even though there is some evidence of genotoxicity, because they felt that a hormonal mechanism was likely what was going on. Therefore they assumed there was a threshold and they computed the ADI and they went forward with an assessment. And it seems to me from reading the papers submitted by the European Commission as well as the arguments we have heard the last two days, they are unwilling to assume that there is a threshold. Sometimes I think the argument has been that because there may be some genotoxicity they are unwilling to assume a threshold, and sometimes I think they are unwilling to assume a threshold because there may be some other effects of these chemicals at low doses, but because they are unwilling to assume a threshold they say they cannot do a risk assessment because they cannot really predict a dose-response curve. Now I think those are the scientific arguments on both sides. I think that the way we phrase questions sometimes leads you to an answer of yes or an answer of no, but I think that is really the fundamental scientific issue that marks the difference between the JECFA assessment and the EC assessment; the willingness to conclude that there is a threshold for these compounds.

Ms Orozco

1024. Dr. Cogliano, I don't want to sound legalistic, but is that disagreement arbitrary? I am sorry, but we have to find ways to assess what has been done and sometimes there is a fair amount of information whereby professionals can disagree, scientists can disagree; other times the amount of information, the quality of the information, might not allow those variations. So what would be your assessment?

Dr. Cogliano

1025. I don't want you to put the word arbitrary in my mouth because I know that means something to lawyers and I don't fully understand what it means, but I would say it is a long-standing area of disagreement among scientists for many years about whether there are thresholds for carcinogens by different mechanisms. And the reason it is a controversy, I think, is the assumptions that scientists bring to risk assessment. There really are no data, we have heard that you cannot scientifically firmly establish that there is a threshold, but there are a lot of clues that a lot of scientists conclude that there is a threshold. But I think it really is an area of legitimate scientific disagreement that has gone on for many years. I don't wish to characterize that as arbitrary, I think it is more a matter of professional scientific judgement.

Ms Orozco

1026. … of course, legitimacy or reasonableness …

Dr. Cogliano

1027. I don't think that there is a set of studies that can be done that will convince everybody one way or the other of a threshold or lack of a threshold.

Chairman

1028. I think this is also related to the so-called long-term latency period and cumulative effects arising from the cumulative exposure to the hormones at issue. I don't know whether or not the DNA repair mechanism is effective enough to deal with these kinds of long-term adverse effects. This is one thing I would like to hear from the experts. Dr. Boobis.

Dr. Boobis

1029. Well, of course experimentally when we are looking at the carcinogenic potential in animal models we dose the animals for what we call the lifetime, I mean it is not actually the full lifetime but it is a very substantial portion of a lifetime, two years in rats and 18 months in mice, and during that time any latency should be revealed. It takes into account accumulation of damage, DNA repair and any other components that might lead to a progression of effects, and indeed cancer is a multi-step process. It is well established now that you need several different overlapping stages before you get a malignant tumour and therefore these are encompassed within the scope of an experimental model. In the epidemiology studies one would have to look over a period of several decades to be able to account for such latency if the endpoint of concern was cancer.

Chairman

1030. What if DNA damage is done because of reasons we are not aware of due to the scientific uncertainty in the contemporary world and the adverse effects appear 30 or 40 years later; are current risk assessment techniques or mechanisms safe enough to deal with these kinds of problems? Dr. Boobis.

Dr. Boobis

1031. The paradigm we have, and there is some evidence to justify the case that this is a reasonable assumption, is that the effects observed scale to the lifetime of the organism, and so that is one of the reasons we use shorter-lived organisms in our toxicological testing. We use rats and mice which live for a couple of years; otherwise we would have to test for a lifetime in a longer-lived species which might be 40 or 50 years. So we are working on the principle that effects that are not evident within the lifetime of a rodent would not be evident, all other things being equal, within the lifetime of a human being. And there is actually very good evidence that that is the case. For a number of carcinogens that IARC have evaluated it takes approximately a quarter of a lifetime after an initial exposure for those tumours to become apparent, and that is true in rodents, it's true in dogs and it's true in humans. So I thing that the paradigm is reasonable that if there is going to be an effect manifest over a lifetime, it will be revealed in those experimental systems and therefore be predictive of lifetime effects in humans by and large.

Chairman

1032. Thank you. Dr. Boisseau and Dr. Guttenplan.

Dr. Boisseau

1033. Thank you, Mr. Chairman. I would like to go back to what Dr. Boobis has just said. If the protocol he has described permits us, where the experimental tests yield positive results, to predict an obvious effect on human beings after a reasonable period of time, why is it, if we are pleading for an absence of thresholds for this kind of oestrogen-related cancer, that the human epidemiological studies that have developed exponentially over the last twenty years have not been able to make any headway in highlighting this type of cancer?

Chairman

1034. Thank you. Dr. Guttenplan, please.

Dr. Guttenplan

1035. Actually, two points. You mention DNA repair in long-term tests. When DNA is damaged, DNA repair usually occurs relatively rapidly within hours and days. If the cell divides before repair occurs, you have a mutation. At least – I should not say that. If it divides and if the damage is of such a type that division does not produce an accurate reproduction of the original DNA molecule, then a mutation can result. Mutation is permanent, it cannot go away, and so once that has happened, there is some increased level of risk. But, as I mentioned before, most mutations are innocuous, most genes in which mutations occur are not going to result in, say, cancer or another adverse biological effect. So DNA repair takes care of most damage, but once the damage has occurred and has not been repaired before the cell divides it is permanent damage. As far as the threshold of oestrogens, and this I sort of throw out to the experts, if one assumes that there is a hormonal cause of cancer as a result of oestrogens as opposed to a genotoxic cause, the hormonal cause is assumed to result from pre-existing mutations, and then those pre-existing mutations, those cells containing the pre-existing mutations, are caused to turnover and divide because of the oestrogen stimulation. Unless there is a threshold for oestrogen stimulation, there should not be a threshold then for the hormonal effects of oestrogen, because the genotoxic effects, the effects of oestrogen, are indirectly genotoxic effects, they are promoting genotoxic effects. Now I don't know if there is a threshold for oestrogen receptors, I just throw that out as a piece of information.

Chairman

1036. Thank you. Dr. Boobis.

Dr. Boobis

1037. There is, and we have measured it. Endocrine-sensitive cells have a threshold for the mitogenic effects of oestradiol, it is absolutely clear, and we are not the only people, there have been many such studies to demonstrate that. I am talking about the mitogenic effects, I mean there are other effects that have been mentioned here and I am not qualified to discuss them in detail, but in terms of the mitogenic effect on, for example, the mammary gland, which is one of the targets we are considerably concerned about, there is a clear threshold for cell division. And that makes a lot of sense, you would not want circulating oestrogen to be stimulating cell division at whatever level it was, it has to be part of this homeostatic regulatory mechanism that allows the body to signal cell division when necessary by up-regulating the level of oestrogens.

Chairman

1038. Thank you. EC.

European Communities

1039. Chairman, we do appreciate the questions you have posed, they have been very appropriate in our view, and we have a number of scientists from our side – since we don't have other questions, we can make a statement in the form of a question, because they would like to intervene. These are important issues. There will be no new evidence, just comments on what has been said to clarify our debate.

Chairman

1040. Comments once again in the form of questions?

European Communities

1041. Yes. – Dr. Boobis, in the comments you have made, you refer to receptor-mediated events as thresholded and then be able to use them to create an acceptable daily intake. It is very clear that in the very low dose range oestrogen binds to oestrogen receptors, and then as the number of receptors are occupied, the receptors are inhibited as the dose of oestrogen goes up, until that response goes away, that is called the biphasic dose-response curve that has been known for 50 years. Then oestradiol begins to bind to androgen receptors, beginning to stimulate and inhibit an entirely different set of genes and an entirely different set of responses. If you begin your dose-response curve at a very high dose, what you will do is come to the bottom of a very bizarre set of events, that is the binding of oestrogen to androgen receptors. You will then use that as your NOAEL and calculate an ADI from it and completely miss the whole bottom part of the dose-response curve that is qualitatively different and completely unpredicted by what happens at the top part, and aside from the fact that you have an endogenous level of oestrogen that the oestrogen is operating against which argues against the threshold issue, could you explain how you can calculate an accurate ADI off of a hormone that operates through multiple mechanisms across a very wide dose-response curve that is never examined in a risk assessment study?

Chairman

1042. Dr. Boobis.

Dr. Boobis

1043. Mr. Chairman, do you wish me to answer this?

Chairman

1044. It's up to you.

Dr. Boobis

1045. I'll have a go. There are three components, one is the question of a threshold. I am sure Professor Vom Saal is familiar with the recent studies using transcriptomic experiments, looking at the totality of a gene expression profile in hormonally sensitive tissue, and there has been a clear threshold for every single gene transcript in those studies demonstrated. It is difficult therefore to understand how one can argue against a threshold. In our own studies using proteomic approaches, looking at the proteins that change within the cell, we have come to an identical conclusion. There are concentrations or doses of oestradiol-17β below which nothing changes – nothing. In answer to the second part of the question, how did we find a dose, a NOAEL where we could proceed to set an ADI. I said earlier it is based on a more holistic evaluation of the data. We are not concerned primarily with an intermediate response, we are concerned with adverse responses. What is the outcome for the organism, is there an adverse effect on reproduction, development, carcinogenicity? Based on such considerations on the totality of the available data we were content that we could identify a no-observable, and I stress this is by definition a no-observable adverse, and again I stress adverse, effect level. And this is the paradigm as adopted by all risk assessment bodies throughout the world. Thank you.

Chairman

1046. Thank you. Yes, EC.

European Communities

1047. Would I be able to ask a question back from that? The point here is that at the very very high end of the dose-response curve you are looking at adverse effects mediated through an entirely different system than the system that oestradiol operates through in a dose range a thousand times or so below the dose range that you are actually testing in your risk assessment, and I do agree that you are seeing adverse effects and that they will go away, the problem is that you then are not aware that there is a whole other set of adverse effects that can occur down below that, and I totally agree that there are different thresholds for turning on genes, and the endogenous level of oestradiol is high enough to exceed every single one of them. And that as you are adding extra oestradiol, you are altering the whole profile of genes that are expressed, and there was a PNAS paper by Toshi Shioda last year that showed that in exquisite detail.

Chairman

1048. Dr. Boobis.

Dr. Boobis

1049. The studies I mentioned were against the background of normal oestrogen levels. There were several papers published in the last three years showing that against that background there is no change from the control level in any transcript. As far as this ultra-low, U-shaped dose response curve is concerned, I would simply say that, as I mentioned earlier, this is one of those areas where there is considerable scientific controversy and I really don't think we can resolve it here; it is a major issue of controversial information. I could point to papers which show other results. Professor Vom Saal can point to many papers supporting his argument, quite correct. But as I say, currently, I think, it is fair to say within the scientific community it is an unresolved question.

Chairman

1050. Thank you. We have no confusion about that. Well, I don't know whether we have to continue this discussion on this particular point that this hour; we have 15 minutes to go before six o'clock. One question for EC.

European Communities

1051. Chairman, if you allow me, I will give the floor to one of our scientists who would like also to make one more point, this is Madam Annie Sasco, who is the expert on epidemiology.

European Communities

1052. OK. So I will be brief. I just want to make a point because it has been asked why did epidemiology fail to find any effect; and I am not sure epidemiology failed completely. Epidemiology, which is a study of the occurrence of disease and risk factors in populations, can be done at two levels. Levels of populations – and this was already discussed this morning when you looked at rates of disease potentially linked with hormonal factors in different countries. And this evidence is consistent with the hypothesis that these products may increase the risk of hormonal-dependent cancer, but there may be alternative explanations. And it's very complex, because cancer is a multi-factorial disease, so even beyond hormones there are also factors, other risk factors, which intervene and play a role. It has long latency, we have to study for example diet 30 years ago to find the effect today, and therefore these population comparisons are just putting in some information that are not definitive. And the same can be said about time trends, and we have seen in most countries of the world we are still seeing increases in hormonal-dependent cancers, but the countries at the top of the scale are countries where these products have been used.

1053. The difficulty with these population statistics leads to the second type of epidemiological studies, where comparison is being done at the level of individuals; so we want to try to find out whether the people who have been exposed to these products are the ones getting cancer today. But when we look at an exposure like the one we are discussing, it is exceedingly difficult to do it, because all countries have been exposed, France as a whole country at the same time was exposed when this product was used, in the US almost everyone is exposed, so it's very difficult within a country to find differences and exposures between individuals, and I guess that is one of the reasons why it has not been attempted, because it will be a difficult exercise. But I think it could be attempted, at least in countries like the US, if we could identify population groups who only eat hormone-free meat and compare them with the ones eating hormone-treated meat. So I think we should not say that epidemiology will never be able to do it, it would be very difficult to do it, but maybe it could be attempted, and only now, because we needed to have 20 years, 30 years of exposure before we can see an impact. But I think for the whole topic, if we look at the effects on puberty, then in a way, from an epidemiology point of view it will be easier to see it, because we have to wait less years and maybe also because the difference is greater.

Chairman

1054. Thank you. Canada.

Canada

1055. Thank you, Mr. Chairman. I am very sorry to make this point so late in the day. Was that an argument, was that a statement, was that an expert testimony, was there a question in there somewhere for the experts? We are here at this point to hear from the experts, not from the EC delegation. We have heard enough, 19 volumes of evidence I understand, could you please clarify the role, even at this late hour, so that the time is not taken up by monologues.

Chairman

1056. I have no intention to further continue this discussion, so in the way of exchanging the views from the experts, the Panel has invited in experts in each delegation. So just leave this matter to the Panel with confidence and trust, and then I would like to give the floor to the US.

United States

1057. Thank you, Mr. Chairman. That was an interesting statement. I would note that the Panel expressly asked this question to the experts in question 26; it asked, which is relevant for this dispute, what the EC did in its purported risk assessment regarding epidemiological studies. And I think that Dr. Boisseau, Dr. Boobis, Dr. Coligano and Dr. Guttenplan all spoke to this issue. I won't put words in their mouths; if they would like to reiterate their answers to that question, they are welcome, but otherwise I would just note that this question has been asked and answered in the written responses.

Chairman

1058. So if delegations have no further questions or comments to be put to the experts, I have the intention of giving the floor to each and every expert to make concluding remarks if they so wish before we conclude our meeting this afternoon. The floor is yours, distinguished experts. Dr. Boobis.

Dr. Boobis

1059. Thank you Mr. Chairman. I have no specific comments. I hope that I have answered the questions put to me as clearly and succinctly as possible. I do believe that the information I provided in my written responses amplifies a number of those questions and hopefully will be a source of information as well to the

Panel in their deliberations next week, and I thank you for your consideration and attention.

Chairman

1060. Thank you. Dr. Guttenplan first.

Dr. Guttenplan

1061. Although I have mentioned genotoxic effects of oestrogens, I would like to point out that in an adult woman, typical levels of oestrogen are 180 to 2,000 picomols per litre, and this is going to occur over their lifetime with the exception of menopausal state and pre-pubescence state. They are only about 2 in girls. So the potential genotoxic damage that is done in an adult would overwhelm that that could be done in a child. However, in boys the levels are even lower, and there I think we have to worry about developmental effects, and there has been less said on that – Dr. Sippell has been the major proponent of that – and I still think that these could be investigated epidemiologically or in some type of study. We might, as Dr. Boobis suggested, need a surrogate, perhaps saliva or urine, but I think it is perhaps the most important issue to address is the sensitivity of children. I should also mention hormone-sensitive cancers in post-menopausal women, it could be another concern. Post-menopausal women have levels of oestrogen that are similar to those of pre-pubescent girls, and if those levels are significantly elevated and you have a hormonal-sensitive cancer, you might be increasing the risk.

Chairman

1062. Thank you. Dr. Sippell.

Dr. Sippell

1063. I just would like to add that after these two days and hearing all the other experts' further comments to their written answers, I think that as much as children are concerned, we know really by no means enough and the data are really insufficient to tell or to be confident that this additional exposure from hormone-treated meat poses no risk. I am very much concerned.

Chairman

1064. Thank you. Dr. Boisseau.

Dr. Boisseau

1065. Thank you, Mr. Chairman. Over these past two days, I have done my best to provide as many clarifications as possible, responding to questions on the methodology used in the different expert groups, in particular the JECFA which I know well. I insisted on the fact that the evaluation is a collective evaluation, conducted by competent and independent experts. This method, even if it has not been formalized or officially adopted, was known to everyone, and used practically throughout the world in the same way for all of the substances that were evaluated. I think that the hormones of which we have spoken were given special attention, and the data used were sufficient to enable us to come up with a risk assessment. Having said this, an assessment can always be updated to take account of scientific progress. Thank you Mr. Chairman.

Chairman

1066. Thank you. Dr. Coligano.

Dr. Coligano

1067. Thank you very much. I found these last two days extremely interesting and stimulating. I think that there are times I'm glad that I am in science and not in law, but I am sure that the rest of you are probably glad that you are in law and not in science. And I think what we are seeing here is the messiness of science as the data begin to accumulate but are not really sufficiently definitive to convince the entire scientific community, the way they are perhaps for something like tobacco smoking. And actually I think that the last comment that the leader of the US delegation made about question 26; our responses are emblematic of where these are. Question 26 was what are the differences between breast cancer and prostate cancer between the US and Europe; are they due to this factor? My own response was that it's one plausible cause but that there are many factors for breast cancer and the epidemiological studies cannot at this point sort out the difference between other dietary factors, physical activity, ethnic differences between the different countries, to be able to attribute causality to any particular cause with any reasonable confidence. So we are at this stage where we have suggestions but we cannot really resolve them, and I think that is what you see the scientists trying to struggle with. And when science is in this phase you will find scientists on both sides of issues, as we just heard about ten minutes ago. The idea of low dose effects of this is one of the major scientific controversies, and you do see scientists point to many studies on both sides of the issue, and it's not like going to be resolved any time soon. But I hope you have gotten a sense of the range of scientific thought, I think you actually can see that among the experts in the written answers and in these discussions. And I hope we have been helpful and I wish you luck in going on to making a decision on this important issue.

Chairman

1068. Thank you. Dr. De Brabander.

Dr. De Brabander

1069. A small final remark, Mr. Chairman. There is a lot said about risk assessment and I realize that indeed I was unable to help you very much on that item because I am an analytical chemist and control chemist, but as I expressed in my answers, I think there is more than human health only, and then the following of good veterinary practice only, there is also the influence of hormones on the behaviour of animals and animal welfare, there is also a concern about the environment. And I think in the future, concern with the environment will be more and more important, wherever it is in the world, and these are items I want to state in my final statement. Thank you.

Chairman

1070. Thank you all very much for your contribution and active engagement in the discussion on the issues at hand. I am particularly grateful for your patience, sitting with us for two full consecutive days, even without having one minute coffee break. It was really difficult for us physically also. I myself, and I think the same is true of my colleagues in the Panel, we have learned a lot from our two-day meeting, even though I must confess that I did not fully digest your comments and replies on the technical issues; but I was very much impressed by the depth of the expertise and breadth of the knowledge you have brought to the area of your expertise, and I think it will greatly contribute to the Panel's work in the future. In the opening statement yesterday afternoon I stated that the Secretariat will provide a summary of the information and a transcript of the meeting for today and tomorrow. The Secretariat will do their best to make a transcript of the two-days meeting, but given the complexity of the issues and the difficulty to digest the terminology used during the meetings, they cannot be quite sure about whether they can make a complete transcript of the meeting. So at this point of time, the only thing I can say to you is that they will do their best to prepare that, but not with a 100 per cent guarantee. I don't know whether my colleagues in the Panel have additional comments before we conclude our meeting. Then I will conclude this two-day expert meeting now and the Panel will be meeting with the parties next week, starting on Monday, 2 October at 10 am. The meeting will be held in the same room as today. The meeting of the Panel with the experts is concluded. Thank you very much for all your contributions. Any point? Canada.

Canada

1071. Thank you, Mr. Chairman. Just a very simple question. Would the parties be provided with the transcript when it is provided?

Chairman

1072. I have been advised by the Secretariat that if the transcript is prepared, then it will be sent to the parties and experts for their comments.

ATTACHMENT 1

SLIDES SHOWN BY DR. SIPPELL

WTO Panel on Hormones

Geneva, 27th & 28th September 2006

Paediatric Aspects

Wolfgang G. Sippell, MD, PhD

Professor of Paediatrics

Head, Division of Paediatric Endocrinology & Diabetology

Dept. of Paediatrics, Christian-Albrechts-Universität zu Kiel

University Children's Hospital

Kiel, Germany

WTO Panel on Hormones
Geneva, 27th & 28th September 2006

- Although this dispute has already been going on for more than a decade, to my knowledge no paediatrician, let alone a paediatric endocrinologist, has been involved as a member on one of the expert committees.

- This is incomprehensible and paradoxical in view of the fact that prepubertal children are indisputably the most sensitive and vulnerable members of the population (smallest body size, longest life expectancy).

- I see my mission here as advocate of and spokesperson for children and their specific needs:

Children are not just small adults, but something very special!
They are our future!

WTO Panel on Hormones
Geneva, 27th & 28th September 2006

Factors supporting the validity of the supersensitive RCBA for Estradiol (E_2) developed at the N.I.H., U.S.A. (Klein et al. 1994)

The novel finding of significantly higher ($\sim 8x$) E_2 levels in prepubertal girls than in boys readily explains fundamental features of human biology for the first time:
(1)

- Earlier onset of puberty in girls than in boys (mean 1 year)

- Faster bone maturation in girls than in boys

- Lower adult height in women than in men (mean 13 cm)

WTO Panel on Hormones
Geneva, 27th & 28th September 2006

Factors supporting the validity of the supersensitive RCBA for Estradiol (E_2) developed at the N.I.H., U.S.A. (Klein et al. 1994)

The novel finding of significantly higher (~ 8x) E_2 levels in prepubertal girls than in boys readily explains fundamental features of human biology for the first time:
(2)

* Higher weight for height/BMI in girls than in boys at start of normal puberty

---

WTO Panel on Hormones
Geneva, 27th & 28th September 2006

 CPP Girls during/after GnRHa Treatment:
Weight Development (BMI – SDS) until Final Height

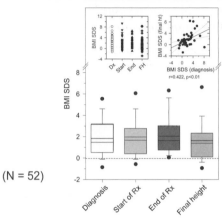

(N = 52)

Heger/Partsch/Sippell, JCEM 1999

WTO Panel on Hormones
Geneva, 27th & 28th September 2006

Factors supporting the validity of the supersensitive RCBA for Estradiol (E_2) developed at the N.I.H., U.S.A. (Klein et al. 1994)

The novel finding of significantly higher (~ 8x) E_2 levels in prepubertal girls than in boys readily explains fundamental features of human biology for the first time:
(2)

• Higher weight for height/BMI in girls than in boys at start of normal puberty

• Incidence of Central Precocious Puberty (CPP) about 10x higher in girls than in boys

• Incidence of Constitutional Delay of Puberty much more common in boys than in girls

WTO Panel on Hormones
Geneva, 27th & 28th September 2006

Ethical considerations

- For ethical reasons studies to investigate whether eating hormone-treated beef elevates estrogen levels in (prepubertal) children cannot be performed (physical/ psychological injury in healthy children).

- Epidemiological studies comparing adverse effects in matched populations of (healthy) children eating beef from hormone-treated and untreated animals would also be unethical.

→ **"Protect children from unnecessary clinical trials!"**

- Declaration of Helsinki
- Good Clinical Practice Guidelines
- EU Parliament Ruling ("Better Medicines for Children")

ATTACHMENT 2

SLIDES SHOWN BY DR. TRITSCHER

Error! Objects cannot be created from editing field codes.

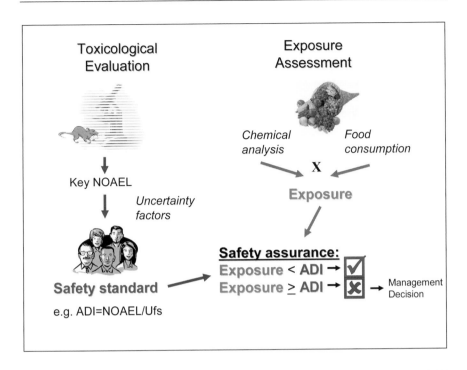

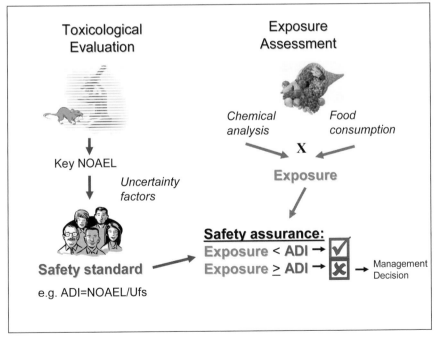

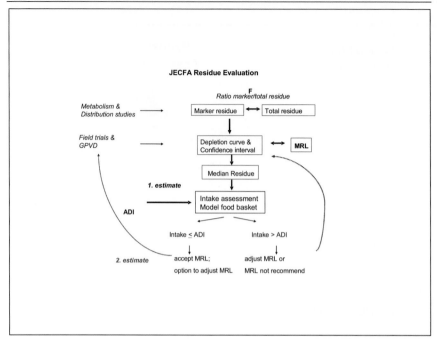